To Cheryl

with all the memories

Haydn

ON HUMAN CONFLICT

M Macdonald

MINERVA PRESS
LONDON
MIAMI   DELHI   SYDNEY

ON HUMAN CONFLICT
Copyright © M Macdonald 2000

All Rights Reserved

No part of this book may be reproduced in any form
by photocopying or by any electronic or mechanical means,
including information storage or retrieval systems,
without permission in writing from both the copyright owner
and the publisher of this book.

ISBN 0 75411 157 1

First Published 2000 by
MINERVA PRESS
315–317 Regent Street
London W1R 7YB

Printed in Great Britain for Minerva Press

ON HUMAN CONFLICT

Introduction
A VERY NECESSARY CAUTION

Many people have indifferent health: this is a factor concerning the human condition that no author should lose sight of. Indeed, you, the reader, may well be one of that group described by some people – burdened as they are with exaggerated delicacy – as having a 'weak constitution'. If so, this book is not for you.

In like manner, but embracing a different range of human weaknesses, there are those who possess an explosive temper. Now why should I make such a vapid observation? Well, you see there are certain concepts in further pages that may well cause trauma. And this could so easily erupt internally, causing mayhem in such organs as the heart, liver and digestive systems. Alternatively, and perhaps worse, it could interact externally, producing excessive spleen. Thus there is a danger of prompting a vicious attack on one's nearest and dearest – even, at an extreme, one's most treasured possessions!

Ah! At this point you will no doubt have tumbled to the fact that I am talking very much tongue-in-cheek. And I must go on to add that this rather whimsical approach will be indulged in from time to time in later pages. But I recognise there is considerable danger in this; you see, when I suddenly change tack and begin to address you in deadly earnest, you may not notice that my literary voice has hardened and that complete sincerity now replaces jauntiness and caprice. Therefore I must insert a caution within a caution. But meantime, back to business... and a rather different position for my tongue.

Moving carefully now into the sphere of mental health, I would also be negligent if I failed to warn those who, finding this world a difficult place, retreat into make-believe and seek to wrap themselves about in protective screening – this is well able to deflect both simple truth and unkind logic. For immediately I must reveal that I am about to explore the worst aspects of the human condition... and that I do so head-on! Moreover, I shall illuminate them in all too harsh a spotlight. And in such a light, make-believe simply cannot survive.

Then again, there are those who, lacking the thick protective screening of those self-isolating beings, nevertheless insist on wallowing in sentiment and are pleased to turn a baneful eye on reality. For this assortment of humanity I hereby display the necessary caution.

Turning now to a less obvious assembly of individuals at risk, and whom I might describe with a certain weariness as 'external optimists', here is a more friendly word of warning. Optimism can be a very precious asset when used with care and discrimination. This discrimination must, however, be spiced with due regard for the capricious nature of life's handouts. Given such caprice (and a less than happy range of possibilities), it is foolish to use optimism as a blocking device or as a mental shield. I happen to believe, in contrast, that every effort should be made to prepare for, and if possible counter, all those 'slings and arrows of outrageous fortune'!

Lastly, for those closely allied to this latter group, and who have great faith in the collective wisdom (sometimes lightly called the 'basic common sense') of the masses, a final warning is obligatory. Common sense lies only in the eye of the beholder.

Has my list been exhaustive? Have I failed to include any group at obvious risk of trauma, I wonder? Perhaps, but then I have at least made some effort to avoid unnecessary distress or suffering. And I am rather sensitive on this point.

You are curious to know why? Well, you see any attempt to make a penetrating study of human conflict demands that the reader has, firstly, a strong stomach, secondly, a constitution sturdy enough to withstand all manner of assaults on their 'moral stance', and, thirdly, the ability to accommodate quite coolly my outrageous way of dissecting the still warm corpse of human history! Moreover, accompanying all of this must come the resolve never to accept or bow to the consensus of the majority solely because it is a majority!

At this point, however, you may have jumped to some rather

hasty assumptions. And I have little doubt that they will all be wide of the mark – in some cases excessively so! Indeed these may be based on the chosen title to this essay alone. So it may be necessary to make some early corrections, in order that you are properly informed, fairly and squarely! It is far better, after all, that everyone puts the correct foot forward from the very beginning.

So then! Do not assume that every page will exhibit a catalogue of woe; I make no grim promise to burden the reader with intimate and chilling details of each and every conflict right down through the ages. Nor, metaphorically speaking, will I attempt to drag my readers face downwards through blood and guts and pieces of rotting flesh, thus to savour something of the outrages perpetrated on humanity. Yes, admittedly, human suffering is the very stuff of our lamentable history – who can deny it? Corpses lie in heaped mounds, litter every continent and damn every century. Even so, you will not be asked to witness the last moments of the dying, hear the strangulated coughs, hold the clammy hands. I am not a voyeur or a sadist; moreover, I have no intention of pandering to the tastes of those who are. Like many who (fortunately) form the backbone of society, I am distressed and anguished whenever I see suffering. And I hope I am now speaking to those who react likewise.

Yet one must always be aware of the possibility that one might be addressing those who do not. In this event all I can say is this: there is a saturation point to horror that finally limits one's emotional intake. And it renders one frigid to all further concern. Indeed, to proceed beyond this point risks a loss of moral balance, even, at an extreme, one's sanity. What is more, this applies equally to those who read endless chronicles of horror as to those who write them!

Therefore, should you have a perverted interest in savagery – and by that token an unhealthy outlook on life – then once again I advise you to read no further. It so happens that my purpose in writing this essay is to search for, then I hope pinpoint, the hidden reasons why mankind turns to open conflict as a means of solving problems; it is not a mere account of the gory details once that conflict is in progress. Cause, not effect! This is a summary of my effort at its simplest!

★

At this point you may well ask why place a health warning in my opening sentences? Well, oddly enough, the causes of conflict exhibit (or indeed can in themselves generate) as great a trauma within the human spirit as the very spectacle of mass slaughter that follows. And if you should find this difficult to believe, all I ask of you is that you keep an open mind until later pages. Moreover, I find it necessary to add yet another cautionary note: this essay can cause grave offence or dismay for it contains the odd quip and at times an uninhibited invitation for a belly laugh!

Now this may seem a scandalous attitude when investigating so ghastly a subject. It may appear to toss aside lightly what are called 'all standards of taste and decency'. Yet in my own defence all I can say is this: the tragedies that can so often overwhelm the human spirit are sometimes so horrific as to be beyond tears. So too can the events leading up to them. And may I remind you once more that it is not my intention to open the floodgates of emotion; rather it is to take a dry-eyed look at the sequence of events that lead up so inevitably to open conflict. And at times that sequence exhibits such an extreme of perversity that it can transform itself wholly into an absurdity. When this happens, one's reactions can have no other path open to them but that of laughter!

Now that laughter may be tinged with anger, with sadness, with irony, yet nonetheless it will be laughter. It takes one back perhaps to one's childhood memories of the Punch and Judy show – that gutsy, pointless, improbable, knockabout puppetry genre that made us laugh despite the utter savagery of the underlying message. You see, when you look at the historical record and at the figures that strutted for those few moments in time on that stage, they become no more than puppets, and in the Punch and Judy mould! It seems incredible that anyone could have taken them so seriously. But then, this is an inherent fault in the human psyche. Many years after, when looking at events in true historical perspective, it is so easy for us to dismiss them as puppets: yet unfortunately for those who lived in that era, the gift of far-sightedness was almost always denied. Moreover, it is a brave person indeed who can stand aside from events and refuse to be buffeted by them – even reject them as a heightened form of reality! It is a braver person still who can speak out loudly and care little for the consequences. For example, that comrade of Alexander the Great (so-called) who denied his leader's growing, if whimsical, belief in his own divinity paid for that outspokenness with his life. There have been others equally brave, both before and since. Unfortunately, most have had less dramatic or less well-chronicled circumstances; nevertheless, they too viewed events and the antics of their deluded leaders with equally cool contempt. They saw everything in far longer perspective and with more penetrating vision. But the greater mass of humanity, in contrast, watched goggle-eyed! Worse, they prostrated themselves whenever necessary. They were all too ready to accept the make-believe of their leader's exalted status. Yet virtually all the figures singled out by the bulk of historians are in reality just gaudily painted puppets. And puppets are hollow things, behind whose eyes is emptiness. No puppet is given the gift of truly uplifting thought, let alone an intellect or a soul. Surely, then, we are entitled to react to the antics of their human counterparts as we do to the antics of Punch and Judy? Especially when they trip and fall on their backsides! Doesn't that entitle us to the odd guffaw, even the occasional belly laugh?

Provided then that the irony we gradually unearth in so many historical situations will produce no more than our honest mirth – that is, mirth generated by a realisation of the futility of most of man's aspirations, his bloated pomposity, and his gross self-deceptions, rather than unhealthy and hysterical laughter – then surely we do ourselves all a favour rather than any harm? After all, good, clean, uninhibited laughter has a wonderful cathartic effect. Thus if we are able to appreciate how easily human self-deception and all too extravagant expectations can be mistaken for super-human foresight and cleverness (which are then used so dramatically to bring misery to millions), surely it helps us to mutter, 'There but for the grace of God...'

Delusions of grandeur, delusions of great talent, delusions embracing the certainty of profound understanding and the ability to control events, are pitfalls all of us can so easily fall in to. Most of us are saved only by sheer good fortune: we are, after all, trapped in anonymity. However, those who happen to find themselves in positions of power, (or indeed assume they have achieved it by their own prodigious efforts), are in mortal danger. Unless by some quirk of fortune they possess that very rare talent – the ability to explode with gusts of laughter at the absurdity of all those grandiose expectations and unrealisable dreams – then they are damned indeed.

*

'The first casualty in any war is the Truth.' This well known observation is itself untrue. There are two main corrections to be made. Firstly, it must be acknowledged that 'truth' in human terms is never absolute. Inevitably it is seen in many different guises, can be approached in different ways, and (to us) appears to have many different facets. Nevertheless, heroic efforts can be made to approach truth as closely as possible. Sadly, however, even when this point is reached, transmitting the truth to others is then exposed to new dangers. The second point to be made is that truth becomes a casualty long before actual hostilities are opened. Opposing sides must be able to slander and vilify each other to such an extravagant degree that all counter-attempts to bring logic and reason to bear are completely overwhelmed.

All animals communicate. This trite little observation may seem an odd way of opening a new avenue of thought. It is after all a statement of the obvious. Indeed it is *so* obvious that a little spasm of irritation may well flutter across that no man's land that lies between your full consciousness and your subconsciousness. But please bear with me as patiently as you can for a moment or two. If I now qualify this observation by saying that all so-called 'higher animals' communicate (with others of their own species) with varying degrees of efficiency and sophistication, then you may think this is only a marginal improvement – it's no 'big deal', as our American cousins say dismissively. And once again I risk testing, or putting too much pressure on, the patience of my readers. Writing, as I am well aware, necessarily takes place in isolation, and is a very intimate yet tentative way of reaching out to others. So if you agree with this observation rather too heartily, you may well sniff at this point and consider whether you should toss this book aside. But again try to suppress this impulse for a little while longer. There is, I hope, method in my madness. For example, if I now go on to say that animals of the human species possess what we suppose to be exceptional abilities to pass on information from one to another, an ability unequalled in the remainder of the animal kingdom, then two thoughts may cross your mind: the first may be annoyance at my having classified human beings as animals, and thereby wholly part and parcel of the animal kingdom; the second may be pleasure due to my inference that at least we are something special and undoubtedly very clever!

Yet this human animal also has some strange intellectual baggage, or perhaps burdens, that it carries about with it throughout its lifetime. One such burden is the awareness that there are two sides to every coin and that 'reality', or 'truth', call it what you will, has many facets. Thus there is one damnable quirk in the human psyche that will insist on spoiling our feelings of self-assurance – our 'feel good' factor. Unsporting thoughts in the back of our minds constantly discomfort us by daring to whisper unkind observations; indeed, they will often insist on seeing the obverse of the coin. That whispering will, broadly speaking, gradually allege that mankind is too clever by half! An unseen finger will dig you quite painfully in the ribs and a disembodied voice remind you: 'Haven't some brilliant minds used this marvellous ability of ours to distribute information and then to record it in less than helpful ways? Haven't they built up a store of knowledge century after century merely to perfect such things as intercontinental missiles, for example? And if that were not enough, haven't they tipped them with nuclear warheads? And still not satisfied, haven't they gone on to experiment with nerve gasses and various forms of germ warfare? As for...' But of course, we either shut out or repress the remainder of the wretched statement.

These are deeply troubling and mischievous thoughts. And try as we might to avoid them, they will insist on dogging us from time to time. But eventually we always suppress them, of course.

If we fail to do so then both you and I will be likely victims of a 'burn-out', or what genteel people call a nervous breakdown. In the worst-case scenario we may even attempt to self-destruct! You see there is both a positive and a negative side to our exceptional ability to communicate: we are apt to find as many disturbing or downright monstrous facts – facts that unhappily have a finger in the pie of existence – as we find pleasurable and promising ones. So what do we do about them? After all, we must hold on to a minimum of self-confidence and self-esteem if we are to find this life in any way tolerable. Failure to do so once more brings about the probability of mental breakdown or, at an extreme, the decision to self-destruct.

Now an important factor emerges out of this, that is if we are determined to survive in this crazy world of ours. Clearly, if we all have this exceptional ability to both pass on and also store information, then we also have the ability to evaluate it: what is more, after such evaluation we subsequently either reject or at least suppress those sections we find worrying, offensive or totally obnoxious.

Arising out of this comes one awkward question and a phenomenon that is so difficult to explain. Why, if it is generally agreed (and most people do) that most forms of human conflict are messy, distasteful and downright dangerous things to engage in, do we never fail to get dragged in? Granted, there are different kinds and degrees of conflict. The least damaging to mankind as a whole is conflict confined to the domestic and quite personal level. It is what one might call 'contained violence', as for example between man and wife, between parents and children, between one sibling and another, between one extended family member and another. This violence occurs (or at least we are tempted to believe) on a fairly widespread scale. Yet it seldom influences the wider social panorama in any truly significant or measurable way. But when individuals band themselves together to form organised groupings, that is a very different matter. Those groupings can, as it were, grow out of nothing! They are formed simply by individuals who, significantly enough, are often total strangers, communicating amongst themselves in very special ways. One of these is to concentrate solely on very restricted information.

Partial truths are then declared to be, and finally seen as, whole truths; worse, what are clearly 'wrongs' are inverted or subverted to become 'rights'. As I say, it often begins with quite small bands of individuals who subsequently get described as 'terrorists', or indeed 'freedom-fighters', depending upon which viewpoint you take. It can also begin with rather larger concentrations of individuals forming what are essentially paramilitary formations, such as the 'Brownshirts' in Nazi Germany or the 'Blackshirts' in Fascist Italy. These were phenomena of the early part of this century, of course, but manifestations of, or very similar organisations of this nature have appeared in the latter half too. These would, and still do, resolutely obey the order of political parties, religious fanatics, or ultra-nationalist groups. Finally, and you hardly need to be reminded of the fact, very special information decked out as 'truth' is passed on to a population at large in times of 'crisis' so as to produce volunteer or conscripted members of a military machine. Suitably indoctrinated, these then form the fabric of a dependable force carrying out a nation's 'will'. This machine often becomes an instrument used for conquest and aggression; it is seldom formed for legitimate self-defence.

So how are people fooled firstly in to accepting this special 'information' and finally obeying calls of this nature? How are they able to deny common sense and simple logic and allow themselves to be taught to act as automations? How are they able to accept that they should initially detest, and subsequently if possible kill, other human beings whom they have never personally met? It is all the more extraordinary in that these human beings, now regarded as an enemy, have never uttered any personal insult, let alone caused them any earlier physical injury.

One cannot escape from the fact that fundamentally the answer is contained in, and embraced by, this one simple word: 'communication'. Moreover, it insists that once each individual has received that information, then a certain course of action is required. Conflicts cannot be fought in any other way.

For example, for eight centuries or more, perfectly good-natured, God-fearing, well-intentioned Englishmen (not forgetting women hanging on rather too firmly to their men's arms) were taught that perfectly good-natured, God-fearing, well-intentioned people who just happened to live on the other side of a stretch of water separating Britain from the remainder of Europe were devils incarnate. The French and Spanish were particularly considered so, but sometimes venom was also directed at the Dutch, not forgetting other kinds of 'riffraff' speaking a sort of Germanic tongue. All of these were, at one time or another, singled out as targets of hatred. William Shakespeare, who, I hope you will agree, was a hypersensitive soul, and not just given to empty bleating of contemporary slogans, attempted to show through the utterances of the characters he created that most human conflict results from serious attacks of emotional diarrhoea. However, he himself is apt to be carried away by the magnificence of the language he uses. And it tends to defeat his own purpose! Most of us in our school days were taught, for example, to recite the famous line from *Henry V* where the monarch utters a wicked stream of verbal diarrhoea yet manages to transmute it into a literary jewel. Please remember that Henry attempts to put spirit into his men before the battle of Agincourt – men who (again, never forget it) are asked to risk and probably lay down their lives on foreign soil for what is essentially an unjust cause. They are, after all, fighting the French for a meaningless and essentially empty dynastic ambition – Henry's personal ambition at that!

Not satisfied with the mere possession of the throne of England, something that should have fully stretched all his energies and sense of responsibility, Henry revived the claims of previous English kings to the French crown. Lineage could be more or less connected back to William the Conqueror, further backed by the fact that numerous members of Henry's previous line had married French princesses. To complicate matters even further, these had brought with them dowries that included tracts of French soil. By claiming large amounts of French blood in his veins, Henry satisfied himself that his claim to the French throne was a just one. That he could persuade others to join him and, if necessary, lay down their lives, is a measure of the 'sacred' aspect of kingship that was commonly accepted in those days. And conceit can have no greater confirmation of its non-corrosive nature (and even transform itself into a benign presence) than when others fully demonstrate their love or esteem for you personally, by putting their very lives at stake! Indeed, Shakespeare very firmly gives Henry the air of nobility rather than conceit when he addresses his army – an army that has already lost over half its number two months earlier during the capture of Harfluer:

> From this day to the ending of the world
> But we in it shall be remembered
> We few, we happy few, we band of brothers;
> For he today that sheds his blood with me
> Shall be my brother; be he ne'er so vile,
> This day shall gentle his condition
> And gentlemen in England now a-bed
> Shall think themselves accurs'd that they were not here,
> And hold their manhood cheap while any speaks
> That fought with us on St Crispin's day.

All this is the most awful tosh. It is emotional blackmail of the most insidious kind – as one would discover if one happened to investigate the historical circumstances, and do so with a cool, clear, analytical mind. And, ironically, although Henry won the battle, he never succeeded to wrest France from the French! Despite later triumphs on French soil and even final recognition as the heir to the French king, he was to die of fever at the age of thirty-five. Yet this rousing speech is, in a very different context, truly magnificent, if only on the purely emotional plane. But Shakespeare redeems himself, at least in my mind, by also uttering the following lines, this time in *Henry I*. As an introduction and before the play begins in earnest, he stages a device, dearly loved by the early Greek playwrights, in which a semi-supernatural figure utters a comment that nails the thematic thread to the mast, so to speak:

A VERY NECESSARY CAUTION

Stage direction: Enter Rumour, painted full of tongues

RUMOUR: Open your ears; for which of you will stop
The vent of hearing when loud Rumour speaks?
I, from the orient to the drooping west,
Making the wind my post-horse, still unfold
The acts commenced upon this ball of earth:
Upon my tongues continual slanders ride,
The which in every language I pronounce,
Stuffing the ears of men with false reports.
I speak of peace; while convert enmity,
Under the smile of safety, wounds the world...

To be entirely fair though, and thinking on a much wider time scale, mankind was not always such an easy prey to rumour or to half-truths, nor for that matter to downright unblinking lying. In point of fact, there is now sufficient scientific evidence to show that our early ancestors were very different. Over a million years ago our forebears lived in constant danger, not this time from members of our own species, but from carnivores far more powerful and fleet of foot than themselves. And these carnivores were also armed with fearful claws and teeth. The only way early mankind survived was by banding together in small extended family groups and then using this exceptional ability to communicate one with another to the best advantage – essentially using it to exchange information that was, to the best of their knowledge, both *truthful* and *accurate*! For example, the sighting of a dangerous carnivore would not only be announced by an initial warning, but also its exact position would be pinpointed verbally, followed by an estimate of its probable intentions. If it happened to be a lion with a sagging belly, already satiated by a meal and merely making its way back to its lair for an afternoon snooze, then this information would be passed on accurately. Conversely, if the lion had a taut belly and was clearly hunting, then this vital information was passed on, moreover acted on immediately. The difference is a profound one. And significantly it was to become, as I shall prove later, one (of two) of the most crucial 'survival factors'. Incidentally, the second of these crucial factors will be dealt with in later chapters; it cannot be introduced here without danger of confusing the issue.

For the moment then, this matter of communication must remain central to our purpose. At the same time we must remember that emerging out of interchange of information must come the further ability to retain basic 'truths' in human memory. After all, since the emergence of our early ancestors and the shuffling steps mankind has since made to the centre of the world stage, there has been an enormous build-up of information, moreover using new ways and inventing new technology. It has now formed a base, something we might be tempted to call 'shared knowledge', though, in all honesty, this seems a bit too much over the top. It certainly does not allow us to insert the word 'wisdom' into the bargain! But essentially – and this is something that must be underlined again and again – until very recently in the evolutionary calendar, mankind thrived solely because of its co-operative, peaceful, neighbourly and good-natured character! Now that's something to set the dogs barking, isn't it! Put another way, our early ancestors only survived *because* they were peaceful and co-operative and shared truthful information with their fellows! By obtaining accurate assessments of danger and passing both information and advice on to others, these defenceless creatures slowly transformed their status. Primitive speech, no doubt supplemented by a wide range of facial expressions and hand movements (speech being something 'anatomically' possible to humans, yet denied other creatures) became their forte. Indeed it formed a significant evolutionary advantage.

So how did it all go so disastrously wrong?

*

Unfortunately, there is yet one more important matter to settle before we get down to actual brass tacks. It concerns this serious business of dissecting and probing the hidden factors that have brought about unending conflict throughout human history. It is this: how do you know that the events I describe, or the statistics I quote, are truly accurate? I could so easily have hidden motives which force me to 'bend' the information in certain ways to suit my purpose. Quite simply, how do you know the content of the pages to come is truthful?

The question of the accuracy and reliability of what I will constantly refer to in future pages as our 'information flow' is a fundamental one. But this is not the time and place to begin a formidable philosophical discussion, following perhaps in the footsteps of Plato, Bishop Berkeley and David Hume. At this particular juncture I take a much more humble and down-to-earth stance. I will merely ask a question you may find either naive or perhaps rather awkward.

It is this: whose eyes do you use when you watch the unfolding of day-to-day events? Do you find this puzzling or perhaps offensive? Many no doubt will. You see, most people carelessly assume it can only be their own. And this is true of course in a purely physical sense. Each individual has been created at the moment of conception as a wholly unique entity. Therefore he or she must achieve input into their stream of consciousness solely through their own sensory organs. And despite vague and often sloppy talk of a sixth sense, most human beings recognise only those of sight, hearing, smell and touch. Yet even out of this small number, human beings (as distinct from others in the animal world) rely heavily on just two: sight and hearing. Again of these two, just one, that of sight, dominates. Of the others it may be true to say that they are rapidly becoming redundant, smell especially so. There are some advantages in this; there are also some dangers. For instance, among city dwellers the possession of an acute sense of smell would prove intolerable. Being exposed constantly to foul air, and thus being made aware of it throughout the working day, would probably bring about a significant rise in suicide statistics. It is therefore bypassed in that section of the human brain which filters out 'unwanted' information. But this also means such people are now exposed to considerable danger. Our sense of smell is after all invaluable, in that part of its function is to warn us of unhygienic or truly toxic conditions. Therefore large sections of humanity must now be knocked flat on their backs, metaphorically speaking, before they recognise danger. However, as people are apt to do, when you are between a rock and a hard place you put up with the circumstances as best you can. They might even reply with the ready quip: 'You win some, you lose some.' But whether city dweller or country folk, there can be little doubt that humanity at large depends heavily on that single faculty we call sight to provide the bulk of our 'information flow'. After this comes that of hearing, while trailing a long way behind comes that of touch, and finally smell.

Can we concentrate on the two most valuable of our senses, those of sight and hearing, for the moment?

Here we find that, as with all other senses, myriad bits of information are constantly being passed back to various centres of the brain. But not all are used. We would be overwhelmed with a gross number of competing bits of information flow if they were. All is duly filtered, evaluated, prioritised. And it is done in a split second. That of value is finally passed on to the full seat of consciousness. This part of the process neuroscientists have now well established. But much of the remainder of the brain's functioning remains a mystery. To date, the important small area which anatomists know as the dorsalateral frontal cortex (a mere subsection of the upper brain) has yielded little in attempts by researchers to understand its mode of working. This is hardly surprising as it contains some ten thousand million neurones! And the sheer complexity of each of their 'wired' connections tends to make even the youngest and most talented of neuroscientists aware that they will reach pensionable age before they begin to make sense of even small sections of its circuitry. Thus, quite clearly, the system is not open to interference or manipulation. Thus you see with your own eyes and hear with your own ears – or do you?

In this strange world of ours there seem to be exceptions to every rule. Breaking and entering as might a cat burglar into the well-organised security system of the brain can in fact be achieved by artifice, though admittedly only partially. This can be done by way of the neurosurgeon's trepanning instruments, or alternatively by using alcohol, drugs or by genuine hypnotism. Entry to the human brain may also be achieved by ways other than what are called the 'normal' senses – and here I refer to extrasensory perception. However, even if and when fully proven, this fascinating aspect of cognition still fails to intrude on the matter in hand. Nor, for the moment at least, can a succession of shadowy inputs called 'instincts'. Unlike extrasensory perception, however, these curious inputs will most certainly become the focus of attention in later pages!

What it is important to emphasise at this point is that each individual inhabits a more or less impregnable fortress situated within its own skull. And this is the domain of a unique sense of 'being', all of which is comforting in one way, disturbing in another. It is comforting in that nobody can really penetrate that inner being, and once there, read our thoughts: it is disturbing in that we are trapped there. We are in fact prisoners; moreover, we have been given a full life sentence without any possibility of appeal. Nor is there any hope of escape; we just have to make the best of our cramped and solitary confinement. From this we will never leave, except perhaps at the moment of death.

Thus we cannot enter into anyone else's lonely and restricted uniqueness, though during the heightened passion and near madness of love, we sometimes think we can.

So then, why should I question whose eyes you use when you watch daily events? Why should I slyly infer that there is a possibility that you may in fact look at life with other people's eyes, hear with other people's ears, smell with someone else's olfactory orifice, or touch with clammy hands that are not your own?

Well, to begin with I do not claim you do so directly. Ah, but indirectly! That is a very different matter. We all do so. And we do it for a surprising part of our daily lives. It is in fact the reason why human beings now dominate all other creatures on this planet. We do not depend solely on our *own* information flow. We readily accept much of the information given us by others. We call this flow 'knowledge'. And by God, what a difference it makes!

At this point do you dare tell me that all the things you know of this world (or think you know) have in fact been verified with your own eyes, heard with your own ears? And it is not just purely physical or scientific aspects that I refer to. All of life, whether it be artistic, spiritual, intellectual, is subject to a continual input and a whole range of different 'info flows' (you see I am already following the contemporary fashion of making snappy little 'buzz words') which we take on board without any kind of protest whatsoever.

The importance of this cannot be stressed too strongly. We constantly take on other people's info flow, and of course we in turn pass on our own to others. It can be trivial or it can be of vital importance. Someone can say to us, 'Corner shop's got new potatoes at really reasonable prices – yeah, really reasonable!' or, 'For God's sake! Quick! The house is on fire!' In the latter case, unless we know the person to be mentally disturbed or a practical joker, we act on that information immediately. And essentially we do so whether we are able to verify it or not. Our daily and quite unverifiable info flow can in fact be prodigious. Oddly too, we tend to value highly those talented individuals who seem able to penetrate other people's thought processes and translate what they find there. The very best of novelists do so and are duly honoured, while professional psychologists and psychiatrists have, as we move to the end of this curious century, at last received grudging recognition.

This matter of taking on board info flows from all manner of sources, moreover second-hand (or possibly at an infinite number of hands), does have its own peculiar dangers or drawbacks, of course. Looming large is the question not only of the accuracy of transmission, but of the accuracy of the basic information in the first place. We must never forget that when we routinely accept other people's accounts of things, then we routinely enter other people's skulls by a curious form of proxy. It is rather like the way an electron jumps mysteriously from one atomic 'shell' to another and then, equally mysteriously, when energy is applied or subtracted, jumps back again. Thus essentially we have to accept that information on trust. And in giving our trust there are many dangers: but we are normally aware of this, of course. We deem some people and some institutions 'dependable' and 'trustworthy'; others we joke about or say nasty things about, such as, 'I trust him as far as I could throw him,' that 'him' in question being a twenty-stone, pot-bellied sneering twit!

However, our difficulties multiply when we are unable to decide whether our source of info flow belongs to one or the other of these well-defined categories. We begin to agonise. We ask ourselves repeatedly: is this source really trustworthy or not? For the most part of our normal working day, however, we accept an astonishing amount of info flow without a moment's thought about its accuracy. Indeed we instantly transfer it into our brain's data bank and never bother to subject it to a test within our own personal dorsalateral frontal cortex. You demur and sniff a little? Well, I grant you much of this info flow is trivial and hardly matters a damn either way; however, a certain proportion is not, and may on occasions be vital to our very existence.

Let me elaborate. First, the trivial things: they begin to flood into your consciousness at the very moment of waking each morning. Your bedside alarm rings, or if you are really affluent and love all kinds of gadgetry a smoothly reassuring yet disembodied voice announces it is seven o'clock in the morning of a certain day of a certain month. And you accept it as gospel to begin with. You do not question whether those technologists who set up the caesium clocks to pronounce Greenwich Mean Time, and to do so to a minute part of a second, knew their marbles, so to speak. Nor do you spend valuable time wondering whether the astronomer royal who incidentally oversees these matters was appointed purely on his well-documented scientific expertise, and not by a nod and a wink from some wretched politician. You may groan at the thought of another hard day ahead, but you are prompted by the necessity to work and the winning of your own self-esteem if nothing else.

A little later, while taunting an indifferent stomach with breakfast, you may hear your radio announce that the Russians have exchanged two of their four brave astronauts manning their space station with two ever-so-cocky American replacements. Now this is something! For those old enough to remember the grim reality of the thirty-year Cold War, a time when the confrontation between what was then the Soviet Union and the USA was at its peak, this information is staggering. There was a time when the interchange of technological know-how was achieved solely by cloak-and-dagger spying, or by internal treachery. And those unlucky enough to be caught at it paid with their lives. The Americans executed their traitors in the electric chair, while Soviet Russia used a basement and a single bullet in the back of the head. To repeat: those of us old enough to remember these ghastly times sigh and thank God that they are now over. And we put this new proof of an 'entente cordiale' in our memory's data bank with a glowing feeling of warmth and thankfulness. If you are not old enough to have experienced those heart-stopping peaks of the Cold War then the process of entry of this particular info flow becomes slightly different. If you are vaguely interested in scientific and technological achievement you assign it to a level in your memory bank that reflects that particular degree of interest. If you detest all things technological, then you yawn and consign the info flow to your cerebral dustbin and eventual oblivion.

My own reaction on hearing this piece of news, and later seeing a visual report on television, was to whistle through my teeth and to leave the remainder of breakfast unfinished. It seemed nothing short of miraculous. Into my memory came the Cuban Missile Crisis and the knowledge that Soviet Russia and the USA were on the brink of unleashing the world's first (and probably last) conflict involving several hundred, if not thousands, of missiles armed with nuclear warheads. And each waited for the other merely to blink. Thus to hear just a few decades later of chummy co-operation between Russian and American astronauts, scientists and technicians is just about as fantastic and unbelievable a piece of information as is possible for anyone to digest. For me it should have posed a problem, for I am normally wary and fastidious concerning every piece of info flow I accept. I am the born sceptic. I view everything critically. But on this occasion I fell for it – hook, line and sinker. You see, I *wanted* to believe it. I wanted to enjoy the warm glow of relief and thankfulness.

Herein of course lies considerable danger. May I repeat an earlier important observation: human beings have risen above the remainder of the animal kingdom *solely* because of this astonishing ability to take on, accept, comprehend and then act on, complicated pieces of info flow that are not their own. These are not processed in their own brains with the aid of their own two eyes and the remainder of the senses. And it provides us with incredible advantages for building up our knowledge of the world about us; but it also presents us with enormous dangers. Life throws up many situations and pieces of info flow which we gratefully accept simply because we *wish* to believe them. In my own case the event described could all have been one gigantic hoax! I have never met the team of newscasters concerned, never judged for myself whether they were honest and responsible individuals(for whom practical joking was totally beyond the pale); I have never met the astronauts or visited the launching sites. I have no knowledge of the science and technology involved in rocketry and space stations, bar the most elementary. It could so easily have been a hoax – the kind governments like to manufacture from time to time to serve some murky purpose that later even they themselves have difficulty in fathoming. Yet I swallowed it. Life often presents us with situations where we either mutter to ourselves, 'Please God this *is* true!' or conversely, 'Please God this *isn't* true!' Much depends on the circumstances. In selectively allowing ourselves to believe some statements that are fed us, as fantastic and as unlikely as they may be, we are in effect not only using other people's sensory apparatus, but, worse, accepting *their* final perception of the event.

Now that famous if dour Scottish philosopher David Hume argued that the entire mass of info flow he personally received *could* actually be manufactured wholly within his own brain, and that the world outside simply did not exist. It is a fantastic vision! It is also an argument very difficult to counter. For myself, when I listen to the music of Bach, Mozart, Beethoven, Schubert or Brahms, for example, I become convinced that I myself could not have created such incredibly powerful and varied outpourings – outpourings that are most certainly of towering genius. And there are sections of their output that are so subtle and so mysterious that my spine tingles and moisture comes into my eyes. Nothing can convince me that I myself could have possibly created works of such sublimity. Therefore, on this evidence alone, I believe the 'outside' world does exist, as fantastic and as unbelievable as most of it is.[1]

Even so, I am still forced to agonise over what pieces of info

---

[1] The case is argued more fully in Appendix 1.

flow I should accept and believe in, and what I should reject as either being imperfectly processed by myself or others, or as simply flagrant lies. More difficult still in this last respect – what is carefully planted by people in some kind of authority over us as 'disinformation'!

Regarding the space station interlude, many friends and acquaintances accepted this news as joyfully as I did. They too, being of the same generation, simply *wanted* to believe it. They too had no prior way of personally evaluating the integrity of the newscasters. They did not personally see the astronauts file into that stunted little craft attached to the rocket, nor did they watch the actual launch. Disturbingly, we all know that it is possible for cameramen and special-effects wizards to create impressive make-believe on the cinema or television screen. Indeed some believe the spectacular 1969 moon landings were a hoax to revive USA prestige, badly battered as it had been by Soviet achievements. All of what we saw, or thought we saw, could have been one gigantic fraud. Yet we accepted it! What other people had processed! Accepted on *trust*! It is rather like the way the bulk of city dwellers drink the water that emerges from their taps without blanching. They know it has gone through the throats, stomachs, guts and excretory systems of countless others. Yet they drink it on trust! They believe it is safe and dependable. They put implicit trust in the work done by the scientists and technologists who devised the treatment plant in the first instance, also in the day-to-day efforts of the technicians who work there. Overall they believe the water authority knows exactly what it is doing and have the appropriate respect for its enormous responsibility. A minority nevertheless buys bottled water! Yet hilariously, they also do this on trust. Who among them personally investigates these safety standards in turn? The term 'spring water' may be factually true, yet the source of that spring may well have been contaminated high up on the hillsides by rainwater filtering through the guts of half a dozen dead sheep caught in last winter's blizzards!

But there is more to this, much, much more.

Chapter I
INFO FLOW

Propositions

If one wishes first to engage and then hold the attention of the widest possible readership of such a book as this, then one has no option but to perform a difficult tightrope act. Moreover, it must take place at the highest of highwire levels of the literary circus, without the welcome and necessary presence of a safety net.

The balancing act demanded concerns the choice of literary style; firstly one can adopt a dry-as-dust academic approach – this is deemed essential if it is to satisfy a fairly small yet important section among one's general readership expecting authoritative presentation, common in the world of academia, or, secondly, one can adopt a racy, undemanding style to reach out to a much wider audience. For the latter a high-flown literary pose becomes a 'turn off'. Indeed they are prepared, figuratively speaking, to run a mile to avoid it. How then does one engage the attentions of both?

The stratagem adopted to avoid what is virtually an impossible balancing act is therefore arranged as follows: a series of 'propositions' and 'expositions' are included within each chapter. And for those who demand impeccable standards and constant offerings before the altar of Logic, thus expecting all the 'i's to be dotted and all the 't's to be neatly crossed, moreover all the syllogisms to be scrupulously followed, then these propositions should take a form (more or less) acceptable to the academic mind. On the other hand, for those far too impatient to be bothered, and, in the Tennessee Williams tradition, find themselves like cats on a hot tin roof, then these pages of script can quite simply be skipped. I hope the style in other pages will be easy to accept and far more persuasive.

*

The following propositions are not self-evident. They are open to debate. Possibly, they will become the subject of considerable controversy.

Even so I begin firstly with a statement that is not open to debate. It is quite simple and uncomplicated. It is this: the historical record of human conflict down through the ages does no more than painfully chronicle an endless record of suffering and misery. Nevertheless, given such a record one would assume that the human race would look for reasons and make every effort to avoid any repetition of the mistakes made. But clearly this desirable achievement has not been realised.

Arising from this observation:

PROPOSITION 1

Mankind has failed to learn anything from history.

EXPOSITION 1A

This is because conventional historians merely recount the details of this saga using but one single viewpoint – the political.

EXPOSITION 1B

Such efforts are sterile. They give no insight into the underlying causes of conflict. All that is shown are the endless antics and posturings of political puppetry.

PROPOSITION 2

To examine fundamental causes it is necessary to use a completely new viewpoint – the biological.

EXPOSITION 2A

The branches of biology that are particularly relevant for this purpose are those dealing with animal ethology and genetics. However, the broad sweep of evolutionary development must always be seen to be the overall basis for enquiry.

PROPOSITION 3

At the individual level and also while forming organised groupings such as tribes, clans, religious sects, ethnic divides or nations, mankind is not always able to control fully its actions. Clearly mankind is partly 'robotic' and in certain areas of activity is untouched by logic or reason.

EXPOSITION 3A

Here the dominant source of behavioural patterns stems from deep-rooted instincts. And being instinctive the reaction patterns so produced are virtually automatic; they are seldom open to the influence of logic – logic being understood as a carefully analysed sequence of reasoning. Consequently, the entire matter moves into the sphere of animal ethology.

EXPOSITION 3B

It can be shown that mankind is in no way excluded from the instinctive reaction patterns common to the remainder of the animal kingdom. Its behaviour patterns moreover must be seen in full evolutionary context. Thus it can be demonstrated that these patterns set up during man's emergence from pre-hominid ancestors several million years ago are so deeply established that they resist modification – at least, that is, on any restricted time scale. Indeed, as we reach what we assume is an advanced evolutionary position our instincts remain intact; they are still passed on from generation to generation by normal genetic processes, and will therefore prove most difficult to counter.

PROPOSITION 4

Of these instinctive reaction patterns, few would deny that the most strongly held is that of self-preservation. However, it is necessary to add that this may be either quite real or false (paranoid). This premier instinct is closely followed by that of 'territorial possession'.

EXPOSITION 4A

Conflict involving either of these may begin at low-level threatening posturings as seen in the behaviour patterns exhibited by most of the remainder of the animal world. In human terms this takes the form of verbal abuse and threatening behaviour that (as in other animals) is stylised and falls short of actual physical violence. However, as in the remainder of the animal world, this stylised behaviour pattern seldom lasts for any length of time. An outcome – subsequent to reaching a venomous stage just short of physical conflict – is usually resolved by the physically weaker backing off, or, more pointedly still, running away. Failing this, and particularly if the contesting individuals or organised groups are (or believe themselves to be!) more or less equally matched, then physical conflict is virtually inevitable.

EXPOSITION 4B

However, it must always be stressed that the instinct for self-preservation can be activated artificially by cerebral shortcomings (or actual disease, such as a brain tumour), and as such may be clinically described as paranoid behaviour. It can also be stimulated artificially by subtle or quite crude misinformation deliberately planted by others on an individual level, alternatively, by organised propaganda generated on an extensive scale by the state, ethnic group, religious sect or political party.

PROPOSITION 5

Automatic response, bereft of any conscious thought, applies equally if one's possessions (or territory) should be wrongly perceived as being threatened. Such possessions may seem at their lowest level to involve the theft of such trivial and replaceable things as fruit and vegetables from a garden, smallholding or farm, or may involve damage to one's car, or theft of machinery from a business (all of which may anyway be insured), etc. However, on a higher and more serious level they might involve one's house, one's business premises or fairly large pieces of territory. On a higher scale still they may involve threats to shared possession of an ethnic group or nation's 'territory' or homeland.

EXPOSITION 5A

For both trivial and more serious 'territorial' aspects of dispute, individual men and women can, and frequently do, lay down their lives. In the same way, at higher levels, organised groups or armies made up of volunteer or indeed conscripted individuals may shed their blood over a period of many years in defence of what is conceived as their shared and collective 'homeland'.

PROPOSITION 6

Each individual's response to the variety of perceived phenomena – a sequence of data subsequently given further attention in that person's thoughts – is dependent on the truth, precision and overall quality of the information flow received.

EXPOSITION 6A

The human response to the shouted words 'Fire' or 'Help' or alternatively the peculiar cry of a baby, is immediate and instinctive. No matter what one's present preoccupation or pressing involvement with other things (possibly the philosophy of St Augustine, or at a very different level 'having it off' with the new au pair), all is brought to a halt and one's senses are put on high alert for further information. If it is not forthcoming, then energetic moves are made for investigation. However, the original information flow may not be entirely truthful or perhaps sufficiently accurate. A practical joke (usually in very bad taste) may have been played on you, or alternatively the matter proves to be very minor and not worth all the frantic effort you have made to investigate it.

PROPOSITION 7

The key to mankind's success, from an evolutionary viewpoint – beginning as an almost defenceless creature over a million years ago, then slowly transforming into the undisputed master of the entire animal kingdom in a relatively short time – lay originally in the ability to communicate complex information from one individual to another. This was done solely by way of the unique formation of the throat, the tongue and the larynx which allow sounds to be transformed into sophisticated speech. This happens to be an ability unrivalled anywhere else in the animal kingdom.

The invention of writing further augmented information flow; this allowed not just a build-up of knowledge but its further retention from one generation to another. More sophisticated methods have recently increased the volume of information flow to an astonishing extent. However, a state of 'absolute advantage' does not exist; there are always some disadvantages to every scientific or technological advance. As has already been touched on, a proportion of information flow may be accidentally or deliberately erroneous. An even greater danger arises from the possibility that we may be submerged under the sheer volume of information we now receive – much of it mere trivia!

But historically it can be seen that there have been times when the information flow has been deliberately manipulated in very subtle ways. Even today, in what are assumed to be sophisticated societies, it may be so cleverly done as to convince the individual, the tribe, the ethnic group, the religious sect, or indeed an entire nation, that such information is wholly accurate, indeed must be acted on with immediacy and with concerted effort.

*

It may be wise to open this essay with the last of these propositions and expositions rather than the first. Indeed it is the author's intention to deal subsequently with the others in reverse order. The reason lies in the fact that matters surrounding the subject of information flow happen to be the least contentious of the issues involved. I hope that at the end of this chapter the reader may be suitably prepared for the deeper and more serious matters that attend the remainder of the propositions!

*

The Internet, commonly assumed to be the most prodigious supplier of info flow yet conceived, will bring incalculable advantages to the whole of humanity, or so we are assured.

Well I for one view such a claim with scepticism. But before giving my reasons, shall we again examine the nature of cognition and the way in which the human mind filters and prioritises the sensory inputs it receives?

I promise you the matter will be kept as simple as possible: to repeat an earlier observation, any attempt to aim for the intellectual heights and to invoke the almost superhuman efforts of such formidable philosophers as Plato, Berkeley or Hume would be excessive and misplaced. A much more humble and, dare one say *whimsical*, approach is required. And in doing so we shall let our imagination take over so that we may probe this matter of gaining and exchanging knowledge in an entirely new way.

Now you might think it tiresome perhaps to repeat a former statement, but nevertheless I will do so. Why? Because it is entirely necessary to underline its significance: you see, mankind alone among the remainder of the animal kingdom – this creature that self-consciously and rather arrogantly calls itself '*Homo sapiens*' – owes its present status in the world solely to just one vital facility – the highly sophisticated and efficient way of exchanging information with its fellows. And here I refer to an era long before the introduction of the Internet – almost a million years ago in fact! Communication even then proved to have been our forte! That is not to overlook the fact of course that other animals too are able to communicate. But they do so in fairly simple terms. There is a very good reason for this: they lack the very special efficiency provided by the anatomical structure of the human throat, tongue and lips. Denied this, they have never been able to achieve the sophistication of our info flow. It was this that provided us, some three quarters of a million years ago (initially), with the basis on which the further development of properly articulated speech and structured language was to depend. Later came another leap forward when writing was developed; later still, of course, a whole clutch of new communication systems. And these were to change the volume of what was once the gently flowing stream of info flow into a raging torrent.

Mankind may have begun as a wretchedly vulnerable creature, lacking the fearsome offensive weapons in tooth and claw of the large carnivores, lacking too the speed and agility of the herbivores in evading danger, but his gregarious nature coupled with the very special use he made of his communication system slowly transformed his status.

At this point though it becomes especially instructive to compare the essential character of the info flow used by our early ancestors with what we now use today. And here I wish to emphasise what I believe is yet another truly vital factor – it is one which has brought great benefit on the one hand yet at the same time poses an enormous threat on the other. Essentially it is this: early man *sought* information from his immediate environment; today it is mostly *forced* upon us.

Don't misunderstand me: here I am not talking of the almost worldwide institution of compulsory education for children. Certainly this is forced on the young, and mostly, so we fondly believe, to their advantage. No, what I refer to is something that affects all age ranges in virtually every area of the world. And it is all-embracing. Moreover, it is something that has happened quite suddenly and recently – to be specific, only in the last century or so. And this is certainly sudden if you think in terms of mankind's pre-hominid ancestral development over one and a half to two million years.

At this point you may sniff, then shrug your shoulders. This signals it hardly matters whether info flow is sought or forced. Either way, it has made the essential difference, hasn't it? Well, shall I put it this way? Until the beginning of the nineteenth century the bulk of the world's human population lived, and never forget it, in scattered communities and essentially as peasant farmers. They were born, provided for, and were buried in the soil they stood on. But by the second half of that same century an enormous change had taken place. Transport by horse and cart was rapidly being replaced by railways, and info flow had been given a boost by a series of remarkable inventions. At the same time, on a much broader field, scientific and technological leaps had further boosted the Industrial Revolution. This was not all. At precisely the same time, new techniques in farming had not only greatly enhanced agricultural output, but growing mechanisation was making the farm labourer increasingly redundant. Almost at a stroke the pattern of life for most people changed, and changed for ever. Population flow from the countryside into towns and cities that had for centuries been no more than a trickle now suddenly became a flood. The farm labourer, like some kind of insect that undergoes a remarkable transformation by the process of pupation, changed from one kind of social animal into another. But unfortunately, being even more exploitable than in their former state, the change both physically and mentally was, as you might say, hardly to their advantage. Even so, adversity is seldom so extreme as to make life wholly intolerable. Incidentally, I should also add that it works equally in reverse: the arrival of good fortune (as humanity commonly sees it) is also less than all-embracing! Nothing in this world is absolute. Adversity can have some unexpected advantages and good fortune is always marred by devilishly subtle disadvantages. And I promise you this extraordinary statement will be paid special attention in later pages. But to return to the migration of huge numbers of people from the countryside into urban areas: previously, the range of info flow reaching the peasant farmer had been highly restricted, and the reason why will be examined later. But as they gradually settled into a new kind of existence one advantage at least became noticeable: the info flow that had previously been so restricted (carefully vetted as it was by the squire and country parson) now gushed out in a variety of unexpected places. Agitators of all kinds shouted their beliefs; pamphlets and posters concentrated thoughts and minds. This led almost immediately to the industrial workforce becoming more politicised. In turn, as you might expect, they were now more able to exert a pressure on the ruling aristocracy. Slowly, a more democratic system of government came into being; more painfully still, workers' rights were acknowledged and respected.

These then we can recognise as the small number of advantages. Shall we now turn to the host of disadvantages? When large numbers of people congregate in relatively small spaces, problems are created. These multiply virtually in direct proportion to the increasing density. And few would deny that looming large on the debit side are dangers to public health and safety. The provision of clean air and water and the safe disposal of toxic wastes becomes, as population pressures increase, a constant battle against epidemics or pandemics. In the nineteenth century many battles were lost. After public outcry, things improved slightly. Hygiene and health were generally now closely monitored, moreover on a permanent basis. But most people concentrated their attention on physical health: few were (and are) prepared to admit that an overview and constant monitoring of mental health should also enter the picture. Thus, being constantly dismissed or overlooked, it was in danger of falling below certain standards. But why? Why should mental instability become more common? Dare I suggest that the ever-increasing weight and range of info flows were now beginning to make their impact? And as the nineteenth century gave way to the twentieth there has been an ever-increasing rise in statistics for mental disorders. Why? Well, to repeat my earlier statement once more: early man *sought* information from the environment; in contrast, throughout our contemporary world entire populations have a vast amount of information *forced* upon them.

Now, if I treat this subject light-heartedly critics may accuse me of being flippant. Yet if I treat it with due academic *gravitas* the majority of readers will begin to find the matter obscure, if not a little boring. So I will plump for the former: I will embrace a studied flippancy despite its obvious risks!

The first task then is to contrast the difference between mankind's attitude to and absorption of his info flows in early eras with that of the modern sophisticated world. To do so shall we make a light-hearted overview, even a caricature, perhaps, of the daily behaviour patterns of the average city dweller in the latter half of the twentieth century?

To begin with, few will deny that they are bombarded with myriad pieces of information, bombarded with it every second of every minute, of every hour, of every waking day. From the time the alarm clock rings each morning that incredible torrent of info flow gradually increases in intensity and volume. For example, after one has stumbled down to breakfast, the morning news items via radio bring one what might be called the 'top of the bottle' (full cream at that!) of the world's woes. This is followed by the least optimistic of weather reports, plus the most diabolical of road and rail congestion round-ups. Digestion of a hurried breakfast is hardly helped by little interludes of nerve-shattering plastic musak aimed no doubt at fortifying the spirit, but having precisely the reverse effect. The trauma of getting to the workplace then commences. During the first half hour (that is, should one live in the suburbs of any large city) the pressures of info flow are subtly increased. And almost all of it is concentrated into and accepted by the two foremost human senses – vision and hearing. Before one's eyes speed brightly coloured boxes made of quickly rusting metal and all too fragile plastic. These boxes, grotesquely believed to enhance our mobility and freedom, are called 'motor vehicles' and constantly move across one's field of vision in a series of accelerations and decelerations. Occasionally though, they screech to a halt to avoid suburban life at its most uncompromising. That is to say they are halted by cats and dogs intent on finding a mating partner on the opposite sides of the highway; sometimes, too, by way of variation, they are halted by pensioners who have survived Dunkirk, the Desert War, or the unimaginable brutality of Japanese prisoner-of-war camps. The latter see a moving vehicle as but a very minor threat compared with the traumas suffered during their younger days. At the same time those who travel by other kinds of dust-covered or graffiti-marked metal and plastic boxes (optimistically called 'public transport') hardly fare better. All forms of transportation have the same characteristics: they are usually painfully gaudy, dust covered or decrepit. But essentially they all emit high decibel levels of pulsating sound, coupled with toxic fumes. Each individual hurrying to the workplace has to evaluate the danger they represent to life and limb (not forgetting one's lungs) by using their personal info flow in different ways. If you travel by motor vehicle, then the dangers are evaluated by gauging distances from the back of the gaudy, grime-covered metal box in front of you, and by the volume of engine noise from behind. But overall you must be sensitive to the squealing of brakes, winking of lights, and tension-building horn blasts. Driving a vehicle that the manufacturer persists in informing you does one hundred and twenty miles per hour can be especially frustrating when you are mostly forced to drive in first gear and at a walking pace. This kind of info flow is of course mockingly superfluous. But like many other such flows in a similar vein, everyone seems to take a perverse delight in offering them. But it does not end there. Another diabolical form of superfluous info flow is evident when the car radio warns you not to be caught in a gridlock on a certain road in a certain area – and it does so at the precise moment you find yourself so caught! Moreover, if and when this problem and trauma are finally overcome, and if and when the workplace at last comes within (cursing) range, you are forced to accept information and 'good advice' from policemen, traffic wardens or perfect strangers with short tempers. As for those travelling by public transport, they hardly fare better. Aggressive bus drivers, suspicious ticket inspectors, pickpockets and muggers abound. Then there are shady-looking characters that could well be psychopathic serial killers out for a morning's airing. All these might well be presented to you by your info flow. Worse, some circumstances or some people you observe fit neatly into your memory bank provided by the horror film of the previous evening. On top of all that there is the ill fortune of meeting wretched people you *do* know! Even if you should find their body language acceptable, their presence is hardly an advantage. You are then confronted by the risk that they may slow your progress, thus making the inevitable record of late arrival at work look like a permanent revision of working hours!

And even on reaching the workplace things hardly improve. The lift may be out of order, you may slip on the freshly washed stairs; your final arrival under the gaze of your immediate superior brings a scowl rather than a smile. Colleagues make infantile jokes, others whom you have always detested make sexual jokes, even passes. Workloads are suddenly found to be increased; files have been lost or removed. Office or workplace machines develop faults yet their repair or replacement is seriously delayed. Deadlines are inevitably exceeded, new one's seem a sick joke, bosses deliver ultimate warnings... and so it goes on. For you to remain sane in such circumstances, the bulk of this information flow has to be either suppressed or totally rejected in some way or other.

Are you beginning to get my drift, as they say? In our contemporary world suppression or elimination of the greater part of our daily info flow has become a vital necessity. One's sanity depends upon it. And, as I have illustrated, it begins at the very point of waking. One is seized with a measure of dread merely by the ringing of the alarm clock. It seems to herald a repetitive daily grind with positive glee. Inevitably, on one of your bad days you begin to question the very purpose and meaning of life. You ask yourself, 'Must it be like this? Why was I born? What is the purpose of existence?' But of course unless you are about to succumb to a nervous breakdown, your facility for partly suppressing or eliminating such thoughts wins out. Often though, these ghastly questions return to haunt one. For example, while driving to the city, the early morning equivalent of the Homeric Odyssey, you may come within hair's breadth of an accident. Shaken, you realise you have barely avoided serious, even fatal, injury. So, in full knowledge that you must repeat this Odyssean venture each day, it is essential once again that you suppress the true awfulness of your position. Some try to be philosophical about it. They do so by dismissing it with the trite observation: 'Well, a miss is as good as a mile.' Alternatively, should you be truly rattled, you try to relieve the built-up tension by merely shouting insults through the car window such as, 'Mate! You would be lethal even with a lawnmower!' But of course it doesn't end there. This is only part of the wind-up. When you finally reach the workplace, you begin to ask whether all that effort was worth it. Yet again you begin to have all kinds of doubts as to the very purpose of life itself. Why were you born? Was it really to spend the better part of your life in this way? You are underpaid, undervalued, under-resourced, and certainly under-employed – that is, intellectually speaking. Millions of those who toil in our cities feel their lives are unfulfilled. Yet they are trapped by the patterns imposed on them by forces outside their control. They see no way out other than by some incredible win on an outsider in the Derby or perhaps via the pools or the lottery. Again it must be emphasised that merely to survive each day the bulk of information flooding into our senses must be either rigorously suppressed or eliminated altogether. And modern men and women have become unusually adept at using this astonishing facility. Those unable to do this simply go under. Doctors' surgeries are crammed with people with all kinds of ailments, most of them intensified or even touched off by various stages of mental stress. Need I say more?

So I hope what I have now established quite firmly in your mind is this: the demands made of us in this nerve-shattering contemporary world of ours impose on us the ability to close our minds to every aspect of daily life (and by God they are many) that appears damaging to our interests. However, the devil of it is that some are only supposed interests, and only as you happen to perceive them. This has its own dangers. One in particular bothers me. You see, I am very aware that much of the material in this essay challenges commonly accepted attitudes and precious beliefs, hence the probability that you will fail to allow a fair hearing for my propositions and arguments becomes almost a certainty.

How can I avoid this impasse? Perhaps the only possibility lies in making a challenge. In other words I am going to say, 'I dare you!' I am going to ask you to turn off that astonishing facility of yours to suppress each and every damaging info flow. Instead I will urge you to establish in your mind something that is becoming increasingly rare in our contemporary world – a completely open, uninhibited and even an adventurous outlook!

Yet in doing so, I most certainly refuse to ask you to suppress certain facilities that I myself find utterly sacrosanct. These are described by those deceptively simple words 'logic' and 'reason'. And I am quite content if you reject what I have to say on these grounds.

But what I am afraid of is that much of what I propose will be all too quickly submerged under a stampede of sheer emotionalism. You see, the history of mankind down through the ages is one of constant overwhelming of logic and sweet reason – overwhelming by the rush of raw emotion. That is one of the reasons why the subject of this essay, namely human conflict, has become endemic. It is not the *only* reason, otherwise what I have already touched on – the highly selective filtering and subsequent wholesale suppression of the bulk of our info flow – would bring this essay virtually to an end. And it would do so before it has really started! You see, it is all too apparent that wars, revolutions and incessant feuding never break out as the result of cool-headed and studied observation. They are never the result of a careful interplay of logic and reason. Yet a book that merely underlines this fact would be a worthless regurgitation of the obvious. Conflict has certainly become endemic because of excess emotionalism and unrestrained passions. However, what is fascinating to me personally is to delve deeper and find out why these emotions and passions are allowed to surface in the first place. More fascinating still is to find out why subsequently they so easily override sweet reason.

And make no mistake – the history of all conflict as I shall retell it will be to underline its absurdity and its incredible waste of effort. Incidentally, this does not mean that I will constantly decry what we call 'patriotism' and 'heroism' under all circumstances. A peaceful ethnic group or nation attacked by an aggressor automatically attempts to defend itself. Logic and sweet reason have no time to be deployed in such circumstances. It is, after all, the aggressor that should have employed them in the first place; moreover, I will constantly show that in the historical record, the defeated or subject peoples sooner or later win back the territory they have lost. Despite this, it is an undeniable fact that otherwise peaceable millions have been, and still are, being persuaded by their leaders to wage aggressive war against their neighbours. And it is all done by artifice. Quite simply, these leaders have learned subtle methods of tampering with the info flow filtering systems of those under their control. Thus millions can be roused into absurdly heightened and aggressive passions by specially treated information which we now identify under the name 'propaganda'. And that propaganda can be so powerful and insidious as to suggest that some human beings must not only be regarded as mortal enemies, but visualised as the scum of the earth. Indeed it is sometimes suggested that they are subhuman, or alternatively the children of the very devil.

However, to begin to investigate at this particular point why various forms of propaganda are able to penetrate into our consciousness and remain there without ejection would be to anticipate later pages. More untimely still, it would break into an imaginative project already in hand – that is to make a comparison of the imposed info flow now battering the very soul of twentieth-century humanity with that of our early ancestors. This happens to be an urgent matter, and this is what I now propose to deal with without delay.

Thus we will leave the fascinating subject of why we so easily accept propaganda until later.

To our stated purpose then...

*

To begin with, we must acknowledge that our visualisation of the day-to-day existence of early man is undoubtedly conjecture. However, we are greatly helped by the painstaking work of scientists specialising in this field, not forgetting that of anthropologists studying the lives of the few remaining primitive peoples on this shrinking planet that still exist untouched by our frenzied way of living. These are now restricted to such regions as the remoter parts of the Amazonian rainforest, the African Kalahari, or the jungles of New Guinea. We cannot of course be sure that our conjectures are near the mark, but probably they are not too wide of it either.

Immediately though, we must dispose of a commonly accepted myth. It is so often assumed that the lives lived by our ancestors ranging from half a million to a million years ago were simple and wholly lacking in trauma. They weren't! Not by what you might call 'a long chalk'! Try to put yourself in their shoes, despite the fact that they lacked them!

To begin with, in all likelihood your vocabulary might have been rather limited, but your data bank concerning items that either ensured or conversely threatened your very existence was as full as any of that of any modern man. For example, you had to know where, when and how to forage for wild fruits, wild vegetables, water-holding tubers or edible insects. You had to know where and when a large carnivore might make a kill and leave some scraps of meat you might scavenge. At a slightly later date, when the bow and arrow were invented, you had to know which plant or what small creature exuded a poison – this could give the tip of an arrow an incredible rise in efficiency by ensuring that partly wounded animals could not escape you. You had to know the where, when and how of so many things. Some you acquired from your own experience, but the bulk of your data bank was provided by the info flow from others, particularly your elders. One other factor: it would also be foolish to ignore the fact that a proportion of your established behaviour patterns were provided by that curious facility we call 'instinct'.

You purse your lips and sniff over this last statement? Well, instinctively, for example, you amplified the basic evolutionary advantages that accrue from natural gregariousness and social co-operation – such as are practised by all members of the ape family. You were not aware of these vital factors, but you practised them nevertheless. You knew nothing of the 'survival factor' utilised when you assembled in an extended family unit, nor the true significance of gradually improving your skills in recognising and naming things and passing on the information to others. Instinctively, too, when faced with danger, you grouped together, brandishing long sticks. Later, these sticks, when dipped in animal fat and ignited by your fire, were used as flaming torches. This was a most effective way of frightening off even the most formidable of carnivores. Later still, while out hunting with your group and confronted by danger, you used well-sharpened wooden spears and accompanied this stance with much excited shouting. But above all you actively *sought* all kinds of information from your environment. The process was always acquisitive and inquisitive. It was never *forced* on one from unknown and highly questionable sources.

The second myth to explode concerns intelligence. It is widely supposed that for a primitive existence to last thousands of years, lack of development of the upper section of the human brain has to be responsible. It seems to compare unfavourably with what we carelessly assume to be our contemporary display of high intelligence. This can be dismissed by examination of the skulls of early ancestors together with those of contemporary primitive peoples. Both the actual skull size and the capacity of the brain contained in it are exactly the same, Indeed Neanderthal Man had a larger skull than ours! So the answer to our supposed greater intelligence and sophistication lies wholly with our capacity to build on the accumulated knowledge of centuries, moreover to be ceaselessly dissatisfied and ever eager to reach out further. Primitive peoples, in contrast, are happy and perfectly content with their lot. They see little reason for change, until, that is, our values and our acquisitive outlook are more or less forced upon them.

Primitive peoples are not unintelligent; neither are they unobservant or lack curiosity. Nor are they indolent at processing the info flow they receive. Their processing capacity equals ours in every respect. It is just that their attitudes to life are completely different. And if we are fair-minded and jettison all our prejudices and preconceived notions then we should regard with admiration the range of information retained by present-day primitive peoples already mentioned, such as the Bushmen of the Kalahari, the tribes from the Amazonian Basin and those from Papua and New Guinea. By any standard it is quite astonishing how much information they gather from their immediate environment. And all of it, remember, is painstakingly *gathered*; it is never actively forced upon them. Remember too that these gifted people sift through all the information coming to them in minute detail. While seeking food or looking for plants or trees with medicinal properties, they examine and identify countless leaf shapes, examine and identify endless characteristics of tree bark. They identify the characteristic pattern and outline of bushes, the colour and texture of fruit, the tracks left (hours or days earlier) by countless animals, the habits, habitats and behaviour patterns of a huge variety of animals and insects. Subsequently they then compare them with their internal data banks built from previous experience and knowledge. Having done so, actions are taken on the decisions made. But essentially they are not pressured as we are. They are not targeted by shockingly intrusive info flow from dubious sources. There are no deliberate attempts to engage their attention, or worse actively change their minds on a whole range of subjects and issues. They are not actively bombarded with it every minute of every waking hour.

Even so, we must be careful not to become so enthusiastic about their way of life that we get delirious and go overboard in admiration. It would be foolish to suppose everything in their lives was (and for the contemporary primitive still is) idyllic! It would be ridiculous to see their lives as eternally relaxed and 'laid-back'. The truth of the matter is that they too would have activities or periods in which the adrenaline started pumping like fury into their bloodstreams. And not only during activities such as hunting. However, once more the information they would have required was *drawn* out of their immediate environment: it did not come out arrogantly and blatantly to meet them. They would have targeted *it*; it would not target them.

Holding on to our realism, therefore, we should avoid the absurd belief that life in those early eras, or for that matter in today's wilderness areas, was (and is) totally without stress, without irritation, without palpable frustration. But we can at least hazard the assumption that stress, irritation and frustration were and are of a far lower order than ours. At the same time we should recognise that self-reliance and individualism would have had a far higher profile – things that are constantly eroded in modern life. You see the further up the so-called 'civilising' ladder humanity climbs, the more these qualities have to be restricted. Sometimes they must be deliberately knocked out of one. Civilisation demands above all a high degree of conformity and co-operation – otherwise all is chaos. It demands the observation of set standards, rules and regulations. It expects a willingness to compromise most of one's own interests for the greater good of the community. Our ancestors and contemporary 'primitives' would have found much of this incomprehensible. In their world, they compromised instinctively, not consciously and with a grudge. Even so, I am aware that anthropologists report at least some degree of regimentation inherent in group loyalties, and this regardless of the simplicity of their lifestyles.

To attempt to estimate these shall we let our imaginations have free rein for a moment? Let us picture a hunting scene, at the same time basing our conjecture on some of the latest investigations of the world's most celebrated anthropologists.

Now suppose an extended family group of some ten to fifteen adult males, accompanied by a handful of adolescents – eager as all their kind not just to learn but to gain kudos and raise their levels of respect among their elders – set out to bag some antelope. Having located a herd, they creep through the bush as silently as possible to bring them within range of their humble bows and arrows.

The leading male, a recognised skilled hunter, finds himself, much to his irritation, being constantly tapped on his backside by his son. Glancing round he observes the wretched boy with a contorted face. A raised eyebrow and a series of silent hand signals draws the information that the excitement has exerted pressure on his son's overfull bladder – he is desperate to relieve himself. But the sound and the odour would alert the antelope, highly sensitive as they are to the slightest of info flows. The communal interest would not be served by the antelopes' escape. A degree of self-discipline, the observance of the rules of hunting and the necessity to disregard one's comfort and self-interest for the common good, now demand restraint. But at least the father realises he should have anticipated such a possibility. He should have taken appropriate steps and have warned his son half an hour ago. Moreover, they both know, as does the remainder of the party, that any large and dangerous carnivore in the area – expert as they are in deciphering incredible amounts of information from traces of urine – would be likely to follow their trail. The hunters would then become the hunted! The father's furious expression therefore demands bladder control for as long as is humanly possible. The party creeps on. A few minutes later the group has silently moved over the ground and is now within possible bow shot. But ideally they should get nearer. Ears and eyes constantly sweep the surrounding terrain for telltale information and possible sources of trouble. Care must be taken not to rustle a single leaf on a scrub tree or bush, not to step on a single dry twig, not to disturb any small bird or other scrub-loving creature. Their eyes must detect the slightest of movements even on the periphery of vision. At the same time they must disregard or filter out such distant commonplace sounds as a zebra snorting, the chirp of a small flock of birds, or the wind rustling the leaves on the topmost branches of the few tall trees. In short, they must rid themselves of trivia.

Arriving within more sensible range at last, the foremost hunter raises his head above the long grass and lifts his bow. As he does so, out of the corner of his eye he sees the profile of another head rise some fifteen yards away. The head of a lioness! It is also hunting. Fortunately she has been so intent on stalking the antelope she has failed to notice competition. Our human hunter has not been seen. He ducks down, turns, and with a fearful grimace signals 'lion'. His reward is unfortunate. It triggers the explosive and double incontinence of his son! The antelope, ultra-sensitive to every sound, dash off. The lioness utters a snarl of frustration. The men instinctively close ranks and crouch down. Then, dropping their bows and lifting their spears like a curled-up porcupine they provide a spiked defence. What is the point of using arrows? Lions are not tasty to eat. And a wounded lion is doubly dangerous! The lioness advances toward them. The spiked display is considerable. Combined with sudden bursts of shrieks from the adolescents and shouts from the adults, it causes her to hesitate. She circles the group. She is puzzled. What she sees and hears does not conform to her normal info flow; worse, after duly processing it she finds it does not agree with anything found in her mental data bank. Deciding this is all very odd and outside her normal range of experience, she pads off to resume hunting more conventional prey.

The adolescents crawl out from beneath their elders' legs. Most are shaken. One of their number is more than shaken. He has lost face; indeed he has egg on his face if not other marks of social stigma. His bid for the early status of manhood has been ruined for some considerable time. And their extended family unit is poorer for having lost one or more antelope for their forthcoming meal.

So much then for levels of conformity, rules and regulation and the info flows experienced in primitive societies. How can we evaluate it and make comparisons with the stress, frustration and danger commonplace in our twentieth century?

Suppose we follow the fortunes this time of a mother and daughter on the only sort of comparable hunt now available. They are out browsing through shops looking for much sought-after bargains, more especially what are misleadingly called 'closing down sales'. How does this kind of stress, frustration and danger compare with that of our primitive ancestors? Whether such browsing is carried out on Fifth Avenue, Chelsea or the Champs-Elysées hardly matters. Arguably, hunting for the basic (or not so basic) necessities of life involves just as much or even greater danger. High on the list are such things as being run down by a bus, car or taxi, then muggings and assault by the mentally unstable. There are also less obvious dangers such as the inhalation of toxic fumes from a mixture of industrial and traffic sources, plus a build-up of all those intense feelings of anxiety that seem endemic to the modern world. The latter are injected into the mother and daughter's info flow by the roar of traffic, the winking of lights and the curious (and possibly unsavoury) sexual glances from male passers-by. Indeed, information of an incredible variety – most of it warning of danger – has to be processed and then suppressed or eliminated. On the other hand there are some advantages. If injury is sustained from any of these sources, then present-day emergency services (provided they are not caught in a traffic gridlock) are astonishingly efficient. Indeed subsequent medical treatment is highly effective unless the injury is beyond all hope. As for minor irritations such as a call of nature, these things can be accommodated by a public toilet – provided, that is, you know where one is to be found. Mere flatulence suffered by child or adult may be amply disguised by the noise of traffic outside the shopping area or the intrusive plastic musak inside. This prevents loss of face. Plus or minus factors of this nature pepper the evaluation of ancient and modern lifestyles, and it is impossible to make a respectable balance sheet of pros and cons that might prove the superiority of one or other. Nevertheless, it cannot be denied that primitive peoples go about their daily lives with a certain confidence and what seems an unperturbed acceptance of life – life as it is. As often as not, also, they do so with smiles on their faces, no matter what the hardships or difficulties. In contrast, modern man and woman seem perpetually worried, unsatisfied, even unsatisfiable. As often as not they go about with a frown or a grimace. Smiles are produced rarely, moreover fleetingly at that. And it all has to do with the sheer pressures of excess info flows. There are not just so many more sources of information – the devil of it is they are capable of reaching, probing and interacting far more urgently with our senses than ever before. Thus they put undue strain on our capacity to filter, evaluate, suppress or reject, for they barge into your consciousness without any kind of 'by your leave'. Indeed messages of one kind or another can now be sent from the far corners of the world by people we have never met, possibly never wish to meet, and with information we may never wish to hear less still to evaluate. All of it is astonishingly varied. All too often it is utterly trivial. All around us telephones ring, portable radios blare, television screens flash, police sirens hoot and ambulances or fire engines shriek. Consider this for a moment: who hasn't been driven almost to the verge of insanity by the accidental triggering of a burglar, fire, or car alarm? Admit it, who hasn't been progressively demoralised to find one's eyes and ears drawn (and this despite all efforts to resist) toward things that normally are none of our business or beneath our notice? Why should we always be magnetised by headlines on someone else's pathetically infantile tabloid? Why are we drawn to the whispered words of someone else's guarded conversation? Why do we listen to the vapid or incoherent thoughts of economists, politicians or political commentators, to the protruding tongues of unknown but exceedingly insolent children? Damn it! We should have ignored them all. Yet we always fail to do so! Remember, only a short time ago (that is slightly less than one hundred years), just a minute section of the world's population was permitted to engage instantly the attention of others. Now everyone is at it! A financial scandal thousands of miles away, in a place nobody can pronounce, concerning a company nobody should have invested in, involving directors nobody should have trusted, causes an instant flutter on stock markets the world over. It drains the blood from the faces of foolish investors and causes a rush to countless toilets. But there can be more tragic results of such instant and invasive info flow. Some poor souls leave their high-rise office blocks or their high-rise homes by the window, scorning the admittedly slower, but safer (if downmarket) exit by lift or stairs. Alternatively, we find the odd souls, in the privacy of their homes, grabbing a firearm (bought illegally from criminals as protection from criminals) then, realising that the target aimed for is several thousand miles away and beyond possible range, turning it in a fit of pique and frustration on themselves. Once again though, these are very minor incidents in the league table of world events. There are far more serious ones. All of them lie beyond the borders of permissible black humour or ironic comment. And they emphasise the incredible havoc or sheer evil that results from badly filtered, badly evaluated and over-hasty reactions to garbled or unsubstantiated reports. Some of this, after all, is pure propaganda with deliberate incitement to make thinkable the unthinkable.

Ghastly examples lie before us. Who can deny that the recent Hutu–Tutsi massacres in Rwanda were touched off by bogus and insidious info flows coming by radio broadcasts from Hutu extremists? Similarly, think of the civil war in Somalia, the insurgency in Mobutu-land, otherwise known as Zaire. Who can deny that the recent fighting in Georgia, Kazakhstan, Uzbekistan, Azerbaijan, Afghanistan – one can go on and on – was the result of instant reaction to a whole litany of lies and bogus claims of atrocities by the 'other' side? Touring loudspeaker vans, radio or television broadcasts were used to fan people's emotions into flame. Those who listened to such info flow were no longer relying on their own personal knowledge of events. Nor did they make a critical analysis which might have countered what they had taken on board. No gross provocation had stimulated their senses – provocation, that is, witnessed by their own eyes or heard with their own ears. They accepted the stream of information brought to them by suppressing logic and reason. The final call to slaughter human beings of differing ethnic or religious group was obeyed by those who listened. They then killed these 'other' human beings despite these wretched people being their neighbours, let alone never having caused them either mental or physical hurt.

Today, those of us who happen to live in what we assume to be democratic and highly sophisticated countries, and who pride ourselves on having a free press, free radio and television stations – more importantly still who believe we have the ability to think and act independently – tend to think nothing similar can happen on our own soil. Yet it is becoming increasingly apparent that fewer and fewer people are using the facility for independent thought. We too are under constant bombardment – if not from blatant lies, then from the utterly trivial! And under this bombardment we find it increasingly difficult to separate out grains of information that are of true worth. They are always submerged and so difficult to capture in our filter systems. Even when we do succeed, and subsequently come to examine and evaluate them, we seldom have the time and opportunity in our hectic lives to stop and think about the implications raised... at least in any kind of depth!

At this point what can we say of the Internet? I see only a greatly magnified threat of being totally swamped by its info flow, moreover swamped mostly by trivia. Perhaps of greater significance still, people tend after all to seek what they *prefer* to hear. At the same time they use their filtering systems to ignore what is unpleasant or downright unacceptable!

Now defendants might retaliate by pointing out nobody is forced to buy all the necessary equipment for access to the Internet, or for that matter to surf constantly through what is available. If people do so, it is because they wish to. They are not *forced*. But I would argue that the compulsion comes from the large corporations who have sunk billions of dollars into the manufacture of such equipment. From every newspaper, billboard and television screen, the message is shrieked at you: you are but a crapulous twit if you fail to become a surfer. And their voices have been so powerful that politicians now insist that all our children become computer-literate and enthusiastic surfers at the earliest possible age!

It is all the more tragic a situation in that only recently have we more or less freed our info flows from the limitations, bottlenecks or deliberate checks of the past. In previous centuries a free info flow was the preserve of those who ruled over us and of the aristocracy generally. Only very recently have we escaped from this bondage of ignorance. And because new forms of ignorance coupled with the deliberate mishandling of data flow now constitute a prime source of human conflict, it is this aspect that must now be looked at in greater detail.

*

Contemporary ignorance versus the mishandling of information flow

Which is least harmful? It is almost impossible to say. Anyway, for that matter, how is it possible to remain ignorant in this information-swamped modern world? Yet one is forced to ask: but ignorant of what? Many people pride themselves on their knowledge of contemporary affairs, yet in truth most of it is entirely superficial. My critics will at once jump on me and ask in turn how can I have the audacity to make such a statement? Surely it betrays excessive and immodest confidence in my own judgement? Well, I base such a statement on the level of conflict that the world continues to see – this despite the lessons that should have been learned from two world wars earlier this century. Nor should we forget the marginally less horrific wars that have occurred since – in Korea, Vietnam, Cambodia, Afghanistan, Iranian-Iraq – need I spell out each and every example? In this way large sections of the world's present population have proven that they are either ignorant of some fundamental truths or that they are easy victims of the mishandling of data flow. In this I include the failure to detect instantly what is often the quite crude info flow of raw propaganda entering their consciousness, alternatively the way in which subsequent filtering and evaluation still fails to reject patent lies.

To understand how this situation has come about it is necessary to make a long detour and begin once again with our primitive ancestors.

*

Now, we have already established that the human animal living more than half a million years ago managed to build up a unique data bank of personal knowledge. Certainly this was narrowly specialised on the plant and animal life around them, but it was nevertheless quite spectacular. How can I claim this? Well, if they had failed to do so, then, quite simply, we, their descendants, would not be alive today. After all, our ancestors were such puny creatures. That is not to lose sight of the fact that their survival rate and lifespan was low. At the same time one should not forget that only those individuals who remained hungry for even more information and on a wider basis would have survived.

Ironically, during the dawn of what is called the 'civilising process' (which happened roughly one hundred thousand years ago), this hunger was never appeased – indeed it was slowly and deliberately suppressed. It happened so gradually that few realised what had been lost. You see, as humanity organised itself into tribal or racial units and these subsequently grew both in the size and complexity of their social structures, so too they became controlled with brutal efficiency by self-styled kings or priests. Again this is not to remain blind to what was achieved despite such control.

Some incredibly long-lasting and sophisticated monolithic structures emerged, of which perhaps the most celebrated were that of Ancient Egypt, Ancient China and that of the Indus Valley. However a high price had to be paid in what we now call 'human rights and freedoms'. The greater bulk of the population became entirely subservient to a tiny minority.

How did this elite achieve this, and over such an enormously extended period? Only by careful control and manipulation of the info flow. For those who ruled by autocratic edict rather than by democratic persuasion, the possibility that underlings might use independent thought based on a growing body of knowledge was always a dangerous threat. Therefore true knowledge was denied and the masses fobbed off with either a flood of trivia or outright lies. What was deemed 'improper' access to, or indeed amateurish attempts to form, independent forms of knowledge was made a treasonable offence. In particular, all early discoveries in technology or in the primitive sciences of the day were immediately declared the preserve of the monarch and ruling classes. As for new technology or scientific observation coming from outside the boundaries of the state, these too were appropriated then jealously guarded and withheld from the masses for as long as was humanly possible. It was this system that gave pharaohs, kings, high priests, courtiers and top officials their actual power. The masses were held in deliberate ignorance of anything truly useful or fundamental. It was this that boosted the ruling classes' otherwise mythical claim to be superior to the common people – the 'blue blood' fable that, astonishingly, lasted almost unchallenged to the nineteenth century! And they were able to organise the accretion of data in a fully systematic way. They were, after all, relieved of the daily necessity to toil away in the fields, in the stone quarries or in the early primitive mines. They had sufficient leisure to gather the information flow, the leisure to process it carefully and then finally all the time in the world to make use of it to their own personal advantage.

Somewhere around 7000 BC, a way of counting objects by representing them with symbols inscribed on clay was invented. Once numeracy was reasonably advanced, a similar technique of using symbols to represent basic tokens of everyday life, called 'pictographs' was developed. Later, out of this the more sophisticated and flexible phonetic word symbols finally appeared. In short, writing had arrived! At this point there can be little doubt that an incalculable leap forward in info flow had been achieved. And here we must ask the obvious question: did the early pharaohs and Chinese emperors have the foresight to pass on such a tremendous development to the remainder of their subjects and thus to the benefit of all? The answer, of course, is 'like hell they did!' It was too precious a thing to be distributed, other than to members of the upper pyramid of society. The masses were left to communicate by speech alone. Certainly speech alone was a facility that could exchange information; however, it was prone to accumulate error when passed from mouth to mouth. Alternatively, when it was stored for a considerable time it could fall victim to fallible memories. Writing not only provided a secret method of communication between those practised in the art, but it was also proof against error – unless, that is, it was endlessly copied by scribes so that inevitable mistakes gradually corrupted the original.

Nevertheless, the enormous step forward achieved by writing – even when in the hands of a minority – proved a decisive leap forward in the separation of man from the remainder of the animal kingdom. Indeed this new form of communication seemed (and still seems to some) to lift mankind out of the animal realm completely, to lift us onto an entirely new plane. What is forgotten, of course, is the intrinsic quality and the ultimate truth of what is written! If it transmits mere trivia or downright lies, then it is immediately devalued. It becomes of no great worth. In fact, it will certainly be inferior to the kind of warning message transmitted by a baboon to its comrades on seeing the approach of a leopard, or the mystical communication by whales over miles of ocean to one another.

So, as we have now anticipated, not all was to be of gain in the field of human info flow. Even some of the earliest examples of pictographs from China, or the Egyptian hieroglyphs, or the later Babylonian and Assyrian cuneiform writing, display crude propaganda and disinformation. Overall, it might simply be called the deliberate propagation of shameless lies.

Most of these relate to the claims of emperors, pharaohs and kings to semi-divine status. And this was often supplemented by greatly exaggerated accounts of their victories over enemies. These were repeated for the benefit of the masses in the only form they could understand – that is graphic descriptions taking the form of sculptured friezes on the walls of palaces, temples and public buildings. Everywhere the divine majesty of the ruler was emphasised. Only occasionally does one find word pictures of humble day-to-day living, as 'enjoyed' by the masses. Thus only here do we have any reliable, unbiased reportage of reality.

This 'precious' attitude to literacy remained more or less unchanged throughout the entire period of the early Chinese, Egyptian, Indus and Sumerian civilisations.

Things never remain in a state of total suspension, however.

The first really notable easing of control came during the rise of several individual Grecian states into the realms of influence and power. Possibly because they were individual and not united into one monolithic state, each localised ruler and his entourage were unable to visualise themselves as 'blue-blooded'. Certainly the concept of semi-divine status for a single family at the head of the social pyramid never took firm hold. Admittedly though, at times certain individuals came very near to this most extreme form of self-delusion. Perhaps the fact that they were more closely linked with their people allowed them to see the advantages of permitting the lower strata access to literacy and even to education generally. Slowly the ability to read and write filtered down to a much wider group of citizens. More surprisingly still, independent thought was encouraged purely for 'intellectual excitement'. Later, the more enlightened of the Grecian states actually set up centres of learning. These were known as academies and vied with each other over the calibre of the masters who taught there. In these not only were speculative questions asked as to the nature of existence, but also answers were attempted. These were then carefully written down and subsequently argued over. And this system brought an astonishing surge in Grecian intellectual achievement. Indeed the 'wonder that was Greece' has remained a source of astonishment and admiration throughout the world ever since.

Yet it would be misleading to suppose that education was limited solely to esoteric enquiry and remained locked in endless philosophical dialogue. More down-to-earth data was gathered on a variety of subjects – especially on technological development generally. Eventually, knowledge on any subject thought to be of true worth was systematically entered into scrolls and carefully stored in libraries.

The collapse of the Grecian civilisation was occasioned by bitter internal rivalries between one city state and another. Their failure to compromise and act as a unified whole (especially after the death of Alexander) inevitably allowed the rise of Rome.

Now you may think I am artificially introducing controversy at this point by stating that the Romans were, in comparison to the Greeks, an uneducated, crude and even barbarous race. But further pages will, I think, tend to prove it. Their one advantage (if it be one) was that they were prepared to subject any individuality they might have had to the demands made by the central authority – whoever that might have proved to be. This gave them the necessary social cohesion essential to the development of military prowess. It also gave them the will to subjugate others. In the early days of empire building their records in the field of education and the achievement of a broadly based literacy were woefully deficient in every way. The elite of Roman society displayed the same attitude of maintaining a precious advantage over the masses as had all the other early empire builders. When the Romans overwhelmed the still-squabbling Grecian states, what they found in the Greek homeland were high standards of excellence in almost all aspects of life. Astonishingly, these were far in advance of their own. It is said that imitation is the most sincere form of flattery, and nowhere is this more fully observed than when the

Romans absorbed Greece into their empire. However, while Roman aristocracy entertained the greatest admiration for Grecian culture and learning generally, they were less inclined to find both stimulation and true delight in intellectual exploration for its own sake. As for universal education, they saw great dangers in allowing the masses such a priceless asset. Instinctively they felt that their hold over the ordinary Roman citizen would be weakened by such a gift. Thus, in the earlier years of Roman ascendancy, academies in the Grecian style were notable by their absence rather than their presence. The filtering down of knowledge to the lower levels of society was either delayed or fully blocked at every stage. Only the top officials, upper echelons of the army and the gradually forming bureaucracy received a proper education. It remained thus for several centuries. Only when Rome became the undisputed master of huge tracts of territory, and acquired much of its material wealth by pillage, not to speak of the labour of countless numbers of slaves, did the insidious blockage of info flow see change. There were three reasons: firstly, what had begun as a small and quite intimate bureaucracy had to be expanded by sheer necessity to control so large an empire – there was no other way; secondly, the aristocracy, now rapidly becoming degenerate and wholly dedicated to an endless round of pleasure, no longer taught their own children. Formerly they had jealously guarded the power given by literacy, numeracy and knowledge generally; typically they had kept it wholly in their own hands. But now slaves, if they were fully trustworthy – especially if they were of Greek origin and therefore already cultured and walking data banks in their own right – were given the boring task of teaching their children. Gradually, by this process, control over info flow began to slip through their fingers. But thirdly, the demands of a growing use of new technology in a wide variety of fields brought with it the need for higher levels of literacy and numeracy. Schools and libraries were finally set up in all the larger towns, and a wider range of citizens allowed access. Even so, one suspects that while this extended down to the middle classes, it still failed to reach the greater bulk of citizens in the lowest. For example, at a time when the empire had reached its zenith in territorial conquest, the lawyer Pliny (the Younger) found that children in his native town of Como had to journey to Milan for their education. His further investigation revealed that the townspeople had failed to organise the necessary funds to pay for a teacher and for the maintenance of a suitable building. Ever faithful to his belief in the power of knowledge to triumph over every adversity, he donated money out of his own pocket to provide the very basic first step – a library. Having set this up, he then attempted to energise his townsfolk's civil pride, or perhaps shame them for the lack of it, by further donating a third of the money to pay a teacher and keep the building in good repair. With typical Roman contempt for mere sentiment and an eye firmly fixed on practicality, he did so on the firm promise that his townsfolk would provide the remainder. Unfortunately, we are not told what proportion of the town's children benefited from this gesture. But at the very least it does suggest that education even in this era was by no means fully organised; thus by this token it was hardly a universal right available to all Roman citizens. Remember too that this was a period that saw the peak of Roman empire building!

Ironically, though, as the Romans were later slowly forced to relinquish some of the outer regions of their now over-extended empire, another factor began to exert influence in the field of education. It came in a most unusual form – it came as a new religion!

Christianity was initially tolerated (more or less) by some of the earlier emperors. Later, when it was found to be the source of a very different kind of knowledge and thereby a significant threat to the state, it was savagely persecuted. Significantly, this new religion had found much of its strength from 'the written word'. And if individual Christians suffered the supreme penalty for holding on to their faith, the precious scrolls carefully hidden away and clearly detailing that faith usually managed to survive. In this manner the new faith saw an ebb and flow, saw persecution and periods of bare tolerance. And it did so for several centuries.

All this changed in AD 313 with Constantine's seizure of supreme power. With his official sanction, the Christian Church crawled out of obscurity and began to organise its own information flow. More significantly still, it slowly took on its own educative role. It too gradually became a repository of knowledge over wider fields than the purely religious one. Nevertheless, both Constantine and a succession of later emperors retained the power to control certain sections of info flow if they happened to have political or military significance. Thus the Christian Church was by no means able to propagate accurate and truthful information in every field. Moreover, it became itself increasingly guilty of manipulating info flows for its own advantage. Some of the early bishops proved equally adept at subtle propaganda as the current emperor and his immediate aides. And the need for propaganda and disinformation proved ever more necessary as bad news began to pour in from virtually all corners of the empire. Uprisings by subjugated peoples, attempted palace revolutions or coups, defections by well known and hitherto applauded commanders in the field, unexpected military defeats, all had to be explained away to the plebeian masses. Over their previous five-hundred-year history of empire- building the periodic changes of fortune had produced setbacks, but these had always been temporary. Sooner or later there would be triumphs to celebrate. But now, as they say, 'times were a'changing'. News from almost anywhere was bad and remained that way. The plebeian masses had to be kept in ignorance for as long as possible. If they got wind of anything, then they had to be fed with disinformation. When truly dangerous rumours persisted – and persisted despite the best efforts to disprove them – the now well-established tradition of throwing elaborate and costly gladiatorial displays or chariot races was used as a distraction. This, combined with the proclamation of pubic holidays, usually helped to calm fears. But now with endless internal uprisings and so-called 'barbarians' keeping up their attacks on the periphery, moreover often breaking through to make brief incursions into the heart of the empire, public holidays had to be proclaimed in ever greater numbers. Incredibly, as the entire edifice began to crumble, holidays at last reached the absurd number of half the days of the year. At the same time, in the Colosseum and Circus Maximus in Rome (not forgetting other enormous theatres built by governors in the provinces), ever more elaborate spectacles were staged. All had one object in mind: to divert attention from the truth and, if possible, propagate or enhance lies. For such spectacles the finest horses and chariots were assembled and the most exotic of wild animals imported from every corner of the then-known world. The latter were subsequently staged fighting one another or, alternatively, against human gladiators. Most spectacular of all, they were used to tear apart unarmed and defenceless 'barbarian' prisoners of war, common criminals or subversive enemies of the state. This was a fate once reserved for Christians. Now, in what had become virtually a Christian state, such 'entertainment' continued, although it is only fair to say that it was opposed by the Church.

As the bid to check the most dangerous of info flows became more and more desperate, unexpected problems arose. Firstly, the number of wild animals rounded up over the years had reached such proportions as to produce shortages. Secondly, with such a large number of immigrants and slaves still being introduced into the population the imbalance was such as to endanger the cohesion of the already-weakened state. These people owed no allegiance to Rome. Indeed, most had every desire to witness its fall. Thus these festivals aimed at pampering the depraved tastes of Roman citizens became increasingly beside the point. As the situation worsened, the slaves, the dispossessed and the unemployed migrants now began to outnumber what one might call 'true' or basically loyal citizens. Cohesion was hanging by a thread. Memories of the revolt of Spartacus, the Thracian gladiator who, with a band of his comrades backed by a large number of slaves, had actually defeated several Roman armies sent against them, could never be erased from people's minds. It had scared the togas off the entire body of the aristocracy. True, the revolt was finally crushed. But the frightfulness of the revenge subsequently taken by the 'civilised' Romans put later generations of both master and slave in perpetual fear and distrust of each other. Another spontaneous uprising was always a possibility. Could something be done to avoid it? Not really. The Romans, above all, were traditionalists, and to an extent they were also fatalists. They were locked into the system they had made for themselves and nobody bothered to look for a key. Thus the public spectacles continued – although they were slowly diminishing in 'quality' and the range of entertainment.

In these desperate efforts to maintain some kind of cohesion, the most fundamental of truths that lay hidden in the vast flow of information reaching the Roman bureaucracy was constantly overlooked. That truth? Something so simple and so gradual as to escape notice – the slow depletion of basic resources.

Now much nonsense has been written concerning the fall of the Roman Empire. Every half-plausible reason under the sun has been advanced. They range from moral decline (a joke as they had no discernible height to fall from in the first instance!), internal bickering (a constant state of affairs anyway), treachery, plagues, rife homosexuality, inadequate control by the bureaucracy – the list is long, tiresome and completely wide of the mark. The truth of the matter revolves around an explosive population growth coupled with the inability of the technology of the day to cope with such rapidly multiplying numbers! The problem was compounded by the continued importation of slaves (a habit impossible to conquer), by the employment of mercenaries and an influx of immigrants from all the quarters of the Empire. The latter were attracted by stories of unparalleled wealth and standards of living. All this resulted in an imbalance of citizens fully loyal to the state. And when basic food and fuel supplies became noticeably sparse, or worse when the occasional drought compounded water shortages, a series of crises arose. Some were temporarily surmountable; for example water supplies in some areas were initially secured by astonishing feats of engineering. The building of enormous aqueducts, however, only staved off the basic problems of supplying water, not food and fuel. The fundamental fact of the matter was that not only the capital itself, but also the towns and cities throughout the Empire had attracted people in far greater numbers than the surrounding countryside and the technology of the day could support. The capital alone had a population of over a million, unparalleled in such an era. To supply the necessary food, fuel, water, shelter, clothing and all that was considered vital aids to civilised living, this city, together with all the other centres of population throughout the Empire had to depend on supplies brought in laboriously by ox-cart or increasingly, as seafaring skills improved, by boat. Transportation difficulties were made all the more formidable as the population continued to grow. Shortages demanded that supplies were now sought further and further afield. With each succeeding century the distances became greater. Finally, a vast swathe of territory was embraced. This ran right round the northern shores of the Mediterranean, beginning in Spain and moving through southern France into Italy itself, then on into Greece, continuing into what is now Turkey and finally curving south-east through what is now Lebanon. Here empire building directed itself due south. A swathe curved into Palestine, curving again through Egypt and finally the whole of what was at that time the fertile shores of North Africa right back to Morocco! All of this territory was raped, century after century, merely to supply the Romans with the kind of luxurious living they felt they were entitled to.

Increasingly, to carry such resources it became necessary to build a huge mercantile fleet. For such a fleet, timber was vital. Beyond shipbuilding, timber was also required for the usual multifaceted construction purposes of public building and housing, not forgetting furniture and utensils. Above all it was the basic fuel for domestic heating, cooking and the ever-growing demands of metallurgy. Thus over the centuries many forests were decimated – the famous cedars of Lebanon among them. This in turn brought Nature's reprisal; an ecological disaster. With the exception of Egypt, which relied on water from the Nile, the destruction of trees gradually brought changes to the climate of the rich grain-growing areas. With desiccation came soil erosion. The ready supply of grain slowly dwindled, while the North African deserts expanded ever closer to the coast. Both food, and fuel supplies, not forgetting the basic resource for shipbuilding, were all hit at one and the same time. The centuries of rape had at last brought their reward. And this was precisely at the time when population levels were exerting the most pressure.

The western section of the Roman Empire, enfeebled more quickly by this strangulation than by the increasing attacks from tribes to the north of the Danube, eventually disintegrated; the eastern portion, however, managed to battle on. Fundamentally, those in control of the greatly enlarged bureaucracy and those at the heart of government in the capital Rome hardly knew what their right hands or their left hands were doing. They had failed to process the vast array of information flow correctly; they had blinded themselves with a mass of trivia, thus submerging the grim truth under the relentless avalanche of data. They were, after all, heirs to centuries of the myth of their own invincibility. Problems had always had the habit of sorting themselves out in the end. The trouble was that this time the relentless pressure of population on one side and the relentless pressure of Nature's revenge on the other could not be resolved by muddling through. Thus the western sector of the Empire disintegrated; nevertheless, as has already been observed, the eastern section tottered on, incredibly enough, for another thousand years. It did so more by luck than by judgement. Its quite unearned good fortune consisted of discovering some untapped resources near at hand. Probing east and further north these eastern Romans began to realise the vastness of the resources in what we now call southern Russia. Very conveniently also, these sources could be reached by very large and navigable rivers. Significantly too, they began to rely more on trade rather than naked conquest!

Even so, the enfeeblement of this once all-powerful and rapacious empire, combined with the legacy of bitterness among the people they had ravaged, gave opportunities to newly emerging powers to occupy centre stage. They came from several directions and at about the same time, which only serves to make the picture a complex one. They came from north-eastern Europe and the Russian steppes, they came from the east in what is now called Mongolia, and they came from the south-east in what is now called Arabia. Arguably, of all three invasions or partial invasions of Western Europe, it is the last that had the more enduring and profound effect on the thousand years that followed. And it was fired and fortified by a vibrant new religion – that of Islam.

Fanning out from Arabia, and gaining more and more adherents to the faith, its followers first conquered Persia to the east, and Syria and Mesopotamia to the north. Then, turning south-westward, they overran Egypt, and what is now Libya, Algeria and Morocco. Crossing the Strait of Gibraltar they then made incursions into much of Spain. Early martial triumphs were later graced with considerable learning. In effect Islam now carried the torch of knowledge. It salvaged much of what had become the widely dispersed and physically fragile remainder of Grecian literary, scientific and philosophical output, then added extensive contributions of its own. It did so mainly in mathematics, medicine and metaphysics.

Meantime, in the western half of the once-mighty Roman Empire, the Christian Church had survived – if by a whisker – the turmoil of successive invasions. In turn Huns, Vandals, Visigoths and Ostrogoths flooded down into what was the former province of Gaul, parts of the Balkans and then the greater length of Italy itself. Incidentally, an offshore island, also once a Roman province and now called Britain, was invaded by Germanic peoples: Jutes, Angles and Saxons. Unhappily, generations of today's children in Britain, France and Italy, on being shown the impressive structures the Romans left behind them – as likely as not in either total or partial ruin – have been taught to believe that such wilful destruction came at the hands of the 'barbarians' who followed. This is a travesty of the truth. The greater part of the destruction came centuries later at the hands of those looking for easily acquired stone from which to build new structures of their own. Bypassing the difficult and time-consuming work of quarrying for stone was, for later generations, a prime consideration. It was not the work of the 'Vandals'.

Turning a blind eye to this and to many other awkward facts that failed to fit into their preconceived ideas, historians down through the ages have persisted in labelling the series of invaders as 'barbarian' and the Romans as 'civilised'. It is a gross perversion of the truth. And as one reads their distorted version of events, one becomes aware of not just a deliberate misreading of the evidence, but a strangely bizarre interpretation of the word 'civilised'. You see, if to be civilised involves acting as the Romans did for more than a thousand years, then I, for one, would be proud to be labelled barbarian. Nothing can or should obscure the fact that the Romans swept round Western Europe and eastward round the shores of the Mediterranean, butchering much of the population and making slaves of those they kindly allowed to survive. Any attempts at rebellion were put down with ruthlessness and appalling cruelty. Public crucifixion was just one method they adopted for prolonging death, thereby suitably cowing the spirit of those who might dare to rise up against them. The Romans perfected (bringing them virtually to an art form) a variety of executions, including being torn to pieces by wild animals. These 'uplifting spectacles' relatives were forced to watch. They were used both in the provinces to serve as a warning, and, as already touched on, in Rome itself as entertainment during public holidays in the huge amphitheatres such as the Colosseum. For those who may have skimmed through my earlier references to Roman tastes in this respect, it becomes a duty to repeat that victorious Roman generals set up a tradition whereby prisoners taken in battle were brought back in triumph to the Colosseum with only one object in mind – specifically to end their lives in front of huge and enthusiastic audiences in the most sadistic of ways. And this was to gratify Romans in their most depraved of tastes. True, at odd times, and as a magnanimous gesture, a small proportion of prisoners were allowed to fight for their lives. They were actually given a weapon and were permitted to use it in desperate defence against wild animals or trained gladiators. But very few survived.

If we turn our attention away from traditional Roman sport and behaviour at such public spectacles and begin to look at personal and private family life, there is hardly much improvement here either. And if the lives of the lower plebeian classes were not well documented and are thus open to a degree of conjecture, then at least those of the upper classes received a good deal of attention from what might be called the 'gossip column' writers of the day. Perhaps though, it is misleading to use the term 'gossip column' as it implies wide publication of deliberately chosen salacious material among Roman citizens generally. What is referred to here is rather different; these are often notes written to friends or relatives, or indeed jottings in diaries; they were not intended for widespread publication. Admittedly here, as in all such reports, one must allow for a degree of exaggeration or pure spite to make the stories more racy and dramatic; but many of the events are broadly confirmed by a number of different hands – all independently of each other.

Based on these one can only say that the upper crust of Roman society had the morals and appetites of alley cats. There is ample evidence too of an astonishing lack of family loyalty. Well-documented reports from different sources tell of all kinds of treachery in which husbands did away with wives, wives poisoned husbands, fathers killed sons or daughters, siblings killed siblings and adult children did away with luckless parents. To repeat, plebeian ranks of society are not so closely documented, but, given the spirit of Roman society in general, such callousness and lack of sensitivity seems widespread. Thus one can hardly hope for much better among the lower classes. All in all, bar a few individuals, Roman society was rotten to the core. Never forget that as a monument to that rottenness, the vast Colosseum in Rome, together with numerous other slightly smaller ones in the provinces, were built for *one* purpose only: this was to maximise the exhibition of unspeakable depravity. Here in these 'amusement parks' vast audiences (the Colosseum could contain 45,000 spectators alone) watched people or animals being torn apart, and did so on public holidays which finally approached half the days of the year! Yet unfortunately today this is glossed over. Emphasis is now given to Roman triumphs of engineering and architectural 'extravaganza' rather than their triumphs of frightfulness.

Yet given all this and more, historians still persist in talking of the Roman 'civilisation'; worse, in the same breath they apply 'barbarian' to the various peoples who had more than a score or two to settle against this rapacious empire. In doing so they only highlight something they are normally at pains to hide – the occupational hazards of academics engaged in what is so inaccurately called 'historical research'. In this pursuit almost all have developed an affliction akin to tunnel vision. And almost all display at least one or two highly characteristic patterns of the syndrome one might call 'political synizesis'![1] This brought on by persistent attempts to draw out basic information from what are, after all is said and done, wholly unverifiable sources. Essentially, the bulk of our twentieth-century professional historians base most of their views and attitudes solely on the works of those in exactly the same profession – Roman historians. And these are far

---

[1] Synizesis: closure of the pupil of the eye.

less reliable than the amateur 'gossip columnists'. The latter, after all, were reporting contemporary events to a private or select audience; therefore, there was a limit to what could be distorted, deliberately falsified or taken from the realms of pure fantasy. The early historians on the other hand were less constrained. It was almost a duty to glorify Roman achievements and be reticent about failures. In many ways their personal success or failure depended on it. Fellow citizens virtually demanded distortions, falsifications and flights of fancy. Thus at best in these documents we find pomposity and unashamed hyperbole; at worst, fantasy. Rome is seen as the centre of creation. Indeed many of these writers exhibit all the sensitivity and self-consciousness of wild boar luxuriating in a mudbath.

It is therefore astonishing that such a high proportion of what is still called 'historical research' and of subsequent judgement of Roman achievements are derived from such sources. Fortunately, though, these bookworm historians have recently been forced onto the defensive. They have been challenged by rather more careful research made by archaeologists in the field. The latter actually go about in overalls and wellingtons and delve into such things as middens and drains! The academics have been challenged too from an entirely new source – from scientists in the recently established field of ecology. With the help of ever more sophisticated methodology and instruments to match, these have achieved a more balanced picture. And in proving the extent to which Roman rapacity brought on an ecological blight in much of North Africa, and in the eastern Mediterranean, such as Palestine and Lebanon, our picture of Roman 'achievement' has been, or should have been, radically altered.

The die-hards so comfortably established in academia, however, reject all those sections of info flow that fail to be compatible with their set attitudes and ideas. It will probably take some time and considerable effort before they may be persuaded to alter them.

In the meantime, even those who are not professional historians still subscribe to the myth of the 'greatness that was Rome'. They do so on other grounds and in other fields. And they will no doubt protest. They will insist that I have failed to consider many other factors that should enter the equation. There are other achievements, surely, they say with confidence. In arriving at an estimate of Rome's civilising influence aren't there the arts and the sciences to take into account – architecture, sculpture, literature, poetry, engineering, philosophy and natural philosophy (or science)? Very well. Readily admitting this, I still insist that even when examining and evaluating these factors, then placing them carefully onto the balance sheet, they still fail to alter my final estimate in any significant way. Roman indebtedness to the Greeks is everywhere visible.

Certainly I would be less than fair if I sought to deny that there are some isolated figures of considerable stature in the arts, plus a handful of philosophers and 'natural' philosophers, or scientists. Among these Lucretius and Boethius should have honourable mention. But nowhere can one find parallels to the massive achievements of the Greeks – and in virtually every area of human activity. This is particularly noticeable in the sciences: among Romans, with the exception of Pliny, we find a veritable intellectual desert. Here, if any of his countrymen present themselves for notice at all, then they turn out to be pygmies. You can mouth the name Celsus and others if you wish; you will still fail to change my opinion.

Looking at Roman achievement in its broadest sense, the only description one can honestly apply is 'derivative'.

As for the word 'civilised', unless the word has hitherto unrevealed elasticity, which I for one would deplore, then all attempts by others to apply it fill me with a mixture of astonishment, anger and a good deal of contempt. For me, the recent work done by archaeologists and ecologists in North Africa alone should be enough to convince anyone of the essential barbarism of the Romans. It fully demonstrates the extent to which the Romans, with their twisted and exploitative outlook on life, were prepared to go. Here, near the ruins of what were once well-populated towns and cities – now, significantly enough, covered by a layer of sand – is all the evidence one needs. Here were once highly fertile areas, capable of indefinite production of food, fuel and all the other basics necessary for truly civilised living. Yet they were all sacrificed for short-term exploitation. The few inhabitants that the Romans refrained from butchering were forced to rape their own resources under merciless direction or as slaves. This was to maximise the flow of resources back into the Roman capital and all the other important centres of Empire. And it was done with unremitting brutality until there was nothing left to rob.

In contrast, how can we summarise the overall character and outlook of invading peoples such as the Huns, Vandals and the like, whose very names have now become terms of abuse? Conventional historians have done such a thorough job of demonising these people that we automatically picture them as mindlessly destructive, foul-mouthed, unwashed, ragged and smelly hordes, destroying every representation of culture and progress in sight. We see them in our mind's eye slashing at every poor Roman male in his spotlessly white toga and ravishing each and every Roman woman cowering defenceless in her home. Not content with this extremely exhausting and time-consuming work, these savages apparently went about despoiling and laying waste to every temple, public building, public baths (naturally!), monument, bridge and viaduct – and did so presumably with their bare hands! They were, after all, alleged to be ignorant of any kind of engineering skills and therefore must have lacked the suitable machinery to move huge blocks of stone! One can go on and on with this catalogue of a presumed orgy of destruction. Yet it is all wildly inaccurate. As already noted, recent archaeological research shows that most Roman monuments and buildings suffered mainly at the hands of the jobbing builders of later generations – and did so for many centuries afterward. These were 'cowboy builders' merely looking for readily available stone or roofing material to build modest farmhouses, byres and the odd pigsty or two. And if they came from a villa, public baths or even an emperor's palace, so much the better.

Only one piece of solid truth emerges out of the mass of mostly false information historians have burdened us with: the invaders were for the most part illiterate. And this one factor alone seems to justify the historian's contempt. To have left no documentation of this presumed orgy of killing, no 'holiday postcard' mentioning the architectural destruction, to have left no juicy titbits regarding their treatment of terrified womenfolk is an appalling state of affairs! It puts the invaders wholly beyond the pale! How can proper research be undertaken on these terms? True, there are some fragments of jottings from those Romans who escaped. And astonishingly there seems to be a fair number of them. There are also observations from those brave bishops of the Christian Church who defended their sacred buildings with incantations and little else. These, incredibly enough, not only managed to impress these 'savages' with their piety but are also alleged to have brought about some moderation of their behaviour. There are in fact quite a number of emotionally charged descriptions. Even so, the majority of historians complain that to retain their honour and credibility, they are duty-bound to examine the picture from different and sometimes opposing angles. They will give the odd sniff and admit that any document written by Romans during these turbulent times will almost certainly be a little over the top. At the same time they will lament that there is nothing or virtually nothing, from the other side. True enough, the odd pictograms have been discovered carved into the remnants of some Roman buildings, but these of course are regarded as acts of vandalism (with a small 'v') and can't be deciphered anyway. But essentially, because the bulk of the invaders were supposedly illiterate, then that alone was enough to damn them. That alone was enough to justify the word 'barbarian'.

Fortunately, recent research into the lives of Huns, Vandals and Ostrogoths and the like made by archaeologists and ecologists rather than historians, once again changes the picture. It causes us to revise our former attitudes – or should do if we are both open-minded and fair-minded. Careful excavation of sites in their homelands, which one can categorise roughly as a wide range of regions to the north and east of the Danube, shows that they had developed a culture and an outlook on life that can hardly merit our contempt. To begin with, ecologists have found that these people seemed to have had an instinctive grasp of basic ecological truths. Their outlook can be summed up as 'long-term sustainability'; this contrasts sharply with Roman short-term exploitation – clearly an attitude completely foreign to 'barbarian' nature. This may have been due to the animistic content of their religion; it may also have been derived from their intuitive conviction that all forms of life were interdependent. Certainly their farming methods aimed at stability and unbroken 'viability'. As for their social life and behaviour patterns, we have observations (ironically enough) actually made by Romans themselves: these show astonishment at and not a little envy of their sense of honour, intense family loyalty, overall restraint in sexual matters, let alone care for the sick and elderly. And all of this was topped by a certain ethical poise. True, as with any race or any group of people, there would of course have been exceptions to the general rule; but compared with the arrogance, vulgarity and coarseness that typified the true spirit of Rome, their conduct was infinitely preferable. And they were certainly just as intelligent. Which begs the question: why were they illiterate? As I see it, they had very different values and quite singular attitudes when deciding on priorities. To begin with they had enormous respect for individuality. Personal freedom was highly prized; even so, their tribal cohesion was achieved without any of the regimentation cheerfully accepted by the Romans. This is an astonishing factor seldom appreciated or even mentioned. But what has this to do with literacy, peevish voices might ask. Well, unfortunately, if you wish to gain proficiency in reading and writing, then the first essential is the creation of sets of rules. Overall it demands the subsequent conformity to set patterns. For example there must be widespread agreement as to what a noun, verb or adjective stands for, and then a set way in which it is spelled. Lacking this essential conformity, everything falls into chaos. Moreover, the process of learning must itself be organised and controlled on a fairly rigid basis – preferably while the individual is young and not hampered by his or her own preconceived ideas. But to these free-living and largely untamed individualists, all of this would have been intolerable. To their way of thinking there were far more pressing requirements and objectives, especially when you were young. Reaching true manhood or achieving the skills and poise of a true woman could hardly be equated with skills in reading and writing; these were visualised in far more adventurous or serious terms. Incidentally, this was one reason why the Romans triumphed for so long in the military field. They were prepared to ignore minor differences of opinion in the political field and would accept directives initially from the Emperor. Failing this they would accept detailed orders from his generals and the chain of command, thus carefully carrying out the agreed battle plan without hesitation or confusion. By contrast their enemies were undisciplined and uncoordinated. Their headstrong behaviour found them all too liable to fall into disarray even in the opening stages of a battle! In like manner they were unable to organise their information flow in any fully structured way. Not that that was wholly to their disadvantage, of course. We have already noted that the Romans were perhaps the first highly organised society in early history to invert their info flow neatly from something that had begun as a great asset into something that became a millstone around their necks. Their bureaucracy became so overburdened with trivia that it obscured the deeper picture. The 'barbarians' were at least in no such danger.

To be entirely fair, though, the inability to read or write does have its disadvantages. Again, as already noted, it hampers the true accuracy of stored data. The knowledge that each individual builds up over a lifetime, when preserved solely within the oral tradition of the tribe, tends, on the death of that person, to become vague, and thus open to misinterpretation. Thereafter comes loss of detail and increasing error. If, in the twentieth century we are now fully aware that the effort to achieve and maintain the proper comprehension of printed text can be bad enough, then surely the proper understanding of info flow handed down orally is open to far greater confusion and loss.

But here it becomes necessary to explode yet another myth. It is not factually true to say that the complex mixture of tribes living north of the Danube were wholly illiterate. Many had begun to invent their own primitive scripts and symbols. Eventually, so-called 'Runic' alphabets appeared, but arrived too late to compete with Latin in any serious way. Why? To begin with, conformity to a basic structure failed to exist. The Norse version had but sixteen characters; the Anglo-Saxon was more flexible with forty; the Germanic or Teutonic, influenced partly by contact with the

Romans, had twenty-four characters. Runic inscriptions nevertheless lingered on, this despite the efforts of Christian missionaries using Latin, and did so well into the fourteenth century. What *is* true then is that the 'barbarians' never adopted a common alphabet, or a common language. Nor did they reach the kind of linguistic sophistication enjoyed by the Romans until well after the western sector of their empire ceased to exist. Certainly they had the ability to scratch simple messages on anything hard such as stone or wood; oddly, though, despite being skilled potters, they refrained from incising messages on clay which could then have been subsequently fired. Why? I am convinced the reason is they simply lacked sufficient incentive. Having so many different languages, or dialects of a language, moreover labouring away in isolation from each other, it was obvious that very little of true worth could have been achieved. And without a basic alphabet, recognised script or lingua franca, all would anyway have dissolved into chaos. To have pooled their efforts would after all have seemed a violation of their freedom! It was beneath contempt to restrict personal choice; it would have been a loss of natural dignity to codify your thoughts in this rigidly systematic way. They could not accept the implied regimentation. You surrender too much when you agree to a common language, coupled as it inevitably is with a common alphabet and a universally recognised style of writing. Shades of our modern world! Today English (or Coca-Cola Americanese!) has virtually become the lingua franca of the twentieth century, but not without protest and much bad feeling amongst those who wish to preserve their own tongue and literary traditions, the French, Germans and Scandinavians in particular.

However, here I am not so blind and so biased regarding all aspects of the Roman world as to fail to recognise any of its permanent achievements. One of the few benefits Western Europe inherited from Roman sources was the beautifully proportioned and unequalled clarity of Roman lettering. In the same way too, came the later adoption of Latin as the lingua franca. Thus when the various invaders – this a century or so after the western Empire collapsed – finally submitted to the indignity of recognising just one written script, it subsequently allowed all

Europe, now split into a multiplicity of different kingdoms, to communicate one with another with relative ease.

In this of course the Christian Church played a vital role. Indeed one suspects that the gradual conversion of the 'heathen' (a contemptuous term in itself) to Christianity once again had much to do with the 'written word', if in rather a different sense. The presence of missionary priests within the close inner circle of heathen kings and their courts owed perhaps more to the service they provided – in essence their willingness to perform clerical duties, than the other and far more sacred duty of spreading the 'word' and teachings of Christ!

To reinforce an earlier observation: this does not reflect on the heathen's intelligence or supposed lack of it. Their priorities were different. It was exactly the same with their distant 'barbarian' relatives in the previous century. Before they invaded Italy and subsequently settled there, becoming in the process more or less Romanised, they were far too busy and preoccupied with other things. All were untamed individualists who simply could not find the time and patience to sit down and apply themselves to what seemed essentially an unmanly occupation. Thus even when, as the centuries rolled by, these petty kingdoms began the process of coalescing into larger units, and the Christian priests exchanged the role of mere 'clerks' for 'clerics' (the semantic derivation is identical), few of the new kings bothered to become fully literate. Right up to the ninth century AD one finds that the dynamic warrior known as Charlemagne, who had become sole ruler of what is now France, Germany and much of Italy, was reputed to be illiterate for at least the better part of his reign. He is said to have become only partially literate toward the end of his life. During all those early years of vigorous campaigning he obviously had little time to apply himself and become proficient. Once again, this in no way implies lack of intelligence. Nor does it suppose that his ability to deal with a variety of different info flows was in any way inadequate. It merely emphasises the advantages of becoming literate at an early age before other pressures associated with manhood crowd in.

At this point we reach what should have been a significant stage in the saga detailing the ebb and flow of human communicative skills. There was now a tremendous opportunity to release the entire flood tide of information without any restrictions or manipulation. There was also an even more important opportunity: for here we come to a critical moment in the structure of Western society. It was also a critical moment in which to deal with the most fundamental aspects of the human condition. You ask why?

Well, with the rule of Charlemagne we have an unprecedented rise in the prestige and influence of the Christian Church. While it is said that the secular entourage at court had better skills in reading and writing than their Emperor, the wily Charlemagne seems to have believed that they were not in the same league as the clerics. Possibly too he clung to the hope that those in holy orders would be by nature more discreet and less likely to use their new-found influence to narrow worldly advantage. At any event, these churchmen now found themselves employed at the highest level with affairs of state. And in commanding such influence came a unique opportunity. Yet tragically they failed to take it!

*

Perhaps it is in the nature of mankind always to be mired in squalid self-interest and the most unworthy of motives. The sickness of the spirit seems ever with us. Certainly this becomes evident within the Christian Church itself during the reign of Charlemagne.

With Western Europe now fully united, a unique possibility existed for a Church that had once been so powerless and subject to centuries of persecution, to use its new position in the most dynamic and effective of ways. It was, after all, virtually the sole repository of knowledge; it had also become the sole educator. In such a position the Church might have been able to influence and finally stabilise the entire pattern of human behaviour in that region. The teachings of Christ on which the Church was founded above all stressed the power of love and forgiveness; they also extolled the reign of peace. The Commandments were a blueprint for a life lived to the full and in serenity. Unhappily those clerics who now found themselves in such a unique position lacked sufficient moral stature; like many more of their calling, both before and since, they had feet of clay. Their vision for the future and their grasp of Christ's teachings were myopic and sadly restricted. The opportunity was lost before they even realised its full potential. Indeed the cruel irony of history at this point is that far from becoming 'the light' for the remainder of mankind, the Christian Church gradually slid into a veritable Dark Age of its own. And it has hardly recovered from this even to this day!

You find this too harsh a criticism? Or perhaps you suspect me of an ulterior motive? Do you suspect a vulgar attempt to employ sensationalism and controversy merely to spice up and suitably dramatise the content of future pages?

To parry such a charge it is now necessary to look at this matter more carefully. You see, what is involved is not merely a squalid tale of clerics jockeying for power; it is far more serious than that. As the suppliers of a primitive kind of Internet, the Christian Church began wholesale tampering with the continent's info flow; worse, it initiated an astonishing attempt to control people's very minds, and to do so from within! In the history of the world to this point such a gross intrusion had never been attempted before! It was fated to fail, of course, but the Church persisted with its attempts for centuries nevertheless.

*

How do I justify this criticism of the leaders of the Christian Church? How do I apply what seems a vindictive term like 'Dark Age' without hesitation or the hint of a blush? After all, most historians use this emotive description for the period *after* the fall of Rome and *until* the emergence of Charlemagne. Indeed in direct contrast, they describe the Church as the *only* light shining in what (for them!) were very depressing circumstances indeed.

Again in direct opposition to my point of view, they believe that the Church was the only receptor and transmitter of what precious little info flow was available. They see it as the sole repository in which was preserved any of the worthwhile knowledge built up from preceding centuries. Incidentally, this tends to ignore the contribution made by Islam, but I will let that pass as this will introduce even more controversy. You see, inevitably it would force us to become bogged down in a fruitless task of weighing the relative amounts of data (and their ultimate value!) contributed by the Islamic 'world' on the one hand and the Christian 'world' on the other. So to avoid much needless complication and to hold on to the main thread of my purpose, it is therefore necessary to look once more at the salient points in greater detail and to examine human behaviour patterns under a specially designed magnifying glass.

*

However, before embarking on this unhappy saga, it is first necessary to examine a significant social development that ran concurrently with it – the arrival of the feudal system.

A thousand years or so prior to the ninth century and Charlemagne's early establishment of a European Union, all the petty chieftains to the north and east of the Danube (which roughly marks the frontier of the then active Roman Empire) lived as they had done from time immemorial, that is, wholly as an integral part of the tribal community. There was no sharp division between ruler and those ruled, unlike conditions prevailing to the south of the Danube. Chieftains lived at a level of personal comfort and overall social distinction that was only marginally above that of their people. Why? Simply because of the nature of tribalism and the limited size of their population. Happily, it encouraged them to mingle freely with all sections of what was a close-knit social group. Thus they recognised most individuals by sight and many by name. Their basic lifestyle was hardly different from them. Unlike the grandeur and magnificence that surrounded most Roman emperors, they lived in what were, in comparable architectural terms, no more than glorified garden sheds. Built of wood, with a thatched roof and one or two holes to allow a little of the smoke from domestic fires to find its way out, the home of the chieftain may have differed only in its length and breadth. Even this was dictated solely by the necessity to accommodate a few retainers; it was not an expression of crude ostentation. It was a lifestyle in which respect or possibly adulation for the chieftain was acquired by force of personality and fighting skill, solely. And information flow was always by word of mouth. In these particular circumstances the people were no worse off for that! It was efficient in its own way because social cohesion was so strong. Information thus spread quickly. Class distinction in the sense we know it today, with its ability to form invisible barriers between sections of society, simply did not exist. All this was to change, however. And ironically it began to change only after the western section of the Roman Empire disintegrated. It was not because Rome established an example during its heyday. Why?

My reading of the situation is this: as petty chieftains crossed what were once well-defended Roman borders they found themselves in what was virtually another world; it was one where the former poisonous delusions of stability, power and grandeur still hung in the very air. It was a very potent poison. Thus within a few decades we find many of these chieftains beginning to acquire the airs and graces of the patricians they displaced. The simple homespun clothing was rejected. With Roman merchants eager to please their new masters, versions of the toga replaced them. As very few villas were sacked, a vague imitation of the lifestyle of the former owners was adopted. In this way social divisions were slowly set up between leaders and those who were led. Social cohesion in the old style took a turn for the worse, especially when what were essentially large tribal groupings began to coalesce into petty kingdoms. Later they fairly plummeted when these were amalgamated into large and recognisable kingdoms covering considerable areas. Yet another factor in the creation of a distinctive class structure was the matter of acquiring collective defence. In a volatile age, where continual bickering between newly formed kingdoms saw armies on the march, the lack of any positive info flow meant that enemies could appear suddenly without advance warning. It became necessary therefore to build a series of small but well-fortified structures within one's kingdom into which both soldiers and the local population could retreat as quickly as possible. Occasionally an old Roman fort would be taken over and adapted, but due to the changing patterns of warfare which demanded new forms of defence, new structures slowly arose. And the stone was as likely as not taken from existing Roman buildings. In due time the strongest and most imposing of these structures (usually somewhere near the physical centre of the kingdom) also contained the domestic quarters of what had now become the 'king'. Slowly a tradition emerged of quite impressive structures being built for the upper ranks of society, yet in contrast mere hovels, often built of wattle and daub, being built for the bulk of the remainder of the population. Thus the former ties with the masses were broken. Class distinctions became rigidly fixed. At the same time the personal freedoms of the individual tribesmen of the former 'barbarian' masses were lost. Indeed, they now found themselves in far worse circumstances than the former long-suffering 'plebeian' class of Romans. And, as we have already noted in previous eras, information flow now became channelled solely toward the topmost class. This social rigidity and exclusivity proved astonishingly strong and lasting. Feudalism, in all of its more deplorable aspects, became fully organised from the fifth century onward, slowly displacing tribalism and becoming the norm throughout Europe. The most successful of the old chieftains (or sometimes the most audacious of upstart military adventurers) had themselves proclaimed kings. They did so at magnificent ceremonies in which, if they had accepted Christianity, they were anointed by resident priests. Significantly, this was a ritual which supposedly conferred God-given rights and powers upon them. Of these, the most important was 'ownership' of all land within the borders of the kingdom. Later, in the form of a personal gift, this land was then parcelled out amongst immediate relatives or individual warriors who had distinguished themselves in battle. Naturally, these were then required to swear an oath of loyalty and allegiance. And such an oath was one that the occupant of the new throne fervently hoped would invoke a certain degree of awe; more important still, one that would be sufficiently binding even in the most adverse of circumstances. It was also understood that this loyalty included the firm commitment to train, maintain and supply men for a standing army whenever necessary. In the name of the king, these feudal barons then in turn handed out land to their knights, who yet again subdivided land to their squires, who in turn saw to it that the common people were more or less fairly distributed over set plots. The latter, at the very foot of the social scale, subsequently became vassals or serfs; they were effectively tied to their hovels and the soil they tilled.

This system lasted ten centuries. And it is hardly necessary to repeat that all info flows of any worth were carefully channelled to the ruling classes, while the commoners were kept in ignorance.

Now ten centuries is quite a long time. How did this appallingly repressive system last for so long? And how did it do so virtually without change? Well of course one would be negligent if one failed to mention that there was indeed opposition from time to time. Inevitably, after suffering at the hands of particularly vicious kings or nobles, the abused vassals and peasantry would occasionally revolt. All failed. The system was too strong. But over the centuries the threat of revolt brought minor modifications and a very slight easing of conditions. Even so, in the main, life for the masses was still intolerable – that is, judged by today's standards. Ironically, the only time the back-breaking and unremitting work done by the peasantry was appreciated was in the arrival of a plague. Suddenly, work done either in the fields producing food in abundance for the king or the local lordship's table, in the forests for fuel for his fire, or timber for his new constructions, underneath the ground for the ores that produced his weapons all came to an abrupt halt. For that moment at least these weary providers of the essentials of life were so decimated that they took on a scarcity value. This became a pressing reason for better treatment and for the provision of more comfortable living conditions. Predictably though, it only lasted until the peasantry obligingly brought forth a new and plentiful supply of children.

Once an ample supply of labour was again assured, things reverted back to normal. As for the gradual rise of the trading classes to form a rather fluid so-called 'middle class' wedged uncomfortably between the land-owning aristocracy and the masses, this is hailed in many history books as an important factor in the further modification of the feudal system. But overall its significance is greatly exaggerated. Had their leverage in the gradual toppling of this appalling system been as powerful as supposed, surely feudalism would never have lasted as long as it did. After all, traces of it still can be found lingering at the end of this century.

Very well then, you wish me to supply my alternative reading of the historical record? I will oblige by stating that as I see it the reason why feudalism had such a long life has just two basic factors: first, and quite simply, the denial of adequate info flow. A secondary contributing factor was the fusion between Church and state, implying within the minds of the illiterate peasantry that God himself had ordained such a system.

To repeat the observation made earlier: Charlemagne's united Western Europe could have seen the beginning of a Golden Age, but of course the greater mass of people saw no such thing. This was largely due to the gross shortcomings in the ethical standards of the new princes of the Church – as distinct from the more humble priesthood it is only fair to add. These princes had the opportunity to organise the transmission of Christ's teaching so that it reached every individual throughout the land. It was a land soon to become known as the 'Holy Roman Empire'. And this teaching should have influenced events accordingly. But 'Holy' was a grandiose and utterly misleading title if ever there was one. At the very outset those teachings were relayed orally and in Latin, which only a tiny percentage of the total mass of people could understand. Moreover, as a sop to counter what would otherwise be a bewildering and meaningless exercise, the masses were 'taught' by a series of pictures painted on church walls or sculptured friezes on any suitable surface: but this was hardly a full equivalent of the Word itself! As an alternative, their adherence to the faith was cemented by resorting to mere mumbo-jumbo; in other words, worship became increasingly complex and heavily dependent on ceremonial. There is only one way of fully transmitting the Word, of course; that is by allowing people to read for themselves the entire New Testament, suitably translated into their own tongue. But here the early princes of the Church had a legitimate excuse. As printing had yet to be introduced to Europe, the production of Bibles was by very slow and laborious copying by hand. Yet even beyond this, those magnificent Bibles quite naturally used Latin only, and the masses were illiterate anyway!

So much then for the vital matter of info flow, or the lack of it!

What then of the fusion of Church and state? This surely should have produced a more equitable, caring and compassionate society, particularly if Christian principles were put into practice from the very top?

What happened in truth was that things reverted back to the kind of monolithic social structures seen at the very beginning of the 'civilising process' a thousand or more years earlier, that is if you can dare call it by that description without blushing. It reverted back to conditions little different to those in the ancient kingdoms founded in the fertile plains of the Tigris-Euphrates, the Indus, and the Nile.

What were those conditions?

Shall we go back even further in time for a moment to consider certain basic features linked with small tribal communities before they coalesced into larger units?

As already touched on, the system of using tribal elders who arrived at a consensus on all social problems worked well. However, there was a proviso: the tribal group could not be too large. It always broke down once the group became bigger. At this point the individual with the biggest biceps and thigh muscles usually took over. Once his leadership was established, the next problem (for him) was to remain in that capacity for as long as possible. And while those at a distance tended to see him as a figure to be admired and venerated, his immediate entourage would see all his small human failings and weaknesses; clearly, years of familiarity do indeed tend to produce contempt. So in the due course of events some members of the entourage would find their leader less than admirable: and so much so that they would attempt to dislodge him. This was, and still is, for that matter, a well-established game. It has proved popular throughout every century since man first stood on his hind legs, and possibly even before it.

Now one really strong man, physically speaking, is often more than a match for several ordinary men. Yet if these conspire together in really large numbers, even the most brawny he-man can find himself in serious difficulties. The only alternative remaining therefore is to introduce a technique whereby one man can literally control millions, i.e. mental trickery. Thus the leader invariably invests himself with some kind of supernatural power.

And this worked quite well in the first primitive 'civilisations'. Indeed it seemed to be the only way in which a large group of people could be directed to work together in a productive fashion. Moreover, on the whole it allowed life to function in a relatively smooth manner. But there were problems, especially when these so-called 'god-kings' died. The eldest of his children, by virtue of being created out of his loins, automatically assumed an aura of divinity also. Neatly, these subsequently filled the vacant position without the necessity for a riotous and bloody scramble – this either by immediate relatives or indeed critical members of the entourage. However, the devil of it was (and is) the genetic lottery that then came into play. No matter how well fitted the father may have been for carrying out duties as supreme head of state, it was by no means certain that these gifts would be passed on. Indeed those qualities often failed to be found in the eldest son. And underlings do expect an awful lot! Beyond looking for superlative qualities in the area of physical strength, they also expected great intelligence, foresight, hindsight, unflappability, dignity, courage, fair-mindedness, good taste, etc., etc. They expected the 'goods'. They expected a superman. This was not altogether unreasonable given that the concept of a 'god-king' was bandied about in the first place. Moreover, on top of all this they expected that the new ruler, if not unusually handsome, would at least possess what is called a 'presence'. There is that indefinable thing known as charisma. All in all this was a pretty tall order, and, as you may expect, it was rarely fulfilled.

What helped, of course, were the trappings: gorgeous costumes and headdresses, stunning places of residence, a glittering retinue in attendance, endless servants, and, especially in early eras, large numbers of concubines. Everything, in fact, that the mass of people lacked, but would actively desire if they had half the chance!

Even so the concept of a god-king and the neat coming together of spiritual and temporal power had its problems, and very peculiar ones at that.

To illustrate this in as simple and as engaging a way as possible, shall we visualise a day in the life of, say, a pharaoh of Ancient Egypt, and eavesdrop on an incident which highlights such problems?

Shall we imagine an apartment of Pharaoh's palace? It is in an elevated position, naturally, and overlooks the Nile. An imposing door leads out onto a courtyard where can be glimpsed a fertile valley that nurtures a large and richly endowed community. The only light filters through a clerestory near the ceiling, which helps to reduce the power of the burning sunlight and allows the illustrious occupants to be seen in more flattering half-tones. Nevertheless it is still rather hot and tends to make work of any kind rather a bind. Worse, the great man himself happens to be engaged on work of the highest importance. It involves reading through a script supplied by the chief priest Ri, and amending or agreeing to a set of imperishable statements soon to be cut into the very stone of all public buildings and temples under their joint control. These statements begin by glorifying the majesty of the god-king and then go on to set out several new laws. In future (for those who can read hieroglyphics) there can no longer be a plea of ignorance of the laws!

But one can't just scrawl any lightly considered message in stone. Second thoughts and an attempt to alter or even eradicate badly expressed information would be a formidable task. He therefore struggles manfully with the old devil Ri's concepts, some of which he ruefully admits are entirely adequate and some (gleefully) less so. With the latter he makes several rough drafts of his own, using several pieces of papyrus. He writes in spurts, then rather crossly deletes those of his thoughts he finds lacking in clarity. After some time, general fatigue, coupled with mental stress, causes him to falter. He sighs and looks out into the distance for inspiration. After a while a little flash of inspiration causes him to pick up the stylus once more. At that precise point, yells and shouts from somewhere outside in the courtyard interrupt his chain of thought. His frown deepens. He seizes a staff and raps the floor. Immediately a servant hurries in and bows low. Pharaoh surveys him haughtily. He issues an order: 'Proceed to the courtyard, and... and...' He stops. The commanding manner is lost in a spasm of indecision and careworn fatigue. He has suddenly recognised the voices. 'No, perhaps it is better... you may leave me.' The servant bows again and goes out. Pharaoh rises from his seat and makes his way through the doorway. His eyes blink in the sunlight. Equally his ears are oppressed by the volume of noise. He holds one hand up to shield his eyes and with the other tries the impossible task of plugging both of his ears. The formidable shrieks and yells come from four boys aged between five and ten who are dodging between the columns and clambering over the smaller statues. They are engaged in the complicated game of slaves in revolt against taskmasters. Pharaoh sighs and watches for several minutes. Then, opening his mouth, he bellows, 'Stop it, I say!' However the game continues, if anything with redoubled violence. He shouts the same command again, but to no effect. He changes his tone – it becomes almost a plea. 'Boys, do you realise I am very busy? I can't concentrate with this noise. Now, just to please me – you know at your age I used to do anything to please my father – boys, will you listen!' The response is hardly encouraging.

The oldest lad bellows, 'Mind yourself, Father!' and hurtles past him dragging his father's latest present – it is a specially built half-size chariot. He is for the moment acting out a stampeding horse that has just disposed of its stupid driver. That stupid driver happens to be his youngest brother, who, thrown out by a violent swerve, now lies dazed on the ground. Pharaoh, greatly concerned, darts forward. Unfortunately at that very moment his eldest son, misjudging the width of the chariot, and also surprised by his father's sudden movement, crashes into him. Man, boy and chariot land in glorious confusion on the ground. The great man disentangles himself and rises fuming to his feet. The stampeding 'horse' rapidly rights the overturned chariot and continues its zigzag career between the columns. Pharaoh utters some curses in his direction then hurries over to the youngest boy. Tears are welling in the child's eyes but he is attempting not to lose face and be called a 'cry-baby'. Pharaoh picks him up and hurriedly looks for signs of injury. Thankfully, but for superficial scrapes and cuts he appears unhurt. The shrieks and yells continue unabated behind him. Turning, he is about to issue another demand when his eyes become transfixed on the antics of the two middle boys. The toy spears he gave them only yesterday – much to his unease and only after endless nagging by all four boys – spears he nevertheless had specially tipped with leather to prevent injury, have suddenly lost their protective capping. He darts forward as one child is about to skewer the other through the lower abdomen. He grasps the spear in the nick of time, breaks it over his knee, then forestalls the expected shouts of protest from both spearman and target by boxing their ears. There is a stunned silence. Even the 'wild horse' freezes in its tracks. Utter astonishment is shown on every face. The great man is as surprised as they are. He has never smacked his sons before. He has never received such awed submission before. He decides to make the most of it. He picks up all the remaining spears and breaks each one with a great show of temper. 'There!' he bellows, then follows this up by indiscriminate slapping of any child he can lay hands on. He then marches over to his eldest son, still rooted to the spot, and still limply holding the chariot shafts. 'Which one of you took the leather off those spears?' he demands. There is no answer. 'Well?' The silence is unbroken. It is in fact rather unnerving. He takes his eldest son by the nape of the neck and marches him to his study. Inside, he closes the door and remains with his back to it to stop any entry. Showing undiminished wrath he bellows, 'You did, didn't you, you little fool!' The boy's face shows hurt mixed with indignation.

'No Father, I swear by the sacred Nile I didn't.' Pharaoh knows when his son lies; he also knows when he tells the truth.

'Then which one of your brothers did?' There was a short silence.

'Nobody did! We just picked them up from where we left them yesterday.'

Pharaoh takes a deep breath and his eyes narrow. He watched them playing with the spears for some time yesterday afternoon. He had to satisfy himself the leather tips were firmly in place and no real injury could result. He remembers the high priest Ri coming to present him with the draft of the new laws in the middle of it all. He had been annoyed by the crafty old devil's subtle questioning of his wisdom in giving in so readily to his children's demands. And as they had this important business to discuss he himself collected the spears (just in case!) and put them in a cupboard, intending always to supervise such games personally. Now suppose Ri had... He sighed. The fusion of the religious and the temporal, the combining of church and state, the virtual duality of leadership has its drawbacks as well as its undoubted advantages. His father before him warned him of over-ambitious high priests who might use underhand methods to tip the very fragile balance of power in their favour. The boys did not see where he put the spears. Only Ri witnessed that. In fact Ri witnessed everything that was important, even very personal things. Damn him! For example, ancient custom insisted he witnessed even the intimate moments of the birth of royal children, something that Pharaoh has always resented. The tradition that Pharaoh takes one of his sisters as his wife – there being nobody else of such exalted rank carrying the royal bloodline – has a long tradition of difficulty; so many children are born obviously deformed, or, if not, frequently die in infancy. The causes are always unknown, and on occasion, if the continuation of the royal bloodline seems in some doubt, then the child of a concubine is substituted in secrecy. In this the high priest always dabbles, even takes a leading role. And Pharaoh suspects that during the emotional upset the high priest could well influence matters to his own personal advantage. Indeed, except for his eldest son, he isn't absolutely sure that the other three are pure bloodline! After watching the birth of his first child, the messy process was sufficiently off-putting to make him decide never to be present again. But there is a price to be paid, of course. A vague uncertainty! Also, a continual worry as to what the old fox Ri is really up to.

He is aware that his thoughts have wandered; his son has touched him lightly on the arm. Staring intently into his face he has now found his tongue again and repeated, 'Father, by the sacred Nile, none of us touched those spear tips.' Pharaoh sniffs, pretending unbelief, but his son continues: 'We just found them in a corner and picked them up, never looked at the tips!' It is the obvious truth. And who else but Ri could have known where they were? He could so easily have asked one of his minions to take them out of the hiding place, pull off the tips, sharpen the naked points, then leave them lying around in a corner for these eagle-eyed children to swoop on.

'Very well. I believe you...' he mumbles. But at that precise moment he hears his sister-wife's voice somewhere in the distance. He shudders. She is always criticising him for being too indulgent with the children. She is always urging him to find proper tutors and full-time guardians, rather than spending so much time with them himself. Women! They never understood these things! He prays she is on her normal routine walk with her own retinue making for the gardens of the palace, and will not attempt to open the door at that juncture. His prayers are answered. She continues on her way and the voice gradually fades. She will never understand that the theory of Pharaoh's divinity is already beginning to wear a little thin, never realise it has to be constantly guarded. And who among the royal household – becoming so intimate as they eventually must with the realities of family life – can maintain a belief in the face of these suicidal offspring of his? Tutors! Guardians! In just a few days they would know the wretched truth! Even the stupidest would question the divinity of the Royal House and its line. He eyes the fine aristocratic features of his son with a mixture of despair and pride.

He has been too damned over-indulgent. He confesses to it almost daily. How many times has he resolved to be firmer? How many times has he resolved to be masterly and commanding?

'When you finally give us some *new* spears...' a petulant voice demands, interrupting his thoughts, 'we'll check each time that they have leather on them – honestly we will.'

'New spears!' Pharaoh explodes. '*New* spears!'

'But why not?' Two eyes stare into his with bewildered innocence.

'Why *not*! I'll tell you why not! Your brother Thotmes almost killed little—'

'Killed!' The interruption comes sharply and immediately.

'Yes, killed! Several of you could be lying dead by now if I hadn't come out to see what all the noise was about.'

'But how can we kill each other?'

'What do you mean, how can you kill?'

'I'm asking you, Father, a plain and simple question. How can we kill each other? We are charmed, aren't we? Thotmes is like me, one of our royal line. And as all our family are descended from God himself we simply *cannot* die. We are protected by Osiris, not like the common people and especially slaves and robbers.'

'You little fool! You are neither protected nor charmed, nothing of the kind!'

'But Father!' The eyes widen. 'You've said so many hundreds of times, even before the altars of every temple in the land. I've heard you with my own ears. And everybody knows Pharaoh lives ages and ages. And when he gets terribly old he goes to sleep and gets put in the pyramid with the servants, horses and chariots and everything he needs until he wakes up again. That is hundreds of years isn't it? Then he comes back to rule Egypt again. Everybody knows that. And little Thotmes said, and Ahtem also, that they wanted to see inside the pyramid to know if Grandfather snores as badly as you do!'

'By the sacred gods...' Pharaoh puts both hands over his ears for a moment. 'Stop it! Stop it, I say. Never let me hear you speak such nonsense again!'

'Nonsense!'

'Yes, nonsense!'

'But Father!' There is incredulity and even horror in his voice.

Pharaoh mops his brow and fans himself furiously with an elegant fly switch. With difficulty he finally conquers his agitation. He goes over to his chair and collapses into it.

'My son, come here.' The boy slowly approaches; although he is now rather too old for such things, he allows himself to be pulled onto his father's knee and clasped round the waist.

'There are things I must tell you...' Pharaoh begins hesitantly. 'But first you must swear on this holy relic that I wear around my neck that you will never tell anyone – nobody, you understand. I will tell your bothers when they get old enough, but certainly nobody else the truth about...'

'The truth about what?'

'No. First you must swear!' The boy eyes him carefully for a moment then slowly and with infinite seriousness touches the relic.

'I swear, Father.'

Pharaoh takes a deep breath. 'Now Rameses, you are my eldest son, and one day I will be put in the pyramid and you will be Pharaoh in my place.'

'Yes, I know! Of course! And then if Thotmes, and Ahtem and little Tutti want to hear Grandfather and *you* both snoring out of tune together, then I shall let them, because then I shall be able to order and do anything I choose.'

Pharaoh groans then tightens his grip round the boy's waist. 'Rameses, my son. I am afraid I must tell you that Grandfather isn't sleeping. Nor will I be. And if your brother pushed that spear into Thotmes's stomach he wouldn't just be sleeping either.'

'Wouldn't be sleeping! What *do* you mean?'

'Because he would be dead! As Grandfather is dead, and as I will be one day!'

'Dead!'

'Yes. Do you really know what the word means?'

'Yes, it happens to people who are not as we are, or as Ri is, or part of our household, or governors of the provinces – all the *special* people. Ordinary people and criminals never come back to Egypt and the land they knew, of course.'

'Good! I'm glad you understand that much at least.'

'That much? You mean... there's more?'

'Yes, there's more, my son.'

'Well then, tell me.'

'I'm not sure you will understand. You are still very young. But I suppose if I want you and your brothers to be more careful in the way you play, and keep yourselves alive, then it becomes essential.'

'We were only playing taskmasters and slaves.'

'But taskmasters don't use spears and chariots.'

'If the slaves revolt they do.'

'Revolt! How often does that happen?'

'Not very often, I admit. But it does sometimes. Remember a year ago those Jews who tried to escape and were executed and pinned up outside the temple to warn others?'

'What! Who told you that? You certainly didn't see it yourself.

Who is passing on such information? Well, out with it!'

'I shan't. Otherwise you will have him whipped.'

'If it's that imp of a boy, that Israelite slave who serves you...'

'No, it wasn't!' The voice takes on an imploring tone, then changes to curiosity. 'Father, those Israelites who were executed, their bodies were just bits of bone after a few weeks, weren't they?'

Pharaoh's voice hardens – 'If I could be sure who among your servants and slaves is filling your head with...'

'Father! Is it true or not?'

'I'll have him flogged to an inch of his life.'

'You might as well tell me the whole truth now. Were they just bits of bone because the Sun God came and stole the skin and other bits of their bodies from them, just leaving the bits that don't matter?'

'I'll have him... oh, very well. I suppose you are getting older. You will have to know sooner or later. Yes, it's all true.'

'But if Grandfather is in the pyramid where the Sun God cannot see him then it's impossible to steal the skin, and so...'

'No! There are other gods that steal the skin, not just the Sun God.'

'Oh! I see...' There is silence as he becomes thoughtful.

Pharaoh coughs apologetically, 'I'm... I'm sorry, my son, that you had to be told that before you are really old enough.'

'So if Thotmes had that spear pushed into his stomach he would die! And despite being put in the pyramid where the Sun God can't see him, his skin and all the other bits would be taken from him?'

'Yes. Or at least they would be without the attentions of the embalmers.'

'Embal... emba... What did you say?'

'Nothing. Just forget it. Death is death! Your brother... I now hope understand... would be dead if I hadn't stopped this silly game.'

'And that's why you got so angry and boxed our ears or slapped us... and broke all our spears, I suppose.'

'Yes.' Pharaoh heaves a sigh. 'But don't let all this spoil all your, your wonderful joy in life. As long as you are reasonably careful you will live long enough to take my place one day.'

A long silence follows, then suddenly the boy's face takes on a pained, even tragic expression. His father tenses and becomes increasingly concerned.

'What is it, son?'

'In... in some of the other very old pyramids is the father of our grandfather, and his father before him and the one before him again.'

'Yes, why?'

'Perhaps when I am Pharaoh, one of our great, great, great... oh, I don't know how many times... grandfather will come to the end of his death and come alive, and then he will want to be Pharaoh instead of me!' His lips tremble, and his eyes fill with tears. 'Father, I did so much want to be like you, and sit on the golden throne, and do so many wonderful things, and now... more than likely I shall never be able to. I have counted up the number of years and it comes to many, many hundreds already, so one or other of our ancestors is bound to be ready to come back to life, and come back to this palace and sit in the high chair. He will take my place, Father. It's bound to happen!' He almost bursts into tears, restraining himself with some difficulty.

Pharaoh reflects for a moment. He comes to the conclusion there are some very unexpected drawbacks in teaching your son to be numerate. Then he curses inwardly the malign effect caused by the half-truths that both he and others have strewn in children's minds. He sighs once more.

'I see you still don't understand the proper meaning of the word "death". Merciful Osiris, help me! Look! My son, you must try to realise that the dead never come back to life, under any circumstances! Never! Do you understand? And no matter how royal the bloodline. They will never come back to this world – maybe to some other, perhaps, but not this one.' He pauses to allow that to sink in.

'But...' His son's lips quiver again. 'Does that mean *you* will never come back either?'

'It does.'

A burst of tears follows. The boy's arms are suddenly flung round his neck. Pharaoh finds it particularly touching. It is also gratifying. Since about the age of five Rameses has never shown such open affection. Pharaoh has to restrain his own emotion as the tears come to his eyes. It is some time before he can continue. 'I hope you now understand, my son, that none of your grandfathers will come back to take the high chair from you. Nor, for that matter, will any of the old high priests return to plot and scheme...' He says this with a good deal of satisfaction. 'But the important part of it all, you see, is this. We must *make* the nobles and the common people believe they *will*!' He pauses to sniff and draw a long heartfelt sigh. 'And more particularly still my retinue here in the palace!'

'They must! Why? If it is all a big lie?'

'Because if they began to suspect Pharaoh was just an ordinary man, they would try to kill him. And what would happen then? They would be always fighting each other to gain the highest place for themselves. They would try to get support from the common people: and those poor fools would be bewildered and all too ready to swallow countless lies. There would be constant civil war and unrest. But if they believe Pharaoh is *more* than a man, and descended from God, then they no longer even begin to have foolish thoughts, let alone ambitions to take his place. They can be tricked into working diligently for him, especially if he promises he will raise them from the dead when he wakes. He can even hold out some hope to the common people – if they too work hard and stop grumbling about it. They will all rise from the dead when Pharaoh blows on the silver trumpets. So because everyone is frightened of death and wants to be resurrected, I can rule them in a civilised manner – from the proudest and indeed the most conniving of the nobles – down to the most humble of the common people in the land. Then crops can be sown and reaped, granaries built, houses, palaces and temples planned, erected and kept in good order, transport of goods run to a proper timetable and distributed fairly – in short, everything can be done with honour, pride and skill. But if the people failed to fear death and no longer believed they would be rewarded for doing good, then they would trample everything underfoot. And we would all live in misery and perpetual chaos.'

'I see... even though it is all one big lie?'

'Yes, and yet, strangely enough, it isn't in a way. You see, it is far better to live in a well-ordered society and try to live a blameless life believing you will be rewarded. You see, during the actual living of it you will get a measure of peace and contentment. This is a reward in itself. Whereas if you live an evil life, then you are forced to endure constant turmoil. You have to look over your shoulder every other moment of the day, and do so even in the company of those you think are your friends. Evil people get their desserts while they live for they never have peace of mind. This is so different from good people. Can you understand this, my son?'

'Yes, I think I can,' the boy stares into his fathers eyes. 'So, there is no life after death really?'

'Well, shall I put it this way. If there is, then so much the better. If there isn't, then there is no point in wasting any tears on it, because you can do nothing to change matters. If you have been good then you will have had the best out of *this* life, and that's all that matters. It is the only sensible belief that has a hope of hanging together.'

There is silence for some time. Suddenly the young voice chirps up. 'Do you think I will make a good pharaoh, Father? Just like you? Everyone knows you are strict, yet not someone who strikes fear into everybody. You are calm and composed: but when you are in a good mood you often play with us and have much fun and joy in life. You are fair and level-headed, not like some of the pharaohs before you, so we are told. You are...' He runs out of adequate words.

'Rameses, try to understand. When a pharaoh dies and a son takes over, nobody knows how things will turn out. It just happens to be one of the few disadvantages with the concept of the god-king and the blue-blooded line generally. Sometimes fathers produce children who, they have to admit as they grow to manhood, they wish had never been born, who, as the Israelites say so poetically, 'bring down their grey hairs in sorrow to the grave'. Sometimes what was once a lovely young child, when reaching manhood turns out to be a misfit, a poor fool, an arrogant fire-eater. In short, a bitter disappointment. And yes, sometimes even a monster. Who can tell? That is why I am fearful sometimes of giving you too many presents, and too much of your own way.'

His son's eyes brim with tears again. 'Surely you don't think I will be a disappointment?'

'Oh Osiris! I sincerely hope not! Though it could happen.' He pauses once more and stares into the distance. 'Look, Rameses, I predict that in a thousand years' time, many peoples will try other systems, only to find that none is perfect. You see, each will have their own peculiar problems, especially so when the most powerful person in the country dies, or for some reason has to be changed. The hereditary system has its failings, but then so will all the others.'

*

Civilisation based on lies, in this instance surrounding the supernatural powers of a god-king, lasted in a reasonably worthy form in Ancient Egypt for an incredibly long period. Naturally, it had its minor ups and downs, but on the whole these were but brief periods. Overall, the stability given by this strange fusion of the spiritual with the temporal, combining the function of a priest with the chief executive of a secular state, was an undeniable asset. As touched on earlier, Egypt's particular geography also helped by providing natural protection. There were large expanses of desert to the west, mountains to the east, huge expanse of thinly populated areas to the south and a conveniently narrow outlet to Asia in the north. Other civilisations were less fortunate, even though they too saw a fusion of religion with the secular state. Despite this they survived for many centuries and had a similar basis for stability and permanence. If their time-span was shorter than that of Egypt then it was due to a less fortunate array of natural defences coupled with unexpected attack by enemies with either very large armies or a superior military technology.

The creation of a European 'Holy Roman Empire', therefore, was a sound enough concept. What it lacked was a supply of individuals of sufficient stature to bring about the reality. The historical record shows that, as a result, it existed only in name. Moreover, if one studies the details of the power struggle between succeeding popes and each of the emperors they crowned, one finds some of the most disgraceful and even infamous of sagas unfolding. Sufficient to say, those individuals with sufficient spiritual stature, and who accepted Christ's teachings to the full, seldom reached high office. St Francis of Assisi, to name but one, neither sought nor received elevation to the upper hierarchy of the Roman Church; he spent the greater part of his life among the poor and downtrodden. Thomas Aquinas spent his in academia. In direct contrast the Borgia Pope Alexander VI exhibited a whole range of vices which were later to bring the entire Church into disrepute. His illegitimate son, Cesare Borgia, who was made a cardinal by his father at the tender age of seventeen years, and who likewise displayed a formidable array of vices, may well have occupied the chair of St Peter at a later date and therefore made the papal line hereditable. However, his headstrong exchange of the red hat for a soldier's helmet, (in particular the more dashing costume of captain general of the papacy), finally nipped this particular project in the bud. His early death at the siege of Viana and his father's poisoning brought all this to naught. Extremes of this kind – saintliness on the one hand and gross corruption on the other – marked the period in which Europe supposedly began as an integrated Empire, yet, in reality rapidly dissolved into a multiplicity of warring kingdoms.

As the stated intention of this essay is to find the underlying reasons for the conflicts that developed among Charlemagne's successors, and subsequently plagued Europe century after century, rather than merely describe them, the reader may delve into the various historical accounts if he or she so wishes. It happens to be one of the most murky on record. That they will be satiated with the lengthy descriptions of every kind of human vice I have no doubt. Unfortunately, these always obscure the fundamental issues, and for this reason I have no option but to move on. It is, after all, once more necessary to concentrate on this vital matter of info flow, or indeed its denial! To proceed, then...

Much exaggerated significance is given by conventional historians to the invention of printing during the mediaeval era. In doing so, many fail to note that, initially, printing was the invention of the Chinese and the honour cannot be (by implication) ascribed to clever Europeans. Several centuries of the denigration of the contribution made by this ancient Far Eastern civilisation have done their work all too well. Hence we tend to be surprised to learn that the Chinese actually produced some fine examples of this technological revolution about the sixth century AD. True, this established just the 'fixed' type process to begin with, but it was nevertheless an impressive start. The greater flexibility of 'moveable' type was also achieved by the Chinese and as early as the eleventh century! Printing of a sort only reached Europe by the fourteenth century, and Gutenberg is finally credited with use of the moveable type in the mid-fifteenth century.

While this undoubtedly allowed a greater number of books and pamphlets to be created, and naturally far less laboriously than by individual copyists working with quills, it did not bring about an explosive increase in info flow. Despite the heady lyricism found in our history books, the reality was rather different. Circulation of printed material was once again limited; the supposed liberation of information, as one may now expect, was again confined to the upper classes. After all, only they had the money to buy books and pamphlets; only they were in possession of literacy and also had the leisure time to read them. Then again, for some of the truly important treatises produced at that time, one needed education in some depth to grasp fully what was contained in their pages. Thus overall the impact made on the greater mass of people was negligible.

Historians also enthuse on the rapid growth of centres of learning in Europe from about the fourteenth century onward. They point out that these replaced the more limited and 'closed' social institutions of the monastic orders, or purely church schools. This too gives a false impression – it implies a great surge of knowledge. What were to become 'universities', in the sense that we understand them today, were once more the privileged preserve of the aristocracy or rich merchant class. Entrance was not open to all. Nor was it on a competitive basis. Ability to pay, or the influence afforded by membership of the nobility, was the premier consideration. Mind you, if you happened to have intelligence over and above this, then it was an advantage, of course, but not unduly so. Also, from time to time, some philanthropists did attempt to encourage the education of those of exceptional ability among the lower classes. But with the leaden weight of membership of such a class hanging, as it were, visibly round their necks, few were able to overcome such a disadvantage.

However, the most serious limitation to information flow came from a most unexpected source.

Up to the fourteenth century (arguably) the Christian Church prided itself on being the repository of the great bulk of knowledge gained in preceding centuries. It was also an educator in its own right. But now it found that knowledge could be a very dangerous two-edged sword.

Much to its dismay it was found that some data – particularly from early Grecian sources – either challenged or sharply conflicted with holy writ. Perhaps one should add at this point a vital adjunct: it would be more correct to say such conflict was artificial – it was not inevitable. It was produced solely by unfortunate interpretations of holy writ by theologians of that era. Other interpretations would have been possible, but they were not pursued. As these theologians were all too aware, a body of dogma had been built up and it was rapidly becoming hallowed. This was surely a gratifying development. So why should this process be obstructed? If parts of this edifice were now in danger of being challenged, even be put in jeopardy, then it was time to call a halt!

There were specific areas of danger – these were almost all in what was then called 'natural philosophy' or in modern parlance, scientific research. They involved mainly the spheres of medicine, astronomy and biology. And, sadly, almost all involved the most respected of Grecian philosophers. Of course the sprinkling of learned Moslems from the world of Islam could be discounted automatically: anything to do with what was now seen as an alien civilisation was beyond the pale anyway! Regrettably this prejudice has lasted to this very day!

At this point it becomes necessary to look at this highly selective process more closely. After all, the sudden brake put on the development of European civilisation by a selective system in which the new technology of printing was freely applied to some areas of information flow and denied to others held back progress for centuries.

Let us begin by examining the field of medicine.

Here many of the leading ecclesiastics were, from the outset, hostile to men who styled themselves 'healers'. They applied this across the board, that is both to the early Greeks and their own contemporaries. To be entirely fair, there were some good reasons for this. Many, after all, were charlatans. And it was not easy to distinguish between those who were and the few who were not. Even fully educated Greeks and Moslems in their own day had difficulty trying to establish the credentials of those who tried to further the range of medical knowledge using scientific methodology.

Generally speaking, the Church's attitude to disease, to birth defects, to high levels of mortality in childbirth (to both mothers and infants) and to wounds received either by accident or in battle, was that they all fell within the province of religious faith. Recovery was a matter of prayer. 'Healers' dabbled in areas that should really be for priests alone. The more intense one's devotion to the Church, the more desperate one's prayers would be. In the case of rich people the more lavish the donation of money or goods, then the greater the chance of recovery. There was one important proviso, however – it had to be God's will. This was a neat way of covering all eventualities. That is not to suggest that the Church set its face wholly against all other forms of healing. There were of course some individuals within the early monastic orders who were skilled herbalists, and these certainly provided a service in administering therapeutic potions. But these institutions were anyway part of the body of the Church, and the potions themselves were blessed. There were also a few skilful individual monks who mended broken bones and who were not averse to using a scalpel in a limited number of conditions. Once again, and simply because these efforts took place within monastery walls and were accompanied by prayer, the princes of the Church found it difficult to carp at such attempts to relieve suffering. Nevertheless, a jaundiced eye, and at times active opposition, was reserved for those 'healers' outside the Church who put greater faith in their own skills rather than the effectiveness of prayer.

In like manner, many (but not all) churchmen found early Grecian investigations into the inner secrets of the body, via the dissection of corpses, particularly abhorrent. It was something that should not be repeated in a truly Christian society. It seems a curious moral objection to twentieth-century eyes, but then we lack their tightly proscribed outlook. Quite simply, this, once again, happened to trespass on their preserve. Any Christian soul at the point of death became the focus of the Church's attention. It was a central part of its function to perform the ritual of the last confession, anoint the dying person, and give comfort to the immediate family. After death, prayers were offered for the soul of the departed, and then a complex religious ceremony took place for the final disposal of the body to the earth. To the mediaeval cleric's mind, it seemed scandalous for any lay person (including those with medical skills) to interfere with this, let alone delay this process. But there are exceptions to every rule. A few clerics took (what was to them) the pragmatic view. They argued that it was surely permissible for those pursuing genuine scientific knowledge to desecrate a corpse, providing the deceased was not of the Christian faith. They were even quite liberal when it came to common criminals or heretics. These, after all, were denied the sacraments; more to the point, they were not destined for burial in consecrated ground. It was firmly believed that they were on their way to Hell anyway. Yet some of the Church's upper hierarchy objected even to this, and not without some respectable logic of sorts being applied. With widespread belief by the common people – and, let it be said, large sections of the Church itself – in witches and magicians, who, it was alleged, used parts of the human body to formulate spells, the entire area of dissection was seen as an ethical minefield. It was ready to prove a disaster area for the unwary. As a result, the hierarchy of the Church maintained rigid opposition to pathology in its broadest sense, and to post-mortem examinations and dissections in particular. They did so for centuries. Medical science, as a direct result, advanced only slowly. Indeed, any information flow stemming from the anatomist's knife had to be acquired more or less in secret.

Moving on to the science of astronomy, conflict arose because of the Church's overly literal interpretation of otherwise harmless forms of poetic licence that littered biblical texts. This led to the view that the Earth was the centre of all creation. So despite the respect the greater body of bishops and clerics had for the Greek philosophers, it was found increasingly necessary to pick and choose which sections of their work to revere and which to dismiss as mistaken and unworthy. As strange as it may seem though, it was considered acceptable for the sophisticated and the now-stratified ranks of the 'princes' of the Church to read 'forbidden literature'. Later they could even discuss amongst themselves the merits or demerits of Grecian philosophic thought. But there was a proviso: such discussions must remain private! This was the sticking point. It was a very different matter to allow such information to pass into the hands of a wider (and by implication), less sophisticated body of laymen. This even failed to exclude royalty and aristocrats! Popes and cardinals considered themselves well above such riffraff, intellectually speaking. After all there were so many subtle aspects to the entire affair. And it was not as if these early Greeks could be gently dismissed with a pitying smile by uttering the word 'pagan'. You see, men the stature of Plato or Aristotle could hardly be held responsible for living centuries before the advent of Christianity. So while they certainly lacked the true 'teachings' of the Bible, they made up for that loss in the damnable forcefulness of their logic. Nor could one forget the astonishing subtlety of argument. Heavens above! How skilfully they could argue their case! Anaximander, for example, who was born in 610 BC taught from direct observation that the starry heavens revolved round the pole star. He then went on to propose that, excepting the 'wandering' stars, this fixed mass of stars was embedded in a spherical vault around the Earth. This in itself was not difficult to swallow. But he also taught that the Earth had a curved surface! And while not yet daring to suppose a complete sphere, he saw it as a sort of curved dish floating upside down on an enormous sea – a sea out of which all life had appeared. This latter statement was an astonishing proposition. Sadly though, it was no more than a uniquely inspired guess. Being slightly at variance with the biblical account of Creation, it automatically became a section of philosophy to ignore, of course.

But worse was to come at the hands of Pythagoras. Born about 580 BC, and initially achieving fame as a mathematician, he had further built on the concept of 'spheres' holding the heavenly bodies, noting, as he did so, that the sun, moon and certain other 'wanderers' had spheres and fixed paths of their own. This allowed future predictions of their movement. Yet crowning it all, he declared that the Earth was spherical! This was utter nonsense! Surely people, animals and all moveable objects would fall off the 'underneath' surfaces, unless they had the ability, like flies and other insects to walk on walls and even ceilings!

Even worse was to come with other philosophers! Xenophon, a contemporary of Pythagoras, not only agreed with this nonsense, but on the evidence of finding seashells among loose rock near the summit of mountains, concluded that these peaks must have slowly risen from the sea. Here we have the first recorded observation that was to lead two thousand, three hundred years later to the science of geology! But this sharply contradicted, or at that time seemed to contradict, the account of Creation in Genesis. For those living in the mediaeval era, each day of Creation was seen as a wretchedly short 'human' day, and wholly within purely human timescales. It was not visualised in cosmic terms, thus embracing a timescale of billions of years! It was presumed God existed in time dominated by the rising and setting of the sun – our sun! His awesome existence was circumscribed and demoted to Time involving the revolution of our earth round our puny and insignificant star, one of average size and only one amongst countless others. We now know that our sun is but one quite unimportant star, one of countless others in our galaxy. In turn our galaxy is only one of many. For early theologians, however, Creation was seen as virtually instantaneous. And the Christian Church was then bedevilled with this pitifully narrow, man-made view right up to the twentieth century. Indeed, there are fundamentalists who still adhere to this view even in the latter half of this century! Incidentally, the bold Xenophon also dismissed belief in the Greek pantheon of gods and goddesses, preferring to adopt monotheism, and this somewhat improved his otherwise hopelessly tarnished image, at least as far as the Church was concerned.

The philosopher Anaxagoras, born about 500 BC, taught that the stars were incandescent rocks, with the sun being also a star, but very much larger and brighter. He believed the moon to be constituted much like Earth and probably inhabited! Philolaus, born about 480 BC, actually believed that the Earth moved through space, in exactly the same way as the sun, moon and wandering stars. This was the most dangerous notion of all. However, ironically enough, the day was saved by Plato, the most impressive of philosophers. Born about 427 BC, he believed the Earth was the unmoving centre of the universe: he also had a mystical belief in the perfection of the heavens. Because a circle also signified the earthly representation of perfection, he taught that all moving heavenly bodies must therefore move in circles. Eudoxus, a slightly younger contemporary, choosing to make careful observations of the orbits and not attempting to deduce them by abstract reasoning, found certain slight irregularities. However, unwilling to compromise the prestige of Plato, he suggested a complicated movement of spheres resulting in a slight varying of the arc of curvature. This saved Plato's otherwise spotless record. Everyone has their blind spots, even the greatest. And Plato had a less-than-deserved reputation, at least in the realms of astronomy. Only in AD 1609, almost two thousand years later, did Kepler discover the movement to be elliptical! However, by that time the Church was already deeply embroiled in the Copernican controversy anyway; indeed, it was beginning to fight what was to become a desperate rearguard action.

Reverting for the moment back to the Greeks to complete our survey of their incredible achievements. Aristarchus, born about 320 BC, taught that the movement of all heavenly bodies was subject to an optical illusion. He argued that the Earth itself moved, and did so round the sun! By ingenious use of geometry, he also estimated the size of the moon relative to the Earth (almost correctly) as one third of the Earth's diameter. Not content with this, he attempted to estimate the distance between the Earth and sun, but was finally defeated by lack of accurate measuring devices for geometrical angles. Amazingly, Eratosthenes, born about 276 BC, actually calculated the size of the Earth, again geometrically, and arrived at a figure for the circumference remarkably close to its actual size.

All this of course was not welcome information for the Church; it could not be accommodated within its dogma. The situation was, however, remedied by Hipparchus, born about 190 BC who became famous for his lifelong quest to make accurate observations of the heavens, though less famous for his erroneous interpretations of them! Conforming to Plato's view, he believed that the Earth was stationary and the remainder of the universe moved around it. He used a similarly complicated series of spheres to prove it. Yet so precise was his map of the heavens (using a method derived from visual parallax) that it was used for navigation purposes, almost unaltered, for centuries. And his work, above all, seemed to confirm the Church's established dogma. What more could one wish for?

In a sense, the Christian Church merely repeated the attitudes of the average Grecian citizen all those centuries earlier.

There was an enormous chasm existing between the commonsense perceptions of the average Greek and what were considered to be the over-adventurous, immoderate, or downright crazy beliefs of many of these philosophers. Only a few of these managed to remain in favour with the general public; some were duly venerated, but many more were not. This is a factor we tend to forget today: moreover it allows us to overlook also that the more unpopular of these pioneers involved themselves in a high degree of personal risk. Therefore we should have even greater admiration and respect, not just for the astonishing heights reached in their achievements, but also for the basic physical courage displayed. We should never lose sight of the fact that much of what they taught could so easily be interpreted as blasphemy. It could be seen either as being disrespectful, or worse, an outright denial of the legitimacy of the entire Greek pantheon of gods and goddesses. By questioning their rightful place in the scheme of things and their involvement in the day-to-day cyclic processes, it was felt that the essential mysteries of life were being explained away. They became mere automatic or robotic phenomena! Had Newton been born into this strange climate of multifaceted veneration of major and minor gods and goddesses, the concept of what amounted to a 'clockwork universe' would have been considered the most extreme form of impiety! For example, everyone knew – and this by using the evidence of their own eyes – that the sun descended bodily into the western sea each evening and therefore into the arms of Poseidon. From thence, during the hours of darkness, it was conveyed or assisted by this god through an underground cavern back to the east, from whence it arose each morning. True enough, some minor deviants believed the sun died each evening and was reborn each morning, but the vast majority of people believed the former. That some philosophers should deny the existence of an underground cavern was bad enough! Surely they saw the sun disappear each day with their own eyes? How could they propose such a ridiculous alternative? This proposition of the world being spherical and simply floating in space was utterly preposterous! Not an inconsiderable number of philosophers were therefore pilloried. Some were exiled. Some suffered the extreme penalty. At best, these 'way out' thinkers were regarded as clever fools and allowed merely to amuse the remainder of society. It was rather like the professional fool found much later in mediaeval European courts whose duty it was to amuse the king and assembled barons. Similarly in Ancient Greece. Put in comparatively isolated spheres and where they could do least harm, they could then indulge themselves in speculative nonsense to their heart's content. Even so, from time to time, some speculations, combined as they often were with a certain respectable rationale (though it is only fair to say, at times with a less than respectable mysticism) could create tensions. At such a point certain philosophers were therefore openly branded as 'troublemakers' and either barely tolerated or actively persecuted.

Centuries later, the now powerful body of the Christian Church fully appreciated such criticism. Indeed, they identified with and replicated the views of the scornful. They were particularly incensed with the worst of these early Greek sages associated as they were with the concept of a spherical world floating (of all things) through empty space... therefore without any visible means of support! It was so crazy as to be beyond belief. How could any rational man delude himself in such a way?

Thus once again, by the careful sieving of information flow of what was thought inimical, and the encouragement of sections which supported the Church's dogma, knowledge of the basic structure of the universe and man's place in it was gravely retarded for some considerable time.

Moving to biology, the brightest star set in the Grecian firmament in this, and for that matter many other branches of science, was of course Aristotle, who was born in 384 BC. His active mind covered a wide range of natural phenomena and his breadth of knowledge, together with the skill used in presenting them (even allowing for input by his students and assistants), was staggering. Fortunately for the Church, in the matter of astronomy he too believed the Earth immovable and the centre of creation. And in biology, much of his classification of plants and animals, while original and showing acute observation, seemed uncontroversial. It was only much later, when it was examined in depth by professional biologists – and even then only by the most perceptive of them – that it became clear that Aristotle was groping towards an evolutionary viewpoint. The fact that the great man himself (at least in the manuscripts that were saved from oblivion) hesitated to draw out the hidden conclusion without further proof probably saved his reputation among the churchmen.

Looking at this question of information flow in general, it can be said that up to about the twelfth century the early Christian Church assisted this flow rather than hindered it. Then gradually, as the centuries moved on, the balance slowly tipped more and more toward subtle deviation and at times blockage. Indeed, after the fourteenth century, an attempt was made for total 'thought control'!

It is a sad story. It is all the more ironic in that the Church, during the era of the Roman Empire, was then subject to long periods of savage persecution. Now, in a position of power and authority, the Church exchanged roles and itself became a persecutor.

As early as 1229 the Synod of Toulouse officially set up the office of the Inquisition. It was charged with the duty of seeking out heretics and bringing them to trial. If it found the accused guilty the Inquisition allowed two options: burning at the stake or recantation. It operated mainly in Italy and France. However, whereas early heretics merely deviated from mainstream theology only in the finer points (and sometimes disputed the accuracy of biblical translations from the Greek), the new breed of heretic no longer quibbled over such hairs; they now bitterly attacked the very administration, conduct and attitudes of the Church itself. In Britain in 1378 John Wycliffe, Master of Balliol College, Oxford, had the impudence to believe that the common people, unable as they were to understand Latin, should at least hear the Bible read each Sunday in their own tongue. To add insult to injury he actually began the first complete English translation. He also sharply criticised the sale of indulgences and the general state of corruption in the priesthood. This resulted in his excommunication. Later he was declared a heretic and the Pope ordered his arrest. Fortunately, protection in high places among the secular nobility and the Pope's divided attention on more immediate political problems saved Wycliffe from the stake. Corruption and debauchery among the priesthood nevertheless continued and indeed became endemic. It was now visible at the very top of the Church among cardinals and candidates for the next Pope. In 1402 John Huss, rector of Prague University, publicly criticised the standards of morality throughout all sectors of Church administration. Hearing of the work of Wycliffe he had the audacity to praise the English reformer. Students and laypersons alike were impressed and he attracted an unusually large following. Faced with yet another demonstration of defiance, the Church promptly excommunicated him. Unfortunately, Huss lacked the English reformer's backing in high places. Nevertheless, he courageously obeyed a summons to appear before the Council of Constance. Here he again stoutly maintained the right of the common people to hear or read the Bible in their own tongue. In doing so he rejected the authority of the Pope. Refusing to recant, he was burned at the stake in 1415. In effect he had become one of the most notable of martyrs in the cause of information flow, and this time embracing the Bible itself. The disgust and anger at his treatment brought serious repercussions. Followers organised themselves after his death; known as Hussites, they began a series of revolts. This caused serious disruption in Bohemia, leading to all-out war in 1419. The Hussites were put down with difficulty, and only after a combination of forces was brought against them. Appalling methods were used to break their spirit, yet the spark of revolt was never fully extinguished. A century later, similar criticisms of Church corruption, this time in Germany, were touched off by a former monk and ordained priest, Martin Luther. With his private pleas for reform contemptuously rejected, he finally reacted in public. In his capacity of preacher at Wittenberg University, he nailed his famous denunciation of corruption to his church door. Showing such defiance, Luther too would have suffered as Huss. However, as with Wycliffe, he too had protection from powerful sympathisers. Subsequently of course a series of revolts convulsed the whole of Europe. And it brought about the second schism in the Christian Church – that is if one sees the Eastern Orthodox Church as the first. Needless to say, given such a situation, the Inquisition flourished. A particularly vicious and active section operated in Spain together with its colonial empire. Trials were held in secret and torture used to obtain confessions. In fact sadistic tortures and burnings continued right up until 1781. They made the word Inquisition synonymous with bestiality and horror, an era which the Catholic Church now finds acutely embarrassing. The measure of embarrassment can be estimated by the Vatican's repeated attempts to shelve responsibility, insisting that in Spain the Inquisition was organised and controlled by each succeeding king of Spain, and not by succeeding popes. Even so, the fact that this horror could continue without effective restraint or open criticism from Rome speaks for itself. Concurrently too, the Index Librorum Prohibitorum was set up throughout Catholic areas of Europe to control every aspect of information flow. Its task was to censor all branches of literature and to burn those books thought to question the authority and legitimacy of the true Church. It did so with great zeal century after century, despite, ironically enough, being steadily circumvented by many Catholics themselves. In fact it tended to achieve the very opposite of what it had set out to do. Books placed on the index began to attract a rarity value automatically! The cardinals had overlooked the quirk in human nature that generates a curious magnetism around anything condemned by authority! Yet the Church persisted with its attempted censorship right up to this century, incredibly enough to 1966, to be precise.

Equally incredibly, there were brief periods where the middle and upper hierarchy (bishops and cardinals) were allowed to speculate freely in areas normally held taboo.

Nicholas of Cusa, for example, believed the Earth spun on its axis and circled the sun. He believed too that there were similar 'suns' in the remainder of the heavens with yet similar systems of planets circling them. On these might be found life-forms in close parallel to our own. He was even allowed to publish a book in 1440 detailing these speculations. Incidentally, he also believed that God was beyond all human comprehension and could only be approached at a distance by mystical and paranormal perception. As a notable mathematician, he further held that only numbers had any absolute value. They alone had intrinsic permanence in their own right and successfully resisted eternal flux and degradation. Astonishingly, despite all these subversive views, he was made a cardinal! Perhaps those in final authority deferred to his powerful intellect and were prepared to make an exception in his case. Whatever the reasons, it must be observed yet again that such interludes were brief and were later seen as mistaken.

Over the long period of its systematic attempt to control people's very thoughts, let alone the free flow of information, the Inquisition claimed some notable victims. Among them was the philosopher-scientist Giordano Bruno. Being an enthusiastic supporter of Copernicus, (the poor timid cleric who had conveniently died before the Church's wrath descended on him), Bruno maintained that the world circled the sun. Amongst other things he also taught that space was infinite, and that planets circled other stars and probably had life on them. The Inquisition arrested him in Venice in 1592. Following his refusal to recant, he was later burned alive at the stake. Galileo, almost his contemporary, but twenty years younger, was suitably intimidated by Bruno's fate. When he too was brought before the Inquisitors, he was persuaded to recant. That does not imply he lacked courage: I suspect Galileo's pragmatism questioned the logic of throwing away his life when he still had many unfinished scientific investigations to pursue.

Given these and many other blatant instances of attempted 'mind control', if we take an overview of the Christian Church's role in the advancement of knowledge or in unrestricted information flow generally, then after the twelfth century, it seems to become progressively darker and thoroughly discreditable. However, with the schism caused by the Reformation there were now effectively two Christian Churches in Western Europe. Thus from this period any overview has to distinguish between regimes that were either Protestant or Catholic. Difficult as it is to generalise, it must nevertheless be said that in the matter of freedom of information flow, the Protestant sectors tended to show greater levels of toleration than their Catholic counterparts. And this may well account for the fact that science and technology in northern Europe (where Protestant regimes were dominant) proceeded thereafter with far greater vitality and breadth of achievement than in the Catholic south. This seems to hold true right through the sixteenth, seventeenth, eighteenth and nineteenth centuries.

A fundamental change came about in the closing years of the nineteenth century, however. This was wholly due to a dramatic change in attitudes to universal education. At this time people throughout Europe were determined to become better informed in every sector of human activity. They also began wondering what the brand-new twentieth century would bring them. Particularly in the sector of information flow, it would seem that for the first time in the long history of restrictions and of crude disinformation, that flow was at last being liberated from the worst of restraints or harmful corrupting influences. To begin with, for the first time in mankind's history (at least throughout Europe and North America) education of all children, no matter what their social station in life, was at last being taken over by the state. It was even offered to the poorest classes without payment! In some countries, child education actually became compulsory. And to further the cause of the hitherto neglected field of adult education, more and more public libraries were being opened. Again their use was offered without payment; moreover, they stocked information over an astonishing range of subjects. Over and above this, not only had the telephone been invented and was sending messages over distances restricted only by length of cable laid, but Marconi was gradually perfecting radio transmission. This held out startling possibilities. Indeed in the very first year of the new century he was to send a radio signal from Cornwall to Newfoundland, thus introducing to the world instant intercontinental transmission of information – and in an entirely new medium.

Consequently Europeans everywhere, as they approached the last minutes of the thirty-first of December, 1899, had good reason to pause to look back over the nineteenth century. And in recognising its startling achievements, they now fondly believed that a 'brave new world' and an age of glorious opportunity awaited them. Surely the sudden and brilliant surge of discoveries in science and technology alone would bring a truly Golden Era? Might it not parallel the astonishing advances made in the Grecian civilisation? Some of the more self-assured of politicians suggested Grecian triumphs would not just be put in the shade, but be totally eclipsed! They shouted, 'Look about you!' Despite the obvious use of hyperbole, many were duly impressed. The Age of Steam had arrived and coal, as a wonder fuel, was not only being rapidly applied to the developing railways and steam shipping, but also used for by-products such as coal-gas and forever expanding industrial and chemical uses. Without doubt it had already revolutionised transport and would develop still further. Faraday, in his famous researches into the properties of electricity, invented the electric generator; later Swan in Britain and (independently) Edison in America invented the electric bulb to form lamps. Stimulated by these discoveries, scientists and technicians everywhere were now investigating new applications of this incredibly flexible way of transmitting and using energy. Power stations were being built and electricity cables were being laid to many public buildings, even to the private houses of the rich in large cities the length and breadth of both continents!

Following closely on the heels of these basic discoveries came photography, a primitive cine-photography, and the phonograph, which was later to become the gramophone. These too were also being rapidly improved and developed. Information was flowing, and *how*!

Moving to discoveries made in the field of medicine, Jenner introduced the concept of vaccination, Lister the use of antiseptics, while that giant of microscopy and bacteriology, Pasteur, not only created the science of polarimetry, but the 'germ theory' and techniques of pasteurisation. Then there was Koch, also a bacteriologist, who invented the artificial culture of bacteria; at the same time his co-worker Ehrlich discovered the vital technique of using aniline dyes to stain them. Perhaps more important still, he discovered and identified the tubercle and cholera bacillus – the essential first step in the subsequent search for a cure to the ravages of tuberculosis and cholera. Ehrlich also discovered part of the cyclical transmission of bubonic plague and malaria, while Laveran and Ross showed ways of their control and eradication. Ehrlich, now working independently, also perfected a diphtheria antitoxin (he would shortly find a syphilis antitoxin and truly launch the science of chemotherapy). As for Landsteiner, he discovered the existence of blood groups, making blood transfusion safe and creating its widespread use. Beyond this came developments in the field of relief of pain, not forgetting the need to render a patient 'docile', thus allowing a surgeon to work unhindered during surgery. Various anaesthetics were discovered by Davy, Guthrie, Jackson, Simpson and Morton. Lastly came the discovery of X-rays by Roentgen, this just five years before the end of the century. It was to revolutionise many aspects of achieving accuracy in diagnosis. It was already giving information on broken bones and was being developed further to discover the presence of diseases such as tuberculosis and internal ulcerations. All these researchers, and indeed many more, totally transformed the science of medicine.

As for the field of pure science generally, there were an astonishing number of brilliant men. Some of these were already unlocking the secrets of the atom, and would allow the next century to be called, with somewhat indelicate triumphalism, 'The Atomic Age'! As a result this new insight into the interior of the atom would bring the hitherto artificially separated disciplines of physics, chemistry, biology and astronomy virtually into an inseparable single science. Fresnel, JJ Thomson, Orsted,

Maxwell, Ramsey, Rutherford, Millikan, Michelson-Morley, Lorentz de Broglie, the Curies, Soddy, Aston, Rayleigh, Barkla, Wien, Boltzmann, Nernst, Bragg, Hertz, Moseley, Planck... and many more had already contributed to the great leap forward, and this before the nineteenth century had come to its end. What would come when the twentieth century fully dawned? Can we permit ourselves just a peek? Well, the scientific world was to find Planck announcing his revolutionary quantum theory in the very first year of the new century, while Einstein, stimulated by the work of Maxwell and Planck, had already started work on the first of many papers he was to submit to *Annalen der Physik*. Incidentally at this time he was almost penniless and about to obtain a humble post as a kind of clerk in the Swiss Patent Office!

Over the previous century the only area where a somewhat sour note had been struck was in the field of biology. In fact it had proved truly controversial – this to scientists and general public alike. The very introduction of the word 'evolution' had shocked a great many, particularly those who possessed excessive self-esteem. And it caused fury among those ignorant of the science of astronomy and geology. Why? It shattered pompous concepts of man's place in the universe. The cause? The publication of *The Origin of Species* by the self-effacing Charles Darwin. His later publication, *The Descent of Man*, merely spelled out clearly and in greater detail what had been implicit in the earlier thesis. Darwin, who at one time had considered becoming a country parson, was too shy and withdrawn to stand up in a crowd and use oratory to promote his viewpoint. Fortunately others did so for him. Scientists – notably in the new discipline of geology, where the estimation of the age and subsequent development of rock formation was pushing the creation of the planet further and further back in time – quickly supported and publicised his theory. The Catholic Church was outraged. Protestant churches too were not, as one might say, 'well pleased'. It does, however, make a significant comment on the relatively tolerant attitude of the British established church, namely the Church of England, in that while some bishops actively opposed Darwin's theory (and did so quite vigorously in public) many more reflected quietly on the matter and adjusted their attitude. They were prepared to modify an all-too-literal interpretation of Biblical poetic imagery. Nevertheless, if Darwin had not been born into the somewhat upper-class and Protestant English gentry, but born in a Catholic country and to the lower classes, his career would doubtless have been very different. One thing is certain: he would never have been buried in a place of honour in the foremost abbey of the land. In sharp contrast, the Vatican even refused Galileo burial in consecrated ground!

Fortunately the controversy concerning the evolution of man, indeed of animals generally and of this planet, gradually died in scientific circles. But it remained of some concern to the general public. The quantum theory, and that of other theories concerning the mysterious nucleus of the atom and its particles, however, raged hotly within the scientific world. Not unexpectedly, it was totally above and beyond the understanding of non-scientists. Equally the theories of Mendel: these were rediscovered by De Vries in 1900 while he was engaged on his own research into evolution. More particularly the mechanics of hereditary transference. These were to raise another storm, if of shorter duration. Thus it could be said that in the year 1900 the infant science of genetics was truly born! With it, of course, would eventually come another great leap forward in our understanding of the very basis of life itself. But to return to the opening years of the century...

Within just three years the Wright brothers had achieved the first powered flight; Bohr had begun to study physics at Copenhagen University; while in 1905 Einstein had published four papers in *Annalen der Physik*, the last of which was rather innocently entitled 'On the Electrodynamics of Moving Bodies'. This was to bring him eventually out of the obscurity of the Patent Office at Bern and make his name the focus of attention throughout the entire scientific world.

But to return yet again to the actual moment of the turn of the century. For so-called 'ordinary men and women' in Europe and North America, whose education had not allowed them a glimpse into the deeper truth and momentous developments in science, their view of the political vistas, as the last minutes of 1899 ticked by, did indeed seem to hold considerable promise. In the USA the immense suffering and destruction caused by the Civil War between the North and South was now only a bad memory. A period of rapid industrial growth had in the interim brought a fair level of prosperity. In Europe the Franco-Prussian war (avenging the latter's defeat at Jena by Napoleon at the opening of the century) was also being gradually erased from people's minds. One could perhaps ignore various Balkan disturbances because there had always been Balkan disturbances: they had been reappearing with monotonous regularity for as long as anyone could remember. As for the petty Germanic kingdoms, they had coalesced under Bismarck's influence to form a united Germany. This appeared to give a gratifying stability to the region. After all, they too, much like the Balkans, had been involved in endless squabbles. Indeed it seemed to balance out those otherwise rather uncomfortable bids for dominance made by either Russia or Austria. Thus weighing up the situation overall in both the New World and the Old (insofar as Caucasian light-skinned people were concerned at least), the closing days of the nineteenth century seemed to give confidence for the future and a sense of well-being. In Britain particularly, all too conscious of her power and her justifiable claim of being the most technologically advanced nation on Earth, politicians in the Foreign Office congratulated themselves on having achieved remarkable success – they had secured a range of interlocking treaties with allies and potential enemies alike! Stability and an end to petty feuding seemed completely assured. They looked at the world with politicians' eyes. With such myopic vision, and using no other viewpoint, what they saw on the horizon was a new era of unparalleled opportunity and even greater glory.

However British people, outside the more exalted of social classes, were somewhat less sanguine. Yet even they recognised stability when they saw it. To begin with, there was an unexpected increase in the size and indeed influence of the middle classes; also, the poor felt their plight was now recognised and remedial action being taken. Bismarck in Germany had instituted pensions and insurance for workers, and British politicians had been duly shamed; indeed the principle was gradually being accepted throughout the remainder of Europe. More promising still, greater democracy and wider voting rights were beginning to achieve results. Incredibly, the 'nobility' were at last beginning to lose their total grip on power. Much to the latter's surprise, it was no longer possible to achieve a position in the forefront of society, or to secure national or international prestige, solely by being born into wealth and influence. The days of wandering round Europe and the remainder of the world with smiling servants constantly uttering 'Yes, m'lord' or 'No, m'lord' were drawing to a close. You could no longer occupy yourself hunting deer in the Scottish Highlands or even small defenceless creatures on your country estate, nor could you attend the occasional society ball and expect this to be sole guarantee of your social status. It no longer secured immediate superiority over others. More oddly still, those just a few notches down on the social scale found that equipping themselves with that particular status conferred by an honours degree at a famous university no longer guaranteed deference either! Faraday, for example, being one of ten children of a blacksmith, was born into the lowest of social classes. In his early teens he was apprenticed to a bookbinder – this on the sole recommendation that he could at least read and write. But a new phenomenon, that some might have called 'uncommon luck', was increasingly evident in this era, and it was one that could even penetrate the rigid class structure. Indeed it allowed Faraday a narrow opening into fame, and by a circuitous route at that! He now became a glorified bottle-washer to another 'rags-to-riches' success story – Sir Humphry Davy. Ironically the latter, a self-taught scientific researcher, himself once the humble son of a woodcarver and sometime apprentice to an apothecary, would not only find his own career pattern being repeated by his new assistant, but surpassed! Faraday's genius, his sheer capacity for hard work, combined with a penetrating curiosity, eventually brought him greater fame than his master. And incredibly, both men made their way in the world because of their lack of higher education! You see it brought unstuffy and uniquely fresh minds to a particular range of scientific problems, problems that had tended to be obscured by an overly academic approach. Indeed it is argued that Faraday's lack of any mathematical training proved a positive advantage in that it forced him to visualise invisible magnetic attraction as actual 'lines of force', as he called them. He was content to leave it to the mathematical genius of Maxwell to construct equations for what was now to become the foundation of electromagnetic theory. He left it to Maxwell again to postulate that, with the speed of transmission of electricity so close to that of light, it must therefore fall within a definite relationship. It inspired Maxwell to predict a whole family of electromagnetic radiations. And he may well have succeeded in finding them but for his early and untimely death. That particular triumph was achieved shortly after by others.

Astonishing and 'uncommon luck' was also evident outside the field of pure science. People with a flair for technology, or alternatively for what are now called 'entrepreneurial' skills, also began to make their way in the world from humble beginnings. Perhaps the premier examples in America were Edison, Ford, and Carnegie. There were, of course, numerous others, but it would be too wearisome a task to name them all. Most were connected with large-scale manufacturing, or with the newly emerging energy source for the next century – oil.

As for the sphere of the arts, some of the greatest names representing the peaks of genius had been at work during this century. They had been producing some of the most impressive and inspired work the world had yet seen. Among them were Beethoven, Schubert, Brahms, Goethe, Dickens, Hugo, Tolstoy, Dostoevsky, Constable, Degas, Monet, Manet and Van Gogh, to name only a handful. These and many more were arguably reaching the same heights, or even surpassing the works of genius in earlier centuries. At the same time some changed the very nature, character, or overall vision of the sphere in which they worked.

And this was not the only area of human activity where significant changes were taking place. Domination by the male sex in almost every sphere of human activity was also being challenged. Women were now mobilising themselves on a crusade for equality, and they were poised to reach and to grasp privileges and rights that hitherto had only been dreamed of. The right to vote was achieved in New Zealand in 1893, a similar right in Australia in 1902. This spurred the Suffragette movement to even greater effort in Britain. Similar movements sprung up in the remainder of Europe and the USA. Women campaigned equally vigorously for equality of opportunity to enter universities, for unrestricted entry to most professions, for entry to Parliament and indeed into government, and for equal pay for equal work.

All in all, as bells throughout Europe and North America rang in the first few seconds of the new year, contemporary writers and commentators on affairs reported that confidence was high. The mass of people celebrating at that particular moment would have supposed that the twentieth century would bring them unimaginable good fortune!

Why then did it all go wrong, horribly wrong! And so soon?

*

Go wrong? Some individuals might be moved to query or even contest that statement. 'Did it really go wrong?' They might press you, and do so with the kind of inflection in the voice that suggests you are labouring needlessly under a fallacy. Much depends of course what age they are, what country they were brought up in, and the quality of their lifestyle. Anyone born after the 1950s in Western Europe, Scandinavia and North America, born moreover into a middle or upper-class family, will have been protected from all those 'slings and arrows of outrageous fortune'. The ghastly traumas suffered by the remainder of the world are therefore too distant. Horror and unimaginable ill fortune fail to impinge heavily and completely on the mind unless experienced personally. Memory does not ceaselessly force back yesterday's terror; it does not flood back into today's consciousness to bring an endless legacy of bitterness and grief. Those born in the second half of this century and into favoured areas of the world can so easily shut out the shocking realities of life that were (and still are) endured by the rest of the world. There is so little effort required to turn one's head away, connect one's ears to that portable musak centre, smother one's taste buds with gourmet delights, feast one's eyes on, then sigh over, luxuries of every kind – in short, lose oneself in the arduous business of truly 'living up' the good life. The woes of the twentieth century? What woes?

Despite the deplorable image the West so often projects to the remainder of the world – the unremitting round of pleasure-seeking, gross self-indulgence and sheer decadence – there are of course many who try to come to terms with a more sober reality. And it is not a matter of informing oneself merely of the details of two world wars. You see when these two conflagrations ended there was still what you might call an interlude or 'riotous peace' because somewhere or other in the world mounting conflict and suffering continued, often bursting into short interludes of open war.

So then, much of the answer lies with the kind of eyes people use – and regretfully will continue to use – to view the various kinds of phenomena of life around them. And after such viewing inevitably comes the very special way in which their cerebral filtering and subsequent processing of information brings them to certain conclusions.

Those conclusions, and the optimism generated in 1899 as the last minutes of the century ticked away, were, as we now know, cruelly misplaced. The new century, far from ushering in a Golden Age, saw human conflict rise to unprecedented levels of ferocity.

It was to cause not just appalling loss of life, but also widespread destruction of historic buildings, sometimes entire areas of lovely old towns and villages over which craftsmen had laboured (in the case of cathedrals) for many decades, if not centuries.

In like manner it was not just on battlefields that the youth and future hopes of nations were blown apart, nor for that matter just in two world wars. In those years of riotous peace between the two world wars and again after 1945, shells, bombs and bullets flew at frequent intervals. But they were not the only dealers of death and destruction: casualties were greatly extended by the displacement of countless millions. Inevitably this lead to the serious disruption of harvests, later to the supply and distribution of food, clean water, fuel and shelter. With widespread food shortages (if not full-blown famines) came the unavoidable aftermath: widespread disease.

Every continent was affected and hardly any area carrying human populations of any size or concentration escaped. The influenza pandemic immediately following World War One, for example, killed more people than the actual hostilities. Everywhere civilians were just as vulnerable to the Four Horsemen as front-line troops.

A mild foretaste of what was to come introduced itself to the British public within the very first month of January, 1900. They were made vaguely aware, even within its first few days, that dark clouds were forming on the horizon. A small cloud had formed a few years previously, but had seemed a very minor affair with some Boer farmers. These troubles in South Africa now suddenly flared up into serious acts of defiance. But news travelled slowly. The Boers had, it seemed, a month previously tweaked the lion's tail. With a British army stretched out in penny packets over a huge empire, there were all too few troops available to deal with the matter. And these had not performed as well as expected. The fault lay not with the lower ranks but with the officers in command. The Government, attempting to hide its embarrassment, informed the public that our brave men, being fully professional soldiers trained in the more civilised forms of warfare, had not been properly instructed in dealing with guerrilla tactics. Cabinet members and senior generals suggested, no doubt with the aid of grave semaphore signals sent by flashing monocles, that they were not fighting a gentlemanly war. The dastardly Boers refused to equip their men with bright red uniforms which would properly aid recognition and make them good targets. It was not cricket. Such men were almost indistinguishable from civilians in their nondescript dress. The Zulus and other African tribes were of course instantly recognisable; they were obliging enough to have different skin colour and go about half-naked. They were also extremely sporting in that they massed together to make frontal charges. This saved wasting an enormous amount of expensive ammunition. The Boers, in contrast, dismounted from their horses and crawled behind every bit of cover, bobbing out from time to time from behind rocks (yes, bullet-proof rocks!) to use the very latest in long-range rifles, probably bought from Germans at that! Incidentally, the presence of Germans in their nearby and recently acquired African territory was a worrying development. It was bad enough having the French as competitors in the scramble for overseas empires without having to take into account the newly constituted German nation also!

In this manner the ground was prepared for the British public to take further bad news. The Government, bubbling with outrage, gradually admitted that several small units of the army, garrisoned in various towns, together with a proportion of British civilians, had been surrounded. The public were stunned. Within days it was rumoured that Ladysmith, Kimberley and Mafeking, which had now been under siege for some time, could not hold out for much longer. Bits and pieces of further bad news had been slowly filtering through during the last weeks of 1899, even so it had not been fully confirmed by the Government. This time rumour had it that small contingents of troops sent to deal with such an affront had suffered serious reverses, had even been wiped out! Later this was officially confirmed. The British public were angry and dismayed. Full details were demanded. Independent newspaper reports, although taking weeks to transmit from South Africa, were now daring to expose what the Government would have preferred to hide: a scandalous lack of professional expertise by senior officers directing the operation. Such independent reporting, aided by the ominous degree of freedom now evident in information flow, was something all Western governments were having to come to terms with. In the good old days, news had been, thank God, transmitted by town crier or by speeches from public figures over whom one had a degree of control. And the human voice unaided could only reach a small audience. Now had come this worrying development of the common people being able to afford to buy daily papers! Bless my soul! In these they not only feasted their eyes on and hugely enjoyed the satirical cartoons, but they actually had the ability to read the printed contents. It was intolerable! Austria, for example, embroiled as always in Balkan disputes, reverted to its old authoritarian ways; with a fond glance back to 1815 and the regime of Metternich, the masters of this now ailing central European empire attempted total censorship. The British, with their gift for finding a devious middle way, attempted to bribe the new press barons into either withholding or at least playing down really shocking news. Of course there was nothing so vulgar as actual money or expensive gifts changing hands, but in the smoke-rooms of fashionable clubs there were discreet offers of elevations to the peerage. This worked reasonably well with some newspaper proprietors but it proved tricky with others. The damnable part of it was that some were already peers! It was unheard of. People with their fingers on the pulse of things had got used to industrialists finally entering the ranks of the elite, in other words becoming indistinguishable from land-owning aristocracy. But they had all come from heavy industry or alternately were jumped-up storekeepers like the recently knighted Sir Thomas Lipton. But who had ever heard of aristocrats in the ink-splattered printing trade? What had been overlooked of course was the explosion in the demand for books, magazines and newspapers. To meet that demand, the technology of printing had developed fast and furiously. What had once been no more than a glorified cottage industry, had now graduated to become a 'light industrial' concern at the very least. But the arrival of electricity as a power source had perhaps contributed more than any other factor to the various techniques employed. This alone had greatly speeded production and lowered unit costs. An electrically driven typesetter was already in operation by 1877 and inventions for various types of rotary-impression machines had come quickly in the 1880s. The rapidly expanding railway network then transported tens of thousands of newspapers from each individual publisher now situated in all the principal cities, and did so with great speed right around the country. Normally, the very rich and powerful had always taken interest solely in the heavy industry sector. After all, only they had the capital to buy new machines and recruit a workforce. The various sectors of light industry usually failed to attract serious attention because the profit margins were seldom impressive enough. Even so it was precisely the rich who had a vested interest in maintaining influence over both the government of the day and public opinion: they could thereby have some control over this dangerous and often riderless runaway beast called democracy. As a direct result, any right-wing Tory government that happened by chance to irritate the press barons found apologies necessary in private. As for a liberal government (either with capital or small 'L') with ghastly leftist tendencies, they had even less leverage over those already ensconced among the nobility. Lloyd George, son of a teacher, and later as an MP a fiery radical, was brave enough at this time to voice support for the Boers. The press however had demonised these descendants of Dutch emigrants so successfully that Lloyd George, in attempting to speak in their defence at a famous public meeting found, his life in danger. He had to be spirited out of the building by a back door, the resourceful police having disguised him in a police jacket and helmet. His younger contemporary and sometime associate Churchill, in contrast, was more circumspect. He constantly rubbed shoulders with the press barons, and, while not giving way on any deeply held conviction, at least managed to hold their respect. Normally he avoided vitriolic abuse. Significantly, in the early years of the century, Viscount Northcliffe held a premier position among newspaper proprietors and all succeeding governments found leverage somewhat limited. When wishing to withhold sensitive or embarrassing information, they had to approach Northcliffe with considerable delicacy and subtlety. No keen observer of the political scene was however particularly surprised when his younger brother Sidney Harmsworth, with whom Northcliffe ran the *Daily Mail*, was later made a baronet. Precisely what services he rendered are not fully proven. Nevertheless it is significant that he received further honours, reaching his brother's rank of viscount later in the twentieth century.

Indeed all governments throughout Europe, no matter what their political complexion, were forced to gain some measure of influence one way or another over the press. They were swept along almost helplessly, not just by the tide of educational achievement now being gained by the masses, but also by the rapid developments in the technology of distribution in all kinds of information. All of them too had to look anxiously over their shoulders, either for evidence of an overall tone of approval or of condemnation voiced by the press in general. Discreet meetings were arranged with editors, or more usually with their owners tugging the strings behind them. Newfangled telephones were used at urgent moments. The days when a very small number of laboriously printed newspapers, distributed with equally laborious means of transport (stagecoach at best, horse and cart at worst), were truly dead and gone. So too was the convenient filter of the local squire, vicar or non-conformist minister, who then passed on his opinions to a barely literate or wholly illiterate public. Likewise was the filtering process by those influential individuals in towns and cities, the masters of the guilds of all the different trades – people and craftsmen and the like.

Throughout Europe then, the true value of effectively guiding the thoughts and opinions of the masses via the newspapers was being actively realised. But often the lesson was being learned by individuals who were by no means part of the aristocratic structure, whether land-owning or otherwise. They now came mainly from the middle and lower classes. For example, Friedrich Engels, born into the German middle class in 1820, had been sent to Britain to supervise work in a small cotton factory at Manchester owned by his father. Being shocked by the overall conditions in that industrialised region generally, he dedicated his life to reforming the attitudes of the day. He began promoting nothing short of revolution by writing, printing and issuing considerable amounts of literature on the subject. Later, in visits to Germany, he collaborated with Karl Marx in preparing the *Communist Manifesto*. As a copious contributor to such specialised information flow, Marx himself, while resident in Prussia, edited the *Neue Rheinische Zeitung*. For his efforts in this direction he was expelled. He came to London after the failure of the revolution in Germany, and with Engels's financial support, continued his work there. If one moves one's attention to Russia, one finds that the Tsarist regime carefully censored as much literature as they could lay hands on, then confiscated the more dangerous. They subsequently reserved what one might call 'political holidays' in the spiritually purifying climate of Siberia for anyone who earned displeasure. Thus a certain Vladimir Ilyich Ulyanov, later known to the world as Lenin, had already been introduced to the invigorating air further north for the benefit of his political health. He had been born into the Russian middle class in 1870, the son of a school inspector at Simbirsk. In 1893 he devoted himself to distributing revolutionary propaganda. After being sent on a five-year spell to Siberia, he returned to the underground editorship of a Social Democrat paper, *Iskra*, which in English translates as *Spark*. Lev Bronstein, or Trotsky, born in 1879 in Elizavetgrad, became a dedicated Marxist in his teens. He also distributed revolutionary propaganda, was twice exiled to Siberia and would later join with Lenin in organising revolution. Joseph Djugashvili or Stalin, born into the poorest class, the son of a Georgian shoemaker, joined the Social Democratic Party in 1898 and was exiled to Siberia five times. Later he became editor of *Pravda*.

Moving south, one finds that in the warmer, if not hot-house climate of Italy, Benito Mussolini, born the son of a blacksmith in 1883, was now becoming politically active. In the early years of the next century he served as a journalist for the Socialist movement. When expelled from it, he would retaliate by becoming its bitter enemy, in the meantime founding the *Fasci di Combattimento*, a wholly new totalitarian nationalist movement, soon to be known as Fascist. Consolidating its influence by editing another newspaper and producing a mass of propaganda, Mussolini was to achieve absolute power in Italy in 1922. Hitler, born in 1889, the son of a customs officer, was to make an even greater mark on the next century. After serving in the trenches of World War One, he reacted sharply against many of his fellow Austrians and Germans who now began finding some comfort in communism. Inspired by Mussolini's fascist dictatorship and its apparent success, he was of course later to make the fullest use of what was to become the world's most highly organised and effective propaganda machine.

Already then, in the first decade of the twentieth century, it was possible for those gifted with deeper insight to see that the triumphant march toward free and uncorrupted information flow was now faltering. Liberated briefly in Western Europe only, and after many trials and tribulations suffered by an assortment of brave individuals (and not a few martyrs) in previous centuries, all of them passionately devoted to its cause, it was soon to be either stifled or cunningly doctored once again.

In Britain, in the first year of the twentieth century, one finds an almost chaotic situation prevailing. Here were demonstrated short bouts of openness alternating with rather longer periods of crude manipulation.

Winston Churchill, then a dashing and highly ambitious young man aged twenty-six, had fully realised that the days of unbridled power of the English aristocracy, to which he proudly belonged, were numbered. Even skilful manipulation of the masses by the aristocracy – still for the most part having undue influence over the government of the day – was almost over. He clearly saw that role passing to the mass media. He had begun a career as an army officer with training at Sandhurst, but became convinced, after seeing active service in India and the Sudan, that any bid for real power no longer lay in that direction. Shamelessly using the influence provided at birth (being the son of Lord Randolph Churchill and a direct descendant of the Duke of Marlborough) he pressed the War Office into allowing him periods 'on loan' as a war correspondent with the *Morning Post*. Making his way to South Africa and touring the guerrilla country he won immediate attention among the masses back home, firstly by being captured by the Boers and then by making his sensational escape. It was to prove an excellent pathway into public life. His name became *the* topic of conversation in every home throughout Britain. Within a year he had left South Africa, and had offered himself as parliamentary candidate for Oldham, Lancashire. This town, significantly enough, had a large working-class electorate. Here he won the seat for the Unionists. Switching later to the Liberals, who, it seemed, had greater prospects of achieving and retaining power, by 1908 he was in the Cabinet as President of the Board of Trade. By 1910 he was actually Home Secretary. It spoke volumes for the influence provided by constant media attention. It was an attention he was to carefully cultivate in later life also.

Not that Churchill should thus be a special target for our sniffy censure. Other young political hopefuls in pursuit of their ambition were doing exactly the same throughout Europe; indeed, the tradition remains alive and kicking to this very day. Unfortunately, though, by immersing ourselves in trivia of this nature we can deny ourselves insight into far more important factors.

A case in point: serious interference with (or manipulation of) information flow was not the only misfortune suffered by the bulk of Western civilisation at this time. There was also a change in attitudes to the prosecution and organisation of warfare!

Few realised this at the time. It was to become, in suitably terse and crude terms, 'Total War'.

Two main factors were involved. Firstly, the technology already existed, if in rather a crude and as yet untried form. Now there were excellent prospects for maiming and killing on a scale never seen before. Secondly, nation states had become so well organised as to be able to conscript huge masses of men into the armed forces. Given earlier Napoleonic and Prussian exemplars, they were no longer forced to rely mainly on small volunteer or 'professional' armies. Every fit young man could be forcibly enlisted into the full prosecution of war – enlisted whether he agreed with his nation's cause or not.

To return to the Boer War for a moment: it is a classic example of the failure of older traditions to apply, and clearly exhibits stumbling steps toward the new. All of these were wholly under the force of circumstances.

The British government of the day, in direct response to universal criticism, now appointed men of proven efficiency to teach those wretched farmers a lesson! Generals Roberts and Kitchener were dispatched by sea with extra troops and equipment; these landed in Africa on the tenth of January, 1900. This would surely put the Boers in their proper place. They eventually did, of course. But it was to take all of two years and a quite unexpected cost in lives, not to mention reputations!

To make an effective response against guerrilla tactics, Kitchener, with his talent for the unconventional approach and effective organisation, reasoned that the Boer raiders could carry on indefinitely – that is unless they were denied the basic sustenance of life: food, clothing and shelter. The simple logic of this was (and still is) undeniable. Although he may not have realised it at the time, he was about to apply some of the first principles of Total War. Superficially it had something in common with the Russian scorched earth policy of the nineteenth century, as applied in the face of Napoleon's advancing army. However, in this instance it was applied *by* the advancing army, not the one retreating. Under his orders, all outlying farm buildings belonging to the Boers, together with their crops, were to be destroyed. Not only that – the resident Boer women and children (any absent menfolk proved they were family members of the guerrillas and therefore the main source of aid), were to be brought back together with their cattle into the most fertile central areas. These areas were then surrounded for miles by manned blockhouses, each within sight of one another, and monitored by ceaseless patrols. The women and children were in the meantime placed into tented camps built army-style in neat rows.

Kitchener's so-called 'concentration camps' did not at that time have the sinister connotation we think of now. Nonetheless, tragic consequences were to gradually unfold, bringing the concept of Total War into clearer focus.

The inmates of the camps were, true to the normal military standards of the time, properly fed, clothed and housed, and given adequate medical plus hygienic facilities. There were several infant deaths within the first few weeks. This was nothing out of the ordinary: infant mortality at the turn of the century was still high, even in the best of conditions within Europe itself. But as the weeks passed, the death toll rose sharply. A catalogue of diseases began to take effect on older children, then adults. Inmates of all ages began to die in steadily increasing numbers.

It has not been properly established whether Kitchener was informed in good time or alternately was too involved in the overall prosecution of the war to give the matter his full attention. At any event, the death toll rose steadily. Then the press got wind of it, and in the oddest way. A very determined young English lady – provoked by rumours and uncertainties about the earlier alleged incompetence of British officers on the one hand, and the wholly dastardly tactics employed by the Boer on the other – set out for the war zone alone. She saw her mission as a dedicated amateur, or perhaps dilettante reporter, who was about to set the record straight. Rumour and innuendo were to be scotched once and for all. Coming by chance on one of the concentration camps she was horrified by what she saw. Reporting immediately by letter back to relatives in Britain, she insisted they should contact the editor of any reputable newspaper. This was done. Once again the Government found itself in an embarrassing position over these appalling Boers. Previously they had been criticised for not killing enough of them (males at least); now they were criticised for killing women and children – prisoners at that, and in uncomfortably large numbers! Remedial measures were taken as quickly as possible. But by that time the death toll had reached truly scandalous proportions.

For those with hidden motives for putting the reputation of the British military in as bad a light as possible, there is no great difficulty in alleging a deliberate policy of extermination. Nobody can deny that these tented camps were erected and organised specifically to contain Boer women and children. Nobody can dispute the final death toll. But the evidence we have today tends to support a series of omissions rather than commissions. A sinister motive seems absent. This was indeed a lurch toward the concept of Total War, but it was accidental rather than deliberate.

To begin with, when a peace treaty with the Boers was finally signed on 31 May, 1902, the British Army had lost 5,774 officers and soldiers killed in action. Yet three times that number (a further sixteen thousand) had died of disease! And these men could hardly be afforded at a time when this volunteer so-called Imperial Army was stretched to its limits over an enormous empire. In fact not only were army medical services totally inadequate, but the entire medical science of the day was unable to assist. Medical researchers were just beginning to realise that the human body could in certain circumstances build up an immunity to disease quite naturally. It did so wholly without outside interference. Metschnikoff in 1884 had just discovered 'phagocytes' or white blood corpuscles, that seemed to perform a service in killing at least some bacteria. But the circumstances in which the human body formed other defences and other mechanisms to either ward off or fully defeat disease seemed baffling in its complexity. As already noted, Robert Koch had discovered the cholera bacillus in 1883. It had become evident that transmission was aided by poor hygiene in crowded conditions. Gaffky, his student, isolated the typhoid bacillus in 1884 and again transmission was proved to be through poor hygienic conditions. It was a tremendous step forward. Yet, as with Koch's every effort to find a cure for tuberculosis (at that time the scourge of Europe), no miracle antitoxins could be found for any of the worst killers. Prevention by sensible hygienic regime was all that could be aimed for. In 1887 a French professor of physiology, Richet, attempted to use the technique of injecting a series of immune serums. His theory was that if an antigen is injected into an animal an antibody will be produced. If a serum containing this antibody is injected into the human body it should give immunity to that particular disease. Unfortunately, while grappling blindly for the correct dosage, he found that when a second injection of an antigen was given to an animal, it often produced fatal shock. This effect was later named 'anaphylaxis'. It became obvious that difficult and time-consuming preliminary tests were necessary so that the degree of sensitisation could be established. Ehrlich too was having great trouble in establishing the correct dosages in his battle to establish the new science of chemotherapy. The medical world therefore was extremely sceptical and cautious. When Behring discovered an antitoxin for diphtheria in 1892 European doctors were not seen battling with each other in the rush for the first of the limited supplies.

At any event, research workers in Germany, France and Britain were now equipped with new techniques of isolating bacteria, and better quality microscopes for identifying them. They were all busy laying the foundations for protection against a host of diseases. But there was a considerable way to go. And while more and more bacteria were being discovered, none could be isolated for some of the most dreaded diseases – typhus, yellow fever and smallpox. We now know the reason: they were viral infections! Unlike bacilli, they were too small to be seen under the most powerful microscopes of the day. Their presence was suspected, but no more than that. The American pathologist Ricketts was the first to prove their definite existence. He gave his life for it in the year 1911, when attempting to identify typhus.

Generals Roberts and Kitchener therefore had arrived in South Africa with men fresh from Britain lacking any natural immunity from tropical diseases. Nor did they have artificial serums supplied by medical science. As in India and elsewhere, previous harrowing experiences showed that good hygiene must be the order of the day. Even so three times more men were *expected* to die of disease than in actual combat. It proved remarkably accurate in South Africa. Shortcomings in medical expertise were therefore clearly to blame. As for the Boer women and children, it was becoming clear that living in isolated farmsteads they had no natural immunity to diseases that were common in crowded conditions. Being suddenly moved to these concentration camps, moreover in contact with guards carrying (yet themselves immune to) many European diseases, was a catalyst for disaster.

Similar tragic lack of immunity had already brought significant consequences in North America. The American Indian population had been decimated more efficiently by European diseases than by bullets. The Inuit[2] too, who saw no military action or gross persecution, were almost wiped out.

Total War was thus almost a reality already by 1902.

Later, as we know, civilian populations were to become embroiled as never before. Not that previous centuries had somehow avoided civilian casualties of course. Entire inhabitants of towns and cities were often put to the sword, especially if weeks or months earlier they had been put under siege and had stubbornly contrived to resist. Nothing infuriates an attacking army more than finding all their assaults successfully repelled. The attackers with their 'blood up', as apologists are apt to term it, on finally breaking through often began a frenzied bout of killing. Defenceless women and children were, as the historical record endlessly shows, butchered en masse. The horror ended only with sheer exhaustion, or when perhaps the more rewarding attraction of looting intervened. Sometimes these massacres occurred despite orders to the contrary. But humane commanders would be powerless to stop their men once the blood lust was on them; at other times such a lust gripped the commanders themselves. A vengeful and quite unambiguous order would be given to wipe out every living soul. Again, historical examples abound from the earliest of times, though one must be careful not to accept mere legend as fact.

Genghis Khan, for example, while certainly guilty of a number of massacres, did not apply it as a universal policy; he was content that the legend alone should precede him. It induced the inhabitants of small towns and so-called cities of that era to surrender without a fight. And often these were spared.

---

[2] Formerly called Eskimo.

Tamerlane, in contrast – if once again we can untangle truth from legend – seemed to have been possessed by an inhuman, if not fiendish, bloodlust; it was one that could never be satiated. The rather better-documented campaigns of Alexander, who was subsequently granted by historians the not altogether merited title 'The Great', had a chequered record in this respect; much depended on his mood or the influence of Bacchus. Julius Caesar, rather a cold fish, almost always conducted his campaigns using his cerebral icebox to temper his decisions. And he calculated everything on the basis of military or political expediency. The Duke of Alva, on the other hand, was a flaring torch who terrorised the Netherlands with the kind of passion that can only be generated by hysterical religious zeal.

Until we reach the twentieth century, most commanders however were aware that a policy of universal extermination was counter-productive. This was particularly so if they were bent on empire building. Moreover, their invading armies, having limited means of transporting their supplies, were forced for the most part to live off the land. It was therefore senseless to kill off the peasantry, together with such people as skilled blacksmiths, foresters and artisans generally, when they provided skills essential to maintaining the physical well-being of the invading army.

Yet in twentieth-century Total War this was to change. Firstly, insofar as professional armies facing each other were concerned, there was now the possibility of annihilating large numbers of men in an incredibly short time. This was as short as it takes to properly estimate their range, in fact. Cannon and gunpowder had given way to field guns, breech-loaded and using high explosive shells. The musket had been replaced by the rifle, and there was talk that the horse, while being essential for the cavalry charge, of course, might well become redundant too. The heavier horse used as a beast of burden, bringing up supplies to the rear, was soon to be replaced by newfangled petrol or diesel machines. By totally transforming supply problems by means of the newly built railways, commanders of armies could now bring thousands of men, spared long and energy-sapping marches, daily to points near a battlefield. Equally, railways could transport masses of weapons, ammunition, food, fodder and material generally on a scale never before contemplated. Yes, everything was changing, sometimes out of all recognition.

The invention of the machine gun alone opened up undreamed-of possibilities of mowing down advancing troops, that is if they were stupid enough to use the conventional mass attack favoured at that time. The men themselves were not stupid; but the officers at the rear, being traditionalists through and through, were. Gatling had brought out a prototype rapid-fire gun quite early in the American Civil War. Hiram Maxim invented a more practical version in 1884. It was subject to rapid wear, overheating and jamming, but other inventors were coming along with fresh ideas to improve its murderous efficiency. A few modifications soon increased this and its reliability overall. These technologists – though unhappily not commanders of men in the field – were aware that whole regiments or even entire divisions could now be annihilated in half a morning's engagement. There was also another change in military thinking: the hallowed, established tradition of laying siege to individual towns and cities now seemed a waste of time – it seemed more effective to blockade an entire nation. The end object in all this was to deny an enemy what was lightly called 'both the will and the means of resisting'. And in this the very basics of life, whether they be food, water, fuel, minerals, indeed any commodity that could possibly assist an enemy, were to be targeted. Bringing an enemy to its knees in as short a time as possible reduced the possibility of suffering heavy losses oneself. Yes, admittedly there was a price to be paid. If civilians suffered, and their overall casualty figures reach levels equal to or even surpassing those of fighting men, then this would of course be regrettable. At the same time there were disadvantages of course: the damage done to what was called the enemy's 'economic potential' hardly made their territory a desirable conquest. No matter: at the end of the day all this could be excused on the grounds of expediency.

To that end inventive minds in different countries were now hard at work attempting to find possibilities of waging war in other unconventional ways. These were mostly technological. Some, for instance, were working on prototype airships to drop bombs well behind enemy lines. Others were probing ways and means to use underwater craft to destroy both naval and merchant shipping.

A steam-driven airship had been designed by French engineer Giffard as early as 1852, though not originally with military purposes in mind. It was not exactly mind-boggling in its capabilities: it was unable to take on headwinds of anything greater than force two, in effect no more than an arial sneeze, which meant it went backwards quite quickly with a wind-force above that. As for wind behind it, progress was too fast by half! In 1884, a balloon, this time using an electric motor, made a circular flight of five miles in light winds round Paris. Now here was something more promising! In Germany, where things were taken much more seriously, Count Zeppelin by 1900 had designed and then laboriously built the first of several successful so-called 'rigid' airships. He went one better by using an internal combustion engine to move the wretched thing more or less in the direction intended. After much difficulty and heartache he gradually achieved far greater range and a degree of reliability. Yet had these early airship pioneers known it, all the considerable efforts expended were to prove a waste of time. In America at precisely that moment the Wright brothers were experimenting with designs for a heavier-than-air machine. Their prototype three years later would successfully take to the air. It did so for slightly less than a minute and covered some eight hundred and fifty feet. Two years further on, with suitable improvements in design, they achieved thirty minutes and covered twenty-four miles! *Mon Dieu!* The indomitable Frenchman Bleriot, inspired by this and not to be outdone, built his own flying machine and in 1909 caused a sensation by actually crossing the Channel and landing safely in Dover. This triumph had a contagious effect. Ambitious young men with dreams of further sensations of this nature were suitably stimulated. They too began building flying machines and feverishly experimented with them – wholly regardless of life and limb. And limbs and lives were duly expended all over Europe and America. Nevertheless, their determination to better Bleriot's incredible feat slowly pushed distance and reliability further and further. But why limit one's imagination to flying a mere fifty to one hundred feet above ground over well-charted landscapes of the different continents? The teenage American physicist Goddard visualised fame in totally uncharted territory. He was dreaming in 1900 of sending rockets extraordinary distances straight up into the sky. Eventually he would inspire others into boldly moving the twentieth century into the space age. A decade later a section of the German military became interested in Goddard's far-sighted publications on the subject. And in 1912 a certain Baron von Braun became the father of a son he chose to name Wernher. By 1930 this young man, also inspired by Goddard's work, was feverishly experimenting along similar lines. Shortly, some enthusiastic generals would hear of his work and give their encouragement. In 1936 the German army would build for him a well-equipped rocket-research station at Peenemunde.

As for developments which would change the direction of war at sea, a primitive submarine had actually been built by an American, Robert Fulton, fully a century earlier in 1801. He did so during a stay in France. Napoleon's successful conquest of Egypt as a stepping stone to invading India had been brought to nothing by Nelson's destruction of the French offshore fleet. The fiery Corsican was not well pleased. Indeed Napoleon was to be continually infuriated throughout his otherwise victorious land campaigns by various (always daringly inventive but necessarily wholly aquatic) operations of the British Fleet. Thus Nelson's unorthodox tactics demanded unusual ripostes in return. Fulton's designs for underwater craft were however hopelessly premature. Barely feasible on paper, they were even less so as soon as anyone attempted to try them under realistic operating conditions. After all, they were denied relatively clean and efficient motive power. Enthusiasm for the very early and seemingly miraculous power of the steam engine at that time had led to the assumption that it could be adapted to propel almost anything. The trouble was that the limited amount of air and oxygen in an underwater craft would be used up too quickly; foul air would kill the crew before that most desirable of preliminary objects occurred – coming within range of the target! Fulton threw in the towel and returned to America. There he built his first successful craft driven by paddles and a steam engine, but this time above water! He had a fleet of such vessels steaming from New York to Albany within a decade. Meanwhile the conventional French fleet, driven by wind power alone and naturally denied Fulton's quite successful developments, had been decimated by Nelson at Trafalgar!

Perhaps though, this became sufficient prompting for further effort. By the end of the century a Frenchman had pioneered the use of a submarine driven by banks of batteries. Its range however was severely limited. His efforts nevertheless created pointers in the right direction. Suitably impressed minds in various countries would pursue this matter and by adding a diesel engine to recharge batteries while on the surface, the submarine became a feasible and indeed fearsome weapon.

These innovations alone were pointers towards a far more efficient and destructive means of promoting Total War. And it would be tempting at this point to examine in greater detail the technological developments in military hardware over the entire range of modern war. However, this must be resisted at least for the moment and left to later chapters. It is, after all, the stated intention of this essay to concentrate on the underlying causes of war.

True enough, one could argue that the existence of any kind of weapon – even those of the most primitive kind – in itself has enticed mankind to put it to good use. After all, our primate ancestors picked up sticks and stones and thereby neatly gained an evolutionary advantage. Further, one cannot deny that such an advantage is also a contributing factor to conflict within a species rather than between species. The argument becomes increasingly absurd if one allows it to range out of hand, however. As has been claimed on earlier pages, our most significant evolutionary advantage has been our facility for active co-operation, not its exact opposite! Those cunning enough to twist the argument will doubtless point out that throughout history man's inventive capabilities could only have been achieved by active co-operation. He has in fact invented things with entirely peaceful applications in mind yet found that they can equally be adapted for war. Again, of course, other individuals have co-operated purposefully with each other deliberately and directly to produce weapons aiding mass destruction. Yet they may not have used them to kill with their own hands; they may have passed on that particular function to others. At the same time they could have claimed that the weapons were for defensive purposes only.

Thus the argument can be skilfully maintained and pushed out into unhelpful 'variations on a theme' in many different ways. After all, in pursuing my chosen theme of the nature and causes of conflict, who can deny that it has led insecure individuals or glory-seeking leaders to believe that new weapons can enhance their personal status or prospects in life? More subtly still, the very fact that unusual or more powerful weapons have been developed must surely tempt some people to probe their capabilities out of sheer curiosity. Naturally the purely 'defensive' rather than offensive argument may be insisted on once again, that is if people have sufficient guile. And it will be delivered with a charming and suitably disarming smile, of course. The gist will be that new scientific and technological developments can be of interest solely for their defensive value. With hand on heart, statements will be made that there is no intention to use them offensively. The simple fact that others have exploited new technology in the past is neither here nor there, they declare. In the modern world defensive capabilities are essential.

There is some truth in this. As with the familiar 'nature abhors a vacuum', there is little doubt that a similar basic urge to occupy an empty area, defensively speaking, visits the minds of men also. It also provides irresistible temptation to beady-eyed empire-building states. A poorly armed or wholly pacific state never fails to focus attention on itself. Sooner or later a predatory nation will be drawn to fill that vacuum.

This is one of the few arguments that have genuine substance. There are many more that have virtually no substance; indeed they move into the realm of casuistry. And in such areas there is hardly any attempt to disguise sophistry. The points made always become more and more fluid, and less and less clear. They reach a point where the original position held becomes so indistinct that everyone loses sight of the essential matter to be resolved. The only other point at which the argument once more begins to have some substance is when someone or somebody broaches the subject of 'pure scientific research'.

Here it is all too tempting to be cynical regarding the word 'pure'. But we must recognise that there was, and still is, a large amount of wholly disinterested research into scientific mysteries done day after day, month after month, with no objective in mind other than discovery for its own sake. The possibility of later applications is at no time visualised or considered. Rutherford and Einstein are a case in point. To repeat, there is no hidden motive – only the joy of discovery! At the same time we would be less than honest if we failed to admit that pure science can very quickly become less than 'pure' in the hands of more worldly scientists and technologists. Those who work in pure science and are truly fixated by its joys are however always defensive and unhappy on this issue. They admit there is all too often a grey area and a degree of ambivalence. To ease their consciences they are therefore stimulated to declare that all discoveries occupy a neutral zone. In themselves they are neither good nor bad. Then follows another necessary admission; subsequent applications however can go either way. So what do we do? Stop all activities in science? Close it down?

Would it be possible to live in a world where sheer curiosity had to be put in suspended animation, so to speak? Jumping on this particular bandwagon, others with less honesty and with hidden motives will move in to muddy the waters once more. They will insist that an important distinction is to be made here. Moreover, it must be constantly taken into account. They will use the old argument notoriously difficult to counter: marksmen using, say, a brand-new and longer-range rifle, when competing at an organised shooting competition, are not automatically murderers; nor are they developing a skill with murder coming later as a possible option. Delight in mayhem and the urge to kill are only produced in a fairly small proportion of individual human minds... they claim.

Once again this is true, of course. Damnably enough I also am painfully aware they could use my own argument to undermine me. They could quite easily pursue the argument further by pointing out that should a large proportion of mankind become habitually aggressive, rather than mainly passive and co-operative, then Total War would be continuous. Triumphantly they could point out that had such circumstances applied in the past, then the human race would have become extinct some time ago. With no doubt yet another smile they would be able to remark that it has teetered on the edge of extinction even with 'intermittent' warfare!

And there is indeed an important point to be made here. Human beings are usually tricked into making war by the actions and the twisted logic of a minority. Weapons in themselves are useless until they are operated by minds suitably prevailed on to use them to the best advantage.

This brings us to the fundamental point at issue. It is this: under what circumstances do normally passive human beings decide to act aggressively? What mental state or cerebral functions are involved? What promotes them to see other people initially as no more than an irritant, yet later begin to notch such irritations ever upward until they reach that of a 'possible source' of conflict? Later still, and possibly over quite some time span, what finally stimulates normally mild and unperturbable individuals to see others as mortal enemies? And here I must repeat that I am carefully considering human beings who by common judgement are wholly passive and sane. They are people who can be proven to act habitually in a responsible and (more or less) rational way. I am not at this point attempting to fathom the reasons why the lunatic fringe act on sheer impulse – and in so doing use extreme violence at the drop of a hat!

To investigate such a matter does however mean making a fundamental change in one's viewpoint.

You see, conflict is seldom stimulated by simple and clearly definable motives. If one is dedicated to finding true causes to this phenomenon rather than being hopelessly mesmerised by its effect, then I am afraid you must use eyes other than the ones you normally rely on. And here I go back to the question raised in the opening sentence of this chapter and ask, rhetorically perhaps, 'Whose eyes do you use when…?'

For any real understanding of this curse the Bible so poetically summarises in the story of Cain and Abel, then even the most subtle of so-called 'philosophical' and overtly political explanations are redundant. Indeed, they were never really valid in the first place. It is to other kinds of high ground we must make for. And there we must continually use very different eyes, moreover refuse to be distracted by the siren voices of conformity that call out all around us.

Chapter II
WAR
Species specific, in the case of *Homo Sapiens*, between communities, ethnic groups, religious sects, nations or political blocks

Propositions

As with all other life forms on this planet, the human animal must find a habitat or niche where the basic requirements for life can be met. This may seem far too simple or obvious a statement at first glance; however, this is deceptive. The very modest demands made by our early ancestors at the dawn of history happened to be no greater than that of any other creature occupying this earth and its attendant biosphere. Yet in a comparatively short time on the evolutionary timescale, man's 'needs' have rocketed upward. They have now expanded to reach such dangerously exploitative levels as to rebound painfully not just on himself, but on Nature and the biosphere as a whole. Moreover the term 'basic requirements' has, with each succeeding century, proved unusually elastic. As various civilisations have emerged, the human animal, with its reliance on ever more sophisticated technology, requiring as it does in turn an ever increasing range of resources, has pushed these requirements beyond the bounds of sustainability.

At the dawn of the historical period these requirements centred on various precious or semi-precious metals, ores or fuels (initially wood). But unfortunately, during the millions of years of geological upheavals that took place while this planet of ours continued to evolve, such resources were not evenly distributed. By chance some areas were richly endowed, while some areas benefited only thinly. Indeed, some were denied what we now choose to think of as 'vital' resources altogether! Therefore problems were created when primitive peoples became technologically more knowledgeable and a proportion of desirable resources were not necessarily found on their territory, or more correctly, the territory that each racial or ethnic group happened to occupy at that time. To obtain what slowly became 'highly desirable' resources, people followed one of four characteristic behaviour patterns: firstly, quite peaceful and mutually benefiting barter or trade; secondly, intermittent and rather crudely staged theft; thirdly, quite savage and outright territorial expansion carefully planned to have a permanent basis; fourthly, if none of these options were feasible, mass migrations.

The first behaviour pattern, obviously the most desirable because it is (relatively) peaceful, (I am after all aware of modern 'trade sanctions' and even 'trade wars') has in fact found expression among all groups and races of human beings over considerable time spans throughout history. But there is a proviso. Essentially that proviso dictates that the ethnic groupings, racial groups, countries or nations, all have some resource for barter within their territory that is either renewable, or, if non- renewable, then in very large quantities. In antiquity, renewable resources such as silk, spices, exotic foodstuffs, perfumes, etc., could be traded almost indefinitely. In later centuries, metals and ores, obtained just under topsoil or indeed fully underground, had to exist in very large quantities and be obtainable without great difficulty. As for timber, used as it was from the earliest eras as fuel and for many other purposes, this could be renewable only if used with understanding and care. Unfortunately the historical record shows gross mismanagement and indeed what amounts to criminal exploitation.

After such renewable or non-renewable resources have been farmed, gathered or mined, these can then be exchanged for those commodities that are either scarce or wholly absent in one's home territory. And indeed a further resource can be found in the skills and energies of people themselves when they are applied to manufactured goods. But again there is a proviso. These goods must be of a superior quality, and/or be technologically advanced.

Otherwise they will fail to maintain their trading value. However, when any of these criteria are not met, then problems arise. They have simple enough beginnings, as when, for example, home-based resources (for one reason or another) become degraded or diminished. At this point the balance of trade with other countries or nations begins to tip further and further out of balance. A full-blown crisis is reached when population pressures finally make unreasonable demands on, or ever increasing consumption of home-based resources. Moreover, the vital tie-up with the technology of the day is inevitably found to fail under the pressure. To compound the crisis, at one and the same time, demands continue to be made for what have now become 'essential' imports from abroad. Here the historical record shows less desirable behaviour patterns – intermittent theft, either by unfair trading practices or alternating raids across borders, alternatively outright and highly aggressive territorial expansion with long-term occupation in mind. Lastly, if all else proves impossible, mass migration.

EXPOSITION 1

Several classic instances can be taken from history of such patterns. Perhaps the best illustrations can be found in our own twentieth century, and not just because documentation is so rich and plentiful but because many individuals will themselves have lived through the actual experiences and can give first-hand testimony.

EXPOSITION 2

In the first decade of this century, highly aggressive European territorial expansion had, after more than three centuries of ever increasing momentum, reached its peak. By 1910, Britain, France, Spain, Portugal, Holland, and even tiny Belgium had all acquired very large tracts or territory on distant continents. These were used not just to decant their own surplus population – a population that the technology of the day could no longer support[1]

---

[1] At that time techniques of food production, food preservation and protection against crop failure by micro-organisms, not forgetting insect predation, were all inadequate.

– but to bring back to the home country a vast range of 'necessary' resources. There was, however, one omission: one European nation had been left out of this unseemly scramble, the newly constituted German nation.

EXPOSITION 3

It is particularly instructive to trace in the historical record the reaction of this new fledgling nation to the pattern of colonial conquests followed by its immediate neighbours.

EXPOSITION 4

More instructive still was Germany's reaction to her discovery that she had virtually no deposits of a vital new energy source: crude oil.

EXPOSITION 5

The reactions of the Kaiser and his generals are to be studied in some detail, as are also the scientific and technological discoveries of the period.

EXPOSITION 6

Evidence will show that the First World War was really, in all truth, the First Worldwide Resource War.

EXPOSITION 7

The Second World War was but a continuation of unfinished business from the First, and therefore must be dubbed the Second Worldwide Resource War.

EXPOSITION 8

The character and behaviour patterns of Adolf Hitler, together with his top-ranking Nazi officials and generals, also repay close scrutiny. Hitler, traumatised by his early manhood as an impoverished amateur artist, never forgot how difficult it could be to acquire even the most basic necessities of life. Later, as leader of his nation, he had an obsession concerning Germany's lack of certain resources – the vital twentieth-century fuel source, crude oil, in particular. Consequently, it will be shown how this obsession determined much of his political policy prior to war, then dominated much of his overall strategy once war commenced. Significantly too, once it became apparent, as his military fortunes declined, that Germany's oil supplies were falling to a quite critical level, he chose to retreat from such tormenting reality. From 1943 onward he backed away into the comforting arms of fantasy. Here Albert Speer's testimony throws a most revealing light on the crucial part played by resources (or the lack of them) during the prosecution of war.

EXPOSITION 9

The Axis partnership, Italy and Japan, were equally devoid of certain 'highly desirable' resources. Above all, they were totally denied the vital resource of crude oil.

EXPOSITION 10

The last option open to any ethnic or racial group – that of mass migration – may be undertaken peacefully, but nevertheless it too has a destabilising effect on the host or series of host nations and can often bring about savage reactions. It is then capable of writing some of the most heartbreaking episodes in the pages of mankind's history.

However, before we can embark on this project some essential groundwork must be undertaken! This will eventually throw new light on human conflict, culminating as it did in twentieth century frightfulness and embracing the whole world.

*

Biological Fundamentals – transcending the political view

Life on this planet, whatsoever evolutionary path it takes – and it is customary to divide these into primary groupings such as plant, animal, bacteria and virus – becomes viable only when it finds a suitable habitat or host.

Here the supply of nutrients, either in liquid or solid form, or indeed a mixture of both, must be found and be (more or less!) assured. But viability also imposes another essential requirement:

the habitat or host must also provide a reasonably safe environment for the particular life form to reproduce, subsequently passing on its genetic material to the next generation.

Now in this proviso there is a fundamental 'difficulty', if one dare call it that! And it is one which many professional biologists themselves ignore. You see there is no habitat or host found anywhere on Earth that can give an absolute assurance for any creature's well-being! Indeed, in the case of animals (in contrast to plants), dangers can multiply very quickly when offspring are born; moreover, these endanger the life of both parent and newborn. Thus animals in particular have evolved not just an astonishing array of reproductive techniques, but also extremely varied skills during parenthood. The struggle to maintain life, and, incidentally, thereby the continuance of the species, is always complex. Indeed that complexity of method, having evolved over millions of years, tends to rise sharply as the creature itself becomes more complex. Consequently, parenthood can be seen to be a relatively simple affair in very small organisms with few cells, yet in larger multicellular examples it can become an astonishingly varied and exhaustive business indeed. There is also a very wide range in the time required to bring offspring to maturity – or alternatively a degree of independence. This ranges from a few hours all the way to twelve to fifteen years, as in the case of the human animal. At the opposite extreme, for example in certain species of turtle (and as has already been noted in Chapter I), parentage 'skills' are virtually nil. Eggs are merely laid ashore deeply in sand to avoid detection, and on hatching the newborn must find its own way to the sea. And it does so, running the gauntlet of a wide range of predators without any parental aid whatsoever! Most species within the animal kingdom, however, have evolved active ways, or show instinctive attempts, to protect their young. Naturally this is linked quite subtly to the degree of protection that the habitat initially provides, conversely, it is also linked to the dangers that accrue either from predators or indeed the inherent rigours the environment itself exerts. Certain species of penguins in the Antarctic, for example, seem to us to have chosen an extraordinarily difficult set of environmental extremes in which to reproduce and care for their young. Similarly, we are perplexed by the various creatures living in the Sahara at the opposite end of the temperature range. And in this respect there is something which one can only call a degree of 'luck-pushing' by parents: indeed this is a basic observation that becomes significant to the central theme running through this essay.

Basically then, the long-term survival of any species of plant, animal, bacteria or virus depends not just on the availability of nutrients but also on the parent's success in passing on its genes to new life and protecting that life to maturity.

As it happens, there is only one exception to the rules that govern the sustainability of life on this planet: this exception applies to the group called autotrophs, meaning 'self feeders'. These can survive quite happily on what would seem quite inedible material such as particles of rock, sand or gravel, using either the energy of light (in which case they are classed as phototrophs) or chemical means (in which case they are classed as chemotrophs). Grouped together, these become of course the basic suppliers of all nutrients either on land or in the sea. They become in effect the initial converters of inedible material into food, on which all other life forms depend.

And having established this we can now move on to the sustainability of life among more complex life forms further up the biological 'ladder'.

Here, as one progresses up each rung, an inescapable fact emerges: crucial to the survival of all living things is an absolute dependence of each level on the one 'below' it. Moreover, it is only partly true to observe that life depends on the mere ability of each level to catch, then kill and devour 'lower' forms. While in no way ignoring the fact that an ecological pyramid consisting of primary producers, primary consumers, secondary consumers and tertiary consumers exists (which in greater detail can be seen as 'food chains' or better still 'food webs'), it so happens that sustaining life is far more complicated than that! Is it really necessary to remind the reader that many (but not all) living things require oxygen to 'breathe' and subsequently exhale carbon dioxide? Unfortunately it very often is. People so easily forget. There is equally the necessity to remind them that conversely, and very conveniently, other life forms, such as plants and tiny organisms on the surface of the sea, require carbon dioxide. Subsequently, by the process of photosynthesis, these then release free oxygen back into the atmosphere! As I say, this is neat and very convenient for all of us! Unfortunately though, this process is so often taken for granted. And this is not the *only* crucial cyclic process that maintains life on this planet, nor for that matter the only factor demonstrating 'interdependence'. The others of vital importance, to name them quickly, are the hydrological cycle, carbon cycle, nitrogen cycle, phosphorus and the sulphur cycle. To further introduce at this point what ecologists call 'mutualism' (the close relationship of two or more species for mutual benefit) will only unduly complicate the issue. The essential point made is that 'interdependence' exists; moreover, it is the crucial factor governing all life on this planet.

This said, it should hardly be necessary to add that as all the myriad forms of life we now see existing on this planet occupy so many different and sometimes totally contrasting habitats, it inevitably follows that 'interdependence' becomes a very complex matter indeed. To repeat: nothing exists in isolation. And nothing exists independently. Quite recently, however, in the history of life on this planet, one life form called 'man' has appeared to have overturned this rule. This creature has achieved considerable mastery over his environment, and he has done so either by clever manipulation of other life forms, or indeed by quite crude and gross exploitation. Thereby, he has multiplied so successfully over a wide range of geographical and climactic conditions that a degree of hubris has developed. This has brought about the dangerous assumption that, despite three thousand million years of evolution, somehow or other the basic structure of biological law no longer applies to him. Indeed this life form called man also shrugs off the unfortunate fact that Nature is quite unfeeling; he merely smiles when he is told that it is totally indifferent about whether any of the incredibly varied forms it has created finally sinks or swims, in other words continues to evolve successfully or becomes extinct.

Fortunately though, Nature does at least provide warning signs before applying such awesome penalties. These warning signs are now everywhere about us. But mankind is so caught up with either the sheer minutiae of daily life, or, alternatively, in the very careful nurturing of his ignorance, that for the most part these warnings are wholly ignored.

It may therefore be necessary to repeat over and over again that 'interdependence' not only applies to all forms of life (bar the autotrophs) but has some astonishing and very subtle implications that must be understood and accepted by all of us – that is if life as we know it is to continue.

*

It is essential to explore aspects of these implications, and to repeat ad nauseam, if necessary, a range of basic facts that must be understood at the outset.

Looking at the sustainability of all life in general on this planet, it must be emphasised that in providing food or safety (relatively speaking), either for existing life or that of the next generation, Nature does not guarantee anything; it merely expects the sheer tenacity of the various life forms to make the best of what is on offer. Not very welcoming for potential customers, you might think! And indeed it isn't in many ways. Often what is on offer in Nature's hypermarket does not amount to very much. And what is displayed can at times be withdrawn! Hastily scrawled notices appear: 'The Management regrets…'! The result can be devastating. Both the provision of food and the hoped-for successful rearing of offspring then fail! However, it can do so either slowly and imperceptibly, so that few creatures notice and are tempted not to bother doing anything about it, or dramatically and spectacularly, often giving very little time for creatures to escape! If by some miracle the life form survives, then it must attempt to find another habitat or host, and essentially what it supposes is another supermarket with a more accommodating management! If its transfer is too slow, or it lacks sufficient determination to survive, Nature merely shrugs and simply allows the individual (or an entire species) to perish.

Now this is not an agreeable situation. Nor is it one which fosters trust and confidence, you may think. That's not the half of it either. Nature also fails to guarantee safety. As a direct result, in its blind gropings to find solutions evolution has arrived at an odd strategy: most life forms tend to produce offspring in far greater number than would seem either necessary or desirable – and this is done quite instinctively without prior thought on the matter. Given this curious phenomenon, it is at this point that I must introduce one of the laws of physics, moreover to use it in a rather revolutionary way. In essence I am going to take one of Newton's famous laws, 'For every action there is an equal and opposite reaction', and apply it right across the board – apply it in a novel way to the realms both of biology and what we choose to call 'human affairs'. You demand brass tacks? You demand them instantly? Very well. I contend that the action of overproduction of offspring inevitably brings about a reaction, or indeed a 'counteraction'. If for a moment we think in anthropomorphic terms (which is admittedly a dangerous thing to do) it is as if Nature, being well aware of evolution's strategy, puts in a wholly ad hoc afterthought and counters overproduction of offspring with a system of checks and balances. It has to, hasn't it? There is no other option. Without this counteraction the evolutionary 'demand' that every life form be 'fruitful and multiply' would quickly end in chaos, end in one almighty crisis! There is after all a limit to the sheer size of this planet, limits also to the availability of primary substances on which living things can exist. That means both food to eat and (never forget it!) air to breathe – that is if a respiratory function happens to be part of one's tie-up with the remainder of the biosphere! So Nature has created these checks and balances in line with, as I claim, Newton's law reformulated into the realms of biology. It demands that no single species goes beyond what ecologists call 'a carrying capacity'. For every action...

Thus inevitably this becomes a crude and wasteful strategy. Evolution creates excess; yet the overproduction of offspring is countered by Nature's immediate and very necessary riposte.

Crude and wasteful? There are some who will immediately object to that statement. Very well, then, shall we give it more detailed examination? Shall we begin with the plant kingdom?

Here we find that, generally speaking,[2] plants produce an incredible amount of 'potential' offspring in the form of pollen or the microspores of seed plants (Gymnospermae and Angiospermae). Plants also have many different and ingenious ways of dispersal and final fertilisation. Dispersal, however, is usually ridiculously haphazard. A high proportion always falls on unsuitable areas – areas that the Bible, in its gloriously poetic imagery, calls 'stony ground'! Incidentally though, the Bible forgets to add that a high proportion also lands on good and highly fertile ground, yet still fails to succeed! Why? Because that ground is already thickly colonised either by its own kind or by others, and, either way, is hostile. This biblical omission has created some unfortunate misunderstandings, which again will be discussed later. But to revert to the main thrust of this enquiry: the production of 'potential' new life by plants is so prodigious as to test one's capacity for credence. Not unexpectedly, one might add, only an infinitesimal proportion ever survive.

Moving from plants to the animal kingdom one finds a similar propensity to produce in excess, though in direct comparison with plants this 'fruitfulness' is not achieved with quite such notable abandon! Even so, there are far more 'candidates' for the next generation than can ever hope to survive. In most male animals, for example, spermatozoa are produced in their sexual apparatus in vast numbers. If healthy and active, each are potential candidates for producing an 'end product' at every ejaculation. Thus if it were possible to count the overall total of these 'candidates' attempting to find a female egg during each time the animal ejaculates, moreover during its entire adult lifespan, then the number would doubtless run into many billions. Ninety-nine point nine percent fail, of course. Thus it is of some importance to the purpose of this enquiry to ask why the males of any species should expend so much energy in the production of spermatozoa when the waste factor is so astonishingly high. Females in the animal kingdom, in contrast, produce far fewer eggs than spermatozoa, but, even so, these are still greatly in excess of the number of 'potential' candidates for future survival. In passing

---

[2] There are exceptions to every rule – nevertheless those exceptions fail to invalidate the generality!

though, one should observe (as always) there are exceptions; for example, in the cases of polyembryony and parasitic Hymenoptera, it has been found that almost two thousand embryos may develop from one zygote (fertilised ovum before cleavage)! Astonishing, isn't it! And in my book, this is wastefulness par excellence! So here too such exertion must surely tempt anyone appalled by this spectre of waste to insert a huge question mark: why! Why such senseless overproduction? Unfortunately there seems no answer. This profligacy exists; we just have to accept the fact. All one can say is that it benefits predators and those creatures that scavenge – living, as it were, on death itself! In the long term it is also a prodigious way of increasing the total biomass on this planet, moreover making it such a different place to the barren surface of the moon, for example. It underlines my concept that to create new life one must have a prodigious amount of death!

But to revert back to the main discussion: despite the sorry fact that so many 'potential' candidates for life (such as spermatozoa) fail to 'make it', and in biblical terms are doomed to 'fall by the wayside', nevertheless most species finally produce offspring. Indeed most still manage to introduce into the world far more than can ever survive. So the process of what one might call 'realistic cutback' is then operated by Nature's system of checks and balances. Consequently, by such a process, somewhere between birth and maturity one finds that many offspring meet a painful end to their wholly short and bemused introduction to this life. Surely this is yet another addition to this (admittedly wholly human) concept of wastefulness?

In fairness to Nature however, as already noted, this is not the full story: the death of any life form does not mean its loss to the biomass and biosphere as a whole. Its constituent parts, right down to that of atomic level, are after all, reshuffled like a pack of cards: they are then recombined, either in the process of being eaten by other creatures, or when they are absorbed back into the soil – the dust-to-dust, ashes-to-ashes cycle.

Moving from animals to bacilli and viruses, our investigation becomes rather vague. This is because scientific research is necessarily far less detailed or advanced; only very recently have ever more powerful microscopes and subtle culture techniques managed to open out this new terrain to systematic study. In the case of the virus, the recent invention of the electron microscope alone has enabled a small number of investigators to gain a foothold into this kingdom! And much still needs to be done. It is however fair to say, as a generality, that with both bacilli and virus life forms there are astronomical multiplication rates, provided, that is, favourable conditions exist. But they too, as with all other of Nature's life forms, must find themselves a suitable host or environment.

Fortunately for us, Newtonian law holds good in all circumstances. It has universal application. Given this constant and excessively fruitful pattern of creation, one would expect to find a totally chaotic situation, indeed with bacilli or viruses eliminating all other forms of life. But, with genuflections to Newton, this does not happen. Even the autotrophs at the foot of the energy/food pyramid fail to be overwhelmed by the sheer explosive growth in consumers. Always the basic checks and balances neatly prevent this. Despite this, one might be tempted to ask yet another anguished 'why'? Why such a convoluted way of doing things? It seems wholly ridiculous that evolution should have adopted the crude and wasteful strategy called 'be fruitful and multiply', only to be thwarted later with Nature's equally painful, equally wasteful checks and balances. Unfortunately, once again, this is how things are, and no questions we might sensibly put, or any logic we might bring to bear, can have any result on the formidable reality of it all. It is there. So we must either like it or lump it!

For the moment though, we must put aside any detailed examination of these checks and balances. Essentially, at this point it is merely enough to know that they exist.

What must be said immediately, however, is that for one animal, namely that called 'man', it is most unfortunate that the establishment of the science of ecology has been so recent. You see, because it is in its infancy the vital message of 'interdependence' it so loudly proclaims is still not properly understood. Nor for that matter does it receive the attention and sense of urgency it deserves – and that even among what one would suppose to be the highly educated and sophisticated people of the West! As for those who remain illiterate all over the world, only a few seem to have a mystical groping for interdependence; even so, these too fail to act on it in any dynamic way! And time is running out. Nature is already sending out a large number of warning signs: these are either being misread or more regrettably still, ignored! Again, one might be bloody-minded enough to ask: 'Why, for God's sake?' Very well. But the reasons are complex and not immediately apparent. Hubris has many causes: they range from a deliberate ostrich pose – what vulgar people brightly call 'head in the sand, arse in the air, just ready for someone to put the boot in' – all the way to highly complex psychological reasons. Among the latter are some unfortunate interpretations of religious texts (as in the Bible, the Koran, and others) that have become the basis for so many different world religions. And these religions have proclaimed that man is unique. So he is. Yet so are all other life forms! Arising from other erroneous interpretations is the claim that man is highly favoured and independent. Again, so he is... to a degree! Who would deny it? But he is highly favoured only so far in that he has been given the capacity to make observations on life – moreover from those observations obtain deductions that should be (but are often not) based on reason. These he is now misusing. Unfortunately too, he has become totally fixated by his own image rather than that of creation as a whole. As for being independent of the remainder of creation, this he is most certainly not! He is, as are all other forms of life, wholly interdependent, indeed gripped just as tightly within the framework of natural law governing the biosphere as the very lowest of other life forms.

Having said this however, certain statements must be qualified. At the very outset it must be stated that 'interdependence', while being the central framework on which all life is built, is not in itself static. It changes gradually in its detailed application. And it does so simply because of the underlying 'thrust' of evolution.

You want an explanation? Very well. Since life emerged on this planet, the process of evolution has demonstrably brought about an astonishing array of life forms into being, each of them of course fitting into this overall system. However, as has already been noted, not all of these life forms have survived: the habitat, the climate or something rare in the environment has changed or has been withdrawn. And it has done so too suddenly for that life form to adapt itself to the new circumstances. Alternatively, the life form becomes too specialised in its demands for a certain kind of food. Whatever the reason, scientific examination of their remains (as fossilised remnants crushed in between rock strata) shows that many life forms have wandered down an evolutionary cul-de-sac and become extinct; moreover palaeontologists have at no time supposed that they have finalised the list. Incidentally too, evolution does not synchronise its march – that is, it does not insist that all life forms should strut down the evolutionary road like a regiment of guards marching impeccably to time. You are surprised? I will repeat this: evolution simply does not have blaring brass bands thumping out spirited music to maintain the strict beat of its marching tempo. It doesn't even have guardsmen – only raw recruits! And these are woefully out of step; some are not even in the march at all! The reason? Well, some life forms are so well designed that they just happen to suit their little niche, and do so exceptionally well. They do not need to change. And if the conditions they live under change infinitely slowly then you get the so-called 'living fossil' of which the ancient fish 'coelacanth' is a good example. On the other hand, of course, some recruits are so eager, undisciplined and unrestrained that they elbow other marchers out of the way and skip ahead – they may even shout 'bugger this' and take to running! And over the roughly estimated three-thousand million years since life began, this somewhat disorderly and ragged march has given us the incredible diversity of life we now find around us!

Now this should be a constant source of wonder and spiritual enrichment to all. But sadly, of course, it is not. It is a constant source of wonder and spiritual enrichment only to some. The minority resist; they are totally dominated by their own egos and remain blind or dismissive of the true nature and glory of creation. Moreover, they remain blind not just to creation on this planet, but creation in its enormity as it has evolved in the entire universe – or indeed succession of universes! To disseminate successfully this sense of wonder, or to combat sterile egoism, is however becoming increasing difficult. Unfortunately we live in a world where mankind is now busy crowding itself into endless termite mounds – those hideous artificial concrete habitats that smother what were once graceful towns or cities. Here, once they are trapped in these appalling places, artificiality of a most dangerous kind rules the day. There is no contact with Nature and with other life forms that can be established in a truly normal and natural way. Everything becomes either increasingly rare or absurdly 'tarted up'. Nature has to be homogenised to make it acceptable; everything becomes grossly de-natured and desensitised. Thus modern lifestyles in themselves become one of the agents responsible for hubris. They encourage mankind to feel set apart from, or even superior to, the remainder of creation. Crazily, they foster the illusion that mankind can blindly obey the instinctive urge to be 'fruitful and multiply' yet at the same time totally escape the subsequent checks and balances. There is no recognition that Nature has been forced to create the Four Horsemen of the Apocalypse just to nullify its own overindulgences!

Thus for urban and suburban mankind – that ever-growing, pathologically insensitive and narcissistic mass, presenting as it does such a tempting target for the galloping Horsemen – it becomes increasingly difficult to understand that throughout the three-thousand million years of the appearance of life on this planet, no single life form has ever dominated the remainder of creation. Put in a different way, no life form has ever pushed beyond a certain limit, what ecologists call the ecosystem's 'carrying capacity'. Granted, it is difficult to estimate with any exactness what that 'absolute limit' is, but at least Nature's warnings give us a wink and a nod when the limit is perilously near.

The devil of it is that the very success of science and technology in probing natural law and in giving man what appears to be 'control' over his world now in the same way tends to bolster a dangerous overconfidence. Indeed the degree of hubris is such that most human beings confidently expect science and technology to conquer all! And it matters little that more than one scientific discipline has proved that many life forms have in the past reached the limit of an ecosystem's carrying capacity and thereby triggered a population crash. It matters little either that it can be endlessly shown that natural law does not differentiate between any of the myriad living things – that it certainly shows no favours and is totally ignorant of the meaning of the word 'mercy'. Somehow or other it is assumed that Nature's checks and balances just do not apply to man.

Given this debacle it therefore becomes necessary to look a little more closely at some of these checks and balances themselves and determine how they operate.

Now for quite some time biologists have supposed that the control of numbers in any one life form is due primarily to the fluctuation (or withdrawal) of the food supply. Coming a close second are the activities of predators: incidentally, this includes various bacilli or viruses – though it is then termed a 'disease'. This opinion is now changing. While the primary precondition for survival, that of adequate food, of course still holds true, a drastic reassessment of predation is now in progress.

To sum up a very complex situation in but a few lines: predation undeniably plays a part yet its importance has been vastly overrated. Indeed this overemphasis has been so marked that its impetus now has a momentum all of its own, long after the brakes have been applied. Recently though, some researchers have struggled to set up the true factor in its place. They state that for the vast majority of life forms, the greatest threat to survival, oddly enough, are other members of that self-same species! Bewildering, isn't it? Indeed, this statement may initially sound so extraordinary as to be judged the utterances of lunatics. Certainly, most otherwise well-informed members of the human race still fondly believe that predation remains *the* significant factor. They will therefore demand an explanation. That explanation is in fact quite simple, so much so that in an era where undue complexity is part and parcel of daily life, such simplicity is suspect and strains one's credibility.

Ridiculous though it may seem initially, the answer is in fact a fully cogent one. It is this: members of the *same* species form by far the most serious source of competition for the basic necessities of life. This embraces not just sufficient food, but, perhaps less obviously (at least for those of us living in temperate zones), sufficient water. In quite large areas of the world – for example, great tracts of land in Asia and Africa, prone as they are to drought – this basic requirement becomes more precious than food. Again, as further extensions to fundamental needs, certain animals require specific kinds of shelter, often natural features such as soft sandy soil for burrowing, or alternatively, perhaps, caves or hollowed-out tree stumps. These serve both as shelter from the elements and an area of safety from predators. In fact, for some highly specialised creatures, these become as important as food and water. And in the event of a quite sudden increase in population pressure, all these basics become the focus of fierce competition. Conflict thus becomes species specific. And in such a scramble, the stronger deny the weaker their fair share. Competition then degrades to open conflict and it becomes particularly vicious of course in an extended drought, when both food and water become so precious. In such circumstances the strong elbow the weaker from their fair share, and do so completely. This sets in motion a chain of events whereby their emaciated fellows lose any chance of survival. They quickly fall prey to predation from other species – either animal or microbial – incidentally giving further ammunition to those who mistakenly use 'survival of the fittest' as the most potent of evolutionary factors.

It is not a pretty picture. Indeed for those human beings who are sensitive to suffering, it becomes grimly evident that Nature shows a very distressing lack of compassion. In fact its overall design or blueprint for living allows for no concessions to finer feelings. It openly displays crude savagery. Not unexpectedly, for those who have deep religious beliefs, stressing in particular that the strong should help the weak, the wealthy the impoverished, the healthy the sick, this spectacle of the remainder of creation acting in precisely the opposite way can arouse considerable feelings of anguish. There are some further aspects to this we must consider too. It can so easily give rise to the belief that in this pattern of behaviour – if in nothing else – mankind is set apart from the remainder of the animal kingdom! Humans alone rise above savagery and possess humanitarian feelings. But do they? Certainly no one can deny that there are many sensitive individuals who not only actively assist the weaker of their own species, but are also greatly distressed by our mistreatment of other species. Regrettably though by far the greater mass of human beings merely utter pious sentiments and leaves it at that. They pay lip-service to the alleviation of suffering and no more. It is a dishonest and self-deluding means of satisfying twinges of conscience. Consequently in constructive terms nothing is done; at the end of the day everything is left to the minority who still retain their passionate commitment. Never forget either that down through history there is an appalling record of the exact opposite – of hatred rather than compassion. For those who have been forced to compete in earnest for the basic necessities of life, the answer has always been war, conquests and massacres. In short, mankind has shown constant exhibitions of selfishness which on occasion reach a level of sheer devilry. There is more than enough evidence to resist all the pious claims for mankind's special place in the scheme of things. In all honesty, the very most one can say is that a small proportion of human beings exhibit compassion for others. No more. Thankfully too, these highly sensitive individuals do succeed from time to time in shaming others. But the vast majority are not similarly sensitised. How else can one interpret the historical record? You judge me too downbeat or cynical? I wish I could be otherwise, but not at the expense of honesty. Produce all manner of saintly, self-sacrificing examples to the contrary if you like; you can even throw them down in front of me with an air of triumph. But you will probably find I am already aware of them. Indeed, unless I am greatly mistaken my own roll-call of the saintly and self-sacrificing down through history will surpass yours. Even so, on balance I still decline to share your upbeat interpretation and your optimism.

At this point you may be prepared to give way just a little. You may attempt to humour me by admitting that the historical record is lamentable. You do this no doubt with a subtle purpose in mind; for you will immediately compensate for it by pointing to recent improvements in the contemporary scene. You may proudly draw attention to the large number of humanitarian agencies now operating all over the world, even detail the measure of success they have achieved. Sadly I must reply that insofar as it embraces the greater mass of donors to such agencies – especially those in a position to help – it is no more than half-hearted assistance at best. At best, most pampered Westerners feel a temporary sensation of unease. Admittedly, during this temporary phase the well fed and affluent may be distressed by reports of starvation or persecution; but these are soon forgotten.

As for their sensitivity to suffering in the animal world, here again many may seem distressed by evidence of savagery; yet it too is temporary. For example, they may see first-hand how small carnivores such as a fox or a stoat will pounce on a chicken or a rabbit and tear it apart while still alive. They might be further horrified to watch, vicariously, through the efforts of wildlife film makers, a large carnivore such as a lion similarly causing indescribable suffering to its prey. In the process they may watch with disgust a female lion bringing down an antelope or wildebeest, by slashing its hindquarters, thereby bringing its desperate gallop down to a mere limping trot. They may continue to watch, fascinated, as it seizes the victim by the neck, and then, while the process of strangulation is still proceeding, see its male lord and master, or perhaps its own offspring, arrive to tear that animal apart while it still lives! George and Joy Adamson in a series of books, pamphlets and other publications, commencing with *Born Free* in the 1960s, opened up a period of unusual public fascination with lions and intimate studies of wildlife generally. In them are various detailed accounts of large carnivores making kills. It is significant that while they themselves were fully accustomed (if not suitably anaesthetised) to the suffering endured by the prey their lions brought down, they too were much dismayed at times by the torture involved. To repeat, particularly when a lioness was accompanied by her almost fully grown offspring, they noticed how these would begin feasting while the mother was still occupied with the process of strangulation. They would be happily ripping off the genitals and lower stomach as the stricken animal feebly kicked at them with its legs. For those sensitive enough to attempt to imagine the agony suffered, the horror is almost overwhelming. But for many, no such imaginative powers exist. They may feel a vague kind of revulsion, but even then it is temporary only. And of course they can make out a legitimate excuse for it all. You see, carnivores have evolved this method of killing over a period of millions of years. It must be the most efficient way of doing so, otherwise it would not have been retained to this day. What is more, it is instinctive. It is not, so far as we are aware, one which is subject to conscious thought, let alone a sense of pity or morality. Therefore there is nothing anyone can do about it. What has been ordained has been ordained. It must simply be accepted. So a certain fatalism takes over. All emotional responses to savagery in Nature are subsequently subverted by naked reality.

However, if we move back from suffering in the rest of the animal world to that of our own, we find complex and sometimes paradoxical emotionalism once again comes into play. And while a degree of emotion is very necessary, sadly it also tends to obscure things. An excess of emotion can and often does prevent us from confronting reality. It clouds the issue and keeps us from acknowledging uncomfortable (if not positively ugly) truths. We get bogged down in a welter of conflicting thoughts. Only if we can extricate ourselves from these will come the realisation that despite being fully conscious of the pain and suffering caused, mankind too can be responsible for extremes in sadistic behaviour. Our very choice of vocabulary reflects this when we speak of human beings 'descending into the realm of animals'. This in turn suggests the loss of what we choose to call 'all human feeling'. It implies either the temporary suspension or perhaps total destruction of a unique facility – that of being able to imagine and empathise with the suffering of others. Uniquely for some, this loss of feeling is of even greater concern than the actual horrors inflicted! It means that the individual can never feel remorse. And remorse is particularly precious because it turns that lost soul back into something resembling a human being once more. In this instance the distinction between human and animal is truly sacred.

Even so, if we are at all honest enough and capable of looking at the matter dispassionately, we are often forced to acknowledge that there are instances where remorse can never become that saving grace. These occur where individuals (sometimes coming together in quite large groups) seem both to employ and enjoy the most sadistic forms of butchery – and keep repeating the experience! Terrorists and serial killers are the most obvious examples. Here such acts become addictive. In these instances their cerebral processes are so wanting in sensitivity and so anaesthetised to suffering and horror that we doubt their sanity. Yet most are not mad in the strictly clinical sense. And worse, in such circumstances – as with the remainder of the animal world – the stark truth of the matter is that nothing can be done about it. We cannot change or even modify their thought processes. They are incapable of feeling remorse. Such human beings become in effect 'mindless killers'. As with a fox, a stoat or a lion, they inevitably become imprisoned in behaviour patterns common to all carnivores.

What are these patterns and how are they achieved? Authorities on animal behaviour agree that the young of all wild carnivores must be taught by their parents the finer points of making a kill. Even so, the basic instinct for killing is already evident in the games the young play in the first few months of their lives. It is well known too that young carnivores which happen to be born in captivity also play these games, but if they are released into the wild they are at a disadvantage – they lack the guidance and further honing of their skills which would come from adults. This is temporary, however. Given time and reasonable conditions, they usually succeed in improving their skills by trial and error. Significantly enough, and underlining my central theme, their greatest danger comes from adult members of their own species. This occurs especially when they blunder by accident into the territorial preserve of neighbours. The Adamsons, for example, experienced great difficulty when attempting firstly to find, then establish, undisputed territory for their immature lions when returning them to the wild. Without such territory they would have been killed by enraged residents – those of their own species!

Returning to human behaviour patterns though, it would seem absurd to suggest that carnivore instincts are also imprinted in ourselves at birth. Absurd or not, closer investigation of our ancestral way of life and recent studies by zoologists undertaken in the field of a range of primates have slowly begun to widen our understanding in this matter. My own conviction is this: we, as omnivores, relying as we do on a wide variety of food sources, have inherited deep instinctive impulses that include ancient echoes from ancestors – ancestors who were undoubtedly skilled in killing. However, in many parts of the world these killer instincts are now mostly redundant. Except for a tiny minority who hunt wild animals such as deer and wild boar, or shoot pheasants and grouse, our survival instincts are turned in very different directions. Even the farming community no longer slaughters its own animals: mechanised methods in abattoirs have taken over. Thus all beef, lamb, chicken, ham and a variety of other animal foods are completely disassociated from the imperatives of survival. They merely appear as if by magic on the shelves of supermarkets, neatly packed and, emotionally speaking, inert. The connection between living creatures and their inescapable fate as mere commodities to be 'farmed' to secure part of our diet becomes remote. We cease to think about it. The lump of flesh is somehow completely dissociated from a breathing, feeling, living thing!

Oddly enough, human children are in closer contact with their ancient instincts. They can often shock their parents with the seemingly callous and wholly insensitive way that they treat animals. Not only animals for that matter either! Unless constantly watched they can, while in an aggressive mood, also seriously injure other children. Again it is a question of sensitivity to things outside themselves. That very necessary facility normally increases as the child grows older. They develop antennae, as it were, to deal with all kinds of external phenomena, and that gradually comes to include the feelings of others. With increased sensitivity comes a capacity to empathise. Unhappily, though, a minority fail to achieve this. As I see it, their development is arrested. Echoes from an ancient past are retained; they never reach a new understanding of human interaction, more especially the need for harmony and co-operation with others. On reaching adulthood, their bodies are fully mature in the physical sense. However, emotionally, and often mentally too, they remain children. For a very small percentage of our population then, this lack of facility to generate any empathy for either animals or other human beings is surely a genetic abnormality. Being genetic it does not therefore require intensive programmes of psychological investigation. Nor should we follow this by psychiatric help and retraining. I believe attempts to rehabilitate this minority are a waste of time and effort. There is only one obligation left. It is quite simple. It is to isolate these people. We must prevent them from making further contact with the wider public generally. Thus any opportunity to find more victims would be frustrated. This should be our principal aim. But retribution should play no part whatsoever.

So much then for the capacity to kill. It clearly lies dormant in us all. Fortunately though, after leaving childhood it never surfaces – that is as far as the vast majority are concerned. There is however a vital proviso. It remains dormant except when circumstances present a serious challenge (or supposed challenge!) to our very survival. Then things can alter radically. Notably too it is the young male in the age group fourteen to thirty who is the more easily persuaded to use violence, or, for that matter, duped to react in this way. Older people take more time and tend to consider the position carefully.

Up to this point we have briefly looked at both the capacity and the mindless urge to kill as is displayed only among terrorists and serial killers – that is, conflict taking place *within* society, not outside it. What then of this latent capacity to kill when it comes to ethnic groups, religious sects, nations, or political blocks waging outright war with an *external* enemy? What is activated at this point to bring it to the surface again? Quite simply, it is the threat, or supposed threat, to survival. Self-preservation is one of the most powerful of instincts we possess. Once activated, almost anything can happen. Some admittedly will attempt to run away from the source of danger, but many more will stand their ground and kill or be killed. Much depends on circumstances. When a mass of individuals forming an integrated and cohesive entity is involved then they tend to stand firm. In such cases entire populations can be whipped up into an aggressive mood either by a genuine threat to their survival or an imaginary one. In each case subtle or indeed crudely inflammatory propaganda can be used by leaders to stir up patriotic feelings to a frenzy. This frenzy can be so potent as to generate a hatred whereby millions can be induced to act wholly out of character. And in such a state they can be induced to endure, and do so with stoic cheerfulness, something normally inconceivable – complete loss of individuality and probable use as virtual cannon fodder. This is all the more extraordinary in that it cancels out the basic instinct for self-preservation. Indeed, as often happens when an enemy appears without much advance warning, and the bewildered target of aggression finds itself at war, its people may be fully conscious of being inadequately drilled, badly armed and incompetently lead into battle yet they are still carried away by an inner conviction of inevitability. Provided the threat they see from 'the enemy outside' is sufficiently potent, they will overlook all the smaller insults to both the logic and reason of the case. Indeed they will prevent the process of debate to enter their minds in any shape or form. In such a heightened state of loyalty both to their fellows and a common cause, they will then zestfully kill other human beings or lay down their own lives in the process. In most instances they have never known or met those individuals who form the body of the enemy. They will have never known them as individuals, possessing the same emotions, feelings and fears as themselves – never known them as fellow human beings. That they too, in all probability, have only the vaguest notion of their motivation to kill is of no consequence. Without the least hesitation battle commences. Both sides do so because of a preconceived concept embracing the word 'enemy' which automatically demands a set course of action.

It all seems so improbable, yet sadly it happens time and time again.

How does this come about? What influences lead otherwise co-operative, sane, responsible and indeed amicable individuals into such madness?

There are several influences, all of them more or less instinctive and seldom within our powers of reasoning. Often, unhappily enough, most lie outside a conscious decision to disobey.

Shall we begin with one I believe to be the most difficult to override, and at times fails to be recognised or even visualised within ourselves: territorialism.

Territorialism

To embark on matters dealing with instinctive urges – urges that for the most part remain deeply embedded within our subconscious minds – it is necessary to go back along the ancestral record tens of thousands of years. In some cases it becomes necessary to go back several million to look at the circumstances surrounding the life of the first anthropoid creatures: these branched out from the primate order to become eventually one of the one hundred and eighty-five other living species within it – the mammal *Homo sapiens*.

Firstly though, it is necessary to consider the territorial behaviour among *all* creatures, and as a unified whole.

To begin with, not all creatures can be said to be 'territorial'. What does territorial mean anyway? Simply, creatures that mark out and defend a small area within their particular niche or habitat; these are territorial. A large proportion certainly do have this instinct, to a greater or lesser degree. Yet, to make matters rather more complicated than they should be, one finds that in Nature's idiosyncratic way of varying its handouts, this instinct is unevenly shared over the entire phyla of the animal kingdom. Among Chordata, for instance, it is only weakly held by that class of animal we call 'herbivores', but more strongly among 'carnivores'. Among that third class we label 'omnivores', and to which this animal called man belongs, the instinct for 'territorial acquisition' is at least as strong as that of carnivores, though personally I would rate it higher. In support of this claim I would point out that 'possession' of territory has moved out of the realm of mere instinct and is now reinforced by a fully conscious 'justification' – this backed by historical, cultural and religious influences. If you would like to put this to the test, then try asking an Israeli or a Palestinian why (and almost on a daily basis) they attempt and duly succeed in killing one another over a matter called 'land ownership'. Incidentally, it would be advisable to proceed with the interview through the slits of an armoured personnel carrier, rather than casually on foot anywhere near the disputed 'territorial' areas.

But once again, let us go back to broad generalities in the animal kingdom as a whole.

To glance for a moment at herbivores, one might observe that, oddly enough, despite having a less developed instinct for holding permanent or even temporary 'territory', many appear to be equipped with offensive weaponry. For example, in maturity a large number of species grow murderously sharp horns. These can be single, double or branched. This is particularly true of males, and in some species, exclusively so. Moreover, they appear to be excellent weapons either for defence or attack – indeed one would further suppose that they could easily achieve the death of an opponent. But this is deceptive. For the most part herbivores use them for stylised displays only, the mere threat usually being sufficient to drive an interloper off the 'rightful owner's' patch. Leaving aside the thorny business of rightful ownership, it has to be said though that male herbivores are inclined to use these weapons more offensively during the mating season. Here the object is to round up as many females as possible and drive them into one's territorial area. Incidentally, the boundaries of these (often temporary) domains are well defined, and, though invisible to us, are marked usually by special scent glands or by urine. Yet even then, the battles between males can hardly be judged murderous. There is much pushing and shoving until the weaker gives in – indeed clearly signals defeat by running away! And while wounding is not unheard of, it is accidental rather than intentional. As for mortal wounds, these are very rare indeed, and again wholly accidental.

Moving to carnivores one finds a different story. These animals are now equipped with murderous teeth and claws rather than horns: moreover, here there is no deception in the ability to kill. Initially, as with herbivores, a carnivore defending its territory against an interloper of its own species will once again use a stylised threat display; however, in contrast (as the instinct is more powerfully held), the threat is followed very quickly by a vicious attack. If the intruder then fails to withdraw in good time, it usually means a fight to the death.

Over the years many myths – totally erroneous in every way – have been built up concerning animal behaviour. For example, there is the condemnatory, 'Only humans kill those of their own kind.' This statement has often been used by otherwise well-intentioned churchmen, social workers and the 'do good' brigade generally; it is used in an attempt to shame the bellicose and belligerent into finding peaceful methods in settling disputes. It would be more effective if it were true. You see, unfortunately it applies only to herbivores. Among carnivores and omnivores, which includes of course the human animal, it is totally false. Indeed, recent studies reveal an even worse facet to instinctive animal behaviour patterns, and one that we find particularly repulsive. Taking the so-called 'king of beasts', the lion, as an example, it is now known that if a newly mature young lion, in his attempt to create territory for himself, intrudes into territory held by that of an ageing and almost toothless male and his pride, then savagery of quite astonishing proportions ensues. If, as is likely, the younger wins, he rounds up all the adult females of his adversary's pride and sets about killing each and every one of their existing cubs And in this murderous assault it may not just be enough to kill – parts of them may also be eaten. This then becomes an act of cannibalism on top of murder. This is to us both horrific and wholly unnecessary. It is as if the victor wishes not only to signal that he has established himself as master of the pride and its territory, but that also at the same time he wishes to eliminate totally all traces of the genetic legacy of its former owner. And it is by no means the only example of cannibalism.

Increasingly over the last few years evidence is building up that this kind of behaviour is paralleled over an ever widening number of carnivore and omnivore species. Firm evidence of cannibalism to date includes the remainder of the large cat family, such as tigers, leopards and cheetahs, then large carnivores such as bears and alligators, moving to birds such as crows and gulls, then small omnivores such as squirrels, gerbils and mice, then an assortment of mantids, red-backed spiders and beetles. And this list is by no means closed. All one can say at this point is that cannibalism is an example of territorialism taken to an extreme.

Having included some omnivores in this list, let us look more closely at those groups classified as being closest to man. Here it has been found that species of ape and lemur also echo this horrifying pattern, triggered as it is by 'territorial' imperatives. Boundaries of their territory are well defined and marked, again by special scent glands or by urine. Territory is closely guarded by males, and any interlopers of the same species are initially given stylised warnings. However if this does not work (within a matter of minutes) then a fight to the death is common. Moreover, should females and their young happen to wander into a territorial space by accident, no mercy is shown either; they too are ruthlessly killed, each and every one. Again in these instances, cannibalism – totally repugnant to us – follows such killing.

At this juncture it is of course tempting to compare this capacity for killing with that of man himself. And the history of our species in no way shows rejection of this overall pattern of behaviour. Fortunately though, cannibalism is thought to occur only in very few instances and it is restricted to the very small numbers of primitive peoples still remaining. There are exceptions, of course. It must be admitted that isolated cases do sometimes occur among the mentally deranged, and even in the most sophisticated and affluent societies. However the 'normal' killing of defenceless people, such as the aged, pregnant women and children, in endless warfare has been well documented and proves to be a well-established behavioural pattern right down through recorded history.

What of unrecorded history? What of early man slowly evolving from ape ancestry?

Beginning with the very earliest stages it is gratifying to see from all the circumstantial evidence so far gathered that he was much more pacific. Here the chosen diet is the critical factor. Early apeman appears to have been vegetarian, with only the most occasional addition of meat – probably scavenged at that! Relieved of the necessity to kill, his character seems to have paralleled that of the gorilla, who, despite a very ignorant and hostile early press, now proves to be a quite good-tempered and inoffensive animal indeed. This is not to suggest of course that the aggressive nature of mankind could be modified overnight by banning the consumption of meat! Forcing everyone to become vegetarian would not necessarily solve the problem. What is suggested is that the very excitement of the hunt and the heightened emotion involved in the physical act of killing another living creature, does tends to coarsen man's nature. They diminish the initial degree of hesitation when circumstances might suggest killing those of his own species. And here one might ask an interesting question touched on in a different context earlier: how many of those living today in the totally artificial Western suburban lifestyle, who trip down to a supermarket to purchase those sanitised lumps of flesh on its slabs, would still remain meat-eaters if they were forced personally to slit the throat of a chicken, a sheep or cow? Furthermore, after watching its death struggle, could they then open out the stomach, dispose of the inedible intestines and cut the animal up into transportable pieces? What is more, I suspect that the act would be even more emotionally painful, if one had actually reared that animal oneself, thence becoming personally involved in its welfare on a daily basis, and building up a rapport!

But to return to early apeman: somewhere in the transition between ape and man, its vegetarianism became less pronounced. Meat-eating, in contrast, became an established rather than a casual part of his diet. What might have triggered this change?

What could have been more pressing than a dramatic climate change? The Pliocene period saw an enormous change in weather patterns on this planet. In Africa, the supposed birthplace of mankind, the rising temperatures, and a drastic reduction in rainfall meant a dwindling of the vast forests. As the Pliocene period lasted twelve million years, those creatures caught in its hot blast were forced to evolve relatively quickly to survive; those that failed simply perished.

Now living creatures can and do make some astonishing transformations when a former agreeable habitat or environment undergoes a disagreeable change. There are striking examples. For instance, a proportion of the creatures that came out of the sea millions of years previously, as amphibians, and slowly developed lungs and various stumpy legs for methods of locomotion, obviously must have had regrets. Eventually deciding that enough was enough, they re-entered their former aquatic existence. Thus all the creatures who now come to the surface of the sea (or for that matter fresh water) from time to time to gulp down air thereby give proof of that astonishing volte-face decision. Dolphins, seals and sea cows were at one time small and obviously rather unsuccessful land-based creatures. Again, the ancestor of the whale was equally small. Its successor has clearly benefited enormously from the change – that is if one uses as criterion of success the finding of vast and dependable sources of food. The correspondingly vast increase in body size is hardly evidence of evolutionary failure! However, the 'semi-aquatic' theory as applied to man by Sir Alister Hardy, later vigorously extended by Elaine Morgan, begins to explain some remarkable changes in apeman that occurred during the Pliocene. Indeed, it explains the changes far more convincingly than does the current wisdom among primatologists and anthropologists who still adhere to the 'Mighty Hunter' theory. In essence this latter theory insists that an ape-like, forest dwelling and essentially vegetarian creature was forced by the Pliocene drought to become a hunting animal – in other words a modified Tarzan-like being on the open savannah. But as Elaine Morgan points out with her own brand of mischievous piquancy (mixed as often as not with devastating irony!), this theory totally ignores the astonishing changes achieved by the female of the species. You see, Tarzan's mate Jane, also lost almost all of the external features of the ape; that is to say she lost the ape's fur, she became fully bipedal, long-legged rather than short, she improved her jawline and jutting nose, grew long flowing hair on her head, etc., etc. But internally there were far more significant changes! She moved her sexual apparatus from her rear to her front so that the male no longer found it convenient to mount her from behind (which is totally inexplicable in the Mighty Hunter context). Frontal sex became, shall we say, more relaxed and a more 'loving' demonstration of a physical act for Tarzan, doing, as he must, what a man has to do. Conversely mounting from the rear became less 'loving'; it also demanded not only that the female co-operated freely, but proved herself capable of a degree of athleticism! She had to contort her body into uncomfortable positions and hold that position for some time. Such contortionism tends to be used now in the post-Aquatic Era only when the male feels frontal sex has become somewhat stale and seeks to find extra stimulation and excitement. Frontal sex is also practised by other aquatic mammals incidentally, so man is not unique! But to return to early Jane. She also deposited fat on the buttocks and thighs. She also... but that is more than enough to mention at this stage! Indeed any *one* of these extraordinary changes must surely tempt the most ardent of Darwinian evolutionists to change overnight into the most bitter of Creationists! To become explicable in any way, surely the 'aquatic' theory offers the only credible alternative. This in essence suggests that an ape-like creature – already living on the coastal fringes of East Africa, or driven there by the Pliocene drought – found the shoreline the sole remaining 'tolerable' niche for its survival. Here, not only was there an abundance of small crab and shellfish generally, but also forays by amphibians such as seals, turtles, and other shoreline visitors. These were all easily killed and provided nutritious food in abundance. But crucially the sea, being salty and not fresh water, provided a means of escape from the vicious predators of the large cat family. At that time these were the most serious of Nature's checks and balances on early woman (forget about disposable early man!) and her child. Instant retreat into salt water (cats are not deterred by fresh water), moreover probably diving temporarily out of sight, would have been found to be an excellent means of escape from even the most crafty of land-based enemies. And over a period of twelve million years, before the Pliocene period finally relented and a less harsh climactic regime took over, this close contact with water does begin to explain evolutionary changes to female physiology that otherwise invite a retreat into creationism!

To my mind it also begins to suggest several other mysterious developments that Hardy and his most persuasive advocate Elaine Morgan failed to touched on – namely the appearance of differing skin colour and the dispersal of early 'mankind' (I now use this term rather than 'man' in deference to Elaine Morgan) out of Africa.

The question of skin colour has of course avoided intensive scientific enquiry for some considerable time. This is because it has involved occasional unpleasant and indeed dishonourable 'racial' overtones.

The current wisdom – with Africa still being held to be the birthplace of mankind – is that our ancestors were all originally dark brown or black in skin colour. Those who eventually wandered out of Africa into the temperate or even uncomfortably cold regions of Asia and Europe, no longer needed protection from the burning sun. However our skins still needed to synthesise vitamin D, a process made easier by a virtually unpigmented skin.

Personally I find this theory difficult to accept. After all, in northern climates we do not go round stark naked all year to allow our skins to synthesise vitamin D and even if, in the short summer periods we shed some of our clothes, then this still fails to explain why the Inuit, Mongolians and Laplanders who presumably never shed anything except a frown on their faces, can hardly be called white-skinned. The only skin they expose to sunlight is that of the face, and occasionally, in relatively 'warm' weather, their hands. Presumably therefore their faces and hands should be differently pigmented from the remainder of their bodies. Has anyone bothered to investigate? Conversely, the Boers, who admittedly migrated from Holland only very recently in evolutionary terms, should at least have begun to show curious developments in their skin pigmentation. Their descendants go about in bare-faced defiance of the dangers of skin cancer, constantly exposing bare forearms, knees and lower legs to the burning sun! Are they now piebald? On the other hand, if the 'aquatic' theory eventually proves correct, then the supposition of black-skinned early ancestors flies out of the window – or more properly gets washed away by the sea. Twelve million years of swimming about for many hours daily in shallow water, coming ashore to feed and sleeping at night in caves does not require very active participation of the skin pigment melanin – the substance that protects the body from harmful radiation. No truly aquatic creature retains a furry coat. Even amphibians usually discard or limit their fur covering. And essentially their skin is almost always lacking in pigment. Why should the human animal be different? Admittedly, we have no means of knowing whether (at this point) there was any significant increase in the risk of tumours arising from cells producing melanin (malignant melanoma); however, the mere fact that white-skinned peoples still survive on this planet suggests that the risk was small.

If one accepts this as a firm basis from which to work, then to hypothesise further as to what happened after the Pliocene is not unduly difficult. A section of these semi-aquatic forebears of ours, finding the climactic conditions becoming more tolerable, ventured back inland. For these (only), melanin cells in the skin were duly activated. But even so, I still believe its role as a protection against harmful radiation has been overemphasised. We seem to forget one very important and widespread role that pigmentation (in a variety of colours) plays in evolutionary experimentation – that of protective camouflage! A dark skin smeared with mud and dust offers far greater benefit to what has now become 'an omnivore with a taste for hunting', than a white skin smeared in a similar way. To this day many primitive tribal people throughout the world practise the art of 'body painting' – is it therefore too fanciful to believe that this is a stylised development of the far more purposeful art of camouflage? Can we postulate that it is more successfully achieved on a dark skin?

But what of that section of white-skinned omnivores that still believed that the shoreline offered a better chance of survival? My hypothesis is this: at the end of the Pliocene the outline of the continent of Africa was certainly different from what it is today; nevertheless, it would hardly have prevented them from either wandering or being driven along what approximates to the Horn of Africa, and up to what we now identify as the Red Sea, or further east to the Persian Gulf. Here they would have found themselves at the crossroads into either Europe, Asia or the Far East. Wandered or driven did you hear me say? Driven? Well, yes. Today we have become so accustomed to white races treating those of dark skin in the most despicable and outrageous manner, that we hesitate when we are suddenly introduced to the suggestion that there may be a reverse side to that particular coin. You see, it is an undisputed fact that all primitive people see any other human being markedly different to themselves as a perceived threat. And they react accordingly! For the section that ventured into the African interior and reactivated their melanin skin pigmentation, what could be markedly more different than another human being with white skin?

Now there will be immediate objections to this, of course, and some critics of my hypothesis may also ask why there was no interbreeding or miscegenation. My answer to this, and it may startle many, is that miscegenation appears to run counter to the evolutionary 'flow'. You demand why? Well, just look about you! Look at the myriad examples of life forms in species other than ourselves. Here we see greater and greater degrees of differentiation and further and further specialisation. None of this could possibly occur if Nature favoured miscegenation. However, the reason most biologists give for such variation (even within a single species, let alone phyla) is that of geophysical change. You see, nothing on this earth remains static – not even the earth itself. Everything continues to evolve. Mountain ranges rise, rivers re-route themselves, deserts shift and forests and grasslands make way for them. And differing conditions within these features gradually bring about detailed changes to indigenous animals. Indeed Darwin's theory revolves round this. One can liken it to the way in which various dialects develop from a basic language. But again, to my mind this is not the full story. How then does one account for the lack of miscegenation among birds? Remember, many of them fly enormous distances and are not cut off from relatives by mountain ranges, rivers, deserts, even entire oceans! Worse, their breeding grounds can be so densely crowded with evolutionary 'cousins', all showing minor variations among each species! Here one would suppose miscegenation must be inevitable.

Take just the example of a variety of 'subspecies' of duck or swans breeding on a single lake. How do Surf Scoters, Velvet Scoters and Common Scoters recognise each other, especially when they are at the height of sexual passion? They are so physically alike that experienced scientific observers often make errors of identification. Yet again, how, during the height of mating passion, do, say, Whooper Swans, Mute Swans and Berwick's Swans sort each other out. Similarly the Light-bellied Brent Goose and the Dark-bellied... One can go on endlessly, and music-hall jokes have been made about the bird-watchers' dialogue consisting of references to the 'greater or lesser' this and that, or the 'rough-legged or the bearded' other thing. Ah, you say with a leer, 'It takes one to know one.' Yet this in itself is an unconscious recognition of a rather mysterious instinct that rejects miscegenation. The fact is that creatures *do* recognise these minor variations. And they surely say to themselves, 'Not to my fancy, thank you very much!'

Now I am aware that students of animal behaviour might retort that it is nothing of the kind; they might well give you a pitying smile and announce that these birds recognise each other by their differing courtship behaviour – in effect different 'dialects' of lovemaking. Yet ask why these courtships became varied in the first place and you may well get a sniff and a cough and a rather cross look before the subject is hastily steered elsewhere. The basic fact remains and sticks in my gullet: as I see it, differentiation among life forms would be impossible if Nature favoured miscegenation! Evolution would grind to a halt. Therefore, with all forms of creation, not excluding mankind itself, there is some deep-seated instinct that begins to create a series of taboos when it comes to 'cross breeding' – for that matter, a taboo concerning its direct contrast, incest. Farm animals are an exception only in that they are artificially induced to make all kinds of curious combinations. Only among mankind are these taboos occasionally broken, and the results usually create a series of unexpected social and cultural problems.

I am well aware, of course, of the consternation that this might cause. The implications are far reaching – not least those concerning racial relations in countries with substantial immigrant populations. This will be dealt with later. But scanning the appalling record of man's inhumanity to man down through the ages, it does at least account for, but never excuse, the lamentable degree of aggression and insensitivity to those seen to be 'different'. Indeed it has proven to be deeply embedded in mankind's makeup throughout all recorded history and, more than likely, before it.

So much then for variation in racial characteristics and the continued fanning out of light-skinned peoples from what is now called the Middle East. Some of these subsequently went south-west and back into that north-east tip of Africa we now call Egypt.

Some went due west along the north shore of the Mediterranean, some due north along the river systems of Eurasia. Others again went north-east into central Asia and some due east toward China and south-east Asia. And during the considerable time involved, mankind remained omnivorous. Yet as skills in hunting evolved there can be little doubt that, proportionally speaking, meat became an important and fairly regular item on the primitive menu.

Incidentally, it should be pointed out that the taste for meat alone was not the sole reason for hunting. In more northerly latitudes especially, the thick hides and furs of animals killed were at least as important as the meat. Initially used for clothing, their use was extended into tented housing using branches as props or adopting a wigwam style. Later, even the bones, gut and other body parts were found to make useful implements and artefacts generally.

Scientific research into lifestyles, however, suggests that average lifespans were just a little over thirty years and that Nature's checks and balances worked with particular zeal in the area of infant mortality. Globally, the total population of mankind as an emergent life form must have remained very small. Obviously in such conditions the 'territorial factor', both as a fully operative human instinct and as a cause of conflict, must have been minimal.

Yet all this changed with the domestication of animals in Neolithic times, approximately one million years ago. It was the first example of the systematic and conscious exploitation by mankind of other life forms, perhaps too the first unconscious attempt to prolong human life artificially. It worked. Life became slightly less rigorous, and, although it was nomadic in character – with the herders being forced to follow their animals to successive new pastures – there is some evidence of average lifespans being pushed out to perhaps forty years. This was accompanied by a decline in infant mortality. It would be misleading, however, to suppose that the diet was profoundly changed, with the bulk now being meat. Mankind, as with most forms of life, tends to be a creature of habit; thus foraging for wild fruits, vegetables and edible greens of a wide variety still continued – much of the evidence being found in careful dental examination of the widely dispersed skeletons of nomadic people.

Following quite quickly on the heels of the domestication of animals came the second major change – the conscious exploitation of plant life – in a word, agriculture!

It is often assumed that this second innovation made a tremendous impact even in its very early stages. I believe this assumption has been considerably overplayed. It also suggests mankind could now be neatly divided into two main groups: nomads, following their animals from one area to another as dictated by the need for fresh pasture (as for example a small number of Laplanders still do today), and agriculturalists, living a static existence, anchored as it were to one quite finite and carefully marked piece of territory. But this division is too sharp. Moreover, it tends to suggest that agriculturalists immediately became vegetarians which is nonsense. It also suggests an immediate opening into the 'good life', which is again totally misleading. Production of crops from virgin territory anywhere in the world even today is unusually promising for the first few years, but then production falls away sharply. Nutrients must be returned to the soil one way or another. This was not understood at first. Therefore, just as nomads had to move from exhausted pastureland, early would-be agriculturalists had to do the same with exhausted soil. Only in very specific areas and under certain conditions were nutrients replaced naturally. These were few and far between.

Eventually of course these specific sites were found in the lower reaches of very large river systems, where the silt from upper reaches is deposited over substantial areas during flooding. Alternatively, they were found in areas where wind-blown soil particles accumulate on a regular basis. Five rivers were eventually found by early settlers to satisfy these conditions – the Nile, the twin rivers Tigris–Euphrates, the Indus and the Yangtze. As for wind-blown soil or 'loess', this was widely cultivated by settlers in northern China. Either way, one important fact should be remembered: silt carried by water or soil particles carried by wind are Nature's example of robbing Peter to pay Paul! One area has to suffer for the other to benefit. So it was in these beneficial areas only that truly successful agriculture could be practised. But even then there were problems. During an odd year, or sometimes a succession of years, rivers failed to oblige by flooding; at other times there were disastrous overreachings. Too little could mean famine; too much saw homes and livestock swept away, with valuable silt ending up as a benefit only to the fish and other aquatic life in the sea. Of all rivers the Nile was perhaps the most dependable; it could be wholly relied on to flood at a certain time of year. Its volume, however, was a different matter. Egypt was by no means a stranger to disastrous flooding. As for wind-blown loess in China, in dry years the lack of rain to anchor it meant that it blew further east into other areas, worse, sometimes even into the very sea!

The arrival of agriculture was therefore by no means an enormous leap forward. So much could go badly wrong – for example supportive technology, or the lack of it. The earliest ploughs were crude wooden instruments held by the strongest man available and pulled by teams of weaker men, women and children. They were just about efficient enough to scratch the surface of the ground. Considerable time elapsed before means were found to yoke animals; even then primitive yokes were so badly designed that they almost strangled the poor beasts! And unlike modern machinery running on fuel won from beneath the ground, beasts had to be fed on scarce resources above ground. Needless to say, working beasts eat their heads off and had to be given extensive use of cultivated areas. Beyond this there were a host of other problems: stones and boulders had to be moved before the crude plough could operate, and subsequently action had to be taken against invading weeds and pests. Even after harvesting there was the problem of safe storage. Here more endless battles to ward off rats, mice, weevils, and general deterioration had to be fought. It was in truth a fight for survival against formidable odds.

Given such endless work and sacrifices, one factor surely gained unusual significance: what was formerly a somewhat vague instinct for territorialism, now became well-defined and highly conscious 'land possession'. Woe unto anyone even suspected of, let alone actually coveting, such hard-won ground.

Yet the greatest threat to such 'ownership' was, paradoxically, not from the enemy without but family members within. It underlines my earlier thesis that for all life forms (bar none), those of one's immediate family group and extended family become the greatest obstacle to survival. You see, if each of these primitive farmers obeyed Nature's command to be fruitful and was successful in bringing on average eight children into the world – what is more, by back-breaking work in the area of food production, bringing them to maturity – then their problems were by no means over. New ones emerged! These patriarchs would be forced to subdivide their land among their male children, then look for suitable suitors for the females. When in turn the second generation produced children in abundance, problems would begin to multiply rapidly. Subdividing your land just cannot proceed endlessly. You finally arrive at so small a patch that any hope of obtaining sustenance from it becomes a mockery. So what do you do? Scatter your surplus offspring to the four winds, hoping to imitate seed dispersal? Problem solved? Perhaps for the patriarch, but not for the surplus grandchildren. Their problems would only be beginning. But before considering these, it is necessary to look at several other emerging factors – problems all of them.

Problem number one: large sections of mankind for the first time in its history were no longer dotted about over wide areas in small groups. They were now essentially extended family members of perhaps ten to twenty persons, forced to live in, comparatively speaking, 'crowded' conditions. This obliged the extended family unit to combine with others to form quite large tribal 'gatherings'. These were organised as a unit by elders, who, after conferring together, would reach a decision by consensus. Yet this too had attendant problems of its own, and will be examined later.

Problem number two: after the Stone Age with its successful manufacture of stone axes, hand daggers, and flint-tipped arrows, other primitive technologies emerged. Pottery and textiles were among them, as was the use of the first metal, copper. But pottery and metalworking necessitated the use of wood to fire primitive kilns. As it was also used in large numbers of artefacts and for building purposes, not forgetting primary domestic fuel supply, it became increasingly scarce in certain areas.

Problem number three: while crowding together had eliminated attacks from wild animals, conversely it increased vulnerability to certain unseen and deadly bacilli or viruses. Occasionally these decimated early groupings, leaving the few survivors totally bewildered as to the cause of such a calamity. This fostered the emergence of unusual individuals who claimed to have some insight into the essential mysteries of life – holy men or priests. Over the years these gradually became a professional class, an organised priesthood. Such a priesthood can be divided broadly into two groups. Firstly there were those who were genuinely curious about the purpose and meaning of life. Their sensitivity was such that the restricted span of human existence, its many shortcomings and its suffering, constantly demanded enquiry into such mysteries. Secondly, however, there were those who were morally unscrupulous – these saw the priesthood solely as a means of gaining power over others. And they rapidly achieved wealth, position and authority, and did so in the most effective and least troublesome of ways – by brazenly demanding it from a cowed community.

Having pointed out just some basic problems, it should become evident that early agriculturalists had by no means created a bed of roses for themselves. Oddly though, groups of 'uncivilised' peoples still living as hunter/gatherers saw from a distance what appeared to be 'lands flowing with milk and honey'. You see, there is a quirk in human nature that underlines the observation 'distance doth lend enchantment'. All too often other people's lives seem so superior to one's own. Envy is then translated into anger. With it comes the pious determination to redistribute such wealth. How else other than by modest raiding? Agriculturalists living on the plains therefore became frequent targets of attack by what one can loosely describe as 'hill folk'. So what do the poor hard-working farmers do in such circumstances? Obviously they put up vigorous defence. But how? Such attacks were sudden and unexpected. The only answer was to have (initially at least) a part-time defence force. Manned by whom? A farmer's surplus grandsons were an obvious source of supply. And these were now supported by the community at large rather than by individuals. Further, if getting them killed in warding off those devilish hill folk was part of the consequence, then a farmer had to do what a farmer had to do. Later, with his emotion fully spent after a period of mourning, the early farmer would see the incident as a crude if rather upsetting solution to the otherwise insoluble problem. After all, making limited amounts of food go round (even under the most favourable of circumstances) is virtually impossible when there are too many mouths demanding a fair share. Scattering part of one's brood to the four winds sometimes worked. But often the winds blew them back again, destitute and starving.

Having surplus grandsons as expendable soldiers and supported by the whole community, however, partly solved this problem. Mankind thus began to apply its own checks and balances to population growth – an activity that was once solely Nature's prerogative!

Isolated in the Nile valley in contrast, early farmers remained secure from sudden attack. They had semi-desert to the west and a line of inhospitable hills neatly combined with the Red Sea to guard their eastern flank. As for the south, incursion by raiding bands for the most part just happened to be very small scale and infrequent. Only the north offered easy access by an enemy. Here a standing army of defenders concentrated. This was one reason why their civilisation flourished and outlasted others. Elsewhere in the ancient world, as already noted, early farmers were by no means so conveniently guarded by natural topography. They suffered accordingly. In these areas they were forced to band themselves together in larger and larger units. More importantly they had to organise fully professional defenders of their territory. But to organise a small army efficiently you need officers and an overall commander. At this point the most audacious of these commanders, having all the necessary credit points in winning battles, bypassed the elders and made themselves sole rulers. This pattern was repeated everywhere except Egypt. At the same time these rulers were supported by the more unscrupulous members of the priesthood. These, as ever, concerned themselves with laying up treasures in this life; it was not seen as necessary to retreat to the wilderness, there to meditate on the possibility of treasures appearing in the next. Anointed by such priests, kingship was given supposedly God-given authority. With this final development the creation of the first city states, each with an individual ruler, became possible, especially in the extensive Tigris–Euphrates valley, the Indus and the Yangtze. Egypt though developed rather differently. It had a single pharaoh and therefore far greater stability. This contrasted sharply with the small city states. Here increasing population pressures forced each of these states to expand. In doing so their boundaries inevitably collided. From this point warfare became not just an intermittent pastime for semi-amateurs but endemic and for professionals.

The significance of population pressure in the establishment of 'reasons' to kill other human beings cannot be overstated and is central to my thesis.

Immediately of course there will be those who will sniff and frown. Many people, conscious of the fact that our world of today is experiencing an unprecedented population explosion, may object to the implication that further devastating wars are inevitable – that is if existing factors remain unchanged. The prospect is too upsetting; therefore it is one they would prefer to deny. Initially they will demand substantial proof. Even then, they will attempt to find as many objections as possible. Yet the unmistakable evidence is there for all to see. Unfortunately though it takes a degree of courage to look at it fairly and squarely. There is after all so much suffering involved. And it overwhelms one. You see such evidence is displayed not just through recorded history, but, as revealed by the efforts of painstaking archaeological research, well before it.

Here in prehistorical eras we find that the Sumerian city states, for example, founded as they were on what was once fertile alluvial soils, happen to provide incontrovertible evidence of endemic warfare. Why? It so happens that the gradual reshaping of the course of rivers in valley basins is continuous, and when an area of fertile land is no longer flooded, it becomes prey to encroaching desert sands. Subsequently these preserve the evidence for thousands of years. By such archaeological quirks of fortune then, forensic research has proven that there was endemic warfare from the earliest periods. Further backing is provided in the later invention of writing – moreover using clay tablets, some of which were subsequently hardened in a kiln. These supplied even more striking commentary. The sacking of early cities and the slaughter of their inhabitants (or their alternative removal as slaves) is recorded endlessly from both these and other sources.

The Stone Age, having given way to the short Age of Copper and then to that of bronze was now beginning to open onto that of iron. And as warfare proved to be the most pressing incentive for the development of new technology, so too grew the demands for a wider list of resources in tandem.

Problems abounded though. During the formation of the Earth's outer crust, Nature, capricious as always, saw to it that mineral resources were not neatly distributed evenly throughout its surface. Instead they were deposited generously in some areas, but thinly (or indeed wholly absent) in others. Therefore having forests to provide timber plus a geological structure to provide metals is equivalent to asking for 'jam on it'. Indeed metals are seldom found in rich alluvial soils. As for timber, its savage exploitation made it an increasingly difficult commodity to obtain. A measure of this difficulty is provided by the 'Epic of Gilgamesh'. This was written on clay tablet and found during the excavations of the Royal library at Nineveh. It formed part of a collection made by Assurbanipal, one of the last and greatest kings of the Assyrian Empire – incidentally, he was also one of the few plunderers of Egypt. These clay tablets are clearly themselves copies of literature from a much earlier period and refer to events that took place almost five hundred miles to the south.

Gilgamesh, in all probability a genuine historical figure, and the conqueror and subsequent king of Uruk in the third millennium BC, is introduced to us as a great warrior and builder. In the usual extravagant terms he is praised for his personal strength, courage and unrivalled energy. Likewise in similar uninhibited macho-terms the epic mentions the indelicate fact that no woman is safe in his presence – not even the wives or daughters of the nobility in his immediate entourage. Introduced later to us is Enkidu, a man of equal strength, courage and boundless energy. However he is totally uncivilised, roams naked in the mountains, having only wild animals as his companions. He is, in a word, a prototype Tarzan! Later these two champions meet and fight it out. After a prolonged battle, Gilgamesh, with what appears to be a skill in an early version of Judo, manages to throw Enkidu. But he does not kill him. Oddly he is struck by his courage, tenacity and manly beauty. What appears to be a homosexual bond then immediately binds the two into an unbeatable duo. This achieved, they promptly go out to find and destroy the evil god of the forest, Humbaba – he who guards the finest collection of cedars anywhere in the world. In this they succeed. Although the epic subsequently goes on to tell of Enkidu's death by some unidentified sickness or epidemic, tells too of the subsequent grief-stricken wanderings of Gilgamesh, it is not too difficult to see a thinly disguised account of an actual historical event. Here a Sumerian city-state and an aggressive hill tribe, at one time in serious conflict, by some extraordinary luck are successful in making peace. Not only this: they actually join forces in an expedition to the upper reaches of the Tigris– Euphrates. The object clearly is the overcoming of hostile peoples of that area and the felling and transportation by raft of precious cedars. Ironically, the deforestation of these upper reaches would later cause flash flooding, giving rise to, or reinforcing, the biblical legend of Noah and The Flood.

Thus we now know that even as early as the third millennium BC certain basic resources such as timber – crucial as it was to such a variety of usages – became, in some areas, already a fast-diminishing commodity. Archaeological evidence points to the establishment of peaceful trading for such commodities at first: inevitably though, as population pressure and a measure of desperation creeps in, the securement of basic resources becomes a military matter – moreover, a prize to be fought for with the tenacity of true desperation!

To repeat then: mankind's history from earliest times demonstrates the correlation between territorialism, population pressure and the availability of resources. On exhaustion of the latter, mankind resorts to warfare.

Yet critics will immediately attempt to pour ridicule on this statement by pointing out that the world had a tiny population in early eras as compared to that of today. They will insist that such a correlation is totally invalid.

But what is carelessly left out of their equation, of course, is the crucial question of the technology of the day. The survival of early city states and their later successive enlargement into empires such as the Sumerian, Babylonian, Assyrian, Hittite Persian, Greek, Roman, to name only those we have considerable knowledge of, were all dependent on the resources that could be made available. These were coupled with very real restrictions imposed by the technology of the day. Remember, crop yields were pitifully small compared with those of today and had to be secured with small primitive sickles. Then again, defence against insect predation was almost non-existent. As for food preservation even the most elementary techniques were in their infancy, let alone measures to frustrate attack by rats, mice and weevil. Thus, if the demand for any *one* basic resource, be it food, water, fuel or an ever growing list of minerals, outstripped the capacity of the current technology to supply – moreover if military means to obtain them by theft from others failed – then famine, followed by disease and chaos, followed. City states and even empires can and do disintegrate. And inevitably in such chaos comes a population crash.

Present too on these occasions are always signs of ecological blight. They go hand in hand. One should add though that after a population crash ecological damage is often stabilised. Given time, Nature is then able to reverse the trend – that is until the sorry business of population pressure begins to build up again. Over the historical record, however, there seems to be evidence of more permanent ecological damage occurring. Tell-tale signs include the enlargement of the world's deserts and the reduction of what were once fertile areas into shadows of their former selves.

To sum up: territorialism, coupled with a population surging beyond the capacity of existing technology to cope, must be recognised as the primary cause of the collapse of empires. It does not have, as is all too fondly supposed, any political or moral agency. What appear to be 'failures' in these spheres are but symptoms; they are not causes. Ecological imbalances also help to accentuate the rate of collapse. And many examples of these can be found throughout the ancient world.

Sadly, of course nothing has changed since. All that has happened is that with each surge in technological development, the bonus is quickly nullified by an equal surge in population. Evidence for this can be seen in the number and severity of population crashes in the last millennium alone.

Moving to the mediaeval era, we see that the effect of almost constant warfare in the Middle East and Europe had its ecological reaction too; it created a population explosion amongst rodents feeding on human carnage! The migration of rats brought bubonic plague in its wake and decimated human populations on both continents. For those lucky enough to escape, however, there were considerable benefits. The sudden shortage of labour among the humble peasantry meant they were at last truly valued for their skills and services. These after all provide the bulk of staple food supplies. As for shortage of labour among servant classes, it meant that the rich had to empty their own chamber pots, cook their own food and wash their own dishes – even lend a hand in saving threatened harvests in the very fields. Now there's a thing! Servants, when they could at last be found, were no longer beaten, half-starved or forced to work for next to nothing. Craftsmen too were no longer swindled or browbeaten to accept the smallest possible return on their skills. Sadly though, this only lasted until excess breeding once more created a surplus labour force. And this pattern of affairs has once again continued right up to the twentieth century.

Reckless overbreeding

At this point we must move from territorialism to consider the problem of surplus breeding virtually as a separate issue. This is because it involves purely instinctive reactions demonstrated largely by the male of the species rather than the female. The latter after all had to suffer the pain, and very real dangers of childbearing: not surprisingly they were rarely as dedicated to large-scale production lines as were the males. In contrast the male instinct includes not merely the wish to dominate the female but also to give the world undeniable proof of his virility. To this very day especially in Asia, Africa, South America and the Far East, males with few children are either pitied or openly mocked. Barren women, incidentally, are detested. Religious, cultural, political and military aspirations all play a part. Despite every evidence to the contrary, a large brood of children is equated with good fortune; the lack of them a dire misfortune. Only very recently in the entire history of mankind have certain racial groups defied this crude instinct, moreover found methods to reduce and control the incidence of conception. All initially have been Europeans or those of European stock inhabiting areas of North America. And these were the first areas in the world to show a marked rise in living standards and longevity. Coincidental? That is an issue to be examined later.

Yet even in what are now sophisticated and affluent countries of Europe and America some dissident voices can be heard. They lament what they see as population 'stagnation': they instinctively criticise a population increase barely above replacement level. Some are religious leaders, some are economists. The former see religious health in terms of the numbers game; they are fearful that their head count might fall and compare badly with those of competing religions. The economists, on the other hand, are obsessed with GDP and the sacred word 'growth'; they fear a slowdown in economic metabolism. Should either of these voices gain greater attention, they could have a mischievous or even devastating influence on the future viability of life on this planet. Why? Both show appalling ignorance of the fundamental biological laws that underpin all life on Earth. Even now these are being gravely threatened. And it exemplifies the acute dangers inherent in the overspecialisation and narrow educational horizons now so prevalent in centres of learning all over the world. Here, devoting one's entire thoughts and attention to a single issue, or creating watertight compartments between disciplines, is seen to be advantageous rather than disastrous. Overlooked completely in this process is the acute danger for mankind. Indeed it is all the more disturbing to find that some of the most prominent of religious leaders trusted and venerated as they are by many millions, have entered into an unholy alliance with a handful of the most influential economists. As the latter are consulted by the governments of some of the most powerful nations on Earth, their joint influence, coupled with fundamentalist religious pressures, must surely have dire consequences. You see, both display by their actions and utterances complete ignorance of well-established biological discoveries. In particular they remain ignorant of the crucial laws of interdependence, together with the fragile nature of the recycling rhythms – that is the vital oxygen, carbon, nitrogen, phosphorus and sulphur cycles. Indeed it seems that whenever even a whisper of these discoveries comes to the ears of these august persons, they presume it to be a mere ad hoc hypothesis! And since these, by their nature, must be temporary they expect them to be replaced by something better! As for the suggestion that all life can come to an end entirely through man's ignorance, rapacity and greed – above all, unprecedented success in breeding – this is totally rejected. This reflects that attitude of the many. The bulk of mankind after all enjoys a total absorption in its own image and has contempt for the remainder of creation. Therefore, warnings made by ecologists, biologists and geophysicists are assumed to be exercises in scaremongering.

As for the fact that starvation constantly faces two thirds of the world's population this is excused as temporary. Such a problem, they protest, is easily solved by better distribution and more modern farming methods. As for the growing list of creatures now either exterminated or in grave danger of extinction solely through the activities of man, this hardly raises an eyebrow. Oddly, while it is always insisted that mankind is a creation of God, a degree of hesitation always surrounds His involvement in the creation of other animals. There is a palpable reluctance and some sort of an effort is always involved. Perhaps this is the result of guilt in remembering the gross exploitation and diabolical cruelty shown to so many other creatures in this world. Meanwhile there is also a wall of silence surrounding the fact that the world population is continuing to double itself in ever shorter and shorter time spans. Shall we look at this more closely. Archaeological research suggests that world population at 10000 BC was about six million. It took about four thousand years to reach twelve million. About two thousand years later it reached twenty-four million; one thousand years later it doubled to ninety-six million. At the birth of Christ it had doubled again to about two hundred, by AD 1000 to about four hundred million! In 1700 it was about eight hundred million. Yet by only 1830 it had shot up to one billion! In just one hundred years, that is 1930, it became two billion! In less than fifty years, that is 1975, it became four billion. If the present growth rate is maintained it will double again by the year 2012. But the spectacle of such explosive increase leaves many quite unmoved. It is again carelessly assumed that science and technology will somehow provide solutions. Their optimism is breathtaking.

Such people take great delight in proving to their own satisfaction that the prophet of doom, and scaremonger extraordinaire of the 1830s, the Reverend Thomas Malthus, who put his ideas into that infamous essay 'The Principles of Population', got it all wrong. The implication of this essay – one almighty population crash sometime before the year 1900 – never occurred. The poor fool, they say, failed to anticipate the tremendous advances in basic scientific research or the spin-off in new technology that it spawned.

They are absolutely correct in this of course: Malthus did not foresee this unprecedented leap. Nor for that matter did he foresee the emergence of a brand-new energy source, virtually replacing the more restrictive use of wood and coal – that of oil. His overall theory that explosive population increase finally nullifies all advances made has had insufficient time to prove itself. Remember, Malthus lived at a time when the Industrial Revolution in Britain was gathering pace. But despite expectations of an accompanying rise in prosperity, there was widespread poverty and appalling living conditions. Could it really be coincidental that at that time ten or twelve children per family were commonplace?

Deeply disturbed as he was by this misery and suffering, Malthus would surely be astonished by the contrast in living standards enjoyed by the vast majority in Britain today; it would be all the more incredible to learn that this has been achieved so quickly, even with another (though modest) rise in population. Yet at the same time he would surely be outraged by the sheer profligacy inherent in our way of life. Unquestionably in his day the old adage 'waste not, want not' had an immediacy and a compelling logic which is totally absent in our twentieth century brave new world. Take merely one example – the way in which we use the world's oil resources. Despite knowing it has taken millions of years (and considerable movements in rock strata) to produce this most valuable and versatile of resources, the prodigious way in which it is wasted amounts to nothing short of lunacy. Every town and city is now choked with traffic. Each vehicle, with its engine engaged either in low gear or stationary, is being used to little purpose and in its least efficient form. Worse, this slow-moving stationary mass is spewing out highly toxic exhaust fumes; these on a hot and windless day seriously endanger people's health. This lunacy is paralleled in the upper atmosphere; here hundreds of aircraft daily spray equally toxic gases into a region where they can do the most harm. At this point is it necessary to remind the reader that this is precisely the area in which the life-sustaining cycles and protective layers (from outer radiation) are more easily tipped into imbalance? And to what purpose? The entire production of several oil wells now provides the fuel for Jumbo jets to carry tens of thousands to attend pop concerts, football matches or race meetings, from one country to another. Often this extends from one continent to another. Moreover a proportion of 'fans' engage themselves in wanton rioting or general mayhem. And with equal mindlessness (though oddly enough without violence) others will fly from the Old World to the New to gawk at a mirror image of their inner being in an 'experience centre' named 'Disneyland'! This for some people, becomes the achievement of a lifetime!

Faced with such a spectacle Malthus would be sickened. Being the man he was, he would be all too aware of the implication that there is no tomorrow, and that one can quite cheerfully bugger any legacy for one's children or grandchildren. Above all he would know that the true significance of his essay has either been totally ignored or misunderstood. Why? The essence of this essay is after all that if unchecked, human populations tend to grow in geometric progression; food and other basic supplies increase at best arithmetically. This is, of course, meaningless to the average person. Explained in a more direct way it can be shown that if (as it is doing now) world population is doubling every eighty years or so, then by AD 3500 it will have grown to six hundred and thirty thousand billion! This would provide standing room only, on all land surfaces – including inhospitable deserts and polar regions. It would also mean the extinction of all other life forms except those in the sea. Even here their survival would be in question as the body wastes excreted by humans would massively pollute the oceans, not excluding the deepest of oceanic trenches. And if by some unimaginable process human beings could still be kept alive and continue to reproduce themselves, then by AD 5500 the total mass of human tissue would equal the mass of the Earth! For those who believe that an escape route can be found by migration to other planets, then even those countless (and perhaps unwelcoming) places would be saturated by mankind by AD 10000. By AD 135000 the ridiculous point would be reached whereby humanity would equal the mass of the entire universe! This, then, might finally illustrate the essential difference between geometric and arithmetical progression. However, then, as now, poor Malthus found an uncomprehending, confused or hostile audience.

But let us return to reality and the current situation. All our newly found wealth and attendant wastefulness could not in any way have been foreseen by Malthus writing as he did in 1824. At a slightly later date not even the astute and far-seeing mind of a Clerk-Maxwell or a Faraday could have visualised the full extent of the advances made as a result of their own basic discoveries, let alone those made by others. From 1834, the year Malthus died, the pace suddenly quickened and became breathless. Yet quite aside from all the scientific and technological leaps and bounds (not forgetting the introduction of an entirely new energy source in crude oil), Malthus did not foresee what I believe to be the most astonishing breakthrough of all: the bold defiance among Europeans of Nature's instinctive urge to be fruitful and multiply! Yes, defiance! The true significance of this is constantly overlooked even today. It fails to be seen for what it is – a unique development in the entire history of mankind.

Ironically enough, failure to realise exactly what has been

achieved is shown among the very people who now religiously practise birth control. It is as if the adage 'familiarity breeds contempt' has been slightly modified to 'familiarity falsifies judgements'! And having so damaged their judgement, it is then easy to believe that the work of a succession of brilliant men and women in further refining the work of Faraday and Clerk-Maxwell has finally achieved our present affluence. People such as Crookes, Mendeleev, Rayleigh, Roentgen, Edison, Bell, Lorentz, Ehrlich, JJ Thomson, Planck, Einstein, Madame Curie, Nernst and Rutherford – which is to mention only a few who were born in the nineteenth century and to leave out those of the twentieth century – are seen as the sole originators of our present triumphs. Yet their efforts in fact would have left us in no better circumstances than those of the early Victorians – but for the crucial efforts of successive millions in practising birth control! This is the true reason for our affluence.

Now I can anticipate of course the howls of protest of those who would dispute this. Ample proof is there for all to see, however. The point is, they choose not to look for it. Myopic vision is at fault, coupled with gross prejudice. This is especially true in the case of many prelates and economists. Yet proof of the overwhelming importance of fertility in the equation can be easily found if one compares the living standards of today's average European with that of people in other parts of the world – more especially where Western-type industrialisation and the wholesale adoption of its technology is rapidly gaining hold. Take just two examples for the moment: India and Pakistan. Here, much diligence and determination has been expended in setting up both heavy industry and high-tech factories. Impressive production figures have been achieved over many decades. But have their living standards shown even a modest improvement as a result? Not one bit of it. As in Victorian Britain, a small minority live in unashamed luxury, while the remainder continues to teeter on the edge of destitution. Comparisons of fertility rates and overall population growth show the reason. It is only a slightly revised version of a primitive farmer's problems in the ancient world. Constantly subdividing his land for his ever increasing brood of children and grandchildren ended in penury, bringing disease and an early death for the majority. Likewise the modern-day Indian or Pakistani factory worker subdividing his wage among his brood of children faces the same daily struggle to exist. Industrialisation has brought about only a marginally increased lifespan and living conditions over that of his forbears eight thousand years ago!

In direct contrast a European or North American worker with an average of only two children is able to maintain a totally different lifestyle. He is able to show every evidence of prosperity and on average lives well into his seventies. A further factor of some significance and one often forgotten is that Western parents can, at the end of a long life, hand over to their children substantial family possessions: these are not subject to endless devaluation, division and squabbling by a host of dependants.

Yet one can dangle these and other examples before the very noses of those prejudiced against birth control, totally blind as they are to the chaos that will most certainly come, and they will obstinately refuse to accept such evidence.

One can only hope there are at least some waverers who are partly swayed. And for these a little more evidence may be required before conviction is achieved. What better then in this instance than to look back at Victorian Britain in the nineteenth century for final persuasion, and do so in depth?

*

Now few will deny that during her long reign Queen Victoria presided over the greatest empire the world had yet known. British dominions and 'protectorates', together with what are somewhat mincingly called 'spheres of influence', were such that she controlled a fifth of the world's land surfaces and a quarter of its people! What is more, to support communications with this far-flung empire Britain had developed an unrivalled ship-building industry. This, by the end of her reign, had produced a naval and mercantile fleet many times larger than any other in the entire world. At 9,304,108 tons it was over *double* the *combined* size of her next two rivals – Germany and the United States. As essential fuel for such a fleet, Britain's rich coal-seams produced such an abundance that she was able to export high-grade so-called 'steam coal' into the bargain. It did even more than that; it fuelled the most advanced forms of industrialisation anywhere in the world. And to redouble this advantage neatly, this enormous mercantile fleet not only took British manufactured goods round the world (where incidentally they found ready and enthusiastic acceptance) but on the return journey, also brought in vast quantities of raw materials. And in truth, much of this was wholesale robbery from primitive peoples and often achieved by their slave labour into the bargain! Yet despite all these incredible advantages, only a minority enjoyed wealth, privilege and political power; the vast majority laboured for a pittance and lived in squalor.

Should we be surprised? From the earliest eras one of the most unpleasant traits in human nature concerns the ability to exploit anything animate or inanimate that appears to be created in abundance – not excluding those of our own species. Conversely, things that are not found in great number are by their very scarcity held to be of great value. Thus if pearls were found in every mussel, or if diamonds and gold nuggets were as common as pebbles, they would have no value for us. The same is true for exotic foods. On the other hand if anything edible, whether it be cereal, fruit or animal, is foolish enough to breed with abandon, then it is exploited to the very limit. Coming to the human animal, no great distinction is made there either. When produced in abundance human beings are seen as exploitable too, and by anyone who happens to find themselves in positions of power. Thus in Victorian Britain the owners of coal mines, factories and heavy industry merely carried on a tradition going back three thousand years or more. Despite some honourable exceptions, most owners exploited their workforce in the most callous and scandalous manner. Even so, there was a point beyond which even the worst of them were unable to go – if only because it damaged their own interests! You see, once you have trained a workforce in certain skills, then it is no longer an advantage to pay them so little that they starve, or for that matter to flout safety standards so grossly that large numbers are seriously injured or killed. Nor, once again, is it to your advantage to work them so hard that they literally collapse on the spot. If you do, then you have to begin retraining large numbers all over again. Granted, with the workforce being so obliging as to churn out masses of offspring, there was no lack of potential replacements. But even so the delay-economics of retraining does not work in your favour. Self-interest rather than pity therefore determines the point beyond which the most unfeeling and rapacious of industrialists were (and still are) unable to go. The undoubted misery and suffering that even this slightly modified exploitation caused was nevertheless still very great.

Overwhelmed by such a vision, social reformers of that period must be pardoned for supposing more equitable distribution of wealth alone would solve everything. They, like many more, either misunderstood, ignored or failed entirely to see the significance of the basic point Malthus had made: unchecked population growth is geometric, food and resource production, arithmetic. Maybe, though, they supposed that mankind's basic instinct to increase and multiply, like that of all other life forms, was far too powerful to check in any realistic way. Birth control was virtually a taboo subject. Certainly redistribution of wealth would have made immediate inroads into the misery and suffering, but the gain would have been temporary only. Within a short time the explosive population increase inherent in geometric progression would nullify everything.

If reformers were blind to this, then political agitators were even more so. As already broached in earlier pages, the German-born Friedrich Engels, by a quirk of fortune, was sent by his father at the age of twenty-two to work in a cotton factory in Manchester in 1842. The shocking conditions both in the factory and surrounding area stoked his passionate reforming zeal. It finally stimulated the writing in 1847 of the highly politicised and indeed revolutionary *Communist Manifesto*. Later, again as already noted, he struck up a lifelong friendship with Karl Marx. Thus in collaboration they finally produced a blueprint for social reformation that became the 'bible' of revolutionaries all over the world. Lenin in particular was to use its guiding principles in his administration of Russia after the success of the 1917 revolution. Ironically though, having gained absolute power Lenin found it difficult to avoid abuse of that power. Stalin, his successor, threw any kind of moral hesitation to the four winds. With a pathological fear of losing that absolute power, he systematically murdered most of his immediate 'comrades' – ironically those who had done the most to make the revolution a success, and not excluding those he had formerly classed as friends. Not content with this, the enormity of such crimes was enlarged still further. By summary execution, brutal treatment in the Gulags or starvation, he eliminated millions suspected even of lack of enthusiasm, let alone opposition to his will. This gross exploitation of other human beings (one cannot slip into the trap of using the expression 'inhuman' because such a trait is observable throughout history and only varies in degree!) was such that the callous behaviour of Victorian industrialists pales into insignificance.

Not that the Russia of the eighteenth and nineteenth centuries under the Tsars was the only country to see the exploited workers try their hand at revolution. Up and down Europe the underclasses, suffering as they did equal privation during the rise of ad hoc industrialisation, made sporadic attempts to overthrow the ruling classes.

Let us return for a moment to Engels. Exemplifying the activities of a dedicated revolutionary, he returned briefly to Germany, there to fight personally at the barricades in Baden during the unsuccessful 1848–1849 uprisings. Acknowledging failure he returned to Britain. Is it surprising that here we find that rioting in what should have been the richest nation on earth was just as prevalent? Our own home-grown agitators and revolutionaries, often vaguely grouped together by the all-embracing term 'Chartists', were equally active and determined. Yet no full-scale revolt was launched despite several favourable circumstances presenting themselves. Why? That question will be answered by a slightly circuitous route. For the moment it is sufficient to say that both Britain and the remainder of Europe managed to escape their own versions of the all-too-recent 1789 French Revolution by the adoption of rather different methods. However firstly it must be said that when attempting to assess the degree of misery and hardship that inevitably come in the wake of ad hoc industrialisation, it is rather easy to become emotional and allow one's vision to distort the picture. In this way one can convince oneself that the workers were exploited to the point of extinction by the most vicious of 'bloated capitalists', as the slightly hysterical catchphrase goes. However, political agitators are just as able to exploit a situation and exaggerate conditions for their own ends as anyone else. As already noted, a workforce driven by starvation and exhaustion, to disease and early death, is a self-defeating exercise for *any* capitalist, however villainous and bloated. It is my own conviction that the greater part of misery happened more by accident rather than by systematic exploitation or callousness. It was caused by a grievous lack of any forethought and planning. The way in which hastily thrown-up industrial centres attracted a population of such unexpected size compounded this. In no way could these be supplied with sufficient food (or even pure water) from surrounding farming areas in so short a space of time. Remember, industrialisation began well before the arrival of the kind of mass transportation we know today. Worse, mechanisation of farming was in its infancy. Obtaining food, basic fuels and other very necessary supplies was a haphazard affair. In no way did it reach any kind of comparison with the organisation and efficiency of the twentieth century. Transportation was by horse and cart over appalling roads, or more often, rutted mud-filled tracks. Refrigeration was unheard of. Even then, if and when supplies did get through, distribution was chaotic. Every industrial area lacked all that was necessary in the way of (in that appalling phrase yet to be coined) 'supportive infrastructure'. And into this chaos came a sudden surge of people of mainly surplus farm-labouring stock, coupled with an influx of Irish immigrants. Why Irish, why immigrant? More pertinent still, why did they become a flood in the 1840s? Well, from 1800 to 1840 the population of Ireland had risen by three million, and the procreative success of its peasantry was such that it achieved three hundred and sixty-five persons to the square mile. It became thereby the heaviest density so far seen throughout Europe! Just after 1840 the Irish talent in procreation was overtaken by that of a fungus called *Phytophthora infestans*, otherwise known as potato blight. Its talents in turn were such that the humble but essential potato, mainstay of the already undernourished peasantry, simply rotted everywhere in the fields. In the appalling famine that followed an estimated one million died. An even greater number hastily emigrated either to America, or, inexplicably as has been noted, to Britain. And in this country they quite naturally swarmed into the rapidly expanding industrial complexes. Ironically at precisely the same time just as many Britons were emigrating abroad! Jokes about the Irish opacity abound, but are simply inapplicable at this juncture. The answer appears to be that not all could find assisted passages or space in the limited sailings available to America. Britain therefore seemed the next best option.

Incidentally, what Irish Nationalists have called the Great Famine and have used as propaganda to vilify the British both then and since conveniently overlooks several awkward factors. As already stated, emigration from the British mainland itself had already reached a peak. Tens of thousands of wretchedly poor and near-starving people were leaving each year for the colonies or the USA, all in a desperate search for better living conditions. In the decade *before* the Irish famine 207,381 people left Ireland for the USA. In the nineteenth century as a whole, 12.7 million British were to emigrate overseas. And not only Britain! In Germany the total was around five million to the USA, Italy two million and Scandinavia 1.7 million. In the Highlands of Scotland a famine was in progress at much the same time as in Ireland. If ever proof were needed that the technology of the day simply failed to cope with the surge in population – and in this instance throughout Europe – this surely supplies it in the most graphic way. The British Government did not command the Irish to produce ten to twelve offspring per family, nor the spores of potato blight to reproduce so rapidly and with such tragic consequences. The attention of the British Government of the day happened to be focused on events far distant. Initially had come military disaster in Afghanistan with over five thousand troops massacred in a retreat from Kabul; then there was war with the Sikhs and famine in much of India, together with troubles in other colonial outposts. This had created a crisis if not a scandal. So Ireland, from which thousands were already deserting, did not appear to pose another problem. Communication with remote districts, and accurate information on the number of people remaining (together with the true effect of the blight) was virtually non-existent. After all, our twentieth-century ease of communication and the use of helicopters to fly over the area was not an option.

When the scale of the famine finally became apparent, aid was sent but in the chaotic conditions prevailing, it was too little too late. Allegations made by Irish nationalists of a deliberate policy of neglect, serve only to shine a revealing light on the levels reached in their blind hatred. Bungling, the British Government certainly was, but vindictive to the point of genocide, definitely not.

However, to return to the industrialisation of Britain in that period. In the absence of any kind of forethought or attempt at planning, the unprecedented influx of what were essentially country peasantry from badly hit areas of England, Scotland, Wales and Ireland, into the mushrooming factories could only bring chaos. Today we have become so accustomed to government intervention in so many areas of our lives – giving rise to the sometimes comforting, sometimes irritating concept called the 'nanny' state – that it is hard to visualise a time when this was absent. Throughout the nineteenth century, in direct contrast, there was a wholly laissez-faire attitude to industrialisation. Owners or managers were allowed to get on with the job without any kind of government planning. Some of the better ones found themselves pushed into activities they had never bargained for; they were persuaded by the appalling conditions to build houses, roads and company stores as fast as was humanly possible. As for those bosses without consciences and with only the highest possible profit in their minds, these of course simply turned their backs on the chaos. This would be unthinkable today. The nanny state is deeply involved in the general welfare of its citizens. It sees to it that they and their children are properly clothed, housed and fed. It even suggests a healthy diet. With children it also, metaphorically speaking, routinely supervises really unpleasant tasks such as 'potty training'. None of this applied in Victorian Britain. There are other factors too which we are all too prone to overlook. The majority of farms round these early industrial sites would be small and unproductive, totally unprepared to meet the calls on them. Nor would they have capital to spend on mechanisation. Perishable basics in greatest demand such as milk, eggs and many vegetables might well have been available at greater distances, but the problem of transport by horse and cart was insuperable. Some meat, of course, could be brought in on the hoof over ancient roads, but it then had to be slaughtered on the spot in the most unhygienic of conditions. Overall, with food in all categories being so scarce, prices duly reflected such scarcity – a factor that poorly paid workers with huge families greatly resented.

Conditions could only improve slowly. Certainly Thomas Telford had begun building roads, bridges and canals at the turn of the century, but there was an enormous area to be covered. McAdam subsequently began 'macadamising' roads in 1815, initially round Bristol. But the major leap in transportation provided by the coming of the railways could only make its unique contribution on any scale after about 1850. Gradual mechanisation of farming and the introduction of new techniques to boost yields also helped. But the climb out of shortage and chaos must have been slow and painful. Men like Robert Owen and Cadbury helped to shame the worst employers into belated action. Even so, these technological advances, combined with the work of reformers and individual acts of humanitarianism, do not explain why Britain avoided revolution. The answer lies elsewhere.

Revolution in France a few decades earlier was precipitated by a succession of bad harvests. Marie Antoinette is accredited with astonishment on being told that the French peasantry were dying for want of bread. Her inspired suggestion was to feed them on cakes. The inspired suggestion by British and Irish politicians and landowners was a little more realistic; they encouraged and at times financially subsidised emigration to less crowded and more productive land overseas. Mind you, troublemakers were transported free with the addition of chains. Indeed transportation became the common sentence for what we now consider petty crime. Beyond this large numbers of young men were recruited into the army, navy and mercantile marine, spending much of their time thousands of miles away. And many never returned. In fairness it should be noted that more succumbed to (then) unrecognised and untreatable tropical diseases than ever died at the hands of an enemy. In contrast, France, while having extensive colonies of her own, was less rigorous in this matter. And her monarchy and aristocracy duly paid the price! Where insurrection is concerned, the Four Horsemen have little respect for power and privilege. Other European countries, such as Holland and what is now Belgium, managed to hive off surplus population to colonies in exactly the same way, following the British example. Thus they avoided the Reign of Terror that finally overtook France.

Emigration therefore became a most effective safety valve in both Britain and the remainder of Europe. And while the solution may seem Draconian and heartless to twentieth-century minds, it undoubtedly saved millions of lives. Indeed affluent descendants of those who were either assisted or forced to emigrate will doubtless see the more positive side of the coin. Yet as no action is without a reaction (using broad application of Newtonian law) it must be added that the Native Indian of North America and the Aborigine of 'Down Under' suffered accordingly.

Let us return however to my thesis concerning population pressure and its direct relationship with endemic warfare.

As the nineteenth century drew to a close it can be seen then that Britain, France, Holland and even tiny Belgium had temporarily solved the problem of explosive population pressures, first by decanting overseas, then by robbing their colonies of timber, minerals and a wide range of resources. These were subsequently brought back to the so-called 'motherland'. There was however one country omitted from this neat solution to grievous problems: Germany. What was once a hodgepodge of individual states had recently become united. This was largely due to persuasive arguments put forward by Bismarck, supplemented as they were with the usual Machiavellian plotting and scheming. The fear of being intimidated or swallowed up by other larger states finally brought all these petty kingdoms into the fold. It was a case of 'Better the devil you know...' But Germany, even as an infant nation, still had problems of population pressure as did all the others. Families of ten to twelve children were just as common in the new fatherland as in France, Britain or anywhere else. Certainly many Germans had emigrated of course, but they were forced to go mainly to the United States – hardly a convenient colony ruled by the fatherland. Nor was there the added convenience of stealing from the natives and sending a wide selection of resources back home! Thus as the twentieth century dawned, German eyes began scanning the continents, only to find that virtually all territories worth taking had already been snatched by her immediate neighbours – not forgetting that damnable offshore island, Britain. On this hangs not one, but two, momentous developments.

Now professional historians almost to a man (there are the odd trifling exceptions such as Toynbee) are quite passionate in their quasi-religious dedication to a strict political interpretation of history. This and this alone is their viewpoint. And it is used in their observations of mankind's emergence as the most dominant creature in creation from as far back in time as the ancient kingdoms of Egypt and Mesopotamia.

For them the political will and the supposedly cunning manipulation of national events alone explains everything. Indeed the more murky and complex those events the better. Thus they spew out crapulous nonsense as to how this or that crowned head of Europe, slyly influenced of course by his immediate entourage, drew up this or that treaty, entered into this or that secret negotiation, dispatched this or that telegram, sent this or that envoy – as if these supposedly august, all-powerful human beings were somehow directing events! The truth is very different. These were mere puppets jerking to strings fingered by an unseen force. That force? Population pressure! And this was inextricably linked with shortage of basic resources.

The historian Toynbee, as has been touched on briefly, was one of the few who attempted to modify this absurdly blinkered approach. He makes a brave attempt to explain the rise and fall of civilisations, but fails to correlate in any truly dynamic way the fundamental relationship between population and available resources. Nor does he attempt to highlight the restrictions imposed by the technology of the day. Others, following Toynbee's rather daring example, have opted to wander into other specialisations such as psychology and psychoanalysis – as if only to prove that they are dimly aware of such extraordinary fields. Thus they establish to their own satisfaction that the Kaiser's withered arm imposed on him an inferiority complex which, as a boy, he strove to hide and conquer. As an adult this tormented man developed a love-hate relationship with his grandmother Queen Victoria and the country she ruled over. Coupled yet again with his envy of her Empire – not forgetting the naval and mercantile power that provided the essential link – he initiated the build-up of German land and sea power. This in turn led to events that shook the entire world in August 1914. However, at this point all historians to a man unceremoniously dump crude psychoanalysis and return to the political closet. From here, in one voice, they declare that the spark leading to the explosive opening of the First World War was actually struck by a wretched little student, and not by the Kaiser at all! To a man they mouth the name Gavrilo Princip. Indeed they go on to add that the said Princip was a member of a secret society. How extraordinary! It is as if they wish to lay claim to some kind of superior intellectual power, firstly in sniffing out, then in explaining, motives deep within the recesses of the human psyche – motives that even Princip himself was unaware of. Well, you have to establish credibility by some means or another now, don't you? And the myth that one solitary individual was responsible for a ghastly war in which millions died on battlefields, moreover caused unprecedented suffering worldwide, is still taught to innocent children in schools throughout Britain (as well as the continent of Europe) to this day!

The simple truth is that the First World War becomes a textbook example of a resource war. The Kaiser should be seen as a rather bungled reincarnation of Gilgamesh, who, after making an alliance with the 'hill men' Austrians, (for hundreds of years previously in fact Prussia's 'southern enemy') now saw advantages in close co-operation and friendship. And subsequently both saw the opportunity to capture for themselves not just primary resources, but also a host of quite unusual new ones into the bargain. These new resources were specifically those that science and technology were now demanding, significantly among them was a commodity called crude oil!

The fact that the young student Princip assassinated Archduke Ferdinand and his wife at Sarajevo is in itself a cowardly, muddle-headed act. It must be clearly condemned. In itself however it did not necessitate all-out war. It is interesting to note that other assassinations such as that of Empress Elizabeth of Austria in 1898, President Carnot of France in 1894, Humbert I of Italy in 1900 and George I of Greece in 1913, did not provoke military reaction. To defuse nationalistic outrage they were all excused vaguely as the work of 'anarchists'. Matters were not pursued further. Yet public opinion could so easily have been stirred up to a fever pitch. All manner of threatening movements could have been made, especially when foreign nationals were found to be involved. But the very word 'anarchist', associated as it was with apparent madmen on the fringes of every society, neatly camouflaged true reasons. That reason? The assassination had been so unexpected that the countries involved were not ready in a material sense for war. In a similar manner the murder of the Archduke and his wife could have been linked with 'anarchists': Austria could have chastised Serbia by trade sanctions and demanded reparations – all short of open war! But this time the preparations for war were at last at an advanced stage. Any stray spark would have been sufficient to touch it off.

What do historians make of it? There is a story that the Kaiser hesitated before giving Austria 'carte blanche'; he drew back from setting in motion a set of irreversible reactions. Yet in a secret meeting two years previously, in December, 1912 to be exact, the Kaiser had come within a hair's breadth of unleashing war. How do historians explain that Count Von Schlieffen, Chief of General Staff 1890–1905, had already prepared a detailed plan to knock out two of Germany's most feared adversaries – France and Russia? He proposed to achieve this by lightning blows initially in the west and then in the east, using newly built railways to transport troops quickly from one front to another. Preparations were even then well advanced. Every physically fit German male was liable for military service. Thousands upon thousands were freshly trained for a two or three-year period then returned to civilian life. However, subsequently they also served part-time in the reserves. This kept an enormous number of men physically fit and well trained, certainly on call at a moment's notice. All in all, it finally amounted to five million men! And as already noted, the fatherland's enemies would be hoodwinked by rapid deployment of men, achieved by the use of this new technology, the steam engine and an efficient railway system.

Construction of the railways, their layout, and even the very timetables were controlled by the military. Incidentally, as a pointer to German awareness of resource deficiencies, a friendship was struck with Turkey and plans made for the construction of a railway from Berlin to Baghdad! With frantic stockpiling, however, Germany was sufficiently ready and poised for what was perceived as a war of successive lightning strikes (but not a war of attrition) as early as 1912. Given that knowledge one must ask, why did the Kaiser hesitate once again two years later?

There is evidence to suggest he did so merely because he felt Germany was still not quite ready. Several either quite new or relatively new resources were in short supply, for example rubber, platinum, bauxite, mercury and mica. These had to be imported and stockpiled. Rubber and bauxite had to come from other continents and by sea. In the event of war these could be only partially obtained from neutral countries. Germany would then have to run the gauntlet of a blockade. Other potentially devastating technological innovations too had not been fully developed or tested; among these were the newly built airships of Count Zeppelin, the submarine and the aeroplane. And for all of these, a brand new resource called crude oil, refined into fuels called diesel or petrol, was essential.

Now attempts have been made by some historians to improve the Kaiser's image by suggesting he wanted peace. This is contradicted by a host of awkward pieces of evidence to the contrary. To repeat, he was, as with all the other supposed personages of power, but a puppet controlled by irresistible pressures. Even if he had never sent the 'carte blanche' to Austria, an all-out war would have been touched off by some other suitable event – this within months or at the very latest a year. To support his now superlatively trained armies, all the necessary bullets, shells, mortars and stick grenades had been manufactured by countless tons. As a further aid to the art of warfare, innovative techniques in mass killing in every shape and form had been tested in secret and were only waiting for proof of their efficiency under full battle conditions. It is ludicrous therefore to suppose one man named Princip was somehow responsible for a conflict that was to involve not just the whole of Europe, but to spill over to much of the remaining world.

Historians, blinkered so profoundly as they are by petty political intrigue, would gain for themselves a liberating new vision if they but interested themselves in just a little science and technology. They might argue of course that specialisation forbids this. They might insist that it is impossible to get a proper grasp of another discipline without devoting all one's time and energy to that purpose. There is a degree of truth in this. Nevertheless, to pick endlessly through the pompous, deluded or fanciful utterances of kings, presidents, chancellors and prime ministers, then move on to the generals, admirals, political agitators, revolutionaries and members of secret societies, is so much wasted effort – especially when the truth lies elsewhere. Indeed it is more than wasted effort – it is a dereliction of duty. Where can they find credibility if the forces controlling these puppets are not only ignored, but as is so often the case, remain totally unsuspected? Thus, rather than concern themselves with the Kaiser's withered arm, historians should have concentrated on other parts of his anatomy: they should have wondered how his production of children (either within or outside marriage) subsequently influenced or failed to influence, the family size of the remainder of his subjects. His grandmother, Queen Victoria, after all produced nine offspring, thereby seeming to put royal approval on large families. Her subjects might well have produced these children anyway of course; but at least it gave them extra justification. Her private thoughts in the matter were unfortunately not transmitted to the wider public. Contrary to fond belief, Victoria was not at all amused by constant childbearing. She was obviously deeply in love and enjoyed sex, but that is a different matter. Contraception was widely assumed to be sinful, and, as they say, 'that was that'. Her subjects seemed to think so too, and happily procreated without restraint. Moreover, this course was followed no matter how poor they were; worse, they did so despite the lack of any state provision for the welfare of such families. German families did likewise, of course.

In a more professional and systematic manner therefore, historians should have interested themselves in the niceties of demography – that is comparing birth rate with death rate, investigating carefully the average lifespan, then finally making adjustments for emigration or immigration. By these and other more sophisticated means they should have some indications of the pressures building up unseen under the backsides of the seemingly all-powerful Kaiser and his ministers. As for the apparently very dull and unrewarding matter of going through statistics of imports and exports, or, more important still, delving for secret papers on deficiencies in certain vital resources, it might finally occur to them such an activity could have a wholly new significance.

To repeat ad nauseam, and thereby risking a degree of irritation, perhaps even the charge of 'overkill': Germany had badly missed out on empire building. Belatedly she *did* make some very late attempts in what was left of the African continent plus the odd island in the Pacific, but these were, resource-wise, quite insufficient. Nor were they truly desirable places to decant surplus population. They were at that time 'white men's graves' with tropical diseases untreatable by medical science of the day. Sending them as an alternative to the United States was not a good answer either. It is just possible that the Kaiser might have deluded himself into supposing that given a massive enough input of German-speaking migrants (and subsequent high birth rate), thereafter this vast country might finally achieve German colonial status! It would be though the back door, as it were, but it would be possession after all! Unfortunately though, as the Americans decided to put a brake on all immigration – no matter from what source – even this vague hope had to be dismissed.

It is instructive though to look at the question of German resources in greater detail, because in the closing years of the nineteenth century this becomes a key issue.

Apart from coal, lignite, iron (but not high grade!), zinc, lead and salt, one finds that Germany had not been well blessed when, millions of years previously and after all the upheavals of the

Earth's crust had more or less settled down, the world had been given the very uneven distribution we find today. It could be said that mischievous chance had given this 'infant' but extremely proud nation just a few toffee apples to keep it quiet, hoping meantime it would not notice some very important omissions. They did notice, however! Like hell! They certainly did by 1900! It was quickly found that Germany lacked, beyond the resources already mentioned (chromium, platinum, bauxite, mercury and natural rubber), other things such as tin, cotton and molybdenum. Molybdenum? This is a resource word many people will gawk at and have difficulty pronouncing! Historians have even greater difficulty in wondering what possible usage it might have. Indeed, any self-respecting academic would be proud to admit ignorance of its very existence, let alone usages! Never mind! Beyond this, Germany had insufficient deposits of copper, antimony, manganese, nickel and sulphur, and relied heavily on imports to make good such deficiencies. Further, in addition she also had to import large quantities of wool and cotton, which most people immediately assume are only related to clothing. Yet looming uncertainly at first, but later with far more gravity, came the most serious omission of all, the fuel source that was to dominate so many minds for the next century – crude oil!

Again at this point it might be supposed that this critical shortage was not fully appreciated until the Second World War. How much truth is in this supposition?

The German inventor Nikolaus Otto produced the first truly efficient four-stroke internal combustion engine – using an electric spark to ignite its fuel as early as 1877. He even manufactured thirty-five thousand such engines before 1900. True, it initially used coal-gas as a fuel, which naturally limited its use to a site near a gas production unit. But later German experimenters, still using a version of the Otto engine, changed to gasoline. Then a certain Rudolf Diesel produced an engine in 1887 using a lower octane mixture which when compressed exploded in the cylinder without an electric spark. Eureka! Having lower revs, this was ideal for heavy transport. Indeed, engineers of the time forecast it would form a most suitable propulsion unit for ships, railway engines and heavy goods vehicles – that is once a few minor modifications were made. Lacking sufficient finance, Diesel looked abroad. The first engine to take his name was actually manufactured a few years later in the United States. In 1913, just months before the outbreak of war, Rudolf mysteriously disappeared overboard from a ship carrying him across the Channel to Britain. It gets more intriguing still! In Britain he was due to attend a meeting in the Admiralty to discuss application of his engine to warships – at that time wholly dependent on 'steam coal' with all the attendant disadvantages of 'coaling up'. Quite a coincidence! It is also an event never fully investigated or explained.

In 1883 Gottlieb Daimler, who had worked as an assistant to Otto, set up his own manufacturing unit to design and build internal combustion engines. Quite quickly he achieved a successful smaller, lighter, high-speed version using gasoline as fuel. It exploded in a single cylinder using an electric spark. In 1885 he produced a two-wheel auto cycle, in effect the world's first motorbike. Two years later came a four-wheeled automobile. At much the same time Karl Benz produced a three-wheel vehicle also with a light engine using gasoline and similarly exploded. A fair number were manufactured and gradually improved before 1900. Then, just after the turn of the century, in 1903 to be exact, the Wright brothers in the USA, using a 12hp gasoline engine, achieved the first powered flight! They covered the glorious distance of forty yards. Yet only six years later, in 1909, Bleriot crossed the Channel, landing successfully and safely in Dover. Development had been rapid indeed.

Now some of the Kaiser's diehard generals and cavalry officers may not have been greatly impressed by the early motor vehicles. An extensive railway system had been built, as already noted, under the supervision of the General Staff to carry men and munitions quickly to German frontiers and preconceived 'zones of operation'. Nevertheless railway lines took time and effort to lay and obviously were not as flexible as motor vehicles. And while they must surely have pointed out that such vehicles were unable to run over fields, jump hedges and ditches, sadly it also had to be admitted that their beloved horses couldn't fly! The accursed gasoline engine undeniably had many applications.

Achieving flight had for the generals one very important function at least – that of spotting the build-up of troops well behind enemy lines, and beyond the reach of conventional telescopes. Captive balloons had been used for this purpose in earlier wars; however, they had proved vulnerable as they were sitting targets for the more ungentlemanly of sportsmen on the opposing side. Count Zeppelin was still experimenting with his airships and had run into problems. Given these setbacks, the General Staff reasoned that if a small and light aircraft of the Bleriot type could cross from France to England, then German versions might well be produced to do even better! Covering a distance of thirty to forty miles, or more, such aircraft could revolutionise the supply of information for tactical planning at the very least. The further use of these early and very flimsy aircraft for bombing was not at first taken seriously. They were after all very limited as to payload. Attention had in any case been focused on very long-range guns mounted on or carried to the front by the railways. These already had a range of ten miles, and there were plans for guns of greater range. For these, of course, new advances had been made in explosives both as propellants, and in their destructive power on reaching the target.

At this point one should be aware that gunpowder, as used down through the centuries, had at last been superseded by new propellants. The cannon ball too had been replaced by shells. In 1846 the German–Swiss chemist Schonbein spilled a mixture of nitric and sulphuric acid while experimenting at home. Having used his wife's cotton apron to wipe up the mess, he put it to dry near the fire. The subsequent explosion convinced him that he was on to something. Had he spilled a larger quantity and used a larger cotton cloth, he would have found himself propelled onto a cloud presumably playing some sort of musical instrument. Certainly an early factory set up later for the manufacture of so-called 'gun-cotton' killed twenty-one workers before methods were found to avoid premature explosions. France, Britain and the USA too were not exactly bystanders in this furious race. They too made improvements in propellants for bullets and shells, including the adoption of rifling and breech-loading. In this Houiller, Chassepot, Vielle, Forsyth, Shrapnel, Whitney, Kynoch and others all contributed. Having greatly increased the range and penetration of bullets, small easily portable rapid-fire guns also received a stimulus with Gatling's invention, later to be improved by Hiram Maxim.

Turning to naval warfare, the German navy took a sudden interest in some remarkable underwater developments in the shape of submarines. The not altogether illogical reasoning behind it was that if Britain was more or less invincible on the surface of the world's oceans, then at least Germany might do rather well beneath them. Actually, as we have seen, a Frenchman by the name of Brun in 1863 constructed the first submarine to conquer the problem of silent and clean propulsion by using compressed air. Its range though was extremely limited. However with the arrival of the internal combustion engine and improved electric motors (Faraday having invented such a motor as far back as 1831), things changed rapidly. The problem of the crew being asphyxiated while underwater by an engine using up oxygen and leaking carbon dioxide fumes was solved by using electric motors powered by batteries. Then, when this power source became depleted, the submarine rose to the surface and used diesel engines for surface propulsion. This achieved battery recharging and gave the crew much needed clean air, at one and the same time. A successful torpedo had already been designed by the Scotsman Whitehead as early as 1864 using compressed air, Originally it had been intended for use by small surface craft (torpedo boats), having only short range and explosive potential. However after further improvement in the 1890s it was sufficiently well advanced to carry two hundred pounds of explosive charge. This travelling at twenty-nine knots and a distance of half a mile, moreover, could be adapted for use in submarines. Underwater devilry thus became wholly feasible well before the outbreak of war.

Experimenting with submarines on their own account the British Admiralty became aware of the very considerable threat posed to both naval and merchant ships. The British Government, forced by the Admiralty to look into the overall logistics and statistics of the thing, estimated that as short a period as three months of successful blockading by fleets of submarines would bring the country to starvation level – beyond crippling the import of resources needed to continue the war. With striking unanimity of thought the German naval staff came to precisely the same conclusion – independently of course. Building submarines and investigating new ways to improve their range and efficiency might well have become top priority, but fortunately for Britain it was relegated to a lower level. The reason? Grand Admiral Tirpitz had a fixation. He was stubbornly dreaming of his fleet of sixty or more battleships. His fixation prevailed. That decision may well have cost Germany the war.

You find that hard to believe? Well, severe losses in British naval forces achieved so easily by fleets of submarines would have broken the tight blockade on Germany. This would have avoided not just the near starvation of the German civilian population, but also a fall in manufacturing capacity, due to lack of vital raw materials. It would also have prevented the people's growing unrest, avoiding what was later claimed by right-wing political activists – among whom was a certain Adolf Hitler – as 'the stab in the back'. Indeed it was this fall in the morale of the fatherland's civilian population that eventually brought about a loss of nerve among the leading generals in the German High Command. And it was this that led to an armistice. Always remember, Germany never suffered an overwhelming defeat on the battlefield!

But to return to the pre-war position: for all these new inventions crowding in on one another a price had to be paid by Germany. The new technologies involved demanded some very new resources, and some were very rare indeed. Worse, many of them, if they could be found within German borders at all, were in such small deposits or quantities as to make their long-term exploitation out of the question. A few failed to be found anywhere and had to be imported in their entirety from abroad. Rubber, for example, essential for so many products, including tyres, had to be imported from Brazil or South-East Asia. The problem of supply was such that the German chemical industry was immediately pressured to find a possible alternative; however this was only achieved much later synthetically using styrene-butadiene. As for the new wonder fuel of the century, Germany actually found some crude oil within the fatherland, but joy quickly turned to concern when it was realised that it was insufficient both in quantity and quality for long-term needs.

The nearest and most promising source of crude oil outside Germany was in Rumania, at Ploesti: here new drilling methods had achieved spectacular results as early as 1880. Efforts were made immediately to import this vital resource, and eyes and ears were turned in every direction to seek other sources. Much to the German High Command's chagrin, their potential enemy Russia had found and developed huge wells at Baku even earlier than the Rumanians had. Envy, unappeased, lodged itself in the back of German minds for a further thirty years and was to influence events in the most dramatic of ways.

Meanwhile there was an awkward problem with Rumania. This small country had, understandably enough, sought neighbouring Russia's protection from aggressive moves by the Turks. In point of fact it had, during the Russo-Turkish war of 1877–1878, become fully allied to the Russian cause. Subsequently, in the turgid mess of the Balkan Wars it had supported Russia's noticeably anti-Austrian–German stance. Conscious of this, the German chemist Bergius was encouraged, in 1912, fully *two years* before the outbreak of the First World War, to experiment in augmenting German oil requirements. He attempted to obtain gasoline from his country's indigenous coal supplies, using hydrogen as an agent. He was eventually successful. Translating his laboratory experiment into a full-scale industry was however a very different matter. He failed to achieve this in any significant way before the outbreak of war in August 1914; indeed he had to wait another decade before his process became fully established. If we weigh up this information carefully it is possible to see that the Berlin–Baghdad railway project no longer smacks of vague opportunism. Baghdad had recently become the terminus in an area where crude oil was known to bubble to the surface, and do so of its own accord! There were other factors too. Having Turkey as a friend also meant that Turkish ports could receive on behalf of Germany almost equally vital imports of rubber from South-East Asia, not forgetting cotton from Egypt. Only at a later stage did the denial of these resources make Germany a world leader in synthetic wizardry.

Is anyone now surprised that just prior to the First World War Germany made every effort to secure Turkey as an ally? Yet as one may now expect, historians with their myopic vision interpreted this in the usual politico-military terms, totally blind to the vital resource factors in the equation.

Overall, it is inconceivable that the German High Command failed to consider every aspect of long-term strategy surrounding resources, especially that of crude oil. Nor should we suspect them of being in any way complacent. With all these promising inventions and their obvious military applications staring them in the face, the German High Command must have realised that the fatherland had a serious deficiency in certain newly discovered raw materials and resources. These were clearly vital to the prosecution of modern warfare. Admittedly there were a few blimpish generals of the old school still attempting to fight yesterday's wars. No country throughout Europe lacked their share of these. German blimps were however outnumbered by up-and-coming younger officers, fully alive to the new possibilities.

Glancing through the many historical essays made by closeted academics on events heading up to the outbreak of the First World War, one cannot but be astonished by their total lack of interest in Germany's position vis-à-vis resources. Not one of these long-winded one-sided essays takes any of the vital military or civilian requirements into account. An overwhelming passion for purely political trivia firstly dominates then obscures everything else. Yet on this central issue of resources hangs not just one, but two, momentous events of the twentieth century.

★

Conflict – the further correlation between population and resources

Having opened up new perspectives on European history prior to 1914 it is entirely necessary to reap the benefit of this new vision, and to do so to its fullest extent. However, if this new vision also pushes one toward somewhat unexpected and indeed uncomfortable conclusions, one should not shrink back from them. Above all, one should never retreat backwards into the welcoming arms of those dedicated to the safely conventional and accepted patterns of thinking.

What are these uncomfortable conclusions? Chief amongst them comes a sweeping reappraisal of Germany's responsibility for the First World War. The unctuous and all too self-satisfied viewpoint taken by all European historians (that is other than German) is that the underlying spirit of Prussian militarism fired this fledgling nation. After the hallowed ritual of duly castigating the Serbian student Princip they turn to newly industrialised Germany. This nation, they unhesitatingly state, was solely responsible for unleashing the dogs of war. Oddly, and as unexpected as it may seem, this view is even taken by some Austrian and German academics too. One has a vague feeling that this curious agreement may perhaps be influenced by their personal political sympathies, more especially if they happened to lean toward socialism or the extreme political left. Be this as it may, the majority have harsh criticism for the Kaiser; they reserve even greater criticism, if not venom, for his circle of political advisors together with top army and navy commanders.

Yet as mere puppets at the mercy of unseen forces that worked away remorselessly behind the scenes, these German overlords merely obeyed a vague sweep of instincts deep down in the subconscious. They were simply carried along by the tide. Population pressure was that tide. In Germany, as elsewhere, it had simply overwhelmed the technology of the day. Millions teetered on the edge of destitution, more especially those parents irresponsible enough to have families of eight to ten children. They saw no hope for the future. Emigration to a foreign country was their only option. But where? Which particular country? Moreover, would they find a generous welcome or implacable hostility? In contrast Britain, France, Holland and even tiny Belgium all had huge colonial possessions overseas into which they could decant surplus populations. Not only this, but on the return journey they could bring back vital new resources and even basic requirements such as timber. That these were acquired by what was virtually theft from the dazed 'uncivilised' and uncomprehending indigenous peoples worried nobody. The morality of such empire building, with its appalling consequences for the native populations, was never questioned. Indeed there was a positive and quite buoyant 'justification' in that both Christianity and civilisation were now being rapidly brought to these peoples. Almost all Europeans shared a firm belief that by colonising these pagan places, light was being brought to those dwelling in spiritual and physical darkness. It raised no series of awkward ethical questions or doubts: there was no public debate either in the camp of the empire builders themselves or the envious Germans watching on the sidelines. And when the Kaiser cautiously shuffled into a programme of colonial acquisition of his own, a wave of hostility, both immediate and outspoken, was shown by the most powerful of muggers on the imperial scene – Britain and France. They were in fact scandalised! German adventurers, with the good wishes of Bismarck, had already succeeded a decade earlier in acquiring (comparatively speaking) small pieces of territory in Africa plus a few odd islands in the Pacific. The African territories though, as already noted, just happened to amount to a 'white man's grave' as tropical diseases were rife; as for the Pacific islands, most were small and scattered and had been spurned even by the Dutch. The question everyone now asked: was there any unoccupied territory? The days when Europeans could wander round the world looking for bits of strange and often unmapped continents ripe for the picking had at last come to an end. Thus the Kaiser's further ambition to enhance his overseas holdings ruffled a good many feathers; the truly knowledgeable among the colonialists knew that all the choice areas, either fully mapped or unmapped, had already been taken. So the British and French now began asking themselves the obvious question: would Germany inevitably be forced to muscle in on their own cherished possessions? The robbers themselves robbed? Competition of this very unfair kind had gone on for two centuries but normally between Britain, France and Spain. Astonishingly, despite this, the arrival of Germany on the scene was judged truly scandalous.

For those of us living in the very different world of the late twentieth century it puts considerable strain on our ability to comprehend, let alone sympathise with, the thoughts and attitudes of our forebears in the opening years of this self-same century.

My application of Newtonian law, ('to every action there is an equal and opposite reaction'), to human affairs, which also adds the codicil 'for every apparent advantage come very real disadvantages', does of course anticipate the eventual outcome. There is nevertheless one important factor to be taken into account. Unlike Newtonian applications purely in the realm of physics, the reactions that take place initially unseen within the depths of the human mind and later dictate a course of action are never so immediate or so neatly predictable. As with the world's weather patterns and the science of meteorology, there are so many subtle influences at work that even the most powerful of computers and entire series of modelled projections fail to achieve true accuracy in forecasting. Only in retrospect do we see the result. A generalised picture solely is obtainable beforehand. Thus a generalised picture of German attitudes to her neighbours in Europe similarly exists at the turn of the century. With that picture in mind, should anyone be unduly surprised by the final direction of Germany's reaction? Can we really claim to be shocked when, with the benefit of this new vision, this vigorous and proud new nation, denied what it saw as adequate living space (lebensraum) overseas, now becomes determined to find such space in Europe itself?

The First World War is therefore just as much the responsibility of Britain, France, Holland and Belgium as it is Germany's.

Now many will contest this view of course. They will be pressured to do so by several conflicting emotions, not excluding that of the crudely nationalistic 'my country right or wrong'. Outright denial of this kind is the only course for the blustering protester. It avoids so much painful soul-searching. They do however make themselves easy targets – their counter-arguments never bother to avail themselves of adequate cover and can be shot to ribbons. Partial denial, on the other hand, is far more difficult to counter. It does after all tend to muddy the issue: people on the defensive or attempting to prevaricate always introduce arguments over piddling detail and are adept at splitting hairs. Nevertheless, I am conscious of at least one rather awkward factor. It may take the form of an allegation – moreover one that critics may well take some delight in exploiting. What is more, it is one that is somewhat difficult to counter. It concerns the awkward charge that I am allowing Prussian militarists off the hook!

Yes, it might well appear that I am excusing or minimising their responsibility and guilt. There is obvious difficulty in denying this. All I can do is protest to the contrary and trust that people will believe me. So I will state quite emphatically the following: I am not an apologist for the militaristic streak running through what is assumed to be the German national character – if such a concept can be at all deemed credible. And you will not find any other extenuating circumstances being slyly advanced in further pages. As far as I am aware, I have no German blood in my veins nor any particular admiration for what are assumed to be the more responsible and attractive features of the German national character – supposedly the ability for hard work and concentration on a particular object. Those who admire Teutonic abilities might also highlight a concern for orderliness, an overpowering love of cleanliness and a demand for the highest of standards. These are often attributed to German people. They may be true; they may be false. I am unable to judge either way. I will admit only to a profound admiration (which at times does verge on what might be considered idolatry) for the concentration of genius in the realms of music. This is found in abundance in Germany. Bach, Handel, Haydn, Mozart, Beethoven, Schubert, and Brahms – especially, in my personal estimation, all hover in an exalted state. Indeed I am convinced that they were able in some mysterious way to make contact with the very essence of that Superior Being responsible for Creation itself.

Certainly one must also have a degree of admiration for the outstanding German contribution to science and technology, though this is tempered by the fact that its application may well on balance be destructive rather than constructive. In this particular respect Otto Hahn and Werner Heisenberg, who, as we shall see later, collaborated (whether voluntarily or under pressure is difficult to determine) only two decades later with an infamous regime, does strike a sour note. This is difficult to reconcile with their undoubted contribution made in a so-called 'pure' science.

However, to move back to the central issue in question – if Germany in all fairness should not be asked to shoulder the blame for the outbreak of the First World War *wholly alone*, then what of the second? More accurately, if Germany entered into a squabble over vital resources in what I now call the First Resource War of 1914–1918, then what of the Second Resource War of 1939–1945?

The second, after all, was but a continuation of unfinished business in the first. On the eleventh day of the eleventh month of 1918 what was achieved in that simple railway carriage just behind the lines was an armistice between Germany and the Allies – not a capitulation. It is essential to remember this. The German forces had been shaken but still remained unbeaten on the field of battle. The collapse had come from within. The spirit of the German people had been sapped primarily by the enormous casualty figures, then further demoralised by shortages of just about everything essential to achieve the minimum standards of living – food, clothing and shelter. Shortage of foodstuffs in the industrial towns and cities in particular had for some time been verging on starvation level. The mobilisation of men into a huge army and not an inconsiderable navy had brought about a shortage of labour in the fields, while the transport system was being overwhelmed by the primary duty of taking supplies to the front lines both east and west. Socialist and Communist agitators who had staged unsuccessful uprisings in the three previous decades and had remained suppressed in the first two years of war had gradually surfaced again. Lenin, at that time active in Switzerland, was, with the connivance of German agents, given passage by rail in 1917 back into Russia; he was visualised as a kind of bacillus carrying the deadly disease of revolution. The Tsar's mishandling of political events, the grave mistakes made by his generals, which resulted in fearful casualties, combined with grievous shortages among the civilian population, had already brought partial revolution – that is, confined to a limited number of towns and cities. Lenin's provision of further virulent infection was indeed to prove decisive in due course. But Germany herself was not immunised against a similar infection. Hardly a family through the land had escaped the loss of a family member and as the general misery mounted so too did the very real threat of revolution.

Turkey capitulated to the Allies on 30 October, 1918; Austria followed on 4 November. Sporadic rioting had already broken out in several German towns. Part of the German fleet mutinied when ordered to undertake a virtually suicidal mission to break the stranglehold of the blockade set up by the Royal Navy. Not that mutiny was experienced by Germany alone. Like a virulent disease it could spread rapidly in all directions! In the previous year French troops had mutinied, refusing to be mown down by enemy machine guns that bombardment had failed to silence. The profligate General Nivelle was replaced by the relatively more cautious Petain, who duly toured the front listening to the men's many complaints. Spells of duty in the trenches were shortened; home leave and time in rest-camps were increased. Petain's humanitarian gestures were to be echoed in 1940 in very different circumstances and brought about very different responses! Liddell Hart comments on the 1917 mutiny using a certain ironic tone: 'Only twenty-three executions were necessary although over a hundred ringleaders were deported to the colonies!' The British too executed an unknown number of their own men either for desertion or disobeying orders in the face or the enemy. We now know that many of these were so shell-shocked that they were incapable of knowing where they were or what they were doing. The truth of the matter was that both the officers in the lower ranks and the common fighting men who saw the appalling slaughter at first hand – whether German, Austrian, Turkish, Italian, Russian, French or British – were totally disillusioned with war. They found it more and more difficult to have a clear view of what they were fighting for. And all countries concerned were close to exhaustion. In this the blockade on Germany was decisive. Civil commotion reached a point where outright civil war threatened. Only the abdication of the Kaiser and the formation of a Socialist Republic saved the German people from the further horrors of internal conflict. Moreover civil war was not the only threat: we should not forget the devoted and undivided attention of the remaining Horsemen of the Apocalypse.

Stepping back from the brink, the mass of the German people still had to suffer the near panic brought about by a worthless currency and the heartbreak of widespread unemployment. Yet there was one positive effect. Many of the more intelligent and responsible of German women (as European women everywhere) were beginning to ask the emotive question: why produce children, more especially sons, merely to serve later as cannon fodder for the militarist? Slowly the birth rate began to fall. Equally disease and rioting thinned the ranks of the less intelligent and the irresponsible, while many of the young and adventurous reactivated a process stopped by the war – they migrated overseas.

By these means the population explosion in Germany was defused. Near stabilisation achieved partly by a new attitude to birth control, partly by a succession of epidemics (a killer 'flu, taking countless people) and partly by emigration saved her from a total collapse. Viewed in any other context the ability of such a nation to survive is inexplicable. Using the eyes of a politician no such welcome pause or stability is apparent. The political scene after all wholly lacked stability. In fact it can only be described as chaotic. Survival being inexplicable, all that can be assumed is the intervention of God and His timely performance of a miracle.

To repeat: this seeming miracle is in truth no more than the neat coincidence of these three factors – birth control stimulated by sheer common sense, epidemic at the hands of one of the Four Horsemen and reactivated emigration by the force of circumstance.

The chaotic political situation needed a miracle but failed to get one. Into the maelstrom of bitterly opposed political factions came a raucous orator with a penetrating stare, possibly (as already noted) with genuine hypnotic powers. Making his mark in the German Workers' Party came Adolf Hitler. Later renamed the National Socialist Party it began to build up a following.

During a spell in prison after the unsuccessful putsch of 1923, he wrote *Mein Kampf*. In it, quite clearly displayed, was a revived concept of 'lebensraum'. It was the old urge crudely repackaged; it openly promised territories to provide extra living space and resources for the German people.

When Hitler finally achieved power the question of vital

resources lay heavily on his mind. In particular he had a fixation with oil. One of his earliest moves was to begin to establish more friendly relations with Rumania. This was tricky. Having fought on the side of the Allies in the First World War, it had been invaded by Germany towards its end. It had provided the then desperate fatherland with much needed crude oil, together with equally valuable wheat and maize. Liberated and independent again, it now seemed essential to establish some kind of rapport. Hitler cleverly wooed the military dictatorship ruling Rumania at that time and began stockpiling oil. At the same time the Bergius process of converting coal to petroleum was given a substantial boost.

As the German military machine was firstly reformed, then gradually strengthened and revitalised, it can be seen that Hitler became further obsessed with the question of oil: it coloured much of his strategic planning both prior to and after the war had commenced. His two allies were if anything even more desperately short of oil. Italy, for example, had to rely totally on what she could import from the Middle East; Japan for her part relied initially very heavily on the USA. Significantly, the first move made by Japan after declaring war was to capture the Dutch East Indies oil wells!

Oil then, without question, became the outstanding factor requiring constant consideration and causing worry throughout the war for Hitler's Reich. This was equally the case for her allies Italy and Japan. However, there were other serious shortages too. These will be dealt with in a moment.

The question that must now be asked at this precise moment is this: did Britain, France, Holland and Belgium still share equal responsibility for the Second War of Resources as they surely did for the first?

Here, the answer must differ. To begin with, their empires were already in decline, with hints of further crumbling to come. Secondly, as with a proportion of German mothers, a rather larger number of women within the Allied camp were also beginning to question their role as providers of cannon fodder. They too asked themselves the leading question: was all the pain at childbirth, then all the care needed to bring their sons to maturity, worth enduring? What was the point if they were only to be exploited and indeed squandered later by the militarists. A new kind of evangelist began shouting the benefits of birth control, together with the further extension of women's rights, from the very rooftops. It made an impact. Birth rates in all these countries showed a steady decline. Anti-war sentiments became strong and pacifist elements within governments pointed out its benefits.

Concurrently, the establishment of some basic social services, including both free and compulsory education for all children, had inevitably put heavy burdens on budgets. With a drop in the birth rate, these now began to ease. Additionally there was the expectation that unemployment figures would no longer continue their unending climb. Certainly the military made off-stage noises of concern at these falling birth rates but Allied governments made no effort to halt this decline. In contrast the dictators of the Triple Alliance made every effort to reverse the trend. Large families were encouraged in every way. Hitler, Mussolini and the Japanese military struck medals, organised children's parades and kissed the mothers' cheeks in dewy emotionalism, slyly acknowledging thereby the sacrifices about to be made. When these gestures failed to give the hoped-for boost, extra monetary and social benefits were given to those women who still remained blind to their hidden purpose. Conversely too, methods were secretly destined to render sterile the unfit and 'racially impure'! Coupled with severe sentences for those advocating birth control (let alone abortion!), a reliable stream of future cannon fodder was gradually created.

Given such a contrast then, it would be fair to say the Allies were no longer culpable in bringing about the Second Resource War.

Meanwhile events moved on. There were ominous warnings of things to come. Initially, Hitler's move to reoccupy the Rhineland in 1936 aroused alarm among the Allies. Pacifist influences however quickly deflected anger and threats of retaliation. The Nazi leader's march into Austria in 1938 in contrast began to change attitudes. It stimulated a truly serious programme of rearming in France and Britain. In the interim, Stalin, although fully conscious of the fact that Hitler feared and detested Communism – indeed had rounded up and quickly eliminated its members in Germany – now entered into a secret pact with this obvious enemy.

By such a pact, Poland was to be invaded and partitioned between them, while the Baltic states were to become a 'sphere of Russian influence'. Trade too was to be vigorously increased. And here Germany gained an exceptional advantage in the import of certain vital mineral and other basic resources – among them oil. Ironically these were to be used to great effect in decimating Russian forces only a few years later. But it was Hitler's occupation of Czecho-Slovakia that finally brought the Allies to threaten direct military retaliation. Most of it was bluff. Behind the scenes there were pleas by two opposing factions – the 'peace at any price' brigade, now allied to a horrified British, and French High Command. For once the aims of both happened to coincide, the latter being grimly aware they were still woefully behind in the rearming programme. This was especially true of bomber and fighter aircraft. There was also a serious lack of anti-aircraft guns for defence against the much-feared saturation bombing.

The invasion of Poland however at last committed the Allies to war. It was commitment stimulated by shame if nothing else. Little could be done, and apart for a very hesitant little sortie made by France, the west looked on helplessly as German troops swept eastward over Poland to meet and greet the Russians marching in the opposite direction.

In the so-called 'Phoney War', lasting from the fifth of October, 1939 to April, 1940, Stalin continued to supply Hitler with vital resources, while the latter now concentrated on his 'lightning strike' against France. This was to begin as early as the twelfth of November. However, a severe and early winter disrupted these plans. Combined with protests by his generals because of their unready state, it caused a series of postponements until the new year. Then a curious incident happened on 10 January, 1940. A German liaison officer flying low over snow-covered territory and unable to see the obvious landmark of the Rhine (covered with ice and snow) went badly off-course and made a forced landing in Belgium. Partly burned but still readable secret documents outlining the plan of the western offensive now fell into Belgian hands. Although officially neutral, there was obvious danger that it might be quickly conveyed to the French. Whether this was a carefully staged decoy or one of those incredible little jokes organised by fate has never been properly established. At any event, a further delay involving what was supposedly a change of plan was now necessary. There was another factor: despite the myth that has slowly built up over the years that the final lightning strike into France was achieved with overwhelming superiority in men, machines and munitions, in fact the Germans had fewer men than the French, linked as they were with a modest but professional British Expeditionary Force. They also had fewer tanks, many of which were also smaller and more lightly armoured than the French. More risky still, they were not over-generously supplied by munitions into the bargain! Only in the air did Germany have definite superiority. Hitler's generals were therefore totally preoccupied with bringing their forces to peak strength and fitness levels. Highly detailed planning, involving parachute troops for attacking forts and capturing bridges and airfields, together with the training of ordinary troops in crossing rivers, was necessary for that coming strike.

Then came surprise. On the ninth of April, the British, at the instigation of Churchill (still First Lord of the Admiralty and not yet Prime Minister), violated the neutrality of Norway by sending in a naval force to lay a minefield.

Churchill's stated intention was to cut off supplies of high-grade iron ore from the Gallivare mines in northern Sweden. This ore was being shipped from the nearby Norwegian port of Narvik.

Hitler's reaction was quite incredible. From a purely military and strategic viewpoint it was, and still is, inexplicable. However the picture changes where resources were concerned.

Rumours of possible violation of both Norway and Sweden's neutrality by the British had reached German ears some months previously. Churchill had a half-baked idea to send an expeditionary force to help the Finns expel a Russian invasion. This involved sending troops over both Norway and Sweden. Shipments of iron ore would obviously be cut. As a precautionary measure Hitler ordered his generals to prepare plans for the invasion of Norway. A reluctant group of planners met on 5 February, 1940. The General Staff were well aware that they could ill afford to divert desperately needed troops, aircraft and supplies at this moment. Their needs for the coming invasion of France dominated everything. Even so they bent under the Führer's will and hypnotic power. The mystery deepens. Historians, however, ignore it.

Hitler was a compulsive gambler. He metaphorically put his shirt on a short 'blitzkrieg' in the west. He expected France would fall within months and Britain would sue for peace. As we know, the first objective was to succeed beyond even his wildest dreams: the second remained a thorn in his side to the end. Given such expectations, why did he react in such an extraordinary fashion to Norway? Was it just the possible loss of Swedish iron ore? Is that really feasible? Such a loss, while an inconvenience, could not be a matter of grave concern. Germany had been stockpiling for years. More to the point, his industrial heartland was feeding a war in the west which was expected to last months, not years. Again conventional historians ignore the matter. Those rare and curious half-breeds known as 'military historians', who concentrate on the finer details of strategy and tactics, fail to illuminate either. Liddell Hart, for example, while almost unique in that he devotes at least some attention to the question of resources, assumes the exceptional purity of Swedish ores to be the overriding reason; yet perversely at one and the same time he underlines German stockpiling plus Hitler's expectations of a short war in the west! No historian, military or otherwise, mentions so-called 'heavy water' or that tongue-twisting item molybdenum.

Now careful study of the records shows that Hitler was always receptive to unusual and sometimes crazy ideas in technology. Some proved to be advances of considerable worth, others less so. The latter indeed ranged down on a descending scale to complete failures. Stung by some failures, Hitler tended to react with indecision. He blew sometimes hot, sometimes cold, on all subsequent projects. Unrealistically, he wanted new weapons almost immediately without any thought to their complexity. Any hint of delay made him blow cold again. The possibility of developing a jet engine, for example, held promise and was given priority for research; then, because of inevitable problems, he switched priority to other things. Incidentally, the British pioneer Sir Frank Whittle, who had taken out a patent, was working on his own version independently in Britain from 1937 onward. Both countries produced the first experimental aircraft using this revolutionary form in 1941. Later, Hitler was to use it hastily in a modified form in his 'secret weapon', the flying bomb. The potentially even deadlier weapon, in the form of the V2 rocket, with different propulsion, was also given priority in 1937. But the 'mad idea' then circulating among scientists, of producing a nuclear bomb, is a much more complex question.

Whether Hitler was himself 'clinically' mad is something open to argument and may never be solved. He certainly had extraordinary dreams of greatness extending, after his early successes, to mastery of the entire world. Of course many people have wild dreams – though perhaps not such extreme flights of megalomania. Most however, at some time or other, come to terms with reality. Hitler rarely did. It often helped him to achieve extraordinary things; equally, it worked in reverse and sealed his downfall. To achieve mastery of the entire world demanded exceptional weaponry. So if Hitler, blowing hot in 1937, could give priority to flying bombs and rockets, why should he miss out on the most fearful weapon of all? Above all, why should his attentions be diverted to Norway at this critical juncture?

Unfortunately it is commonly assumed that German physicists and chemists, unless directly involved with applications of science to the war effort, were ignored or undervalued. Hitler, after all, had no interest or understanding of pure science. He had only a vague appreciation of the great rush in scientific developments at the turn of the century. Nevertheless he appointed scientific advisors in the German Ministry of War Supply who certainly had insight into both. Indeed, these were fully competent to make a guess as to what scientists in the enemy camp might be doing. Certainly the possibilities of an 'atomic bomb' were firmly in the air at this time.

Three influential military figures, Generals Milch and Fromm, and Admiral Witzell, had close contacts with top German scientists at this time. They may well have poured intriguing notions directly into Hitler's ear. The problem was that nobody could give a firm indication of when such a bomb could be achieved. Hitler, blowing cold again, did not in fact give it priority, but there is some evidence that the three men used their influence privately to keep it on a back burner.

As far back as the opening years of the century, 1903 to 1907, Einstein in his famous series of papers had formulated the equation $E = mc^2$. The implications were enormous. But Einstein's genius expressed itself as a theorist, not as a practical worker. More to the point, as a dedicated pacifist he took no part in applying science to weaponry. Ironically, at the time, he was of the opinion that the release of nuclear energy was impossible. Rutherford, whose genius expressed itself differently by experimenting first and theorising after, voiced the same opinion as Einstein. Both supposed that the amount of energy required to split atomic nuclei would necessarily be as massive as that released; thus it had no practical advantage. Both men, slowly and ruefully, were to revise that opinion later.

Meanwhile, the German physicist and chemist Otto Hahn had as a young man decided to gain extra experience first in Britain with Ramsey, then later in Canada with Rutherford. Moving back to Germany, Hahn became Director of the Kaiser Wilhelm Institute in 1928. Working with his assistant Lise Meitner (who being Jewish later fled to Sweden), he began to reinvestigate his own experiments and those of Fermi working in Italy. These involved bombarding uranium with neutrons. In 1938, now working with Strassman, he performed an experiment which actually split the uranium atom. Incredibly, he apparently misread his own findings! If one remembers his early contact with Rutherford, it is not too fanciful to suggest that, still influenced by the great man's opinion, he hesitated to claim he had achieved this astonishing breakthrough. However, he sent results of the experiment by post to Meitner, who was working at that time in the Bohr Institute in Copenhagen. Otto Hahn, because of his hesitancy, did so before considering publication in the usual scientific journals. A startled Meitner, with her nephew Frisch (another Jew fleeing Germany), immediately thought the unthinkable. Within days, Frisch repeated the experiment. This not only verified the splitting of the uranium nucleus but also the release of substantial amounts of energy into the bargain.

Just ten days after receiving Hahn's paper, on the 16 January, 1939 Meitner and Frisch sent their findings to *Nature* in Britain. Two days later Niels Bohr hastily went to America. Here, at a scientific conference, the astonishing news was exchanged in even greater detail. The wider implications were then furiously debated. At that conference was Fermi, who, having married a Jewess, had fled Fascist Italy. Prior to all this, Leo Szilard, also a refugee from Germany, had fled (initially) to Britain where in 1934 he conceived the possibility of a chain reaction. Theoretically, he proposed that a neutron splitting a nucleus would release two neutrons and that they in turn would each release two more, thus creating a continuing process. Having moved to the USA in 1937 he was sufficiently startled and in turn horrified by Hahn's experiment to contact fellow refugee scientists Wigner and Teller. They in turn contacted Fermi and finally Einstein – yet another Jewish refugee, now working at the Institute for Advanced Studies, New Jersey. The result was the famous letter written on 2 August, 1939, partly drafted and then signed by Einstein to President Roosevelt. It did not reach him until the eleventh of October; however the letter noted that work by Fermi and Szilard had brought him to the opinion that a powerful explosive device, in effect a nuclear or so-called 'atomic bomb', was a distinct possibility, moreover that Nazi Germany had sufficient scientific expertise to make that a reality in the near future.

Meanwhile, back in Germany, the interchange of scientific information, as with the remainder of the world, was still being achieved by publication in scientific literature. Thus the sudden withdrawal of further papers from America and Britain on nuclear fission sent urgent messages to the Nazi controllers of the Ministry for War Supply.

Personally I find it inconceivable that Hitler was not informed at this stage. Although understanding nothing of the technicalities or formidable obstacles entailed, he at least must have been persuaded, either by Milch, Fromm or his special scientific advisor, to allow some resources to be diverted for such a project.

How else can one explain the subsequent setting up during the invasion of Poland of a remarkably talented group of physicists in Berlin itself?

They included, beyond the obvious figure of Hahn, the remarkable theorising skills of Heisenberg, combined with the more practical Geiger, Bothe and Weizsaker. These were directed overall by a staunch Nazi, Erich Schumann, who had previously taught military applications of science at Berlin University.

In a remarkably short time this team independently reached Szilard's theoretical assumptions of 'chain reaction'. At the same time they accepted Niels Bohr's theory that natural uranium is composed of approximately 99% isotope U,238, only 0.7% U,235 and but a trace 0.006% U,234; further, they accepted that only U,235 can be split successfully. Even then there was a further condition – it had to be *slow* neutrons! The main constituent of uranium U,238 happens to allow itself to be split only by high-energy neutrons: it is therefore unsuitable for a fully controlled chain reaction. However, the separation of U,235 from natural uranium posed immense problems – these for both German and American scientists. The latter, having far greater financial and technical resources, not unexpectedly gradually pulled ahead. And in the matter of finding a way to slow down neutrons, two methods were thought possible; firstly using a moderator of pure graphite and secondly using deuterium oxide, otherwise known as 'heavy water'. Hahn and his colleagues tried graphite but were unsuccessful and turned to the only alternative – 'heavy water'. In the USA, in contrast, Fermi, now given the task of creating an atomic pile, successfully used graphite to slow neutrons to thermal velocities and eventually achieved fission. Incidentally, heavy water too was successfully used, but at a later stage.

Now at that time the only commercial production of heavy water – a specialised process in itself and quite distinct from that in a mere laboratory – was severely limited. Heavy water, or to give it its full scientific description, deuterium oxide D_2O, rather than H_2O, demanded extraordinary measures to achieve adequate supplies. Found in tiny traces in normal water, it requires enormous amounts of energy and repeated electrolysis to be extracted. This was being achieved at that time by just one factory in the whole of Europe: the Norsk Hydro project at Rjukan in Norway. Here, at what was at one time Norway's biggest waterfall, with a head of two thousand feet, cheap electricity was producing just a meagre ten litres of this elusive D_2O per month!

Surely Hitler was informed of this factory and its vital contribution to the possible production of an 'atomic' bomb? To repeat, invading Norway at a time when all attention and energies were being focused on the coming attack on France was sheer madness, militarily speaking. Hitler took enormous gambles in the political field, yet in military matters at the beginning of the war at least, he was much more realistic and cautious. Odds were narrowed down to as small a margin as possible. So loss of iron ore would be an irritant only. But heavy water? As it happened, Norway also possessed large deposits of molybdenum, essential amongst other things for the production of specialised steels, electrodes, filaments and, when added to oils, for lubrication in engines. So, does the Norway adventure which was eventually to tie down much-needed men and material and prevent their use in other theatres throughout the remainder of the war, now take on a different complexion?

In point of fact, from 1940 onward every effort was made by the Germans to increase the production of heavy water in Norway. Progress however was slow. Then in February, 1943 nine men of the Norwegian resistance, having trained for months in Britain and subsequently parachuted in, cut through the outer perimeter, avoided the guards and placed explosives at the separation plant. By this heroic action the plant was destroyed. One thousand litres of prepared heavy water trickled very expensively away. Attempting to rebuild later, the Germans were foiled by air attacks. The bombing of Berlin also seriously interrupted work on the newly built atomic pile. Work in America in contrast went on in safety and without serious delays.

It is now common knowledge that Germany lost the race in the production of the kind of weapon Hitler would have found most effective in achieving his dream of world domination. The margins by which he lost, however, are not. Historians sleep happily in their beds, never questioning or even realising the narrowness of the margin. Nor do they have nightmares conjuring up the scenario that would have faced the world had German scientists been less hampered. They forgot too how Hitler's threat of using 'secret weapons' at first created derisive mirth in Britain and America. When the first flying bombs zoomed over the Channel, however, these smiles faded. They faded even more when unseen and unheard rockets began arriving. There was some defence against the former, and a proportion were destroyed over farmland before reaching London. Against the rocket there was no defence. One thousand and fifty rockets fell on Britain. Casualties were substantial. Morale in London at least was seriously affected. Had they been armed with nuclear warheads... it is beyond even thinking about!

Evacuated from Berlin to the foothills of the Swabian Alps, and in the protection of a cellar carved out of a cliff, German physicists had built an improved atomic pile. They were within days of reaching the critical point where chain reaction would have commenced when on 22 April, 1945, Allied forces broke in.

As a sequel it is interesting to note that just two months later, on the sixteenth of July, an American desert area saw a vivid flash. Rising into the sky came the typical formation of a mushroom cloud. The first atomic bomb had been exploded in the make-or-break trial run. Only three weeks later the centre of the city of Hiroshima was a desert.

Controversy still surrounds this act. Critics tend to forget that the Japanese fought on land, sea and in the air with a tenacity beyond that even of the Germans. Opposition to Hitler simmered throughout the war despite being ruthlessly crushed from time to time. Not so in Japan. The fanatical dedication by the Japanese people to their Emperor was such that there was no underground opposition. And as the Americans hopped from one Pacific island to another and ever closer to Japan, the resistance became ever more desperate. Few Japanese ever surrendered, only the most shell-shocked and disorientated. Most were prepared to fight on to the bitter end. Thus 'kamikaze' pilots crashed themselves into American aircraft carriers, destroyers attempted to ram battleships and humble soldiers held out for years even after Japan officially surrendered. The loss in Allied lives in attempting to defeat Japan by conventional methods would have far exceeded the civilian casualties in Hiroshima.

Nevertheless, my personal belief is that a warning should have been given. Exploding the first atomic bomb in the sea near Hiroshima would have demonstrated what was in store. If the Japanese had then ignored this threat, then, regrettably, the bombing of Hiroshima would have been justified. But to drop a second bomb on Nagasaki only three days later, especially when the Emperor was preparing to announce surrender, was inexcusable.

To return to the saga of the German race for a nuclear bomb. It would be thoroughly misleading at this point to leave the reader with the impression that German physicists were about to achieve their goal. The hideout in the Swabian Alps was still no more than a mere laboratory. An enormous effort would have been necessary to convert what was no more than a successful experiment into an industrial complex capable of producing enough fissile material for a nuclear warhead. In particular there was the problem of finding the resources and money necessary for building massive new industrial plant underground where they would be safe from bombing. Here the treatment, purification and separation of natural uranium to give isotope U,235 would need to be carried out without interruption. Again it was a question of priority. Massive bombproof concrete shelters for building and repairing submarines and extensive coastal fortifications were being built in France. This was done by slave labour from conquered countries. Diverting this labour to building underground plants capable of manufacturing material for a nuclear device could have been achieved if Nazi heads of the political apparatus, or Hitler himself, had insisted on it.

This saga is of absorbing interest in its own right.

As it happens, it is equally misleading to repeat the constantly aired opinion that American industrial muscle and scientific expertise had left the Germans woefully behind. German scientists temporarily lacked two crucial advantages: firstly a clear political directive and unstinting financial support and secondly a certain range of technical apparatus. Shall we take the latter disadvantage first?

In the University of California, nine years before the outbreak of war in Europe, the research worker Ernest Lawrence had greatly improved particle accelerators. These had been invented earlier by the British researchers Cockcroft and Walton, and had already been given further startling modifications by the American Robert van de Graaff. But Lawrence had now designed and built an even more efficient device he called a 'cyclotron'. It proved spectacularly successful in giving nuclear particles (such as protons) greater and greater acceleration by causing them to run in a spiral motion round a large magnet. He was thus able to improve vastly on Rutherford's pioneer experiments in bombarding atomic nuclei. By 1939, on the eve of the outbreak of war, quite a few American universities had even larger versions of Lawrence's cyclotron. These actually totalled thirty-five in number; all of them were now busily engaged in probing the secrets of the atom. In contrast the Germans had no cyclotrons, although they had belatedly begun constructing a prototype. But the second disadvantage was the most crucial.

In 1942, with initial German success on the battlefields beginning to falter, Albert Speer made his entry onto this scene. The death of the Minister for Munitions, Dr Todt, in an air accident, prompted Hitler (no doubt using his famous intuition) to appoint his architect and brilliant administrator to the post. The Führer's passionate love of architecture had earlier brought him into contact with this young man, and he had been impressed by Speer's efficiency. After he became the Führer's personal architect, something approaching a friendship developed between them; it brought Speer out of obscurity and placed him suddenly in that tiny circle of intimates allowed immediate access to Hitler. This emergence had been so spectacular that it caused much speculation. There was whispered talk of the Führer grooming him as his eventual successor. Speer himself, initially at least, had no aspirations. He was perhaps the only member of the immediate entourage who could be considered truly sane. He had that most remarkable of gifts – an ability to maintain a degree of detachment despite a meteoric rise. From his elevated position he could still look reality fully in the face. All other top Nazis, such as Goering, Hess, Himmler and Goebbels, lived in realms of fantasy that to us today – taking a detached and wider viewpoint – raise serious doubts as to their sanity.

Hitler quite openly showed his personal friendship for his new minister. Immediately those attempting to engage the attentions of the Master of the German Reich attempted to use Speer. A certain General Fromm was one of the first.

It seems at first an odd way to go about things. Why approach this sometime architect, now arguably the fourth most powerful man in the Nazi hierarchy (and still rising), rather than the Führer himself? As we shall see, Speer provides part of the answer in his autobiography *Inside the Third Reich*.[3]

To anyone who is non-German and is convinced of the well-publicised belief in German efficiency in every field of human endeavour, then the entire matter strains one's credibility.

Strange as it may seem, we find that almost everything had to be done in an indirect way. The Führer was difficult to approach. He had very limited time available, and was notoriously of uncertain temper. Normally, one had to make contact with each individual on the ascending rungs of the ladder that the hierarchy precariously stood on – and do so one at a time. Even then, with so much back-biting and murderous rivalry in the upper echelons, nothing was certain in this fear-ridden dictatorship. Yet Fromm was Chief of Army Armaments, and as Hitler took a keen personal interest in all army equipment, he had constant and easy access to the Führer. More significantly still, he had been given a key post as Commander of the Home Army, a key post in Hitler's eyes that is! Ever conscious that his top generals might engineer a coup, the command of army troops (as distinct from Himmler and Goering's private armies) within the Reich had to be placed with someone he sensed he could trust. Why then should Fromm, with something as crucial as an atomic bomb project, go to Speer, who was trained as an architect with no scientific background? Why should he avoid going directly to Hitler? And where was scientific adviser Schumann? It surely suggests that Hitler had earlier enthused over the possibility, then, sensing long delay, had, in a tantrum, brushed it all aside again. There was another factor involved too. A wonder weapon's true value could only be

---

[3] Albert Speer, *Inside the Third Reich*, London, Weidenfield and Nicholson, 1981

accentuated by making pointed (and defeatist?) remarks about the downturn in German military fortunes; this was a very dangerous thing to do given Hitler's temper, balanced as it was on a hairspring. Fromm was certainly grimly aware that the Führer's lightning 1941 blitzkrieg against Russia, with its over-confident expectations of shattering the Russian army at a single blow, had failed. Fate had intervened with heavy rain in the summer, bogging down all wheeled transport; it had then gone on to provide an early and severe winter for which the German's were woefully ill-prepared. The entry of America into the war in December, 1941 further accentuated Fromm's fears and his prognosis of eventual defeat.

Speer does not relate how this general engineered a special relationship with him in his new role as Minister for Armaments. In point of fact Air Force General Milch and Admiral Witzell – engaged as they were in the design of new aircraft, ships, submarines and ancillary weapons, not forgetting scarce resources for their crucial supply – had equal call on his time. It must surely have been Fromm's grasp of overall strategy and assessment of Germany's dire position that now gave him a sense of desperation. This then must have provided sufficient motivation for closer contact with this rising star.

In Speer's *Inside the Third Reich* we find the following:

> I met regularly for lunch with General Friedrich Fromm in a *chambre separée* at Horcher's Restaurant. In the course of one of these meetings at the end of April, 1942, he remarked that our only chance of winning the war lay in developing a weapon with totally new effects. He said he had contacts with a group of scientists who were on the track of a weapon which could annihilate whole cities, perhaps throw the island of England out of the fight. Fromm proposed we pay a joint visit to these men...

A brief digression at this point is not so much wasted effort because it illustrates several important aspects relevant to our theme. It embraces conflict *within* the human mind – one which reacts to, rather than produces, external conflict. It has to do with divided loyalties. Both men were confronted with the most difficult of assessments and an agonising choice. Was the Führer now fully in control of his senses, or was he gripped with an insatiable lust for military glory? And was this a lust so overpowering that he had the entire planet in his sights? If so, was he prepared to use the German people as a mere tool, or more to the point as mere cannon fodder, for his purpose? Was he prepared to use them to gain this fantastic dream regardless of cost and all manner of sacrifices? After each occupation of the surrounding states he had declared himself satisfied, yet almost immediately orders were given to prepare a new campaign. The Russians had been badly mauled, but the lightning strike had ground to a halt, defeated by the weather. Yet despite being in a bad way the Russians could always withdraw further into their vast country. If Hitler were to put out peace feelers once he captured one of his main objectives – significantly, for our theme, this was the oil fields in the south – and Stalin was prepared to barter them for an armistice, then could things remain in suspended equilibrium? Could they be suspended until such time as a wonder weapon could be produced? Or indeed several wonder weapons?

An armistice is not as fanciful and as unlikely as it may sound at first. The bulk of Russians, overrun by the German army, hated Stalin, his commissars and his secret police. Stalin's callous disregard for basic human rights far outdistanced that of Hitler. And he too dreamed of conquering the world with his special brand of communism. In the occupied territories, and especially among many thousands of Red Army prisoners, substantial numbers were volunteering to put on German uniforms to settle their score with Stalin and all he stood for. Treated properly, the vast majority of Ukrainians, Belorussians and Lithuanians, who now found themselves behind German lines, would have gladly accepted new masters. Unfortunately, Himmler intervened. The obscenities committed by his SS soon put paid to the realignment of loyalties. Significantly Hitler too, whose belief in his own political genius had never wavered, remained blind to the possibilities. Not only did he allow Himmler a free hand in Russia, but he encouraged the excesses. It was yet another of his incredible blunders. The commissars and communist intelligencia whom Himmler and Hitler now wished to exterminate had long since fled eastward, anticipating the wrath of their own people –

more than that of the Germans. Himmler, with his entirely erroneous and twisted racial views, in the process of hunting for them, annihilated thousands of innocent people. He was gradually to turn a population wearily prepared to co-operate at worst, and fully collaborate at best, into bitter enemies.

Just two or three years' cessation of hostilities on the Russian front would have changed Hitler's fortunes completely. France had now accepted occupation of part of her territory; Petain and the Vicky regime were fully collaborating in the remaining area. French factories and workers were being quickly reorganised to feed the Reich war machine. Within Germany itself, jet engines and rockets were already in an advanced state of development. With a Russian armistice, every effort could have been transferred to these projects.

In that hard winter, with all German forces at a standstill, both Fromm and Speer must have asked themselves the agonising question: would the Führer regroup in the political sense rather than military? Could he make a deal with Russia as he had France? Or would Hitler rashly pursue his goal with conventional weapons and without such a halt? Denied this vital temporary respite, would the German people be called on yet again to make endless sacrifices for the Führer's quite extraordinary ambition? If this last assessment was correct, then where did their basic loyalty lie? With the German people, or with that one individual with a magnetic personality – this single individual exuding such certainty in what he called his 'destiny', and who had such a strange and unaccountable hold over them. These were questions both men must have asked themselves time and time again.

Fromm was to remain loyal to that single individual, despite everything; Speer lapsed but was to hide the redirection of that loyalty right up to the bitter end.

Meanwhile, in April, 1942, the issue was only just becoming focused in both their minds. Fromm had obviously taken a considerable risk. If Speer had seen this as defeatism – possibly leading to disloyalty – and duly reported to Hitler, the good general may well have had the Gestapo knocking on his door. We tend to forget today that all high-ranking officers and party officials were not merely fearful for their own lives, but also had to consider their wives and children too. Himmler, the SS and the Gestapo were ruthless in their dealings with those considered traitors. But Fromm obviously had faith in his judgement of Speer's character. This faith was not to be gravely misplaced. Had he known it though, Fate was soon to be unusually malign. It was already beginning to engineer this general's downfall. On active service many miles away on the Russian front, a certain Count von Stauffenberg, scion of one of Germany's most respected of families and a brilliant young staff officer, was now being quickly promoted. He had already transferred to Army High Command and was secretly preparing for a spectacular intervention. This young man had become sickened not only by Himmler's treatment of Russians within the conquered territory, but also by the Führer's conduct in the prosecution of war in general. He too had come to believe that this so-called benefactor and inspired leader of the German race would never be satiated. Stauffenberg was slowly being convinced that the Führer was prepared to use every German throughout the nation, in callous disregard of all their suffering, merely to satisfy an impossible dream. This officer was even now tentatively sounding out others similarly disillusioned. His aim was to form a group to achieve the Führer's overthrow or assassination. But it was to take considerable time. Fully two years later, after being gravely wounded on front-line duties with a Panzer Division in Tunisia, Stauffenberg was given a desk job in Berlin. He now had the rank of Lieutenant Colonel and initially served as Chief of Staff to General Olbright, second in command of the Home Army! Previous attempts at Hitler's overthrow or assassination by other officers had come to nothing. All of them had been bungled in one way or another. Olbright, already a conspirator, and a deputy to Fromm, was in an excellent central position. Both Olbright and Stauffenberg now guardedly attempted to sound out Fromm. Utterly convinced though he was that Germany had already lost the war, Fromm gave the impression that he still found his oath of allegiance to Hitler unbreakable. Hitler knew his man!

Here amply demonstrated is both the strength and the weakness of German military character. Stauffenberg and Olbright, sensing that their commanding officer could not be trusted, wisely refrained from making any open invitation. He was not asked directly to become one of the conspirators, this despite his being in a key position to achieve all their ambitions. Fate intervened once again and in one of its most diabolical of moods. In June 1944 Stauffenberg was promoted to full Colonel and appointed Chief of Staff to Fromm himself! In this position he had direct access to Hitler two or three times a week. Having lost an eye, part of one arm and having other injuries which were slow to heal, his not too arduous task was to supervise and report on the retraining and reorganisation of badly mauled units withdrawn from the various front lines. These worn out and often wounded troops were temporarily placed under Home Command. When judged fit enough, the Führer required these wretched men, who had already gone through so much horror and hardship, to return to duty. There, used as last-ditch reinforcements, they were to plug the gaps in the Russian front.

Stauffenberg now made several attempts to set a pre-timed bomb near Hitler. All of them were foiled by the Führer's abrupt change of timetable. Finally on 20 July, 1944, at Rastenburg GHQ, the young colonel placed a briefcase containing a bomb under Hitler's map table, within six feet of his legs. Fate then allowed one of the several staff officers, also in the room and attempting to study the map in greater detail, to intervene. In all innocence this officer moved the briefcase away. In so doing he allowed the blast that took place a few minutes later to take his own life but save that of the Führer! Fate also allowed Stauffenberg – at that time convinced that Hitler had been killed – to complete the three-hour aircraft journey safely back to Berlin HQ. Here, after a fatal delay, he and the other conspirators put their takeover plans into action.

They marched into Fromm's office; this was a very necessary action so that they could take over the control centre of the entire Reserve Army. Here, told of the supposed assassination, Fromm hesitated then demanded proof. Not being satisfied he made a phone message to Rastenburg. Here he was told Hitler had survived. Refusing to take part in what was now clearly a mutiny, Fromm was taken prisoner together with other dedicated Nazi officers. Locked in a room these found an escape route. Returning with the aid of an armed guard, they turned the tables on the would-be saviours of Germany. The chief plotters now found themselves taken prisoner. Anxious to prove his loyalty to Hitler – that singed and shaken leader, saved miraculously by Fate merely to commit suicide a year later – Fromm conducted an immediate court-martial.

Within an hour he helped Field Marshal Beck to put a pistol to his head, then had General Olbright and his Chief-of-Staff Stauffenberg, 'this colonel I no longer know,' summarily executed in a courtyard outside. Ironically though, this act was not sufficient to save him from the Führer's vengeance in the bloodbath that followed. Judged to be a 'fence sitter', Fromm was given the dubious honour of being executed by firing squad, rather than suffer torture then slow strangulation on a meat hook. This was the fate accorded the remainder of the true or even suspected conspirators. In preserving the Führer and ensuring another year of further suffering for the German people, Fate outshone all its previous malign complications of circumstances in these final episodes of slow Nazi downfall.

But to return to the rather less dramatic, yet in many ways far more important, events of June, 1942. At a meeting hurriedly arranged by Fromm, Air Force General Milch and Admiral Witzell, together with Speer, were introduced to a group of nuclear scientists. Speer records in *Inside The Third Reich* that among the cream of German scientific elite present were the subsequent Nobel Prize winners Otto Hahn and Werner Heisenberg. The latter gave them a generalised picture of German nuclear research to date, not excluding bitter criticism of the Ministry of Education's lack of funding. Heisenberg also threw caution to the wind by bemoaning the loss of so many science graduates to the armed services. He contrasted this with the liberal finances available to nuclear research in the USA, together with deliberate concentration of ample scientific personnel. The crucial role played by such technical apparatus as the cyclotron was also aired – an area where Germany was now woefully behind current American expertise. Much of this information taken from technical journals still available in the USA[4] had shown that overall the USA now had a substantial lead in nuclear research. This was particularly painful and unwelcome in that German scientists had led the world in this particular field only a few years previously. Heisenberg ended what had become a virtual exposé of the Reich's mishandling of scientific research by emphasising the enormous consequences that would ensue from such errors.

Speer was very quickly taken on-board. With his rare and very valuable gift of being able to cut through masses of data, there to detect and then analyse the fundamental aspects of any issue, he realised the necessity for urgent action. Immediately he sought further information. At the end of this painful 'lecture' he relates how he had asked Heisenberg to clarify the position regarding the actual manufacture of an atomic bomb. The future Nobel Laureate answered honestly and directly. While on a theoretical basis the production of a bomb was feasible, the technical problems involved in turning theory into reality was a very different matter. These were formidable! He stressed that even if those in the topmost echelons of the Third Reich gave the project their maximum support – massive financial aid, technical know-how and manpower – then an atomic bomb would still take years to develop. At the very minimum it would take two years but given any further delay in prioritising the project, probably much longer.

Speer, being already aware that the Führer's wildly enthusiastic support for all and any kind of 'wonder weapon' would plummet once any delay was mentioned, now found himself put in a difficult position. Convinced it would be possible to direct sufficient resources, convinced too that German scientists could overcome all subsequent technical obstacles, he knew even so that it would be almost impossible to achieve Hitler's consent. Whether he openly discussed the problem with Fromm is unclear, but his hesitation must have been apparent. Either Speer or the good General may have begun considering whether the project could be camouflaged by other activities, with Hitler being kept in

---

[4] Author's note: undoubtedly supplied by agents as an embargo had been put on all scientific literature.

ignorance of the true effort expended. At any event we suddenly find in the next sentence...

> Nevertheless, General Fromm offered to release several hundred scientific assistants from the services, while I urged the scientists to inform me of the measures, the sums of money, and the materials they would need to further nuclear research.

Hahn and Heisenberg did so a few weeks later. Speer records his astonishment at the modest requirements; he suggested they take considerably more. In the interim, however, he was obviously having second thoughts about the difficulty of hiding the truth from Hitler. Given that a number of those in the high echelons of power, among them Martin Bormann, were clearly busy sharpening knives to stab this rising star in the back, it was a risk not worth taking. Judging that the war could hardly last another two years, he realised that the bomb would not be ready in time anyway. Such a wonder weapon could not be just rejected out of hand, nevertheless, and on his own authority. The only person who could make a final decision, and indeed take full responsibility for that momentous 'yea' or 'nay', was Hitler himself. Speer records:

> I was familiar with Hitler's tendency to push fantastic projects by making senseless demands, so that on 23 June, 1942 I reported to him very briefly on the nuclear-fission conference and what we had decided to do.

These last few words are misleading. They tend to suggest that Speer had already stopped the project. What he actually means is that he has given it qualified approval and a substantial increase in resources. Thus he must have been totally astonished to find that several people already had their fingers in the pie. Hitler had also received reports on the atomic bomb but from very odd sources. Speer goes on:

> Hitler received more detailed and glowing reports from his photographer Heinrich Hoffmann, who was very friendly with Post Office Minister Ohnesorge. Goebbels too may have told

him something about it. Ohnesorge was interested in nuclear research and was supporting – like the SS – an independent research apparatus under the direction of Manfred van Ardenne, a young physicist. It is significant that Hitler did not choose the direct route of obtaining information on this matter from responsible people but depended instead on unreliable and incompetent informants to give him a Sunday-supplement account. Here again was proof of his love of amateurishness and his lack of understanding of fundamental scientific research. Hitler had sometimes spoken to me about the possibility of an atomic bomb, but the idea quite obviously strained his intellectual capacity.

Speer wrote a skeleton section of his memoirs during his long prison term immediately after the war, then filled it out after his release. He could at this point safely make scathing remarks on Hitler's lack of capacity for deeper understanding, but unfortunately he omits far more vital information. He only touches on SS involvement and this opens up fascinating speculation regarding the shadowy Himmler, who ran what was a separate little empire of his own. Hitler and Himmler often held meetings in absolute secrecy with no other person present. Immediately we must ask the question: had Himmler advised the Führer to invade Norway two years previously? Himmler's enthusiasm may have been thwarted by Hitler's initially glowing expectations, typically growing cold again as soon as technical delays in production were mentioned. He may nevertheless of his own volition have seen to it that 'heavy water' remained high on the list of Germany's military necessities after Norway had been taken over. Perhaps the jumbled and disorganised way in which Hitler accepted advice will make a final answer impossible. As for the momentous business of making a firm decision at that particular moment and giving a clear 'yea' or 'nay', Hitler neatly evaded it. All Speer received was the comment 'there was not much profit in the matter'. Thus he threw the ball back into Speer's court.

Significantly, what Speer does record is that Hitler would have had no hesitation in using an atomic bomb against Britain. As early as 1939, while watching a film of dive-bombing in slow motion, the Führer was fascinated by a short montage of a plane diving toward the outline of the British Isles:

> A burst of flame followed and the island flew into the air in tatters. Hitler's enthusiasm was unbounded. 'That is what will happen to them,' he cried out, carried away. 'That is how we will annihilate them!'

However, in the very next sentence Speer goes on:

> On the suggestion of the nuclear physicists we scuttled the project to develop an atomic bomb by the autumn of 1942...[5] after I had again queried them about deadlines and been told that we could not count on anything for three or four years. The war would certainly have been decided long before then. Instead I authorised the development of an energy producing uranium motor for propelling machinery. The navy was interested in that for its submarines.

Nuclear submarines in 1942? You bet they were! Another wonder weapon to deal a heavy blow! Produced in quantity it would have guaranteed Britain being knocked out of the war. At that time Britain imported *all* its crude oil and a significant proportion of food and raw materials from America. It had no Bergius plants for converting coal to petroleum products! Britain's sole contribution to the war at that time (apart from partly blockading Germany) was as an unsinkable aircraft carrier, from which stinging bombing missions were increasingly being launched.

Meanwhile in America, on the heels of Einstein's famous letter to President Roosevelt in August 1939 a consortium of scientists, including the Italian Enrico Fermi, together with many Jewish refugees and several top researchers on loan from Britain, were working with the cream of US researchers.

By 1940 McMillan and Seaborg were already bombing ordinary uranium with high-energy deuterons and had achieved the early alchemists' dream of transmutation. They produced a new element possessing a higher atomic number of 93! They gave it the name 'neptunium' and incidentally were later given a Nobel

---

[5] Author's note: this was anyway totally unrealistic.

award. But more momentous events followed. Neptunium isotope Np 238 is radioactive. Emitting beta radiation it changes spontaneously within a few days (without human intervention) into another trans-uranic element with the next higher atomic number: 94! And that number happens to be an element we now know as 'plutonium'. And plutonium is another candidate for producing an atomic bomb! Plutonium is also produced by way of an atomic 'pile', which, I should point out, German physicists were, with Speer's backing, still allowed to proceed with – if in a much more restricted capacity.

The question as to whether the Germans would have produced a nuclear bomb within time to have a decisive influence on the war is therefore far more subtle and complicated than most people realise.

To sum up: Hitler's dream of conquering the world had far more substance than we are inclined to allow. If he had delayed the outbreak of the Second Resource War by just two, or possibly three years, which in the historical context is quite a short time, he may well have achieved his ambition. Within such a breathing space he would have had the opportunity to develop fully several technological breakthroughs, giving him total military superiority over all other European states including Russia. The jet engine (applied to both fighters and bombers), the flying bomb, the V2 rocket, the ground-to-air missile, the nuclear submarine – all would have been virtually ready to put into operation. The advantages of concentrated effort in a country not yet in a state of war, and still able to import large quantities of raw materials from abroad, moreover not having to face the serious disruption caused by bombing, would have been enormous. Merely by demonstrating the existence of these wonder weapons to ambassadors and their military attachés of the countries that at that time were still only *potential* adversaries – Britain, France and Russia – would have caused rapid changes in attitude. In the face of these weapons alone, they would have been forced to enter into some kind of accommodation with the Nazi regime. The further knowledge (if still only a longer term threat) that nuclear bombs could be carried to a target via flying bombs, rockets or piloted jet aircraft would have clinched the matter. After all, scientists in the Allied camp could have confirmed it: nuclear research had reached a point where the development of such a bomb was not just theoretically feasible, but an actual probability. Nor would the USA, despite being on another continent, have remained safe. Nuclear submarines and von Braun's V2 rocket further developed into an intercontinental missile would have brought them within reach of the horror of total war.

Hitler could then have achieved his dream – irony of ironies – without spilling one drop of German blood. Nor should we forget that lovely old medieval villages, towns and cities all over Europe would have escaped wanton destruction. The work of countless craftsmen, who over centuries had given loving attention to so many artefacts within them, would then still survive today.

The more closely one looks at Germany's position, given that Hitler had taken that fateful decision to go to war in 1939, the more one must cast doubt on his sanity. The greater too the blame that must be laid on the shoulders of the top military. They must have known how finely balanced were the scales between success and failure. A coup engineered by senior officers, the majority of whom had never committed themselves to the Nazi party and its doctrines, a coup moreover carried out before the attack on Poland, could have changed the entire course of twentieth-century history. Yet somehow or other they were mesmerised by this former corporal. To repeat: the sheer force of conviction this man possessed concerning his 'sacred destiny', combined as always with his penetrating stare, may well have had a genuine hypnotic effect. Indeed it seems this is the *only* respectable theory one can advance after the year 1942 when, in the looming face of disaster, these men continued to serve him virtually right up to the bitter end.

Albert Speer's story, and his own record of faithful service (almost, but not quite, to the very end) is in itself a baffling and extraordinary saga. Speer, despite his cool, collected and balanced outlook, his ability to see through all the propaganda and delusions of the era, did in fact join the Nazi Party. Reflecting on that fateful action during his twenty-year imprisonment, he could find no logical reason for doing so. Only emotion carried him away. The first time he attended one of Hitler's meetings in a dirty, rundown beer hall with a party of his own students, he recalled Hitler speaking with urgency and 'hypnotic persuasiveness'. The content of the speech he forgot almost immediately. But he could recall vividly how later, after the meeting finished, when his students asked him to discuss the speech over a glass of beer, he refused.

> I felt I had to straighten things out in my own mind to master my confusion. I needed to be alone. Shaken, I drove out into the night in my small car, stopped in a pine forest near the Havel, and went for a long walk.

Time and time again, in the next fifteen years, Speer was to ask himself why he had become such a prisoner of this man's will. Why had he continued to serve in the full knowledge that Hitler was leading the country into a maelstrom of suffering and misery from which there would be no escape? He never found a completely convincing answer.

His memoirs are fascinating nevertheless, if only for the insight he brings to Germany's weaknesses in the field of resources as the war progresses.

As already noted, Germany had a range of critical requirements, many of which had to be imported from considerable distances overseas. Previous armaments ministers had hastily stockpiled as much of these as they could, but only a sufficient amount for a war of short duration. Of all the most critical items, Speer was aware that crude oil constituted Germany's Achilles heel. The lightning strike on France and her capitulation had failed to bring about the expected peace-feelers from Britain. Indeed the seriously ill and woolly-minded Prime Minister Chamberlain had been succeeded by the aggressive Churchill. Aware that the Royal Air Force was now the only weapon available to strike at Germany (and that, equally, Goering's air armadas were now the greatest threat to Britain), he ordered both greatly increased resources and industrial manpower be given fighter and bomber construction. A committee studying Germany's resource problems was already in existence and Churchill was well aware of their findings. They had, with fair accuracy, estimated what specific materials and quantities Germany had already stockpiled.

In petroleum they arrived at a half million tons yearly from Germany's own oil wells, plus a tiny amount from Austria and Czechoslovakia. However four million came from Bergius plants. They estimated that twelve million were needed for the war effort as a whole. Therefore at least eight million had to be imported from Rumanian oil wells, notably at Ploesti. These, incidentally, were well beyond the reach of all aircraft from Britain at that time. Thus the Bergius plants treating coal and heavy oil with hydrogen to form petroleum products were an obvious target. Churchill directed that they should be attacked. The bravery of RAF pilots apart, it proved a time-wasting directive: the navigation and bomb-aiming equipment at that time were ludicrously unequal to the demand. When photographic air reconnaissance finally got into its stride and cameras and techniques of taking pictures improved, chiefs of staff were dismayed and even deeply embarrassed by the results. Great care was taken not to leak reports of these failures. When attacking industrial targets such as Krupps in the heart of the industrial Ruhr (far larger than Bergius plants), these were found to have received the odd hit more by luck than judgement. The shattering truth dawned that only one bomber in ten arrived within five miles of its target. Having arrived, its crude bomb sights seldom enabled a hit on (a properly identified) target. The greatest percentage of bombs fell in open country or on the homes of civilians!

Hypocritically, given their own record, Hitler and Goebbels claimed that Britain had commenced terror bombing. They suppressed the fact that the carefully designed German Stuka dive-bomber, which, as its name suggests, uses a diving technique to deliver its bomb load and does so with very high accuracy, had already been used to devastating effect. Fortifications, airfields, munitions dumps, not forgetting key industries in Polish towns and cities, parts of France and the Dutch cities of The Hague and Rotterdam had suffered direct hits. Britain possessed no dive-bombers. The Americans too, when they entered the war, used high-level bombers with equally crude bomb-aiming equipment. Their only dive-bombers were heavily committed with their Pacific Fleet against the Japanese. Speer, as he records, had few worries in his first year as Minister concerning accurate bombing.

Both British and American air forces merely produced pinpricks on German resources and production of armaments. Had the British known it, the appointment of Arthur Harris as Air Marshal Bomber Command in February 1942 was to aid Speer enormously. The Reich minister was able, because of the policy of widely dispersed bombing fanatically adhered to by Harris, to make a spectacular increase in German war production – this in almost every sphere for the next two years, including the crucial supply of petroleum! 'Bomber' Harris, in his pig-headed insistence that bombing alone could bring the German war machine to its knees, paralleled Goering's bloated over-confidence. This had elevated itself into the realms of pure fantasy during the 'Battle of Britain' and was proved wholly in error. Britain could not be knocked out of the war by bombing alone. Equally nor could Germany. Bomber Harris was thus responsible, with the benefit of today's hindsight, for seriously delaying final victory. He prolonged the war for arguably at least another year, and was thus the cause of quite unnecessary loss of life among the Allied forces as well as countless German civilians. His fixation with bombing towns and cities could possibly find some excuse in the first year of massed RAF raids under his direction. Navigation and bomb-aiming equipment was still pitifully inadequate, and it required huge built-up areas to catch a proportion of bombs that otherwise fell in open fields in the countryside. These may have killed a few old cows already destined for slaughter but little else. However with the subsequent rapid improvement in navigation systems and special 'pathfinders', Harris had less and less excuse for 'area bombing'. His arrogance and blindness were such that he opposed and almost succeeded in blocking the supply of long-range aircraft to Coastal Command at a time when they were desperately needed in the fight against U-boats. At this time Admiral Doenitz and his 'wolf pack' tactics were sinking record numbers of Allied shipping in the Battle of the Atlantic. Oil tankers were an especially vulnerable target. Yet Harris seemed oblivious to the fact that without American crude oil supplies his bombers would be unable to fly. He also resisted for as long as possible (despite directives from his superiors) bombing carefully selected targets such as factories producing ball-bearings and railway locomotives. It would be tempting to investigate the saga of the scientist–inventor Barnes Wallis and his attempt to convince the Air Ministry that his 'bouncing bomb' could destroy German dams. These dams and the water held in their reservoirs supplied vital hydroelectricity and water supplies to industrial heartlands. Reviewing the Barnes Wallis story is a temptation that must be resisted because of inadequate time and space. The attack was however eventually made and carried out with exceptional skill and bravery. Speer's reaction should be noted:

> On May 17, 1943 a mere nineteen bombers of the RAF tried to strike at our whole armaments industry by destroying the hydroelectric plants of the Ruhr. The report that reached me in the early hours of the morning was most alarming. The largest of the dams, the Mohne dam, had been shattered and the reservoir emptied. As yet there were no reports on the three other dams...

Speer hastily went by air to inspect the damage, and 'surveyed the scene of devastation from above'. Sheer ill-luck had however prevented the RAF from inflicting even greater devastation. If the three other dams had been breached also then the attack would have had enormous effects. But it was serious enough. Speer goes on: 'My report on the situation which I soon afterwards delivered to the Führer's HQ made a deep impression.' Subsequently he relates the incredible efforts then put into effect to repair the damage. Experts were summoned from all over Germany and he ordered seven thousand men to be taken off the building of the Atlantic Wall in France and rushed to the Ruhr to make good the damage. With his usual gift for a fundamental analysis he comments that the British, using just a few bombers, came closer to achieving a truly serious blow to German armament production (and indeed to industrial production in general) than the combined effort of thousands of bombers previously. Yet he also marvelled at the British Air Command's poor grasp of strategy, in that on the same night they had divided their forces to destroy the Eider Valley dam. And the latter dam, as he notes with relief 'had nothing whatsoever to do with supply of water to the Ruhr'.

Indeed he was so impressed by this strategic attack – despite its only partial success – that he attempted to persuade Hitler to stop the tit-for-tat terror-bombing of London and other British cities. He pressed his case to switch to British west-coast ports, which he correctly guessed were 'strained beyond capacity' by the convoy system. The German Air Force was, however, too heavily committed in Russia. Thwarted, but turning his attentions to that front, Speer noted that the Russians had built just a few gigantic hydroelectric schemes rather than many smaller ones. If these were bombed, he realised, tremendous disruption would be caused to the Russian war effort. With his prodding, Hitler actually passed on a directive to his corpulent Commander of Air Forces. Astonishingly, Goering was persuaded to rouse himself and make a half-hearted attempt; but it eventually came to nothing. This error had far-reaching effects! Meanwhile, by superhuman efforts the breach of the Möhne dam was closed by 23 September, 1943, and as Speer comments 'in the nick of time before the beginning of the rains'. As one reads his actual script one can almost hear him heaving a sigh of relief; indeed in a further line he pours scorn on the British planners under Bomber Harris who failed to press home their initial success by bombing the rebuilding effort. The breach in the dam could not have been closed for another vital six months if rebuilding had been delayed into the autumn rainy season. He also notes wryly that a few incendiary bombs would have set fire to the wooden scaffolding.

Unbelievably, British Bomber Commands visible obtuseness persisted even at this point! Despite the enormous propaganda boost enjoyed throughout Britain by the exploits of the 'Dam Busters' Harris himself was not to be redirected from his obsession with area bombing. Moreover, he did his best to convince his counterpart in the American Air Force operating out of Britain not to he diverted either. Meanwhile Speer was still bemoaning his lack of success in redirecting German policy and he quite rightly justifies his opinion when the British for some unexplained reason temporarily broke with area bombing and launched five consecutive attacks on a single strategic target. Again from *Inside The Third Reich* we find:

> While I was trying to convert Hitler and the General Staff of the air force to this policy our Western enemies launched five major attacks on a single city – Hamburg.

He goes on to describe the horrific scenes when the first attack put the water mains out of action so that the firefighters had no means of tackling the multiple areas of blaze. When the aircraft returned the following night (and yet again on succeeding nights) he recounts how the 'huge conflagrations created cyclone-like firestorms' and how the very asphalt in the streets caught fire. This in turn caused yet more human suffering and casualties. Large numbers of people were suffocated in their cellars or turned into human torches in the streets. The horror was so complete that Speer likened it to the effects of a major earthquake.

Writing his memoirs on scraps of paper in his prison cell and filling our these accounts after his release, Speer was now free to be highly critical of Hitler's reactions without fear of the consequences. A few lines further on he describes how the Gauleiter of Hamburg teletyped Hitler repeatedly 'begging him to visit the stricken city'. The Führer refused. Mindful of the necessity to bolster at least a residue of morale among the survivors, the Gauleiter parried the refusal. He suggested Hitler should at least meet with (and possibly decorate) those the rescue services who had displayed notable heroism. Speer recounts laconically 'but Hitler refused even that'. It was typical of the Führer's attitude to suffering. Incidentally, elsewhere in his memoirs he mentions how Hitler and his entourage while travelling east by rail to his command centre of Russian operations, were faced by a somewhat similar situation. Stopping momentarily at a station, his special train drew alongside the carriages of a mobile hospital unit filled with wounded from the Russian front. The survivors of months of ferocious fighting now found themselves suddenly looking directly at their leader, dining in every comfort in his luxuriously equipped carriage accompanied by his elegantly dressed military staff. Hitler's immediate (and instinctive?) reaction was to pull down the blinds!

But to return to Speer's observations and opinions regarding strategic bombing. Here we must always be mindful of the fact that he had an unique overview his position in the hierarchy allowed him to estimate accurately the true extent of German vulnerability.

Hamburg, as a port, with large warehouse facilities and numerous industrial complexes was heavily defended. True enough, as with the other large cities with similar defences, such attacks cost the British and Americans heavily in aircraft and aircrew lives. As both were difficult to replace it put a huge question mark against the already dubious supposition of winning the war by bombing alone. Equally though there were debits on the German side. Speer, in his usual efficient way of probing the situation with statistics, noted Germany's heavy military expense involving ten thousand anti-aircraft guns, searchlights, night-fighter aircraft and day fighters. All of these would have made a significant difference if they could have been employed on the Russian front. Besides tying down thousands of servicemen, a third of the optical industry was involved in producing gunsights and the electronic industry was similarly laden in producing radar equipment and telecommunications. As for wastage in ammunition by the anti-aircraft batteries, this was phenomenal. Speer was fully aware of the contribution ground-to-air missiles would have made had they been available and not still at development stage. Their use would have been decisive. The already heavy losses suffered by British and American bombers would then have become catastrophic; indeed the air offensive would have ground to a halt had these been ready in time. Speer also comments on tank production at Friedrichshafen and ball-bearings at Schweinfurt and their vulnerability to air raids. His warnings to Hitler finally increased the number of anti-aircraft guns around them if nothing else. Yet Speer, untypically, had allowed his emotions to overturn his cooler logic. He records: 'Hamburg had put the fear of God in me.' For a short time he actually believed that within three months armament production would collapse if such attacks continued. He had omitted to take into account the heavy loss suffered by the Allies. It forced them to pause not just to refit and retrain aircrew, but also to attempt to provide high performance and long-distance fighter aircraft to cut down on losses from the German night fighters and daylight air defenders. He had also overlooked the toughness and dedication of the German industrial workforce, whose morale was not to be destroyed. At this point he also skates rather too lightly over the huge number of foreign workers and concentration camp inmates forced to work in heavily bombed areas; they had no possibility of throwing in the towel. There was no option but to stay at their workplaces, no matter what rained down from the sky.

Hitler, as always in such situations – able as he was to wholly discount all the suffering – turned on the dejected Speer and, referring to the armament industry as a whole, merely said, 'You'll straighten all that out again.' Which Speer duly did. Within weeks things were already recovering. There was however a further short jolt that gave cause for concern, though the Allies once more failed to follow through the only policy that could have had a profound effect. As Speer duly noted:

> We barely escaped a further catastrophic blow on 17 August, 1943, only two weeks after the Hamburg bombings. The American air force launched its first strategic raid. It was directed against Schweinfurt where large factories of the ball-bearing industry were concentrated. Ball-bearings had in any case become a bottleneck in our efforts to increase armaments production. But in this very first attack, the other side committed a crucial mistake. Instead of concentrating on the ball-bearing plants the sizeable force of 346 Flying Fortresses divided up. 146 planes successfully attacked an aircraft assembly plant at Regensburg, but only with minor consequences. Meanwhile, the British air force continued its indiscriminate attacks on our cities.

The attitude of Bomber Harris, with his puerile 'you started terror bombing – we'll finish it' attitude, only served to bring gallant RAF aircrew down to the level of frightfulness achieved by the German Reich. It forced brave men to act dishonourably throughout the war. And all to no purpose! The unforgivable bombing of Dresden when Germany was on the point of surrender, and which surpassed even the horrors of the firestorm suffered by Hamburg, should have put Harris in the dock at Nuremberg with the other Nazi war criminals. The charge against the top political figures and generals at that long trial was that they had waged war with total disregard for human dignity and human rights; they had brought to countless millions of civilians unendurable levels of suffering. Harris too was guilty of precisely that.

But to return to Speer's testimony. In it he recounts how digging into earlier stockpiling and substituting slide-bearings for ball-bearings bridged the gap made by the severe drop (67%) in total ball-bearing production. Given Harris's policy and respite from further attack, plus desperate measures to restart production, things slowly began to ease again. Speer states: 'What really saved us was the fact that from this time, and to our astonishment, once again the enemy ceased attacks on the ball-bearing industry.'

Hitler himself took a keen interest in the resource position though occasionally he deliberately falsified the importance of a particular item or commodity for ulterior purposes. For example, in November 1943 a Russian counter-offensive threatened to retake Nikopol, which was a centre for the mining of manganese. Hitler insisted that all available divisions be thrown into the battle to prevent its capture. When his HQ staff protested that from a purely military point of view this was unwarranted, moreover that the troops were badly needed elsewhere, he flew into a rage. He shouted at his staff that without manganese the war would soon be lost. Within three months, he declared, Speer's magnificent efforts in the armament ministry would be brought to nothing. An hour later Chief of Staff Zeizler privately telephoned Speer to confirm whether this dire reading of the resource position was correct. Speer immediately summoned experts in the steel industry to hammer out the position exactly. They found that even with the loss of Nikopol, existing stocks, combined with various procedures for making savings, would be sufficient for another eighteen months. Speer immediately sent a teletyped message to Zeizler and a reassurance to Hitler also. He stressed that the situation did not require extreme concern. Two days later when Speer arrived in HQ, he records that:

> Hitler snarled at me in a tone he had never used toward me before: 'What was the idea of you giving the Chief of Staff your memorandum on the manganese situation?' I had expected to find him well pleased with me, and managed only to reply, stunned, 'But Mein Führer, it's good news after all!' Hitler did not accept that. 'You are not to give the Chief of Staff any

memoranda at all! If you have any information kindly send it to me. You've put me in an intolerable situation. I have just given orders for all available forces to be concentrated for the defence of Nikopol. At last I have a reason to force the army group to fight! And then Zeizler comes along with your memo! It makes me out a liar. If Nikopol is lost now it's your fault! I forbid you once and for all' – his voice rose to a scream at the end – 'to address memos to anyone but myself. Do you understand that? I forbid it!'

Manganese in truth was the least of Speer's worries. In the memorandum which he had also given that very day was an inventory: he listed the stocks, imports, present consumption (and estimated number of months they would last) of all the important resources required for the armament industry. He carefully excluded imports from Nikopol, Finland, Norway, the Balkans and Turkey, alluding to the possibility that Germany's enemies might well sever supplies. The list included, beyond manganese, nickel, chromium, wolframite, molybdenum and silicon. From the statistics he had produced he concluded that chromium was now their greatest worry:

> Should supplies from Turkey be cut off the stockpile of chromium is sufficient for five and a half months. The manufacture of planes, tanks, motor vehicles, tank-shells, U-boats, and almost the entire gamut of artillery would have to cease after this deadline.

Speer comments that Hitler turned away, totally unwilling to consider the matter. Returning to realms of fantasy he began discussing with Speer's assistant Saur the production of a new tank!

Within a few months the strain on Speer and the hectic way in which he dashed around unplugging bottlenecks in a host of industrial plants in both Germany and all the occupied areas became so great that he fell seriously ill. During his spell in hospital he became alarmed that his enemies in Hitler's entourage were hatching a plan with the connivance of the doctor in charge; he was convinced they would quietly see to it that he would fail to survive. The story is fascinating in itself, but it has no place here.

It is sufficient to observe that Speer, with the help of friends, managed to bring in another doctor.

Returning to his ministry on the eighth of May, 1944, only four days later, he had to deal with the greatest crisis of all: fuel! Up to that point, thanks to Bomber Harris continuing to evade repeated instructions from RAF chiefs of staff to attack the Bergius plants, the output of fuel was completely adequate for all Germany's needs. However, the American air force stationed in Britain had a better grasp of strategy. On the twelfth of May, with a force of almost one thousand bombers, they attacked several fuel plants in central and eastern Germany. Speer records that he will never forget that day. Next morning he inspected the tangled wreckage of one of the plants. It was however possible to rebuild and repair given a superhuman effort – provided no more attacks were made. He flew to Obersalzberg and gave a report to Hitler and Field Marshal Keitel. In it he expressed the candid and utterly realistic view that unless the attacks were prevented or, alternatively, the Allies failed to press home the attacks, then Germany was doomed:

> The enemy has struck us at our weakest point. If they persist at it this time, we will no longer have any fuel production worth mentioning. Our only hope is that the other side has an air force general staff as scatterbrained as ours!

The effect of this dramatic statement was however partly deflected by the ever comforting Keitel:

> Keitel, who was always trying to please Hitler, hastened to say that he would be able to bridge the gap with his reserves. He concluded with Hitler's standard argument: 'How many difficult situations have we already survived?' And turning to Hitler he said: 'We shall survive this one too, mein Führer!'

Speer makes no immediate private comment at this point. His earlier summing up of the character, intellectual capacity and consistent failure of Hitler and his staff to come to terms with unpleasant realities makes it unnecessary. Once again it was yet another retreat into pure fantasy, this time on Keitel's part. One wonders indeed if he was wholly sane. His knowledge of the impending use of 'wonder weapons', including jet aircraft, the flying bomb and V2 rocket, must surely have been the *sole* source of any possible optimism. Yet Speer had already privately concluded by the careful analysis of statistics a truly significant fact: the rate of production and the actual bomb load carried by these wonder weapons when launched against Britain could not possibly compete with the bomb load now being dropped on Germany – and this by conventional aircraft only! He realised equally that he himself had, during his years in total control at his ministry, allowed his analytical gifts to be carried away by Hitler's purely emotional stance. Reading Speer's memoirs one immediately feels his suppressed bitterness in being forced to rectify or buttress up an entire string of errors made by the Führer at this time. We see in particular how over these crucial years he had been pressured into diverting far too many resources to the V2 project – essentially an offensive weapon. This had been to the detriment of defensive weapons, now so badly needed. The ground-to-air missile was a case in point. These could have proved decisive in the air battle now raging in German air space. Having far greater accuracy, and at that time no known system of defence (such as was later achieved by deflecting them from their target by use of flares), Allied aircraft could have been virtually annihilated over the Reich's coastline before they penetrated inland. Ultimately though, Speer could hardly blame himself and take full responsibility. Hitler was solely to blame for the crisis. Not only did he override all advice from his air force generals (and air aces such as the legendary Galland) who begged for these anti-aircraft missiles, but he also seriously delayed the emergence of the jet fighter. Ever thinking of an offensive potential, he insisted on its redesign to a light-bomber version! Regarding the introduction of jet engines and newly designed airframes, Britain too for that matter also lacked sufficient drive and vision. It likewise had failed to give enough scope and backing to its own talented designers and engineers. Whittle's project had also failed to receive sufficient priority. Placed in its tentatively designed airframe, the first British jet-engined prototype called the Gloster rose into the air as early as 1941. Test flights were on the whole successful – few modifications were necessary. But here again not enough manpower and resources were diverted to make this jet fighter fully operational, or to manufacture it in quantity. It could so easily have made a spectacular impact on the actual course of the war.

Speer, at the heart of things in Germany, had daringly disobeyed Hitler's orders to concentrate solely on jet bombers; he had secretly allowed the fighter version to proceed, though at a far lower level of priority. Being in the background however, it achieved very slow progress. Meanwhile, the obvious upper hand gained over the conventional German fighter by the Allies had brought on several of Hitler's famous rages. He suspected loss of nerve and even cowardice on the part of his pilots. This was his reaction to each and every reverse. The errors were not his own; he had been betrayed by incompetence, loss of nerve and possibly even treasonable cowardice in the face of the enemy. After experiencing Stauffenberg's bomb, and the failed coup, almost every setback was now blamed on treachery. It was the most twisted and cruel reaction of all. He never allowed himself close enough to the front line to observe personally the devotion of all those men fighting so desperately on land, sea and in the air. His attitude to the fighter wing of the air force was documented with startling clarity by Speer. We find out that the fighter ace Galland, now promoted to Commander General, had asked Speer to fly with him to the Führer's headquarters, there to give support to his urgent request. Hitler had just issued a directive; the outfitting of the air force with two thousand updated (but still conventional) fighter planes then nearing completion was to be transferred wholly to Normandy rather than be used in defence of the fatherland. As Galland well knew from experience, here they would be wiped out despite the improvements. The jet fighter, seriously delayed by Hitler, was the only possible response. But that was still not fully ready. Meanwhile aviation fuel supplies were being seriously depleted.

On their arrival at headquarters Hitler met them immediately. His conscience was troubling him. Having broken his promise (given in July) to have the vital Bergius fuel plants protected by fighter planes he was in no mood to have the situation conference, then being held, further soured by Speer and Galland's plain speaking. He merely arranged to see them afterward.

When they finally met, Speer brought out his usual series of statistics and related his prognosis regarding the seriousness of the situation. He spelled out the dire consequences if bombing could not be countered effectively. As he spoke he watched Hitler, for the moment still silent and attentive, becoming ever more emotional and angry. His facial expression and the way he chewed his fingernails were always a warning of an outburst to come. Speer records:

> When I finished, thinking I had amply proved every available plane should be employed to combat the bombers, Hitler was no longer in control of himself. His face had flushed deep red; his eyes turned lifeless and fixed. Then he roared out at the top of his lungs: 'Operative measures are my concern! Kindly keep to armaments! This is none of your business!'

This was, strictly speaking, absolutely true of course. Nevertheless, Speer could not avoid an overlap when making his desperate attempt to protect fuel supplies. It seems incredible that Hitler could remain blind to the simple logic that without fuel everything ground to a halt. Yet Hitler had long spells in which his recourse to fantasy brought him total denial of reality. There was one further factor. Ever jealous of his authority, and hypersensitive to anyone who might seem to question it, he made it an issue of willpower. In such a mood he now dismissed the two men and turned on his heel. His fantasy world was not to be pierced.

Dejected, Speer and Galland spent the night in quarters allocated them. They were about to board a plane the next morning when a staff officer brought a message from the Führer. They were to report to him immediately. Speer's account at this point gives us a vivid picture of Hitler's hairspring temperament. Far from recovering his composure and regretting his outburst of the previous day the Führer had overnight burnished his sense of outrage. He was now even more violent. As Speer records he '...spoke faster and faster stumbling over his own words...'. In fact Hitler had now reached a stage where he suspecting treachery on all sides. The reverses his once triumphant Third Reich were now suffering were not the result of both his own and his henchmen's mistakes: within his disturbed mind all such reverses were now the lack of fortitude, will and even the courage of the armed forces – indeed of the German people as a whole. It was a frightful and wholly unfair verdict. Hitler's spite was now aimed particularly at the fighter wing of the Luftwaffe. Speer's reports that he roared at the two figures standing before him, 'The fighter arm is to be dissolved. Stop aircraft production! Stop it at once, understand? You are always complaining about the shortage of skilled workers, aren't you'. Beside himself with rage he went on to order the astonished pair to redirect all the specialised workers in aircraft production into a totally different field – the manufacture of 'flak' guns! This was the current slang term for anti-aircraft guns using scattered shell-bursts. It was an incredible demand. And in terms of the massive disruption involved it was also wholly impracticable. Still stumbling over his own words the Führer used a convoluted logic: he justified his absurd directive on the grounds that 'every day I read in foreign press reports of how dangerous flak is. They (the enemy aircraft) have some respect for that, but not our fighters!' Poor Galland, an ace pilot of well-proven courage, who had furthermore gathered very wide and first-hand experience of every kind of air battle, attempted to bring some sanity into play. He began to point out that fighter planes would have far greater success if they were concentrated inside Germany, rather than scattered in penny packets throughout occupied territory. Speer further records, and again laconically, 'but he never got beyond the first words. Again we were abruptly dismissed, actually thrown out.'

We can detect transparent bitterness in Speer's tone. Yet fate once more had its little joke. The sheer pressure of events eventually made Hitler change his mind. The shortage of ammunition for the guns, rather than the guns themselves, resolved the issue. That shortage embraced chemical production now badly disrupted by strategic bombing. The Führer, eating his words, finally ordered Speer to resume fighter production. As he had already evaded once again the original direct order, Speer was able to supply a proportion of planes. The despairing Galland was given at least a partial opportunity to demonstrate German courage in defending the fuel plants. Speer at this time was even on the point of manufacture of the first few fully airworthy jet fighters – but only just!

Yet a new factor was emerging. It was to worry Speer even more. He found that Germany's defence against the bombing of Bergius plants was becoming all the more intractable a problem in that enemy bombers were now being protected by massive escorts of fighters. Previously any fighter protection had been restricted by their lack of sufficient range; this problem had now been solved. The American Mustang fighter powered with a Rolls-Royce engine and fitted with long-range tanks was not only now faster and able to out-manoeuvre all German aircraft, but had the astonishing range of one thousand, five hundred miles! This could take it to the eastern borders of the Reich. Already in April 1944, with the Allies having conquered a large portion of Italy, the American air force, flying from bases there, had struck directly at the Ploesti oilfields in Rumania. Fortunately they did not keep pressing the attack.

Then in May – and the raid that had prompted Speer to fly to Hitler's HQ – almost one thousand bombers, protected by over one thousand fighters, had been met by a mere four hundred German fighters! In the mêlée, sixty-five of the latest Messerschmitts (conventional) were shot down and the bombers pressed on to their oil-related targets. It is only proper to add that forty-six American bombers failed to return to base, but their fate was at the hands of conventional anti-aircraft guns rather than the fighters. These losses were judged bearable and the raid successful. Compared with far heavier losses which had been sustained in previous sorties without an escort, it gave every hope for further strategic strikes in the future. It is also relevant to note that in June, after forceful direction by his superiors in Supreme Headquarters, Bomber Harris reluctantly bombed Gelsenkirchen oil-related targets by night. Ninety-three British bombers were lost out of a force of eight hundred and thirty-two sent over a period of three nights. German night fighters scored by far the greatest number of casualties. For the severely pressed German air force this was heartening, but Speer knew that the long-term position was hopeless. Yet somehow – and almost mechanically – he soldiered on. Meanwhile, Bomber Harris, true to form and threatening resignation unless allowed to revert back to previous policy, once more began scattering bombs over a wide area. No doubt the excuse he could put forward was that oil-related targets were too heavily defended. Even so, he achieved virtually nothing except a slightly smaller loss of aircrew and aircraft, and drawn-out misery for all concerned. The Americans remained convinced of the soundness of hitting truly strategic targets. Yet this too still failed to proceed with sufficient vigour until the following year. This time though they had a legitimate reason...!

On the sixth of June, 1944, a massive invasion force had landed on the Normandy beaches. The liberation of France had begun! Every Allied plane was diverted to bomb with as great an accuracy as possible – hopefully avoiding the loss of French lives – large sections of French rail track, railway sidings, locomotive sheds, bridges and roads to prevent the rapid arrival of German reinforcements. These were in fact to be delayed from reaching even the fringes of Normandy for several crucial days, with Hitler adding to Field Marshals Rommel and Rundstedt's frustration by insisting that this was a feint and that the real invasion would begin at the Pas de Calais. With just a toehold on the beaches it was vital that sufficient men and supplies were landed. These then had to push back the existing defenders as far back inland as possible to give the invasion sufficient weight and impetus. Without the initial requirement the entire force could have been pushed back into the sea again. The Americans bombed the further reaches of the communication system with fervour, accompanied by masses of fighters. RAF Fighter Command performed magnificently just ahead of the front line, strafing anything that could be seen on rail or road. Bomber Command under Harris, when asked to attack strategic targets further into France and on the flanks down either side of the coastline, did so with the greatest reluctance and only under direct orders from Supreme Headquarters. To prevent any German motor torpedo boats or submarines attacking shipping supplying the beachheads, most of the French ports were attacked. Sadly it was later found that few threats to our seaborne forces were lurking there and the ports had received an unnecessary pounding. And inevitably, bombs overshot. The lovely old towns surrounding the ports of Le Havre, Cherbourg and St Malo in particular were virtually reduced to rubble. Later the ancient town of Caen was devastated. It was thought to be infested with Germans preparing a Russian-type defence, such as they themselves had ruefully experienced at Stalingrad. Fearing it would seriously hold up the advance, orders were given to bomb. In actual fact the bulk of the German troops were on the outskirts. It was just one more tragic incident, and an error which could have been avoided given more carefully organised contact with the French resistance fighters.

Shortly after, the famous breakout by General Patton was followed by the partial encirclement of the Germans retreating through the Falaise gap. Here strategic use of air power once again demonstrated its effectiveness. Trapped in a small concentrated area, great slaughter ensued. The German army escaped complete annihilation only because of the failure of the Allies to effect fully an encircling movement.

Subsequently the zone of operations moved slowly east over France. Paris was liberated and the Allies moved on toward the German frontier. The Reich once more became the main target. The Americans now gradually intensified their bombing of Bergius plants, oil fields and indeed anything oil-related, such as plastics and synthetic rubber. Bomber Harris, asked to join in, again threatened resignation; he insisted on going back to scattering bombs over the widest possible area.

The final death throes of the German Reich are captured vividly in Speer's account. Such determination to continue the long, drawn-out agony is unbelievable given the hopelessness of the position. With the might of a revitalised and re-equipped Red Army pushing in steadily from the east and American, British and Free French pushing in from the west, we half a century later might well ask the bewildered question: why did Germany continue resisting to the very end? Why did those top generals and military planners, who were in full position to know the truth, persist in obeying the Führer? After Stauffenberg's bomb and the bloodbath that followed, one must remember at least one of the factors already stated: they were not just fearful for their own lives but those of their immediate family too. Speer, for example, had a wife and six children to consider. The dreaded shadow of Himmler, always vaguely in the background, kept many on the straight and narrow. There was however another factor. They were so near to reversing their fortunes finally with the 'wonder weapons'. The jet fighter – though in handfuls – had at last taken to the air. A rocket-assisted plane had also appeared, although it demanded almost superhuman skill to control. The heat-seeking ground-to-air missile was almost in production. In the naval sector a torpedo reacting to the sound of a ship's engine was ready. Snorkels had already been fitted to some U-boats. As for the war in general a remote-controlled flying bomb had been tested, which was far more accurate than the V1. The latter were somewhat eccentric and could veer off-course. Beyond that a new and very deadly nerve gas had been prepared and was available by the ton, let alone even better versions of the Tiger tank... the list was extensive. Speer noted with irony that his main problem was knowing which new weapon to concentrate on and which to set aside! Full-scale production of just two or three of these weapons would have made a substantial contribution to their far better fortune. Now it was all too late! He bemoaned the fact that because of Hitler's constant interference and sudden changes of plans, endless time had been lost. And that time was truly precious. But above all, everything was grinding to a halt because of desperate shortages in fuel. Even when, after the most desperate of efforts, plants were partially repaired and the precious range of petroleum products began flowing again, fuel supplies could not be rushed to where they were most needed – low-level bombing by light aircraft and fighter planes using rockets made it impossible. They blasted or shot up everything on the roads, railways and even the canal systems. Movement of any kind was now restricted to night-time, and even then flares could illuminate sections of transportation routes. Most of the larger cities were in ruins, and the supply of the very basics to those still living – existing rather than living, and as rodents in the cellars of once fine homes – was intermittent or non-existent. Pure water, food, and heating fuel such as coal were all at a premium; much depended on where one lived.

The Führer at this point suddenly demanded a scorched-earth policy. More correctly he demanded the destruction of those factories, power stations, bridges, warehouses, reserves of vital commodities, farms, livestock, shops and humble homes that still remained relatively undamaged. Anything and everything within the path of the advancing enemy had to be erased. The people themselves were to struggle back as best they could into the centre of Germany. When an incredulous and horrified Speer asked where they would find shelter and the basic necessities, the Führer just walked away.

The ring around the Reich now tightened and the once-proud Wehrmacht and Panzer units were denied fresh supplies of ammunition because supply lorries had run out of fuel. They were now being decimated. Old men and young boys were being drafted into makeshift units, given the briefest of training and then thrown into the battle. It was becoming a nightmare of Dantean intensity.

Six children and a loving wife had deterred Speer from active disloyalty to Hitler. Survival of the German people now finally demanded a higher sense of loyalty, despite Himmler's shadow. In the midst of such chaos a coup was out of the question. Assassination was the only remaining option.

He planned to use the secret nerve gas Tabun, hoping to introduce it into the air conditioning of the Führer's bunker. When his amateurish efforts came to nothing, one senses a fatalism born out of exhaustion. With it came the dead weight of an increasing sense of guilt and hopelessness. He went about like a sleepwalker, with only occasional flashes of lucidity. Meanwhile Hitler, surrounded by the remnants of his political and military staff, hermetically sealed in his bunker against the smallest sniff of reality, moved counters representing non-existent Panzer divisions around on his map table. Was he clinically mad? Or had the concoctions given him by his personal physician further deepened his susceptibility to hallucination?

Were those surrounding him equally mad? Goering, as was well known, had intermittent binges on alcohol; in addition he had also become something of a drug addict. Hitler in contrast was strictly teetotal, and as a vegetarian obviously conscious of his diet and maintaining a healthy lifestyle. Anyone who was tempted to use psychological crutches such as alcohol or drugs during a downturn in fortune immediately earned his contempt. He failed to understand how anyone could lack the will to resist.

How could they be so cowardly as to require stimulants of this nature to make life, even if weighed down by enormous pressures, bearable? There were astonishing contradictions in Hitler's character. He could have a strict range of scruples and sense of morality in some sectors, yet be uniquely deficient in others.

Although he was a man impossible to know with any measure of intimacy, Speer came as near to the Führer as anyone could hope or expect. During his subsequent long years of imprisonment he had ample time to reflect on the matter of Hitler's sanity or insanity. Yet he could come to no proper conclusion, this despite his proven ability to penetrate well below the surface of things. And there is a further related question: what was the nature of Hitler's hold over those in closest contact with him? Again there is no firm conclusion.

What are we to make of a composite picture of the Führer drawn for us from a variety of sources and not just from Speer's memoirs?

Many high-ranking officers repeat the same story: they testify that, while away from Hitler's HQ and in full contact with the fighting forces during the years of reversal of fortune, they were able to look reality fully in the face. Shaken, they would determine there and then exactly how they would present the brutal truth to Hitler on their return. Yet as soon as they stepped back in the Führer's presence and gazed directly into those strange staring eyes, they faltered and fumbled. Within moments their resolution would crumble. Incredulously they would hear themselves mouthing half-truths or downright untruths. Here a sometime army corporal, who had admittedly served bravely enough in the First Resource War, was somehow paralysing their willpower. He was forcing men who prided themselves on their honour and sense of duty to act dishonourably; he was forcing them into total disregard for a higher duty!

Speculation has been made in earlier pages regarding the possibility of Hitler having genuine hypnotic powers – whether consciously or unconsciously. Bizarre as this may seem, it cannot be dismissed out of hand. But this is not the only factor. What of his extraordinary willpower and belief in his singular 'destiny'? This is something he had (supposedly) had from an early age.

It is difficult to trust the testimony of those who knew him as a child or teenager. They would after all be less than human not to be influenced by the knowledge of what he was later to become. And this would falsify in one way or another the freshness and integrity of their original observation. Indeed, even if we accept it with care, the mystery is still only partly solved.

He was by all accounts extremely shy and withdrawn throughout boyhood. The household was dominated by his father, a crusty sometime border policeman, later to become a low-ranking customs official. Alois Hitler had married twice before and he was considerably older than Adolf's mother, Klara. It was a complex family set-up. There were half-brothers and sisters from the two earlier marriages that constantly engaged the father's attention. The fact the Alois and Klara's first child was conceived before marriage suggests that lust rather than love had cemented the union. The first child of this third marriage died in infancy. So did a second. Adolf was the third child; he was to be followed by a younger brother who died at the age of six. The fifth and last child of this third marriage was a daughter, Paula. She actually survived Adolf.

It is doubtful if Alois had any real love for this particular son. And there is little evidence that Adolf held him in any regard other than as master of the household. His mother compensated for this vacuum by almost worshipping her rather sickly-looking son. At the age of sixty-five Alois suddenly died while taking a morning walk.

Adolf was then thirteen years old. Since the age of eleven he had been in rebellion against his father who wished him to follow in his footsteps as a petty customs official. The realisation of his mother's now straitened circumstances caused him to weep, if nothing else.

Klara moved to a small apartment near Linz with Adolf and Paula. Here she managed with the greatest difficulty to pay for a further three years of schooling for her son. But his poor academic record and neglect of his studies forced her to concede that further 'forced' education would hardly serve the interests of either mother or son. At the age of sixteen Klara attempted to find him a job. But Adolf refused to knuckle down: for him there was to be no common round of employment. He fancied himself as an artist. For the first time Klara found her love for him intermingled with dismay and irritation. But the teenage Adolf would have none of her entreaties, complaints or coaxing. It says much for her basic trust and indeed undiminished love that over the next three years she supported him in his dreamy idleness, intermittently broken by spells of sketching and reading. Significantly there was no thirst for either ancient or contemporary literature of recognised merit, certainly none containing profound comments on the human condition. Tolstoy and Dostoevsky, who at that time were making quite an impact on the western European reading public, failed to attract him. Clearly they meant nothing otherwise they could not have failed to alter his contempt for 'the uncivilised Slavs'. He read history, political history; endless dreary tomes describing the activities of puppets deluding themselves that they had control of the affairs of men. For variation he would switch to romantic Teutonic mythology; this was at least recognised as fiction, whereas the history tomes were not. In Linz he sometimes stood at the back of the opera house listening to outpourings from Richard Wagner. He found himself attracted to this music, though composers of a greater stature left him cold. The reason is not too difficult to find. Wagner, a romantic dreamer and sometime participant in political riots, had a long struggle for recognition of his gifts too.

To digress, profitably I hope, for a moment. Born, like Hitler, with the crippling misfortune of a cerebral dysfunction that would give rise to an ego of incredible proportions, Wagner refused to accept any limitation as to his musical stature. In his later works, and no doubt to compensate for a subconscious sense of his failure to reach the ultimate heights, he tried to give his work a spurious profundity by retreating into obscurantism. At this point I must anticipate the shocked surprise and howls of protests of those who attend productions of *Tristan and Isolde* and *The Ring* cycle; I am aware of course that there are many who regarded them as a pilgrimage and a palpable religious experience. Hitler certainly did. I must also remind you that I am expressing a personal view, and emphasise that I am referring to Wagner's later work. Even so, this may still not mollify those who rate Wagner a genius of the first rank. Fairly spitting with repressed indignation they will no doubt insist he is fully entitled to rub shoulders with the truly great. Even so I will not be moved by their opinion. I will persist in judging him as second rank. You see I continue to see a pseudo-profundity which he carefully hides by obscurantism. Subconsciously like Hitler he attempts to repress the remnants of a boyhood insecurity – an insecurity which was to become further embedded in his character during early manhood. This had been developed while finding such difficulty in making his way in the world. It contrasts so sharply, for example, with Schubert's character and outlook. He too struggled to find recognition for his far greater gifts, and in worse circumstances. But Wagner chose to revert to the use of sheer willpower in his bid to achieve the stature of the truly great. In doing so his output became more and more forced and artificial. In the end it merely attained bombast. Are we surprised the Führer found it so compelling?

By using music to become a suitable vehicle for the brutal symbolism of the libretto Wagner himself had chosen – a deliberate excursion into a maelstrom of emotion – he created a grandiose 'loudness' and even an unashamed vulgarity. True profundity does not require the clash of Titans to announce its presence. A profound vision is often enormously subtle, but it should never be deliberately obscure. Wagner, together with later composers at the turn of the century, stimulated a fashion in obscurantism – or, more to the point, found a refuge there. And it is a fashion that has become more and more absurd and destructive as the twentieth century has proceeded. Indeed it has continued to bump its uncomfortable way along the path of sterile intellectual posturing. The fashion has been paralleled in poetry, literature, painting and sculpture. To separate oneself from the supposed intellectually inferior (if not cataleptic) members of society our contemporary posers find obscurantism a remarkably effective way of achieving airs and graces. It puts them in an unassailable position; you see lesser beings are always unsure whether or not they happen to have a cultural 'blind spot'. And everyone has some blind spot somewhere or other of course! To be entirely honest, and as painful as it may be to admit at this particular moment, my own blind spot may well embrace the music of Wagner. It is only in making comparisons with other musicians of the very first rank that one can have any hope of a reasonably sound judgement in the matter. And it has nothing to do with the scale of the work, its complexity of instrumentation or the sheer size of the forces employed. To repeat, profundity can be achieved with astonishingly small resources. It can be achieved by a sextet, a quintet, a quartet, a trio, a duo or even, as demonstrated so convincingly by J S Bach, a solo instrument. Again the seemingly childlike simplicity of almost any one of Mozart's mature piano sonatas underlines the point. Technically speaking they can be played by amateurs or aspiring ten-year-olds; musically they demand the skills of the cream of the pianist elite. So too the demands made by other composers – for example the apparently reserved and emotionally restrained cello or violin sonatas by Brahms, the Schubert trios, the late Beethoven quartets. These are all small scale, that is if one judges them in terms of the number of instruments used, their tonal range and dynamics. However in musical conception their content is enormous! In such compositions there is a spiritual vastness. Truly, in all of these works, penned as they are by those of true genius, one finds a quiet yet true profundity. Can it then be so surprising that Adolf Hitler in those early days of his astonishing career sensed a particular affinity with Wagner, sensed too how he could hide a youthful lack of self-confidence with a dazzling show of emotional pyrotechnics? Is it so surprising either that when he attained the pinnacle of success as Führer of the German nation he attended stagings of late Wagnerian opera as an all too eager, all too self-conscious pilgrim? Is it so astonishing to discover either that, when in private, his thirst for inspired music extended to the dizzy heights of Franz Lehar's *The Land of Smiles* and *The Merry Widow*?

But let us return to his teenage years. The mature Adolf refers to them in the propaganda exercise *Mein Kampf.* This was written while serving a prison sentence for an attempted coup, therefore its statements must be taken with caution. Of his teenage years he writes: I quote, 'They were the happiest days of my life.' Such happiness was not to last. In October 1907, at the age of eighteen, he journeyed to Vienna hoping to take the entry test that would give him a place as a student in the city's Academy of Fine Arts. Here his rapidly maturing ego received a devastating blow. He was rejected! His draughtsmanship was considered insufficiently mature. He tried a second time a year later. Again rejection. He was so shaken that he requested an explanation from the rector. Perhaps as an act of kindliness, and to soften the blow, the man's reply suggested that Adolf's ability lay rather with architecture than drawing and painting. As no fully authenticated examples of his artistic work exist, this suggests that he found the straightforward sharp and angular outlines of buildings far easier to translate into formal representation on paper as compared with the far more subtle living-and-moving outlines of the human face or body.

But a far more serious shock awaited him. After returning that first time from Vienna to Linz illness visited the household. His mother had been unwell for some time. Now she seemed to have taken a turn for the worse. In the following months, helped by his sister, he found himself forced to undertake spells of nursing. As already noted, his second attempt in 1908 to gain entry into the Academy had failed; three months later, on 21 December, his mother died of breast cancer:

> It was a dreadful blow... I had honoured my father, but my mother I had loved... her death put an end to all my high-flown plans... poverty and hard reality compelled me to take a quick decision... I was faced with the problem of somehow making my living.

Over the next four years he lived in squalor and misery in Vienna. And although he is rather coy in describing those years in any detail – describing himself as working 'as a day-labourer then as a small painter' – he seems to have finally scraped a pitiful living by making watercolour sketches of some of the fine Viennese public buildings. Presumably these were then sold as tourist trinkets to any shop that would accept them.

The outbreak of the First World War, the First World Resource War, changed all that. He volunteered immediately and his enthusiasm was such as to gain special permission to serve (despite by accident of birth being Austrian) in a Bavarian Regiment.

In such a regiment he served first as a private then as a corporal: he did so with distinction. Much of the time he was given the particularly dangerous duty of dispatch runner, notably in the absence of telephone communication between the trenches. He was wounded twice and decorated twice for bravery. In December 1914 he was given the Iron Cross (second class) and in August 1918 the Iron Cross First Class. This was an honour seldom given to the ordinary soldier; it was usually reserved for officer ranks. His ego had, it would seem, not yet developed to a point where he valued his life as priceless. This would come later. At such a point he believed the entire destiny of the German people rested on his shoulders. Meanwhile on the eleventh day of the eleventh month in 1918 came the Armistice. It was announced by an army chaplain in the hospital where he was recuperating after being temporarily blinded by a British gas-attack at Ypres. It was one of the most bitter moments of his life. In *Mein Kampf* he records that he broke down and wept. It was the only time he had done so since his mother's burial; he was devastated by what he saw as Germany's shame and humiliation.

Who would have supposed of this insignificant-looking young man that, just twenty years later, he would actually become Head of State and issue orders to commence the Second World War – and do so without emotion requiring tears! What is more, he did so despite knowing exactly what sacrifices and horrors war entailed.

But twenty years earlier two further 'wilderness years' were to continue. Demobilisation of a large proportion of the army had thinned out the ranks of the survivors of this ghastly war. Adolf, however, had no home, no profession or trade, no wife, no family, no prospects. What could he be demobilised into? Only vagrancy. Remaining in what was rapidly becoming just an apology for an army, he was realistic enough to see that it at least gave him a bed for the night and some pitifully inadequate rations. A year later, during a spell of duty in Munich, he took part in overturning a communist regime of disillusioned former fighting men. These men, hardly different from himself, called themselves the 'Soldier's Council'. This kind of opportunist takeover was happening all over Germany and also in Austria at the time. The right-wing officers of the Reichswehr were however determined to maintain some kind of order and, if possible, some traditional values. Moreover, they also hoped to set up a government suitably strengthened by members of the old aristocracy. In this instance, in Munich at least, they were successful. But the foundations were still very shaky. A putsch of one kind or another was a constant threat. Adolf, genuinely sharing their outlook, once again must have impressed his officers: he was given a post in the Press and News Bureau of the Political Department. Here he was employed virtually as a spy, infiltrating some of the many tiny political organisations springing up at that time. It was after all important for the officers of the Reichswehr to know who might have active subversion in mind. He also attended lectures with the remainder of the rank and file on right-wing political philosophy. It corresponded somewhat to the efforts of Soviet army commissars in Russia at that time who were attempting to politicise men during the reorganisation of the Red Army.

Recorded in *Mein Kampf* comes the first turning point in his fortunes. During a lecture by a visiting academic who happened to touch on the positive contribution made by the Jews to German trade and industry, Adolf sprang to his feet. With a great rush of emotion he made an impassioned speech to denounce such an opinion. It made some impression on his officers. They now posted him to a regiment, promoted more or less to the position of educational officer. Hitler comments:

> All at once I was offered the opportunity of speaking before a larger audience and the thing that I have always presumed from pure feeling without knowing it was now corroborated: I could 'speak'.

Here in *Mein Kampf* he announces the discovery of his true talent: oratory!

In September 1919 he was also asked to obtain information on (and form an opinion of) the aims and membership strength of a political group called the 'German Workers' Party'. Was it right wing or was it left wing? Did it have subversion in mind?

What followed was almost pure farce. Attending one of their meetings in a dingy Munich beer cellar he found about twenty-five people listening to boring talks on economics. At the end of one of their meetings, infuriated by remarks made by what he presumed to be another 'professor', he sprang to his feet and made another impassioned speech. It turned heads. Later the chairman and founder member, a certain Anton Drexler, thrust a pamphlet into his hand. The following day after reading it and failing to be in any way impressed, he received a card informing him that he had been, in absentia, accepted as a member of the party!

> I didn't know whether to be angry or to laugh. I had no intention of joining a ready-made party, but wanted to found one of my own. What they asked of me was presumptuous and out of the question.

Nevertheless, out of curiosity more than anything else, he decided to attend the committee meeting to which he had been invited, there to give his reasons for refusing to join this 'absurd little organisation'.

Duly arriving at a dingy room he was to meet just four young people, one of whom was Anton Drexler, the author of the pamphlet. These now greeted him with great enthusiasm, assuming he had accepted membership. 'Really I was somewhat taken aback,' he says. But out of politeness he sat through the burlesque of this tiny party attempting to ape a large organisation. He listened to interminable reports and letters read out. The treasurer, for example, revealed that the party had seven marks fifty pfennigs and received for his efforts a hearty vote of confidence. It was to Adolf an appalling performance. Yet he sensed he could perhaps make something of these shambles:

> After two days of agonised pondering and reflection, I finally came to the conviction that I had to take this step. It was the most

decisive resolve of my life. From here there was and could be no turning back.

Sheer willpower was from this moment on to transform this man into a figure the entire world would know, and possibly will never forget. He was by a process of cerebral metamorphosis to emerge from a cocoon that had sheltered his withdrawn and basically insecure personality into something entirely different – a magnetic figure, full of bombast and confidence. And yet subconsciously he would never quite forget his earlier larval form as represented by his boyhood and early teens: the shy, insecure, dreamy would-be artist.

It is my conviction that it is this basic insecurity that subsequently drove him to build a grandiose façade around his immediate circumstances and his own person. It was essential to achieve what seemed full security. A security on his own terms! At each step along the way, as his political standing slowly grew, it forced him, as it were, to pinch himself to discover whether he was truly conscious or whether he was dreaming. The insignificant, shy, withdrawn pavement artist and sometime corporal, was used to obeying orders, not giving them. With the iron discipline of the German Army still fresh in his memory, and with the instinctive reaction to an order – doing so immediately, unquestioningly and at the double – it was surely odd to find himself now issuing orders. Pinching himself and finding it was after all reality of a kind, it stimulated him to secure even greater control over what were now subordinates and to dream even wilder dreams.

Now everyone born into this life realises sooner or later the fragility of existence. For everyone there is the tacit awareness that there can be very cruel and unexpected interruptions to our basic sense of well-being and optimism. Out of the blue, people can be struck down by illness, disease, accidents, psychopaths, fires, explosions, earthquakes, floods – there are so many harrowing possibilities. Yet the vast majority accept that constantly worrying about this overall fragility attending human existence (and indeed that of every living thing), is just so much wasted effort. It also somehow suggests that a constant sense of insecurity reveals an element of mental imbalance, or perhaps a form of cowardice. On the other hand, to create for yourself an in-built sense of security does not necessarily mean that you become either careless, irresponsible or fatalistic. With a due measure of common sense, you take reasonable precautions against illness and disease by practising personal hygiene, perhaps adding a balanced diet and sensible lifestyle. You take sensible precautions against fire and burglary with some obvious and rather basic safety measures. You take precautions against all manner of accidents that attend daily life with a sharp eye, and a concentrated and alert mind. Day after day you go about your well known pattern of existence with a reasonable degree of inner confidence and security. You have, if you are a balanced personality, an awareness that you are but a minute speck in the universe and the totality of existence: you are but an insignificant little piece of biological mechanism given that essential breath of life by the Creator. You are in the vastness that is the universe, something far less than a nobody. You are a conglomeration of cells holding together somewhat uncertainly as one living organism. And you are aware that one day you will disintegrate into its distinct and separate atomic parts, 'dust to dust, ashes to ashes'. Nobody possessing just a modicum of humility and the realisation of their true insignificance worries about their status or how other people regard them. But there are of course those born with cerebral malfunctions who are unable to accept this. They just cannot acquire that final essence of dignity or stoicism that self-depreciating mirth concerning one's own foolishness can bring. Adolf Hitler was at heart a gravely insecure individual, astonished that he should have survived the years of penury in Vienna, the years of slaughter in the trenches, the bullets that struck down the marchers at his side in the recent putsch he had led. Surely, deep down, he must have found difficulty in believing his luck! How could he account for it? One word – destiny.

As you might expect, destiny is an awkward word which becomes illusive when one attempts to define it in the truly academic sense. People often give it their own interpretation anyway. Sometimes it involves God, sometimes what they call Fate. Hitler's definition is uncertain, both in his own mind and ours. Yet it had to supply a degree of visual evidence of his personal attainment and rise from obscurity. In the early days of the German Workers' Party – itself to be metamorphosed into the German National Socialist Party in his hands – he designed and organised the wearing of quasi-military uniforms, the so-called 'brown shirts'. He followed this by the swastika emblem, the tasselled pennants, the eagles and the flags. Then came magnificent staged spectacles. The young architect Albert Speer was initially to have some hand in this, thereby gaining Hitler's notice and approval. It was pure theatre – Wagnerian theatre at that! The party leader in his military-style uniform marched onto a podium there to become the centre of attention of the ranked masses. And on such a podium he would rant on about his destiny and Germany's destiny, coupled so tragically as they now were. He used to the full his gift of oratory; it hid the lack of substance contained in his speech. It was all overlaid with great surges of inspired emotion.

No truly balanced and 'secure' person would have needed such an excess of outward show. Perhaps at this point in Hitler's career one could excuse it as being the means to an end. To become the absolute ruler of Germany he still had a long way to go. Numerically, his supporters, coming as they did from the extreme right wing, were still counter-balanced by extremists from the left wing. In between were the mass of apathetic or confused German people with no special political convictions. All they wanted was a stable currency and a reduction in the grim statistics of unemployment. Significantly, the acquisition of a rundown newspaper by Hitler, and its subsequent provocative style had brought with it a jump in circulation. It now became as important as the showpiece rallies. It communicated a vague exposition of his ideas to those unable or unwilling to attend the tableaux. It was vital in spreading his actual words and his image to as large an audience as possible.

In 1923, his short term in prison after the failed putsch brought, at least in his own eyes and those of the growing ranks of followers, a semi-martyrdom status. It also had enormous propaganda potential. Indeed it made his case a talking point throughout Germany. Party membership received a boost. The rallies became bigger, the uniforms of his immediate cronies more glittering. The length of Hitler's harangue became longer; the thunderous applause louder. The thousands attending became tens of thousands. Yet when these speeches are closely examined and put under rigorous analysis nothing can be found to have changed. They are still of quite insubstantial nature; they merely camouflaged their lack of content by storming emotionalism and verbosity. But the hitherto uncommitted people of the fence-straddling political centre were beginning to swing his way.

It is tempting at this point to be side-tracked into a parallel study of Stalin's early life and emergence from obscurity. There are so many interesting similarities. Stalin, the son of a drunken and violent Georgian shoemaker, had been born in 1879, just ten years earlier than Adolf. No love had been lost between father and son. By all accounts the man could be brutal either drunk or sober; he treated the boy with as much consideration as he would an animal. The mother compensated for that very special kind of loss. Moreover, by utter devotion she brought her son safely through every kind of childhood illness and danger to maturity. Indeed she endured even harsher circumstances than poor Klara Hitler. Thus Joseph Stalin's boyhood insecurity was later to show itself in the pathological mistrust of all his associates once he reached power. His treatment of them varied from harsh terms of imprisonment to summary execution. It far exceeded in numerical terms the treatment meted out on malcontents and fully proven conspirators by Hitler in his early years. It even surpassed the bloodbath of Hitler's later period. When Stalin became First Secretary of the Communist Party, possessing in such an innocent title far greater power than any of the most autocratic of Tsars, his subconscious feelings of insecurity were such that within a few years he had murdered all the most able and efficient comrades within the political apparatus and most of his top army commanders. He did so on the mere suspicion of lack of loyalty, and without any attempt on his life. The execution of his best generals was an act that later almost cost him the annihilation of the Red Army at Hitler's hands. Similarly, he too came to believe himself chosen by destiny to conquer the world; he too believed that his every decision was infallible, that his every measure was wholly just and logical. No ordinary mortal, so he believed, could have raised himself up by his own bootstraps, and by such an incredible confluence of circumstances. How could anyone become the leader of what was potentially the greatest power on Earth without the secret and subtle help of destiny? As I say, the parallels are absorbing and tempting.

Such a divergence nevertheless must be resisted.

Shall we return to Adolf Hitler? He finally achieved absolute power more by trickery than the wholehearted approval of the German people. But having gained that power and all the trappings that went with it, there was no real satisfaction. He now turned from what was a highly improbable dream fully accomplished to an impossible dream no man should ever have the nerve, presumption or monumental foolishness to attempt – conquest of the world.

But first, to do so he had to subject to his will a powerful body of men – the upper echelons of the German Army. The former corporal would now need to bend the stiff-necked, stiff-backed generals and field marshals to his purpose!

Military historians and the biographers detailing the lives of some of the most colourful or legendary of the top commanders, such as Guderian, Rommel, Doenitz and Rundstedt (not forgetting some of the actual biographies by men such as fighter ace Galland, General Kesselring, Field Marshal Manstein, Major Skorzeny, General Westphal and others), present a confusing picture of events. Some tend to emphasis that when Hitler cleverly engineered an oath of allegiance taken by all officers and men, and made to him personally, this in itself, they believed, became the most significant factor. The deeply embedded sense of honour alone cemented the relationship. This kept most of them helplessly in its grip. Yet this suggests that they lost their powers of reasoning and ordinary common sense. It is something hard to swallow. Again, before this oath had been asked for, there was a period when the key men in control of the military apparatus assumed that Hitler would be a temporary aberration, as it were; they believed he could easily be deposed once he had diverted the necessary resources and money into the now rapidly expanding fighting forces. But their analysis of the political scene was of course hopelessly complacent. Himmler, with Hitler's full authority and backing, was already setting up a power base of SS fighting units equipped with the latest weapons. These were entirely outside the control of the General Staff. Goering was doing much the same with an elite section of the air force. The Führer was also a master in understanding human psychology. He sensed the underlying factors that quite subconsciously brought about elation or dismay; he knew what brought on envy, and endless jockeying for position – exposing, as it did, petty ambitions and a motley of human weakness. It is difficult now for us to understand how intelligent men could be manipulated by promises of promotion, promises of extra thousands of men under their command, promises of finding personal glory on the battlefield.

Again, few dare to suggest openly or indeed consciously that Hitler had genuine hypnotic powers, yet if one reads their testimony of events it is difficult to dismiss that conclusion. It becomes all the more pressing for consideration when the years of the Führer's unbelievable good fortune and triumph are followed by ill fortune – indeed one disaster after another. What held these men to him?

Speer attempts to answer, but tends to become too occupied with an associated factor which he and others call 'will-power'. This becomes for him especially noticeable as the Reich went into the last stages of decline. Speer comments:

> His will (power) often seemed to me as heedless and crude as that of when a six-year-old child whom nothing can discourage or tire. But although it was in some ways ridiculous, it also commanded respect. This phenomenal confidence in victory in a period of repeated defeats cannot however be explained on the grounds of his energy alone...

Speer goes on to consider the power of autosuggestion:

> I can only explain Hitler's rigid attitude on the grounds that he made himself believe in his ultimate victory. In a sense he was worshipping himself. He was forever holding up to himself a mirror in which he saw not only himself but also the confirma-

tion of his mission by divine Providence.

Unfortunately Speer's text from this point suffers from the English translator's acute difficulty: the problem is not solely in finding exact equivalents for each word, frequently impossible anyway as every translator acknowledged, but the spirit of the meaning in German. The following text should therefore be read with special awareness that it is an 'approximation'. In the midst of his own difficulty to fathom Hitler's beliefs, Speer plunges on:

> His religion was based on the 'lucky break' which must necessarily come his way; his method was to reinforce himself by autosuggestion. The more events drove him into a corner, the more obstinately he opposed to them his certainty about the intentions of Fate. Naturally, he also soberly understood the military facts. But he transmuted them by his own faith and regarded even defeat as a secret guarantee offered by Providence of the coming victory. Sometimes he could realise the hopelessness of a situation, but he could not be shaken in his expectation that at the last moment Fate would suddenly turn the tide in his favour. If there was any fundamental insanity in Hitler, it was this unshakeable belief in his lucky star. He was by nature a religious man, but his capacity for belief had been perverted into belief in himself.

Here the reader should again apply due caution over words such as 'religion', 'faith', 'lucky break', 'Fate', 'lucky star' and 'Providence'; they should not be taken casually or at face value. It is important to relate them to the broader context and spirit in which they were written. That no two persons would define any of these words in the same way should be remembered too. As for Hitler's definition, it is anyone's guess what his concept of a Higher or Superior Being, or of Providence may have been – let alone whether he saw himself as an integral part of that Being and an ultimate beneficiary! In this respect there are suggestions made in some memoirs that Hitler and a few of his close associates, notably Goebbels, entertained an interest in the occult and studied astrology, or at least consulted astrologers. Firm evidence of this is not readily come by. The only comment one can make is that should it be true, then high echelons of Nazis would have done far better to study the genuine scientific enquiry we call astronomy. Perhaps the realisation of the vastness of the universe and of Time would have forced them to accept the measure of their own insignificance. And the very shortness of human life compared with the inconceivable breadth of Time alone should have both deflated their egos and demolished their outrageous conceit. But then, with men of such limited intellect, the sphere of astrology rather than astronomy would be the obvious solace to turn to. For evidence, albeit limited, we must turn to the diaries of Count Lutz Schwerin von Krosigk, though it is pertinent to add that those who had any contact with the good Count dismiss him as a fool. At any event his diaries note that he spoke to Goebbels by telephone in the last weeks of the squalid underground existence in the bunker under the ruins of Berlin. One day the Reich Minister for Propaganda was ecstatic. On the thirteenth of April a world radio news broadcast announced the death of Roosevelt. For Goebbels, this had transformed the situation. To us it underlines the degree of fantasy attained by the Führer's retinue and the readiness to clutch at straws. Apparently Goebbels shouted over the line that it was 'written in the stars that the second half of April will be the turning point for us'. Why Roosevelt's death and the immediate takeover of his successor – who anyone in his right mind would assume to be equally dedicated to the final defeat of Germany – should make any difference is not explained.

Meanwhile Speer goes on:

> Hitler's obsessive faith inevitably influenced his entourage. One part of my consciousness certainly acknowledged that now everything must be approaching the end. But despite that, I spoke all the more frequently – though to be sure I spoke only for my specific area of 'restoration of the situation'. Strangely this confidence existed apart from the recognition of unavoidable defeat.

On the twentieth of April, which happened to be Hitler's fifty-sixth birthday, the Russians were about to encircle Berlin. At a conference he was urged by his generals to leave for the south. He would not give a definite answer. Himmler, Goering and

Ribbentrop discretely left that very night. Hitler went back to his map table and began moving non-existent Panzer forces into position for the final battle of Berlin.

On 22 April Russian tanks broke through the suburbs. The Führer's rage was indescribable, according to the remaining entourage who survived the war.

That evening Hitler finally decided to remain in Berlin. He ordered Generals Keitel and Jodl to go south to take command of those forces still intact and capable of continuing the fight. Once more he returned to the map table.

The full details of the following days, as recounted by those who survived, are so fantastic that one can read and reread them and still remain in disbelief. The brutal truth and ultimate reality failed to penetrate the minds of those present until the very last hours.

After exhaustive enquiry, one or two salient facts seem to be established. On 30 April, 1945 Hitler finally accepted that the position was without hope. At about 3.30 p.m., as had hastily been agreed, his mistress Eva Braun swallowed poison. A few moments later Adolf Hitler put a revolver in his mouth and pulled the trigger. By his prior order, the bodies were carried above ground, petrol was poured over them and they were immediately burned. Goebbels then tidied up a few matters that were (for him!) still important, such as the Führer's testament which appointed Admiral Doenitz as successor. Ironically, it had been discovered several days earlier that Himmler had prematurely appointed himself Führer! Worse, he was secretly negotiating a surrender with Count Bernadotte, nephew of the King of Sweden and president of the Swedish Red Cross. As for Goering, Hitler's original chosen successor, as astonishing as it may seem, that indolent hulk had suddenly galvanised himself into action. With indecent haste he too attempted to take on the empty title. The fury of Hitler in that last day had been such that he ordered that both should be arrested and shot as traitors. He had however forgotten that they were now in the safety zone of their own military 'empires' where his writ no longer operated. Hitler's hastily revised testament had thus named Doenitz and had even singled out names for ministers in his 'government'! Once

Goebbels had finished this incredible charade he summoned the resident doctor. A lethal injection was given to each of his six children. They were aged twelve, eleven, nine, seven, five and three! This accomplished, a SS orderly was ordered to shoot his wife and then himself in the back of the head. This was done. Their bodies were also taken out, but due to heavy shelling they were only partly burned. Identification was subsequently carried out by a Russian forensic team. The remainder of the staff – quite a large number as the bunker was extensive and served as a military headquarters – then attempted to get through the Russian lines as best they may. Some survived. They were to add their own testimony and personal version of the macabre details of the last few days at the Nuremberg trial; others simply vanished, presumably blown to pieces by Russian shells. A week later Admiral Doenitz surrendered unconditionally as the Allies had demanded.

The Second Worldwide Resource War had at last ended. Europe, no stranger to conflict down through the centuries, now had experienced the most destructive and the most inhuman development of Total War the world had yet seen. And it was not just the slaughter on the battlefields or the extensive casualties among the civilian population; the concentration camps had been overrun in those last few days, and the most horrific sights revealed to the world.

Some fifty years later there are now some fascist sympathisers who deny that the mass murder of Jews, Russians and Poles ever took place. Others act as apologists and dispute the actual numbers. Many more pray that the figures have been exaggerated, simply because they are unwilling to believe that human beings can descend to such a level.

It is not part of my purpose to sift through the evidence and attempt to give a convincing answer, even less to split hairs. To pinpoint the fundamental causes of conflict is my chief concern. While cause and effect are inextricably linked, and can often begin a new cycle, the balance must still lie with the former. In any case, there are ample scholarly expositions and research at hand, and many millions of words have been committed to paper. It is often better that people make an effort to uncover the ghastly truth in their own way, rather than have it laid too neatly before them.

Returning to the causal factors of such a major conflict then becomes particularly important and pressing at this point because there is a danger that in summarising the rise and fall of Adolf Hitler – summarising above all both the power and the weaknesses of a totalitarian state – the impression may have been created that I am inadvertently overturning a significant part of my own thesis. I have after all stated that political leaders are but puppets, twitching to each pull of the control strings held by three dominant impresarios on the human stage: population pressure, basic resources and the technology of the day. And the Nazi party machine under Hitler seemed to have an enormous measure of control over all three – indeed unprecedented control compared with earlier regimes. Evidence abounds that on achieving supreme power the Nazi propaganda machine under Goebbels secured a vice-like grip over all information flow. It was a grip that surpassed all others in world history. It will probably never be equalled again because the technology of information flow has diversified considerably since that era.

Because of this, shall we begin with an examination of whether or not Goebbels achieved what was desired when it came to determining population growth?

As noted earlier, following the 1914–1918 war, the slaughter and the strategy of slow attrition attempted by each side caused a backlash. A high profile anti-war lobby grew up in all European countries. Perhaps more importantly, the fight for female emancipation had begun to move from purely political areas into the biological. Women felt that they had the right of control over their own bodies and over their fertility. Why should they produce children one after the other, and without pause, remembering all the hardships, pain and danger it entailed, merely to see the product of years of love and devotion blown apart in a split second? Why should any of their leaders, consumed by vanity and the pursuit of absurd ambitions, have the right to use them as cannon fodder? With the voices of the courageous pioneers of birth control beginning to be heard, and despite all the wrath of so many scandalised macho males and churchmen, the birth rates declined. This was as noticeable in Germany as elsewhere. Emigration to the USA and to South America, which had been halted during the war, also resumed again, although in smaller numbers. In the chaos that inevitably followed the Armistice of 1918 the Weimar Republic was faced with ruinous inflation and mass unemployment. Conscious of this, it is all too commonly assumed that Hitler's initial popularity, following his overturning of the Republic, stemmed from his ability to stabilise the currency and bring full employment. This is a distortion of the truth. The German love of order and aptitude for hard work was already beginning to achieve the results sought – and this some years *before* Hitler's seizure of power. The rapid decline in fertility rates, which is the truly fundamental factor in achieving stability, does however take some time to make its vital contribution. Unhappily it just happened to coincide with the Nazi takeover. Hitler therefore enjoyed the fruits of its influence! At the same time his hasty programme of public works, of autobahns and of rearmament masked any understanding or appreciation of that contribution.

That he was very much alive to the pressures exerted by population is nevertheless proved by his constant references to lebensraum in *Mein Kampf* and his various speeches. It is all the more ironic in that being childless himself (as far as has ever been established), he clearly regarded zero population growth as an impossibility. Therefore, and quite logically, he also saw conflict with surrounding 'lesser' and 'inferior' racial groups as inevitable. Doubtless he would have been happy if the so-called inferior races could, of their own volition, have achieved zero population growth. Again though, he saw this as an impossibility. Surely it would be flying in the face of Nature's (and God's?) basic command: be fruitful and multiply.

Having gained full control of the German nation, the stream of Nazi propaganda was, as one may now fully expect of the proponents of a Master Race theory, directed towards an increase in the German population. The benefits of the previous years of a sharply reduced birth rate had already brought the emigration of 'pure' Germans out of the fatherland to a mere trickle. Now, those of impure blood, especially Jews, were encouraged to leave, helped by ominous warnings of the loss of full citizen rights and whispers of worse to come. Many heeded the warnings, Einstein and Teller amongst them. After initial hesitation and a period of disbelief, they finally packed their bags. Many others, without due sensibility to unfolding events, stayed to ride it out... and suffered accordingly.

The question that must now be asked is this: to what extent were Hitler and his associates successful in reversing the trend towards smaller families among all the true Aryan folk? Well, not as successful as you may think. The trend was certainly halted and began to climb again, but only slowly. Despite all the propaganda Goebbels had poured out, German women seemed to have an instinctive fear for the future and for their children. The cannon fodder the Führer required for his purposes did not materialise in the flood he either expected or desired. Nevertheless, with better health care, excellent medical facilities and hygiene, moreover freedom from serious epidemics – a freedom attained by brilliant scientific researchers with a significant proportion of Jews amongst them ironically enough – the average life expectancy rose. Overall therefore the German population figures certainly showed an increase, but *not* due to an artificially stimulated birth rate.

Many people still believe that when the Führer opted for open warfare, firstly by invading Poland, and then after a brief adventure in Norway turned and struck at France, he did so with overwhelming numbers. This, to repeat once again, is far from the truth. In point of fact Hitler had fewer front-line troops employed in the actual assault than the French and British forces opposing him. What he *did* have was technical superiority in the weaponry used and the *way* in which they were used. He had also stockpiled sufficient resources for a lightning strike – but not, to emphasise earlier observations, a war of attrition. Fuel supplies constituted Germany's Achilles heel. The problem had only been partly solved by the Bergius process. The triumph of the Reich's chemists in producing artificial replacements for the most crucial commodities, for example high-grade synthetic rubber, was not always crowned with similar success. Attempts to synthesise a range of other resources met with certain drawbacks.

Significantly, many languages round the world now adopt the contemptuous German word 'ersatz' to denote any synthetic substitute that is sub-standard. As it happened, many within the synthetic industry were mesmerised by its early success in creating products that could approximate, and in a few cases actually improve on, the natural substance. But unhappily the broader economic picture usually proves that the natural product is superior and cheaper in the long term!

At this stage, the intriguing point to be made is that while Hitler had an unusually keen intuitive grasp of the fundamental influences exerted by population pressure, resources and current technology expertise, it was restricted to that of Germany and her immediate neighbours – it did not embrace entire continents. He embroiled himself in a world war, yet he remained in his thinking a parochial Central European. He failed to acquire a broad enough vision to encompass the relationships between the entire planet's population, its resources and each individual country's current technological expertise. In particular he badly underestimated the advantages given by sheer space and untapped resources, as enjoyed by the Soviet Union and the USA. Dare one also include what was at that time a weakened but hardly insignificant British Empire?

To remain fascinated by or trapped exclusively into an examination of conflict in the first half of this century would however be a dereliction of duty. It would seriously impair the wider scope, and the wider picture that this essay attempts to achieve. Mankind's capacity for conflict has unfortunately not been in any way satiated by the two conflagrations just studied. Remember, the year 1945 was a landmark in that it signified the opening of the so-called Atomic Age. A flash and a mushroom cloud announced to the world the precise time of its murderous arrival over the city of Hiroshima. The second flash over the city of Nagasaki spelled out the message that those who possessed such awesome power would not hesitate to use it, and do so repeatedly if necessary. Without question it brought an even more apocalyptic immediacy to the concept of Total War. Not that the subsequent development of more devastating types of nuclear explosives such as the H-bomb have remained the only source of mass destruction, of course. From 1945 onward scientists have developed 'germ warfare' and 'nerve gas' weapons with an equal if not greater ability to erase all forms of life from this planet. And it is because of these that it is now a far more urgent task than ever to trace the elemental forces that lead to human conflict. All the more so in that by luck rather than judgement the world has avoided yet another, and final, conflagration. Nuclear war between the two power blocs, the Soviet Russia and the USA, was avoided only by a hair's breadth in the so-called Cuban Missile Crisis. Perhaps in view of this, and the further fact that all the subsequent examples of open conflict in the latter half of this century have been – at least in comparison with the Two Resource Wars – relatively 'minor' and certainly non-nuclear, I will now, in all future references, persist in calling this period the Riotous Peace. The end of two Total Wars has certainly failed to give Total Peace and it is therefore necessary to make some distinction.

Shall we now go on to consider this latter half of the twentieth century?

*

For some young people, and indeed some older people, lacking any interest in science, and having only a sketchy 'general knowledge' of life in general, Albert Einstein was the creator of the Atomic Bomb. This is of course fallacious. In a superficial way, perhaps, one could accept that Einstein might be thought of as the grandfather of the bomb. He did after all conceive of the interchange of mass and energy in his famous equation $E = mc^2$. Yet to repeat observations made on this subject in earlier pages, both he and Rutherford actually believed that the release of vast amounts of energy by nuclear fission was a theoretical possibility only. In their view vast amounts of energy would be required to produce fission and therefore it would be of no practical use. They were both forced to revise this opinion later, of course. Even so, Einstein, a committed pacifist, took no part whatsoever in the subsequent project to attempt nuclear fission, specifically in relation to production of a bomb. Nudged by others he merely lent them the weight of his name in the famous letter to President Roosevelt. And the secrecy surrounding the project was such that he had no inkling of its rapid progress. He was to hear the astonishing news, like millions of others, solely through the cryptic announcement of the attack on Hiroshima. The mathematician Banesh Hoffmann, who collaborated with Einstein at the Advanced Institute, Princetown, New Jersey, reports on the man's reaction:

> Einstein's secretary heard the news on the radio. When Einstein came down from his bedroom for afternoon tea she told him. And he said, '*Oh weh*' which is a cry of despair whose depth is not conveyed by the translation 'Alas'.

Once again we are faced with a translator's constant difficulty and fundamental inadequacy. Perhaps one might compare it with the cry of desolation one sometimes hears in the music of Schubert. It does not occur often, otherwise one would find oneself constantly in tears. The loveable and kindly Schubert re-emerges with a smile, like sunshine out of a storm cloud. There is, fortunately for us all, no spiritual insecurity in his make-up; thus the cry is involuntary and limited to rare occasions. Einstein, knowing that his theoretical enquiries had first suggested to the world of science that the release of vast energy was possible, may well have felt intense despondency, even a tinge of remorse. His creative genius had, without his consent, been used to further something totally alien to his humanitarian outlook and overall philosophy. He may well have been ruefully aware that in the realms of music, genius was never repaid in this way. Those great masters he loved so much, and whom he knew could give the world such joy, would never find their work lending itself to such macabre invention. In failing health he redoubled his efforts to bring some kind of sanity back to a world still bedevilled by endless territorial disputes, endless political posturing and chicanery. In Europe and elsewhere many sensitive and caring individuals banded themselves together to form anti-nuclear protest groups of one kind or another. It was well meaning, but somehow fatuous. They were after all, metaphorically speaking, attempting to persuade (and solely by philosophical debate!) psychopathic Mafiosi armed with machine guns and grenades to revert back to pistols or swords. They even advocated a policy that if one of the followers could be persuaded to disarm unilaterally, then it would at least prevent proliferation. Apparently the adage 'nature abhors a vacuum' had never made much impact on their thinking, still less its possible translation into human affairs. As for attempting to find basic causes of human conflict, an activity which should have been their fundamental concern – this was assumed to be beyond any human achievement!

Meanwhile the world had only a few short years to wait for conflict to erupt once more. Just five years after the end of the Second Resource War, a state known as North Korea launched an unprovoked attack on South Korea.

As the communist regime of North Korea was (and still is) particularly secretive, with a closed society resenting any outside observation, the relevant statistics for its birth rate, death rate and average life expectancy, are not available. Nor is an overview of its resources and technical expertise. That they were able to put (in relation to the size of their country) very large numbers of men into their armed forces suggests a high birth rate and a large surplus of males. This view is reinforced by the way in which these men were hurled against the South. But why did this conflict begin in the first place?

Since the beginning of the twentieth century Korea, as a complete entity, had unwillingly fallen victim to Japanese colonial ambition. However, with Japan's defeat and occupation, the Allies (at that time including Russia) partitioned the country into what were to be temporary 'occupied zones'. Russia took a zone north of the line of the thirty-eighth parallel, while America took the south. Korea was to be made an independent state eventually – or so it was hoped. But in effect the Russians quickly set up a communist regime in the North, and supplied it with arms and military advisers. The Americans in turn organised what on paper was a democratic republic. Unfortunately it rapidly became virtually a dictatorship under the autocratic Syngman Rhee. In 1949 the Americans withdrew completely. So did the Russians. On 25 June, 1950 the North invaded the South.

The army of the South, surprised and outnumbered, began retreating down their long peninsular. US President Truman immediately appealed to the UN and the Security Council. The Council demanded that the invasion be halted and that North Korea return all forces to the thirty-eighth parallel. When this demand was ignored, Truman ordered American forces to enter South Korea. Unfortunately, US and British forces stationed in occupied Japan were unready for such an order: they managed to obtain only a toehold in the far south. Finding them in danger of being driven into the sea, General MacArthur hurriedly planned a counterstroke. Two months later, in a well-executed amphibious operation, he landed substantial forces high up on the western coast. From here he drove rapidly inland, cutting off all supplies to the North Korean army in the south. It was now the turn of these forces to withdraw in confusion. In fact the retreat would have become a rout, bringing about the complete collapse of the North, but for Chinese intervention. So-called 'volunteers' in large numbers, all of Chinese origin now appeared unexpectedly on the flank of a somewhat overextended US advance. It caused an immediate military and political crisis and it had worldwide implications.

In Europe, the Soviet occupation reaching, as it did into the heart of Germany, coupled with the conversion of neighbouring states into Soviet satellites precipitated the Cold War. The closure of access to Berlin, which had beleaguered the US, British and French (symbolic) zones of occupation was parried by the Allied response in organising the Berlin airlift. This confrontation had brought a blast of icy air to international relations. Even worse, Russia's successful achievement of her first nuclear test in 1949 had traumatised the West. Stalin's ambition of promoting the inexorable advance of communism throughout the world, backed by ever increasing Soviet military might, suddenly presented an immediate threat. General MacArthur, the most prominent and acclaimed military figure in America, appeared to believe that striking China a severe blow then and there, possibly with nuclear weapons, would present Russia with a suitable warning. It would underline the West's resolve to hold back the communist tide.

After all the US still had a military advantage. But what kind of advantage?

Well, Von Braun had been whisked off immediately, as soon as he had been captured, to America. He was now assisting American scientists in the design, testing and production techniques of the first ever intercontinental missiles. The nuclear submarine, first envisaged by Hitler's naval architects, was also taking shape on draughtsmen's boards and would rapidly become a reality. In fact it would become the most formidable weapon not just in the US navy but also the British. Submarines armed with missiles would put the entire vast Soviet Empire within range. Meanwhile, nuclear bombs could only be carried by aircraft – even if they were now jet aircraft. This problem had to be addressed. The US immediately engaged itself in building airfields and bases for long-range bombers in a wide variety of countries ringing the Soviet Union. Yet America herself was still out of range of Soviet attack. In this sense she had the edge in military advantage, but for how much longer? It was evident that the Soviet Union too would soon build nuclear submarines equipped with intercontinental missiles of their own. How soon?

Perhaps the full extent of the private interchange of views between Truman and General MacArthur will never be known. Even from what is known, it would seem that the General had aggressive tendencies that Truman found increasingly alarming and unacceptable. It also became a clash of personalities. After considerable hesitation, Truman 'pulled rank'. As the President and Head of Armed Forces he relieved the General of his duties! It caused a sensation not just in America but around the world. Military analysts will no doubt debate to this day whether or not Truman's decision not to attack China prevented a Third World War, with all its unforeseeable consequences. China and the Soviet Union still had, outwardly at least, strong ties between them. Stalin, though ailing, was still alive and the rift between these two communist states had yet to develop. Attacking China directly risked immediate involvement with the Soviet Union. Truman nevertheless faced a dilemma. America and her allies would be committed to a conventional war in Korea probably for years, and China had huge manpower resources. Indeed, Mao

Zedong was to throw in his Chinese 'volunteers' with a liberality that caused major difficulties for the allies. But Truman finally set his face against attacking China itself.

The Korean war was to last three years. And as the battlefield moved energetically up and down considerable swathes of the Korean peninsular, the civilian population suffered severely. An estimated four million civilian and military casualties resulted. One million Chinese soldiers perished.

On 27 July, 1953, an armistice was signed at Panmunjom, putting the dividing line between North and South Korea back exactly where it had existed three years earlier! One quite savage and destructive war had ended in stalemate, but a major conflagration had been avoided.

One would suppose that the human animal the world over at this point would have had a surfeit of conflict; numbed senses should have become totally weary of the tumult of war. Not one bit of it! Population pressure saw to it that the seeds of conflict, sown initially in the human mind, and there activating bottled-up resentment, were soon to turn into active physical expression throughout Asia and Africa.

Before making a survey of these, it is necessary to step back a few paces. In 1947, just three years prior to the Korean war and in the realisation that colonialism had come to an end, Britain had granted India independence. Mahatma Gandhi's brave and protracted struggle had finally succeeded. Using his impeccable moral code of non-violent non-co-operation, he had produced a feeling of quite logical inevitability. Sadly though, violence was to grip the internal heart of India herself. The cause stemmed from religious intolerance. And as religious conflict is an issue in its own right, it will be dealt with separately on further pages. However it must at least be touched on at this point. Why? Population pressure has a vital influence on religious intolerance; the two go hand in hand. But one tends to obscure the other, and the result is endless confusion in the public mind.

In the meantime, fasting almost to the point of death, Gandhi prevented what was already a massacre of serious proportions from developing into one that possibly might have been unprecedented in history. Even so it failed to stop the partition of

India. The mass evacuation of millions of Muslims into newly created Pakistan continued, and with it the reverse movement of Hindus into the south. Tragically, by insisting on Hindu–Muslim brotherhood and friendship, Gandhi was to be murdered by a Hindu extremist on 20 January, 1948. Without his immense influence, India and Pakistan were to be involved in a series of border incidents and territorial disputes, culminating in intermittent warfare, that has continued to this day.

Historians viewed this period with their normal tunnel vision. Using as ever the political standpoint, they are of course forced to mark both the late 1950s and the decade of the 1960s as a period when European states finally accepted that the colonial era had come to an end. Britain, so they announce, had begun a process that was to be followed by France, Spain, Portugal, Italy, Holland and Belgium. They overlook the fact that Spain had, several centuries earlier, already begun to lose her colonial acquisitions to other European robbers – but never mind. The fundamental reason for the end of colonialism is not political, it is biological. The morally indefensible argument concerning empire building and colonialism had certainly been lost, but this had no impact. Only because population pressure in Europe had declined were Europeans no longer *forced* to look for territory abroad. But all of this was, as one may expect, neatly masked in the welter of fine words. The deep emotions of reformers was countered inevitably by the tumultuous barracking of die-hards. Ironically, population pressure in the reverse direction – that is among those whose freedoms were now on the verge of being won – was now being built up. With greater irony still, this was being assisted by greater control over epidemics and pandemics introduced by Western medicine, coupled with Western (partial) control over public hygiene!

The French were the first to feel that pressure. It occurred in what at that time was called French Indo-China, and which in a very different post-colonial era becomes instantly recognisable as the area containing Vietnam, Laos and Cambodia. Here Europeans began vaguely to hear of French difficulties in the early part of 1953. It was to culminate in the siege and military debacle of Dien Bien Phu. Shall we examine this significant period for a moment or two?

Since the Second Resource War, sovereignty had been hopelessly confused because the Japanese occupation of Vietnam during the war had brought a temporary liaison with the Vichy French government and its resident French garrison. These forces surrendered to the Allies on 14 August, 1945. However, before the Free French government, battling as it was to restore conditions in France itself (where incidentally it was arresting all Vichy officials and collaborators), found the spare time and energy to send politically 'sound' officials and military to Vietnam, a partially successful communist coup was engineered by Ho Chi Minh. Assisted by both the new communist takeover in China and the Soviet Union with arms and general supplies, Ho Chi Minh set up his power base quite naturally in the north. For Europeans this tended to mask the fact that communist cells and their sympathisers existed throughout the south also. To hold back the tide of communism British and even Japanese troops under British command were used as a temporary barrier. They formed a defensive line to protect the south. Later the French took over and arranged a truce. It failed to hold. France now found herself attempting to put the clock back a century or so.

Military operations, ending in the siege at Dien Bien Phu, brought heavy defeat for the French. It was to become the opening of a complicated saga that would later embroil the USA. In all the confusion of the purely political events that followed in the intervening years, nobody seemed to notice that Vietnam had one of the highest birth rates in the world. Nobody bothered either to note the grim correlation between unsustainable population growth and the inevitability of human conflict. This had been demonstrated time and time again in every region throughout the world and down through every period of recorded history. History should teach us its lessons. Either it is a very poor teacher, or we are appalling students. I suspect the latter. Vietnam was a tragedy waiting to happen. And happen it did of course, in time.

Meanwhile, France, already in political turmoil at home, and recoiling in anguish over the ninety thousand killed and wounded in Vietnam, found additional trouble just across the Mediterranean. Her colony of Algeria, considered part of metropolitan France itself and having large numbers of French settlers, was being subjected to what Europeans saw as terrorist attacks by native Algerians. These were calling for independence. The Moslem majority quite naturally saw them as 'freedom fighters'. The term, as always, is interchangeable depending on one's nationality and religion – itself but an accident of birth. Again the very high birth rate among native Algerians was the unseen and unrecognised basic factor in what was to become a very bitter and bloody conflict. That further conflict should continue to this day amongst Algerians themselves, even after eventually obtaining their freedom, continues to surprise and shock Europeans. Yet again this displays ignorance of the underlying demographic details. Algeria too has a totally unsustainable population increase.

Problems of the post-colonial era were not confined to France. As 1956 opened the British in Cyprus found themselves bemused spectators of the growing unrest between Greeks and Turks. However, attention was diverted by the Soviet semi-invasion of Hungary and the trouble of the Suez canal. Here, what was claimed as an international waterway happened to run through what had long been claimed by Egypt as her sovereign territory. And Egypt now pressed her claim.

This matter would never have had the international impact that it did but for the fact that an enormous tonnage of oil tankers used the canal to bring precious crude oil to virtually the whole of western Europe. Such use avoided what would otherwise be a very long and expensive journey round the entire continent of Africa. What now resulted was the well known Suez Crisis and short war. Slightly earlier, the conflict between what was now the state of Israel and the remainder of the Arab world had gradually grown in intensity. Whatever the rights and wrongs of the case for a Jewish homeland, the Arabs inevitably saw a steady stream of immigrants into this tiny strip of territory as a threat to the existing Palestinian Arabic inhabitants. With an already high density of population, given the area's restricted resources (if only that of pure water!) there seemed to be no room for more. Egypt, the strongest member of the Arab League and a recipient under President Nasser of Soviet arms and technical assistance, had for some time taken over the role of most menacing of potential adversaries – a position formerly held by Jordan and Syria. Seeing an opportunity opening up, Israel secretly timed a counterstroke to coincide with the British and French invasion of Egypt. The US refusal to sanction this action halted yet another attempt to put the clock back. It was seen as a colonial aberration: the remainder of the world got on with life as usual. Meanwhile Cyprus gave endless cause for concern, while on another continent a certain Fidel Castro engineered a successful revolution in Cuba. Then terrorist/freedom fighting in Algeria reached new heights.

In 1961 the Berlin wall was constructed. In 1962 China and India had a brief war, and on 22 October of that year came the Cuban Missile Crisis. As already noted, the world teetered on the edge of nuclear war. Fortunately it was averted. In 1963 came truly serious conflict in Cyprus which spilled over into 1964. On 16 October of that year China exploded its first nuclear device and in December fighting reached its height in Vietnam. A little further away, Indonesia and Malaysia found reason for conflict on their own account. In 1965 came a serious Pakistan–India interchange; in 1967 there was the Israel–Arab Six Day War. The year 1968 saw the Soviet invasion of Czechoslovakia and the Nigeria–Biafra war. Then, to everyone's disbelief, came a Soviet–Chinese border conflict! Earlier rumours of serious division were now seen to be true.

Opening a new decade, in but a year the world saw East Pakistan attempt to break away from West Pakistan to form Bangladesh. In the brief but bloody interlude, India became involved. Further east there was heavy fighting once again in Vietnam. In 1973, at last, because of bitter protest at home, the USA withdrew. At the height of the conflict over half a million US servicemen were engaged and over two and a half million tons of bombs, including defoliants and napalm, were dropped yearly. The casualties on all sides had been severe. Also in 1973 the Israelis came near to disaster in the Yom Kippur War, while in Chile, President Allende was killed and General Pinochet took over. Incidentally in the USA people started hearing the name Nicaragua. They duly turned to a world atlas to look it up, only to discover it was on their own doorstep. Cyprus made headlines again in 1974 when Turkey invaded and effectively cut the island in two. The following year Lebanon erupted into civil war. In 1975 came the infamous Khmer Rouge takeover in Cambodia and its leader Pol Pot wiped out almost two million of his own countrymen. Again in the five years that followed up to 1980 there were endless incidents in Africa and terrorist outrages throughout the world too numerous to quote.

The next decade, the 1980s, started badly with the outbreak of the Iran–Iraq war. It was to last all of eight years. There also came widespread unrest whipped up by Islamic fundamentalists trained in Iran. It ran from Egypt right along the north shore of the Mediterranean to Algeria and beyond – all of which is explained immediately if one looks at the figures for the birth rate and the overall growth in population vis-à-vis available resources. But nobody does of course.

In the Iran–Iraq war, which is said to have cost well over a million lives on each side, hostilities ended only because of exhaustion and lack of resources. Second-hand weapons willingly sold by all the great powers, not forgetting many who were not so great, were beginning to dry up. People in the West began to have bad consciences. Questions were asked about arms sales, and answers became more and more difficult to find. Some arms dealers were murdered and no suspects rounded up; some Western designers of high-tech weaponry were murdered and no suspects found. It all got murkier and murkier. It was not that during these eight years the rest of the world just sat back and looked on. When one riotous breach of peace was solved another broke out in its place. Afghanistan, graveyard of so many military reputations, now again saw conflict. It erupted when Soviet Russia sent in troops to prop up a shaky communist regime. At the same time Cambodia and Lebanon saw intensification of internal struggles. As for Africa, here once again the entire continent showed uninterrupted and tumultuous discord. Should one mention the continent of South America? Should one reel off the names of states where internal discord saw periods of military dictatorship? Dare one mention Argentina, Chile, Colombia, Panama...? One could go on, but it all gets too tiresome to relate in any detail.

In contrast, throughout western Europe during the decades of the sixties, seventies and eighties, there were young people reaching their twenties, and many more moving on to their thirties and forties who had never known at first hand what it was to be at war. All of these were now watching their television screens mesmerised. Concerned with the human condition, they turned to each other wide-eyed, and with that ever-bewildered silent framing of their lips, asked: '*Why?*'

Cameramen, risking their lives, repeatedly showed horrifying scenes. Yet the reporters and commentators who tried to explain how these came about, trapped as they were with the political viewpoint, gabbled on about this particular political faction or that political leader, this agreement broken, or that threat made, this territorial claim accepted, this denied – as if these squalid little manoeuvrings subsequently dominated events. They left the viewer baffled by the complexity of it all. Never, at any time was there an investigation into population increase, never an examination of the basic resources that a country was forced to rely on. Nobody bothered to make enquiries into agricultural potential, or deposits of various ores, or indeed the skills, adaptability and work ethics of its people. Oddly, Japan, even more than Germany and almost alone in the world, with so few natural resources, relied almost solely on its people's skills plus their adaptability and work ethic. But how many could copy her example? Having become so dependent on importing one vital energy source, that of crude oil, this country's future will always be precarious unless another energy source can be found. Dependable energy resources are always the crucial factor.

What then of events nearer home and directly involving Europe and America? What of events once again involving a vital energy source, crude oil?

In August 1990 Iraq invaded Kuwait. All over Europe and America millions began to fear that their affluent lifestyles, and fond hopes for the future – dominated as they were (and still are) by the ease with which they used the car, the lorry, diesel locomotive and the airliner – would be seriously affected. The USA, once a net exporter of oil to countries all over the world, had over the previous half century been so profligate with this substance that she stopped exporting and began to import. Today she could be described as a voracious importer, going about the world buying up supplies anywhere and everywhere. Even in 1990 Arabian oil was a prime source. Britain, on the other hand, initially comforted by the rapid (and all too wasteful) exploitation of North Sea oil, suddenly woke up to the fact that it had (and still has) to be blended with heavier oil from the Arab States before it could be properly refined! Prodded by their worried electorate, politicians on both sides of the Atlantic began jumping up and down in fury, fearing a stranglehold on supplies. Does anyone need reminding of the consequences of such tension? Maybe not, but nevertheless a great deal of hypocrisy surrounds events that followed. What is known as the 'Desert Storm' onslaught was, in the parlance and shameless double-talk of the day, 'liberation of the weak and oppressed'! Liberation of weak little Kuwait against mighty Iraq and the aspirations of the monster Saddam Hussein. The last part of this did at least come near the truth. What is more, Saddam did his level best to play up to the demonic role the West had cast for him. He did everything that a man holding the reins of absolute power usually does to defenceless people. Yet, truthfully, if any war was more nakedly and unashamedly a resource war (in subtle contrast to a free-for-all 'lebensraum' war) then it beggars one's memory to think of one.

In September of that same eventful year, ethnic Albanians living in Serbian Kosovo began rioting. It was an event that passed virtually unnoticed. All eyes were, after all, turned eastward toward Kuwait.

Although no one realised it at the time, the death of Tito a decade earlier had in effect sounded the death rattle of Yugoslavia itself. With hyper-inflation rampant, a worthless currency both internally and on the world market and with three hostile religious groupings – in a country that Tito had rammed together by force – all these were pointers to Yugoslavia's final demise. Self-styled 'foreign correspondents' employed by the more reputable newspapers or television channels and implying that they were journalists with lively minds quick to sniff out or anticipate events, should, if they were truly professional, have been alerted. They should not have needed exceptional olfactory sensitivity to 'sniff out' impending disaster. Demographic factors alone had already destabilised this shaky federation. Beyond this, Serbia, Croatia, Bosnia and Slovenia all had a long history of internal conflict; they also had long and bitter memories. While British, French, Polish, Dutch, Norwegian and German populations, who had survived the Second Resource War, were prepared to forgive (if not forget) each other's sins, the various Yugoslav federated states still harboured internal enmities. Indeed they burnished their memories! Each and every atrocity committed in the Second World War and even before it, still remained in people's thoughts.

To every foreign journalist looking for easy copy for jaded home consumption, the initial rumblings heralded the usual story of yet another incompetent communist regime falling apart. Then an apparently disconnected event concerning Yugoslavia's immediate neighbour caught the eyes and ears of the world's media.

In March 1991 several thousand Albanians, crowded onto leaky vessels of all kinds and began crossing the Adriatic into Italy. The world's press and television cameramen immediately scrambled for a story. Albania, after all, had been the last bastion of unashamed and rigidly maintained Stalinist communism. Arriving breathlessly at the ports of arrival, with expectations of dramatic pictures and copy, they were held back by Italian police. They were informed that the would-be immigrants were, for the moment at least, forbidden to land. Not that it mattered all that much. Whether contact was made with these refugees or not, the preconceived slant for the story was already formulated. To a man they immediately trotted out the repetitious hoary old story of 'escape from a corrupt and discredited communist regime'. Given no other possible explanation it was of course believed. Nobody was aware of a population explosion in Albania or of earlier attempts by other Albanians to cross into the comparatively 'rich' neighbour Yugoslavia. And even if they had known, no correspondent or cameraman was prepared to sit for months on the Albanian/Yugoslav border. In the cold and spiritually debilitating gloom of various mountain passes, it would have been a soul-destroying exercise to interview small groups of Albanians trickling over the frontier. For a start there were no taverns or public houses. That alone was a serious obstacle. And having no source of refreshment, there would be little hope of a line-up of garrulous peasants waiting to exchange stories for a few Deutsche Marks – the only dependable currency! The only alternative would be to carry wine bottles laboriously in a haversack to lubricate their tongues. But why should Albanians trek over the mountains in the first place? If they had asked that question the answer would have been quite simple. It was nothing political. Just grinding poverty. Why grinding poverty? But you just can't ask fundamental questions like this. It just isn't done! So no correspondent bothered his head to delve into the statistics of the Albanian birth rate, death rate, and overall population growth – let alone resources available. If they had, they would have found the birth rate far outstripped that the remainder of Europe and was on a par with some of the highest Asian and African percentages. Further investigation would have shown moreover that such an increase was wholly unsustainable given the basic resources produced by Albania and the work ethic of her people. So how did young Albanian parents still in their twenties and thirties react when they saw their infants menaced by starvation? They were, quite naturally, young enough and determined enough to do something about it. They were not prepared to allow their infants to become just another statistic in the very high mortality rate. So they started out in tiny groups for those mountain passes. And the trickle over the years and decades gradually amounted to a substantial number. But this is not dramatic enough to be judged newsworthy. Thus none of the news-hungry media printed the most potent item of all.

To this day, no estimate has ever been made of the total numbers of refugees who finally arrived in Yugoslavia in the sixties, seventies and eighties, nor is there a guide to their ethnic grouping! Ask the average member of the European public the ethnic composition of Albania and you will be rewarded by a blank stare. If you tell them that Albania is two thirds Moslem and the remainder either Roman Catholic, with a spattering of Greek Orthodox, agnostic or atheist, all you will get will be a disinterested nod or a shrug. So what is the point in making the effort? Why bother to find the exact proportion of these ethnic groups who struggled over the mountains into what appeared a rather better future? When Serbs began jumping up and down, protesting that their 'holy' territory Kosovo was being swamped by Moslems, they were ignored. Indeed it was suggested by bemused commentators glancing at them from a distance that for emotional Serbians this display was quite normal. One can imagine what was said. 'Oh yes, vigorous exercises of this nature are an integral part of their national pastime.' Someone with a warped sense of humour might even have suggested that Serbians could be encouraged to jump up and down even more vigorously – moreover rigged out in national costume – provided they were given a little money. With your camera at the ready you could then capture this age-old folk custom for posterity!

Meanwhile Italy's government continued to dissuade Albanians from flooding into their country, and were severely criticised by the remainder of Europe for doing so. Apoplectic Serbians were ignored. Someone somewhere happened to notice that five thousand ethnic Greek-Albanians had fled to Greece in the interim. How extraordinary! Everyone was genuinely astonished, then sighed and shrugged it off with, 'Oh well, years of oppressive and incompetent communist dictatorship, you know!'

Then on the seventeenth of March, Serbia suspended the provincial Kosovo constitution. The use of the Albanian language for official purposes was declared illegal. Shortly after, would you believe it, Slovenia and Croatia declared their wish for independence. With a substantial Serb minority in Croatia, the Serbs now immediately protested. Austria and Germany made noises supporting Slovenian independence, and tension heightened. The entire matter should have been thrashed out in the relative calm of the forum of the United Nations, but as usual it became bogged down by political subterfuge. Again, nobody bothered to point out that the Yugoslavian army was composed largely of Serbs, or that heavy guns and armour just happened to be on Serb territory. When Serbia yet again repeated the exhausting exercise of jumping up and down – this time shouting till they were purple in the face that the Serbian minority in Croatia could not be abandoned – they were once again ignored.

A dazed European population finally woke up one day to find their television screens filled with ugly and heart-rending pictures. A state of war had actually opened up on their own continent. Europe! A war in Europe! Serbia had launched a vicious attack. Within a very short time her army had quickly occupied up to one third of Croatian territory. The fact that prospecting for oil in that area had produced some modest results, oddly seems to have had no influence on the decision to make such an attack. More to the point, reports of the wholesale execution of civilians and the destruction of the beautiful and historic town of Vukovar shocked everyone. People stared at their television screens again, then turned wide-eyed to each other and framed the word 'why?' on their lips. They repeated this agonised question yet again when the little architectural jewel Dubrovnik was shelled. The Serbs did so of course for no other reason than that it was *such* a jewel and had previously brought in masses of foreign exchange from appreciative tourists. The principle involved? Just a vindictive 'the resource we haven't got, now you haven't got.'

Such awesome and implacable hatred seldom fails to generate similar feelings among opponents and be reciprocated at a similar level. Atrocities – but this time committed by Croatians against Serbs – began to be reported. Shortly after, Bosnia happened to choose the worst of times to make noises about independence. The river of blood became a torrent. With it came the destruction of thousands of homes, crops, farms and livestock. The term 'ethnic cleansing' was rapidly introduced into European figures of speech. Moslems in predominately Serbian areas were massacred and their mosques dynamited; Serbs in Moslem areas suffered a similar fate and their churches were burned to the ground. It seemed to go on endlessly. Only exhaustion combined with lack of food, embargoes on petrol and diesel and the threat of greater military involvement by America and Britain finally secured a truce. Writing as I do in 1997 I predict that this truce will of course be quite temporary. It will last only until sufficient cannon fodder has had time to be built up given the present high birth rate and until sufficient military hardware has been stockpiled. This is never very long in achieving, that is if time-honoured Balkan traditions are adhered to. Very little justification will then be required to restart the conflict. The explosive mix will be ready and waiting for the least spark to touch it off.

Now, except for this ghastly episode – discounting the Soviet rapid invasions of Czechoslovakia and Hungary which were not strictly full-blown conflicts and did not incur widespread casualties – Western Europe has enjoyed virtually a half-century of peace. Given the previous ability in the first half to blast each other to pieces, I think you will agree that this is quite extraordinary. As it is man's instinctive nature to dominate and exploit every living thing within reach – not excluding members of his own species – it is nothing short of miraculous. But then there has been another miracle to account for it. Nature's command to be fruitful and multiply has been defied. Everywhere, except for the Balkans, average family size now barely rises above replacement level. The norm is 2.4 children in most countries and even lower in a select few. Unequalled prosperity and the ability to use high-value currency to buy food, fuel, ores and a wide variety of resources relatively cheaply all round the world, suggest that the current European lifestyle can be sustained virtually for ever!

Or is that a little overoptimistic perhaps? Personally I believe it is crass complacency. But doubtless most people will already have found my views on a variety of subjects rather peculiar anyway. So while they will not risk being thought outrageously overconfident – to subscribe to the belief that Europe will enjoy such good fortune for ever – they do have an inner glow that suggests it will last, well nearly, for ever!

Is their view justified?

★

The answer to this is complex. You see, it does not merely involve economics and the decisions of very wise-looking groups of professors skilled in their mysterious art to guide us on our path.

It involves other factors. And anyway, the basic economics of our situation are simple enough.

Our present extravagant lifestyles depend solely on the basket of European currencies enjoying high exchange rates with the remainder of the world. At the moment European countries – and for that matter all countries where white so-called Caucasian races form the predominant proportion of the population – enjoy very favourable exchange rates indeed. We have become so accustomed to this that we find it difficult to believe such a position can ever change. The economic superiority of white races has for the moment been challenged successfully only by the Japanese, though you can throw in for good measure a few small 'city states' such as Hong Kong and Singapore if you like. These are, for the moment, the only non-Caucasian peoples who have comparable lifestyles. But why do we expect it to remain so? For most Caucasians, the vague answer seems to be that we have superior technology and will doubtless have the edge over all others in the future. Assuming for a moment that this might have some substance in it, the next question to ask is: how do we retain that 'edge'? A ready reply is thrown back at you with an expression of surprise or even pity at such naivety. 'By producing first-class scientists and technologists of course!' is the sharp response. If you pursue the matter further and ask: 'So continued superiority now becomes an educational matter rather than an economic one?' then after an uncomfortable pause you will get a rather uncertain murmur of agreement.

Before turning to this troubled area embraced by the emotive word 'education', hedged about as it is with so many facile assumptions, shall we turn back to purely economic matters for a moment?

What is there to prevent other non-Caucasian peoples from copying the Japanese example and making serious inroads into our current manufacturing and trading achievements? What is there to stop them biting quite sharply into our share of world markets? Does such an awesome possibility see us in the classic pose supposedly practised by the ostrich? Or does it totally fail to register in our minds? If it does register then perhaps it is inclined to press our gift of imagination beyond its bounds. No matter.

Either way, the external optimists will immediately rush in and declare that if such an unlikely thing were to happen then all we would have to do would be to devalue our currency a little. This will slowly bring us an advantage: it will make our manufactured goods cheaper and therefore fully competitive once more.

This is true as far as it goes. But there is a reverse side to this coin, and hardly anyone turns it over to take a brief peek at it. You see, while lower exchange rates certainly provide an advantage for exporters, it is by no means advantageous for importers. And here I do not refer to what are really luxury imports such as cameras, camcorders, audio-visual items, computers and the like, but basic raw materials. For that matter it is not just for raw materials either, but also certain foodstuffs. After all, a wide variety of foods cannot be grown in our climate and for a century or more we have come to accept imported and sometimes quite exotic delicacies almost as staple items in our diet. But to return to raw materials proper. Some can partly be supplied from our own country yet there is a need to top up from other sources. Other items are wholly absent. Grouped in both categories come such essentials as timber, copper, bauxite, manganese... need I spell out a long list? Our manufacturing industries, on which our export potential depends, must have these basic raw materials. As for food imports, does anyone begin to sniff or quibble over the proposition that our workforce must be adequately fed? For certain raw materials in short supply all over the world, prices may become uncomfortably high – that is should a currency become devalued. Factories that by ill luck happen to depend on such raw materials will find themselves in a precarious position. The workers will not be too happy either. A devalued currency means that they will be forced to pay more for *all* imported foods and goods without exception! They will begin to demand higher wages to compensate for this devaluation. The factory owner or owners cannot put up the price of manufactured goods leaving their gates because of the risk of becoming uncompetitive. Wage rises therefore must be at as low a level as possible. Poor workforce relations that may then result could end in strikes. Failure to resolve them may cause weeks of closure. If the supply of goods from a certain source dries up, then world markets react quickly. Other factories in other parts of the world quickly fill any vacuum that opens up. If this pattern is repeated too often the position for any industrialised trading nation becomes serious.

Thus the overall economic position of nations currently enjoying good lifestyle cannot in this respect be casually assumed to rest on solid foundations. It is in fact fraught with uncertainties. But there are even more important factors to consider.

The world is now rapidly losing all those primitive races who were once so naive. For centuries they have been blissfully unaware of the real value of their foodstuffs, their timber, their minerals and their ores. No longer! They are also becoming more knowledgeable about the personal risks involved in securing some of these commodities. For that matter even poorly educated Caucasians themselves are beginning to refuse to put their lives at risk without adequate protection. This requires some extremely expensive machinery plus the undertaking of complicated health measures. For example, it should hardly be necessary to quote the risks posed by such an innocuous substance as coal. We all know the incredible risks coal miners used to face, not just from underground explosions and the horror of entombment should pit-props collapse, but from years of exposure to coal dust causing lethal lung diseases. There is also awareness of the carcinogenic perils faced by miners of certain forms of asbestos, not forgetting workers subsequently using this material. But studiously ignored are the perils faced by miners of the ore uranite, and of workers extracting its uranium, to feed the nuclear industry. Here it should be noted that in the race to manufacture the atomic bomb in the 1940s hundreds of Canadian miners contracted a variety of cancers. And casualties were only being slowly reduced in the fifties, sixties and seventies by slightly better protective measures. With the discovery of rich uranium deposits in South Africa and Australia, much of the work was done by wholly uneducated miners from the black races, and with only a sprinkling of whites as supervisors. Need one mention that the appalling health hazards were never divulged to this workforce? Only recently have some measures been taken to remedy the situation partly. These are still far from satisfactory. As for such minerals as cinnabar (from which mercury is extracted), bauxite, iron ore –

once again it would become tiresome to go through an entire list of substances – essentially workers exposed for long periods merely to the dust of these substances are now proved to be at risk to a wide range of diseases. Even dust inhaled during the manufacture or shipping of foodstuffs such as flour can have serious health hazards! Yet the continued supply of all of these commodities – moreover at distinctly undervalued prices – goes on apace and the West still takes it all for granted. The day has yet to come when Western populations will wake up to very changed circumstances, though anyone with half an eye should see that this situation cannot go on much longer.

When the change comes, as it surely must, prices for all these commodities will rise sharply and our exchange rates will fall. We will then have a rather tricky situation on our hands, to say the least!

Now some may take comfort from the supposition that since Western population levels are falling then such economic downturns might be absorbed without too much difficulty. They will attempt to use my own exposition of the advantages that accrue from having 2.1 average family size, or less. They will endeavour to 'hoist me on my own petard' as elitist dons are apt to say with a faraway look in their eyes. It matters little that nobody knows what a petard is, or precisely what agonising pains and contortions are visited on persons so hoisted – most people grasp the meaning of this expression intuitively. Their expectations of my discomfort are however misplaced. Their initial supposition is wide of the mark. Falling populations are a myth! People constantly confuse statistics for falling birth rates with those of overall population levels. The plain fact is that Western population levels are *not* falling! They are continuing to rise – if slowly. It seems that the average person has no concept of the intricacies and wide range of factors involved in obtaining a proper demographic picture. Birth rates must be balanced with other factors such as death rates, longevity, immigration and emigration. All of these must have proper place in the equation. It may be tiresome to have to repeat, but repeat I must until the truth finally makes its full impact. Overall population levels are still rising in Western nations. Yes, birth rates are falling, but so too is the death rate and emigration rate. Thus our average lifespan has been increased and so too has the inflow of immigrants and asylum seekers, often with attitudes to birth control very different to our own. These factors then conspire together to give a final figure of population increase. Therefore we cannot absorb any downturn in our economy by the falling demands of a supposedly shrinking population.

Shall we return to the main economic picture? Here it is necessary to repeat slogans churned out by politicians at times of difficulty, painfully trite or infuriatingly condescending though they may be. To stay competitive, the West must produce goods and services that are both high quality and keenly priced. But increasingly this becomes an economic tightrope on which we are forced to walk almost indefinitely. And it demands a very skilful balancing act. As touched on previously, Western labour forces quite naturally wish to retain a high standard of living, and equally naturally, demand large wage packets. This tends to price the goods they produce well above those of Eastern equivalents. Not unexpectedly this creates problems for company owners and directors throughout the West. Indeed some of these problems have proved so formidable that some owners and keen-nosed entrepreneurs have parted company with the West and set up factories in what were once called with a patronising tone 'Third World countries'. To prevent further bad feeling among all concerned these are now called 'under-developed nations'. Here workers are docile and the wages paid almost embarrassingly small. The pretence used, when undertaking such a dramatic move from West to East, often embraces the word 'humanitarian'. These factory owners or entrepreneurs either openly or tacitly make remarks suggesting that they are all troubled by a sensitive conscience: this, so they announce, has stimulated them to leave the comforts of the West. They claim they are duty bound to take their skills and a little capital, and use them to give new hope to those in the East. Only the most naive of Westerners now accept this. The unvarnished truth is that the opportunity for becoming a millionaire in the West seemed (and seems) to be receding, while the prospects of becoming a billionaire in the East puts a sparkle in the eye and becomes, by an ethical doublethink, more and more enticing. However, the Western workforce and their trade unions already know – and much to their cost – that such philanthropic gestures on behalf of factory owners have lead to a not inconsiderable number of redundancies. In some instances entire workshops, complete with all machines and equipment, have been bodily transported east. Both workers and trade unions have reacted with much energetic jumping up and down, shouting and waving, but, in the end, hopelessly and helplessly. They comment on the situation with unprintable language in private and many sour words in public, but all to no avail. Unemployment in Britain, Germany, France, Spain and Portugal has, over the last decade, risen steeply. This has been particularly noticeable among the unskilled and semi-skilled. Even skilled workers are often forced to retrain and move to different types of employment if their sector happens to be hit. For example Germany has been the home for almost a century of the world's leading manufacturers of cameras, lenses, sensitised plates, films, microscopes and binoculars. But such revered names as Leitz, Zeiss, Rollie, Voigtlander, Plaubel, Linhof and Agfa, together with many other more specialised manufacturers, were all forced to move either a portion of their workshops abroad, or arrange for a considerable number of parts to be manufactured there. They then merely assemble the finished product in Germany and stamp their brand name on it. This pattern has been repeated in other countries and in different industries.

As for the more patriotic of factory owners who have remained in their country of origin, they have been forced to continue their tightrope balancing act. They must attempt to keep down wages and general costs on the one hand and scour the world for the cheapest raw materials on the other. Undoubtedly though, their greatest concern has been for the level of wages, for in most industries these outgoings are in most cases proportionally well above the costs of raw materials, machinery upkeep and running costs.

This has brought an almost unanimous shout of concern from heads of industry and commerce: indeed their shrill cry has been heard for some considerable time. 'We need a more highly skilled and smaller workforce.'

Consternation or even horror is the reaction from all and sundry. Nowhere is this well-justified horror better observed than among the faces of politicians. Highly skilled, *smaller* workforce! This cry has been received as if it contained a string of the most abusive and indecent of expletives. You see, if this objective is pursued with vigour, then it will cause enormous problems for governments, no matter what their political complexion. The words 'highly skilled' cause a reaction similar to that seen among political protestors when sprayed with tear gas, whereas the single word 'smaller' causes chest pains and every indication of an approaching heart attack. Those words grouped together are so potent and horrific as to be virtually beyond bearing.

For any group of politicians proudly holding office, whether great or small, and whatever kind government, then the prospect of rising levels of unemployment is a factor only marginally less traumatic than going to war or finding a pandemic on one's hands. In some senses it is both a form of war *and* a pandemic of course! Rising unemployment means an ever increasing burden on the taxpayer, who in turn – as it is always painful to remind everyone – finally foots the welfare bill. The recurring and most baffling of problems is how to reduce unemployment by finding 'real' jobs – that is, not temporary work on mere trinkets or trifles and things that nobody wants. Essentially one must provide goods or services that people either at home or abroad urgently need. And it is all the more difficult and baffling in that bosses of giant industries and even employers in small ones keep using wretched comments such as: 'We must have a skilled, honest, responsible, flexible, highly intelligent and well-motivated workforce.' They have the greatest difficulty, so they keep reminding everyone, in finding such people. They are sick and tired of attempting to employ large numbers of unskilled, dishonest, irresponsible, illiterate and ill-motivated so-called 'workers'. Such people quickly bring about the collapse of any industry or commercial enterprise. Above all, they keep mentioning that ghastly jargon term 'R&D'. And they keep going on about this until the cows come home.

Demystified and suitably spelled out in readily understood terms as Research and Development, this, they insist, must be pushed to its limits! It is the only way to remain ahead of competitors. And it has nothing to do with economics. It is wholly in the educational sector. It demands the most concentrated input from our universities, research centres, and technological institutions. It is here that crucial discoveries made in so-called 'pure' science are subsequently translated into 'applied' science, and thence into the realms of technology. Ultimately, one sincerely hopes (but that hope is frequently disappointed), these discoveries are then used for the benefit of all.

The devil of it is, discoveries cannot be made to order. The ability to manipulate shafts of light and use them to penetrate Nature's secrets, there to make a basic discovery on which endless ramifications and applications depend, is not something that can be acquired simply by prodigious and concentrated work. Certainly these factors are always needed: but it also requires that mysterious something, which, for want of a better word, we often call genius.

Shall we look at this factor more closely for a moment? Of all industrialised nations, Japan demonstrates how vital R&D truly is. Maintaining the technological 'edge' has for them been even more of a life and death struggle than for us. Having had until quite recently a population explosion that lasted for two centuries, and which took place in an off-shore island lacking so many natural resources, Japan at first attempted to build a colonial empire and decant its surplus people overseas, just as we did. The loss of these colonial possessions in their own Resource War, which began last century and continued into this one with the invasion of Korea and China, finally ended with the flash over Hiroshima in 1945. Occupied and humiliated, Japan, a proud and highly structured nation, was forced to rely solely on the last resource remaining – the astonishing work ethic of her people. Since 1955 her manufacturing output has had to be of the highest quality and at the forefront of technological achievement. To achieve this, then quite clearly the education of her people had to be intensive and thorough. Mistakenly (in my view) the Japanese created an educational system which was both rigid and mercilessly competitive. They did so in the expectation that it would produce a population with extremely high levels of intelligence. More important still, they expected it to be interspersed here and there with individuals with that mysterious quality which translates as near as possible to our word 'genius'.

As in the West, two very serious misconceptions are present and are likely to persist through thick and thin. Shall we deal with this little matter of 'genius' to begin with?

It has long been my belief that genius is not a matter of intelligence that has been heightened to some extraordinary degree; it is an attitude of mind. There are many highly intelligent research workers in laboratories all over the world: moreover they give their particular object of study the kind of lifelong intensity of devotion that in the realms of any one of the world religions would qualify them for the status of sainthood. They have done, and will continue to do research work of the highest standards. Yet they fail to make that vital breakthrough which achieves a fundamentally new perspective on the mysteries of creation. Sometimes it is a question of luck; sometimes they are anticipated by others working in the same field. In such cases all the honours and the glory goes elsewhere. But most often, as already indicated, it is an attitude of mind. And having made this statement it becomes immediately necessary to amplify it.

First, however, it is essential to note that the field of science requires a very lengthy and highly structured edifice on which to build. Japan, as all other nations, has had, throughout its history, its fair share of individuals justly requiring the use of the accolade 'genius' in all of the arts. The field of science is a different matter. It has not as yet acquired its fair share here. There is a very good reason for this. For centuries Japan remained almost a completely isolated entity, cut off virtually without any contact with the remainder of the world. Those adventurers and would-be traders who visited its shores had an indifferent if not hostile welcome. Intercourse of any kind was frowned on and at times wholly forbidden. This continued until the year 1853. In the interim Europe had built up a scientific edifice of considerable size and complexity. Its foundations stretched back to Ancient Egyptian, Greek and Moslem civilisations. The advantage was overwhelming.

In contrast Japan's isolation, while in many ways benefiting the arts in that they remained highly individual and in many ways unique, allowed her no scientific foundation worth mentioning. And her development in this sphere suffered accordingly. A further factor has been the way in which Japan has chosen to build its educational structure – with undue emphasis on rigidity and competition. There is also the matter of the influence of this carried on into adult life and the work ethic of the entire nation. This tends to be artificially forced on the Japanese people rather than grow naturally and 'organically', so to speak. The workforce has a certain robotic quality. It does not seem to be composed of individuals of mere flesh and blood. The workers in some of the huge paternalistic industrial companies are so highly organised that even their short refreshment breaks during the day are often interspersed with what are virtually compulsory physical exercises and aerobics. Doubts about the wisdom of such rigidity and regimentation are now beginning to surface among the Japanese themselves, but the matter fails to be debated with vigour or pursued to any depth. All this will be examined in a moment. But first let us spend a little time on the trauma suffered by Japan when her isolationism came to an end, more or less in the 1840s.

To begin with it was forced on her, rather than accepted of her own volition as desirable or indeed necessary. Westerners began landing on her shores with a certain air of brazenness and a deliberate flaunting of their technological superiority. It forced her to reconsider her position. At the outset the Eastern concept of personal dignity and of loss of face proved especially troublesome. The Japanese nobility especially were traumatised; they began asking questions of each other. Was Japan really a backward country? Was it still lost somewhere in the Middle Ages? Lacking any reliable information of the outside world, few answers were forthcoming. All efforts toward self-appraisal of her real status were to remain uncertain for some time. In the interim how could one assess her relationship and stature with the remainder of the world? Her ruling aristocracy, as with those in any other nation, always held themselves aloof from their own countrymen, yet they were now forced to feel their way in relation to strange and possibly uncouth people from fabled lands. As with all those unsure of themselves, their self-appraisal oscillated sharply between feelings of inferiority and superiority – inferiority to the

West in general, but superiority to neighbours not too far away. After all, there had been some tentative contact previously with some of these, and they had at least a vague grasp of their military and economic status.

As already touched on, the turning point came with the American Commodore Perry's uninhibited flaunting of US naval power. This brought about a trading treaty with Japan in 1854. And it finally ended the unchallenged influence of the isolationists. Almost immediately Japanese pride now insisted on a complete reversal of attitude. Frantic efforts were made to assimilate every aspect of Western science and technology. Shipbuilding especially saw a tremendous upsurge in activity; warships were required for defence while merchant ships were desperately needed to import resources necessary for the great leap forward in industrialisation. Japan had a little coal – the power source of the nineteenth century and underpinning all European industrialisation – but it was of poor quality. She also had some deposits of copper, lead, manganese, iron, gold and silver, but these were insufficient for the enormous surge forward. To repeat an earlier observation: her greatest resource was the work ethic of her people. Unfortunately though, at this precise moment a population explosion prompted her to take the path toward aggressive empire building. And should any Europeans be tempted at this point to become judgmental and begin making derogatory if silent comments in the privacy of their own thoughts, it may be necessary to remind them that aggressive empire building was already a policy adopted by Britain, France, Spain, Portugal, Holland and Belgium – and for exactly the same reason. Moreover, it had been in operation for some considerable time.

At any event, from 1894 onward a war with China brought her control of Formosa, Southern Manchuria and Korea. Further rapid industrialisation was achieved to such effect that in 1904–1905 Japan was able to obtain a crushing defeat of Russian naval and land forces operating on their Pacific coastline. At the same time Japan consolidated her territorial claims and made inroads into several small Pacific islands. Just one hundred years after emerging from her long centuries of isolation, and now buoyant with unbroken success, Japan assumed she was strong enough not only to invade the remainder of China and a group of smaller neighbouring states, but also to defeat one of the strongest nations in the Western bloc into the bargain: the United States!

A brief diversion becomes necessary at this point, although it is still within the boundaries of my basic theme concerning human conflict. It has to do with attitudes of mind and this curious Eastern concept of loss of face. This is very different from the Western idea of the 'red' face denoting embarrassment. There is, believe me, a world of difference! This will be made clear in a moment or two.

To return meanwhile to the central issue. Europeans took good care to seize territory only from the technologically naive. They boldly went into distant countries with small bodies of men armed with rifles and cannons, quite confident that they could wipe out thousands armed with mere bows and spears. And not unexpectedly it worked. Sometimes of course they fought each other over the spoils, but on getting bloody noses they usually thought better of it. After patching up a hasty truce they found other territories to engage their attentions. In fact disease proved a far greater threat to seekers after empire than any of the natives or indeed other robber nations.

Now if one were to observe somewhat tartly that something must have been badly wrong with Japan's educational system in the late 1930s – excluding of course the rapid strides being taken in science and technology – in that she decided to go to war with the USA, then it is probable one may well be accused of making a snide joke out of a deeply serious issue. But in reality it goes to the heart of the matter. What is education for? What does one hope to achieve? Does education give us merely some kind of explanation for our curious way of living in this extraordinary world? Does it interpret just a little of the strangeness and complexity of natural phenomena and nothing more? Very well, then! Let us examine this at face value. How could the leaders of a supposedly well-educated nation such as Japan show such stupidity and unrealistic hopes by going to war with what was clearly a Western super-power? They were not attempting to conquer an ancient civilisation that had somehow lost its way, as they had experienced in China, for example. How could they even begin planning any coherent strategy when this superpower was clearly allied (if not yet openly) to Britain, Canada, Australia, New Zealand, and the remainder of the free world into the bargain? May I observe that it is not as if the education of the pre-war young of Japan should have included advanced lessons in philosophy; it is not as if they should have been introduced to complex ideas concerning morals and ethics. After all, no nation in the West has attempted such feats anyway. Forget such idealism! What I am actually highlighting are elementary geography lessons! Elementary facts that any ten-to-fourteen-year-olds should be apprised of during their schooldays. You see in such lessons most children should become vaguely aware firstly of the vast *size* of the land surfaces of the US, secondly of the huge population that inhabits it, and then thirdly the favourable or unfavourable relationship to the existing resources available. Even the most superficial introduction to world geography should surely have embraced the fact that the US had a wealth of natural resources, further that it contrasted sharply with that of Japan herself. Crucially too, the US had a glut of that absolutely vital resource: oil. This she exported (at that time!) all round the world. Indeed a large proportion came by tanker over the Pacific Ocean straight into Japanese ports. Were the Japanese not informed that almost ninety per cent of this vital energy source had to be imported? Incidentally too, why should a trickle of Japanese emigrants have begun making their way across the Pacific in the opposite direction, grimly intent on finding a home in the US – and that from the beginning of the century? These elementary facts must surely have entered the thoughts of the Japanese government and the military, a fusion of which, incidentally, became pronounced from the 1920s onward.

It is an incredible position. And I, for one, would dearly love to read the Japanese geography textbooks of the 1930s era; more intriguing still, get an eyeful of the information available to the military planners from 1938 onward. Was their information deficient, or were they *so* emboldened by their years of unbroken success as to be wholly blind to reality? Were they living in a closed mutual-admiration society much like the upper echelons of the Nazi party at that time?

How does one cope with the fact that a Japanese War Office survey, just prior to the Pearl Harbour assault, showed that stocks of oil recently built up could only last for three years in peacetime and only one and a half years in war conditions? These estimates alone should have tempered the military ardour and extraordinary self-confidence of the Japanese High Command. One must ask again: why then did they pursue such a suicidal impulse? Impulse is the only word one can use. It cannot with any logic be called strategy.

Can it be at all credible that the US's refusal to allow any further immigration of ethnic Japanese into their country helped to trigger such impulsiveness? Can it be that America's growing reluctance to allow further 'lebensraum' activities into yet more Chinese territory caused a blind fury? Was that fury so potent that Prince Konoye sought and achieved an alliance with Germany and Italy? Is it credible that, despite being perceived as a mortal enemy, just a year later a neutrality pact was made with Soviet Russia? Could further nibbling territorial expansion and the final US threat of withholding oil supplies finally have convinced the Japanese military that they had not only 'lost face' but fully half of that face had actually been shot away? Of course the Japanese puppets, supposedly in command of the destiny of their country, were just as pressurised by the explosive influence of population increase as had been the Kaiser, and, later, Adolf Hitler. Even so, is it credible to be pressured to such an extent as to commit what was tantamount to ritual suicide on a national scale? Hitler, as has already been observed, was at least able to create some faith *in*, and some sort of credible strategy based *on* his 'secret weapons'. And as I have already demonstrated, given but a year or two's grace for proper research and development, they would have made an enormous impact on his bid for world domination. In this light, his attack on France and then Russia and the fatal opening up of two fronts when Britain refused to recognise defeat, could not be judged suicidal; he had, even when his armies were in full retreat, some justification in believing that flying bombs and V2 rockets would tip the balance. In contrast, the Japanese High Command had no such wonder weapons – or at least no evidence of any kind has since surfaced. On the existing historical record I refuse to believe that the human flying bombs (kamikaze pilots), using what little remained of Japanese fuel supplies, can receive serious consideration as formidable secret weapons!

So then, how could the Japanese education system have failed to supply Japanese leaders with this simple, but admittedly unpleasant 'background knowledge'? Elementary information from a modest geography textbook should have quickly suppressed the initial mad impulse to fall foul of the USA and her allies.

Must one be content therefore with the conclusion that those simple resource factors were glossed over? Were minds so attuned to other things that they refused to accept them? Having no access to documents or reports made by the Japanese High Command, I must allow others to answer those questions – that is if they accept that such questions should be asked in the first place. And many of those dedicated solely to the political saga will refuse, of course.

Predictably too, those who *do* refuse will certainly be scandalised by further permutations I now offer on this theme. But this is not done out of any desire to create controversy artificially; it is done out of a deep conviction that it allows us to take further steps into the heart of the matter.

To repeat: Japan set out, just one hundred and fifty years ago, on her all-out bid to achieve massive industrialisation and modernisation. Moreover, she did so with a determination to reach parity with anything achieved in the West. Hopefully she thought she might achieve even more – not just parity but superiority in output and sheer excellence in both heavy industry and what are now called 'high-tech' areas. Thus the need for excellence in her institutions of learning was obvious. And over that span of one hundred and fifty years many highly gifted research scientists and many able technicians duly emerged from these sources. Yet only one scientist, Hideki Yukawa (and possibly Tomonaga?), can be said to have achieved just that little extra in excellence, that little jolt that raises it to a higher level – a level such is achieved by men and women of sheer genius. Of course Japan's lack of any scientific edifice on which to build accounts for such a void during her isolation from the remainder of the world. But what if we start our enquiry *after* her reconnection? What if we compare her record with an offshore island of roughly the same size, and, as it happens, slightly smaller population – namely Britain of the nineteenth century. During that time emerged Joule, Faraday, Clerk-Maxwell, J J Thomson, Rutherford, Soddy, Bragg, Harden, Wilson, Barkla, Aston, Jeans, Eddington, Moseley, Chadwick, Watson-Watt... and the list is by no means exhausted. Ah, but some people will quickly say, 'A genius is born and not made.' As already stated, this happens to be my view also; but given the laws of Nature, and the statistically stable nature of the genetic lottery in particular, I must remind you that they happen to work in exactly the same way all over the world. I should remind you also that by way of statistical chance alone, Japan should have produced a handful of individuals of scientific genius at the very least. Genius had after all already touched her musicians, poets, writers, artists and sculptors. Producing men and women with scientific insight amounting to genius likewise is fully within the bounds of genetic probability. Yet to date the Japanese are well behind in their production. Why for heaven's sake? As I write these lines, no doubt some malicious amusement is about to be savoured at my expense: tomorrow morning the mass media will announce a series of incredible new breakthroughs achieved by not one, but half a dozen, Japanese scientists! Sod's law, as they say! Nevertheless, meanwhile I have no choice but to pursue my theme. And I must continue also with my permutations. So! One can only speculate that individuals of genius have indeed duly appeared out of the wombs of many Japanese women, yet for some curious reason they have failed to develop their potential as such. Why? Is it feasible that the educational system is itself at fault? Very well, having grasped this particular nettle...

What could be wrong with the Japanese system? Two words may suffice: undue rigidity! There seems (to a distant observer such as myself at least) so little scope for individualism and rebellion. Here I'm not speaking of physical rebellion: I am not alluding to the scandalous number of assaults and verbal abuse currently suffered by teachers in Western schools. What I allude to is intellectual rebellion. Most of the world's great scientists have been shy, dreamy, rather solitary, self-effacing people: yet at the same time they have been fearlessly individualistic in outlook. They have been able to take great leaps forward and acquire unusual insight simply because they were able to defy conventional wisdom. The rigidity of the Japanese system, and the mentality it produces, surely militates against intellectual rebellion; it produces efficiency but not creativity. In this respect, for example, what does one make of the fact that the fifteen-year-old Einstein found his school in Munich – and the degree of regimentation in Bavaria was less pronounced and constricting than the Japanese – so intolerable that he insisted on being transferred to a school in carefree Italy!

In due time we will doubtless find numerous Japanese scientists entering the halls of fame. But I rather think they will do so by finding means to circumvent their current educational system; alternatively, the system itself will have been modified.

To return now to European education and this vexed matter of achieving a smaller but better educated and properly motivated workforce. With it, I regret to say I must underline something else that will raise the hackles of many: if genius cannot be produced merely by intensive education and ample resources, then neither can improved education achieve slightly notched-up levels described as 'high intelligence'! Such people too are born, not made!

Do I hear a sharp intake of breath and some muttered expletives?

Now most people who endeavour to seek out the truth, particularly those who delve into the more unpleasant questions that life tosses into our path, are normally brave enough not to be put off by any disturbing revelations they might uncover. And being brave and uncompromising they may agree with me that those emotionally ravishing words, 'Man is born equal,' are wholly untrue. It is just so much wishful thinking. It has been given poetic form and quasi-religious status by idealists who have mistaken an uplifting dream for actual reality. Men (including woman, naturally!) are all born very unequal – very unequal indeed!

In my view, most human beings are born not just on the wrong side of the blanket as far as privilege and social status are concerned, but they are also often denied so many of the gifts genetic inheritance has in its power to bestow. Such gifts handed us – or indeed denied us – at birth are either wholly visible as our lives develop, or remain partly hidden. The latter have to be proved in one way or another as the years go by. The plainly visible gifts such as fine physical stature, exceptional facial and bodily attractiveness, abundant good health, unequalled energy and so on immediately give the individual so bestowed an advantage. Every known kind of human society places considerable value on outward physical attractiveness. An artistic gift too, if it is fully recognised and in good time – is equally valued. But what of those other and very unwelcome kinds of inheritance? What of those unwanted disadvantages also handed out at birth? Or what of those faults that slowly develop as an individual matures? Whether we admit it or not, all human societies tend to accept that they are grave disadvantages. And, having come to such acceptance, they rarely do very much about it. For physical illness and defects, many societies do, of course, grudgingly give money via taxes to set up national health services. Here some conditions can be treated or alleviated. To a lesser degree also mental defects. Again those with small facial blemishes, birth marks or minor physical deformities can undergo cosmetic surgery. Laser treatment or minor corrective operations too are now performed as routine. But for the vast majority of males and females born neither handsome, beautiful or bodily near-perfect, nor on the other hand sadly disadvantaged by ugliness, poor health or body deformity, such people merely accept what they have been given and get on with their lives as best they can.

Yet if one places intelligence within the list of miserly genetic handouts there is an immediate outcry! Absurd, isn't it! And the bulk of that outcry will come from politicians! Now why should this be? Well, you see, this matter concerning intelligence and education has become a political football. It is jealously dribbled from one party to another. Nobody is ever allowed to take it from them – well, not if they can possibly help it. Even so among the general public there are also some would-be philanthropists and would-be social martyrs who desperately try to capture the ball for themselves. Both these groups refuse to believe that there is a continuum of infinitely fine gradations of intelligence from genius right down to... to what? A semi-cataleptic state? Yes, unfortunately. Monstrously unfair though it is, some are born so cruelly restricted in cerebral development as to be barely able to respond to normal stimuli or utter recognisable words – this even when reaching adulthood! Faced with such bitter reality, society has quite rightly excised those repulsive words 'moron' or 'imbecile' from its vocabulary. It has substituted a more kindly 'those with learning difficulties'. This is as it should be. Nevertheless, nobody should deny the existence of a continuum of infinitely fine gradation of sensitivity to perceived phenomena (my definition of 'intelligence') between such heart-rending states of cerebral deprivation and those of pure genius. If people do, then it is a very special insensitivity all of its very own. It is a dangerous insensitivity into the bargain. It is idealism run riot; it is complete refusal to come to terms with reality. For such idealists, the compulsory attendance of children at school and the application of education in itself by some miracle supplies intelligence. They will spurn my belief that all education can do is to *encourage* a child to reach its full potential. They will ridicule my further belief that, when having reached that potential, it is impossible to push that individual further! This is anathema, and of the most abhorrent kind! You see, it ruins their bright-eyed vision, ruins their best-laid plans for the future, ruins it utterly and perhaps rather cruelly!

There are other facets to this too. There are some who, while admitting all too reluctantly that intelligence is a gift bestowed or withheld at birth, will nevertheless smile sweetly at you and say knowingly, 'Ah, but everyone has hidden gifts! They only need to be teased out with a little loving care, you know.'

Now this has some truth to commend it. Unfortunately for us all, it is only a half-truth. And half-truths are dangerous because they can mislead people into believing they are complete and fully formed ones. Yes, everyone has gifts. What is omitted from this statement however is something very important: they may not necessarily be used to benefit society, or uplift the soul of man. You raise an eyebrow? You ask me what I mean by that?

At this point it is necessary to make another statement which may cause offence. While flippancy in any shape or form in some of the previous pages would have been unforgivable and in the worst of taste, it may now become more acceptable. It may help to lighten an all-too-sombre and intense atmosphere in future pages. And having been so sombre, why not employ it immediately? Where better than when discussing 'hidden gifts and the uplifting of the soul of man'? Especially when it concerns half-truths. So then – hidden gifts!

Well, some emotional cripple, for example, might well be born a twentieth-century Vermeer or a Rembrandt! Unfortunately in our current artistic climate with its worship of the deliberately obscure, the cognoscenti positively spits at them. They execrate such people; they become the painterly equivalent of 'revisionists' and traitorous 'counter-revolutionaries'. The cognoscenti are seen to stand enraptured before a single blob of paint on a white canvas and talk of 'emotional values'! Is it then such a wonder that traditionally gifted would-be Vermeers and Rembrandts are frustrated? Is it so extraordinary that they are reduced to forging masterly 'new' Vermeers and Rembrandts – moreover doing so with such skill as to fool the so-called experts and sell them for millions at auction? Or in a very different field, who can deny that Robert Maxwell (as so utterly distinct from Clerk-Maxwell) had gifts? Gifts are gifts. He had a gift for grossness, loquaciousness, fantasy, for brow-beating others. These were such that combined with an incredible belief in his own importance, he could, when he so chose, 'charm the very birds off the trees' as they say. That these birds were bald-headed vultures sitting on monetary thorn-bushes escapes the attention of most people. That they were in fact heads of international banks renowned for their tight-fistedness, astuteness and acute smell for carrion makes Maxwell's gifts all the more incredible. Remember, all bankers without exception are normally wholly proof against charm. Such people were nevertheless persuaded to extend Maxwell's bank overdrafts into tens of millions! This strains our credulity to breaking point. Wow! Now this is undeniably a gift of some magnitude. All else pales before it. And it makes it all the more difficult to come down to more conventional gifts. I mean to say, who gives a tuppenny toss about, say, a boy shepherd playing his fiddle, or guitar, or penny whistle, or what have you, while guarding his sheep, yet in the interval getting to know the intimate nature of every creature on four legs around him? And not just every creature with four legs, but also those with wings, even amphibians that both walk and swim! Who cares that he can philosophise (not without merit) on the nature and meaning of life into the bargain! A wonderful gift, yet totally scorned by today's factory farmers or soulless employment agencies. Yes! Everyone has a talent for something. Again, what about the gifts of oratory given Hitler, Mussolini, Lenin and so many more? Do these assist mankind to get through the difficulties that life persists in throwing in our path, and do so decade after decade? At a lower level of significance, a cat burglar may have gifts such as a head for heights and an incredible facility for opening skylight windows. Again one must ask: is this helpful in making everyone's journey through life just a little less traumatic or painful, if you see what I mean?

But to return to education. Beyond the matter of mere intelligence and this vexed question of hidden gifts, when it comes to other important factors such as attention span, patience, curiosity, sensitivity, co-ordination of hand and eye, retentive memory, the ability to dream (wholesome!) dreams and to subject oneself to self-criticism, possessing the gift to see ourselves as others see us, once more we are all very unequal. Again, politicians the world over, despite having gone through educational systems themselves (or because of it), firmly believe in one of two doctrines: those on the political right believe anyone can pull themselves up by the bootstraps, provided they have determination and capacity for work! They will even tell you the true story about humble Margaret the daughter of a corner shop owner, who married a humble thatcher. On the other hand, those on the political left believe that provided the young are well taught and have equal opportunities, then their future achievements are guaranteed. Ditherers between right and left try to put a foot in both camps. Either way, these are holy writ. Shall we examine this belief in detail?

Now the human brain is only partly formed in the womb, and, like some other parts of the body, develops later by further multiplication of cells. A marginal increase in brain size goes on after birth until early teens. However, it is not possible to alter its fundamental composition! And this holds true no matter how truly laudable the work of neurosurgeons in correcting abnormalities, or the dedicated resolve of teachers throughout primary and secondary education.

The brain consists of several main segments – four in all. Firstly comes the cortex forming what Sir Charles Sherington, the celebrated researcher, called rather prosaically 'the roof brain'; below this comes an assembly we can temporarily call, rather unpoetically, the midbrain; while at the base, and making a connection with the spinal cord, there is the crudely called 'old brain'. A further swelling sticking out at the back of the latter is another structure known as the 'cerebellum'. The first three are evolutionary in their development and can be thought of as Neomammalian, Paleomammalian and Reptilian, but nobody is quite sure as yet about the evolutionary position of the cerebellum. All these four compartments carry out certain functions. The cortex is where fine intellect resides and all those decisions made by the interplay of reason take place (more or less), the midbrain seems to control the emotions, and I hope we know what those are, while the old brain regulates basic automatic functions such as heartbeat, breathing, blood pressure, dilation of blood vessels, and so on. The cerebellum is still something of a mystery, or, one should say, is more mysterious than the others. Research is still making painful headway on all four. To complicate matters still further, all four are interconnected and constantly send messages to each another.

Looking at them in greater detail, we find that in some compartments are tiny cells, or neurones, which have extensions called axons. These are often several feet in length and can transmit electrical impulses in the most astonishing ways. It gets more complicated still!

The very thin, crumpled 'roof brain', or cortex, alone has about ten thousand million neurones; the cerebellum has some forty thousand million granule cells, while nobody is yet quite sure about numbers in the other compartments. As unbelievable as it may seem, the brain as a whole consumes about one third of the body's oxygen supply! The cerebellum (alone) makes the inside of a computer chip look positively crude, having as it does a mind-boggling combination of basket cells, climbing fibres, molecular layers, Purkinje cells, parallel fibres, recurrent collateral layers, Stellate cells, deep cerebellar nuclei, granule layers, gogli cells, granule cells, medullary layers, mossy fibres and as yet many more unidentified bits and pieces!

If for the moment we think of the brain rather crudely (and purely for simplification purposes) as somewhat similar to our domestic electricity systems, with the sort of circuits, sockets and fuses you might find in the average house, then a tiny malfunction in any of them is enough to cause problems of one kind or another. As we know by experience, these domestic irritants can range from a flickering light to frequent blowing of fuses. Of course at an extreme, it becomes something more than an irritant: the wretched house can go on fire! Similarly with the human brain. Clearly some malfunctions can be quite small and can go almost unnoticed, or are at least tolerated. Others may be of such a serious nature as to demand our immediate concern. At an extreme we are faced with trauma and some very hasty action on our part.

But it doesn't stop there. Unfortunately with the human brain there are even more complications. It is not only 'electrically wired', but it has a chemical input too! A wide range of behavioural abnormalities, for example, can be caused by a chemical imbalance at birth. They can also develop slowly by a rather restricted or unwise diet during childhood – or for that matter at any time later. And improper chemical balance can be at the root or a wide variety of 'learning difficulties' which is another way of saying that before birth or after birth, the development of the brain (and the cortex in particular), has been interrupted or retarded. As for overindulgence in alcohol or the use of drugs during one's teens or later adult life, surely nobody now requires to be told that these are factors that can cause either temporary or permanent imbalances. You can be stoned out of your tiny mind (or proportionally tiny cortex) by booze or by syringe, simply by the artificial introduction of toxic substances. And it takes some time before the body's defences can deal with it and eject it from the system. A brain fuddled by alcohol or drugs can make a person incapable of supplying one of those eternally suspicious members of Her Majesty's Police with the answer to such ludicrously simple mental tests as adding two and three, or retaining the ability to recall the day of the week or month of the year. It can also result in completely unacceptable physical behaviour such as abusive language, urinating here, there and everywhere, vomiting here, there and everywhere, or becoming unusually aggressive – right up to the point of causing others what is called grievous bodily harm. At an extreme of course it can result in manslaughter or murder. Chemical imbalance is therefore a factor of some importance. Happily though, and unlike attempts to make repairs to our electrical 'circuitry', remedial action in the chemical field is possible. In fact it becomes progressively more effective as researchers push out the boundaries of our knowledge. A deficiency in, or imbalance of, an infant's diet, once investigated and pinpointed, can often be brought back to normal. A prolonged chemical imbalance running through childhood does however make for more permanent damage. Serious malnutrition, in which a wide range of trace elements in the diet are wholly missing (and over a long period), is a very different matter. Here, as so often happens in the so-called underdeveloped areas of the world, it can mean stunted brain development and therefore permanent loss of intelligence. As for industrialised nations the ingestion of toxic particles too, via, for example, water which runs through lead piping or the inhalation of exhaust fumes from leaded-fuel vehicles, is a prime example of toxicity that can seriously affect brain development. But in all of these cases the addition of missing trace elements, on the one hand, or the withdrawal of toxic substances on the other, can bring about significant improvements. In the case of self-mutilation of one's brain, such as is wilfully performed by alcoholics or drug addicts, then the breaking of the addiction can restore most of the cerebral functions to normal. Unfortunately though, other parts of the body, such as the liver, may well have received permanent damage by that time. But this is to stray from the point in question.

Some cerebral abnormalities are *not* brought on by self-abuse, or by innocent ingestion of toxic substances, or by dietary deficiencies but rather from genetic or radiation sources. And these often result in a brain tumour. Fortunately, these will occasionally yield to a surgeon's knife or a laser beam. The point to be made however is that it would be wishful thinking and certainly all too premature to expect neurosurgery to come to the rescue and deal with all cerebral abnormalities. For the foreseeable future it would be foolish to expect semi-miraculous progress in this area. There is far too much research needed before reaching a degree of perfection where infinitely tiny 'welding' or repairing may be achieved on what might be somewhat simplistically thought of as 'broken', 'blocked' or otherwise damaged electrical 'circuitry'.

Despite all this, politicians the world over view education in an absurdly naive way. Even as I write, European and American governments are attempting to jump on the pantomime horse now laboriously pulling the educational bandwagon – or indeed on the bandwagon itself! Their stated objective is to put more and more money into every school and college in their respective countries... as if this alone guarantees the desired result! The delusion is not just common among politicians of course but has gradually spread to populations as a whole. It has taken on the nature of an epidemic if not a pandemic. And it has the added attraction that money has never been flung at education before.

The proof of this is evident if one looks at the fabric and basic equipment of most schools. Endless years of cost-cutting in the maintenance of the buildings, has left them at best shabby and down at heel, at worst structurally dangerous. A brief inspection of internal conditions shows that equipment is well worn, markedly out of date or totally inadequate in both quantity and quality. Many parents now band together on a private basis to organise fundraising schemes for schools, particularly at the primary level.

So with the politicians now having made such an astonishing commitment, everyone lives in fond expectation of great things to come. It is in fact an exercise in 'great expectations' and Dickens, if he were alive today, would surely find wonderful material for his pen.

But delusions go far deeper than that. They involve something quite fundamental. And to expose them I am forced to use sleight of hand, for most people are unusually touchy and sometimes hypersensitive in this area. Therefore, in deference to such sensitivity I propose to move from the direct consideration of education to that of farming! Farming? Yes, farming.

You see there is a similar kind of 'great expectation' in some areas of farming. Well, a very special sort of countryside pursuit involving an equally special kind of farmer – the amateur farmer! This peculiar species is one who, having fled the horrors of city life, and a dreary existence behind a desk, now thinks of making his fortune – and of course at the same time enjoying a different version of the good life – by becoming the owner of a dairy herd. Having made a fair pile of money in the city without undue effort, he is convinced that by throwing money at his new venture in the countryside he and his family can enjoy all the obvious benefits this kind of living now offers. He is convinced that by buying a few cows and opening a gate onto some rich pastureland, then sho-shoing his herd inside, that the rest is pure bliss. You employ somebody to bring them in each day to the stalls, attach the milking machine to the udders, and that's that. Oh, sorry! At the end of the day your obliging farmhand does the nasty mucking out, of course. And that's all there is to it.

Of course, for your green-welly brigade, everything seems to work well for the first few months. It may even stretch over a year. The amateur farmer fills his lungs with good clean air, the wife starts raiding all the top garden centres, buying all that is necessary for creating a beautiful garden, the cows all look happy and contented, the birds sing, and daughter Natasha is quite delirious on her new pony. Provided the milking machines continue to work well, and your farmhand puts his back into it, there seems to be no earthly reason why your former streetwise city dweller can't sit on the patio imbibing some rather expensive wine while he watches for the arrival of the village postman with all the expected subsidies and cheques.

Real farmers know differently, however and wait with a little smile of anticipation fluttering round their thin lips. For the first year, perhaps, things go reasonably well. Then the inevitable happens. Perhaps the winter will have been long and hard, with extra low temperatures, and the bills for extra feeding will start coming in. Each of these are as long as your arm; indeed, they are far longer than your bank manager – still smiling through clenched teeth and mechanically protesting that he has your interests at heart – is entirely happy about. Alternatively the spring, when it finally comes, is too wet and with almost no sun. This means that the grass is poor and the land waterlogged. Conversely, the winter rains may have failed, temperatures are unusually high, and the sun is shrivelling everything, including the milk yield. This also means extra feeding has to go on far longer than usual. That's just the grass part. What of the cows? They have had the usual sort of illnesses plus one or two unusual ones. Even the healthy ones seem somehow in less good shape than normally. Then there's the question of the young stock coming on. And that's a matter of genetics – plus one hell of a lot of luck into the bargain!

Genetics! The amateur farmer fondly believes that genetics, in so far as it concerns him, is a simple matter of picking the cows with the best record of milk yield, body weight and general health, and having them sired (artificially of course; can't have Natasha watching that!) to a really good bull – and Bob Maxwell's your enormous uncle.

Sadly, in reality, genetics is a grassy minefield just waiting for the unwary welly boot to boldly walk over.

You see, breeding animals of *any* kind, not just high-yield milking cows, involves putting a set of purely human ideas of 'desirable characteristics' into operation. And human ideas are always flawed. Why? Because almost inescapably they take the human point of view. They embrace further exploitation of the animal as the basic aim, while the actual welfare of the beast comes very low on the list indeed. For both the animal and its would-be exploiter, it is a tragedy waiting to happen.

Now since more people in our current industrialised society tend either to own or breed dogs and cats rather than cows, and are therefore slightly more knowledgeable and at home in this area, shall we consider the genetic howlers visited on our canine and feline friends for a moment?

Take dogs. Those who breed or happen to own so-called 'pure' strains such as Pekinese, Boxer, Bulldog, Labrador and Alsatian – yet again I will not tire you with a long list, will know much to their cost that what are deemed desirable outward characteristics from a human point of view, are anything but desirable for the dog itself. Out of the blue come some highly undesirable internal characteristics, such as blocked nasal passages, badly aligned teeth, inflamed eyes, infected ears, intestinal problems, arthritis, heart trouble, fits, liver trouble, etc., that do not present themselves in any obvious way when one is making a superficial overview of the breed. They all look so attractive. Yet you find the more 'pure' the breed the more frequent the incidence of illness, and the more enormous the bills from veterinary surgeons into the bargain. No, all is not plain sailing in the dog-breeding world. And much the same goes for cats. As for cows...!

The perennial optimist will no doubt chirp up breezily here: 'But haven't farmers done reasonably well on the whole? I mean, wouldn't they be out of business if their well-trained eye for a good animal, whether it be a cow, sheep, pig or what have you, was that badly off course?'

Yes, it must be admitted that farmers have had a crude but quite workable system of improving the variety of living things they exploit, moreover not just a wide selection of animals but also vegetable and cereal crops. Success in general terms has been theirs in point of fact for many hundreds, if not thousands, of years. And it has been achieved by a crude rule of thumb. You select 'promising' animals, vegetables or cereals, and then, to put it politely, encourage (or force) them to exchange what we might call 'genetic material' in the time-honoured fashion. And the results? Well, you tend to get even more promising offspring with a bit of luck. Subsequently you then thank the Good Lord and repeat the process. The terms 'tend' and 'luck' are significant, however. You see, there is always a proportion of offspring that are something of a disappointment. Why should this be? Here we must partly retrace earlier ground.

The Austrian monk Gregor Mendel, after a series of exhaustive experiments commencing in 1857, found that inheritance had some strange and highly complex factors. These were hidden away from casual observation, and were far more elusive than those broad expectations contained in the rule-of-thumb approach. He discovered something quite extraordinary: inheritance does not consist of a process of blending various characteristics! No? Why not? Using simple visual characteristics as the tallness or shortness of quite ordinary plants such as peas in his garden he found that when genetic material was interchanged, the offspring did not attain medium height as one would expect; the new plants were either tall or short. Big deal! Our American friends would voice a withering kind of sarcasm at this point. For Mendel it was of vital significance. It is still difficult for many of us today to see in this apparently puerile or empty-headed observation anything of real importance. It is rather like asking the apparently stupid question, 'Why do things fall?' Individuals who have asked themselves this question, and for that matter many other questions of apparently equal stupidity have gone on to acquire worldwide fame. To help those who remain puzzled by Mendelian subtlety it may be helpful to put it this way: suppose you had two pots of paint, one jet black and the other brilliant white, and then you poured them into an empty pot and mixed them briskly, what would you get? Mid-grey, surely. Inescapably grey. Wouldn't you be astonished if you saw jet black, moreover almost of the same intensity as your original? Unable to believe your eyes, you find a fresh empty jar and repeat the experiment, pouring equal amounts of jet black and brilliant white, and get the same result. You do this several times, only to produce virtually jet black. Then suddenly with one experiment you find you have brilliant white! It is much the same when mixing two characteristically different genetic 'types'; they do not blend. You get either one or the other! Incredible, isn't it? Mendel called the most often repeated type 'dominant' and the least repeated 'recessive'. As it happened, it was fortunate that Mendel experimented with plants and based his findings on simple characteristics such as tallness and shortness (amongst other things)! If he had chosen animals he may well have become overwhelmed by the sheer complexity of results: he would never have achieved his breakthrough. He could also have taken a helpful shortcut by considering the most obvious factor of all – when a male animal mates with a female, you don't get a blend of something in between, in other words, a hermaphrodite. You get either a male or a female offspring. Yes, yes, I know there are exceptions to every rule. I know all about X and Y chromosomes. I also know that among human beings a man and a woman can sometimes produce an oddity. But given that there have been less than two hundred cases of genuine hermaphrodites being born in Britain during the whole of this century, you can forget about it. Nor can transsexuals and homosexuals be classed as true hermaphrodites. As I say, Mendel fortunately asked what appears to be a ridiculous question: he asked why blending failed to happen. Of course so did Newton, when he wondered why things 'fell'! All basic discoveries are made by asking seemingly absurd questions. The answer in the good monk's case was that 'cross breeding' between tallness and dwarfism did not produce as one might expect medium-height offspring, but tallness! Years of experiments showed tallness persisted and was 'dominant'. Shortness conversely was recessive. Ah, but the recessive gene was not lost! It remained hidden away as you might say, dormant for generations. Then, when you least expected it, it popped up again. This time the answer, as Mendel showed, was that if both male and female happened (by chance) to have that recessive characteristic, then in combination they no longer produced the dominant characteristic but its opposite.

Mendel's paper of 1866, when read before a group of biologists, produced nothing more than an enormous yawn. What was this man going on about? Indeed his findings were not rediscovered (posthumously) until the twentieth century. However they have now been eagerly built on, thus forming the new and extremely exciting science of genetics. Advances in the last thirty years in particular have given spectacular insight into a wide range of hereditary phenomena over an equally wide range of living creatures. It has also opened up insight into inherited diseases – even forensic investigations. Incidentally it has also settled some messy human paternity cases. Husbands who suspected their wives of being unfaithful now found scientific reasons why, for example, two blue-eyed parents could have produced a brown-eyed child, why two blond parents a dark-haired child, two white-skinned parents a brown or almost black child! Somewhere in their ancestry were brown-eyed, black-haired, brown or black-skinned individuals! All these are characteristics that can resurface on a 1:4 basis. This is the classic Mendelian effect. A further feature that Mendel did not discover however was that of 'mutation'. There is no discredit in this. These are mistakes in the copying of genetic information brought about usually by radiation – this from either natural or artificial sources. Mendel died in 1884 and the discovery of X-rays and radiation, by Roentgen and Becquerel (moreover how these agencies could have an effect on living cells), had yet to be achieved.

So then, what can one summarise from basic Mendelian principles as applied to agriculture, more especially the breeding of animals? The simple rule remains intact. If you breed like with like you tend to get... well, very much the same, or slightly 'enhanced'. Therefore an Aberdeen Angus cow sired to a similar bull doesn't produce a Jersey offspring and a rustic oath to go with it. On the other hand, if by accident you forgot to close a gate, and you allowed a prize Aberdeen Angus bull to wander into a field with a Jersey cow, then you would produce, well, the coarsest and most explosive of rustic oaths most certainly, if nothing else!

So what of the human animal? Do I hear yet another sharp intake of breath, then a muttered comment? Even when it is filtered through clenched teeth there is recognisable fury coupled with horror. There it is again. It sounded something like, 'I knew it! This bugger's going to bring up eugenics!'

If I heard that comment correctly, then I can only reply, 'Hang on to yourselves a moment,' which I am told is the command of the professional stripper, the sort that frequents higher-class pubs up and down the land. However, being strictly teetotal I must take this information on trust. I also understand that this command is made with a lewd grin and body language which suggests that all will yet be revealed.

But first, as a very necessary introduction to my act I have to go back to my previous comment concerning the workforce of the future.

Although all governments throughout Europe and North America will indignantly deny it, they have already been seriously worried (and no doubt partly compromised), by those equally lewd suggestions made by leaders of industry and commerce.

Those lewd suggestions? That they require a much smaller but highly trained workforce. Smaller! To repeat once more, this is a vile contraction of a seven-letter word into one of four, at least where a politician is concerned. You see, politicians of all political complexions, be they bright red, charming yellow, or with blue rings round the eyes, are, in the privacy of their own thoughts, shaken to the very core. Why? The answer should be obvious. In every civilised country quite incredible amounts of money have to be spent on what in Britain is reassuringly called 'social security'. No doubt there are also similarly soothing and hopeful equivalents in other countries. And these costs are rising inexorably. In point of fact they have gone through the roof, and have done so for many years. Indeed they have outstripped all other items of expenditure in the annual budget. Thus the vision gradually forming in a politician's mind's eye is of an ever greater haemorrhage of money from the Exchequer as more and more people, especially those in the semi-skilled or totally unskilled sector come onto the lists of unemployed. Worse, it becomes a vicious circle. With more unemployed and fewer in employment, then the greater the burden of taxes on this shrinking group. Incidentally among the very rich with their special tax-avoidance accountants, this must be written as 'shirking group'!

Now, suppose there was a truly sharp recession in world trade. Moreover, what if such a recession happened to be more intense and lasted longer than any that we had seen before? This kind of scenario is the politician's equivalent of a ride on the most terrifying of coaster-rollers, or is that roller coasters? It doesn't just send chills down the spine; it becomes a bowel mover of great potency. Indeed it must surpass any laxative known to medical science. And it doesn't even need a doctor's prescription. You see, in such a scenario, unemployment levels rise so sharply that the Exchequer is unable to meet the bill for social security benefits. Calamity! In such circumstances there is no alternative but to reduce the amounts paid to all those millions of claimants. And hell hath no fury like claimants scorned. Indeed it will stimulate such levels of fury among the unemployed that staff at benefit offices will be physically attacked. Subsequently, when this produces no useful effect (let alone monetary benefit), the mood will undoubtedly spill over into the streets. Pilfering from shops, muggings and house burglary will all rise drastically. As governments will have already cut police and armed forces to the bone, and as jails have long since been bursting at the seams, the possibilities of uncontrollable rioting will become ever more apparent. In the worst scenario, when (as has already happened) heads of recently privatised industries award themselves obscene salary increases — then sack possibly up to one third of their workforce to pay for it — this becomes such a provocative act that the sheer frustration, anger and resentment of the unemployed will reach boiling point. If millions have to face austerity, then very well — it might be bearable if the whole country is seen to pull together. If everyone without exception puts their shoulder to the wheel... as the clichéd expression goes. But if the bottom end of society finds themselves thrown as it were into ordure, while the top end of society actually becomes ordure, then undoubtedly all hell will be let loose! The rioting and looting of shops will be intensified. Key workers such as those at electricity power stations, or those endlessly repairing these paper-thin objects called water mains, or employed in transporting our untested and bacilli-nurturing food, will either be seriously delayed or wholly prevented from reaching their places of work. Having reached that point in disorganised rioting, there could well be further escalation into organised rioting. This may then be assisted by enthusiastic input from criminal gangs using well-tried mafioso tactics. It is not beyond the imagination of any man — even those politicians with the meanest of intellects and visionary forecasting — to see the developing nightmare. It is a scenario where the entire country is being paralysed. And unless truly drastic action is taken it would be followed by a gradual slide into disintegration and total chaos. To repeat; this is a bowel-moving scenario all governments have secretly, and in their very worst of moments, been forced to contemplate.

How does one fend off such a horrifying possibility? The simplistic answer now used by politicians is contained in just one word — 'education'! What a marvellous word and what an uplifting concept this is! Everyone is so much in favour of it! You get an uncontrollable chain reaction, just as you would if you had split the unstable nucleus of an unstable atom, and without a moderator at that! Wow! Uplift! By God what uplift! Your are on an emotional winner from the very start. Yes, you avoid rising unemployment by putting 're-' in front of education and making it 're-education'. You re-educate the semi-skilled, and the unskilled. You promote all kinds of schemes under the general title 'Never be a work-shy wimp!' and so forth and so on. You then set up schemes using the very latest techniques in work-finding, using, as it behoves you when looking for such elusive and elementary particles, an up-to-date electron microscope. Beyond this you even pay people to attend these schemes – even pay people to teach them how to write begging letters or place ticks in the correct boxes on the inevitable forms. It just doesn't matter whether there are any real jobs available out there in the real workplace. You just live in hope, like Mr Micawber, that something will 'turn up'. Outwardly though you remain buoyant and make sure that the media portrays your as an able and caring politician. Yes, you are seen to be doing something, except, mercifully, getting down on your knees in the privacy of your bedroom and actually praying for such miracles.

Outwardly then, you prove without a shadow of a doubt that you are not trooping into the House one day a week just to bellow and barrack from the back benches. Nor for that matter do you just sit in Whitehall watching the world go by from behind a ministerial desk. You may even prove you are not contemplating (no doubt with some disgust) your own navel.

Yet, as odd as it may seem, contemplating your own navel, would, if done properly and with intensity, actually be of greater benefit. In fact it would prevent you being so foolish as to waste time and energy on such schemes in the first place. Secretly, many politicians, again in the privacy of their thoughts, will agree with this. Without being seen to undermine the 're-educationalists', they become instead just educationalists with a big 'E'. So, what do they say in public? 'Listen! Education must begin earlier,' they enthuse. 'It must of course begin in the most obvious of places, with the very young – in our primary schools.'

Again they are on to a winner. There is an emotional intensity that can be fabricated all too easily at the very mention of the word 'school'. Combine the word 'school' uncomfortably close to the word 'education' and you've hit the jackpot. This is our salvation! God, watch my lips! 'School' and, yes, *and* 'Education'. Our children's future must and will be safeguarded. The watchword now becomes 'school with education', or, if you prefer it, 'education with school'! A magic combination of principles. Very soon now we will see on the podium in many public places politicians of the left, right and centre blasting out these emotive words. The public will be enraptured. A Freudian slip might induce one to write 'enruptured'! Politicians will have to wait for the frantic applause to die down. Finally, they will frown and say, 'Ah, but all is not well with our schools. Look how our educational system is failing us!' There is a hush. 'Things must be improved, and will be.' But the remainder is drowned in truly thunderous applause.

Admittedly that applause does reflect just a little of reality. Something or other is failing us most certainly. And people are genuinely worried. You only have to look about you. What does everyone see? What does everyone read in the *Daily Expletive*, the *Pseudo-Sunshine*, the *News of the Unworthy*? What constantly affront us almost each evening on our television screens? Children out of control! Children apparently leaving school unable to – I simply do *not* believe it – read or write!

Children, and it appears to follow quite logically, are very badly served by our teachers.

Yes, a certain percentage of children are out of control. Statistics for appearances in juvenile courts prove that, if nothing else. So what are the percentages for incompetent teachers, you ask. Incidentally some headmasters and headmistresses aren't all that great either, you add. Ah, where are the statistics? There aren't any? Really? Why? It's so difficult to categorise incompetence. Ah, I see! Oh, I've just noticed some scraps of paper that someone has unearthed by accident concerning teachers though. Ah! What are they? Oh, just figures for early retirement, mental breakdowns, and injury suffered in classrooms. Teachers or pupils? Don't be silly. Mind you, all these figures seem to show a sharp increase. Extraordinary! Come to think of it, in my day, you know, it was actually the *kids* who wanted early retirement, who had mental breakdowns and suffered injury. My God! Do you remember old Slasher Johnston? If someone so much as coughed more than twice... whereas these days they openly break wind then turn to the remainder of the class to ask whether it was juicy enough. But then that's progressive education for you, isn't it? No discipline, you see.

True! In this day and age nobody, neither parent nor politician, dares form the word 'discipline' with their lips openly, for fear of some crusading soul taking them to the European Court of Justice – and that at its bare mention at that. So they are on safer ground to mouth 'religious teaching'. That may stick for a short time until it has to be retracted again because of the fury of atheists who will have none of it. In its place comes 'moral teaching'. But who teaches morals? Immediately there are shuffling noises and a group of priests, mullahs, pastors and rabbis come forward; sometimes even bishops, ayatollahs, moderators, chief rabbis, archbishops and cardinals step out of the closet and declare themselves. 'We teach morals,' they chorus. And with true piety and forgiveness they allow a few humanist philosophers to join them into the bargain. All get short shrift, of course. There are coarse expletives and shouts of, 'Do me a favour!' Then come verbal blasts about being completely out of touch with young people. Leading writers, or sometimes competent journalists from the broadest of broadsheets, will ask decorously, 'How can you old windbags possibly claim to have any influence on the spiritual life of the nation?' To counter this charge (and no doubt very soon in the near future), we will see such taunts actually galvanising a string of clerics to attend rock concerts and rave meetings. White of face, yet still wearing a mechanical smile, they may even jerk their heads to the beat of what passes for music, though in truth of course it will be involuntary. It will just be unnerved reaction to the level of decibels pumped out by huge loudspeakers and the intensity of the drums and flashing lights in their faces.

Not content with pointing spiteful and ill-informed criticism on teachers and clerics, our politicians will then turn their attention to the police. Soaring crime rates among teenagers can always be blamed on excessive internal administration among mere constables and lack of time actually spent on the beat. Alternatively, they can be blamed on sheer incompetence, or lack of imaginative organisation by chief constables. As with teacher bashing, once again the general public will give a standing ovation to anyone engaged in bobby bashing. They are, after all, genuinely shocked by rising crime rates, particularly among the young. They see in their newspapers endless reports of the young deliberately choosing to attack the least able of citizens to defend themselves, that is, the very old and the incapacitated. They see distressing cases of pensioners, many of them survivors from the Second World War, who went through hell and back to keep freedom and justice alive for these very children, being knocked to the ground and their money stolen – worse, being derided for their frailty. We hear of young boys and sometimes even young girls committing murder of the old and frail. More shocking still, we hear of the murder of members of their own peer group, even younger children!

Decent members of society view all this with bewilderment – bewilderment no different to that revealed while viewing the tragedy shown on their screens in former Yugoslavia. Again and again comes the whispered question, 'Why?'

Beyond a failing educational system, lack of religious and moral teaching, the word 'deprivation' inevitably gets an airing. Desperate as they are for answers, everyone pounces on it. Yes, yes of course! 'Deprivation'! Marvellous word! It's all the fault of an all-too-wide difference in monetary rewards. Why should a garbage collector doing truly essential work get a pittance while dealers on the stock market, who are no more than gentlemen gamblers, make fortunes weekly? Then there's the baneful influence of the class system, and the unearned status given so many fools and charlatans. All these items are trotted out. But if 'deprivation' is a serious contender, how does this explain the fact that crimes of 'mugging' are just as prevalent among (as opposed to 'of') the very rich as the very poor? Here mugging committed by the rich on the not-so-rich is admittedly done without physical hurt; but it certainly involves mental hurt. The upper-class muggers who go to their city office each day dressed in Savile Row's finest should, out of mere respect for the profession they pursue, be wearing jeans, sweaters and balaclavas pulled down over their faces. However, when committing barefaced mugging I suppose it becomes a point of honour to remain barefaced. Certainly, fraud in the banking industry, and commerce generally, has now reached epic proportions. Worse, it is committed by those who society knows to be already rich by any normal standard. Faced with such outrageous behaviour, how can one possibly use the excuse 'deprivation'? The word is just about as applicable as the term 'fun-loving' to a sex-crazed, genitalia-flaunting baboon. Why does everyone therefore suppose that antisocial behaviour is the preserve of the so-called 'lower classes'? Could it be because the amounts of money involved are so astronomical that nobody can quite believe that such barefaced mugging can happen? Peter Clowes, at one time head of Barlow Clowes Investments (yes, investments – it's not a misprint), was charged and convicted of fraud and theft involving over one hundred and thirteen million pounds! That was mere petty cash compared with (currently) unnamed Pakistani businessmen who were involved in the recent collapse of an entire bank, the so-called BCCI scandal. And almost weekly there are reports of fraud, though admittedly involving just a few million pounds, by already very wealthy accountants, banking officials and company directors. Fraud nevertheless. So in heaven's name, why? Why is the City so riddled with corruption that endless government edicts, and every effort by the Serious Fraud Office, have all failed to make serious inroads into the matter? The Robert Maxwells and the Peter Clowes of this world, despite every effort to rid ourselves of them, are still very much alive. Indeed, people in this mould are still kicking the financial ball about with as much gusto as ever. Thus the question of class clearly has damned all to do with it – the lowest classes merely appear to contribute more to mugging or shoplifting because, percentage-wise, they form a larger mass of population. Conversely the rich merely appear to contribute less because, as already noted, they make it a point of honour not to wear balaclavas. So what can we make of it all? Surely for both groups, such behaviour has to do with personal attitudes to life and inborn degrees of sensitivity?

Shall we look at this in greater depth. If a person just happens to be born with a complete lack of sensitivity as to the very existence, let alone welfare, of other people (as is clearly the case with those cast in the mould of a Maxwell or Clowes), then their cerebral functions, as donated by genetic inheritance, simply make them that way. In some instances they should be pitied rather than vilified! Does this statement promote a fit of fury or astonishment? Does it suggest that I wish to present saintly credentials while attempting to absolve all forms of criminal activity, and do so simply by using the all-too-ready excuse of cerebral malfunction? And does it further suggest that such malfunction involves either genetic inheritance or perhaps unfortunate mutation coming from natural radiation or man-made sources? Then no doubt you will be further infuriated by an answer which partly admits this and partly repudiates it. Put it this way: do we blame someone for having a deformed leg or a withered arm? Since these are external and easily noticed we give people with such disabilities our sympathy and support. Unfortunately though in this day and age it may be necessary to qualify this and say that sympathy is the reaction expected of decent and caring people. Yet for those same caring people, internal and invisible abnormalities within the brain which cause milder forms of cerebral dysfunctions – as distinct from severe and very obvious ones – seem to inhabit a different category. For the most part, these are treated quite differently; certainly without much sympathy. People require the mentally unbalanced to wear an armband or some other identification tab of their hidden deficiencies before they are prepared to advance the smallest measure of concern and consideration.

So does this mean we are being absurdly inconsistent in all this? Does it sound perverse to say that in many ways we are, but in others we are not. No doubt some will think that it is perversity personified. Yet there is no inconsistency here. It is one of those mysterious things we often come across in life; it is called a paradox. You need an explanation? Well, to begin with we have boundless admiration for those who are able to rise above their disabilities. This tends to make us less sympathetic to those who cannot. In this we tend to forget that it is often possible to rise above a purely physical handicap, whereas it is almost impossible with one that is cerebral. We tend to forget too that even with physical abnormalities, the gifts of determination and fortitude are not shared out equally across the board. Some happen to be gifted; others are not. And for the latter there are so often quite unseen and unsuspected extenuating circumstances. Even so, the bulk of human society still tends to eulogise one type and denigrate the other. You wish me to give examples? Very well. And I shall do so necessarily with physical handicaps. Moreover I will do so with better known heroes and (apparent) villains so that the merits or demerits of each are obvious. This avoids useless debate as to their degree of achievement, or lack of it. Do I make a sound choice when, after pulling several names out of a hat, I begin with the wartime flying ace Douglas Bader? Do you agree he gained universal admiration and praise for his astonishing record of courage and audacity? For those who are rather young and have their admiration quotient severely limited to pop hooligans and highly aggressive sportsmen, it may be necessary to add a little more information. Bader lost both legs in an early flying accident. Nevertheless, he overcame this disability after years of painful effort. And he did so to such an extent that he passed as fit for flying duties. Subsequently he flew Spitfires during the most desperate of times during the Second World War. What is more, his squadron scored many victories. Even when he was shot down over France and made a prisoner of war, he gave his German guards endless trouble through his attempts to escape. His entire life exemplified the triumph of sheer tenacity and buoyancy of spirit under the very worst of circumstances. Shall we now take a very different case. Kaiser Wilhelm, with his withered arm, is to this day detested by most Europeans – not excluding many Germans themselves. He is seen in a discreditable light for having allowed his boyhood feelings of inferiority to influence his political and moral judgements in later life. Nor can we forget that he did so, materially at least, in the very best of circumstances. But are we being fair? His puppet existence, and the pressures exerted on him by the procreative talents of his subjects have, I would now hope, been fully explored. He was not in control of events, no matter how powerful his position may have seemed outwardly. Over and above this he was surrounded by a fawning royal court;

worse, in the early part of manhood at least, by equally sycophantic military commanders. Would any of us in his place, and with such impaired judgement, have avoided such a fate? Yet we cannot help but enthuse over Bader's example and think badly of Wilhelm. We are, after all, only human. Other examples may suffer our partiality in much the same way. Which then brings us to the difficult question of recognising extenuating circumstances – and doing so in all manner of crimes! More difficult still is the further matter of appropriate punishment.

Kaiser Wilhelm, as far as I am aware, did not kill anyone by his own hand. Nevertheless he is implicated to a greater or lesser degree in the deaths of millions. Bader probably did kill by his own hand, though the evidence is circumstantial. Combat in the air is after all notoriously hard to follow through with certainty, and a proportion of pilots bale out or survive after crash-landing. Nevertheless it would be fair to say that Bader attempted to, and probably did, kill a number of unknown Germans. He was convinced it was his duty; he was also fortified by the knowledge that the German cause was evil. Yet the mental acrobatics we perform so efficiently to dismiss all our normal (peace-time) attitudes to killing and see Bader as a hero and Wilhelm as a villain are considerable, all the more so if we believe passionately in the commandment 'Thou shalt not kill'! Nevertheless we accomplish such a feat with ease. Indeed we would condemn as perverse or mentally unstable anyone who was unable to do likewise, and in this instance I believe justly so.

But these are exceptional cases. What of the more common criminal acts carried out during periods of peace? These involve not just one's fellow nationals, but in many cases members of the same social class or even neighbours. What of those who murder, rob or defraud, in an effort to appease the demands of a formidable and totally insensitive ego...?

Here, let me say immediately that despite what may have appeared as many hints to the contrary, I happen to believe that people who take away other people's lives or subject them to deep trauma must themselves either forfeit their own lives or, alternatively, lose their liberty for a very long time. Surprised? Does this seem out of keeping with much of my preceding utterances? Well, to be honest I sometimes find it difficult to square this with myself, having as I do a basic conviction that 'to know all, is to forgive all'. Yet some crimes are so extreme that even if we knew all the circumstances, it would take super-human understanding to forgive everything. Some crimes simply demand capital punishment. However, it is the concept of 'punishment' which is mistaken.

Let me say immediately that this word has no real meaning in my vocabulary. For that matter, sheer vindictiveness or revenge have no place in my stance either. Nor do I support the view that the death sentence and long prison terms act as deterrents. I take such a stance solely in that the ultimate penalty is a crude but very effective *preventative* measure. I am exercised by the thought of criminals repeating their crimes. This and this alone is the only cogent reason for such a belief. I am convinced that we have a duty to protect society. Thus if I must choose between the life of a serial killer and that of a future victim (or the injury or death of a member of prison staff, during rioting or attempted escape), then the choice is obvious. One cannot risk the lives of those who, like prison warders, do this unpleasant work for us. It is after all a considerable degree of risk and over a prolonged period of time. In some cases it is perhaps twenty to thirty years! Nor, for that matter, in the event of a killer's escape, can we risk attacks on unprepared and defenceless members of the public. When the risk is substantial then I believe the life of such a criminal must be forfeited. It simply isn't good enough for the remainder of society to blot out mentally the possibilities of escape, then allow members of the prison service or the police to take such daily risks on our behalf. Those who think otherwise are hypocrites, unless they are prepared to volunteer for such service themselves. The safety of the innocent must override all other considerations. Such a viewpoint (and such admittedly crude preventative methods) is of course based on the belief that there are rarely any cures in the cases of truly vicious prisoners. This is said in the knowledge that only a very tiny minority of criminals ever realise the true extent of their guilt. They are, in other words, incapable of reform. Cerebral malfunctions will guarantee that they remain at all times a danger.

Of course, like many more, I have reservations about supporting the death penalty because as it has been proved, mistakes have been made. That an innocent person should suffer the extreme penalty is unforgivable. This said, there are however some instances where guilt is beyond question. There are cases where a murderer is caught red-handed, and the act of killing is clearly predetermined. It is in this small minority of cases that the death sentence should apply. It should go without saying, however, that it should *not* apply where the evidence is in any way uncertain. Long prison sentences should be looked at in exactly the same way. It is not a matter of revenge; there must be safe methods to protect society at large from further hurt.

Anyone who has studied patterns of criminal behaviour for some time will realise that individuals who deliberately plan criminal acts have either lost or probably never had the ability to overcome the tyranny of 'self'. Their lives are heightened illustrations (or perhaps one could call them infamous sagas) of complete domination by the ego. For such individuals, other people exist almost as fantasy beings. At best they are seen as mere 'accessories'. They become no more than rather tiresome objects to be categorised crudely as either of help or of hindrance; they are just so many depersonalised 'things' that must be used or swept out of one's way in the pursuit of extravagant needs or desires. And the achievement of such needs and desires is always paramount. Always there is an utter fixation with 'self'. It blocks out all other considerations. It is impossible for such people to step back mentally a pace, as it were, to see the destructive nature of their unrestrained self-interest.

Since I have used the word 'sensitivity' it may be necessary to define it further. In direct contrast to unrestrained egoism, such a word means the ability to be (to a greater or less degree) conscious of the outer world beyond the self. It entails being truly alive to the reality of the pluralism and uniqueness of other life forms. And those other life forms will have, as an unavoidable result of their total individuality, needs and desires of their own. Thus when the life form happens to be one of the species of 'higher' animals with heightened awareness, or indeed another human being, then our response must be doubly sensitised. In the latter case it may be possible that this individual has needs and desires that may complement or run parallel to one's own; equally it may disagree with, or ever become violently opposed to one's own. Nevertheless, one has to respect that position, despite discomfort or very real anguish.

Sensitivity, thus defined, gives us in itself an overall sense of morality. But unfortunately it is something that cannot be developed or taught. The facility for this kind of cerebral activity is either gifted at birth or wholly absent. Its later achievement is impossible if it fails to be there in the first instance.

Now many will express indignant and vociferous denial of this. Many will claim to know individuals who have successfully reformed themselves. And I do not doubt such claims. But this, once again, is an attempt to prove that the exception invalidates the generality. You might as well tell me that not all people who go blind remain blind for life. You might insist that you personally know someone who has recovered their sight even without medical intervention. Who would be foolish enough to deny such a possibility? However, it would be equally foolish not to include the following proviso: the basic elements of vision still remain. I do not doubt that some very unusual eye conditions can make a natural recovery. Similarly an eye surgeon can, in a very small proportion of cases, perform intricate operations to recover loss of sight. But it can only be done if certain basic 'assets' are there in the first place – the optic nerve being the irreducible essential. If this is not present, or has been destroyed, then nothing can be done. And I trust you can understand what I mean when it applies to the broader issue. There will always be a small number of criminals who appear to have a 'road to Damascus' conversion. However these will always prove to be the result of a reactivation of cerebral functions *already present*, not a miraculous creation of something wholly new. And any number of quite commonplace factors could be involved in such reactivation: firstly, if cerebral functions are disrupted by chemical imbalances these can be remedied by accidental or deliberate treatment; secondly, actual physical injury to the brain as the result of a fall, for example, may wholly rectify itself over a period of years; thirdly, there may be successful withdrawal from drink or drug abuse; fourthly, there may be the successful removal of a tumour using the skills of neurosurgeons. These and many more will account for such conversions. However, all of these unfortunately form a tiny proportion among those who repeatedly reoffend. Figures issued by the Home Office in Britain and similar departments in Europe and America are more than adequate comment in this respect. That society should therefore, and despite such knowledge, expect our schools (for pity's sake!) to make some contribution to instilling a moral code is not just wishful thinking – it is a dangerous delusion.

Having returned by what seems a circuitous route to the matter of education in general, can we now ask what society's other expectations of education actually are?

Providing a moral framework for children to build on is by no means the only delusion exhibited by parents and society generally. So what are these additional deluded expectations? Perhaps the simplest and least complicated of all is that children will eventually become well adjusted, contented and responsible individuals on leaving school. Briefly then, schools should just turn out 'good citizens' – this and nothing more. So what qualities would this entail? For most people, sensitivity to others would be the very first requirement. And there can be no doubt that this is an admirable quality. But, to repeat, this is a God-given gift. It is not something that can be taught. Moreover, even when present, it is never equitably distributed. Some have been given generous quantities, some more limited. Some seem to lose out altogether.

So much for sensitivity then. Can we move on? What other expectations are there? Immediately comes a host of alternating and often confused suggestions. Parents who are themselves unable to read or write, and cannot add or subtract without the use of the fingers on both hands, demand that their children become at the very least both literate and numerate on leaving school, although they have only the vaguest idea what these terms mean. They hear these words on the lips of other parents, and, being human (and just in case they are missing out on anything), they demand such attainments too. Beyond this basic expertise, they expect their child to be proficient in other 'streetwise' practicalities, if one can call it that. Among these is 'geography', meaning that their offspring can point with a finger to the approximate position of, say, London, on a map; alternatively, if they are not Londoners, point to their own home town or city, plus the usual venues for the more important of football matches. Parents make these absurd demands because at some time previously, they have no doubt been alternately amused then mortified to find the child's finger wandering hesitatingly over the Outer Hebrides while attempting to find London. Secretly too, as Londoners, and supposedly therefore at the centre of the universe, they may have afforded themselves considerable grief by entertaining a desire to visit Liverpool. This, they vaguely suppose, is a port somewhere to the west, moreover they confidently believe that this city has produced the most towering of musical geniuses this world has ever seen. To do so, they have, with equal confidence, mounted a train going to the West Country – ultimate destination, Penzance!

Then again, at the other end of the scale you have indignant parents who demand that their child show proficiency in the use of calculus, which they claim (lying) was their own achievement at the age of twelve. Expectations are as low or as extreme as the often unrealisable aspirations of both miracle-seeking and status-seeking parents. Indeed the entire exercise becomes confused and even meaningless the further one delves into it.

So then, why not ask teachers themselves what qualities they would wish to see amongst their pupils? Further, why not ask them what, in an ideal world, they would subsequently wish for if they had the opportunity to enhance such qualities in reasonably agreeable surroundings and reasonably well-funded educational programmes.

At once one finds that the answers concentrate on a surprisingly small number of basic requirements; what is more, all teachers reach unanimous agreement! First and foremost, all look for and highly value in any child an in-built and quite natural curiosity. Essentially this is a wide-ranging curiosity that embraces creation in general. What is meant by that? Well, such a child does not concentrate on trivial phenomena such as the regular appearance of snot on the end of a neighbour's nose. It does not endlessly debate whether the bulge in Hubert's pocket represents a packet of sweets, cigarettes or an unusually precocious sexual development. A wide-ranging curiosity, then, in its more valuable and open-ended sense. Oddly though, this is assumed to be an inherent gift donated to all children! It is the very birthright of children, so we are told, to 'be curious'. Yet this too is a myth. If only it were true! Teaching would overnight become, as they say, a 'mere dawdle'! Incidentally too, a natural curiosity in itself tends to diminish the stranglehold of the ego and gives the individual a more realistic picture of his or her relative unimportance in the scheme of things. But a sharp and penetrating curiosity is, like many other qualities, just a gift that is unfairly shared. It is present in ample proportions amongst some, rather sparingly given to others, and wholly absent in a not unsubstantial minority.

Can we move on? What other qualities do teachers value? After this initial gift of curiosity comes the ability to concentrate the mind. Let us be more specific here. It is the ability to concentrate on single issues to achieve a set purpose. But equally, of course, it should include the facility to resist total fixation with any. However, once again this seems to be an inherent gift and not something that can be taught or superimposed in any way. Some children can concentrate without difficulty, some have rather a struggle and are easily distracted and some are wholly deficient and move into a dream world of their own – after about two seconds flat! For a teacher looking into a sea of faces, ranging anywhere from twenty to thirty, it is not easy to pick out those who 'are away with it'. It is almost impossible to study each face and at the same time concentrate on one's own delivery of what is hoped to be an interesting and lively lesson.

Beyond the ability to concentrate, there is also the question of attention span, which is not quite the same thing. For example, an intelligent twelve-year-old being taught elementary science may suffer considerable trauma on being told a piece of stone is not quite the inanimate object it was thought to be. Not only is it composed of vibrating molecules which vary the speed of vibration according to temperature, but the molecules themselves are composed of atoms whose inner particles are far from stationary! These particles or 'electrons' are arranged in 'shells' revolving round a nucleus at fantastic speeds and in a variety of different paths. This depends not just on the kind of atoms they are, but incidentally on whether they happen to be in the upper part of the periodic table, and also radioactive into the bargain!

Now an intelligent pupil may concentrate avidly on this information, indeed so much so that he or she may be shocked to the very core. This pupil will realise for the very first time that it is really nonsense to talk of animate or inanimate things. The significance of this may become so profound that it causes loss of attention on further parts of the lesson. Unhappily though, some pupils may be diverted to think up unkind remarks concerning less intelligent class members. They may dwell on the inanimate composition of a detested fellow pupil's grey matter, and in doing so will fail to hear even more traumatic information. Concentration has now overridden the attention span to such an extent that the pupil fails to hear that the atoms found in a pebble or a piece of stone are no different whatsoever to those making up the molecules of living things! Among living things are humans themselves. Therefore the atoms in a stone are no different from those in you or me!

Now perhaps only two or three pupils in an entire class will have balanced their concentration with attention span. Maybe one of these will be sufficiently moved to mutter, 'Merciful heavens!', or words to that effect. You see this information is just as significant as that previous to it, yet many of the class will miss it! A somewhat partisan concentration has allowed some information to penetrate and be absorbed, but over-concentration on it has interfered with the absorption of the remainder. Indeed it will have prevented this further revelation. And it is truly traumatic to find our bodies are composed mainly of carbon, oxygen, hydrogen and nitrogen with tiny traces of iron, phosphorus and magnesium thrown in! To any young person successfully absorbing all this information for the very first time, the implications are truly staggering. Here is demonstrated the unity of all creation. Here a tiny opening has been made for a pupil to observe and wonder at the mysterious nature of atomic and subatomic particles. Here is the path that may lead some pupils to grapple at some later stage with a scientist's concept of unity and possibly the belief in a Superior Being of infinite subtlety. But how many pupils have to be physically helped out of the classroom after such a lesson? How many will have been so traumatised as to be incapable of speech or normal locomotion? All too few. The vast majority will take such information on board with pursed lips and a sniff – full trauma is reserved only for trivia. Schools are not seen as places where awe-inspiring information may be gained. This comes only in the playground; for instance when some filthy-tongued, lewd-gesturing, lead singer in some God-awful rock band has given the drummer a black eye, kicked the manager in the groin and run off in some kind of tantrum. Only then do young people become traumatised. Some even briefly consider suicide! How can they continue life without constantly seeing and hearing such an exalted being? And these are the reactions of the reasonably intelligent! What of those who have not been so gifted, and are classed as having 'learning difficulties'?

Here the ability to concentrate is very restricted indeed. The attention span is equally low. If, as in some schools, pupils are not streamed according to aptitude, then brighter ones begin making very coarse remarks concerning the not so bright. Young people generally are, as you may have noticed, notoriously cruel and unforgiving of each other's disabilities. Remarks will be made with suppressed giggles. It will be suggested that so and so has an attention span comparable to that of the life of a K-meson, which physicists calculate at one ten-billionth of a second or thereabouts. But given such lack of attention span, then what can any teacher reasonably do in such circumstances? The general public and their elected political figures, having little sympathy and less knowledge of the realities of classroom life, merely assume that teachers are incompetent. They turn on the entire profession, use insulting language and call for wholesale sackings. Reacting to this, teachers, out of a sense of injustice and sheer frustration, may attempt to explain their difficulties. And in doing so they may be incautious enough to mention the problem of attention span. Worse, they might be doubly incautious perhaps to repeat their pupil's jibe concerning the K-meson. At this point some aggressive politician may well consult an encyclopaedia for data concerning the more exotic of nuclear physicists' findings. Here he might find something suitable, and subsequently berate teachers with the waspish comment that if the attention span of a pupil can be compared to a K-meson, then this is far longer than the time involved in the interaction of a pi-meson and proton (a trillionth time as long, in fact!). Therefore, why don't teachers just get on with some similar 'interacting' and stop this perpetual moaning, groaning and protesting! Teachers in turn, should they be sufficiently daring, might then well ask what one does with fourteen-year-old Elvis Hasem who has an attention span lasting an entire morning, though unfortunately directed solely at the cleavage and upper thighs of nubile Susy Lovesit – a pupil ordered to stand almost daily in a corner for insolence? These are the realities of daily life within our educational system, and of which most people are wholly ignorant.

But beyond concentration and attention span, there are other qualities teachers value. These are good co-ordination between hand and eye, a reasonable memory, reasonable patience (for the young, difficult indeed!), a lively imagination... the list can be extensive. Yet ask yourself in all honesty whether such things can be taught, or whether they are, in fact, gifts that are either present or absent in varying degree.

The overall conclusion that any fair-minded person must come to is that our educational programme is failing us not because of the quality and expertise of the teachers, but because of the falling quality and intelligence of those who are taught! The fault then, if one may be allowed to soliloquise for a moment, 'lies not within ourselves, nor within our children, but within our genes'.

So how does one go about improving genetic material? The answer, would you believe it, is summed up in one word: 'eugenics'.

*

There – the dreaded word you have long suspected me of concealing (perhaps even lacking the courage to mouth openly) has at last been uttered. And what a foul word it is – or at least appears to be – when linked with so many ghastly associations in both recent and ancient history.

Foremost amongst these, of course, comes that most horrific of episodes in our own century that will forever be associated with Nazi Germany. The name Adolf Hitler is instantly and indissolubly linked with this very special kind of infamy; it should however also include another, Heinrich Himmler. It was the latter who as Reichsführer SS may have either suggested the policy, or, if it was Hitler's alone, eagerly supported it and was certainly its principal executor.

It comes as something of a shock to most people to find that so-called 'eugenic' policies were not by any means confined to the Nazis. They emerge from time to time right down the echoing corridor of history. For example, even in this century and before Hitler came to power, a little-known programme was being carried out by doctors working in mental hospitals in the United States during the 1930s! And these two instances alone are enough to 'queer the pitch', as they say.

What must be made clear immediately however is that both Nazi and American doctors began initially by totally misunderstanding the basic principles of genetics. Having done so, they then amplified these errors by applying them to eugenics. This in turn twisted the purely semantic definition of eugenics – found in any dictionary, and in all innocence described as the scientific improvement of a race – into something wholly evil. Thus any individual in public life and with a reputation worth guarding, whenever confronted by this word, rears up like a frightened racehorse and gallops off in the opposite direction. Nobody, but nobody, is prepared to mouth the word or to investigate the subject in any depth. Is it of any surprise that the matter has remained in limbo for half a century? Are you in any way disconcerted to find that nobody is prepared to root out facts and determine whether the fearsome aura is warranted or not? Well I am, and to make matters more pointed still, I am prepared to do something about it.

To begin with, shall we immediately dive in at the deep end and take a closer look at Adolf Hitler's understanding of the word? In doing so, it is also necessary to examine the interpretation of the more shadowy Heinrich Himmler standing behind him.

In this quest once again Albert Speer's observations give us an intimate picture rarely found in other sources. Fortunately it was Speer's habit to jot down scraps of conversation that came from the lips of the man he revered during those early days. Even in the last years, when that reverence was diminishing and hostility was taking its place, the jottings continued. However, the following is taken from happier times, that is several years before the outbreak of war and when Hitler was in an expansive mood. Oddly it shows that the ruler of Germany had a certain intuitive grasp of genetic inheritance (if unconscious) which, as we will see later, opens up a gap between himself and Himmler.

Speer was sitting with the Führer and a handful of cronies in a very relaxed and intimate atmosphere. They were talking of women, marriage and children, when the following was uttered by Hitler:

> A highly intelligent man [meaning especially himself] should take a primitive and stupid woman. Imagine if, on top of everything else, I had a woman who interfered with my work. In my leisure time I want to have peace of mind... I could never marry. Think of the problems if I had children! In the end they would try to make my son my successor. Besides the chances are slim for someone like me to have a capable son. That's how it always goes in such cases. Consider Goethe's son – a completely worthless person.

This is an astonishing insight into the Führer's attitude. His mistress Eva Braun was, true to his words (and Speer's judgement), a somewhat empty-headed, quiet and what is called a rather 'mousy' person. She never attempted to meddle in Hitler's work or 'destiny' as he often grandly called it. In having an undemanding and undemonstrative partner, Hitler followed the pattern of many artists, poets, musicians and creative people generally. Putting the bulk of one's time and energy into one's work becomes difficult or impossible with a demanding or headstrong woman. Then again, an intellectually brilliant woman can make a hypersensitive man very uneasy. Poor Eva Braun was neither. And she certainly had to be content with very little. There is no evidence either that she ever became pregnant by her lord and master. There is much speculation as to whether or not Hitler was capable of fathering a child anyway; probably the truth of the matter will never be known. He may have been impotent or contracted a venereal disease, this either while on army service or during his early days as an amateur artist in Vienna. Speculation can cover a far wider variety of possibilities than this. It doesn't get us anywhere, however. There might be a clue in the above passage in that there is a certain feeling of contempt for women in general running through it. This may have stemmed from an unfortunate incident in his youth. But in respect of our thesis what is even more revealing is his grasp of the complexity and the uncertainty attending genetic inheritance. He illustrates it succinctly when mentioning Goethe's son. Again it is an intuitive grasp; Hitler was not given to studying the scientific basis of anything, least of all inheritance. At that time too, genetics was still an infant science and the complexity of inheritance was still only partly realised. Yet the Führer accepts that as in the case of Goethe's son, having a genius for a father in no way guarantees exceptional gifts passed down the line.

Moving on from Hitler's concept and thoughts of genetic inheritance generally, it must be said that even when both father and mother are ranked as geniuses, the guarantee is absent here also. All one can say is that statistically the chances are good – no more than that. And significantly enough it works in reverse order, of course; having witless or semi-imbecile parents does not guarantee that the offspring will be mirror images either. It is just possible that they may produce a genius, though once more, statistically speaking, this is highly improbable. They will tend to produce offspring as feeble-witted as themselves, or at best a marginal improvement.

In this respect it is astonishing to find that Hitler's intuition also stood him in good stead when it came to Heinrich Himmler's concept of racial inheritance. The Führer failed to see eye to eye with much of his SS leader's outlook. He did so to such an extent that he even made fun of him behind his back. Despite Goering having been named officially as the Reich's deputy leader, everyone knew and accepted (not excluding Hitler himself) that Himmler was in fact the second most powerful man in Germany. Speer was understandably astounded when, among his cronies at least, Hitler could undermine this *éminence grise* in quite a cutting way. The following is an example of his caustic approach to Himmler's mythologising of the part played by genetic inheritance in the German race and the SS in particular. To further his aims Himmler had organised teams of archaeologists to uncover as much as possible of Germany's ancient past. Exhibitions were being staged around the Reich of a wide range of objects uncovered, and with a degree of veneration that Hitler found ridiculous. Himmler also attempted to achieve a mystical relationship with the past in the most curious of ways, by establishing links with his body of SS storm troopers. This prompted Hitler to comment:

> What nonsense! Here we have at last reached an age that has left all mysticism behind it, and now he [Himmler] wants to start it all over again. We might just as well have stayed with the Church [Hitler was baptised a Roman Catholic]. At least it had tradition! To think that some day I might be turned into an SS saint! Can you imagine it. I would turn in my grave...

Speer did not venerate Heinrich Himmler. Hence we are denied similar fascinating glimpses into the mind and attitudes of a man who made most people's flesh creep. Beyond a few remarks here and there, including incidentally an account of one very disturbing private visit that Himmler made Speer (later described in detail) we have no commentary. There are few commentaries from any source, in fact.

Always fearful of an army coup, Adolf Hitler, on taking supreme power in Germany, had given Himmler a directive to build up an independent army. As already noted it was to be wholly answerable and loyal only to the Nazi leadership; it was most certainly to be outside any form of control by the High Command of the regular army. It became in time a state within a state. Contrary to common belief, it comprised two distinct units: the first was a body of spiritual psychopaths who composed the staff of the early concentration camps, then later staffed the specially designed extermination units; the second was made up of quite normal men forming an efficient fighting force with the most up-to-date weapons and equipment including state-of-the-art tanks and artillery. Perhaps more importantly still, they were encouraged to build up a remarkable *esprit de corps*, which later gave them a reputation for unusual efficiency and punch on the battlefield.

It was this second branch of the SS that Himmler attempted to mythologise as representing the finest inheritance from the past. It fitted his overall purpose: the Third Reich was to become in both his and Hitler's dream world the cradle of a new civilisation in which 'pure-bred', white-skinned Aryan or Teutonic people would eventually inherit the entire planet. Himmler had a particular penchant for tall, blue-eyed blonds, so-called Nordic types. Perhaps subconsciously he was aware of his own unfortunate physical appearance in this respect! These fine physical characteristics he contrasted sharply with non-Aryan people whom he believed were wholly inferior. He had also in this respect a hysterical detestation of Jews, gypsies, the insane and homosexuals: this may well have surpassed even that of the Führer's. His simplistic view of genetics embraced the conviction that if he encouraged his elite SS troops – who as already mentioned were almost hand-picked for their external characteristics – to 'have it off' with supposedly virtuous, and similarly blonde, blue-eyed Nordic maidens, then he would be blessed with legions of similar children. As for internal characteristics, more especially those controlled by the brain, his expectations were rather more vague. Being advised, this time by professional geneticists and psychologists (rather than pseudo-scientists and cranks), that these were more difficult to 'manufacture', he was forced to leave such things to chance and allow Nature to do as it would. He had no option anyway! Fifty years later, teams of geneticists and psychologists are still unable to predict which individual offspring from parents gifted with high intelligence will be similarly blessed! Statistical analysis is still the only guide. But Himmler at least entertained the fond hope that such children would grow up to click their heels, give the Nazi salute, and be ready to die for both him and the Führer, just like their parents. Unfortunately for him, and for those equally ignorant of the laws of genetics, even such a modest hope is by no means certain. Genetic inheritance is excessively complicated. It is particularly so where internal cerebral formation and the function or dysfunction of its myriad parts are concerned. And the ridiculous part of the entire idea is that even if he could have achieved what he wanted, it wouldn't have been much use to him! Admittedly, the male offspring would have tended in the main to be blue-eyed blonds, who one day would have grown up to be tall, blockheaded, semi-robotic do-or-die soldiers; and in this at least he may have had part of his wish fulfilled. Alternatively, if they were female, they would eventually (after a period of training and exposure to propaganda in their early teens by the Hitler Youth Organisation) have performed other vital functions: they would have become open-legged maidens, ready, willing and eager to produce yet more cannon fodder for the glorious Reich! But modern wars are not won by cannon fodder! They are won primarily by scientists and technicians allied with the skilled upper echelons of the military machine. Moreover, the latter must be able to use new weapons and new ideas most effectively – use them to horrific advantage! Fortunately though, or perhaps unfortunately, according to your individual viewpoint, scientists and technicians, working in combination with gifted and unconventional generals such as Guderian, Manstein and Rommel, cannot be produced so easily, certainly not to order. The irony of ironies for Hitler and Himmler was that their inverse eugenic 'solution' for Jews, gypsies, the insane and homosexuals – that of their wholesale murder – finally made certain that they would never win their European war. Hinging on failure in Europe came the further certainty that Hitler would never conquer the entire world. Why? It so happened that a proportion of German scientists were either fully Jewish or partly so. And even the latter were therefore 'tainted', as Hitler and Himmler judged, with mixed blood. Conscious of the deteriorating situation, many of those of such 'undesirable blood groups' saw the warning signs in the early 1930s and fled. Similarly in Italy. For example Enrico Fermi, as we have already noted, had a Jewish wife. Crucially then, if Einstein, Szilard and Teller had not been forced to leave Germany, subsequently finding new pastures in America, they would not have contacted Roosevelt. It is then conceivable that the project to produce the 'atomic bomb' would never have got under way as early as it did. That is not to suppose that the United States lacked first-rank scientists of its own – far from it. What is very probable is that the timing would have been seriously delayed. Einstein's signature on that letter, encapsulating as it did all of his worldwide prestige carried a conviction and a special sense of urgency. It may have carried less significance under any other name. Thus if the project had been delayed, Germany could then have had more time to assemble its 'pure' Aryan scientists. These, together with the quite massive resources necessary, would have won the 'atomic' race. To repeat once again: the outbreak of war need only have been delayed by two years. It would have been enough.

There is irony too in other matters concerning the overall efficiency of his military machine. That irony is to be found in the willingness of the vast majority of officers and men, both in the SS and the national army, to obey Hitler's orders, and to do so to the letter, no matter how mistaken they were in overall strategy or tactics. They did so for years, without any kind of serious protest. Hare-brained ventures were thus undertaken which spread the men and machines much too far and too thinly. These eventually cost the Führer dearly because he did not have highly trained men and high-grade machines in place where and when he most needed them. Having them tied down in Norway, North Africa and Greece is a classic example. In the last years of the war in particular, the lunatic order 'no retreat' made total capitulation inevitable. Had the German military as a whole used more of their own initiative and 'courage' in rather different directions, then the war might well have gone very differently. It may quite well have ended in stalemate, total exhaustion having overtaken all countries concerned!

So much then for Hitler and Himmler's understanding of genetics and its application to eugenics.

What now of the concept as embraced by medical staff in mental hospitals or clinics in the United States? Here a series of programmes was put in place by some (but not all) states to sterilise the mentally abnormal. The concept grew out of the conviction that children born of mentally handicapped parents would be equally handicapped. This in itself, as already noted, is not necessarily true; to repeat, the genetic lottery is such that there is actually just a faint possibility of producing genius. Certainly though, the statistical probability of handicap is very high. Thus it is unfair to demonise those doctors for their concern for the future. They had, after all, the not unrealistic vision of an intolerable burden being put on the state. They saw an ever increasing number of abnormal parents and children producing a chaotic situation within their health service – one which society at large, no matter how willing, would eventually be unable to support. To deny the mentally handicapped any children is however too harsh, and unacceptable. A sense of outrage would have been avoided if they had merely been limited to one or two. Then again comes the difficulty of defining 'abnormal' or 'insane'. True, there are extremes where no such difficulty exists, but in the continuum between the clearly insane and the supposedly sane, there are some very subtle shades of grey indeed. So where does one draw that dividing line?

Crude attempts to group these doctors in the same category as Nazi medical staff is nevertheless grossly unfair. The latter sent the insane to gas chambers or gave them lethal injections. Incidentally they also experimented on Russian prisoners of war to determine the point at which the human body can no longer survive in extremes of heat or cold, mimicking in effect the extreme battlefield conditions in North Africa and that of the Russian winter. In direct comparison the American experiment was motivated by concern for the overall health of society. This should surely set it apart from the Nazi programme, motivated as it was by sheer evil.

Despite this, the legacy of revulsion surrounding the Nazi episode in particular has left us with half a century of undiminished horror. As already observed, the very mention of the word 'eugenics' raises most people's emotions to levels bordering on hysteria. Thus any discussion attempting to divorce the emotional element is immediately suspect. It lays one open to the chance of being a crafty apologist, or worse, attempting to engage in a subtle exercise of rehabilitation.

This happens to be the greatest misfortune for us all. You see, we have two stark choices: we can ignore the trend now observable throughout the greater part of the world, which demonstrates on the one hand that the feckless and irresponsible tend to reproduce well above mere replacement level (while the caring and responsible barely reach it) or we can attempt to redress the balance. If we fail to, then the scenario for the world's future will involve far more terrible visitations by the Four Horsemen than have ever gone before. And it would be complacency of the most dangerous kind to suppose that Europe and North America would not be included.

Suppose then we act rationally and attempt to do something about it. What course do we take? Is the answer to encourage the caring and responsible members of society to have larger families? Can we study this carefully for a moment.

There are three main difficulties in this course of action. While it can be shown statistically that in life's genetic lottery 'good citizens' tend to produce children who also become true pillars of society, nevertheless they also inevitably produce a small proportion of children who are bitter 'disappointments'. True, one must again emphasise that they are a small proportion. But how do these compare with the reverse side of the coin, that is the accidental production of good citizens by the feckless and irresponsible? Remember, they too – this time by happy throw of the genetic dice – will produce 'recessive' surprises. Admittedly these are also in small proportion. But how do both of these 'recessive' characteristics balance out? Will they equal each other and therefore cancel out any advantage or disadvantage? Will they be unequal? If so, will they tip the balance marginally or significantly?

All this becomes somewhat academic however when one approaches the second difficulty. And this overrides all other considerations. From previous arguments it should now be obvious that all nations should be attempting to bring their population levels down, rather than contrive to put them up. This is particularly urgent for the rich and highly industrialised areas of the world where demand for a highly intelligent but small workforce is so pressing. Urgent too because the need by industry for a wide range of resources, many of which are imported from abroad, is proportionally so high. The latter factor in particular should cause us all concern. As many of the hitherto poor countries in the remainder of the world begin to develop their own industries, the demand for raw materials will become ever more intense. Competition for these resources will become nothing short of murderous in the near future. The recent Desert Storm episode alone should illustrate this! Thus, in these new conditions there will be a sharp levelling off downward rather than upward in the overall living standards of formerly rich countries. To maintain anything like their former affluence it will be urgently necessary to cut family size slightly below replacement level rather than increase it. Smaller populations, with less pressure in resources, is the only possible way to achieve stability and peace in the world.

The third and final factor concerns what everyone now refers to as 'green' issues. The pressure of human numbers all over the world is now exerting an influence on the ability of the vital cyclic rhythms to function unhindered – a function they have hitherto carried out so reliably for millions of years. This has been discussed earlier and does not require further comment. It is merely pertinent to remark that while caring and responsible citizens are normally sensitive to 'green' issues and always attempt to minimise their personal impact on the environment, nevertheless because of their sheer number they too produce irreducible pressures. These cannot be discounted. Inevitably they contribute to overall levels of pollution, and, despite every effort not to, they intrude into the habitat of other life forms thereby causing their destruction. With the ever continuing extinction of what were once well-established species of flora and fauna throughout the world, the final warning applies no less to the 'greens' in society: 'Ask not for whom the bell tolls; it tolls for thee.'

Having touched on the contribution of caring people to the coming crisis, what about the uncaring? How can one reduce their influence? By eugenic means? Is that feasible? Supposing for a moment that it is: what are the actual problems of attempting to apply eugenic principles to the feckless and irresponsible members of human society?

Immediately the assumption is that such principles apply only to those in the lowest of social classes. This is wholly false.

Previous comments on the Robert Maxwells and Peter Cloweses of this world should have already steered readers away from that particular pitfall. True, the thematic thread being followed at that particular point was concerned with criminal behaviour. However, don't you agree that 'upper-class' criminality is also closely linked with fecklessness and irresponsibility? The two go hand in hand. Any programme involving eugenics therefore applies to *all* classes. It applies equally to the very rich, not forgetting the comfortable middle classes; it is by no means confined to the poor. The social worth (or lack of worth) is the paramount quality looked for, not monetary worth. Those who acquire fortunes by dishonest means never fail to pamper their sexual needs. Their formidable love of self insists that they procreate indiscriminately and without restraint. They are thus just as undesirable in society as a common cat burglar or a pimp dispersing his genetic seed in a similar way. This should be understood at the very outset. At the same time though, and to underline an earlier observation, one must guard against the erroneous view that the insensitive, the irresponsible and the criminal will always produce offspring that are the mirror image of themselves. It must be emphasised repeatedly that the complexity involved in the constant reshuffling of the genetic playing cards – especially where cerebral characteristics are concerned – by no means guarantees such an outcome. Certainly there is a statistical probability; sometimes too this is reinforced by nurture. It is after all a sad fact that children of criminals may themselves become accessories to crime or its active participants. This is not because of their defective judgement but because of the baneful influence of one or both parents. And it has nothing to do with the class structure. Such a parent or parents may well be found listed in *Burke's Peerage*, may have a home in the stockbroker belt, may live on a luxury yacht moored in Cannes, or indeed any other permutation you may care to suggest. It is not a necessary condition of antisocial behaviour that one should live in squalor and have an address on a run-down suburban council estate or in an inner-city hovel.

But clearly the entire matter of determining which individual might be grouped as antisocial, and which individual might not, is fraught with difficulty. Initially these will centre first on detection and then on adequate proof. This alone may seem so formidable that most people will immediately decide that such a programme would be impossible to implement – at least in a truly democratic society. Are you surprised when I say I tend to agree with this view? So what do we do? Merely allow things to go on as usual? Can we remain complacent, carefully overlooking the fact that morality is declining sharply throughout Europe and North America, that crime permeates all sections of society, and that prisons are bursting at the seams? Must we continually look around us in astonishment and ask why? Why, despite the general level of affluence, despite our ever increased spending on social services, despite the safety nets preventing the worst of hardships, do criminal acts continue to rise? More worrying still, they have nothing whatsoever to do with deprivation or with social class!

Any society that remains complacent on such a central issue will surely deserve everything that will eventually come to it. Again comes the agonising question: what can we do? Set about a furious programme of prison building, alternatively devise a programme of early release and send all those unreformed prisoners back into society? The latter has already been attempted in several European countries, and also some of the states in the USA. Because of the high incidence of reoffending it is now causing outcry. Undoubtedly, the vast majority in society wish to see the first alternative implemented. But is this any sort of answer in the long run?

The problem seems baffling. But equally, can we continue to wallow in our complacency? Can we continue to allow criminal elements in society to produce offspring well above the replacement factor, while the decent and caring produce just two or three offspring at most?

Yet if a eugenic programme is too complex and difficult to administer, then surely there is another answer. What about considering as a last resort a simple population policy that advocates just two children per family across the board – this regardless of credentials in social wholesomeness or unwholesomeness. When you are, as they say, between a rock and a hard place, you must seek a very rapid sideways movement – if at all possible! If a criminal's procreative talents are restricted to just two children, then at the very least we have created what is commonly called a level playing field! At least his progeny are not constantly outnumbering those who are honest, hardworking and caring members of society.

Now no government on this planet has as yet put in place and then firmly kept to a population programme to any significant extent. There are always, however, exceptions to every rule. China is that one and highly important exception; but this will be discussed later. Western nations generally, for example, have supposed that there is little need. As they see it birth rates have been falling steadily. They remain unconcerned by the fact that largely through better health care and longevity the total population levels are still rising, if slowly. Eastern nations (bar China) still largely dominated by religious and cultural pressures, also lack the moral courage to do so. Both East and West therefore remain unconcerned by the elusive (and almost impossible to define) overall 'quality' of their citizens and the children they are producing. Once again, is it possible to continue to ignore this vital issue?

A population policy of two children per family across the board, when properly and firmly implemented, becomes in itself eugenic in its overall effect. This being so, how could such a policy be put in place, initially among democratic nations of the West and then, by the principle of leading by example, among the nations of the East?

Of course one can anticipate the howls of outrage coming from those who see what are called Basic Human Rights (set in suitably arrogated upper-case letters!) being brutally violated. Many will belong to religious sects. These take what they believe to be unquestionable authority from holy texts. All of these texts were however written in a time when infant mortality was extremely high, and life expectancy unusually low. It was a time when the Four Horsemen were extremely efficient and untiring as they galloped from continent to continent. Early historical records show that beyond the usual ravaging wars there were widespread plagues of great potency. Nor should we forget the less spectacular, and rather plodding (but equally lethal!), infectious diseases among children in general. Yet, in the twentieth century, when everyone insists on benefiting from disease control and therefore achieves a considerable measure of death control, you must balance it out; you must also adopt birth control into the bargain. You cannot have your cake and eat it. It's that simple. You have to choose between allowing the Four Horsemen unlimited access to your family and surrounding area, or alternatively drastically limit your family. You must do that no matter how desperately you yearn for the patter of tiny feet all around you. If you fail to do so, you are in effect about to murder either your own, or other people's, children. You cannot take a double-barrelled shotgun in an attempt to ward off the Four Horsemen, but you can and must take steady aim at the stork. This is the brutal reality of life.

Currently in Britain the record for the biggest family, to the best of my knowledge, is held by a Protestant cleric on the island of Skye in the Inner Hebrides. The present total is eighteen children, and on an assembly line of sorts manned by one woman – his wife! To achieve this feat considerable participation is of course required by many other members of Highland society. Although children are clearly the gift of God, and He has in this respect seen fit to provide this particular couple with superbly efficient reproductive apparatus, nevertheless the angels do not also deliver the very necessary Giro payments from heaven. These come from much lowlier places. Equally earthbound are the services of the district nurse, doctors and a variety of other social services. Sheer earth-bound necessity has also caused council workmen to knock three council houses into one so as to house this family, and make enlargements in the local school. It seems the angels had also overlooked the desirability of educational facilities, as indeed they had over other useful things. In fact further additions were found necessary at the local hospital, local shops, roads and road transport. Other facilities must be left an open question, for I have no further information on the subject.

Now suppose the majority of the inhabitants of Skye followed this example. Suppose all had families the size of a football team, plus a few dedicated supporters. Would the care and attention given by society to this one family once again be available to all? The mind boggles. The health service, to begin with, would need to train and assemble an army of midwives and doctors – all in indecent haste. At the same time new clinics and hospitals would need to be built, high-rise apartments furiously assembled, water and sewerage (especially!) laid... the list would be extremely large and varied. The peaceful island of Skye would very quickly transform itself into something more akin to the skyscraper character of Hong Kong. And who would be required to pay for all this? Not the islanders. Their tax-paying abilities, based as they are on crofting, are virtually non-existent. The burden would fall on the tax-paying population of Britain as a whole – that is supposing they were able and willing to do so. It presupposes also that they would religiously keep themselves in a responsible frame of mind by limiting their own families to just two. If they should fail to do so, then Nature's laws concerning population balance must sooner or later come into operation. A population crash and all the suffering associated with it would be inevitable not just on the island of Skye but throughout the entire British Isles.

That such distressing laws of Nature were actually set in place by the Creator might be questioned by some. No doubt some questioned this during the Irish famine in the previous century, questioned it again during the lesser known ones in the Outer Hebrides, and again in the Inner Hebrides (including Skye) and much of the Scottish Highlands at much the same time. But if you question whether the Creator formed this planet and the remainder of the universe as He did, moreover with similar wisdom set in motion all the laws of physics and of biology in the form we see and understand them today, then you inevitably bring into question whether He is actually omnipotent, omnipresent and omniscient. Quite a formidable exercise on your part! It is certainly more than I'm willing to undertake. To begin with I really can't think of any other range of possibilities. You see, if the Creator is wholly omnipotent, it is difficult to imagine what other agency could have been involved. Some of course may wonder who is in operational control of the Four Horsemen. They may posit the Devil if all else fails. And should they believe in such an agency, then they must also ask why an all-powerful God might allow so much of that power to slip through His fingers. It is not an inconsiderable loss of control, after all. To allow the Devil a very good chance of destroying all life on this planet without exception is quite something. And this prospect is very much closer than most people realise. It is a prospect moreover brought about by our own self-conceit, our overpowering love of self and the sheer volume of our unrestrained desires or supposed needs.

However, let us return to perhaps less overtly philosophical regions and more down-to-earth considerations! To begin with, there is this problem of formulating a population policy. Here, let us take Britain as basis for study. It is after all an offshore island and most people are able to see certain restrictions applying to land surfaces when they are jealously marked by the sea. This is in direct contrast to nations situated on continents where borders are perhaps rather fluid, mainly due to wars or long-standing territorial disputes. A finite land surface has similarly finite resources, and this concentrates the mind more quickly.

To restate an earlier observation: British governments over the post-war years have never formulated any policy on population. Let me qualify this: there is no policy openly and honestly declared, although there are some undercurrents from time to time that seem to suggest one.

The British consider that they have brought the art of 'muddling through' to a peak of perfection. They rely on this art constantly. They look down their noses at the Continentals and Americans who, being extremely jealous of their success, attempt to do much the same. The latter however are confidently classed as mere amateurs. Thus, having such a long tradition in the field, the British assume they can muddle through the desperate problem of population in exactly the same way as they have done with endless wars, insurrections, plagues, the voting system, the suffragettes, the Irish and recurring epidemics of 'flu. Unfortunately though, the population problem is not so amenable to a little judicious muddling. It cannot, as with 'flu symptoms, be helped by the odd tumbler of hot toddy!

How then may we begin to tackle the problem coherently and rationally?

Before doing so, shall we take a brief look at an oblique attempt at a population policy dressed up to look like something rather different? It constitutes a classic case of muddle, spiced with

British subtlety.

It had to do with the Social Security Department's belated discovery that a huge amount of money was being claimed by single-parent families, this despite having a marriage certificate recorded in earlier years. This presupposed a working father at the helm originally. Mark you, having a recorded marriage is quite distinct from some single mothers who have only the vaguest notion of who the father might be. Or if they do know, they wouldn't tell anyway.

Now a proportion of the more socially responsible of these missing fathers had already made a contribution toward their offspring. They did so by making a down payment. Sometimes, rather than money it was transformed into the form of bricks and mortar – the house in which the family already lived. These fathers were a minority, however. Many more did indeed leave the bricks and mortar to the former wife, but it was, figuratively speaking, suffused throughout with either wet or the dry rot spores of an enormous mortgage. Others simply decamped with no forwarding address and no further contact whatsoever. Many of the latter, to add insult to injury, (not merely to the former wife but also the taxpayer) having left one love nest then promptly set up other structure. This too vaguely resembled a nest, possibly with love but probably without. Here procreating began all over again! Worse, a proportion of these were unemployed and possibly unemployable. Presumably having to nurture carefully their energies to produce further offspring, normal work was out of the question. They did so of course because of the basic instinct to procreate. They may even have hoped to produce mirror images of themselves. Beyond this there may have been a patriotic sense of duty in procreating in as short a time as possible. Why? well, obviously in the knowledge that the tabloid press could note their prowess and present the story to an admiring and grateful nation. You see, a man has to do what a man has to do. And you can't gainsay that now, can you? Or can you? Well, extraordinary though it may seem, ex-wives and taxpayers did, and, for that matter, still do. And they get very hot under the collar about it indeed.

So to counter growing unease at this trend the government set up the CSA, or the so-called Child Support Agency.

Now the CSA in due course found the task of tracking missing fathers an exceedingly difficult one. They had large offices and staff waiting, moreover only too willing to act as latter-day Solomons – for, as you might expect, such a process needs considerable wisdom after you have traced your target. You see, after working out payments due to former wives and children, you must also find ways in which money can be extracted from fathers. But initially they found missing fathers extraordinarily elusive, indeed so much so that they had nobody to practise their Solomon skills on. So rather than sit about twiddling their thumbs, they turned to other matters. They set about making infinitely complicated enquiries into the financial payments already made by clearly documented and already traceable fathers. And despite many of these having a history of reasonable generosity, they pursued them with vigour anyway. Possibly, this was in the hope they could persuade them to extend such generosity further.

Meanwhile they put the task of seeking the wholly irresponsible and elusive on the back burner, so to speak. This infuriated the reasonably generous, who promptly took to the streets, held marches and rallies, and stood for hours shaking their fists outside the Houses of Parliament. Disconcerted by this rumpus, the CSA finally began what it was originally set up to do – the more difficult task of contacting some of the more elusive brigade. After some considerable time and trouble some of these were actually traced. But here they met even greater exhibitions of fury. These middle-aged Romeos were now on their second or sometimes third attempt at building a love nest. Moreover they were often engaged in producing their second or third rounds of children. These were outraged at the very thought of being asked to contribute to the maintenance of those children they had ditched. Taking their cue from the responsible fathers, they too held marches and rallies and in the mother of all demonstrations, they shook their fists and jumped up and down outside the mother of all parliaments. The extent of the wrath exhibited reached such levels of fury (and was so completely unexpected!) that government ministers and the CSA lost their nerve. All the original zest and pioneering spirit evaporated; they became defensive and dispirited. As well they might! The government found that the energy expended in creating this department and the effort involved in finding literate and numerate people to run it was now rapidly costing far more than the amount saved by the taxpayer. Somehow it had never been anticipated that an unemployed and unemployable man with (say) eight children by several different women, or what the Scots call with delicious decorum 'bide-y-ins', might already have given his 'all' as you might say. Clearly, men who consider that they have given the best of themselves by contributing their sperm to needy women resent further calls on their services and energies. Some too may claim a form of inverse patriotism by saying that they initially forced an uncaring government to create the CSA in the first place! Therefore, weren't they being instrumental in keeping a large number of persons in full and active employment there? Surely these would become redundant if their task was made too easy? However such tactics and such patriotism did not (and still does not) appear to be appreciated. The CSA has come in for sharp criticism: its future now hangs in the balance.

This then is the British way. And in this saga we find the merest hint and the most subtle of suggestions that a population policy of sorts is being pursued. There is the muffled hint to sections of society which suggests that having children by different partners and then engineering a disappearing trick is not exactly playing the game. It just isn't cricket, whatever other game it may be. It is however never openly suggested that having four or more children, even by one partner, is being unpatriotic and unhelpful. It is never explained why we already have an overcrowded island. It is never explained that having four or more children exerts population pressure, simply because it moves outside simple replacement levels. It is never explained that those optimists who point to the carnage on our roads as excellent moderators of that increase are being overoptimistic. It is never stated that our total numbers are still rising. No – procreation of any kind and in any circumstances is too delicate a subject for the British government. It is a throwback to the Victorian era when propriety was everything. Everybody knew of course that, underneath it all, the realities of life bubbled merrily away. But it was indelicate to refer to it. Sex and its adjacent activity, procreation, were too close for comfort. Worse, both sex and procreation were the subject of mirth, and no politician likes to be closely associated with mirth. Yes, they like to show they are human by cracking the odd joke or two, but it is a very different thing for people to laugh at you rather than with you. It is not at all funny to have a joke rebound on you. Sex and procreation are the daily standby for stand-up comics, television script writers and the tabloid press generally – and no politician wishes to be associated with such rabble. Thus it will take a very serious crisis on the population front indeed before that attitude changes. As in the darkest period of the Second World War, when the British tried to keep up their spirits by making innumerable jokes about it, leaders may again be tempted to raise two fingers in the air and be cheered to the rooftops. Who knows? Stranger things have happened. Incidentally, it is a moot point whether Churchill knew exactly how his famous victory sign would be interpreted by ordinary folk. Did he chuckle away quietly to himself, or did he remain blissfully ignorant to the end? But to more important matters...

Now suppose, by some incredible change in attitude, a British government becomes seriously alarmed by rising crime rates, rising unemployment, rising social security requirements. Suppose it becomes convinced of eventual bankruptcy. Suppose it also begins to picture the fury that erupts when Social Security offices are closed and boarded up – and the subsequent scenario I have already painted. What might it then do in the way of setting up a completely open rather than furtive population policy?

To begin with it is essential to lead by example. Thus all cabinet ministers should be chosen for their personal sense of responsibility in the matter and be seen to have no more than three children. Any member discovered to have 'undeclared interests', as they say (that is, mistresses or connubial stand-ins bearing offspring), must therefore be asked to resign. This example should extend right down through the ranks to junior ministers and the usual range of 'sidekick' researchers and advisors.

Having set such a rigorous and open example, a democratic

government can then set up a policy with confidence. This should be achieved ideally by persuasion. But it must be clearly stressed that a target of two children and an absolute maximum of three applies right across the board. This means royalty, admirals, generals, air marshals, top civil servants, industrialists, bankers and all those at the centre of interest in what is suggestively called the 'entertainment world' – all the way down to the humblest and most private of citizens. Any overtly eugenic stance, and the difficulties associated with it, would then be avoided by the fact that it would apply to the entire population – this regardless of their honesty, regardless of apparent sanity or insanity, regardless too of their sense of responsibility and patriotism, or lack of it. At the same time it would be senseless attempting to achieve these targets if the further question of immigration was left out. This cannot remain in the classically British state of muddle and confusion that it is in now. This problem will be examined more fully in a moment or two. Essentially though, immigration, whether legal or illegal, must be firmly halted. The countries currently decanting their surplus population must be encouraged to put their own houses in order – it sends entirely the wrong signal if they are able to continue to decant their surplus without active signs of disapproval. Indeed it would make a mockery of efforts in Britain to check or even lower its overall population – only to make room for others! As for asylum seekers, they should be given temporary entry only and be returned to the country of origin as soon as circumstances permit.

Once there is some hope of population stabilisation, then at last 'green' principles have some chance of realisation. The lunacy of building houses and factories on good agricultural land, or over ever decreasing areas occupied by wildlife, could then be outlawed completely. Similarly the further extension of motorways on any kind of land whatsoever. Factory farming, with the grave dangers inherent in its system of sudden bacteriological or viral invasions, could be slowly phased out; it could then be replaced by more labour-intensive 'free' methods. The jaunty criticisms made by critics of 'green' farming – that it would be far too expensive – would be outweighed by the resulting prevention of the more immediate forms of food poisoning. Dare one also add the likelihood of currently invisible and less obvious long-term ones? The list of advantages of population stabilisation is extensive, and it would be tiresome to begin detailing each and every one at this point. Overall, every effort should be made in every government announcement to highlight the advantages of stabilisation (possibly even a slow decrease), and at the same time every effort made to expose the sheer madness of a slow but inexorable population increase.

If a trial period of persuasion fails, what should be done? Fiscal policies eliminating benefits after the birth of a second child should be introduced immediately. For those with strongly held religious beliefs, and particularly those with (somewhat incorrectly called) 'fundamentalist' attitudes, then the burden of financing extra children should be dropped neatly onto the toes of those who advocate unrestrained procreation in the first instance – the churches concerned. Moreover this should be achieved wholly out of their own private funding.

Turning to those who have total contempt for government edicts of any description, and also lack religious beliefs of any kind, then a policy should be introduced whereby all individuals convicted of embezzlement, fraud, assault, injury or murder should be sterilised if they already have more than one child. While nobody should be denied – no matter what their criminal record – one child, they should automatically forfeit their right to have more. It must be explained to society as a whole that criminality is basically a cerebral dysfunction in which the love of self reaches excessive proportions; this, coupled with insatiable desires and insensitivity to the needs of others, has a basic genetic input. It is seldom due to an unfortunate genetic mutation, to a childhood injury, or to a temporary chemical imbalance. Locking people away in prison is not an effective way of preventing their further criminal activity; in the long term it is only a temporary solution. The possibility of passing on the worst of genetic inheritances to offspring is too high a risk and too great a burden for society to continue to bear. Clearly, no human society anywhere on earth can continue building prisons and staffing them with properly motivated officers at the rate currently demanded. When the feckless and irresponsible reach what might be called, in the parlance of nuclear physicists, 'critical mass' then a chain reaction and the explosive disintegration of that entire society becomes unavoidable.

Shall we now turn to the ethnic minorities already settled in Britain who will claim that their religious and cultural traditions forbid them to accept a two or three children maximum? Here it should be explained that since the reason for their migration from their country of origin was desperate overcrowding in the first instance, it is illogical to create the same problem here. They can hardly claim that their motivation for entering Britain was the beauty of what is left of our countryside, the vestiges of charm and character remaining in our cities, or the delightful uncertainties of our weather. Therefore to make any kind of contribution in their host country to overcrowding, bringing as it does the sort of chaotic situations and low standards of living prevalent in their countries of origin, simply defies simple logic. Indeed it represents a degree of irresponsibility that is doubly unacceptable. It is also dangerous. It creates a climate of persistent and irreversible racial tension.

Failure to co-operate, or any evidence of lack of understanding and indifference to the depth of ill feeling created, should be countered by offering three choices: deportation back to the country of origin, further migration to a country still without a birth-control policy or, finally, agreed sterilisation after the birth of the second child. Weakness in operating such a choice can only end in disaster for everyone concerned.

To re-emphasise an earlier observation: mankind, as all other carnivores and omnivores, is a 'territorial' animal. Millions of years of obeying a biological instinct deeply embedded in his nature cannot be neatly excised and thrown away in an instant. When a host country, either rightly or wrongly, begins to feel its way of life and traditions are being threatened, that is, compromised by the influx of very different (perhaps even alien) traditions, then a potentially explosive situation develops. For those who may immediately (and very foolishly) raise the highly emotive cry 'ethnic cleansing' – as if it were some utterly new social virus now infecting the latter part of the twentieth century – it is pertinent to observe that it would be more sensible to ponder on the matter first and then begin reading a little history. Even the most cursory glance at man's turbulent past will show that 'ethnic cleansing' is a crime endemic to *Homo sapiens*. It has been practised by every race on this earth since the very beginning of recorded time. You need elaboration on this point?

Very well, we have one very graphic example from the Bible. In the Book of Exodus we learn that the Pharaoh of Egypt, alarmed by observations that the Israelites were 'fruitful and increase greatly', was thus persuaded to set up 'taskmasters over them to afflict them with heavy burdens'. Oddly, when this failed to influence their reproductive rates in the manner expected, he attempted to engage the support of the Hebrew midwives. 'When you see them on the birth-stool if it is a son ye shall kill him; but if it is a daughter then shall she live.' This was a curious, if not foolish, move on several counts. To expect midwives – themselves part of that same ethnic minority – to kill their own kind seems an extraordinary exercise in wishful thinking. Possibly the pharaohs of that era had undue confidence in the range and effectiveness of their authority, but failing this it defies plain common sense. If you can look at the matter of killing children quite dispassionately (as he obviously did), then it seems strange that he was not aware of some basic facts. For example, if just one or two male infants somehow escaped this fate, then fourteen to fifteen years later they could impregnate a very large number of females. In contrast, if he demanded that all female infants were killed and just one or two escaped, then the reproduction rate would fall dramatically. Again, unless this particular pharaoh was unusually obtuse, simple logic should have told him that it takes nine months in the normal way of things for a female to produce a child, yet over a similar period a single male can impregnate an astonishing number of females. If such a male remains undetected over a number of years, then working either part-time, on night work only, or on a piecework basis, possibly with brief holidays to recuperate, just one individual could father an entire army. Conversely, if you attempt to kill every female infant, and allow all the males to live, you make a truly dramatic impact. You see, if a stray female or two escapes slaughter the outcome is very different. These poor creatures, after being bowled over in the rush, might well wish they were dead – if you understand what I mean. In fact Chinese peasants are said to have adopted this appalling and very primitive method of birth control for many centuries. Female infanticide is even rumoured to have persisted right up to and during the Communist regime of Mao. But it was only practised during famines! As soon as the situation eased, then the menfolk redoubled their procreative efforts on any adult female remaining. This accounts for the fact that the Chinese have the dubious pleasure of claiming to be the most populous nation on Earth.

However, to return to the curious Egyptian solution. When, as might be expected, Pharaoh's furtive ploy with the Hebrew midwives failed, he turned to his own ethnic group and commanded of his people that they search for all Israelite newborn and perform the deed themselves. 'Every son that is born to the Hebrews, ye shall cast into the Nile, but every daughter shall live.' This however is but a marginal improvement in effectiveness. Perhaps Pharaoh had in mind that most Egyptian men would subsequently take over the role of mating with Hebrew women, thus destroying their ethnic identity and individuality. Who knows? The irony of ironies of course is that Pharaoh's own daughter, on finding the Hebrew Moses in a basket providentially caught amongst the Nile's riverbank reeds, was overcome by motherly instincts. Defying authority she saw to it that the infant was spared. In the fullness of time, to use Biblical language, Moses became the man who led the Israelites out of Egypt. Strangely though, the people he led did not seem to be just females with a sprinkling of very old men among them. So perhaps the King of Egypt's commands had had far less impact than supposed. Possibly too, melting hearts were not restricted to his daughter.

This then is but one example among many from early history. More modern examples of attempts at 'ethnic cleansing' – abound. They can be found during much of the Spanish conquest and subsequent occupation of Mid and South America, during the virtual extermination of the Native Indian in what is now the United States by immigrants from Europe and during the white Australians' dealings with the Aborigine. More recently still, it is in evidence in the Rwandan Hutus' attempt to cleanse the Tutsis (and vice versa) and the Israelis' attempt to cleanse the Palestinians (and vice versa). Possibly the worst example of ethnic cleansing to happen since the upheavals of the Second World War occurred when Britain gave India her independence. To repeat earlier observations: at that moment Ali Jinnah, leader of the one hundred million Muslims, who were outnumbered mainly by Hindus on a three-to-one basis, insisted on partition. He created Pakistan. In doing so he touched off ethnic cleaning in both camps. The saintly Gandhi, preaching universal brotherhood, attempted to prevent the horrors most realists anticipated. Encouragingly enough, Gandhi's inspired teaching and his resolution to begin a public fast to the death halted some of the early rioting and killings. Yet the deep-seated primitive instincts within all humanity finally triumphed. Partition saw between nine and ten million Muslims moving north over the newly constituted borders within days, with a smaller but still substantial number of Hindus moving south. With unbelievable viciousness, half a million Muslims were then slaughtered in east Punjab alone. Overcrowded trains, already in the process of taking the refugees toward the new border were stopped and defenceless men, women and children were hacked to death. Equally, Hindus on foot or in oxen carts travelling south were also set on and murdered, though it is thought on a smaller scale. That such incredible ferocity and hatred could be shown to people when they were already moving out of disputed areas indicates the true power of these repressed primitive instincts. And nobody has been able to provide accurate figures for the casualties sustained. Figures vary from just over a million to almost two million. Gandhi, nominally a Hindu, and still preaching universal tolerance, was murdered by a Hindu extremist shortly after. In the space of just a year it is estimated that fourteen million people finally uprooted themselves and moved to safer areas! Nor has it stopped there!

Bloodshed has continued from time to time ever since. Small enclaves of Muslims and Hindus (and even smaller enclaves of Christians) who either refused or were unable to move, thereby finding themselves still living on the 'wrong' sides of the border, have suffered attack and unprovoked killings to this day.

Unhappily it is possible to find many more examples of ethnic division combined with vicious attempts at extermination throughout the world. Often though, such 'cleansings' are carefully given another name. Whatever term is used to describe the driving away, reducing, or even complete wiping out of other ethnic groups, it may be necessary to remind the reader yet again of its biological basis. Similar behaviour patterns are seen amongst most of the so-called 'higher' animals. This phenomenon can only be understood when it is fully seen for what it is: a deeply held instinctive response that arises out of the concept of 'territory'. Further, those who attempt to find wholly new territory, and, in doing so, move in among a long-established resident population, are usually at a grave disadvantage. Unless their combined physical strength – and, in the case of the animal called man, their basic technological skills – is wholly superior, then the attempt will fail. Nature always gives the resident animal that extra sense of legality in the matter of possession. This summons up the most formidable determination, born of outrage, to defend such territory. Thus throughout the animal world, not excluding that of man, it is the resident who normally wins the eventual battle.

And the exceptions to the rule? There are always exceptions, of course. The ongoing Israeli–Palestinian conflict, now spanning fifty years, is unusual because of the length of the confrontation and the inability of the one to subdue the other. This is because both sides claim that their territorial rights have been denoted by God himself. And you can't claim greater authority than that! Nor, directly leading from this claim, can you ignore your greater sense of moral right either. Inevitably, utter determination and an overpowering sense of outrage come when the other side disputes it. Horrific things have been done over the years in the name of God. They are still being committed by both sides. Deep down in their heart of hearts, although they often deny it, both Israelis and Palestinians wish to cleanse each other off the face of the earth.

A somewhat similar conflict is going on in Northern Ireland and for almost as long – though if you look at the turbulent history of Ireland one could say that it has actually lasted far longer, centuries in fact. Invasions by the English have in this case muddied the waters. But basically quite a time ago some Irish –

much like the Jews of the Diaspora – migrated overseas, and in this instance into southern Scotland. Then after some time they seemed to regret it. With nostalgia for their earlier territory they took it on themselves to move back into Northern Ireland. Unlike the Jews, however, they had changed their religion marginally in the interim! Although still Christian, they became Protestant rather than Catholic. Both acts have been bitterly resented by the Southern Irish. And attempts to infiltrate the North were met initially with repressive measures by the Protestants.

As a counter to this, the IRA and its splinter groups mounted a terror campaign. This increased the divisions between both sects and created a climate of bitter hatred. Protestants began intimidating Catholics living in their midst, forcing them to move out and burning down their houses if they refused. In areas where Catholics were in the majority, the process was reversed. In what seemed to be the only way to prevent a civil war, British troops were employed as peacekeepers. This proved a costly error. If a UN force composed of men from almost anywhere else in the world had been used, their activities would have been seen as even-handed. Being British the troops were inevitably suspected of partiality toward Protestants. Catholics refused to accept that they were maintaining law and order. Bombings and shootings increased rather than diminished. When the troops themselves began to suffer casualties, the position deteriorated further. It eventually resulted in 'Bloody Sunday'. Troops, believing they were under fire, lost self-control and began shooting indiscriminately. This tragedy brought the conflict to its most savage peak. The conflict widened to the British mainland. Bomb outrages, hitherto somewhat rare in England, were stepped up. Used against what were euphemistically called 'military targets', they resulted in killings of unarmed off-duty soldiers in barracks, bandsmen giving concerts, and, in one particularly horrific incident, of their wives and children on a bus. Civilians in government were not immune either. An attempt, which came very near to success, was made to kill the prime minister and the party hierarchy during a conference at Brighton. For two decades such killings became quite indiscriminate. People attending Armistice Day prayers at a memorial to the fallen in both wars were not spared either.

Protestants, now forming their own terror groups, tracked down those they suspected of IRA membership and performed summary executions.

The record of maiming and killing over a period of three decades has produced nothing but misery for all concerned, and a long period of stalemate.

Demographic indications, which of course everyone ignores, nevertheless appear to show that the Catholic minority in Northern Ireland, having a higher birth rate than the Protestants, will soon become the majority. Thus in a democracy, where the majority call the shots, the Protestant determination to remain part of Britain will find itself outvoted. Integration with the remainder of Ireland will be inevitable. All that bloodshed and misery will then have been for nothing.

Given such demographic predictions, one would expect attitudes to change and attention to be focused on birth rather than death. For example, in the staunchly Catholic areas of Belfast, Derry and all those other small towns near the border, it is common for the end walls of house blocks to be covered in large murals depicting masked men with Armalite rifles; surely it would now be far more effective to repaint them with depictions of naked men and woman (suitably masked of course) having sexual intercourse? The message could be further clarified by accompanying it with the ringing slogan: 'Give her one for Ireland!' Better still: 'Give her half a dozen for Ireland!' There is some evidence however that the dictates of public decency might be violated. While it is perfectly acceptable to have murals tacitly encouraging the taking away of life, it would probably be considered indecent to allude to the creation of life!

Not that the final integration of Northern Ireland into the South will then solve matters overnight. Should Protestant terror groups refuse to accept the position, and continue the conflict, then all that will happen is that the government of the South will find itself shouldering the burden rather than Britain. Dublin will find it necessary to enlarge the small Irish Army greatly, which, lacking high-tech equipment, and experience, will find itself in a serious position. As for the financial burden in maintaining a military presence, not forgetting the finding of compensation for all the damage and loss of life due to bombings, this could cripple the Irish economy. The Southern Irish could of course attempt a programme of ethnic cleansing of the North, but this would not sit comfortably with their position as members of the European Union. The Union does expect a measure of decorum among all those accepted within its fold.

The conflict in Ireland is a sad and ever-recurring microcosm representing far larger tragedies and exhibiting even greater viciousness in many places throughout the world. Almost every other day horrors are reported from Algeria, Afghanistan, Sri Lanka, Azerbaijan and Palestine.

Given such conflict, then surely it is counter-productive to sweep ethnic and racial demographic issues under the carpet; sooner or later they refuse to be so treated.

Unless discussed openly and bravely, without either hypocrisy or ludicrous attempts to camouflage fundamental issues, they will rapidly become more pressurised. The longer everyone attempts to adopt what is often called a 'politically correct' stance, the more explosive the final outcome.

Now if we begin to examine the current position in Britain, we find there have been prolonged and frantic efforts to disguise underlying tensions. This is both foolish and dangerous. To repeat the earlier observation: it matters little whether a host country is mistaken or not when it feels it is being swamped by alien cultures or religions. Mistaken or otherwise, there will be a surge in instinctive 'territorialism'. If the years go by and nothing is done, such a surge will finally become unstoppable.

It is all very well for pronouncements to be made that we now live in a multicultural, multiethnic society. You see, many feel that this has been foisted on them surreptitiously. In such a fundamental matter, previous governments should have made it an issue requiring a referendum. Had such a question have been put to the test, and it was the will of the people, then so be it. However, a referendum has never been called. Frantic brush-sweeping and sleight-of-hand carpet lifting has been the only reaction or response. Nor does anyone publish accurate statistics on legal immigration let alone illegal – which by its very definition and nature is impossible to quantify with any hope of accuracy.

Those who one might define as 'hosts' — and here one must identify them in almost ridiculous terms as being of 'ancient' and Caucasian British stock — are now beginning to feel pressured. At the moment they merely 'suspect' that they are being swamped. An entirely different attitude will be found among Asian, African and Afro-Caribbean people. These find such continued immigration, legal or otherwise, both comforting and necessary. After all, it gives them added confidence and political clout. And these two opposing viewpoints are so incompatible as to become dangerous factors in racial tension.

Despite the usual complacency, recent demographic statistics show a continued, if small, rise in the British population totals over the last three decades. Automatically the Caucasian hosts will take a deep breath, sniff and, with a sour expression, immediately attribute it to legal, illegal or asylum-seeking immigrants from overseas. The immigrants will respond, almost as an automatic reflex, with the cry of 'racism'. This may be true. But it is simplistic to suppose that it solely embraces the colour of people's skins. Denied accurate knowledge, British Caucasians suspect their country has become the dumping ground for migrants from virtually every region of the world. It goes beyond colour prejudice. Resentment is building up against young, blond, blue-eyed Caucasian Russians, Poles, Lithuanians and others from former Soviet bloc countries, in exactly the same way as it is against dark-skinned people from Asia and Africa. Young unemployed males from former satellite states within the Soviet empire, desperate as they are to find better living conditions in what to them is the fabled West, are just as liable to attempt to get legal, illegal or asylum-seeking status as others from anywhere on Earth. The only difference is that they are less likely to be noticed in the crowd of other Caucasians; thus their presence does not register so easily.

The crux of the matter is the sheer scale of the numbers involved. Quite simply, the flood-gates cannot be opened onto a small island such as Britain, or for that matter on Western Europe as a whole. On the world scale, Western Europe is already high on the list of population density in relation to finite size. The hard reality of the situation insists on limitation. To allow the present situation to continue unchanged merely encourages demographic worldwide irresponsibility. The dumping or decanting of surplus populations will continue uninterrupted anywhere and everywhere around the world unless a firm stand is adopted.

Throughout the history of mankind there has never been such a desperate need for each sovereign state to settle its own problems of surplus population. Gone are the days when open spaces seemed to offer such opportunities. They can no longer, as the West did throughout the seventeenth, eighteenth and nineteenth centuries, start a process of empire building and colonisation. World populations have exploded since that era, and all possible areas, bar the polar regions, have been occupied.

But let us return to Britain. To repeat, the feeling of being swamped is becoming more and more common and stress-inducing because it is not allowed open and healthy debate. Once again, let us be perfectly honest here – such a feeling is of course common among the English, Welsh and Scottish, who are all white-skinned Caucasians and can claim a long line of forebears as residents going back many centuries. The reverse is felt among those not classed as Caucasian. It is unavoidable and indeed understandable that they become apprehensive as a result of any talk of a halt of intake of further immigrants.

Legal and illegal immigration, together with asylum-seeking, is therefore unquestionably a subject that demands long and hard scrutiny together with complete transparency.

Shall we look at asylum-seekers initially. This is a particularly difficult sector to resolve because emotion inevitably triumphs over common sense and brutal reality.

To do so we must begin by scrutinising the criteria for entry as drawn up by the Home Office. Incidentally, one notices that transparency is not an observable trait encouraged or fostered by that office. Therefore the following definition is one that is paraphrased from the few announcements that filter out from this august body. Briefly then, a person or persons may apply for consideration as an asylum seeker if he or she (or family group) faces intolerable persecution, extending to threat of death, in their country of origin.

Now unfortunately tens of millions of people all over the

world fall into this category and do so each and every year. Currently, the most obvious are Tibetans, Kurds, and East Timorians from Asia generally, while from the continent of Africa come Algerians, Hutus, Somalis, and people from what is sarcastically called 'Mobutu-land'.

And it is not as if one can see an end to this appalling picture of repression and ethnic cleansing. Tomorrow morning or the next day, news may come in from other parts of the world announcing yet more trouble spots.

Yet despite meeting the criteria for entry as asylum seekers, many millions are unable to do so because they just happen to lack easy access to embassy or consul officials. Perhaps more importantly they lack the money to both reach and then take the next flight out from an airport. No doubt the British and other European governments are secretly relieved that this is so. Otherwise the weight of numbers would be intolerable.

Nevertheless it does leave the door partly open. It leaves it open to those who *do* have access to embassies and a little money. Unfortunately, the majority of these are basically economic migrants; it is dissatisfaction with their living standards that has brought them into generalised conflict with their government. Unlike Tibetans or Kurds, they do not suffer obvious repression. Certainly they will claim otherwise and with great passion, yet no evidence of structured and systematic persecution is observable. As a result the task of distinguishing between genuine asylum seekers and economic migrants is highly problematic. It becomes all the more so when some of the latter are so desperate that they are prepared to mutilate themselves with burns or apparent torture marks to fool immigration officials.

In genuine cases of repression, particularly where they extend to an entire race or ethnic group, the sheer numbers involved make it impractical to encourage mass exodus. The only sane solution is to involved the United Nations. This body, whenever possible, should send in a peace-keeping force and create a buffer zone. But, as we well know, this is a solution yet to be given absolute priority, and this even among the leading UN members. Over a period extending from its very inception, the UN has never fully coped with such a vital function. The reason? It has never been properly organised or indeed financed. The only army the UN has successfully mustered is in its offices in the New York headquarters; here its only battle has been to keep its head above water in the flood of self-created paperwork – little more. Meanwhile ethnic groups in different areas all over the world, because of their failure to limit their populations, are attempting to cleanse each other by periodic massacre in the hope that survivors will then take themselves off into neighbouring countries.

Fundamentally, despite being the authors of their own misfortune (by their failure to adopt sensible birth control programmes), millions are looking for any opportunity to escape horrors already on their doorsteps, or indeed seen moving toward them. And the reason they will choose the West, ironically enough, is that these areas are perceived to have achieved (comparatively speaking) rock-like stability. Nor does it escape their attention that high standards of material comfort exist. It contrasts sharply with a world where fluidity, chaos and destitution predominate. The West seems a truly fabled place. Yet no thought is given as to how the West has achieved this blessed state. It is merely assumed – and it is the most plausible of all errors – that such superior lifestyles and such enviable stability have been achieved solely by its superior technological expertise! Ironically, the bulk of Westerners themselves believe this myth. The truth of the matter is very different. Success in limiting population growth is by far the most potent factor. But this escapes everyone's attention.

This then is the basis for the mistaken belief that continued immigration into the affluent and stable West can have no harmful effect. Each immigrant, thinking quite naturally only of their own individual case, assumes that they are a negligible addition to Western numbers. Desperately seeking stability and affluence, they refuse to consider that they may be agents in destroying both. And this mistaken belief is further highlighted by their tendency to have a higher birth rate than their hosts. They see no harm in this. It is never considered to be the most damaging factor of all in the sphere of race relations. Nor in the longer term is it considered harmful to the ultimate fortunes of their adopted country.

In truth all that will be achieved, if this trend continues, is the spread of misery and destitution over the entire world. Widespread migration of peoples into neighbouring countries or into different continents is now the greatest threat to peace and stability throughout the world. Yet because it is usually such a gradual process, nobody considers the enormous impact and the increasing pressures building up over each succeeding year.

Additionally too, there is a further factor in all this. There is a deep-rooted feeling among those who were formerly colonised and abused by the West that they have the moral right to restitution. Why shouldn't such restitution take the form of colonisation in reverse? They feel they have a right of entry into those countries who became wealthy at their expense. In their eyes, to reverse the process is but common justice.

Unfortunately, of course, two wrongs seldom make a right. Successful colonisation by Asians and Africans of Western countries such as Britain, France, Spain, Holland and Belgium, who were once their harsh and repressive masters, will not bring common justice. It will bring only bitter conflict and widespread misery. The present generations of Europeans are not responsible for the sins of their empire-building great grandfathers. And they find it difficult to accept that they should be continually held accountable. The same is true with the descendants of those who at one time formed the ranks of Hitler's conquering armies. Why should the sins of fathers and grandfathers fall, generation after generation, on young German shoulders? If those countries invaded by Nazi Germany chose to perpetuate hatreds and a sense of injustice then they would prove not just counter-productive, but also in time create injustices. The ghastly outcome of burnishing long-passed hatreds in Yugoslavia alone exemplifies this.

Thus in many cases there may well be a refusal to accept blame. And under such circumstances tensions can only increase and racial divisions widen.

However, for those who refuse to consider such a baneful scenario, and who cling to the hope that somehow we can all muddle through, it may be necessary to look at some of the existing conflicts throughout the world. Perhaps this will suitably influence their attitudes.

Here it may be necessary to remind those individuals most critical and resolutely opposed to my central thesis of an earlier statement. It is this: there is a direct correlation between areas of the world with very high birth rates and areas with recurring conflict. The two go hand in hand. It is an unfortunate trait in human nature to attempt to blame others for one's own failings or stupidity. And here the irresponsibility of those who insist on having large families is no exception. Endlessly they blame their current governments for their destitution and misery. Not for one moment do they begin to accept that they themselves are the agents responsible. In countries where governments fall short of reasonable standards, and where ineptitude, inertia or corruption is rife, these are precisely the people who indulge in spontaneous rioting. Sometimes it is directed toward the regime in power, but as these are usually well protected by troops or militia, it usually redirects itself into ethnic conflict. It is no more than a mark of the frustration building up. Scapegoats must be found. Who better than those who appear different? Where better than to enter into conflict with those who have (at least to you) ridiculous customs, different dialects or language and above all do not share your religion.

Inevitably, in attempting to maintain law and order, the regime or government begins a round-up of suspected troublemakers. Frequently such conflict then becomes endemic. If home-made weapons or outdated arms come into the hands of troublemakers, they may organise themselves into militant groups. Under such circumstances the regime then renames the troublemaker a 'terrorist'. And at this stage an entirely new dimension opens up.

Here they then fulfil the criteria set down by the British Home Office of individuals suffering persecution and threat of death. And such is the absurdity of the current entry rules that leaders of such groups often find it safer and easier to organise opposition to their regime from abroad. Thus at the present moment Britain has had protests from several foreign governments. These sharply criticise our policy, alleging that we harbour terrorists seeking to overthrow their elected (often democratically) regimes. It is indeed a crazy world, but the anomalies thrown up by our asylum-seeking criteria are even crazier.

To illustrate this, shall we investigate the situation in just one such country, Sri Lanka?

Now people in the West have a vague idea that this is an off-shore island lying at the tip of Southern India and little else. The name does however recur at intervals on our television screens or in the media generally. Always it is associated with some quite grim item of news. And it reminds us that a particularly vicious conflict is still ongoing. Notwithstanding, the reasons for such a conflict are (at least to most Europeans) obscure. We are aware that the north is the stronghold of people called Tamils while the south is home to people called Singhalese, and little else.

If we attempt to sieve through the little information available to us, it would appear that in the sixth century a group of Singhalese tribal people from the north of India invaded the island and colonised it. The native inhabitants, the Veddas, fled to the jungle and only a handful survive today. The Tamils, a later invasion again, came from Southern India. Currently they form about twenty-two per cent of the population, while the Singhalese form about seventy. Presumably some other minority groups, plus the remnant of the Veddas, make up the remainder.

Now most Europeans are at least aware that the Tamils who live mainly in Northern Sri Lanka are in open revolt against the South. They have after all been in conflict for almost three decades. The focus of the struggle appears to be self-rule: they demand that their stronghold should become an independent state. Why? In the 1960s they accused the South of treating them as second-class citizens and denying them their fair share in government. What was that government? As far as Europeans can make out, peering as they must at such things from a distance, it seems to have been an elected assembly based on the democratic model. To arouse the ire of the Tamils then, clearly some reasons for the perception of unfairness must have been present. But why do the Tamils insist on retaining a separate identity? And why do so in such a distinctive way? Why are two peoples from the same continent and not racially dissimilar in any obvious way, unable to form a cohesive and peaceful whole? There seems to be no answer except, as with all conflict-prone societies anywhere in the world, an underlying religious one. They embrace two distinct religious groups, in this case Hindu and Buddhist.

During the 1960s the remainder of the world first became aware of open conflict when bomb outrages were committed in the capital Colombo. The death toll was heavy. It was a time when Tamils mingled freely with the remainder of the population throughout the island. Notably too, many Tamils with moderate views were appalled by the turn of events. Unable to find those responsible, and assuming that they had found refuge in the North, the Singhalese made sweeps into the Tamil stronghold. Accusations of brutality by the police and military soon surfaced. The truth as always is difficult to establish. Human nature being what it is, it would seem that stung by original bomb outrages, excesses by the Singhalese may well have occurred. At any event, bombing in the South was repeated. The Singhalese retaliated with more sweeps into Tamil strongholds attempting to seize suspects. The Tamils took revenge by slaughtering Singhalese people in outlying villages. Thus the cycle of violence was firmly set in place.

At this point any disinterested observers would have supposed that it would have been better if the South had seen fit to grant the Tamils their own regional government. It would have prevented further loss of life, endless suffering, and a further drain on resources. The island had visions of creating for itself tourism on a substantial scale; to that end it had begun building a series of holiday complexes. Bad publicity linked with the ongoing conflict nipped such hopes, like an early frost, neatly in the bud.

It is perhaps easy for Europeans to propose Tamil self-government, but less easy for the Singhalese directly involved. Certainly the South has not seen fit to do so, though once again the reason is obscure when one considers the enormous cost and disruption that has resulted.

Despite ever increasing military operations, and several attempts to overrun the North completely, the Tamils have always bounced back. Again, to any distant observer it would seem that the expenditure of effort forced on the South to achieve complete conquest is hardly worth all the suffering and misery demanded.

Failing an agreed partition, the only solution would appear to be the creation of a buffer zone set up between the two warring parties. The United Nations should have been approached long ago, and a UN force of peacekeepers sent in to maintain it and, ideally, break the cycle. This was achieved after all in Cyprus. So why not here?

There are similarities to be noted between Cyprus and Sri Lanka in that conflict in both cases originated in a religious and cultural divide. North-eastern Cyprus was populated mainly by people of Turkish origin, who are Moslem, and the south-west by ethnic Greeks who are Christian. The Turkish sector received aid, spiritual, political and material, from Turkey, the Grecian sector similarly from Greece. The parallel in Sri Lanka is that the Tamils receive aid from cousin Tamils living immediately across the narrow straits in Southern India; both are Hindu. Oddly the Singhalese received military aid for a brief period from the government of India under Rajiv Gandhi. The bitterness of the Tamils was such that it cost him his life. He was assassinated soon after by a female Tamil 'human bomber'. In the Cyprus/Sri Lanka comparison, the demographic picture is not too dissimilar either: the population 'doubling time' is forty-six in the case of Sri Lanka and fifty-three in Cyprus. It is always necessary to add the usual proviso, 'if present trends continue'.

Now on these two relatively small islands, neither of which is unduly blessed with natural resources, such a population increase is not sustainable indefinitely. It has also been the basic cause of conflict in that failing to integrate their populations due to the religious divide, each sector feels pressurised to expand into the other's territory. In the case of Sri Lanka the weight of numbers and the need for more agricultural land is stimulating Hindu Tamils to extend their territorial living space further and further south, while the same pressure is pushing Singhalese Buddhists north. Unless both sides adopt a population policy of zero growth – which, as you may have guessed, neither is prepared to do – then the situation ensures the very bloody conflict will continue. If you happen to be deeply cynical then of course you may think this is one way of keeping the population within bounds, but it is hardly pleasant or civilised.

How does this affect Britain? It doesn't or shouldn't, except that it was once a British colony. Here once again the sins of our forefathers (or rather their immoderate procreative drive necessitating large-scale colonial conquests) have the habit of coming back to haunt us.

At any event, not very long ago a group of Tamil males arrived in Britain and asked for political asylum. It was refused. Such a refusal (the details have never been fully revealed) would probably have been based initially on the grounds that they were in revolt against a democratically elected government; secondly, they had ample means of access to sanctuary among their own kith and kin in Southern India. Whether this was fully explained to them or not still remains unknown. If they suspected they were being flown back to Colombo and straight into the hands of the Singhalese, then their lives were certainly in danger. If, as is more probable, they were being flown to Southern India, then what took place shortly after can only be called a very ingenious Tamil ploy in arm-twisting. But ultimately the Home Office was to blame for the following curious incident.

Just prior to deportation from Heathrow airport, the Tamils stripped down to their underpants. They did so in front of a large audience of other bemused travellers, then threatened to strip further unless their deportation order was rescinded. Probably by prearrangement, a Tamil sympathiser phoned the media. Within no time at all, reporters and television camera crews arrived on the scene. The immigration officials suddenly found themselves facing batteries of camera lenses; these were pointed at intervals to their worried faces and then to the scantily clad Tamils behind then. The previous training and experience of the immigration officers had evidently failed to anticipate such circumstances. A hurried conference was called and the officers departed for a short time. It was a meeting to which the reporters were not invited. Nor subsequently was any information handed out. In all probability a consensus was reached observing that the criteria for entry to Britain made no mention of strange sects called nudists or would-be nudists. Nor did the Home Office mention their persecution in foreign countries. Until a direct ruling was asked for and received, therefore a legitimate extenuating factor seemed to present itself for reconsideration! Within a short time, not underpants but deportation orders were dropped.

Now why did the mere threat of exposing male buttocks and genitalia have such a paralysing effect on the normal functioning of logic and reason? It is not as if the Tamils had found it necessary to prove that their bodies were formed in exactly the same way as British males. It is not as if they found it necessary to certify that they were just as 'human' as everyone else. Nor for that matter were they under any obligation to prove (again like British males) that Nature had fully endowed them with the equipment to impregnate women. As far as Tamil females were concerned, it was never in doubt. The mere fact that in Sri Lanka they were fighting for extra space for their rapidly rising population constituted proof enough. True, to repeat an earlier observation, there was the question of persecution. If they had been flown back to Colombo, and directly into the hands of the Singhalese, then certainly their lives would have been in danger; but if they had been redirected to Southern India and their Tamil cousins, no such threat would have existed. In the former case, exposing one's all to the general public at Heathrow is an extreme anyone would be prepared to go to if one's life depended on it; in the latter case it was just psychological arm-twisting. Thus through the Home Office's lack of transparency, the resolve and the judgement of their own immigration officials had been opened to ridicule. This ruse alone should be enough to show how fundamentally flawed and unworkable are the present set of criteria. The Home Office, of all people, must surely have known that the situation in Sri Lanka over the past three decades had displayed periods of horrific violence on both sides. They may attempt to excuse themselves by pointing to interludes of relative calm. But these were due to exhaustion. During such time, both sides used them to regroup. And in such a period they indulged themselves in a little harmless procreation to ensure a future generation of cannon fodder. Subsequently, after finding sufficient weaponry and ammunition, they then engaged themselves in population control in the time-honoured way.

This is but one example of evasion of criteria for entry into Britain; it is by no means the most bizarre. We can expect many more in the world's ever expanding and pressurised mass of human beings. Doubtless, far more subtle means will be employed to manipulate the criteria for entry in future. Given that conflicts of one kind or another will continue to occur (or for that matter existing conflicts will intensify) and to do so each year somewhere or other in the world, who indeed would wish to find work as an immigration official?

All in all then, the sheer practicalities of attempting to provide an asylum-seeking programme must be seen for what they are: an exercise in muddling through of breathtaking proportions.

For that matter, the same logic applies to legal and illegal immigration; no country on Earth can continue to remain year after year a host to new arrivals given the relentless nature of human conflict, moreover the constant movement of terrified refugees and the sheer numbers involved.

Despite knowing the potentially disastrous effects such muddling through can have on race relations and the tensions slowly building up, nothing is being done to bring some kind of logic into play. Again this hinges on the lack of any fully open and clear policy concerning population stabilisation generally. In the absence of such a policy – a policy in which a British government states with absolute clarity that it hopes for population stabilisation and will in future operate a range of measures to bring this about – then the 'muddle through' policy will prevail indefinitely. And the crux of the matter is that illegal immigration is almost impossible to quantify with any accuracy. Everybody is reduced to guessing. For extreme right-wing and fascist groups, this is a gift to be exploited. At the same time, the ethnic minority, understandably enough, remains sympathetic to further immigration. Whether it is legal or not, they feel safer with a growth in numbers of their own kind. This is a basic instinct that applies to every immigrant group throughout Europe; indeed, in every host country throughout the world. All show reluctance to co-operate, either directly or indirectly. They will continue to provide 'safe houses' and financial support to those of their own kind. In this they are merely obeying a deep-seated instinct in all of us. Such social bonding is a survival factor going back half a million years. But here it will also be necessary to repeat yet again that unfortunately they also remain blind to the inevitability of a crisis should such a trend continue.

Oddly, as has been experienced in Britain and the remainder of Europe, many immigrants become recklessly hostile in their attitude to criticism. Again this is to be expected given that there is no official policy by any European government on the desirability of population control and indeed overall population stabilisation. Yet this type of retro-muddling is appreciated by the British in typical fashion: it provides an endless source of mirth! After all, if you feel powerless to do anything about a situation, all you can do is laugh it off. Unfortunately though, this becomes increasingly difficult as problems multiply. Perhaps the laughter gets a little strained when, after the occasional racial riot, utterances are made by politicians containing the cautionary words 'as we live in a multicultural society it is our duty to eliminate all sources of racial tension'. The laughter then turns somewhat sour with the realisation that such multiculturalism has been imposed without any kind of mandate, solely by a vociferous body of woolly-headed idealists.

Clearly these have never fully considered the basic and quite simple practicalities. Nor, for that matter, have they understood the implications surrounding biological instincts. These are the sort of people who have either no interest in the science of animal behaviour – with its forbidding academic title 'ethology' and equally forbidding technical language all of its own – or, alternatively, who refuse to believe that 'territorial acquisition' and subsequently 'territorial defence' can apply to supposedly rational human beings. Be that as it may, had a referendum been taken and a majority had in fact voted for multiculturalism, then the position would have been markedly different. In its absence we are left with a feeling of disquiet, and this both among ethnic minorities and the host majority. As a direct consequence, when so-called 'racial incidents' occur, the lack of widespread agreement and a fully relaxed atmosphere that is so easily attainable when goodwill is freely given, can make the incident artificially tense.

Resentment is fanned still further when high-profile individuals from ethnic groups begin criticising decisions to return illegal immigrants to the country of origin. In this highly emotive area, some civil rights activists seem to lose what appears to be basic common sense and this only serves to inflame passions still further.

Shall we examine their point of view for a moment so that the underlying motivation can be investigated and properly understood? Currently there are several men and women in the public eye who have categorised themselves as human rights activists. These are the subject of considerable media attention, particularly during racial rioting or when hunger strikes are staged at immigrant detention centres. And during interviews they use the concept of multiculturalism with confidence – despite its shaky foundations and lack of clear-cut mandate. Some of these are professional lawyers and some are not. However, they more or less speak with one voice. For purposes of brevity shall we rather irreverently caricature just one? Further, shall we make it female and fabricate the name, Miss Ain't-no-Flies-on-me, due to her extravagant posture of confidence before the cameras?

What one must understand from the outset is that despite my irreverence and my somewhat overdrawn caricature of her, I nevertheless believe that this person has her own kind of integrity. That her viewpoint might be mistaken in no way diminishes that integrity. She does not deliberately falsify her beliefs. Nor does this warrior take it upon herself to defend the indefensible merely because she has a passion for impossible causes. Her confidence is derived from her mode of thinking. It is so different from Caucasians; moreover, she has the unshakeable belief that she occupies the moral high ground. Indeed her stance, on closer examination – and if I interpret it properly by reading carefully between the lines – has an impeccable logic. It is this: it is absurd for the average British white person to assume that the migration of a wide variety of racial groups is a modern phenomenon. Such movements have been going on since the beginning of recorded history, and even before it!

Now who can deny that? Thus if she happens to be speaking in the south of England and therefore to mainly Anglo-Saxons, she may be bold enough to remind them (either openly or tacitly) that they themselves were immigrants at one time. This will of course take the wind out of their sails! And in the confusion that follows few will have the presence of mind to speak up and point out that there is an important omission here. Although her statement is undoubtedly true, she has forgotten to register the further fact that it also caused both the unhappy hosts and the newcomers several centuries of conflict, misery and suffering. The coming of Angles, Saxons and Jutes was resented. Pitched battles were fought. Later various modes of ethnic cleansing were adopted by both incomers and protesting hosts. Who were these hosts? They were broadly speaking Celts. These in particular, having already been 'disturbed' by the Romans, fled westward; the survivors, becoming partly 'Romanised', were conscious that the ethnic forebears had been forced to move into Wales, Ireland, northern England and Scotland. And they resented being pushed around still further. Incidentally, these remain to this very day suspicious of, and often hostile to, what have now become 'the English'. Numerous incidents currently reported in the latter half of the twentieth century prove that the Celts still object to further forced contact or incursions by the English when the latter move west or north – and do so whether they be in the shape of their holiday homes, language or customs, or whatever. The Celtic fringe may be small and somewhat self-conscious, but where they live and have put down their roots is regarded as their 'territory'. Again, nobody will remind Miss Ain't-no-Flies-on-me that since the bulk of the English, Welsh and Scots (but significantly not the Irish) have at long last become more or less peaceful inhabitants of Britain they have by the end of the First World Wide Resource War (1918), also achieved very slow population growth. A coincidence? But it has been done only by making the sacrifices demanded: they have denied themselves their basic urge for larger families. They have done this in the belief that only small families ensure a viable and reasonably prosperous future for all. But is this sacrifice now to become so much wasted effort? And unfortunately nobody will have the presence of mind to add that since the Anglo-Saxon episode all those centuries ago, the world has become densely populated with no open spaces remaining – at least in tolerably agreeable climactic-zonal areas. For that matter too, nobody will add that it now becomes urgently necessary for all nations to put their own houses in order. They should not attempt the easy way out. They should not attempt to relieve their population pressures in the short term, this simply by decanting surplus people to anywhere in the world that will receive them.

Not that these words would necessarily change this formidable lady's mind, of course. She probably sees the instinctive human urge for masses of children as the unchangeable norm; probably she sincerely believes that it is not open to radical change. She also sees such a norm evident among truly 'vibrant' races; this she contrasts with former imperialist 'has beens' and in doing so notes that the use of birth control is a phenomenon restricted solely to 'decadent' races. Privately she judges these to be in sharp decline and believes it is a fate of their own making. The Malthusian theory of exponential growth, if she has ever heard of it, means nothing to her. As for the drumming of horses' hoofs, bearing those four repulsive horsemen, she confidently dismisses them as mythological.

However, suppose for a moment that she is challenged regarding the long-term effect of persistent illegal immigration. And suppose we invent an incident for the purpose of furthering our understanding of her viewpoint!

Very well, here is the invention: in some distant country a group of young males, finding as they do the endless misery of bare survival in their country of birth too much to contemplate, attempt to break that mould. Understandably they are weary of back-breaking work. They fear this may persist as an unbroken pattern to the very end of their days. Being 'vibrant' males they have already in their teens taken child brides and have several children. These they must now care for, which is an added burden. But they reject the only sensible escape route − a vasectomy after their second child. Instead they seek a rather different alternative: the help of a professional 'tourist agent'. And after both they and their parents undertake to repay this man over a decade or more for his trouble, a method is devised for these young hopefuls' illegal entry to Britain. However, owing to the fact that simple devices such as special compartments in lorries and buses have been discovered far too often for comfort (while the ruse of posing as a ship's crew then quickly disappearing when unloading cargo is no longer an imaginative variant), it is decided that other methods need be tried. In this instance a small and rather innocent-looking fishing trawler is chartered in France or Holland – that is after the young men have reached these points by the usual cheaper and well-tried methods. The immigrants are then landed at the dead of night on a deserted British beach, well away from all evidence of human habitation.

Unfortunately though, in this instance they happen to choose a recently designated nature reserve for migrant birds, ducks and geese. Worse, this area is watched round the clock either by professional ornithologists or by 'twitchers' from camouflaged hides, using night-vision binoculars and specially adapted cameras. They do this to prevent foxes and other carnivores (not forgetting the odd two-legged egg collector) from diminishing the rarer birds' chances of survival! Calamity! Under such circumstances the charge of illegal entry is absolutely clear-cut. It is impossible to claim these people are bona-fide students or tourists. But this in no way intimidates such a lady in leaping to the immigrants' defence. Not even the unkind mirth generated at her expense concerning such an unhappy choice of landing place. Nothing puts her off. When asked why she criticises their arrest and imprisonment, and in particular supports their subsequent hunger strike, she merely demands to know what the assembled media would do – provided, that is, they were human enough and had sufficient imagination and empathy? What if they found themselves in the young men's shoes? How would they react to such a predicament? There is an uncomfortable silence. She reminds them that these poor hopefuls have travelled several thousand miles at great risk and discomfort only to be caught at the very last moment. What then? They are subjected to cruel mockery. At this, the assembled media begin to squirm. Her display of moral superiority and outrage is impressive. She asks yet another emotionally charged question: what have the immigrants got to lose after all? Their position at home has always been wretched; they have been subject to semi-starvation since the very day they were born. At this very moment their country is facing severe food shortages. They might as well die here as anywhere. She then berates the assembled journalists and camera crew for their lack of common humanity. She claims they have more sympathy for immigrant ducks and geese than immigrant human beings. Again the originality and force of her emotional plea initially causes surprise; then it discomforts all assembled. It prevents coherent response and certainly any attempt at further probing questions. Nobody has the heart to point out that migrant birds, ducks and geese only spend a few months each year in Britain, then return to their country of origin. Nobody subsequently adds that in that country and during transit they are often decimated by trapping or shooting, or fall victim to Nature's own series of predators. You see everyone is morally compromised by a suggestion of inhuman unconcern. Thus their minds are unable to function rationally. Raw emotion continues to overwhelm any truly logical response. Sensing her unassailable position the lady presses on. She repeats her assault and asks, 'If you are human at all, how can you fail to have sympathy for young men, forced as they are to try any desperate method to escape destitution?' Everyone assembled now feels spiritually diminished. It has so reduced their moral stature as to resemble that of a small piece of ordure. Feet are shuffled and coughs are heard during the silence, Again, on seeing such discomfort Miss Ain't-no-Flies-on-me redoubles her assault. She has them on toast. How can anyone, she demands with a dramatic gesture, put the welfare of mere birds above that of their own species? Well! Why don't you answer? Thoroughly shaken, only a few of those assembled attempt it. They stutter and stammer excuses. They cite, as their only defence against such emotional ravaging, illegality. What a paltry defence it is! They are a pushover. She demands whether man-made laws override every feeling of human compassion. The interview is virtually at an end. Confusion and shame are all around her.

Thus all fail to ask the good lady a simple question: does she think that there might *ever* come a day when the host country simply cannot accept more immigrants? And regarding mere animal life, does she believe that no creature on this planet has any absolute right to life whatsoever? The answers she might give to both questions would surely be very revealing. But alas they are not asked. Can we imagine what they might have been if someone had had the presence of mind to ask her? Being so confident of her moral superiority, she might have retorted that as far as the first question is concerned then Jeremiahs have confidently predicted population collapse for years. But has it happened? No! Mankind has shown steady increase. Therefore, why shouldn't the process go on merrily just as before? Science and technology are wonderful, aren't they? As to the second question, she might hesitate for a moment before resolutely declaring, 'If I have to choose between making more space for human beings and space for wild creatures, then I am firmly on the side of the humans.'

Whatever else the redoubtable lady might disclose, surveying the scene so proudly from her moral height, she will certainly hide her ignorance of current demography and therefore the need to address some rather cold, clinical facts. Reality can be constantly obscured by emotionalism if you are adept at the game. What she will not disclose is that while being vaguely aware that human numbers are increasing sharply worldwide, it is against her humanitarian principles to study the matter closely. That would be defeatist. Therefore she will have no knowledge of each individual nation's current demographic details, more particularly its population 'doubling time'. Nor could the scientific discipline of ecology be thought of any value or interest. You see, if either of these subjects had been of equal concern, then in all probability it would have already altered her understanding of life (in its totality!) in the first instance. She would be aware immediately that there is such a critical thing as 'balance' in the biosphere, what is more, that we are reaching a point of 'imbalance'. Should this point be passed then it is not just man's future viability in question, but *all* life in its entirety. It is this kind of sobering introduction to reality that may have subsequently changed her entire outlook. But of course she will have none of it. And this applies not just to Miss Ain't-no-Flies-on-me, but to many of those who so bravely and proudly term themselves 'human rights activists'. Their objectives, while being praiseworthy in purely human terms, are nevertheless tragically flawed when seen in the context of wider and very sombre realities.

But let us return to the gates of the detention centre where the lady is still demonstrating and still being interviewed. Having suggested that the Home Secretary and all the immigration officials are closet imperialists and fascists, she adds that she could hardly expect more of fourth-generation, fourth-rate 'white' imperialists. In this she has successfully lowered the morale of attendant press and television still further by implication. Aren't they also white? Didn't they have great grandfathers who went about the world in pith hats using Lee-Enfields and carving out vast swathes of territory? But what both they and Miss Ain't-no-Flies-on-me constantly overlook is that it was the population explosion in Britain in the eighteenth and nineteenth centuries that caused empire building in the first place. That population explosion was one which the British technology of the day could not contain. It forced an expansion outward and into aggressive colonisation, just as twentieth-century population explosions in Africa and Asia are now forcing people to move in the opposite direction. As for 'territorialism', coupled with distaste for miscegenation, both of which are factors common to and instinctive among all races, these are either unknown or only vaguely understood. This is all the more ironic in that Britain was eventually forced to evacuate her colonies precisely because each of the indigenous races retained their territorial instincts and distaste for racial interbreeding. And their animosity gradually achieved results: independence!

Unfortunately, the good lady will not expose herself to this kind of reality. Her rhetoric is potent and it virtually smothers all attempts to probe her sense of logic. Perhaps though, one reporter may be so incensed at being labelled a fourth-rate imperialist that he may summon up the courage to ask what he considers a cunning question that may expose a weakness. He asks: 'If our country is so racist and repressive why are so many immigrants desperate to get in?' The lady hesitates, which is unusual, so he dares to open his mouth still further and asks, 'Don't you agree that immigrants might be more welcome if they then accepted our values and customs – particularly in the matter of smaller families?'

This brings the lady's temper quite suddenly to white heat. 'On what evidence do you make this base suggestion?' she demands. She does so knowing full well that there are no published statistics to prove the accusation. He thus becomes a mere blob of butter she can spread on toast. When he hesitates, she bawls, 'Well? Produce facts, not spurious fiction!'

Baffled and angry he shouts back, 'Look at our inner-city schools. My God! In the playgrounds you hardly see a white face.' He has lost it completely!

With his vile prejudice now exposed to the world she smiles and lowers her voice. 'Call that evidence? Ho! Anecdotal, my dear sir! Just anecdotal...'

To viewers watching such an interview via television, that most intimate and persuasive of all mediums, the issue is no longer in doubt. Both the moral high ground and what passed for an argument appear to have been won by this crusading lady. Is it so surprising? The plight of illegal immigrants, some of whom have lost their lives attempting the various difficult and dangerous methods of entry, cannot but generate an emotional response. Everyone feels either defensive or a degree of remorse. It seems so uncaring, so lacking in compassion to pack them off to detention centres, treat them as criminals, then finally put them on a plane home. Our lives here in the West seem so secure and so excessively pampered compared with theirs. What will entry of just a handful more matter? There's room enough, surely? This then is the view generally expressed.

A rather different view, however, is taken by those in government who are forced to face and then apply themselves to basic practicalities. Here the difficulties pile up. Immigrants have to be housed, fed and given all the other things a modern society now regards as basic necessities. Thus money must be found for extra homes, schools, hospitals and what is called 'social infrastructure'. That means you must continue to commandeer more and more productive agricultural land to extend our towns and cities. Here you meet stiff opposition from farmers, many of whom have a family line of yeomen who have worked that land for centuries. They highlight the lunacy of such a policy. So you turn to areas of relatively poor scrubland or open heath. Immediately wildlife conservationists protest. Both have a valid argument. For how much longer can one intrude into cultivated or wild open spaces that constitute the food basket and the 'lungs' of an industrialised society? It is indeed lunacy to cover highly productive soil in concrete, or destroy the tree cover and habitat for what is left of our wildlife. Our countryside cannot continue to disappear in this way indefinitely.

Then there is the problem of money. How do you persuade the taxpayer to shoulder the burden? Somebody has to find the wherewithal for increased demands on the social services, health, education, roads, electricity, water, all the many-faceted requirements of modern civilisation. And it is not as if there is some end in sight. The prospect goes on indefinitely year after year.

But nevertheless sympathy for these young men triumphs. We are, for the moment at least, still affluent and our conscience troubles us. Tomorrow – well, perhaps it will take care of itself.

*

Sadly, we live in a world where few understand the underlying biological implications. The newly emergent science called 'ecology' is still very much an infant. Unfortunately too, it is deemed something of a bastard – a misbegotten offspring of biology at best. Because of this, it is seldom referred to in polite circles. As for the impolite, they have either never heard of it or have no idea what it is all about. The very name 'ecology' baffles them. As for the possible impact it might make, you would do better making enquiries from one of the rapidly disappearing natives of the Borneo jungle: they at least know what interdependence of all living things means at first-hand. They live in a real jungle not a concrete one. Bafflement therefore is the typical reaction of the supposedly well educated and sophisticated inhabitants of Europe and North America. For suburban man, Nature is merely something to be exploited.

It is tragic that the bulk of humanity today lacks the ability to see this astonishing and often very beautiful planet of ours, other than in wholly self-centred terms. Admittedly it is not easy to be objective, non-partisan and selfless. It is particularly difficult for those living in cities to try to adopt this new vision; it is almost impossible to see the world as a series of interlocking ecosystems all obeying basic biological laws. At a superficial glance these ecosystems seem so different: they involve dissimilar things such as oceans, land surfaces and the almost invisible surrounding atmosphere. Yet within each myriad life forms of incredible complexity all have their being. Moreover, each has evolved differing characteristics. They have done so in response to climate variation and chosen habitat. This is the summation of natural selection – an ongoing process! Yet all of these ecosystems in some miraculous way appear stable. It is so reassuring, so much so that we tend to forget or, alternatively, remain ignorant of, the fact that they are by no means proof against change – catastrophic at that! And the central message broadcast loud and clear by this new science of ecology is that the greater the diversity of life forms within any one of those interlocking ecosystems, then the more certain are its fundamental health and viability. Conversely, the more restricted or limited that diversity, then the more unstable, unhealthy and therefore questionable that viability.

Fortunately for us all, the health of the biomass as a whole is not greatly endangered when a small proportion of these ecosystems fall sick. Provided the factors that cause sickness are not permanent and are eventually removed, most ecosystems will gradually recover. Like newly born islands (those bare volcanic eruptions rising steaming out of the sea) life in all its different forms will gradually begin to colonise them all over again. There is an important proviso though: there must be healthy ecosystems fairly near at hand to supply colonists in the first place. Sadly this is of no concern to the average city dweller. They have no eye to see, nose to smell or ears to hear the plight of suffering ecosystems. Should their 'metabolism' become sluggish, their outer form sickly and their smell nauseating, who bothers their tiny mind about it? This is nothing to the bulk of suburban folk. They do not hear an inner voice whispering, 'Ask not for whom the bell tolls…'

*

John Donne's lines would seem to resonate in pessimism, even suggest despair. Yet as it happens there are some rays of hope remaining. And I shall focus on one, although for the bulk of self-assured, self-preening Westerners it may prove to be a shocking or perverse choice. You see that ray of light for me falls on China!

Now for some, the very name produces aversion and distaste. In their eyes it is a country presided over by an appalling regime. Indeed the majority of Europeans and North Americans glimpse it only in vague outline, enveloped as it is in a fog of prejudice and misunderstanding.

Yet the present Chinese government has carried out the most audacious experiment ever attempted in the history of mankind: the resolute decision to prevent the further expansion of its population. This involves defying the most basic of human instincts: unrestricted procreation.

Even so, the one-child-per-family policy, in the eyes of the West, is just another Draconian measure imposed by a distasteful and authoritarian regime; it is also a horrifying denial of human rights. And they see no irony or contradiction in their view.

For those who blurt out this opinion, expressing as it does an immediate gut reaction, there is a vital question they should ask themselves. What other alternatives are open to the Chinese? For a country bursting at the seams what is to be done? Do they propose that China should seek a few little territorial conquests perhaps? Could she persuade, possibly with the aid of a little military muscle, her neighbours to 'modify' their borders to give her people 'lebensraum'? The seemingly thinly populated areas of north-western Mongolia perhaps? Ah, but that is Russian territory. South-west into India? Hardly. Well then, what about territory to the south? Vietnam perhaps, or Laos, Burma, Thailand, Cambodia? But aren't these well populated already? Well then! Why not jump a continent? Australia has large open tracts with virtually nobody on them, hasn't it? It has, but! But what?

You see it is so easy to criticise China from a distance. It is so easy when one has no personal responsibility in the matter. It is so easy when one is never faced with the terrifying reality of such a huge population and the need to grapple with this ghastly problem of 'lebensraum' oneself.

A brief look at recent Chinese history, more especially from the middle of the century, just after the success of the communist takeover, may however be instructive.

In the 1960s, despite Chairman Mao's various policies to tackle the gravest problem of all, that of feeding his people, his efforts to improve agricultural techniques and boost food production were singularly inept. And even during the few years that he actually achieved a marginal increase, the sharply rising population wiped out what was gained. The Malthusian nightmare was fully enacted! On average one million people died yearly of starvation. That was in good years. In the bad ones, either through drought or disastrous floods (or indeed Mao's personal interference), the number rose dramatically. In two years, between 1961 and 1963 for example, an estimated nineteen million died.

There were two alternatives for Mao at that time. He could send his armies marching over borders to conquer new territory, or risk internal chaos and counter-revolution. He came very close to both. That he refrained from launching China on a serious programme of territorial conquest, yet still survived internally, was nothing short of a miracle.

In the decade preceding, as has already been noted, the USA, together with her allies in the West, suffered years of acute paranoia. This was generated by a horrifying vision: the gradual communist 'takeover' throughout the world! To be quite objective and fair, there was some good reason for concern, but not for the excesses that such paranoia suggested.

Shall we backtrack for a moment and retrace ground already covered?

At the end of the Second World War the immense efforts the USA had put into the production of the atomic bomb gave her military high command a brief period of euphoria. She had become the most powerful nation in the world. Such euphoria was to be shattered only four years later. That the Russians could have manufactured then tested their first nuclear device so quickly came as a tremendous shock. It also made the unrestrained march of communism an even greater threat. And the menace came in two main directions: from Russia poised behind her satellites such as Poland, Hungary and Czechoslovakia, thus sweeping directly into Western Europe from the east, and from China, in the opposite direction, infiltrating the entire south-east continent of

Asia. True enough, China did not possess nuclear know-how at that time, but there was the suspicion that Soviet engineers and technicians were already helping her construct those facilities. Meanwhile America attempted to maintain her lead. Frantic efforts were made to break into the field of intercontinental missiles with the help of the captured German rocket expert Werner von Braun. Never content with doing things by halves she also pressed forward with the development of the even more powerful hydrogen bomb. But the race was an uncertain one. The Russians had captured some rocket technicians too! In the meantime China appeared to make her first attempts at territorial expansion. She invaded Tibet. She did so on the grounds that it had been for centuries part of her own territory anyway. International condemnation came thick and fast. China paused as if in surprise, then looked around as if wondering what all the fuss was about. Later, ominously for the West, there was a brief war with India over disputed border territory. This China won hands down. The world looked on in dread, wondering whether the 'yellow hordes' of Western imagination would then sweep on deeply into Indian territory. Again international condemnation seemed to have an effect. This time there was also a distinct possibility of USA retaliation – under the guise of a United Nations mandate. The secrecy surrounding Mao's inner circle of government, and the attitude of his immediate advisers (and possible successors, some of whom were later 'purged') were such that there is no clear picture of Chinese policy at this time. One can only suppose that the threat of nuclear war forced Mao to hesitate. The vital decision to take the only alternative – that of population control – was however not taken immediately. When, or how, and by whom, still remains unclear. The attention of the world was in any case diverted by the communist North Korean invasion of non-communist South Korea. As we have clearly seen in previous pages, the US government and military began to think seriously of the 'domino effect'. A hurried resolution by the UN (which Russia failed to veto because of an earlier protest 'walk-out') gave the USA and her allies a mandate for military intervention. Again as we know, the Korean war lasted a very bloody three years. It did so because of a later intervention by

Chinese 'volunteers'. These were hurriedly sent to prevent North Korean defeat. The move caused serious argument and division between the American President and his top military advisers. President Truman and Second World War hero General MacArthur in particular found themselves in direct conflict. Truman desperately wished to limit the war: MacArthur saw outright war with China, including the nuclear option, as inevitable. This eventually brought about his sensational dismissal.

Truman's viewpoint was partly influenced by evidence of a cooling in Russo-Chinese relations and the possibility of a permanent rift. Indeed Russia had drawn back from full military support of both North Korea and China. Initially this had developed because Mao had shown a rather surprising reluctance to accept Russia's undisputed leadership of the communist bloc. Ironically, Mao had not only criticised Russia's interpretation of the communist creed but had also proved remarkably uncooperative in the matter of a disputed border region between them. And indeed the rift gradually widened rather than healed. At the same time Russia was aware of an imbalance in the arms race. It seemed essential to concentrate efforts to produce a battery of long-range ballistic missiles capable of bringing the threat of nuclear war to the mainland of the USA. In this she still had a certain leeway to make up.

To repeat earlier observations, mercifully, a US nuclear strike against China was avoided. Nuclear strikes against other communist regimes were also avoided, when later another 'domino', in the shape of South Vietnam, was attacked by North Vietnam. And incidentally, not even a US military defeat finally provoked the nuclear option!

Was this because in 1964 China had finally succeeded in manufacturing then testing her first nuclear weapon? Possibly. But China had poor relations with Vietnam anyway and her attitude to provoking further confrontation was unclear. Again this period is shrouded in deliberate Chinese silence and we may never know the inner thoughts of her leaders at this time.

The death of Mao in 1976 brought a new leadership and with it some vital changes in attitudes. Agricultural communes had already proved a dismal failure; they were quietly dismantled and later it was tacitly admitted they had failed. Private enterprise, with the peasants being allowed to hold small strips of land and sell produce on the open market, was at last sanctioned openly. A pragmatic approach to industrialisation was also adopted. Yet above all the realisation that every effort in greater food and industrial production would still be nullified, because of remorseless population increase, at last received full attention. A rigorous population policy was finally implemented.

A decade later the world suddenly heard talk of a Chinese economic miracle. Devastating famines were no longer a recurring pattern, more astonishing still, production of hitherto unheard of 'luxury' consumer goods, such as fridges, washing machines and television sets, had been put into operation. These products were now beginning to make an appearance on the home market. Housing for the people – the population still rising, but now due to greater longevity rather than other factors – was being supplied; new, well-planned cities were springing up. Export trade with the remainder of the world was booming.

An incredulous West looked for reasons. Irony of ironies, once more the hoary old 'triumph of capitalism' coupled with 'rejection of discredited communist doctrines', was trotted out. The implementation of the one-child-per-family programme was either totally ignored, or, if mentioned in passing, was referred to as 'an unfortunate remnant of communist repression'!

Such blindness should have taken everyone's breath away. It did no such thing of course. The 'triumph of capitalism', repeated endlessly as a theme with variations, and composed on the spot by journalists, was accepted as the only possible answer.

Relations with the West subsequently improved dramatically. Then suddenly, without any kind of warning it all soured again, and equally dramatically. The very mention of the name T'ien-an Men Square is now enough to summon up all of the West's old revulsion. Every possible prejudice is revived, every expression of acute distaste and distrust put into play. The ancient myth of the cruelty and inscrutability of Eastern despots has been hurriedly exhumed and found miraculously to be very much alive and kicking. But can there be any variation in the interplay of logic among human beings anywhere on earth? Surely from a purely anatomical point of view the human brain is constructed without any variation: it operates in exactly the same way, East or West. But this seems to have been overlooked. Why should thinking processes carried out in the East be any different from our own? Certainly there are minor variations in attitudes caused by traditions and culture, but in pursuit of rationality the cerebral processes should be immune.

Shall we look at the T'ien-an Men incident again, but this time without our normal baggage of prejudice?

After Mao's death came a gradual re-evaluation of his record as leader. There was a gradual rejection of his supposed superhuman qualities that foolish propaganda of the period had created. There followed a slow liberalisation of attitudes and a softening of the hitherto sharply defined outline of authoritarian rule. But the difficulty is that once you set off down this path, it is apt to take on a momentum of its own. And Chinese students, like students everywhere in the world, quickly sensed a change of atmosphere. They keenly sniffed the air with anticipation. And they insisted on doing so much more eagerly and more openly than their elders. It is perhaps the birthright of the young to be buoyed up by unquestioned optimism. Yet they, more than others, are tempted to be carried away by their own soaring spirits. They lack the deeper insights given by full maturity and the even greater courage demanded when faced by the greatest tyranny of all: reality. And unfortunately they became entangled emotionally rather than objectively with the concept of 'democracy' at the very outset.

Never having experienced it, the students in China were never aware that being man-made – and therefore operated by fallible and sometimes downright dishonest men – it too has its limitations. Consequently their enthusiasm was both boundless and at the same time naive. You see in a country of (at that time) 1,105 million people, democracy, if at all worthy of the name, is almost impossible to achieve. Democracy, in any truly recognisable form, can only flourish among rather small nations with highly sophisticated checks and balances. In a huge monolithic structure it is impossible. The only alternative is to portion it up into semi-autonomous states federated to central government, as in the USA. China had none of these preconditions. Admittedly, in theory it was divided into provinces presided over by devolved government. The so-called 'People's Congress' indeed represented the various provinces, but in practise under Mao at least, it had no real power. It was merely a rubber stamp. Not that the Chinese have anything to be ashamed of. No government anywhere in the world can hope to reach a consensus in central policy-making using such a huge body of delegates. It is not just cumbersome but chaotic. Even if one looks at Western regimes that may be justly described as fully democratic, one finds that overall policy and decision-making is in the hands of a few ministers of central government. These are seldom more than twenty in number. Subsequently even this small group is subject to an inner cabinet or council of a mere handful. Here collective responsibility may be taken – though as often happens even this handful in itself may be temporarily dominated by one individual gripped by a massive ego. At the end of the day the only difference that truly matters when comparing democratic states with communist ones is that the former can rid itself of a regime that no longer retains its confidence. It does so by using a system where a genuine opposition party or parties exist and where a general election and majority vote can effectively kick out the party in power. Communist states, on the other hand, are stuck with their leaders – unless there is a secret 'palace revolution'. There is no effective and openly acknowledged opposition. But to repeat: China in 1989, on the eve of the massacre at T'ien-an Men Square, was nowhere near the transitional state able to make such a radical change. It was neither possible nor subsequently workable.

Those in control of the Chinese communist party of that time were either aged revolutionaries who had gone through all those terrible war years (and almost equally turbulent years of peace!) or young administrators who had never imagined the possibility of their authority being questioned. That the students should choose to fabricate a replica of the Statue of Liberty in the capital's main square and demand almost instant 'democracy' was in itself an affront to the party's dignity and authority. It was all the more serious when the students refused to disperse after a warning. This was totally beyond comprehension. It appeared to these old men that the vehicle of liberalisation had suddenly gone wholly out of control. Attempts to use the brakes had shown only the presence of 'design faults'! They were faced by the horrifying vision of a braking system refusing to function. Thus dispersal by force was the only option. Tragically it became dispersal by unnecessary force and hysterical overreaction.

Even so, a state of panic does not absolve those who, in the grip of heightened emotion, commit murder against unarmed civilians. It may have been forgivable if they were an armed mob intent on bloodshed on their own account, but they were not. To be entirely fair though, we know nothing of the chain of events over the last few hours leading up to that decision. Was the information supplied by the Interior Ministry inaccurate or deliberately alarmist? If the latter, what was the nature of the order finally given? And how was it interpreted by military commanders? Finally how did the behaviour of the officers and lower ranks on the spot reflect the intentions of those commanders? Incidentally, exceptions can be found in every sphere of events. That the army – and oddly enough in its lower echelons too – was not made up of mere automatons has been clearly proved. We all have that remarkable and quite indelible memory of a lone student walking out into the path of a line of tanks. The commander of that lead tank was no cog in a machine, blindly obeying orders. The column stopped and repeatedly tried to negotiate a way round the lone figure. At no time did we see the column continue on its way and brutally crush him. Surely this has a poignant message of hope for us all? True, we have no other evidence that similar hesitation was shown before the killings began in earnest. Indeed all the suggestions are negative. Perhaps one day, though, a fuller picture of these tragic events will come to light. That said, there is one further factor that has never been fully investigated. It is this: if the students' demands were for a fully Western style of democracy – one which included the right of each individual to procreate without restraint – then the matter takes on a very different complexion indeed! Horrific though the loss of life on that occasion may have been, it would have been nothing compared with the loss of life that would have followed had China reverted to the free-for-all procreative errors of the past!

Thus looking at the matter from this very different angle, it must be seen that the panicked reaction of the leadership, though unusually harsh, had an element of justification. They would have had a nightmare vision of a sudden end to their remarkable achievements. All that they had done to bring calm and relative prosperity to a country that had suffered so much and over so many years was now being put in jeopardy. Can we imagine ourselves in their position? Would our reaction have been any different?

Now there is a curious quirk in human nature that seizes on and delights in the perceived faults of others. In the privacy of our own thoughts many of us are uncomfortably aware of our own imperfections. Therefore, a sense of relief is achieved by gloating over the record of those who have sunk far deeper into the quagmire. Criminologists assure us that even among prison inmates this quirk is evident. For example, a burglar may, by sheer good fortune, have avoided physical injury to his victims – thus he feels superior to those guilty of robbery achieved with violence. A burglar who has committed violence feels less guilty than those who have committed murder. Those who have committed only one murder feel morally superior to those found guilty of multiple murder. Those who have murdered 'mere' adults feel superior to those who have murdered children. It is all incredibly grotesque, but it happens. In contrast, if we consider those outside prison walls and who live in a free society, how much more contemptible are those who, while seeking power and influence for themselves within that society, put on a tinsel halo and decry the records of others? How easy it is to make use of this moral aphrodisiac, never having experienced the infinitely more serious traumas suffered by China.

Almost certainly, with the wisdom of hindsight, the Chinese leadership will regret the use of such unnecessary force. And one would hope that they are human enough to recognise their tragic mistake – moreover be suitably burdened with a bitter conscience. In mitigation, however, the West should recognise that, with the demonstration appearing to get out of hand, far too much seemed at stake. The possible overthrow of the regime was at risk, and none of the octogenarians felt able to gamble their hard-won achievement of stability with the possibility of country-wide chaos.

Predictably of course, there will be those who will refuse to see this episode in this light. With some zeal they will point to China's poor record since that day. Indeed if reports are true then thousands will have been imprisoned, and probably in the harshest conditions. Beyond this, a proportion may well have been executed. Certainly many of the leading dissidents went into hiding and a number of these have not been accounted for. Some of those who made it into Hong Kong gave details of the physical hardships of the journey. Clearly this alone may have been too testing for some. The difficulty of penetrating through to the truth of the matter, when the authorities remain so secretive, makes it the more open to 'creative' accusations.

As for China's retention of the death penalty for certain crimes, predictably human rights activists naturally claim – and do so rightly – that this is now an unacceptable and positively barbaric form of retribution. They will claim that it is increasingly recognised as unacceptable, given that the world is slowly becoming more civilised. Unfortunately though, this is a claim that goes too far. It would be better if it were really true. Currently it is wishful thinking and only partially true. In all honesty the only claim one can make is that sensitive and intellectually gifted people in various parts of the world are increasingly setting their faces against such punishment: the broader masses still favour such barbarism. Moreover, in countries where executions have been abolished, there is increasing agitation for its reinstatement. Ignoring this, those who harbour a long-established prejudice against China will remind you that the present regime executes 'criminals' by firing squad for a whole series of crimes. This includes minor cases of drug peddling and any kind of organised corruption involving the social fabric of the nation; and it does so right up to the more usual cases of (what Americans call) first-degree murder. Further, they will point out that this penalty is not applied sparingly and in extreme cases; it is applied liberally right across the board! Liberally and with vigour! More vigour, and less than very necessary care.

Pressing their case even further, the most persistent of China's critics will pose this emotionally charged question: how many of those executed each year were in fact young students dedicated to the cause of democracy and freedom? And they will raise the emotional temperature by adding, 'These students have been categorised as common criminals? Their only crime? That of being judged 'politically subversive'!

Now without question these accusations must be taken seriously. They cannot be dismissed as trumped-up charges or as fantasies. Nor should one see them as all-too-convenient sources of ammunition for those implacably prejudiced against China.

However, in the matter of capital punishment it should be remembered that in the USA itself (where significantly enough many of these accusations originate) quite a number of the fifty states still retain the death penalty. True, it is used more hesitantly perhaps, moreover after lengthy appeal procedures, and only in cases of 'first-degree murder'. Even so, it *is* used. Furthermore a growing number of executions have been carried out over the last decade. Undermining their critical stance, together with their right to stand on the moral high ground even further, is the ample indication that many states currently without the death penalty will reverse their attitude in the near future. Throughout the USA there have been two decades of sharply rising crime rates. And the incidence of horrific murders has alarmed the population to such an extent that pressure groups have been formed in every 'uncommitted' area to demand the reintroduction of capital punishment. To repeat: this growing trend can only dent the American claim to occupy the moral high ground. It cannot but diminish Western credibility in criticising China on this issue.

Even so, to Western eyes, and especially where 'minor' cases of drug trafficking are concerned, the Chinese viewpoint does seem excessive. But are drug trafficking and organised crime really minor offences? Could this be a superficial and all-too-hasty judgement? Are we far too complacent on this issue? Can we retain such criticism and condemnation on deeper examination? Shall we look at the issue of drug trafficking which is linked to the Mafia (or its Eastern European and Russian equivalents) and the West's conspicuous failure to counter it more closely?

Here, in my view, we are shockingly complacent. Criticism of China only helps to bypass the fact that most Western nations will one day find themselves in crisis. They have still not woken up to the severe threat posed; there is no realisation that it involves the entire way of life and moral health of their populations. They pooh-pooh the stark reality. And that reality embraces the chilling scenario of utter chaos should the trend toward greater and greater drug dependency continue. Entire nations could be reduced to helplessness and disintegration.

And what of rising murder rates? Here hidden in the cold statistics is one other factor concerning capital punishment which few are aware of. It is this: I would hazard the prediction that as governments in both Europe and America are unable to keep abreast of their prison-building programmes, capital punishment may be reintroduced universally, not because of any change in the moral argument, but purely for economic reasons. It may be the only practical solution left! If you can't build secure accommodation fast enough, and find the money and staff to maintain it, then you end up with an open-ended and virtually insoluble problem. For certain categories of killers, especially those who are either mentally insane or of infantile mental development, there is no hope of a 'road to Damascus' conversion. And as these may have been convicted in their late teens (and thus given a sentence extending to fifty years or more), then the problem lasts over their entire lifespan. As this category of prisoner is slowly increasing, the ever mounting costs, both in terms of overall finance and the undue strain put on prison staff, may well become too burdensome a weight on society's shoulders. In such an event the already grudging acceptance of that burden may evaporate. Executions may thus become 'economically expedient'! The question of morality is then thrown out of the window; it becomes in effect mainly academic.

However, reverting back to what the West sees as the ugly story of Chinese authoritarian rule: what we are actually faced with is a chronic lack of fully authenticated information. So much of what we know, or are supposed to know, is no more than conjecture – worse, mere hearsay.

Crucially, the West needs accurate information. It needs to

know the degree of success, or alternatively the difficulties and indeed lack of success, experienced by the Chinese leadership in imposing their unique population stabilisation policy. The urgent question is this: do the bulk of Chinese people fully accept that strict limitations of their procreative urges are necessary? Do they fully accept it as the only logical solution to a desperate problem? Alternatively, do they find it just another unpleasant experiment embarked on by leaders with dubious motives and what appear to be absurd expectations?

We have no evidence either way. All we can do is speculate. And by doing so of course we invite China's critics to rush in! With glee they immediately open up an enormous field for emotionally generated controversy, none of which is based on fully authenticated observation.

It may be necessary to repeat therefore that the Chinese experiment is by far the most audacious yet carried out in the history of mankind. Its implications in combating the fundamental causes of war, famine, disease and insurrection are profound. Given China's appalling population problem, such an experiment should be viewed with relief and every good wish for success. Furthermore, if it *is* finally crowned with success, then hopefully it should become in turn an example to be followed by other pressurised states in the remainder of the world.

Nevertheless it is essential to remember that it is still an ongoing experiment. Doubtless there will be some errors or unexpected difficulties within such a programme. Few can claim that error never attends new and uncharted ventures. Thus a more open response by China to the questions and the doubts of the remainder of the world would be doubly welcome. Reticence shown in the past has been due to the persistent criticisms of human rights activists, mainly from the West, most of them with certain religious affiliations and a curious understanding of the sanctity of life. They see most forms of birth control as murder: at the same time they ignore the irrefutable logic which shows that unrestricted procreation leads to a population explosion and inevitably to war. What is war but murder? And it notches up the scope of killing by including both infants, their parents and grandparents! Surely such an attitude is bereft not just of simple logic but also of what is often called 'basic common sense'. Birth control essentially involves the prevention of semen with its countless spermatozoa making successful entry into a female egg. The vast majority of spermatozoa are doomed to die anyway. So why should prevention of just one reaching its goal be judged reprehensible? As for the question of a proportion of failures in birth-control techniques necessitating the later requirement of an abortion, why should the killing of the foetus in the early part of its existence be considered more horrific than the killing of countless adults and their children, born or unborn, during war? This is wholly beyond my understanding. These high-minded but emotionally ravaged people have of course viewed the Chinese 'one child' limitation with particular horror. That this is wholly misplaced has yet to permeate their logic-defying judgement. They seem totally unaware that unless such measures are taken then a Third World War is inevitable.

It is this rejection of simple logic by the West that tends to make the Chinese shrug their shoulders and retreat further into isolationism. Absurdly enough, this in turn is mistakenly seen as a retreat into the depths of a troubled conscience! To compound this farcical situation, isolationism in itself becomes a further target for abuse by her critics. In such circumstances, one can only pray that simple logic will one day win out. The current vicious surge of prejudice and vindictiveness can only do immense harm to all prospects of peace for the future.

However, in such difficult circumstances it must be recognised that lacking Chinese openness and assistance, all we can presently do is speculate. For my own part, given the current evidence for an economic miracle and the sheer volume of manufactured goods reaching the West, I must suppose that the implementation of the one-child-per-family programme has more or less been successful. Shall I correct this statement: I suppose it has been successfully implemented in China's cities! I am less sure of rural areas. Overcrowded cities impose a logic of their own. Moreover, the more sophisticated and educated that city dwellers become, then the more they are likely to accept and understand such logic. Away from the big cities, greater space seems to imply no such restrictions. And unsophisticated and poorly educated peasantry may still have age-old customs which are all too deeply rooted. I can only speculate therefore that control of human fertility in such areas may be more problematical.

If my guess is near the mark, then there are certain questions that require an urgent answer. Foremost of these concerns: what are the type of birth control techniques that are being used? Are they similar to the current contraceptive techniques advocated in the West? Are they oral, using an equivalent of the Western contraceptive 'pill'? Or are they mechanical using the condom? More likely still, are they a combination of both? But more urgently comes the further question: what if such methods of contraception fail? Are abortions then mandatory after the birth of the first child? Are they achieved across the board by compulsion? If so, do the Chinese people accept this stoically? Or alternately do they find it traumatic? If so, do they resist it to any significant extent? Particularly, where isolated country areas are concerned, is compulsory abortion evaded? Is this on any (proportionally) serious scale?

Questions such as these are, as I say, merely open to conjecture in the West; they can so easily lead to accusations that the Chinese are hiding something nasty in the woodshed. Recently, for example, there have been accusations that the peasantry have been actively encouraged to hold on to one of their age-old customs: infanticide! In particular this involves killing infant girls rather than boys.

To my mind, and if these accusations can be substantiated, then they suggest that abortions have been evaded. It also suggests that the mothers – whether they be single parents or indeed within a reasonably stable marriage – are still unable, for one reason or another, to look after the child. Orphanages set up by the state to care for such children are now being suspected of a deliberate policy of neglect! A team of Western reporters has actually accused the Chinese government of cynically allowing disease and malnutrition to take its course, leading inevitably to an early death. Male infants, on the other hand, apparently receive better treatment and tend to survive. This is indignantly denied by the Chinese leadership. They protest that it is ludicrous to suppose that it is a formulated policy. If neglect can in fact be proven, then it is localised. They insist that this can only be an isolated instance of the failure of orphanage staff to carry out their proper duties. It is in effect a criminal neglect of duty. In an enormous country, and with tenuous links between central government and the more remote regions, the population generally (let alone orphanages!) was, until very recently, prone to all kinds of shortages. This could be true. All one can do in the meantime is keep an open mind. On the face of it though, the very presence of orphanages itself poses a question. In a country where constant recurrences of famines and disease are now a thing of the past, and where a strict policy of one child per family is apparently adhered to, it does suggest evasion of that policy in country areas. Indeed it may be more widespread than initially supposed.

But can we afford to adopt a holier than thou attitude? What is the West's record in caring for the defenceless? What is the West's record – and no matter what the sex? Here the defenceless are no longer found in orphanages. Thankfully, due to the widespread practice of birth control, few unwanted children remain. Desperate childless couples, having joined large waiting lists and assessment programmes, immediately snap up any unwanted newborn children. Some are even pressured to go abroad! Indeed 'defencelessness' these days has moved from children to the very opposite end of the life cycle – the very old. Here, due to longevity and the prevalence of dementia, severe pressure has now been put on the overall care of the aged. In the West, accommodation in old people's homes is in great demand. And it has caused a number of problems. So if we heed the biblical command to concern ourselves with the 'mote' in our own eyes rather than those of others – in effect to examine our own consciences – what do we find? Are we prepared to ignore our own record in this respect? How many staff in old people's homes have been found criminally negligent? How many have cynically assisted the old and defenceless to die prematurely? How many have been charged and found guilty of murder in our own courts? How many 'homes' have been closed down after belated inspection, this following many years of complaints by relatives which were conveniently ignored? Can we put our hand on our hearts and say to the Chinese that our control over, and inspection of, homes for the defenceless has always been of the highest order, untainted by scandal or corruption? Sauce for the goose is sauce for the gander. To make the matter more pointed still, we must remember that organised help for the defenceless aged is usually undertaken by local government – it is not the duty of central government. On the face of it this should be more efficient and allow for closer inspection of such 'homes'. Yet our record until very recently has been abysmal. Scandalous conditions and criminal behaviour by so-called 'carers' have come to light, and more often by accident rather than efficient inspection. Yet we still criticise the Chinese central government which attempts to rule an immense country by remote control. And they do so with an array of civil servants, all of whom are human and composed of the usual proportion of less than honest and non-efficient individuals. What would be our attitude if Chinese journalists and photographers began poking round and investigating our eventide homes?

Shall we put this aside and now attempt an examination of the overall conditions of Chinese life. An obvious question: do we find signs of evident dissatisfaction, or even widespread rebellion in the face of the Chinese government's authoritarian rule?

Bitter opposition usually expresses itself in attempts at mass exodus. In the case of former East Germany, the communist government combated mass exodus with heavily fortified borders manned by trigger-happy guards. Even so, there were endless examples of desperate attempts to find sanctuary in the West. Yet given the enormous population in China and the impossibility of putting an Iron Curtain round her immense borders, all one can say is that numbers of those seeking sanctuary appear to be very small, indeed minimal. There are of course constant attempts to get into Hong Kong but these are largely economic migrants, not political discontents. Then again, a proportion of those who appear at first sight to be seeking political asylum are, on closer inspection, not really genuine.

An example of pseudo-asylum seeking has recently been reported from the USA. It may be instructive to look at this incident in detail.

A freighter called the *Golden Venturer* (an inappropriate name in this case!) was seen to beach itself on a sandbank off New York City harbour. A nearby police boat investigating the stranding saw a number of people dive into the sea as it approached. Later it was found that the ship had two hundred and sixty Chinese attempting to enter the USA illegally. Six bodies were washed ashore and eighteen survived an icy sea. These were taken to hospital suffering from acute hypothermia. In all, two hundred and seventy-three were detained and an unknown number drowned. The Indonesian captain and crew were arrested. Commenting later on the incident, New York's Director for Immigration said that the would-be entrants were from Fukien province and had paid up to thirty thousand dollars each to be taken to the USA. He added that twenty-four vessels had been intercepted off New York in the last five years and blamed organised gangs of criminals in both Hong Kong and New York for setting up profitable businesses based on 'carrying human flesh for profit'. The last part of his comments were however the most pertinent to our discussion, and I quote verbatim: 'Most immigrants had been coached to apply for political asylum on the grounds that the Chinese government was limiting their families *to one child* each.' Obviously his audience was not well informed. He found it necessary to add: 'Beijing has adopted the one-child policy to limit population growth.'

If we examine this incident it seems unlikely that any Chinese male could find thirty thousand dollars for such an uncertain venture. In a country where average wages are low and the exchange rate between Chinese currency and the US dollar makes for doubly unfavourable circumstances, then this in itself suggests that these men had shady backgrounds. Probably they were common criminals on the run from the Chinese police. Rebellious students and political activists, with genuine reasons for seeking asylum, have no such contact with criminal organisations. In their amateurish attempts to escape they are usually caught – well before leaving!

This then should be some indication of the changing conditions in China. It should also underline the difficulties in determining the true motives of the relatively small number of apparent asylum seekers[6]. And it is, in this respect, an interesting exercise to contrast the lack of evidence of mass exodus with a near neighbour of China, namely the Philippines. Here, given the area of its land surface coupled with the percentage of people to the square mile, this country is still experiencing a violent population explosion. Circumstances are such that the Philippine government is actively encouraging people to leave its shores, and by any and every means possible. Significantly too, this is not a communist regime. It has for long periods been ruled by rightwing dictators embracing the usual military connections, or, as a minor variant, mere puppets controlled by the military.

In a country composed of a large collection of islands of varying size, eighty per cent of the people are Roman Catholic. These are held tightly in the grip of one seemingly magnetic personality, Cardinal Sin. No, this is not an irreverent and mocking invention on my part but his actual name! And this revered personality, metaphorically breathes fire on sinfulness, particularly in the realm of sexual matters. Arising out of this, the good Cardinal sees fit to continue fierce and unrelenting opposition to all forms of contraception. Are we therefore surprised that the Philippines has, for decades, seen millions after millions living in destitution, dirt, disease and squalor? While a small minority live in luxury the vast majority of its citizens have to fight daily for existence, and must tolerate the most revolting slum conditions anywhere on earth. The solution? The government has the answer – decant them overseas!

Unfortunately, as countries round the world are beginning to resent this, making it more and more difficult to accomplish, clever ways have to be found to get round obstacles. Indeed some Filipino businessmen closely allied to government have found quite lucrative ways of doing so. For example, in Britain, there is a weekly magazine aptly titled *Exchange & Mart* in which secondhand goods are advertised. These range all the way from cars and general household goods, to pets and business opportunities. There is also what might be called a 'lonely hearts' section. Here

---

[6] Since these lines were written, some Chinese student-leaders who have achieved asylum in the West have naively celebrated their freedom to have as many children as possible!

though, one suspects that the advertisements are aimed very definitely at the second-hand Romeo rather than the Juliet market! For example, advertisements extol the charms of 'beautiful yet submissive Eastern girls', which incidentally is surely a contradiction in terms. Any beautiful girl, no matter what nationality anywhere in the world, knows her own worth! And submissiveness seldom enters the equation. At any event, for what are clearly third and fourth-hand Romeos, with bitter experiences of British womanhood, comes the invitation to pick out from a large colour brochure a likely girl for what is coyly called 'marriage or companionship'. Applicants, having picked, then pay a substantial fee and are flown out to the Philippines to inspect their choice in person. Here they are given a 'generous' five-day interval. With a marriage ceremony finally performed and more money duly paid, it only remains for the husband to demand a passport for his bride and a similar right to bring her back to this country.

Unfortunately though, over the years many husbands who finally succeeded in this ploy found that their brides deserted them just weeks or even days after landing in Britain. Possession of a passport and transport to another country was the girl's primary objective. After that she considered herself free to earn herself money in any way suitable to her tastes and inclinations. This dictates that she disappear into the anonymity of the nearest large city. Often, at a later date, irate 'husbands' who happen to be successful in tracking them down, resort to physical violence to relieve their feelings. One temporary fifty-year-old husband recently hit the media headlines by murdering his beautiful yet submissive Philippine girl. And the situation can also be reversed, and even more cruelly! Philippine girls who have found employment as housekeepers in some Arab states have, in trying to defend themselves from attempted rape by their masters, found themselves injuring the said master. They are then subject to the laws of Islam. Flogging of the woman (again this is not a misprint – it does not involve the man) usually results. In one case of attempted rape, where the woman picked up a kitchen knife and used it to good effect, beheading (of the woman) was the penalty under Islamic law.

In this crazy world of ours, however, the Philippine government escapes criticism: the Chinese regime's attempt to avoid a Third World War and bring some kind of dignity and hope into their people's lives is castigated as evil.

Incidentally, in Britain, nobody as yet has challenged the owners of *Exchange & Mart* to explain or try to defend their moral stance in this aspect of their commercial zeal. Such commercial activity is surely more akin to that of a cattle market rather than a genuine exercise in uniting two people in a truly loving and caring relationship.

Is it really necessary to make any further comparisons with, or comments on, this matter? In its policy of population control, China has, in the most fundamental of ways, occupied the moral high ground. In contrast Cardinal Sin, his bishops, priests and laity carefully turn their gaze from painful reality and merely wallow in specious religious sentiment. They refuse to accept that their policy ensures that the Philippine people will continue to remain in endless squalor and misery.

Chapter III
IDENTITY

Words are such strange things. Sculptured by the tongue of primitive man they must have been, in the earliest of eras, few in number and very basic; they undoubtedly represented just the most simple and immediate of his observations. Some of them may well have survived, despite being corrupted, bastardised or otherwise mangled by countless centuries of use, and for all we know they may still represent the most basic of things. However, in all the centuries that have rolled by since that era, there has been a vast accretion of tongued sounds; and this has resulted in an enormous vocabulary in each of what has now become an enormous range of languages and dialects.

Significantly for us all though, about eight thousand years ago words were given further substance and a curious authority by being given a written form. And whether as incised marks in clay, or curious scratches on parchment, silk or papyrus, under the hands of ancient scribes they took on a new life. Moreover, scribes began to extend words beyond merely simple descriptions of people and of things; they began to extend them to all common phenomena met with in everyday life. Indeed they began to try to embrace abstract concepts. They began groping and stumbling after tight and tidy representations of what were essentially will-o'-the-wisp abstractions, things such as 'responsibility' or 'honour' or 'lawful' or 'God'! And this act of invention – that is, creating a word out of thin air to represent strange, astounding, dubious, confusing, or awe-inspiring facets of life – has its drawbacks and its dangers. You see, any attempt to synthesise a representation of a natural phenomenon and its pressing 'reality' (in itself a word open to endless philosophic questioning) tends to give a wholly pseudo-authority to far too many words. This becomes all the more serious when they are entered into what have now become standardised dictionaries.

Take for instance the first two words I used for the title to this essay, namely 'on' and 'human'. Now the first word 'on', consisting of but two letters, is so utterly simple in its usage as to suggest directly primitive origins. It may have come to us straight out of the distant past with very little alteration. The second word 'human' is also entirely straightforward and not open to further comment. The third word 'conflict' is, however, rather different. Would it surprise you if you were told that it is more complex than you would at first suppose?

At first sight this short word of but eight letters embraces a concept we all think we understand, yet on closer scrutiny it becomes more vague and subject to misinterpretation. You see, unfortunately it is open to 'mutation', even subtle merging with other concepts. It is more fluid than it should be; indeed some people bandy it about so carelessly that it reaches a level of imprecision that I, for one, find unacceptable. You raise an eyebrow? You wish me to explain further?

Very well then. For example, I could have chosen to entitle this essay rather differently. I could have chosen *On Human Aggression* rather than *On Human Conflict*, and in this form many would have supposed that the last two words were synonymous. But there *is* a distinction, if only a subtle one. You see, 'conflict' is not just a rather bland substitute for the more spiky and abrasive 'aggression'. It just isn't. Shall I explain it this way – a young child often shows quite sudden and wholly unexplained bouts of raw aggression. It goes red in the face, screams and punches anyone within reach. If you are not the parent you sniff and think privately, 'You've got a right one there chum'. Even the ever loving parent is often duly shocked, puzzled or embarrassed. Similarly adults of retarded development may display behavioural traits reaching the level of a five-year-old child, and not a very bright one at that. They too are often prone to sudden inexplicable rages and aggressive behaviour. And if, as so often happens, they find themselves in a court of law, then they are often described as being of 'diminished responsibility'. Nor at this point must we forget otherwise highly intelligent adults. A small minority, despite having doctorates or scoring 'genius' marks in some wretched mastermind competition or other, nevertheless display periodic evidence of quite batty, disturbed, or even schizoid behaviour. All of these groups show 'aggressive' tendencies. So would you agree that the word 'conflict' is not really applicable here – this mainly because such people do so out of the blue and without discernible cause? To repeat this slightly differently, let me say that they do so without the application of logic and prior thought. Conflict, on the other hand, and in the sense I have already used it, has a cause and is the result of (at least) a certain degree of conscious thought. It is, in legal terms, 'premeditated'. Of course such meditation may well prove faulty, but that is another matter entirely. You get my drift? So then conflict is 'causal' (related to or having a cause) and not casual. Putting the letter 's' in a different place makes an enormous difference. And with a rapid little genuflection toward those who insist on the academic application of proper philosophic techniques I will admit that with 'conflict' being causal, it often has an 'effect' too. But nevertheless I will mutter under my breath, 'Not necessarily so.' You see, a conflict of interest, a conflict of purpose, a conflict of understanding (such as is posed by a genuine paradox) and many other kinds of conflict are often contained wholly within one's thoughts – at least, that is, the thoughts of civilised people. They are unseen. They bubble away deep within the labyrinth of the cerebral processes; they remain essentially part of very private inner conflicts. And they may remain there for some considerable time without surfacing; sometimes they never surface. True, at the odd time there may be curious facial expressions. There may be a frown or a spasm of pain. But this could equally be caused by flatulence, don't you agree? On the other hand, nobody can deny that inner conflict may also transform itself into an aggressive stance, and certainly, at the end of the day, manifest itself in physical violence.

Overall then, most cases of inner conflict leading to outward forms of aggression are fully causal. They are born, nurtured and often burnished in the first instance by a harsh word, an insult or indeed an imagined insult. Indeed in this form they fully demonstrate cause and effect. But even here I insist that it is not inevitable.

Far from inevitable, in fact. Why? Because the sheer survival of man, not forgetting many other species of the animal world who happen to be gregarious, depends on the ability to suppress the surging of inner conflict and its associated possibility of aggression. To repeat earlier observations: without it, we, and many other animals, would have failed to survive. We would never have proceeded beyond the most primitive of stages. The success and indeed the very existence of gregarious species demands the cultivation of the very opposite of aggression: it demands harmony and co-operation! And the greater the density of people or animals packed within a single area, the more essential does co-operation and harmony become. Indeed without it, both we and they are doomed.

Of course you don't need to remind me that our lives are not therefore wholly filled with sweetness and light. You will always get individuals who, for one reason or another, fail to see the overall necessity, who fail also to accept fundamental reality. There are always those who fail to conform. They become, in that most descriptive of words, 'anti-social'.

There are for instance the solitary types; but they seldom cause trouble. But there are others who do cause trouble, much trouble. Much more threatening to mankind's welfare are those who either secretly or openly reject the system – usually for personal gain. There are a variety of such people, and we label them anarchists, revolutionaries, terrorists. Mafioso and the like. They seem born with a grudge against organised human society. The vision of the vast majority making endless compromises to achieve a workable level of harmony, co-operation and social cohesion – in a word, all things constructive – fills such people with contempt. For them, the entire structure of society is something akin to a mansion house filled with all kinds of treasures; foolishly, though, somebody has forgotten to equip it with a decent security or fire-alarm system. And these people are prepared to rob, vandalise and sometimes attempt wholesale destruction of that edifice on a grand scale. Oddly though, they still expect hard-working farmers, truck drivers and shop assistants to be good-natured enough (or perhaps simple-minded enough) to maintain food supply to *their* tables; they still expect engineers and technicians to work quite normally to supply *their* water and electricity, expect doctors to attend *their* wounds or cure ailments, expect oil-rig workers to extract *their* all-essential fuel – in short expect a host of people to remain sweetly responsible and co-operative. Such 'pillars of society' should not only supply them with day-to-day needs, but do so with a smile or take the consequences.

Equally there are the small-time conmen and thieves who work away unsystematically and individually. These merely wait for fortuitous circumstances. They wait for the lucky break and the odd chance to relieve other people of their money or treasured possessions. These too would be scandalised if farmers, truck drivers, shop assistants, electricity and water workers and all the rest suddenly became truculent and uncooperative, even downright bloody-minded. In short all criminals would be mortified if others adopted their kind of antisocial behaviour.

Thus, as modern life becomes more and more complex it becomes evident that we rely even more heavily on social cohesion. We must pray for at least reasonable levels of overall sweetness, pray for it to last as long and for as uninterrupted a period as is possible. We pray for it most fervently of all of course for infants, children and defenceless people generally. And from the very outset and the earliest periods of mankind's history, this must have been the dominant consideration. If it had not been, then once again, humanity simply would not have survived. Passing on the baton of life more or less successfully from one generation to another is, after all, a basic instinct. And it is the vital determinant as to whether or not a species survives – any species! Failure to protect and nurture the young, either among human or animal species, quickly brings about extinction. Thus jovial optimists might be tempted to say that we learn, or rather ingest the survival value of sweetness and light from the very cradle; we do so by way of (well, metaphorically speaking of course) our mother's milk. So when it comes to the child's turn to reach adulthood and all the responsibilities it entails, there is an automatic adoption of sweetness and light. It begins, so the eternal optimist pronounces with conviction and a hint of a leer, even during courtship – in fact the very preliminaries of mate-selection.

Automatic and instinctive? Well, I prefer to take a more realistic and sober view. Courtship, with its fervent protestations of love, leading to and including parenthood, if it is indeed to be equated with sweetness and light, is only partly instinctive. I believe all forms of human harmony are in part at least contained in a very artificial learning process. Moreover it is often kicked at and resisted. And it begins in childhood. There is a further unfortunate factor too: when finally acquired, it is much more a 'preserve' or a characteristic of the female of the species rather than the male. We must never allow mere sentimentality or emotional diarrhoea to blind us to this reality. And there are facets to all this that cannot be quickly passed over to avoid embarrassment or preserve primness and decorum. You see it must be noted that even during courtship, when the smiling or protesting swain mutters all those sweet nothings, the underlying motive in his mind is often very different from hers. In most cases it has never been better described in contemporary parlance as just a ploy to 'get a leg over'. This is often for him the only object or goal. And he may even think of it in terms of a league game. Moreover it is done without much regard for genuine sweetness. Preferably too (if it happens out of doors at least) it is achieved in the poorest of light. And it is not just my automatic use of the academic tradition in inserting an addendum at this point: you see, whether or not he is successful in inserting parts of his anatomy into the female, it is evident that courtship of this kind hovers round the term 'rape'. Harmony, co-operation, sweetness and light can certainly attend courtship; indeed in a proper loving relationship it becomes 'sine qua non' for marriage and long-term commitment. But to pretend that it is always present is to become a stranger to truth and to remain blind to day-to-day reality. What I am getting at, and I trust will gradually be proved, is this: there is undoubtedly an element of instinctive behaviour initially in this adoption of 'sweetness and light'. It becomes the genuine survival factor achieved by gregariousness. However we must never forget that the greater part of the subsequent adjustments, compromises, and sometimes very real sacrifices we all have to make in curbing our personal needs and desires – curbing them for the common good of the community we live in – is learned! More significantly still, it is usually done the hard way! It is not imbibed with our mother's milk. Throughout the centuries we have gradually learned to fit ourselves into this system as best we may. We learn even as children. We learn sometimes with a careful explanation of the principle involved, sometimes with a sharp word, a clip round the ear or a smacked bottom, depending on circumstances. These circumstances do not relate solely to the nature of the crime committed. For example if a five-year-old throws stones at a greenhouse because he is enraptured by the sound of breaking glass, he is often unable to understand what all the subsequent fuss is about. A smacked bottom seems outrageous to him. Similarly it involves the attitude of the parent and the ethical or psychological mores of one's parent's social class. Thus depending on these, both the crime and the punishment are looked at and indeed administered rather differently.

At this point it should be said that in case histories drawn up by social workers, psychoanalysts, police and criminologists while studying the more deplorable examples of antisocial behaviour, it is found that in the majority (but not all) of serious cases, the individual has suffered a disturbed, violent, loveless or, alternatively, overindulged childhood. These are the most common factors. This is particularly true for the most serious of crimes involving what is called 'grievous bodily harm' or actual murder. As for historical cases of mass murder, there is some evidence that individuals the stamp of Hitler and Stalin, for example, were brought into this world by what can only be called 'rape within marriage'; certainly they were subsequently treated brutally or alternatively ignored by their fathers. In direct contrast, however, they were also overindulged as far as possible by their mothers. In this way they got the worst of all possible worlds. This in no way excuses the crimes they committed later, of course. Nor for that matter does it guarantee that each and every child so treated, will grow up to be a monster. There are, after all, genetic variations within the human cortex that can nullify many, if not the majority, of all environmental influences. But as a general principle, the quality of nurture often has a significant role to play in an individual's initial understanding and future attitude to life. This can later change under the bombardment of experience, or resist such trauma until the last day of life.

Ideally then, the procreation of all human life should be achieved under conditions involving love and harmony. If it is not, then it usually bodes ill for the future welfare and development of the child. The obvious question we must ask ourselves at this point is this: why then does procreation occur without these essentials? Why does it often occur at an opposite extreme, that is even in hatred and disharmony? Apart from what is called 'common rape' there are a variety of reasons. Failure of contraceptive techniques or materials is perhaps the main source. Sometimes though, the female is just gripped by a temporary 'broody' feeling, while the male is either drunk, sex mad or attempting to give proof of his virility. Either way the resultant child starts life at a serious disadvantage. It is difficult enough bringing up a child each and every day teaching it to be a responsible and caring member of society when love *is* fully available; it is almost impossible when love is restricted or wholly absent. Equally though, it should also be remembered that possessive or overprotective love can prove just as destructive. And in this vital matter of parental responsibility for the quality of life in future generations lies our greatest danger – even our very survival as a species. Here I state in all sincerity that it is essential, if human society is to survive in any half-decent way, and not teeter inexorably toward chaos, that procreation be achieved with true love. It must never be an empty and disingenuous protestation of it. Worse, it must not be achieved on a descending level of loveless involvement, leading to common rape. To repeat: any child born without love and subsequently nurtured in the worst possible way will almost always become a misfit. It may even become a deviant, or societal leech on society. Worse still and, at an extreme, it may become a destroyer of society! In short, these children will always be outsiders. They will begin life in conflict; they will probably end it in massive acts of aggression. And this is why, in probing for the cause and nature of conflict, procreation becomes central to my theme.

Thus to look at this vital area more carefully and in greater detail, it is now necessary to return to this rather tricky matter of vision. We must ask yet again: with whose eyes do the greater mass of people look at life? And following on inevitably, whose information will they process?

*

To repeat earlier observations in my effort to hopefully drive the message home: the structure of any community, whether it be large or small, is basically an aggregation of extended families forming a clan or tribe. The bigger the community, the greater the aggregation of clans or tribes forming ethnic groups. And so it goes on up the scale until it reaches that of a recognisable nation. Moreover, from time immemorial, direction or control has been in the hands of individuals who, depending on the size of the community and its circumstances, have called themselves tribal elders, tribal chiefs, squires, knights, barons, kings, presidents or emperors. Alternatively, power has sometimes been in the hands of prelates or religious figureheads of one kind or another; in these instances we talk of bishops, cardinals, popes, high priests, imams, ayatollahs... the list is extensive. To describe these various grades of controlling power we say that they exert 'political' or 'spiritual' control over our lives, depending on whether the regime is broadly secular or wholly clerical. Unfortunately though, in the latter case the control can never be wholly spiritual; inevitably it becomes involved with secular matters. Thus in practice our lives are dominated by people associated with the word 'political'. Consequently most people's aims and motives are derived from such an outlook. The spiritual input is usually small or relegated to the background. In like manner the bulk of people within such a regime tend to use only the politician's eyes; they use similar info-filtering and adopt the same kind of cerebral processing. Thus everything is seen in political context, often to the exclusion of all else. Even historians who subsequently pick over the debris of the historical record insist on using the eyes of the political animal – equally to the exclusion of all else! And it has brought us into not just total visual imbalance, but also into an appalling mess.

Earlier pages have shown how thoroughly mistaken and even tragic the consequences have been. They have also attempted to explain how easy it is to fall into this trap, given that we are forced to take on board much of our information flow on trust. After all, we are unable to verify it all personally. We are not superhuman. We lack either sufficient time or the opportunity. Over and above this we are very often denied the full insight into abstruse areas; this is because these demand an ability to decipher jargon and achieve a breadth of knowledge only available to the professionals in the field. Not unexpectedly many sections of society in despair have thus thrown away what few safeguards they had. This is all the more regrettable in that at one time they did at least possess their individual abilities to use reason and logic. They also had the use of their own personal filtering systems together with the benefit of their own securely hidden thoughts. In short they had sufficient individuality to rely on their own cerebral processes. And it has all been a tragic mistake to assume that these processes are no longer up to the task, moreover that we must timidly accept the word of the professionals in all their various fields.

Down through the ages individuals here and there have fought to retain independence of thought and outlook. They have refused to follow what were accepted 'truths' and the prevailing attitudes – all of which were reflected back in mainly political form with hardly a tinge of the spiritual. The earliest non-conformists we know of, however, tended to challenge contemporary religious beliefs; these were grouped under the generalised word 'prophets'. Later, protesters took the political content fully on the chin, so to speak. They were not prophets in the ordinary sense, merely writers of prose. Sometimes too they were poets, playwrights and philosophers. Very occasionally they were professional court fools, sometimes scientists, sculptors and painters. Nor should we forget musicians, though in so abstract an art it is more difficult to translate the message with precision. Beginning with the Ancient Greeks we have Aeschylus, Sophocles, Euripedes and Aristophanes, who set up a tradition of informed criticism of both the political and spiritual attitudes of the day. Socrates paid for such criticism with his life. His enemies formulated the trumped-up charge that he had corrupted youth and mocked the gods. Later, in other countries and under other regimes, brave people would also take their stand. And while it would be impossible to name every spirited individual who has criticised the established political outlook since the astonishing Grecian period, it is difficult to refrain from saluting such people as Swift, Donne, Voltaire, Goethe and Dostoevsky at the very least. In the sphere of music Beethoven perhaps (as one of three towering masters in the field) makes what is essentially a cry for spiritual wholeness complete with freedom from political chicanery and repression. He reinforces this cry and brings it out of the realm of pure abstraction by angrily deleting Napoleon's name as dedicatee on the title page of the *Eroica* symphony. Nearer our own time come Ibsen, Shaw, Wells, Aldous Huxley, Brecht, Camus and Sartre. To digress for a moment, incidentally, in a wholly opposite direction, an interesting (but in the end somewhat unsuccessful) attempt has been made by Albert Speer, as a close associate of Hitler, to explain how even perceptive people can lose their precious individuality. He exemplifies how easily one can lose integrity, how easy it is to be dominated by the sheer willpower of others. Unable to divest his inhibitions fully, and those dark truths lurking in the inner self, he struggles to explain his inability to penetrate and unmask the true nature of the man he served. Despite having been at the right hand of the Führer for eleven years, and serving faithfully almost right up to the very end, Speer never unravels the final mystery of this man's extraordinary hold over others. One can only suppose that Hitler – unlike the vast majority, who openly reveal endless uncertainties as to their purpose in life – projected absolute certainty, in his own words 'faith in destiny'. To the outside world Hitler exuded rock-like confidence. He was unshakeably convinced of some 'divine' purpose. It was this strange aura of certainty that could overwhelm others. Further, those staring eyes, coupled with that strangely strangulated note in the voice, seemed to have had a genuine hypnotic effect. Whether Hitler was himself conscious of his power of hypnosis, or alternatively quite unconscious, and merely using it intuitively, is neither here nor there. Many of the German High Command, professionals to a man, with records of undoubted courage and initiative (made personally in the face of carnage on the battlefields), nevertheless themselves remained strangely mute and sycophantic in this former corporal's presence.

That power simply existed. As with other extraordinary examples in the historical record, perhaps some day the mystery will be solved. This is not as implausible as it may seem. After all, our ancestors would surely find our ability to send messages and moving pictures through thin air from one side of the world to the other quite incredible. To them it would invoke pure black magic. Similarly, in the years ahead our successors will surely forgive us for our failure to believe that personal magnetism is equally non-mystical and has a purely rational and scientific explanation.

But let us return to the dominant hold of politics in human affairs. On the one hand a political explanation is always advanced for every supposedly giddy height we have reached in social achievement, yet conversely a political remedy is also held out as the only medicine for every social ill on the other. With it comes the insistence on subtle political dimensions in every sphere of human affairs. The tyranny is further compounded by the insistence that human populations within any regime must use the eyes, ears and nose of their political masters, and none other!

The object of this essay is to show that not only is this a gross violation of human freedom aiming at the total destruction of the very gift of individuality, but also that every attempt has been made to prove that other eyes, ears and noses must now be used to provide an essentially new viewpoint. This is vital if we wish to understand the root causes of so many of our present ills, let alone all the dangers that face us in the foreseeable future.

*

So then, once again down to business.

The first and foremost of these attempts has involved, and will involve, the new vistas opened out by dedicated individuals working in the fields of biology, ecology and genetics. And again I propose to plunge into these without any further excuse or 'by your leave'.

What I intend to do is to bring into the very centre of your consciousness a wide range of information flow that has recently been opened up. Moreover, I trust that the reader will evaluate what is set out using their own God-given capacities for rational thought – not forgetting the aptitude to accept or reject what they find irrational. One can ask for little else except patience and the plea that if I have made any errors then they have occurred either out of ignorance, lack of precise information or my own stupidity. It is essential to remember that we all have a very special encumbrance and wretched birthright: we all inherit fallibility. Therefore we must always be aware of the presence of error and not be unduly surprised when we find it. By the very nature of things nothing we do or touch is free from it, and of course it is always so much easier to see other people's errors, less easy to detect one's own. This is often a question of not being able to stand back far enough. One is too involved with one's own thoughts to obtain a fresh eye and be sufficiently searching and alert. But provided that errors are minor, and not serious enough to undermine the entire credibility of my outlook and judgement, then what is transferred from these written pages to the reader will have been worth all the effort expended. Equally it will have been worth the effort reading it. But you must always remember my caveat!

*

Initially I will restate three fundamental biological hypotheses that have stood the passage of time. These are now accepted by the overwhelming number of scientists working in this discipline. Firstly, mankind is part and parcel of the animal kingdom. Secondly, mankind is a primate, closely related to others of that group, particularly in the hominoid section. Undoubtedly we are an offshoot from common ancestors such as gibbons and apes; and as such mankind might with due sarcasm be called a Yuppy Ape. Thirdly, mankind belongs to that group of primates who may be described as being essentially gregarious.

The last of these declarations is hardly open to doubt. As a result I do not expect it to stir up any kind of controversy. This is not true of the first and second declarations, however. One hundred years ago these were the subject of fierce and even bitter controversy. They provoked intense debate not just among the established churches and laity of that era, but also among highly competent and professional biologists themselves.

Much of the dust has of course settled since then. Virtually all professional biologists, with the exception of the odd maverick, now accept these declarations. They accept them indeed as fact and cease to give them a second thought. The majority of individual churchmen, of the Protestant persuasion at least, now accept them too, if somewhat reluctantly; however, some remain more guarded than enthusiastic. But one should never overlook the fact that there are some religious groups and certain sections of the general public who continue to raise objections. These are either fundamentalist die-hards, or persons of an insufferably pompous nature who never question the validity of either their corporate or personal self-esteem. They consider that monkeys and apes (not to speak of the remainder of the animal kingdom) are wholly inferior creatures, scarcely with any right to life. They suffer other creatures to inhabit the same planet as themselves only if they happen to be domesticated or exploitable, or both. In the case of wild animals, which seem to have no exploitable potential, they tolerate them only on a temporary basis – simply because they happen to be there! But they hope to accelerate the rate at which they are presently being exterminated. In short, human beings are seen as standing wholly outside the animal kingdom. They are certainly superior in every way. Moreover, they have such intelligence and wisdom as to be almost divine.

Being all too aware of this, and rather than suffer undue deflection from my purpose, I will therefore begin by dealing with the uncontroversial 'gregariousness' of the human animal first.

As has now, I trust, fully been demonstrated, our social cohesion affords us a very definite 'survival factor'. But such a factor has not been fully covered in any systematic way. So it is perhaps incumbent on me to enlarge further on this aspect for a moment or two.

At the outset then, mankind is now so firmly established as the dominant species on this planet that it is perhaps all too easy to forget that this premier position is of fairly recent achievement. As already noted, our early ancestors were, in comparison, almost defenceless: they had what can only be described as a 'precarious' hold on life. They were surrounded by many species of creatures who were more fleet of foot, far more powerful, and had more fearsome killing capacities. This was achieved by large jaws lined with huge teeth which could slice muscles, tendons and arteries at a single bite. As if this were not enough, early man had to find a night's shelter in cold, damp caves, or alternatively encircle a small 'dormitory' area with bits of spiky thorn bushes or piles of stones. Before the Aquatic period food was difficult to find, moreover open to endless competition from other creatures. It was in particularly short supply during drought or extensive bushfires. It seems something of a miracle, especially to modern comfort-seeking and somewhat decadent Western minds, that we ever pulled ourselves through that early period. Modifying this view slightly are anthropologists currently studying representatives of our Stone Age ancestors, such as the Amazonian Indians, the Bushmen of the Kalahari, and the people of remote parts of Papua New Guinea. All these anthropologists report with admiration and astonishment the toughness, unexpected skills and sheer tenacity that these last representatives of our early ancestors exhibit. However, one factor needs our special attention. The most dangerous time for any of the precursors of *Homo sapiens* in this crucial make-or-break era was during his or her birth and early childhood. Dangers were multiplied because an already vulnerable species was brought closer to extinction by the very helplessness of the human child. It cannot, after all, pick itself up in the very first hours of birth and begin to stumble and later run after its mother as do many other species. It cannot even cling to its mother's fur as can all other primate infants – indeed these are subsequently carried about hardly impeding the mother's agility. In contrast a human infant is wholly dependent on the mother for food, transport and protection – this for a period that is seldom less than three years. Following such a time it then requires at least a further ten years of overall care, protection and training. This comes at the hand of its parents, siblings or extended family group. One can only repeat that it is astonishing that our species ever survived! Given our very low status in the animal kingdom, our very limited numbers and the host of acute dangers that attended the hunt for food and avoidance of large carnivores, our survival is nothing short of miraculous. This is especially so if you look at puny man and fragile woman individually. But we did not survive individually! We survived – never forget it – because of teamwork and info flow that were unequalled by the remainder of the animal world. In the earliest eras close co-operation with one's extended family group was crucial. It is still important today, of course, except that the survival strategy has changed direction. We no longer need fear to protect ourselves from other members of the animal kingdom: now the danger comes from members of our own species! Ironically too, in the age in which gregariousness and social cohesion have achieved such a density ratio, it has become a factor that tends to work against us! Our only serious competitors, other than ourselves that is, are unseen and tiny. They are microbial and viral. And these are able to attack us much more effectively than ever before!

But let us return to the dangers attending birth and early childhood. It would appear that our earliest motivation was to add to, rather than just maintain, the traditional social behaviour patterns of the primates generally. And it arose from the peculiar difficulties surrounding childbirth. Because of a sharp reduction in the adult female's mobility each time she neared labour then subsequently gave birth, there was pressure on the remainder of the family group to find a safe haven. Moreover they had to remain there for some considerable time. There would also be a division of labour established on a systematic basis, seldom found amongst other primates. Having either learned the art of making fire artificially or by taking flames from bushfires and keeping them alive continually, the first duty of the immobile female, (beyond that of looking after her child) would be to maintain that fire. This would in turn facilitate both experiments in primitive cooking and be a useful defence against animal attack. The males would then spend the greater part of their time foraging for food some distance away. Incidentally, despite the myth of 'man the mighty hunter' having been exploded some time ago, it is still commonly supposed that the males spent the best part of their time hunting, continually risking their lives in the effort to maintain a diet of meat. In fact dental examination of early skulls shows this to be wildly inaccurate. There was a heavy dependency on wild fruit, tubers, vegetables and nuts, with meat comprising only a quite small percentage of the total diet. However what *is* important is the early appearance of the division of labour. With it, inevitably, by dint of constant repetition, came the acquisition of uniquely developed skills. Such social organisation, demanding as it does co-operation and harmony, was probably well established by the time of the ancestor of true man (probably Australopithecus), up to two million years ago. This would predate toolmaking and the full use and control of fire. Man's only defensive strategy at this time would have been his gregarious nature and – if the behaviour pattern of the gorilla and chimpanzee is anything to go by – the use of long sticks. Today's male chauvinists who refuse absolutely to assist in any work around the house, and refer to it contemptuously as 'women's work', will doubtless derive great comfort (and further authority) when they discover that the division of labour may well have a five-million-year history. Unfortunately, this will be offset somewhat by the further discovery that it applies only to women nearing the end of a pregnancy or actively engaged in the care of young children. Females not so immobilised would gather the vegetarian part of the diet just as effectively, and possibly even more efficiently, than the men. Probably though they would have hesitated to participate in hunting for meat. Male chauvinists would also be disconcerted to find that in the remainder of the animal kingdom, where many species also have a system of division of labour, the males often participate in 'female duty sectors' and are not contemptuous of 'women's work'. Many species of birds for example will show male–female co-operation during the incubation of eggs, with the male taking over to sit on the clutch, thus giving the female a well-earned respite. Similarly, after the hatching of young, the male will be equally attentive in feeding and in general care and attention. Again, certain insects of course have highly complex social organisation. And despite division of labour, the males often take a vital role in securing the protection and welfare of the young also.

Nevertheless, in the case of man, there is at least some justification in apportioning tasks, and this is not excluding making sharp divisions on the basis of sexual differences. Until very recently, significantly enough before methods of contraception became widely used, women were faced with endlessly recurring pregnancies. On this basis it is not so illogical that the 'little woman' was expected to remain at home accumulating household skills – skills that over thousands of years slowly embraced an ever widening variety of 'duties' such as spinning, weaving, sewing and cooking. For that matter it is not too illogical either to find that this became traditional; and this remains true whether she was in fact engaged in child-rearing or not. Even barren women were expected, consciously or unconsciously, to retain their 'femininity' – thus they remained wedded to traditional female occupations.

However, the overall factor that no one should lose sight of concerns the subject of this essay: the phenomenon we call conflict. As already stated, my objective is to examine causes of conflict and to follow them through even in trivial 'low level' forms. Indeed? Follow even what stand-up comedians refer to as the 'sex war'? you might ask in disbelief. Yes, this despite what may at first appear to be only trivial male–female misunderstandings. What may seem trivial though often develops into something far more significant. And it becomes the point at which all self-control and restraint is lost. This then inevitably leads to open aggression. Certainly in the male–female relationship there is always a degree of tension. Fortunately though, for those who are generous enough to accept each other's faults, a regime of harmony, sweetness and light prevails for much of the time. Even for those a little less generous – and this applies to the majority of both human and animal relationships – the pair bond rubs along reasonably well and without undue discord. Even so, at the lower levels of tolerance we would be less than honest, or dangerously blind to reality, if we failed to recognise that a large proportion of relationships are not co-operative and harmonious. And no matter how we attempt to excuse it or minimise it, the reality is this: there has been and probably always will be a degree of conflict between the human male and female. This is doubtless because of differing attitudes and different interests. We might argue how or why this has come about, also why men seem to have been dominant and exercised a degree of authority over women for perhaps two million years. The fact is these things exist! They have always existed, and probably will continue to exist. Why? Simply because a significant proportion of couples will always remain unable to accept and thereby tolerate each other's faults.

In the Western world, where for well over a thousand years the Christian Church has insisted on the sanctity of marriage, it has succeeded in camouflaging the true extent of conflict within marriage. Only since the mid-twentieth century has a relaxation of the tight influence of the Church become evident. This has been coupled with a modification of attitudes to divorce, and a similar relaxation in the legal system – more especially relating to the grounds for, and financial settlements for, divorce. Thus a much truer picture emerges. And it shows indeed a considerable lack of co-operation and harmony. Demonstrated fully is the inability to use just a modicum of toleration and goodwill. Duly reflected in this are the current figures for divorce in the Western world, which are quite staggering. As for the remainder of the world, with its differing religious beliefs, attitudes and customs, it is more difficult to generalise. However, it would be fair to say that grouped as a species, mankind does not show any significant variation in behaviour patterns, no matter which area of this planet it inhabits. So while there will be many pair-bondings that remain happy and fulfilled over a lifelong period, there will also be a significant proportion scattered throughout the world that are anything but!

All this once again seems trivial when one examines it on an individual level. Such conflict is however of considerable consequence, as soon as one begins to examine its influence on social cohesion in its overall context. Not least are the complexities and sheer weight of the problems brought in its train. You sniff and purse your lips? If I further contend that these problems will in time be recognised as the actual Achilles heel of the democratic system in the Western world – actually become the main reasons for its catastrophic collapse – you will do more than sniff; you will assume that my cerebral functioning itself has suffered catastrophic collapse! You may even decide that you have been duped into attending the ravings of a madman.

If you have patience, however, I will attempt to explain

further. And I will do so without any foaming at the mouth, or examples of deranged or distorted reasoning. Indeed I hope I will exhibit due respect for, and every possible use of, reason and logic throughout.

Very well then. To begin with, you will no doubt agree with my earlier statement: our earliest ancestors survived only by the skin of their teeth. They were faced with appalling odds. Logically then, you must also agree that countless generations since have faced only slightly diminished difficulties and dangers. And they have in turn succeeded in passing on the baton of life solely through exceptional parenting skills and devotion to duty. Clearly then, our present-day survival is wholly due to their unusual tenacity and self-sacrifice in this vital sector. But that does not mean that each and every human adult was (and still is) a superb parent. As in every other section of the animal kingdom, careful observation shows that parenting skills can vary enormously. And here I do not refer to varying techniques adopted during courtship or procreation, let alone parenthood in *different* species, but *within* species. In other words, species-specific parenting. For example, in some species even the most rudimentary forms of parenting are non-existent. Many female fish merely scrape out a hollow among small pebbles, or find a cavity in amongst coral or in a rock, then fill it with an astonishing number of eggs. These are then fertilised by the male, and that is all there is to it! It illustrates the absolute minimal level of attention. In fact subsequent parental care is thrown to the winds – more correctly to any predator who happens to be about. Survival of these species depends on the incredible numbers of potential offspring produced and not on care and attention. Many amphibians are similar. Turtles, for example, come ashore, lay large numbers of fertilised eggs in sand, then abandon them completely to their fate. As for frogs, has anyone failed to notice the thousands of tiny mites in frog spawn carelessly abandoned to fend for themselves? It is an example of the initial fecundity demonstrated by some species. But subsequent survival is a matter of luck. Sheer numbers constitute the survival factor involved. Again most species of snake, and lizards, while initially showing some parental instinct by assisting in the incubation of their eggs, promptly leave them after hatching. They too allow them to fend wholly for themselves. However, in contrast at the opposite end of the scale, you have some fish, together with many species of bird and a wide variety of mammals, which are devoted and indeed self-sacrificing. Salmon are an extreme example of the latter. They fight through almost insurmountable obstacles during their migration from the sea into inland waters to spawn. Having done so they then die from exhaustion. Many birds will use desperate measures to defend their eggs or chicks from predators. Alpha baboons defend their troop to the death against leopards; giraffes and elephants put their young in the centre of a defensive ring and vigorously protect them from lions. Within all of these animal species, there are, however, a minority – just a few individuals here and there – which somehow or other fail to come up to standard. There are some poor mothers and worse fathers. Much the same applies to the human species. Some females are so incompetent, lazy or feckless that people commonly say they 'disgrace the name of womanhood'. Males, in this category of disgrace are even more numerous. They tend to wander much further down the scale of irresponsibility. And it is at this point that we come to the crucial factor involved in the overall survival of the species. You see in all other sectors of the animal kingdom, and where dedicated parenthood and nurturing of offspring *is* an integral part of the survival factor, then the offspring of the incompetent, lazy and feckless parents do *not survive*! The significance of this cannot be overstated. You see, until fairly recently in the two million or so years of mankind's 'parenting' history, this was true of our species also. The children of incompetent parents seldom reached maturity.

Now here of course some readers will immediately realise the direction in which these statements are leading. A nod is as good as a wink. Others will need to have it spelled out for them. Why? Because they look at the matter with the wrong sort of eyes, unsuitable filtering systems and an array of cerebral dysfunctions. Worse they remain firmly attuned to the political viewpoint and find it impossible to adjust to the biological.

Very well then – here is the inescapable conclusion spelled out. Even so, I will avoid the crude mouthing of 'survival of the fittest' because I firmly believe it is both inaccurate and misleading. For me the fundamentals of biology, embracing reproduction and the genetic laws that underpin it, can be pronounced in the simplest of terms as 'survival by tenacious parenting'. A bit of a mouthful. Nevertheless this is the key! Tenacious parenting! It is of crucial importance. And because offspring *tend* to inherit many of the characteristics of their parents, deleterious genetic material such as poor parenting until very recently was not carried through into following generations. So 'survival of the fittest' is too imprecise a battle cry in this fundamental sector of the survival of a species. Yes, yes, for those who happen to know a thing or two about genetics you have no need to nudge me and begin whispering certain scientific facts in an unusually kind attempt to save my reputation – I am very well aware (as proved in earlier chapters) that genetic inheritance is so complex that it does not ensure that children are a carbon copy of their parents. Indeed such is the incredible complexity of genetic reshuffling, using as it does all of its huge hand of cards, that 'direct' inheritance of either good or bad characteristics is always uncertain. And there are myriad possibilities or recombinations and permutations; moreover, genes can influence each other even *after* the cards have been shuffled. So no such certainty exists. Nevertheless the *tendency* is there. If it weren't, just think of the consequences! The age-old 'art' called farming would prove impossible – that is in any truly structured and dependable way! Before the formation of the science of genetics, farmers simply worked on the crude rule-of-thumb principle that if you selected 'a good 'un' and mated it with another 'good 'un' then you mostly got yet another 'good 'un'. Possibly you even got 'one real beauty'. In other words, despite your exaggeration you got a very welcome improvement of the offspring for your pains. Occasionally of course you got a 'bad 'un'. But you made sure in one way or another that the failure had little chance to 'roam'; that it was never allowed to reproduce, in other words. For thousands of years farmers have gradually improved their productive capacity on this planet by this fairly straightforward principle. It applied both to growing crops and producing livestock. Then just prior to this century came Mendel with his theory of 'dominant' and 'recessive' genes. And these factors gave a vigorous kick-start to the science of genetics.

So then, early genetic research began to explain just a little. Yet immediately it made the entire field extremely complex and only fully understandable to gentlemen farmers with college education. For those without such an advantage, it became increasingly necessary to call in 'them as knows a thing or two'. Today governments now very wisely supply them in the shape of agricultural advisors.

In the case of human reproduction, however, despite the very same crude principle being operative until very recently, it was thought both unnatural and unnecessary to call in anybody – least of all a medical geneticist. Human reproduction was somehow sacred ground. But times have changed. A fair number of people now consult such geneticists if there is a suspicion that they may pass on a serious genetic disorder. Yet these are still of a purely *physical* nature. What of mental disorder, or even 'character disorder'? After all, if you mate two irresponsible, feckless and lazy individuals with one another, then you will *tend* to get much the same characteristics in the offspring. Yet somehow it is still nobody's business. But in the very near future it will become very much people's business – indeed everybody's business! And here comes the 'crunch', as they say! To repeat: all creatures on this planet – other than man and domestic animals – who happen to be bad parents seldom see their offspring reach maturity, let alone achieve parenthood in turn. They die young; sometimes very young. This is the inevitable 'reward' for poor parenting. Therefore injurious genetic inheritance is not passed on. Only the most hard-working, responsible and tenacious of wild creatures see their offspring both reach maturity and also pass on the baton of life. For more than two million years the same basic evolutionary law applied to mankind also. But recently all that has changed, and changed significantly.

However, before further pursuing this vital matter, which involves what is clearly unwise meddling in Nature's basic evolutionary regime, it is first necessary to define what *is* incompetent, or substandard, parenting. Furthermore, it is important to establish the extent to which it has even now begun to damage Western society – and this before we concentrate on sheer survival in the future! Unfortunately, we find at the very outset that assessing the current damage is by no means a simple affair. It does not embrace merely the parent's basic duty of supplying the bare essentials of life: simply food, clothing, shelter, the so-called material necessities. You see, because of the intervention of the state in securing these basics (when or wherever needed), the emphasis has now swung sharply to what one can only call 'emotional essentials'. The first of these is love, the second intelligent interaction and the third, respect for the child's own individuality and personality. To paraphrase the Bible, yet the greatest of these is love. And it must be love that is uplifting both to the giver and the receiver; it must never be stifling, capricious or dependent on reward. And this transcends all class structures and financial circumstances. Unloved children can be found enduring a regime of misery just as often among the families of the rich as they can in the middle classes or among the poor. However, no matter which social class such children are born into (given that all the basic physical necessities are supplied by the state) they do of course reach maturity without undue difficulty. Outwardly, at least, they are 'sound in wind and limb', which is something you might say of a healthy pony. Yet mentally they are all, almost without exception, scarred for life. Not surprisingly too, an astonishing number come into conflict with the law. And it is instructive to look further into the circumstances surrounding this very special irony, an irony because the state, having become the overall nanny and a most conscientious guardian of all children, is subsequently forced to transform itself into something very different – policeman, judge and jailer.

Scanning background reports that are often requested by judges, or alternately case histories drawn up by sociologists or criminologists, one finds that there is a common factor endlessly repeated. Moreover it transcends all the peculiarly class-conscious moral restraints one would expect to find in each social group.

Shall we examine a range of typical histories? Perhaps it may be instructive to start in the upper class initially.

Here among the well-heeled or truly rich we find that almost all the offspring who come into conflict with the law exhibit one factor in common: they have self-centred parents totally dedicated to their own pleasure and the 'social whirl'. Pater and mater are stoutly committed to personal enjoyment, no matter what the basic needs of their children. Indeed one finds that from the earliest possible age their offspring will have been shunted off to a parental substitute: this takes the shape of a professional nanny. Moreover, when (almost inevitably) the child bonds with that substitute, the natural mother subsequently throws a tantrum, triggered of course wholly by jealousy. The upshot of this? Prompt dismissal of the nanny! Not that the natural mother now presents herself as the new object of bonding. Not a bit of it. Another nanny is appointed. It is no more than a blocking exercise. Unwilling to spend precious time herself seeking and giving love she is simply determined no one else shall gain the child's affections. And such a pattern can be repeated several times if necessary. Whether the child survives this trauma or not is immaterial. The parents have no time to notice anyway. If it happens to be a boy, when he reaches the age of six he is packed off to a prep school. Here he is of course a boarder, and even during holidays may only see his parents very briefly. Thereafter he is then bounced like a rubber ball into a public school. The effect of this treatment is to produce an emotional cripple. Don't misunderstand me: I am not gunning after the schools. I am only examining the small proportion of cases involving pupils who later tangle with the law. Incidentally, if anyone believes that expensive schooling (and the ethos they claim to inculcate) in itself guarantees impeccable adult conduct, they are either blimpish fools or incredibly naïve. All schools, without exception, have a small proportion of pupils who will later bring them discredit. In truth, all that a school can do is show the way towards responsible citizenship. The very word education, derived from the Latin 'ducere', to lead, is an accurate assessment of the process involved. One can lead, but not force. Schools bear no responsibility if an individual deliberately rejects their guidance. Whether they are state schools in rundown crime-ridden estates or famous and exclusive training stables for the rich there will always be a percentage who will do just that. But it is the parents who are the real villains in the piece, because they have slammed the door on receptivity in the first place.

However let us return to the child. Having no experience of any family cohesion or close parental interest, let alone unbroken and dependable love, the now physically mature adult assumes that the world is a barren place lacking in any true loyalty, joy or fulfilment. Therefore not only does he owe society nothing, but life will have little meaning or purpose. Subconsciously attempting to find such a purpose he will suppose that it can only be embodied in the quest for unending enjoyment. The case history from this point will show dependency on drugs or alcohol together with an appetite for promiscuous sex. There will also be evidence of complete indifference to the feelings of others. This is hardly surprising: there will be no sensitivity to, or recognition of, hurt or harm done. This seemingly unsavoury and unhelpful range of qualifications for entry into society does not nevertheless form a barrier. Indeed entry may even be gained into responsible positions. Such is the influence afforded by his family name, plus the ability to surf the upper-class network, that it will automatically secure him a well-paid position. This will include high social status. In all probability the sphere available will be either in industry, banking or commerce. And having thus established himself, he now consolidates his position for a few years. Eventually, as one might expect, no satisfaction is found in this. The fixation with self and the pursuit of pleasure is so dominant that he will inevitably search for a fast track to a higher position and even greater status. There is a craving for the kind of outward expression of success that society crudely recognises, and this is usually expressed in monetary terms. Acquiring money rapidly and in unusual quantities becomes a substitute for the lost love and attention as a child. Demanding early gratification, he embarks on a series of frauds that go undetected for some considerable time. When finally brought to court, then significantly enough, should his attention be drawn to the misery and hardship suffered by his victims, he shows no regret or shame. Remorse is completely foreign. And such case histories are found repeated time and time again.

As for the females of this species, who are often identified with the tag 'poor little rich girl', these are at least never expected to go through the charade of working for a living. They are expected to marry 'a living'! They attend all the best parties and social functions where they may expect to meet males of the required status. In the interim, these emotional cripples also become dependent on drugs and alcohol. As with the males, they too become noted for their promiscuous sex life. Their confrontation with the law though is normally less grave than that of their male counterparts. Admittedly in a fit of pique, she will sometimes commit the odd act of grievous bodily harm on a rival or ex-lover. Fortunately, since her victim is of the same worthless class as herself the remainder of society hardly loses by it. And it is only a typical expression of her jealous rage. Most of the other offences are just curious, silly or bloody-minded, such as hurling abuse at all and sundry while tipsy, shoplifting, defrauding a charity while sober, acting as a high-class drugs courier – and so on and so forth. Her one redeeming feature is that she will seldom have more than two children. She thus limits the genetic 'fallout' on the remainder of suffering society.

Notching down now to the middle classes:

In this particular social group the children of selfish fun-loving parents do not of course have nannies. In lieu of these they are left with part-time childminders whose qualifications for such a title are at best elastic or creative. At worst it is often the product of pure fantasy. Sometimes the minder will have physically or sexually abused the child; more often though the minder is what one might call 'childproof'; that is, it has properly organised itself to ignore all the little bleeder's needs. Thus the infant is merely put in a so-called playpen, as if it is some kind of zoological exhibit. There it is left hour upon hour to fend for itself. If it survives this treatment and reaches the age of two or thereabouts, it is plonked before a television and magnetised as far as possible by what is assumed to be (fully censored) 'good for it' children's entertainment. On reaching school age the offspring cannot be dumped into a boarding school; the parents do not have the resources. The youngster remains in the household. But its presence is ignored as far as possible with no interest being taken in its further upbringing or educational progress. Later, if it happens to be intelligent, the emotional cripple (using its own initiative and without any parental encouragement) often gains good academic qualifications and enters a profession. Here, after a process of consolidation, it takes a leaf out of the upper-class book of success stories and seeks a fast-track route to riches and social status. Again this represents (unconsciously perhaps) the final elimination of a childhood vacuum: the craving for admiration and affection. In due course into the courtroom dock steps the young solicitor, the accountant, the bank employee or local government official. Here he is accused of embezzlement, false accounting, or some kind of complex fraud generally. Again when attention is drawn to the financial suffering and trauma caused to others, there is no reaction.

Turning now to the lowest end of the social scale...

Here the parent's desperate pursuit of 'the good time' in all likelihood again involves heavy use of drugs or alcohol. When faced with children showing every evidence of shocking neglect, it is the state that immediately takes on the role of nanny. But it does so in an impersonal way; the result is that the child is taken into care at a very early age. At this point they are either farmed out to foster parents, from whom, if lucky, they actually receive some proper care and affection, or alternatively they land in a children's home, where they seldom do. Here, although these homes are well run and well resourced in the purely materialistic sense, the percentage of children who later find themselves in conflict with the law is extremely high. Burglary, drug trafficking, prostitution, mugging and vehicle theft figure endlessly on the list of those formerly in children's homes. It makes depressing reading.

To sum up: bad parenting in all three social classes dominates all these case histories. The percentage of other factors is so small and so diffuse as to be hardly worth examining. Yet the degree of attention and resources any government is forced to give to criminal activity in this age group (sixteen to thirty-five years) is disproportionally high. And not just in combating such activity! Merely attempting to address the hurt subsequently suffered by its victims, is now reaching unsupportable proportions. Decent and responsible people everywhere keep asking: 'Why?' Surely in any country with a high standard of living and with an immensely expensive national welfare programme, true poverty is a thing of the past. Crime should be diminishing, not increasing. Just one hundred years ago, people who happened to be judged paupers faced parochial work houses. Those savouring such hard times would find today's handouts generous beyond their wildest dreams. Once again comes the bewildered question: 'Why?' Why does the incidence of crime continue to rise? Why is it, when nobody is really starving, naked or homeless (yes, admittedly there are a tiny percentage who are temporarily in this latter category), that year after year, the statistics show an inexorable rise? And despite an accelerated prison-building programme all available accommodation is bursting at the seams. After all, it is not as if such a rise is commensurate with the current demographic increase: it is rising considerably faster than this. And it is requiring such a disproportionate amount of available money, time, effort and organisation just to keep pace with it. Most ominous of all, crime is becoming organised. No longer do criminals act for the most part independently.

To drive home earlier observations, I believe that if the other worrying trend continues then obviously the entire viability of any civilised society is threatened. Recent events in Italy provide us with a chilling example. Here the penetration of organised crime known as the Mafia reached every level of Italian society during the 1960s, 1970s and 1980s. It brought virtual paralysis to the normal processes of government. Each time the state organised countermeasures the Mafia reacted with astonishing self-assurance: the prosecuting judges, lawyers, magistrates, senior police and paramilitary officers were all murdered! In cold blood! Such a degree of penetration by organised crime can be likened to cancer cells slowly spreading to every part of the body. Its invasive powers are such as to reach to the very heart of government. In Italy it involved cabinet ministers, and allegedly, at least two prime ministers. Beyond government circles, the Vatican itself was not immune. Scandals involving the criminal activities of several top bankers have revealed links and close involvement with at least one cardinal and a handful of bishops. Ironically, these had been nominated by a succession of popes as being the most trusted and suitable of clerics to control the Church's banking interests! Perhaps the truth in this latter scandal will never be revealed: the bankers in question have either committed suicide or were murdered. Again, much of Eastern Europe and, more recently, large areas of Russia – all now in the throes of establishing some form of democracy – also find themselves moving toward what one might call the 'Italian experience'. Organised crime undertaken by gangs, as distinct from uncoordinated acts carried out by individuals, has increased to a point where most Eastern European states have been forced to set up special units on paramilitary lines to tackle it. Sadly, it seems that former totalitarian states have a far better record in controlling crime. No doubt this is because having being steeped in criminality themselves they understand the criminal mind, and are prepared to adopt suitably ruthless measures without any qualms whatsoever.

However, as soon as they are replaced by a democratic system the vulnerability to Mafioso-type takeover is immediately exploited by the criminal class.

Initially the much-vaunted freedoms achieved by democracy so often give a superficial aura of health and moral vitality, yet this aura can camouflage serious weaknesses. And few are prepared to acknowledge them openly. This is mainly because everyone insists on seeing such problems in socio-political terms, and to the exclusion of all else. Thus the Western world is faced with a scenario spelling in large letters the word *crisis*. Indeed, if present trends continue then there may come a time when governments of each individual state can no longer hold back the tide of criminality. In such an event, what do we all do then? Just throw up our hands in the air with a gesture of impotence? Do we admit to ourselves that the entire system is disintegrating and then take the only option remaining – the adoption of measures used by former totalitarian states? Or what of the measures taken by fundamentalist states? We could try measures used by the more extreme of Islamic regimes. We could, after all, persuade ourselves that we are fighting a 'holy war' against crime. It's them or us, isn't it?

Shall we look at Stalinist examples? These are still fresh in many people's memories. And first-hand accounts of the effectiveness of that penal system are vividly etched in our consciousness by such people as Alexander Solzhenitsyn and Arthur Koestler. Information is detailed and profuse. We would hardly need to start from scratch. For those who would prefer a more open system and believe that justice carried out in public has a greater deterrent effect, then there are Islamic models to follow. In the latter they do everything openly (in fact in public): they cut off the hands of thieves, give a hundred lashes to those found under the influence of alcohol or drugs, execute by beheading or firing squad, adulterers, drug traffickers and murderers, indeed anyone found undermining the moral code. Huge crowds watch this spectacle. The Soviet system, of course, also concentrated on those undermining its peculiar codes, but it was much more secretive. Millions simply disappeared into the Gulags. Only a tiny proportion – those subsequently judged harmless – were allowed freedom after half a lifetime in captivity. And executions were at least done in private in a cellar with a bullet in the back of the head.

But do we really wish to revert to this barbarism? Surely this is unthinkable in any civilised society. Therefore, rather than attempting to seek solutions *after* crimes have been committed, is it not preferable to discover *why* they were committed in the first place? Preventative measures are so much better than attempted cures. So what, for heaven's sake, is the cause of all this criminal activity?

After a half century in which the welfare state has been firmly in place, people keep looking toward their politicians to supply answers. Naturally those answers in turn are always political. And they are as varied and as inventive as cowpats in a field, yet are not nearly so enriching of the cerebral soils they will eventually sink into.

But there is a biological answer. It is this: we are actively breeding a criminal class! We are breeding them, ironically enough, with the very best of intentions. We do so through the tireless efforts of the welfare state. It is as if we had set up the most advanced and costly of programmes for the production of a certain type of living species – say, just for the sake of illustration, thoroughbred horses! And to do ourselves proud we build countless well-appointed stables all over the country at enormous cost where each animal is sired not to the best bloodstock that can be found anywhere in the country, but to the very worst.

Subsequently we attempt to train this entire stock to achieve the most demanding steeplechase or Derby standards! You protest? You feel disgust at my analysis – at what you now suspect may be my prognosis? Or maybe it is just contempt for the author's inferior intellect? Very well, no doubt you are convinced you can advance far more considered or logical reasons. Yet I hazard a guess that it will be one of the very many that have already been aired, moreover aired tirelessly, loudly and with great passion. Each of the soapbox orators so involved will deny that many of their pet theories have already been put into practice and have been found wanting: they will insist that these measures were not given sufficient time or perhaps applied without necessary vigour! Haven't we heard that before? Do I hear at this point another involuntary grunt or even an expletive? Does this signal your frustration or fury?

Given that it is unkind and ungentlemanly to allow bad feeling to fester without some attempt to remedy or defuse it; given too that an atmosphere of tension rarely allows the interplay of sweet reason, shall we then investigate this further? Can we review some of the most common opinions, more particularly those offered by people who believe that they have their fingers on the pulse of things? For those with a political viewpoint tinged by spirituality this is a favourite: an ever rising prison population is the inevitable product of the loss of a religious faith. It fully reflects our moral decline and the growing reign of godlessness. This is no doubt true. So then how do we arrest such a decline? Immediately one discovers that nobody can suggest a truly effective solution. There is no known method of successfully introducing the concept of an all-seeing, all-loving, all-powerful deity into the thoughts and souls of the criminal fraternity. Prison chaplains and prison reformers have struggled manfully (and indeed womanfully) for decades, if not centuries. The basic problem is that the vast majority of inmates are beyond all hope. They have become part of this fraternity in the first place because their cerebral processes repeatedly deal with each and every piece of information flow in a hopelessly warped fashion. Their entire outlook is deformed by a massive ego; they are incapable of thinking of anything other than themselves. Their thoughts and their very souls are protected by impregnable defences. If they have any vision of the purpose and meaning of life then it is either hopelessly twisted or seriously myopic. Their information filtering systems are meshed in such a way as to allow only certain material through. And then when their meagre flow is finally processed, the powers of reasoning applied are wholly inadequate or defective. All but a tiny minority are beyond all hope of saving. Therefore it is better to accept reality and refuse to waste further time on reform. The only preventative measures to be applied in these instances happen to be solely in the biological field. So we must pass over all suggestions involving a programme of religious conversion and move on to the next sector. Here we begin delving into the purely political arena. And at once we find several widespread beliefs. Perhaps the most convenient (in that it has a vote-winning potential) concerns what is called 'inequality'; it is a particular favourite of those with an impeccably socialist upbringing. In voices ringing with emotion and fervour they proclaim that criminality is generated because there are so many socially disadvantaged groups, ground down as always by greedy capitalists. But this ignores the awkward fact that a fair percentage of the prison population, despite having little capital, has precisely the same attitudes and methods as the greedy capitalists; deception or strong-arm methods! And does this mean that the entire body of the socially disadvantaged automatically becomes criminals? It is all so much hogwash. When will people learn that criminality knows no boundaries between classes, 'ground down' or otherwise.

Other postulates? Hereafter the suggestions will come thick and fast. They range ever further and more wildly. The favourite ones are the following: criminality is the reward of a sexually permissive society, alternatively the growing influence of drug or alcohol addiction, lack of respect for all authority – they will go on and on. There will be a chorus of approval at some point, and it will appear that a consensus has been reached. However, despite final success at the diagnostic level, when it comes to a decision on remedial action, consensus is lost again. Agreement can never be reached because there are no realistic hopes of its effectiveness. So once again other causes are looked for.

Some suggest the baneful influence of high-pressure advertising; this, they insist, cleverly boosts pseudo-needs and desires. Therefore it demands quick and wholly illegal solutions in order to meet them. Yet this overlooks the fact that the rewards *for* crime are also advertised – and this often very dramatically! It is achieved daily in the tabloids. There is an endless reportage of court proceedings involving the more revolting of crimes. It is done in suitably breathless tones of hyped-up drama. Then again, even the uncongenial regimes within prisons themselves are advertised in one way or another. This is done most spectacularly during prison riots. Alternatively it is achieved in the figures for suicide or fatal attacks on inmates. Yet all this has clearly failed to deter those teetering on the edge of criminal activity. It has about as much effect as high-power advertising on the dangers of smoking, drug and alcohol abuse, or for that matter sexually transmitted diseases. The supposed powers of the advertising industry in this instance have been greatly exaggerated.

Inevitably then we are forced to move on and examine other very common proposals. Among these, one finds severe criticism of the mildness of the tariffs Parliament has set for a range of crimes. This is combined with totally inadequate sentencing. Yet if one points out that judges are either consciously or unconsciously prompted to do so – being the only realistic solution to overcrowded prisons – most people show disbelief. They are unable to accept such simple logic. They insist that if you move from inadequate prison terms and begin to notch them upward toward adequate or indeed truly deterrent ones, then you find prison governors suddenly exhibiting the most extreme behaviour. They jump up and down, screaming and shouting, maybe even blowing their brains out in desperation. Why? The system is so overcrowded already that it is unable to absorb the present intake, let alone an increased one! So we find we must move on again; we must attempt some other diagnoses and suggest other solutions.

Now some people firmly believe that a taste for law-breaking begins in childhood and is the result of a lack of discipline at home. This, they insist, is exacerbated by a lack of discipline in schools. However, as the parents of difficult children are often themselves difficult, and have been known to react violently to such suggestions, distributing black eyes and damaged noses to anyone within reach, most people prefer to take softer options. Thus, as has been noted previously, teachers alone have become the favoured target. They are after all so defenceless. But this too has problems. Not unexpectedly the morale throughout the teaching profession is now at an all-time low. After all, what sanctions do they have against disruptive or wholly violent children? With corporal punishment banned one finds that even accidentally touching a child is now neatly interpreted as assault, worse, sexual assault. Budding little mafiosos currently hone their skills by deliberately manufacturing such charges. Faced with a lack of discipline, headteachers use the only remaining sanction: exclusion. This has brought fury from both parents and police alike. Inevitably it throws the problem back on their shoulders. Excluded, children tend to use their time profitably in shoplifting, or attacking elderly and defenceless pensioners. Special units are now being organised to address this problem. Violent pupils are given supposedly remedial treatment, which at least keeps them off the streets under some kind of supervision. But these units are too few and far between; worse, they are again being overloaded. In Britain and many other European countries, the numbers of children on exclusion orders has risen to an all-time high. The main reason for such exclusions is assault by pupils on teachers – not vice-versa. Indeed the incidence of verbal abuse and serious physical assaults on teachers has involved hospital treatment and sometimes even the services of morticians. Overall, it has meant that nervous breakdowns and requests for early retirement have reached almost epidemic proportions throughout the teaching profession. How does one reverse the trend? Reintroduce corporal punishment, put all teachers through a course of karate and various other methods of self-defence? Or adopt the measures found in some states of the USA where armed police patrol school premises? Should we in Europe go partially down the American road at least, and perhaps recruit former paratroopers or SAS for special discipline duties within each school? Once again, while many can quickly concur on an initial diagnosis, when it comes to finding a method of treatment and hoped-for cure, all agreement is subsequently lost in bitter argument.

To move on to the next commonly held knee-jerk reaction: many see the problem as the result of too few police actually on foot patrol in the streets. However ludicrous or trivial a proposition this may seem, they back it up with the slightly more credible accusation; they allege that every officer in police forces throughout the land is now a mere clerk weighed down by mountainous piles of paperwork; they further allege other time-wasting duties such as endless hours waiting to giving evidence in court. Warming to their theme, they will further claim that the upper echelons within the police force are hopelessly inadequate as organisers; some will even darkly suggest that top officers are in league with the big fish of the underworld. Moreover, in order to mask this, they pursue only the minnows. A few individuals, not to be outdone in holding way-out views, and trusting that they may have the most eye-catching potential, protest there are too *many* police on the beat! And this is why there are proportionally too many successful convictions of small fry, and none of the really massive killer whales. They contend that there should be more concentration on intelligence work. For instance, it must be discovered how people with no visible or legitimate means of support nevertheless enjoy extravagant lifestyles, live in mansions, drive Ferraris, have yachts at Cannes, own racehorses and dine regularly at the top restaurants or hotels. Here a mere salute from the gorgeously uniformed doorman costs the equivalent of the average person's weekly wage. These are the people whose homes should be raided at four in the morning, not pitiful little narks! Why do police use what precious little energy they have breaking down the doors of some miserable mugger or common jerk on a council estate? They demand this with tremulous voices and misty eyes. Why indeed? These allegations do have a degree of rueful logic about them.

Inevitably, following this comes a free-for-all debate on crime and punishment – or more correctly, crime and retribution, for this is what most really want. Others will muddy the waters still further by demanding that most eyebrow-raising, jaw-dropping question of all: what earthly good is done by putting people in prison anyway? Isn't it tantamount to handing out very generous scholarships to universities of crime? Surely with such scholarships criminals will be taught the finer points of their trade – more advanced methods of fraud, robbery, murder and mayhem in general. They might even be persuaded to do post-graduate research on combating advanced forensic techniques, such as microscopic dust examination and genetic fingerprinting!

This is true of course up to a point. And if one asks what they propose as an alternative to prison sentences, then you find that they advocate either the most Draconian of solutions, such as hanging, flogging, birching (castration for sexual offenders), or, alternatively, a benign but greatly extended community-service system, with criminals making direct restitution to their victims. Should one point out that this will take an even larger chunk out of national resources, there is an initial silence followed by fierce debate. Should you insist that the requirements for recruiting, training, organising and monitoring a whole army of community-service officers will greatly outweigh the cost of our present prison service, then there is indignant (but somewhat unconvincing) denial. It will be followed by a savage accusation that you are secretly one of the 'hang 'em, flog 'em' fraternity anyway.

Overall, the number of opinions given in this matter of crime and punishment are truly staggering. It would require a full-length book to cover them all. Moreover, it would be beside the point, as many of these apparent solutions have already been tried, either here or in other countries, and found wanting.

Significantly though, none have come anywhere near the formulation of methods derived from a biological viewpoint! That is, after all, the root of the matter and the basis of this essay – at least that is if we continue to search for the root causes of *all* conflict and refuse to distinguish between subversive internal conflict within a state or community and external conflict with an obvious and clearly visible 'foreign' enemy.

*

Brass tacks? You demand them? Yes, very well. But first it is very necessary to cover some preliminary factors and to scotch some of the inevitable misunderstandings before they take firm hold.

Retribution, for one. To repeat earlier conclusions: the

common denominator found when examining the case histories of the majority who tangle with the law is gross fixation with the self. The ego is like some ghastly brain tumour wedged in the most inaccessible and inoperable of places. Its influence on all cerebral activity – especially during the process of stimulating curiosity, controlling or selecting information flow, then filtering and prioritising it – is wholly repressive and dominant. It determines that most criminals are devoid of any ability to visualise the legitimate needs and desires of others. At an extreme there is even an inability to accept their victims as flesh and blood just like themselves. They do not see them as inhabiting the real world in any shape or form. Indeed what passes for 'reality' is itself either warped or confused. Then again, not just people but events too are seen as ghost images that flit through the consciousness without making any real impact. In acts of mayhem, their victims are not visualised as a collection of living and breathing entities capable of feeling hurt, anguish, pain and suffering. The fixation with self, intertwined with its real or imagined needs, obliterates all.

Unfortunately though, gross egos are not some kind of component to facilitate evil which are carefully created by the criminal himself (or herself!); therefore as such the gross ego cannot legitimately draw our condemnation and wrath. It is a genetic abnormality, handed down usually from parents. Sometimes, such is the genetic complexity involved that it can skip several generations and come from grandparents or ancestors. And as an abnormality it should be treated like any other, that is with sympathy and understanding.

Yet it is so difficult to do so in these cases. Damnably enough, such people can look so normal and friendly. Al Capone himself, once he had removed his enormous cigar, plus that give-away hat tilted over one eye, looked like such an awfully nice fellow. In contrast, people with very real physical afflictions such as deformed arms and legs, or alternatively suffering from cruel conditions such as spina bifida and other such crippling genetically transmitted diseases, can be recognised at a glance. But deformed egos? Gross fixation with self? How do you detect it at but a glance? You see part of the problem is that with the deformity being mental rather than physical, it takes quite some time and effort to detect. True, those born with behavioural defects brought on by cerebral palsy are instantly recognisable – and instantly receive sympathy. But gross egotism? Gross insensitivity? These always seem to be in a totally different league. Yet these too really are serious mental handicaps, despite our hesitation or sometimes our absolute refusal to accept them as such.

At this point though, and to promptly scotch any possible misunderstanding, I must make a very clear statement: I am not making a plea for the closure of all prisons, nor, as a direct consequence of this, the vast expansion of psychiatric units. And most certainly I do not propose extending the already existing programme optimistically called 'Care in the Community'. Prisons are still necessary. But not for the purpose of retribution. They are necessary solely as isolating systems. Their only purpose is to keep criminals from contact with the general public: they must deny them the opportunity to commit further crime. And in this I am not showing disrespect for the discipline known as psychiatry, or making any attempt to belittle the valuable work done by doctors committed to this service. I merely believe that there are limitations to what can be achieved – this despite recent advances in treatment. Nor do I quibble over the degree of success achieved. I accept that it has been substantial. I am aware that there is now a wide variety of very effective drugs available, further, that there are promises made by pharmacologists that the range so far developed is by no means exhausted. Nevertheless, all reports made on the subject suggest that treatment by drugs does not achieve a permanent cure. It merely *controls* the condition. It is effective, moreover, only in extreme cases where pronounced mental instability is evident. And if I read the statistical picture correctly, then while control of extremely violent or depraved behaviour is a very welcome advance there are still grave potential dangers. For example, if for some reason the regime of carefully administered (and correct dosage of) drugs is interrupted, then the patient all too often reverts back to his or her former state. Given this awkward drawback, it would seem that society cannot be subjected to unacceptable risks of this nature, especially when treatment is attempted in relatively open psychiatric units within the community. Tragic cases of serious assault, not excluding murder, by outpatients have already given the tabloid press all the sensationalism it could possibly require. Individual doctors responsible for allowing these patients back into the community are now targeted and, wherever possible, crucified in print. Thus while most people accept that former so-called lunatic asylums should have been closed, their substitutes, despite having more success in many ways, have also brought too many risks. The pendulum has swung too far in the opposite direction.

But what of the much larger category of individuals within society who offend against what are broadly called 'commonly accepted standards of morality and decency' in general, such as muggers, bank robbers, burglars, fraudsters, rapists and the like? These are clearly not 'deranged' in a clinical sense? Here we find ourselves in a grey area and possibly one where we can make serious errors.

If one can detect antisocial behaviour before a serious crime is committed – and detect it with accuracy – the question one must ask is: should intervention begin at this point? If accuracy cannot be guaranteed should remedial treatment be introduced *after* conviction, when individuals are already locked away? The grave danger in both cases is that the state could manipulate the system. It could specifically select those it finds 'politically undesirable'. True, there is less danger of this in a fully democratic regime. But under repressive regimes it becomes very different. Stalinist-type states quickly manipulate such systems and send all suspected political deviants to psychiatric units. Here they receive very special remedial treatment indeed! Thus who can guarantee that any state will remain fully democratic and will not slide unwittingly down that particular slope? Given that nobody can, then it puts us on the horns of a dilemma, as some people would put it somewhat dramatically. But there are other more direct factors involved. In this grey area, where criminal behaviour is so difficult to define and where the distinguishing between clinically sane or insane is almost impossible to resolve, we are faced with an attempt to gauge 'degrees of responsibility'. Here we are forced to ask ourselves that most difficult of questions: is this particular individual conscious of what he or she is doing and therefore 'culpable', as they say, or are they acting unconsciously? If so, they cannot be fully responsible. If the answer given is 'sane and culpable', then most people will find it extremely difficult to offer the criminal a modicum of understanding. As for sympathy, that seems virtually impossible. Often the best we can do is to mutter to ourselves that wise dictum 'to know all is to forgive all' then sigh a little and summon up a sad smile.

But there are those, especially victims of crime, who cannot do this. They might with difficulty finally accept that gross absorption with self coupled with a corresponding total lack of sensitivity is an inherited abnormality; even so, forgiveness is a different matter. This they find almost impossible to cope with. They tend to place blame on both the criminals and their parents, despite it being wholly inappropriate. Who can blame them, when their vision of the circumstances is so clouded? Tragically too, genetic roulette can play some other cruel jokes. Some parents, for example, are wholly blameless. They may well be law-abiding and loving. They may well have shown ample sensitivity together with a high degree of tenderness and devotion to their children. Yet they may find to their dismay that one (or possibly more) 'black sheep' have been introduced into their family. With disbelief they find themselves with a child or with children who display strange characteristics sharply at odds with what they might hope for and indeed expect. How can this happen?

Using for the moment a somewhat circular route as an explanation, one can point to somewhat more trivial forms of genetic surprises in unexpected eye, hair and skin colour. As noted previously, this alone caused considerable anguish prior to the work of Mendel and the second decade of the twentieth century, when the science of genetics began to provide explanations. Parents who both had blue eyes, blond hair, and white skin would be shocked if they found that one of their children had brown eyes, dark hair and dark skin. It immediately raised the suspicion of infidelity – usually female infidelity! However, with post-Mendelian research into the matter, we now know that no hanky-panky was involved. The explanation is a genetic throwback. Indeed it could extend back among ancestors for possibly several generations. It involved what Mendel fully explained as the fortuitous combination of hitherto 'recessive' genes. But these are trivial cases. Far more serious and indeed lethal examples of genetic inheritance can be passed on in the casino in which genetic fortunes are made or lost. These can provide real heartbreak. One of the first to be identified by scientists was the disease 'sickle-cell anaemia'. A disease first notified and described in 1910 among African Americans, it had to wait until the mid-century before its genetic source was fully realised and proven. Recessive genes, if unknowingly brought together by the lottery of male and female sexual combination, can suddenly produce this disease, despite both parents being healthy. But disease and physical abnormality can also be produced, perhaps, even more tragically, outside quite natural sources. They can occur because of genetic mutations caused by man-made and quite artificial agencies. And these can have their malign influences either prior to or just following a child's conception. There are a range of such possible sources: accidental exposure to radiation by one of the parents during localised or long-range radio-active fallout (such as the Chernobyl incident), exposure to accidental leakage of radiation while working in military applications (or installations) or in the nuclear industry, an overdose of X-rays, possibly cumulative over years during hospital treatment, ingestion of one or more toxic substances now sprayed on so many crops or entering the food chain by other means, adverse reaction to medication or vaccination perhaps while travelling abroad as defence against tropical diseases, heavy cigarette smoking, exposure to toxic substances at the workplace or airborne in a highly industrialised environment... there are so many possibilities.

Whatever the cause, the result can be heartbreaking. And while medical science now offers some hope for remedial treatment in a small number of genetic disorders – particularly those affecting lungs, heart and kidneys – there are almost none for the brain. Certainly, neurosurgeons can operate on something as tangible as a brain tumour, where many (but not all) have a genetic source, but something as intangible as the intricacy of the connection between many millions of neurones, all of which affect a child's cognition and behaviour patterns, presents an insurmountable problem. Moreover, at this point one can add that there is nothing wholly tangible that attends the formation of an abnormal ego, certainly nothing that can be cut out like a tumour. As for attempting to look for possible breaks in the 'wiring system' of all the countless million cerebral connections, this would be a hopeless task.

In short, the correction of mental abnormalities leading to criminal behaviour is both now and for the foreseeable future well beyond the reach of current neurological or psychiatric expertise. It is thus doubly tragic if we attempt to apportion blame in all areas of mental abnormality.

To sum up then: the level of conflict within Western society as a whole, derived as it is from criminal behaviour, is not seen as a significant threat to survival. Or at least not yet! But there is a degree of complacency in this view. For those who have examined this possibility in depth there can be no such ease of dismissal. The very survival of the ancient ancestors of mankind – a distinct species of primate we now call Ramapithecus over ten million years ago – depended on these creatures' ability to work together co-operatively and harmoniously. With evolutionary development into Austalopithecus and later into *Homo erectus* some two million years ago, that vital behavioural trait was further honed. And it allowed us to build the first true civilisations.

Since then, our gradual triumph over all other animal competitors and predators has however meant that mankind has increasingly turned to conflict within his own species. And it takes two main forms. Firstly there is war, an expression of conflict directed in an outward direction between large ethnic or tribal groups and (normally) the immediate geographical neighbour. Criminal behaviour, on the other hand, is conflict directed inward within society and at quite intimate levels. In the latter case, could it be that because of such intimacy, the old adage applies, 'familiarity breeds contempt', or rather, in this case, complacency?

Thus the activities of the criminal upper-class for instance, which are usually in the field of massive fraud, are not seen as a threat to an entire nation's stability. Yet decades of such fraud can bring the ethical judgement and self-regulating ability of banks, conglomerate industries and large commercial enterprises into question. Later, when this slides into disrepute, it still does not immediately tax the mind of the average citizen. The fact that the Italian Government has been in an almost permanent state of crisis during three decades fails to register in the minds of people in other European countries. A little more concern however does penetrate through when involvement becomes personal from time to time. Shall I present an example. The crash of BCCI, with branches in London and other parts of the world, happened to hit one close-knit community quite directly and hard. The crofting and fishing community of the Outer Hebridean Isles of Lewis and Harris woke up one morning to find that their island council (corresponding to a county council or regional council) was in crisis. Their council treasurer, attracted by high interest rates, had deposited a substantial sum of money with this bank. He had lightly supposed that the Bank of England regulations and subsequent scrutiny of all other banking sectors in the country did what they were duty bound to do: regulate. Unfortunately, the people of Lewis and Harris live in an area remote from the sophisticated info flow enjoyed by the banking fraternity in the south. More unfortunately still, average individual earnings and commercial activity generally are among the lowest in Britain. Indeed they attract special EEC subsidies to keep their community viable. Thus the council treasurer in good faith had attempted to find the highest interest rate for the money deposited. He did not investigate the record and standing of the bank closely. Nor did he have any knowledge of the lifestyles of the several Pakistani businessmen at its head. These, as the Irish say with a glint in the eye, were 'living the life of Riley'. Inevitably then, on the collapse of the bank, the Hebridean islanders found themselves having to contribute (via suddenly increased taxes) to a shortfall of millions of pounds, estimated at the time to be well over five million. Such a sum would no doubt seem small in the eyes of county councils further south with huge populations and financial clout to go with them; but this presented a savage blow to the sparse island communities. As a direct result, not only was the council forced to make many of its workers redundant, but it was also faced with the closure of smaller community schools. This meant redundancy for teachers, plus cutbacks in a wide variety of social services. The immediacy and seriousness of the situation was thus brought home in a salutary way. In contrast, the diffuse nature of losses suffered by many small businesses and retired couples in and around London and the Home Counties, while being equally traumatic, failed to have a real impact on the nation as a whole, simply because it *was* diffuse and therefore had no immediate and dramatic consequences. Recently too, Barings Bank was faced with collapse for rather different reasons. In this instance, however, it seems to have been a case of gross negligence rather than criminal fraud. And should you now gain the impression that bank failure is an isolated British phenomenon, dismiss it immediately, because you would be wildly mistaken.

In France, another bank teetered on the brink of disaster recently. Again it was in the hands of negligent rather than crooked Frenchmen, though in this case while 'living the life of Riley' they happened to be too preoccupied with its delights to bother with such boring things as attending investigative board meetings. These lapses allowed massive loans to be made to dodgy developers coupled with all too voluble and persuasive entrepreneurs. These latter gentlemen subsequently disappeared very quietly and unnoticed into the undergrowth. This in itself would have been no loss. Unfortunately they went their way clutching suitcases of banknotes and any valuable, transportable and resaleable objects such as art, jewellery and watches that they could lay hands on. Millions of small savers, pensioners and shopkeepers all over France would have suffered acutely but for the government stepping in behind the scene and preventing total collapse. Even so, thousands were made redundant in the various building sites and industrial schemes that became bankrupt in the aftermath. The echoes of this particular scandal still reverberate in France to this day. Certainly unemployment among construction sectors of the workforce remains unusually high.

The Italian banking scandal has already been mentioned. But these banks were not the only institutions to cause widespread trauma – and this during a period covering five decades. Government investigation into the business dealings of some of its core industries such as Fiat, Olivetti and several world-famous fashion houses resulted in a number of court cases. Many remain unresolved. Principal figures and vital witnesses have either sought refuge abroad, or refused to give evidence because of threats made to their lives. Some have indeed been murdered.

In fact any European country one would care to name has had some financial scandal or other at regular intervals (almost yearly) throughout the latter half of the twentieth century. The remainder of the Western world, such as the USA and Canada, is hardly to be excluded. Given that this fraud-prone Western world actually congratulates itself on having a far lower rate than elsewhere, then perhaps you will agree that the scale of the problem worldwide begins to assume quite staggering proportions. Doubtless the so-called 'Tiger economies' of the Far East will see chaotic situations in the near future.[1] Any economy that quite suddenly appears to grow at a rapid speed without the aid of a fundamentally proven boost – such as the discovery on its territory of huge untapped resources of oil, natural gas, chromium, gold, uranium, or indeed any highly valuable resource you care to name – is doing so probably as a result of massive fraud and will collapse sooner or later.

There is a further factor involved here. It concerns the major stock exchanges of the world. Today, each nation's economic situation is made much more volatile by so-called 'improvements' in their organisation and methods. Newly installed computerised systems, whereby a system called 'Sets' matches buyers with sellers, now enable shares to be bought and sold far more quickly than ever before. It is estimated that with this new system in London alone, over eight hundred million shares can change hands in a single day! Thus even the hint of some minor financial scandals or government overreaching itself, will initially cause a fairly localised stock-market flutter. It will do so whether such rumours are true or not. The flutter can then so easily begin to gather a momentum of its own. Selling gathers speed and, like a snowball, gains body and weight. Panic sets in. Frantic dealing on one stock exchange will have repercussions not just on neighbouring markets but worldwide. Such fluctuations seem of no real consequence to millions of people who have never owned

---

[1] Since these lines were written such a collapse has occurred.

a share in their lives. To these financial innocents, transactions on this scale are baffling in their complexity. Yet they are affected nevertheless; it is so subtle that it is not immediately apparent. They begin to notice only when taxes increase and unemployment begins to rise. Remember too, at this point, that this is only the result of 'improvements' in financial dealings.

It is the same with crime stemming from and largely involving the middle classes. Being diffuse in its effects, it fails to make sufficient impact on the minds of the average citizen. Thus its potential seriousness and long-term threat to the viability of the nation as a whole is underestimated.

Again in the lowest class, the true nature and seriousness of the threat is minimised because familiarity breeds complacency. Overall, the vision of a community or nation as a cohesive entity is never considered. And the dangers that accrue to undermine that cohesiveness are restricted because of their lack of any high vantage point from which to observe the full scenario. Such a vantage point and such a scenario are only appreciated by the departmental heads of the various welfare and social services, not forgetting police and prison coordinators. These, being in direct contact with treasury officials, then pass on their problems to the politicians. The buck stops at individuals within the cabinet. It stops more especially at the feet of some poor fallible being attempting to bolster his self-confidence, courage and reputation for good judgement; this individual must pass himself off to the country at large as a far-sighted and virtually infallible, Chancellor of the Exchequer!

Yet the final bill paid by each country as a whole for criminal behaviour over a wide range of antisocial activities is far greater than most of its citizens can ever imagine or quantify. The ramifications are far too varied and subtle. Moreover, that bill is rising inexorably. Clearly such an outlay of time, effort, money and resources cannot be maintained at its current rate for very much longer.

In further pages an attempt will be made to press the biological viewpoint still further, because only this can enable us to establish new diagnostic techniques and a much more accurate prognosis. However, details of this urgent remedial action must wait until later. There are after all other causes of human conflict and it would be both foolish and remiss of any author – moreover cause a serious thematical imbalance in any essay – to dwell on just one factor and pass over the discussion of others at this stage.

*

Propositions

PROPOSITION 1

The premier evolutionary survival factor handed mankind was the ability to communicate with other members of his own species in a far more complex and flexible manner than any other species in the animal kingdom. This facility was accorded by the unique formation of the throat, with its projection of the thyroid cartilage coupled with its unusual larynx, and also the development of muscles controlling the lips and the tongue. However it is the author's belief (a theory difficult to flesh out with details until further research work by specialists investigating pre-hominid evolution becomes available) that following very closely behind comes what one can only call 'self-sacrificing' or 'tenacious' parenting skills.

EXPOSITION 1

Early man was almost defenceless in the face of carnivores far more powerful and fleet of foot than himself. More significantly still, early woman, during the later stages of pregnancy and for some time after giving birth, was put into a far more perilous position than the male. That any of her infants or herself could have survived these circumstances puts considerable strain on one's credibility. More pointedly still, that any of her infants could then have grown and survived to reproductive age, there to pass on the baton of life – and indeed secure the survival of the very species – seems nothing short of miraculous. But then we are living in an age where the civilising process has made us unduly dependent both physically and mentally on the massive protection given by our carefully structured and highly organised societies. In contrast the rigours of early life demanded a toughness, a degree of self-dependence (or independence) and a resilience that we in a decadent age can only marvel at. That early man, and even more so early women, were able to combat successfully all their formidable problems and the very harshness of their existence is fully proven by the simple fact that if they had failed then we, their successors, would not be alive today.

EXPOSITION 2

It is true that a variety of other species within the animal kingdom also show great tenacity and indeed at times self-sacrifice when guarding and rearing their young. But in each case they do not quite reach the standards shown by human beings – nor, for that matter, do they extend their parenting skills over such an unusual time span. The contrast is even more startling when one tabulates the number of other species that seem less than careful while rearing their young. And it becomes glaring when comparisons are made with those species that leave survival of their young entirely to chance.

EXPOSITION 3

It can be shown that the human animal has, over its million or more years of evolutionary development, become hostage (I use the word carefully and deliberately) to several behavioural patterns in which firstly an unusually strong emotional bonding is made with infants, and secondly, severe trauma is automatically felt when their well-being or indeed their very lives are threatened. No other animal shows such extremes of passion or trauma in similar circumstances.

EXPOSITION 4

These behaviour patterns were of primary importance not just as initial survival factors but later in establishing human beings as masters over the remainder of the animal kingdom. However, now that the human race has become so successful and its numbers have increased so dramatically this very factor, ironically enough, begins to work against us. Our deep-seated instincts, often backed by unquestioned religious beliefs – dovetailed as they so often are with the military ambitions of mentally unbalanced leaders – now insist that children continue to be brought into the world well after mere replacement levels have been reached. Thus the population explosion in areas of the world least able to sustain such increase now threatens not just peace and stability right round this shrinking globe, but, in its wake serious environmental and ecological degradation. This coupled with the development of weaponry of mass destruction puts an enormous question mark around the survival of *all* life on this planet.

EXPOSITION 5

While these deep-rooted instincts concerning reproduction and the survival of the young can be seen to rise up into our conscious minds virtually automatically, that does not mean that reason and logic are powerless. It does not ensure that they fail to make any impression or have any influence on our subsequent actions. The success of many nations particularly in the Western world, in checking population increase and thereby bringing stability and high standards of living to its citizens, proves that mere instinct can finally be tethered or at least led down less chaotic and dangerous paths.

EXPOSITION 6

It is commonly assumed by envious Eastern nations that the affluence and social stability of Western nations is achieved by scientific and technological expertise and nothing more. Europeans, plus a large proportion of Caucasians of European descent (as distinct from Hispanics and Blacks) now living in North America, not forgetting the Japanese on the opposite side of our world, have become role models to be copied. Ironically too, the bulk of people within these rich nations also take this view. This is a tragic miscalculation. Affluence has been achieved only by reducing family size to replacement level. Evidence will be given to highlight this claim.

EXPOSITION 7

In direct contrast, evidence will also be given to highlight the reverse. Examination of population statistics around the world will show that there is a startling correlation between high birth rate combined with the 'doubling time' of a population and the incidence of social unrest – at best! If we pursue the correlation between high birth rate and doubling time at its worst, then we find that it displays a grim picture that includes outright mayhem, civil war, aggressive expansion of borders, ethnic cleansing or full-blown genocide. The evidence is compelling and impossible to disprove.

To repeat ad nauseam if necessary – and especially for those with fundamentalist religious beliefs who refuse to look a heartless and indeed brutal reality fully in the face – our evolutionary heritage is now working wholly against us. If, as with many other creatures on this planet, we cared little for the fate of our offspring and left it merely to chance – that is Nature's checks and balances – whether they survived or not, then we would no longer find ourselves in the critical situation we are in today. Yet as already noted, this is not an option for us. However, arising out of this, let me remind you that crisis is not relatively minor or transitory; it involves the destruction of *all* life on this planet! Nevertheless we are programmed by several million years of evolution to form unusually strong bonds with our children, moreover suffer far greater trauma than all other creatures when their lives are at risk.

The following table, which is provided by the Centre for International Research of the US Bureau of Census, the Statistical Division of the UN, the World Bank, and lastly, Population Concern, makes for a grim analysis of the situation. The table gives many of the relevant factors beyond mere birth rate and 'doubling time'. These are of course wholly necessary to give an overall assessment. Even so, it is the author's personal conviction that the birth rate remains the vital factor. Undoubtedly it, and it alone, has enormous influence on subsequent behaviour patterns that humans show. Moreover, the high mortality rates amongst infants and young children generally that were such a common feature in previous centuries, and were commonly accepted as the will of God, are no longer such a crucial levelling factor. Expectations have risen enormously throughout the world. It has done so not just in the so-called 'developed' areas but the 'undeveloped' also. The well-proven achievements in medical science, mainstream science and technology generally have entered the awareness of virtually every race and ethnic group throughout this planet. The only exception has been those few truly 'primitive' peoples living in the back of beyond. Here, Nature's checks and balances are accepted without question. But this is not the case with the remainder of humanity! Indeed the provision of the basic necessities of life is now considered a 'human right'. Sadly though, this is an expectation that can only be achieved by a complete reversal of so many entrenched attitudes and trends, crucially demanding a last-minute defusion on the population explosion. All else is but pious fantasy, delusion, and irresponsible make-believe.

The following statistics are for 1994. They show a range of figures covering virtually every country and nation throughout the world: among them are birth rate, death rate, doubling time (at current rate), infant mortality rate, and total fertility rate. These statistics have been abstracted from a much larger sheet of figures which include percentage rate below 15 years and above 65 years, life expectancy of male and female, % of urban population, % of women using contraception, government view of contraception, and lastly per capita GNP.

You think this is more than enough? Sadly it is not. Unfortunately, figures for emigration out of, or immigration into, each sovereign country are *not* given. This is regrettable as it can have an enormous impact if such mass movements of people go on year after year. Yet clearly such statistics are difficult to finalise with any degree of accuracy. Sometimes, even if the effort has been made, they are so complex as to be misleading. Emigration and immigration tend to proceed in waves, sometimes with considerable gaps in the time sequence. And it might be temporary or permanent. For example, some affluent countries issue work permits for non-nationals for short periods of time; this can sometimes be even on a seasonal basis, such as at harvest time or for summer work in hotels and tourist industries generally. As for illegal immigration, this, by its very nature, is virtually impossible to quantify. Unfortunately, however, it is a factor that can be the most destabilising factor of all.

It is equally unfortunate to the untrained eye that these statistics may mean very little until one makes some vital comparisons. For example, the birth rate per thousand for the UK, Denmark, the Netherlands, Germany, France, Spain and

Italy hovers between ten to fourteen births per thousand. The population doubling time (naturally assuming present conditions prevail) in the UK is 281 years, in Denmark 533 years, in the Netherlands 169 years, in France 182 years, in Spain 630 years, while Italy tops it all with 2,310 years! Germany is problematic because of the recent reunion, plus the flow of refugees and immigrants. One can then contrast this with Albania, such a short distance across the Adriatic with a birth rate of 23 per thousand (PT) and a doubling time (DT) of only 39 years (thirty-nine years – this is not a misprint!), or, even worse, Gaza, with 56 PT and a DT of only 14 years. Israel is not far behind with 21 PT and a DT of 47 years. Iraq, significantly enough given the present confrontation with Saddam Hussein, has 45 PT giving it a DT of 19 years (nineteen years – again not a misprint!); Turkey 29 PT and DT 32 years; Iran 44 PT and 19 years; Pakistan 40 PT and 25 years; India 29 PT and 36 years; Bangladesh 37 PT and 29 years; Lebanon 25 PT and 34 years; Sri Lanka 21 PT and 46 years; Rwanda 40 PT and 30 years; Eritrea 42 PT and 27 years; Ethiopia 46 PT and 22 years; Somalia 50 PT and 22 years; Algeria 32 PT and 28 years; Egypt 30 PT and 31 years; Indonesia 25 PT and 43 years; Malaysia 28 PT and 30 years; Philippines 30 PT and 29 years; Burma 28 PT and 36 years – one can go on and on, with the correlation becoming more and more pointed still! Remember, the bulk of European countries have, on average, a doubling time of well over two hundred years and, in Italy's case, two thousand, two hundred years!

Table I: *World Population Statistics (1994)*[2]
(Abstracted from United Nations Statistical Division, World Population)

	Birth rate per 1,000	Death rate per 1,000	Doubling time in years	Infant mortality rate	Total fertility rate
Northern Europe					
Denmark	13	12	533	6.6	1.8
Finland	13	10	257	4.4	1.8
Ireland	14	9	120	6.3	2.1
Lithuania	14	11	210	17.0	1.9
Norway	14	10	193	5.8	1.8
Sweden	14	11	255	4.8	2.0
Britain	13	11	281	6.6	1.8
Western Europe					
Austria	12	10	385	8.3	1.5
Belgium	12	10	330	8.3	1.6
France	13	9	182	6.7	1.7
Germany	10	11	-	5.9	1.3
Netherlands	13	9	169	6.3	1.6
Switzerland	12	9	231	6.2	1.5
Eastern Europe					
Belarus	12	11	693	12.0	1.7
Bulgaria	11	13	-	15.9	1.5
Czech Rep	12	11	2,888	8.5	1.7
Hungary	11	14	-	13.3	1.7
Poland	13	10	257	13.8	1.8
Romania	11	11	-	23.3	1.4
Russia	11	12	-	18.0	1.6
Slovakia	14	10	182	15.6	1.9
Ukraine	12	13	-	14.0	1.7

---

[2] The reader may well like to make their own correlation between high birth rate and internal instability or outright conflict with neighbouring states, by underlining in red any country having a total fertility rate of over 3.0. Such an exercise is highly instructive when news bulletins break a story on new conflicts – yet fail to give any convincing reason why.

	Birth rate per 1,000	Death rate per 1,000	Doubling time in years	Infant mortality rate	Total fertility rate
Southern Europe					
Albania	23	6	39	32.9	3.0*
Bosnia	14	7	95	15.2	1.6*
Croatia	10	11	-	11.1	1.4*
Greece	10	10	1,155	8.2	1.4
Italy	10	10	2,310	8.3	1.3
Macedonia	16	7	84	24.5	1.9
Malta	15	8	95	7.9	2.0
Portugal	12	10	462	9.2	1.5
Slovenia	10	10	1,155	6.6	1.3
Spain	10	9	630	7.9	1.2
Yugoslavia	14	10	198	16.5	1.9*
North Africa					
Algeria	32	7	28	58.0	4.2
Egypt	20	8	31	62.0	3.9
Libya	42	8	21	68.0	6.4
Morocco	30	7	30	57.0	4.0
Sudan	44	13	22	85.0	6.4
Tunisia	25	6	36	43.0	3.3
West Africa					
Benin	49	18	22	87.0	7.1
Burkina Faso	50	18	22	132.0	7.2
Ivory Coast	50	15	20	91.0	7.4
Gambia	48	21	26	90.0	5.9
Ghana	42	12	23	81.0	6.0
Guinea	46	21	28	147.0	6.0
Liberia	47	14	21	126.0	6.8
Mali	52	21	23	110.0	7.3
Mauritania	46	18	24	117.0	6.5
Niger	53	19	20	123.0	7.4

* These figures are distorted by emigration rates (not given) and by warfare.

	Birth rate per 1,000	Death rate per 1,000	Doubling time in years	Infant mortality rate	Total fertility rate
West Africa (continued)					
Nigeria	44	13	23	87.0	6.5
Senegal	43	16	26	80.0	6.0
Sierra Leone	48	22	26	143.0	6.5
Togo	49	12	19	94.0	7.0
East Africa					
Burundi	46	17	24	105.0	6.7
Eritrea	42	16	27	-	-
Ethiopia	46	15	22	110.0	6.9
Kenya	44	10	21	66.0	6.3
Madagascar	46	13	21	93.0	6.1
Malawi	47	20	25	134.0	6.7
Mozambique	45	18	26	147.0	6.5
Rwanda	40	17	30	117.0	6.2
Somalia	50	19	22	122.0	7.0
Tanzania	48	15	21	102.0	6.3
Uganda	51	21	23	104.0	7.4
Zambia	46	18	24	107.0	6.5
Zimbabwe	41	11	23	59.0	5.3
Mid Africa					
Angola	47	20	26	137.0	6.6
Cameroon	41	12	24	81.0	5.9
Cen Afr Rep	44	20	29	142.0	5.6
Chad	44	18	27	122.0	5.9
Congo	42	16	27	116.0	5.5
Zaire	48	15	21	93.0	6.7
Southern Africa					
Botswana	36	9	26	43.0	4.6
Lesotho	31	12	36	79.0	4.7
Namibia	41	8	21	66.0	6.0
South Africa	34	8	26	49.0	4.4

	Birth rate per 1,000	Death rate per 1,000	Doubling time in years	Infant mortality rate	Total fertility rate
North America					
Canada	14	7	98	6.8	1.8
United States	16	9	98	8.3	2.1
Central America					
Costa Rica	26	4	31	13.7	3.2
El Salvador	33	7	26	45.0	3.9
Guatemala	39	7	22	57.0	5.4
Honduras	38	7	23	50.0	5.2
Mexico	28	6	31	35.0	3.2
Nicaragua	37	7	24	57.0	4.6
Panama	23	5	38	21.0	2.9
Caribbean					
Cuba	15	7	91	10.2	1.8
Dominican Rp	28	6	31	43.0	3.3
Haiti	42	19	30	111.0	6.0
Jamaica	24	5	37	13.2	2.4
Puerto Rico	18	8	67	13.0	2.2
Trinidad	18	7	60	16.7	2.7
South America					
Argentina	21	8	53	25.6	2.9
Bolivia	37	10	26	75.0	5.0
Brazil	25	8	40	66.0	3.0
Chile	22	6	41	14.6	2.5
Colombia	25	5	35	33.0	2.7
Ecuador	31	6	28	53.0	3.8
Paraguay	34	6	26	48.0	4.4
Peru	28	8	34	81.0	3.5
Uruguay	18	10	89	21.1	2.4
Venezuela	30	5	27	20.2	3.6

	Birth rate per 1,000	Death rate per 1,000	Doubling time in years	Infant mortality rate	Total fertility rate
Western Asia					
Armenia	21	7	49	18.0	2.6
Azerbaijan	26	6	36	25.0	2.7
Bahrain	29	5	29	25.0	3.7
Cyprus	20	9	86	10.0	2.7
Gaza	56	6	14	43.0	7.7
Georgia	17	9	86	16.0	2.2
Iraq	45	8	19	79.0	7.0
Israel	21	6	47	8.1	2.8
Jordan	38	5	21	34.1	5.9
Kuwait	35	2	21	16.0	4.9
Lebanon	25	5	34	28.0	2.9
Oman	53	4	14	24.0	6.9
Saudi Arabia	36	5	22	24.0	5.5
Syria	44	6	19	44.0	6.9
Turkey	29	7	32	57.0	3.5
Arab Emirates	23	4	36	23.0	4.1
West Bank	46	7	17	40.0	5.7
Yemen	48	14	20	115.0	7.6
South Central Asia					
Afghanistan	49	22	25	168.0	6.9
Bangladesh	37	13	29	116.0	4.9
India	29	10	36	79.0	3.6
Iran	44	9	19	66.0	6.6
Kazakhstan	20	8	59	27.0	2.5
Kyrgyzstan	29	7	32	52.0	3.6
Nepal	39	15	29	90.0	5.5
Pakistan	40	12	25	109.0	6.1
Sri Lanka	21	6	46	19.4	2.5
Tajikistan	35	6	24	40.0	4.5
Turkmenistan	33	7	26	45.0	4.1
Uzbekistan	33	6	26	35.0	4.0

	Birth rate per 1,000	Death rate per 1,000	Doubling time in years	Infant mortality rate	Total fertility rate
South East Asia					
Cambodia	46	17	24	112.0	5.8
Indonesia	25	9	43	68.0	3.0
Laos	44	16	24	107.0	6.3
Malaysia	28	5	30	14.0	3.6
Burma	28	9	36	98.0	3.8
Philippines	30	7	29	40.0	4.1
Singapore	17	5	56	5.0	1.8
Thailand	20	6	50	39.0	2.2
Viet Nam	30	7	30	36.0	3.7
East Asia					
China	18	7	61	31.0	2.0
Hong Kong	12	5	99	6.4	1.2
Japan	10	7	267	4.4	1.5
Korea North	24	6	37	30.0	2.4
Korea South	16	6	67	15.0	1.6
Mongolia	34	7	26	48.0	4.5
Taiwan	16	5	68	5.7	1.7
Oceania					
Australia	15	7	85	6.6	1.9
Fiji	25	5	35	15.0	3.0
New Zealand	17	8	76	7.3	2.1
Papua	35	12	30	72.0	5.4

Table II: *Area and Density*

Country	Land Area	Population (per square mile)
Afghanistan	251,770	71
Albania	10,580	322
Algeria	919,590	30
Angola	481,350	23
Argentina	1,056,640	32
Armenia	11,500	320
Australia	2,941,290	6
Austria	31,940	250
Azerbaijan	33,400	221
Bahamas	3,860	70
Bahrain	260	2,148
Bangladesh	50,260	2,320
Barbados	170	1,566
Belarus	80,200	129
Belgium	11,750	863
Benin	42,710	123
Bolivia	418,680	20
Bosnia	19,740	233
Botswana	218,810	7
Brazil	3,265,060	48
Brunei	2,030	140
Bulgaria	42,680	197
Burundi	9,900	610
Cambodia	68,150	151
Cameroon	179,690	73
Canada	3,560,220	8
Cape Verde	1,560	262
Central African Republic	240,530	13
Chad	486,180	13
Chile	289,110	49
China	3,600,930	331
Colombia	401,040	89
Congo	131,850	19

Country	Land Area	Population (per square mile)
Costa Rica	19,710	165
Ivory Coast	122,780	113
Croatia	21,830	220
Cuba	42,400	261
Cyprus	3,570	208
Czech Republic	30,590	338
Denmark	16,360	319
Djibouti	8,950	64
Dominica	290	259
Dominican Republic	18,680	416
Ecuador	106,890	99
Egypt	384,340	153
El Salvador	8,000	655
Guinea	10,830	36
Eritrea	48,260	72
Estonia	17,410	89
Ethiopia	376,830	147
Fiji	7,050	108
Finland	117,610	43
France	212,390	273
Gabon	99,490	11
Gambia	3,860	275
Georgia	26,900	203
Germany	134,930	602
Ghana	88,810	191
Great Britain	93,280	626
Greece	50,520	205
Grenada	130	716
Guadeloupe	650	649
Guatemala	41,860	247
Guinea	94,930	67
Guyana	76,000	11
Haiti	10,640	661
Honduras	43,200	123
Hong Kong	380	15,297

IDENTITY

Country	Land Area	Population (per square mile)
Hungary	35,650	288
Iceland	38,710	7
India	1,147,950	794
Indonesia	705,190	283
Iran	631,660	97
Iraq	168,870	118
Ireland	26,600	135
Israel	7,850	692
Italy	113,540	503
Jamaica	4,180	586
Japan	145,370	860
Jordan	34,340	123
Kazakhstan	1,049,200	16
Kenya	219,960	123
Korea, North	46,490	496
Korea, South	38,120	1,166
Kuwait	6,880	185
Kyrgyzstan	76,600	59
Laos	89,110	53
Latvia	24,900	102
Lebanon	3,950	917
Liberia	37,190	79
Libya	679,360	7
Lithuania	25,210	148
Luxembourg	990	407
Macedonia	9,930	211
Madagascar	224,530	61
Malawi	36,320	263
Malaysia	126,850	154
Mali	471,120	19
Malta	120	2,954
Mauritius	710	1,540
Mexico	736,950	125
Mongolia	604,830	4

Country	Land Area	Population (per square mile)
Morocco	172,320	166
Mozambique	302,740	52
Namibia	317,870	5
Netherlands	13,100	1,174
New Zealand	103,470	34
Nicaragua	45,850	93
Niger	489,070	18
Nigeria	351,650	279
Norway	118,470	37
Oman	82,030	23
Pakistan	297,640	425
Panama	29,340	86
Papua	174,850	23
Paraguay	153,400	31
Peru	494,210	46
Philippines	115,120	597
Poland	117,550	328
Portugal	35,500	278
Puerto Rico	3,420	1,056
Romania	88,930	256
Russia	6,592,800	22
Rwanda	9,530	805
Saudi Arabia	830,000	22
Senegal	74,340	110
Seychelles	100	691
Sierra Leone	27,650	167
Singapore	240	12,440
Slovakia	18,790	255
Somalia	242,220	41
South Africa	471,440	87
Spain	192,830	203
Sri Lanka	24,950	717
Sudan	917,370	31
Swaziland	6,640	126

Country	Land Area	Population (per square mile)
Sweden	158,930	56
Switzerland	15,360	457
Syria	71,070	197
Taiwan	13,900	1,514
Tajikistan	55,300	106
Tanzania	342,100	87
Thailand	197,250	301
Togo	21,000	203
Trinidad & Tobago	1,980	650
Tunisia	59,980	145
Turkey	297,150	208
Uganda	77,050	257
Ukraine	233,100	221
United Arab Emirates	32,280	52
UK – see Great Britain		
United States	3,539,230	74
Uruguay	67,490	47
Uzbekistan	172,700	128
Venezuela	340,560	63
Viet Nam	125,670	582
Yemen	203,850	63
Yugoslavia	26,940	390
Zaire	875,520	49
Zambia	287,020	32
Zimbabwe	149,290	75

NOTES

The above information has been abstracted from a much more extensive chart produced by the United Nations Statistical Division giving figures for 1994 (when this essay was in an early stage of preparation). Very small states with a tiny population have been omitted. For a complete cover of all countries or recently emerged new states, readers can contact Population Concern, 231 Tottenham Court Rd, London W1P 9AE (tel: 020 7631 1546).

Unfortunately the data sheet does not attempt to show recent population losses or gains from warfare, famine, pandemics or emigration. Equally it does not attempt to show recent immigrant numbers in host nations. In the case of Germany where only a few years earlier East Germany was re-united with the West and where large numbers of immigrants have entered from other countries a blank space indicates that even a broad assessment is problematic. Other blank spaces among the list of countries denote lack of reliable information. Again, data supplied by highly secretive regimes such as that controlling North Korea for example must be taken with caution as the figures could be manipulated to suit political purposes. Lastly, the figures for Yugoslavia (now defunct as a state) are misleading in that Slovenia and Croatia have a low birth-rate and doubling time, whereas Bosnia, Serbia and Kosovo have very high. Yet this is not expressed in the figures due to massive refugee movements and emigration to the remainder of Europe or the USA.

Regarding the data for land area and population ratio (average) per square mile, all subsequent inferences must of course be related to the geophysical nature of that area. Many countries have large inhospitable sections where human numbers must necessarily be restricted. They range from deserts with few possibilities of tapping water supplies, to mountain ranges or arctic conditions. At the other end of the scale small 'city states' like Hong Kong have a completely artificial and precarious existence in that water, fuel and food supplies are at the mercy of outside suppliers.

Can it therefore be sheer coincidence that all countries that have a birth rate higher than fifteen per thousand and a doubling time of less than fifty years show evidence of instability at best, and a tendency to descend into sheer chaos and disintegration at worst?

Even as I write (1995), severe clashes are taking place between Israelis and Palestinians, with outrages committed by both sides. Again, in almost every state in Africa, where birth rates and doubling times all compete for worldwide premier positions, the incidences of rioting, civil war and tribal savageries are so repetitive as to find a permanent place on our television screens. They add daily to the chronicles of misery, horror and degradation already burdening our twentieth-century historical record. In North Africa, Algeria has entered into a horrifying contest between fundamentalists and those with pro-Western attitudes or sympathies. Bubbling under the surface are similar fundamentalist pressures along the whole swathe of North Africa, from Morocco to Egypt.

In Europe itself the dismemberment of Yugoslavia continues as the ghastly war involving Serbs, Croats and Bosnian Muslims is temporarily and by outside intervention brought to a halt. Neighbouring Albania too, with such a high birth rate and such a short doubling time, is in a state of turmoil. Lawlessness is rife and rival political factions teeter on the edge of open conflict. This eventually can only lead to yet another civil war and/or mass emigration into neighbouring countries. Many Albanians are already in Bosnia and Kosovo, while others attempt to find work in Germany and Austria, and indeed in another continent across the Atlantic, in the USA[3].

Predictions for further conflict can be made with a high degree of accuracy merely by listing all those countries or regimes where currently the population doubling time is less than fifty years. And that list is horrifyingly large!

★

---

[3] In the interim between submitting this manuscript and its publication, the final crisis in Kosovo has erupted.

Conflict and race: the phenomenon of racial hatred

The world of science has difficulty with race. It finds it almost impossible to accept that such a concept can properly exist. And if it does then it doesn't mean very much. Why? Simply because no reputable research worker has yet devised a reliable way of dividing up mankind into fully distinctive racial groupings. It seems impossible to find, then define and tabulate clearly defined characteristics.

Science has very pernickety ways. It goes about things methodically and extremely carefully. If it didn't, it wouldn't be worth two brass farthings, of course. Being quite exacting in everything it does is the key to its success. Yet despite demanding such fine limits of tolerance and showing prissy exactitude when publishing scientific papers, it subsequently goes on to do something laymen find quite astonishing: it sets up its concepts and theories much as a young pimply-faced attendant at a funfair sets up coconuts for people to shy at! It then stands aside and watches to see if anyone with any skill can knock them off their pedestals. The longer a concept or theory can defy everything thrown at it then the greater the respect all other scientists have for it. It underlines a basic and highly important fact: all human knowledge is provisional. It is never absolute.

For those working in the fields of physics and chemistry (particularly), the introduction of a new theory demands extremely rigorous forms of presentation. It demands very subtle ways of defining observable phenomena in written form. This is then assisted more often than not by mathematical equations. Coupled with all of this are high degrees of precision with all measurements. Indeed measurements of one kind or another are vital; they play a central role in scientific methodology. Without them physicists and chemists feel distinctly unhappy. It would be rather like demanding that they should walk down a busy city street stark naked. But when one comes to the field of biology, there is a slightly different approach. You see many areas just don't lend themselves to measurement in highly precise ways. It has too many blurred outlines. Take the sphere of classification alone. How, in the process of identification, do you measure (with any kind of precision) infinitely small creatures observed under a microscope which are not just moving about, but changing shape as they do so? And as you go up the scale, how for that matter do you measure an ant, a bumblebee, an elephant or a tree? Sheer necessity demands that – initially, at least, in the area of classification of plants and animals – there must be a rather coarse visual check set against a previously agreed stereotyped image. And how do you come to an agreement on that stereotype? If you succeed in doing this, how do you come to an agreement on its probable grouping and ancestry?

Things were rather chaotic before Linnaeus set out his system. However, with later improvements and refinements the broader categories at least became better defined. Biologists in general, and botanists and zoologists in particular, nevertheless still cast envious glances over their shoulders at the physicists and chemists with their more precise and 'scientific' use of measurement. Indeed for most biologists throughout the eighteenth and nineteenth centuries, classification still needed that further stamp of authenticity. Visual interpretation simply wasn't good enough. So increasingly it became sine qua non that measurements were to be included in their findings – one way or another.

This worked reasonably well with plants and animals in all the properly defined classifications, but when one came to certain fuzzy areas all the trouble began. And what trouble it was!

As has been noted earlier, the evolution of plants and animals either progresses very slowly or takes sudden leaps and bounds. As you might expect, it was the latter energetic development that caused all the trouble. Environmental changes or the occupation of new niches often necessitates fairly rapid adaptations. But genetic mutations from chemical or radiation sources can also cause change. Members of the same species, according to the circumstances they find themselves in, can therefore show fairly rapid diversification from either source. So you get that very unsatisfactory concept called 'subspecies'. Here there are just *tiny* variations; even so the creature is already beginning to stray from the 'norm', which makes it an elusive concept if ever there was one. Now it is not generally realised that the very word 'subspecies' can work some scientists up into a lather. It is a classification many hate; indeed some prefer not to recognise it at all if they can get away with it. They like to deal with 'full speciation'. The argument is that adaptations and mutations will achieve complete 'speciation' if they go on long enough. Therefore only full speciation should be recognised – and only when differentiation is such that it shows distinct branching from the ancestral line. In other words, not only is it altered in a recognisable way, but the life form may no longer be able (or willing) to mate and produce viable offspring from members of its ancestral line. The very definition of 'species' and 'speciation' thus involve the procreative barrier – the inability of male and female of differing subspecies (yet of the same ancestral line) to mate and give birth to really fit and 'randy' offspring.

Even so, problems arise particularly with animals in the wild when species are prevented from mating by natural obstacles, such as a range of mountains, a desert or a large river. Are they just a subspecies or have they achieved full speciation? Putting specimens together artificially, and then waiting to see what happens, is not really fair as they might mate out of desperation, not out of choice. Among ruminant hoofed mammals (Cervidae) commonly called deer, with ancestral lines running back through antelope and cattle, you can get the large Red Deer and also several slightly smaller ones, such as Roe Deer (Capreolus capreolus). And these live in exactly the same habitat. This is rather disconcerting at first sight, for you would expect interbreeding. Then again Reindeer (Rangifer tarandus) and the American Caribou (Rangifer caribou) can also be introduced artificially into the same habitat, but these will not mate under normal circumstances either. Grey squirrels (Sciurus carolinensis) introduced from America into Britain will not interbreed with our native red squirrel (S. vulgaris); indeed they are gradually driving their smaller cousins further and further north because of their superiority both in collecting food and their breeding capacity. So what about extremes in abnormal circumstances? Well, some species of whale hunted to virtual extinction by man, have become so desperate in the search for mating partners that several cases of hybridisation have been reported. But among life forms over the broad spectrum, this is a most unusual phenomenon. Hybridisation seems to be one of those things Nature very definitely frowns on. Because of this, and the important question it raises, it is necessary to investigate all aspects of interbreeding more fully.

What I personally find intriguing is this: why should subspecies with only very minor variations and perfectly able to mate, from a purely physical point of view, prefer not to do so? It is a fascinating question. And it becomes all the more intriguing in spheres where closely related creatures are crowded together in the same habitat. Take some species of birds for instance.

As it happens, here the business of classification between species and subspecies becomes more disconcerting still – all the more so because they positively thrive in exactly the same habitat. Why should this be? Why don't they interbreed like mad? What prevents them? Why do they refuse? And why does the creation of subspecies go on unabated?

True, a series of genetic mutations from chemical or radiation sources will account for some initial differences, but why then do they refuse to mate with first cousins or second cousins in the subspecies context? For example, making any visual identification between a whimbrel and a curlew is problematic for the average city dweller out on a country walk. The differences are so small; it would suggest that if a male of one and a female of the other were in the mood, there would be no good reason to prevent courtship and mating. Again, for the casual observer the identification of a mute, a whooper or a Berwick's Swan, though easy enough for the professional ornithologist, fairly exasperates those amateurs with no previous insight. Equally, the *reason* for their marginal differences becomes a source of wonder. Then again, variation is just as small between a Brunnich's guillemot and a common guillemot, between a black-eared, a pied and a black wheatear. Looking through binoculars and seeing them in silhouette, differences are impossible to identify. Only when you can get really close and see the tiny variation in colour in just one small area of head or wing-tip is identification possible. And one could go on and on in the same way with a huge list of 'subspecies'. For some subspecies, even the professionals have to look carefully and look long.

So what of human 'subspecies' such as common or garden

Englishmen, common or garden Excitable Welshmen, common and dour Scots? What about white-haired, blue-eyed English, dark-haired, blue-eyed Welsh, red-haired, blue-eyed Scots and brown-haired, brown-eyed English... and you now tumble to the fact I am attempting to 'send up' this business of classification of course. You realise I am making a mockery of this very serious business of the identification of racial types – something which would be quite infuriating to those who love and study birds. To a 'twitcher' or professional ornithologist, you can't even begin to study the life history of birds without settling the question of identification from the outset. Yet when I return to the human species and begin mentioning words like Celtic, Nordic, Iberian Semitic, Indian, Negro and Malay racial groups, then I am in danger of getting into the hottest of hot water! I can be suspected of harbouring a racist outlook before even I complete a sentence or train of thought.

It was not always so. In those far-off days before governments began introducing what is called political correctness, it was quite normal for people to talk of different races without everyone risking raised blood pressure, glancing over their shoulders and lowering their voices. Indeed, scientists themselves began to take an interest in the matter.

In the early part of the nineteenth century, attempts were made by research workers to find some method of classification of racial types. For them it simply wasn't good enough to talk glibly about this race or that race, unless you had something solid to go on. Yet those workers who attempted to put the entire business on a proper scientific footing had initially great difficulty in finding an appropriate methodology. After considerable effort and scratching of heads, they thought they had found at least one or two that could be reliable. How mistaken they were! Over one hundred years later and after the most painstaking work, they were all proved not just wrong – which was bad enough – but also unscientific! Deplorably so!

Now for any scientist who values his reputation and wishes to retain a modicum of self-esteem, the charge 'unscientific' is shattering. He or she has no objection whatsoever to putting a concept or theory on display for others to take potshots at. They may be disappointed when errors are found, and perhaps even peeved when their particular coconut comes tumbling to the ground, but provided the scientific method was sound in the first place there is no shame attached. That another scientist should carefully study findings and then level the charge 'unscientific', however, is the most abusive and insulting epithet that can be thrown at any researcher's head. But this is precisely what happened in the case of racial characteristics.

For example, in the opening decades of the nineteenth century it was thought that a person's race could be determined from skull measurements. Fixation with mathematical formulae prevailed. A complex system called the cephalic index was devised. It was then used quite happily, as already indicated, for the next hundred years, moreover by a range of research workers in a variety of countries. They even set up what seemed at that time to be clearly defined criteria. This covered many different races. Even so, in due course, the basic methodology proved hopelessly deficient.

With growing controversy over the entire subject of race, some scientists were determined to make a fresh start. At the beginning of this century they looked about them and thought they had found a superb new method. This involved using the newly introduced science of blood grouping. At that time it was proving vital to the medical world's understanding of successful blood transfusion in accident and emergency situations and in general surgery. Surely this would now prove a better line of investigation? Given a little time and careful analysis, why shouldn't blood groups provide useful markers? Many years again were spent sampling blood from a wide variety of races before this too proved a waste of time and effort – at least, that is, insofar as positive identification and markers for racial groups were concerned. Then toward the end of this century came the invention of so-called 'DNA fingerprinting'. Here, once again, it was hoped that this brilliant new tool might be fruitful. Once more it was not to be. Hopes were once again dashed. Many things were learned, but a foolproof method for determining racial groupings was not among them.

Genetic fingerprinting

As its name suggests, genetic fingerprinting has become a truly formidable and (almost) foolproof new tool in the identification of individuals. It has proved of unique importance in investigations made by forensic laboratories. Most secretions from a human or animal body, including naturally, that of sperm, form the basis on which sophisticated tests can be carried out. However when applied to the thorny question of identifying different races it raises almost as many questions as it answers. As I see it – and I may be proved wrong by the experts – the difficulty lies with providing a 'norm'.

The revolutionary factor concerning genetic fingerprinting depends of course on the central assertion that each individual person produces a unique genetic 'print out'. However racial groups being composed of a large number of individuals can not in themselves produce a 'fixed' print out.

Because each individual is unique, then there are unavoidably a fair number of mutations from the 'norm' – the norm that supposedly makes up the broad pattern of 'pure' racial characteristics. Thus one is faced with the difficult question as to how many variations one can allow before that individual falls outside the 'basket' of genes constituting the norm. Then again there is an added difficulty when one is faced by subtle influences supplied by the environment. Depending where an individual lives, or perhaps more importantly, where they work over a long period of time, there is the possibility that they may be exposed to above average radiation from natural or man-made sources; exposed also to ingestion of chemical pollutants. Mutation may thus be unduly accelerated. This is particularly so if males and females exposed to similar environmental influences produce children. Under such circumstances even groups of people repeatedly sharing the same gene-pool due to strictures applied by geographic, ethnic or religious isolation will show greater and greater variation from the supposed norm.

Now failures of this kind tended to make scientists believe that if, after *so* much effort, racial characteristics could not be described and measured in scientific terms, then they simply did not exist.

Yet ordinary people in their scientific ignorance, happily talk of this race and that race, much as they talk of last week's football match or the scandalous price of fuel or a common loaf of bread. They find it very real and obvious. Artists and sculptors too seem to find subtle yet very real distinctions in racial characteristics. It enables them to exhibit a piece and achieve a nod of recognition, confirming that this portrait or bronze head is of a Malayan, a Chinese, an Inuit, or a European, without any requirement of a title or label. Perhaps some day computer graphics may do even better by giving measurable contour lines that fully define racial characteristics in the human head. But these days are not yet with us.

So does race exist? Or is it just a figment of our non-scientific and all too fevered imaginations?

Predictably, someone will immediately bring up skin colour as the most obvious marker. But this is incidental. It is perfectly possible to find a range of differences within an assembly of white-skinned humans, as one can in our light brown, dark brown, or so-called 'red' or 'yellow' cousins. But how could such differences have come about in the first place? This is the crucial question. If we are all of the same species and can interbreed, (moreover we have, as proof, perfectly viable offspring), then how is it possible that differently pigmented skin and skull shapes still exist when races have intermingled for thousands of years? Why aren't we all an amorphous mass of olive-skinned beings, with virtually identical skull shapes – all quite indistinguishable from one another?

To make any headway in this matter we must yet again go back to our early ancestors.

As noted earlier, and until such evidence comes along to suggest otherwise, we have to assume our forebears emerged from the southern part of the continent of Africa. Banding together in extended family groups of not more than perhaps twenty persons was an early behavioural trait. Incidentally this is seen in a wide variety of animals, not just in primates. Providentially, this proved to have very definite advantages in the business of survival. When speech became well developed, and one supposes that some humans became more articulate than others, then the survival factor for these individuals particularly received a considerable boost. Skills in foraging for wild fruits and hunting, already well developed, received that extra edge. They did so from the ability to pass on information, rapidly and effectively, when and where it was needed. Even so, I stick to my own theory that the most crucial survival factor of all was that of good parenting.

Now the female of the human species – as is not too difficult to imagine – happens to be deeply concerned with the tricky business of finding a male partner. But not just any man! Ideally he should be what might be called a 'decent and upright' candidate. He should be someone who will, she hopes, metamorphose from a rather ignorant and immature oaf into a truly responsible father, the father of *her* children. As noted earlier however, candidature for parenthood is of rather lesser importance to the male. While he has a vague feeling that he should look for someone who might make a good mother, it is the anticipation of the sexual act itself that is usually uppermost in his mind. He is not too concerned about the host of responsibilities that can so easily flow from copulation. He might knuckle down to that later, but on the other hand he might not. It is very different for the female. You see, few indeed desert their children. When you have babies you are emotionally stuck with them if nothing more, so to speak. So finding a suitable and dependable father is very much a serious business.

True, the qualities females look for may vary a little with circumstances. These qualities may also seem in retrospect to have been ridiculously optimistic, but she looks for them nevertheless. Uppermost in her mind is the eventual welfare of her babies and the opportunity for them to develop 'sound in mind and limb', more important still, reach maturity without undue hazard. To this end she may form what to others may seem very unsuitable and certainly very unromantic attachments. She may, for example, keep close company with a man who may be physically repulsive. And for that matter he may not be very charming or in possession of social mannerisms either. But you can bet your boots that this man will have power and influence. In earlier eras he would have been either the most successful hunter, or the most skilled fisherman, or the most victorious warrior – even someone gifted as a primitive potter, sculptor or artist. The latter would have revealed that a slightly more romantic side of her nature had dominated her choice. But for the female with purely mercenary motives, and no more than a conniving baby factory on two legs, such a cookie would try to find favour with the man with the most cattle, the largest hut (with waterproof thatch!) or the finest collection of beads, in later centuries gold coins! In this she would be following her deeper instincts. She would be sacrificing her lust for handsome young men (alas impecunious and irresponsible) for the greater good of any children she would hope to bear.

As the centuries rolled by, the extended family groups tended to grow into tribes – all essentially co-operative and cohesive, offering as many survival benefits as possible.

Unfortunately though it was not all advantage. The larger the tribes became, more disadvantages would creep in. It is an expression of Newtonian law encroaching on human affairs: advantage in one direction means a disadvantage in another. There is no such thing as 'pure' advantage! The success of the large tribe was Janus-faced. The more successful you became, both in securing your food supply and in carefully warding off predators, then the more you cut down on the death rate of two opposite age groups – the older members of your tribe and the younger. Thus numbers began to rise substantially and tribal boundaries became too constraining. Immediately the other side of the Janus face begins to show. Tribal boundaries were crossed. And then all hell broke loose. As with all other territorial animals, such crossing of boundaries meant savage reprisals from occupants. Confrontation would begin with stylised 'threat' displays. If these failed to produce the desired effect, real battle would begin. Unless the invaders were far larger in number or had superior weapon technology, they would be beaten back by the defenders. Both would lose a proportion of their fighting men. And with population size having been neatly culled, a status quo would be established. Territorial boundaries would then be respected until the next surge in population once again called for encroachment.

At this point we should note that there are highly important biological implications when reasonably firm territorial boundaries are established and respected over a period of time.

Such a thing as a 'gene pool' begins to have significance. What is a gene pool? It is a restricted source of genetic material interchanged between individuals of a tribal group each time males and females procreate. Having no outside input, it creates distinctive characteristics that become the norm within that group. However, in using our new Newtonian definition – that no advantage can be created in one direction without disadvantages in another – we have to consider assets and debits.

Suppose the gene pool contains such characteristics as long limbs, large ribcage, large-capacity lungs, strong heart muscles and excellent eyesight. Such a group of people will become skilled hunters, adept at tracking wild animals over long distances. But on the debit side they may well begin to accustom themselves to an unbalanced diet. They might become overly dependent on meat and negligent in seeking wild fruits and tubers. This may eventually have a negative effect on their general health, with their arteries furring up and strain being put on the heart. Their neighbours on the opposite side of the territorial boundary, in contrast, might be small-boned, with small ribcages, lower lung capacities and rather poor eyesight. On the plus side, they may be more articulate, with a wider vocabulary, and possibly more intelligent. These may be less skilled in hunting but will have a more balanced diet and rather less chance of developing heart disease. Being more articulate they may, however, be more argumentative and quick-tempered. The incidence of internal squabbling and fatal wounding may thus be greater. Each gene pool will thus be seen to possess genetic factors giving advantages and disadvantages. It is so tempting to think that if the two tribes could in some way unite under one leader, subsequently pouring one gene pool into another, this would produce an excellent mix. Unfortunately of course, as Mendel showed, genes cannot be poured into a container and mixed in the way that black and white paint stirred together becomes grey. Some genes are dominant and some recessive. To make matters worse, there are so many genes and so many combinations and possible reshufflings! In fact the entire outcome would be most difficult to predict. Certainly throughout history, tribes have amalgamated to make larger groupings. They have done so either by political agreement or as the result of warfare. And in the latter case the victors would often take away women and children as spoils of victory. Whether interbreeding (miscegenation) is achieved under either circumstance, be it peace or war, then the gene pools would certainly be enlarged! Ah, but with imponderable results! Imponderable? What about an informed guess, you might ask? Well, the more optimistic of geneticists believe that almost any gene pool intermixing tends to be beneficial; the more pessimistic, on the other hand, believe that inputs may well bring more disadvantages than advantages. The entire subject is fraught with all manner of complex issues. Take diet alone. Racial groups have adapted their digestive systems over thousands of years because of specific crops grown and proportion of meat eaten. Changes, brought about by forced or peaceful migrations, therefore can have unknown long-term effects. Looking at adaptations to certain climactic conditions or a habitat where thousands of years of over-dependence on certain foods is marked, the problems could be severe. Certainly, mankind is fortunate in being omnivorous and therefore not too specialised in overall terms. As we know there can be severe problems for animals – either herbivore or carnivore – who overspecialise. The obvious example is the giant panda, living on a very restricted diet of bamboo shoots. Such animals are doomed to extinction should their food source rapidly diminish. But on the other hand, to jump immediately to the conclusion that specialisation per se must be avoided at all costs (and therefore the larger the gene pool the better) would be foolish. One only has to think of the highly complex effects visited on the immune systems of all animals (including man). And here I do not allude to the mere effects of contagious diseases. True, the North American Indian tribes, for example, were decimated far more efficiently by contact with the bacilli and viruses brought by the white man, than by bullets. But this has nothing to do with the actual interbreeding between red and white. Here, data is sketchy and incomplete; even so the results insofar as they relate to advantages and disadvantages to the human immune system, seem to show many negative aspects.

Sweeping aside all the highly complex effects interbreeding has on human organs, the immune system and health generally, then

IDENTITY

supposing it might be proved beyond a reasonable doubt that interbreeding has more advantages than disadvantages, there is still one area of the body that can nullify everything: the human brain.

During evolution the human animal, it is necessary to repeat yet again, spent over a million years existing in small extended family groupings of around twenty persons, seldom more. Its successful emergence from the most adverse of circumstances was due to active co-operative between individuals and high standards of parenting. But when these small groups began merging into larger and larger tribal units, the vital survival factor of co-operation began to break down. And the evolution of the human brain simply failed to catch up with the sudden evolution of human social structures.

Anthropologists studying the few so-called 'Stone-Age' representatives of our ancestors still surviving in the jungles of Borneo note the system whereby gatherings of tribal elders settle disputes. And in truly serious disputes, or in a violent rupture of tribal law, the entire community assembles and listens intently to the elders debating the matter. Witnesses are called and their testimony is again heard by all. Interruptions are allowed by any of the assembled onlookers if they believe what has been alleged is inaccurate. The community operated as an organic whole or as a 'biological entity', if you prefer to think of it in that way. The system of employing elders came about because of the gut feeling within the community that several minds debating a problem are superior to one, moreover that the old tend to have greater wisdom than the young. Generally speaking it does indeed ensure that a wise council and a sensible decision usually prevail. It also ensures majority approval.

Seeing that almost every aspect of life in the depths of the Borneo jungle, in the Kalahari desert and the most remote parts of the Amazonian basin has remained virtually unchanged since the Stone Age, there is every reason to believe that similar social systems operated among our ancestors at least until eight thousand years ago. They too would have been headed by patriarchs and elders. And these would have overlapped into larger tribal groupings during the emergence of the early primitive herdsman and agricultural civilisations, more especially of the Tigris–

Euphrates, Nile, Indus and Chinese 'loess' soil systems. But as soon as these early civilisations established themselves and population levels began to climb, a significant change took place.

Now much of this has been noted earlier. Tiresome as it may seem, it is necessary to repeat sections of these chapters for not only does their significance need underlining, but also there are new and quite crucial aspects which arise out of them.

To begin with it is important to underline that the comforting psychological assurance of belonging to a naturally formed social and biological entity was already beginning to break down when tribal groups became significantly larger. Worse, with population levels quickly becoming unsustainable because they had reached the limits of primitive technology, came severe scarcity of resources. This forced many more raids and longer incursions into the territory of others. Rising levels of conflict meant that the consensual rule of the elders was rapidly superseded by the autocratic rule of one man – the most successful of the young warriors. This almost universal adoption of autocratic rule in turn destroyed the intimacy and cohesion enjoyed by the smaller tightly knit communities. Physical contact between the leader and those led would have become more remote, when, to protect and enhance his position, the leader would assume airs and graces. Gradually all the grandiose trappings of kingship came into being. Decisions too would be made by this individual in physical isolation from his people. These would often be arbitrary, capricious or downright repressive. Distancing oneself from the 'common herd' is part of the continuing process toward autocratic and absolute rule. This kind of leadership, as already noted, is nevertheless a very chancy business. It is often subject to challenge from ambitious underlings. Indeed it follows a wider pattern seen throughout Nature. In fact it is routinely observable in the remainder of the animal kingdom when ageing dominant males are first challenged then displaced by more physically powerful youngsters. To combat the likelihood of overthrow, the human alpha ditched reliance on sheer physical strength and resorted to artifice and sheer cunning. Archaeological evidence points to these petty kings engaging the services of tribal shamans at a very early date. By these means they added to their personal armoury the quite potent protection of magic and sorcery. Later, as exemplified by the emergence of the small city states in Sumer and elsewhere, kingship became hereditary and was attended by a well-organised priestly caste. Sometimes, as in ancient Egypt, the long-term preservation of the stability of the state was often endangered by the priestly caste themselves. Some engineered a palace revolution on their own account. Later generations of pharaohs guarded against this and doubly protected themselves by neatly combining both roles: they became priest-kings. Later still, when Egypt formed a fully viable civilisation, the priest-king became a god-king! And you can't engineer a much safer position or higher status than that!

In evolutionary terms, all this happened comparatively suddenly. It is therefore small wonder that the common mass of people had difficulty adjusting themselves! Moving abruptly from tiny communities of hardly more than twenty individuals they now had to cope – which involved intense psychological strain – with tightly packed societies numbering thousands. In some instances they had to cope with tens of thousands. The sudden loss of the social intimacy that had lasted several million years was nevertheless cunningly balanced by the new system. Here the cementing agency of a revered (or feared!) head of state was neatly dovetailed into an accommodating, if complex, religious system. And its extraordinary political stability and social lasting power is nowhere better exemplified than in Ancient Egypt. This said, there was, as we have already seen, another factor in Egypt's favour. As has been demonstrated in earlier chapters, it happened to be fortuitous and in this case geographical. It should be fully recognised and admitted that Egypt's natural defensive position prevented incursions from outside. She had deserts and mountain ranges protecting her to the east, west and south. Only from the north was any attack in strength possible and a standing army could be concentrated in this region. Undoubtedly this aided her longevity. In comparison, other early civilisations to such as Sumerian and Indus were much more open to attack. So despite having almost similar autocratic rulers – equally neatly bolstered and protected by a well-established religion – they suffered accordingly.

More importantly to our examination of the development of racial characteristics, the arrival of these early civilisations certainly meant that larger gene pools were established. But once again they were kept more or less 'pure' by standing armies protecting clearly defined territorial boundaries. The occasional conquest of (or by!) other states would however seem to frustrate the proper establishment of a distinctive racial line – obviously these brought in 'new blood', so to speak. But this is a superficial and hasty assumption. Interbreeding may well have been common in earlier more primitive eras, but not when human society became more sophisticated. Conquered peoples were now brought in as slaves, and used wholly as such. They were set apart from the remainder. A taboo was usually set up forbidding sexual intercourse between the 'superior' people and the 'inferior'. This taboo could only be broken by the ruling elite, who would sometimes take the more attractive female slaves as concubines. One must remember that this was an era when one of the many perks accorded kingship was the right to break (and do so flagrantly!) all the taboos you imposed on your own people. Sometimes too, Sumerian kings or Egyptian pharaohs would graciously extend the privilege of keeping concubines to other members of their entourage – at times even to governors ruling the provinces. But the mass of people would be kept strictly apart from 'impure' blood. This applied equally to early examples of economic migrants. The biblical story of Abram (later renamed Abraham by the Almighty) and his wife Sarai (later renamed Sarah) who came into Egypt from the Negeb as migrants escaping famine, has unusual significance in our examination of such taboos. In this story we find that Pharaoh himself was attracted by Sarai's beauty, but was forced to suffer for it. If we take the subsequent saga literally, then we find that the early authors of the biblical book of Genesis were anxious to prove that God himself was displeased at the prospect of Abram's line being 'sullied' with Egyptian blood. To the modern mind this is hardly what one would expect of an omnipotent God. Since He is the Creator of all things and all peoples, then logically one expects Him to treat all races even-handedly. But then these extraordinary anomalies insist on arising only if you happen to be fundamentalist in your beliefs. If you insist on an entirely literal reading then you create all sorts of problems for yourself in this particular area. Having convinced yourself of God's supposed partiality and the creation of a 'chosen people', the ramifications (and problems) are endless. If however you are not of fundamentalist persuasion then there is particular significance and indeed some revealing passages in these pages from Genesis from Chapter 12, verse 10 onwards. Indeed the saga speaks volumes for the attitudes of the time. To examine these in detail at this point would nevertheless interrupt our immediate purpose. It would be better to pursue the matter more closely when the relationship between conflict and religious beliefs is subjected to more detailed observation in later pages. In like manner we will examine the later saga of Moses, and the captivity of the Jewish people. Here again we find further illuminating commentary on attitudes towards the 'purity' of racial lines. This episode, revealing as it does remarkable Jewish fecundity despite all the rigours set on them by their Egyptian masters, is significant in that it illuminates one of the most common causes of racial tension: fear of the host country being outnumbered. Obviously, this also highlights factors which are relevant to the theme of this essay. But once again examination in greater detail must be left for a later chapter.

Meanwhile the input of religious beliefs remains relevant in that it has an important part to play in the maintenance of gene pools, and, directly arising from these, of course, the formation of racial characteristics. This is the direct consequence of the tacit or indeed openly stated taboo against interbreeding with other racial groups. And it includes not just those professing different religions, but also splinter groups within the same religion.

For those who feel I may be putting undue emphasis on the importance of such taboos, it may be necessary to remind such readers that they still exist. To this very day, intermarriage, or indulging in sexual relations with members of different religious (or ethnic) groupings, still arouses the strongest of passions. In Britain alone, particularly among immigrant groups, there have been several instances of parents (fathers especially) severely injuring or murdering daughters who have committed what, in their eyes, is the most unforgivable of sins: sexual relationships outside their racial group. For example, Hindus are rigidly opposed to relationships with Moslems or whites, and vice versa, Tamils with Singhalese and vice versa and Sikhs with almost anyone. In their ancestral India and Pakistan, the breaking of these taboos by Hindus, Moslems, Sikhs and Tamils can cause widespread rioting and serious loss of life. Again in the Middle East, it is unthinkable for an Arab to marry a Jew and vice versa. Many more instances can be found around the world. And just in case British Caucasians should feel a sniffy superiority creeping up on them, let me remind them that any Northern Irish Protestant having a sexual or even mildly amorous relationship with a Northern Irish Catholic (and vice versa) can cause serious repercussions. On our own doorstep here again we find cases of severe beatings or murder. And once more, these have been chronicled at regular intervals throughout this ugly conflict.

Of course religion alone is not the sole 'protector' of gene pools in this respect. In the deep south of the USA, from the end of last century's civil war until fairly recently, numerous summary lynchings of black males merely suspected of making sexual advances on white females have been documented decade after decade. Mixed marriages between black and white were also virtually banned by the apartheid regime in South Africa – no matter what religion was involved. It is tiresome to extend examples further for they occur in virtually every region where racial groups intermix. It is sufficient to note that in seeking the causes of human conflict, the factor involving racial miscegenation must take one of the premier positions on our list.

This being so, it may be fruitful to examine this issue in the wider context of instinctive behaviour within the animal kingdom as a whole.

To begin with we must ask a very necessary question: what is instinctive behaviour? How does one define it? You see, most people casually assume that all species among the remainder of the animal world act wholly on instinct: only human beings bring conscious thought (a much vaunted cerebral activity supposedly dominated wholly by rationality and logic) to bear. Yet this is a fallacy. We too are greatly influenced by our instincts. Indeed we can be influenced to such a degree that at times they can suppress or wholly reverse carefully debated and fully rational decisions. And these are after all reached by the seat of consciousness in the roof brain or cortex. Oddly enough, people commonly speak of having 'gut' feelings and press their hands to the pit of the stomach, as if our instincts reside there. This suggests that they are quite separate from the brain. But in fact of course our instinctive behaviour resides within the space allocated by the skull for *all* of its decision-making functions. Instinct is truly part of cerebral activity even if (speaking in evolutionary terms) it takes place in the 'old brain'! More importantly still, neurologists and psychologists are still in fierce debate regarding a clear-cut decision as to whether our instincts are advantageous to our general well-being or disadvantageous. One can cite endless examples either way. It is of particular relevance in an age where mankind's supposed intellectual gifts and technological expertise have brought about a crisis – the distinct possibility of ending all life on this once beautiful planet of ours in 'either a bang or a whimper'!

To define instinctive behaviour becomes even more difficult if you wander into the quagmire of its close association with 'reflex action'. The two are not synonymous although the outline of one may well blur into the other. A bright light flashing into one's eyes causes an involuntary blink; a doctor tapping one's knee with a special drumstick tool causes an involuntary kick. Both stimulate an automatic response from one's physical reflexes. On the other hand, an instinctive response has to do with rather longer cerebral functions of the brain. It moves toward or becomes intuitive in that it influences the mind. It is not physical, although the mind may well instruct the body to make a purely physical response later. Perhaps the only definition that makes sense is a negative one – instinctive behaviour is that which arises without due use of logic and the process of reasoning.

Having said this, it now becomes necessary to define what science finds indefinable: racial characteristics. How can we do this when, as already noted, the whole august body of science has refused to believe that they are measurable? How can we grapple with these problems when influential people simply declare that they fail to exist?

Our difficulties are compounded by imprecision in semantics on the one hand and of blurred outlines on the other! Yet to leave the matter wholly unresolved smacks of cowardice.

Can we at least examine an area of zoology where racial characteristics are in fact discussed – if under a different name and only where they apply to animals other than man? You see by even using the word 'subspecies' where it applies to birds, fish, amphibians and a host of land animals (even if it is done with distaste by scientists), then at least it gives us just a little hope in this respect.

Indeed why shouldn't we start with speciation itself?

*

To most people with just a modicum of curiosity concerning the world they find themselves inhabiting, moreover the way in which the incredible profusion of life forms have come into being, the entire spectacle of the biosphere proves endlessly fascinating. Before the speculations made by the early Greeks (Aristotle in particular), we were all Creationists; that is to say mankind believed that all living things had been created in an instant! What is more, it believed that they remained true to their original form over the march of time. For that matter, mankind also believed that the landscape they inhabited, the mountains, the valleys, the plains, the river system, indeed everything they could see around them, had also been created in an instant and similarly remained constant and true to its original form. Doubts came to the surface both in Ancient Greece and some centuries after the 'glory that was Greece' had passed away. But progress was slow. Several lively minds among a group of Moslem philosophers questioned the perceived wisdom of their day, and so did some Christian clerics such as Nicholas of Cusa during the revival of learning in the monasteries. But they seldom had any impact, or, if they did, they were a nine-day wonder quickly forgotten.

It is often carelessly assumed that Charles Darwin was the sole originator of both the concept and the theory of evolution. This is very wide of the mark on both counts. A full century before both Alfred Russel Wallace and Charles Darwin put pen to paper and began making tentative notes about it, several lively minds had resurrected the tentative thoughts of the Grecian philosophers. They had even begun to pursue the matter. The evolution of the Earth's surface and the basic framework for the science of geology were in fact born at the hands of the Scottish physician James Hutton. Convinced by his study of rock formations that they had undergone slow development and were not created at an instant, he began to make extensive notes on his findings from the 1750s onward. He published his *Theory of the Earth* in 1785. He also began work on a theory of biological evolution which anticipated Darwin's theory of natural selection! However, he died before finishing it. His papers then remained undiscovered for two centuries.

Hutton's pioneering geological work was later championed by Lyell, who published several volumes of *The Principles of Geology* during the 1830s. These greatly exercised the imagination of the young Charles Darwin. Introduced in this way, Darwin rapidly became a close friend of Lyell and each stimulated the other in forming an ever clearer picture of the immense timescales involved – not merely in the formation of this planet (or indeed the emergence of life on it) but as required by the formation of the entire universe. The latest findings of astronomers of the day, more especially when they touched on tentative hypotheses for the gradual formation of the universe, were carefully noted. Evolution was becoming, in this sense, all-pervading. Everything was seen to be in a state of flux. Although at that time it was difficult to prove, many astronomers were convinced that the stars themselves were born, slowly reached maturity, then died and were reabsorbed into new forms.

British scientists were not of course the sole leaders in the evolutionary field. In France and Germany minds were also active in postulating or propounding various theories. They too embraced gradual development throughout all aspects of the universe, as opposed to rigid Creationism.

Opposition from both clerics and laymen holding the traditional fundamentalist viewpoint however stiffened and became progressively more bitter.

The aristocratic Frenchman Georges-Louis Leclerc, better

know as the Comte de Buffon, began a natural history of living things in 1752. He too was tentatively putting forward a theory of gradual evolution – only to draw on his head great abuse from his critics. The English language was later to be enriched with the word 'buffoon', derived, it would seem, from the general attitude in France to his painstaking efforts. Another French aristocrat, Baron Cuvier, who became a notable anatomist studying comparative classification, was rather more cautious and avoided the wrath of fundamentalists by putting forward an explanation of successive catastrophes to account for change. God was therefore seen as a sort of evolutionist Himself! Being dissatisfied with His earlier work, God destroyed it not once but several times. Finally *He* created the more complex forms that we see today. And this clever hypothesis did to some extent modify the wrath of the opposition. Indeed the more intelligent fundamentalists saw it as an escape route that could explain away what was otherwise inexplicable. Without it there were some very awkward pieces of evidence of universal flux and unending (if slow) change that taxed the ability of the most able in their ranks to find excuses.

Yet another French aristocrat (maybe the famous and slow-maturing French wines played a part in their fascination for the evolutionary process!), Chevalier de Lamarck, made a stab at a biological evolutionary theory. It proved to have immense influence on the scientific thought of his day. He propounded 'inheritance by acquired characteristics'. In it he suggested, for example, that the giraffe had begun life as an ordinary sort of antelope. Over the years it established a niche for itself by eating the leaves from trees. Thousands of years of stretching upward toward ever higher branches gradually acquired, for each following generation, longer and longer necks. It complemented this with added length to its front legs, and a specially adapted tongue and digestive system.

It was extremely plausible. It further served a purpose in becoming in effect a vital touchstone for Darwin. Almost exactly fifty years later, in his own theory, he established a subtle variant. And in many ways it is almost impossible to understand Darwin fully without having a conceptual image of what is now the discredited Lamarckian version. Indeed it supports one of my own theories that it is impossible for the human mind to conceive of any natural phenomenon whatsoever without being able to juxtapose an opposing version. For example, it is impossible to conceive of daylight without being aware of darkness, impossible to conceive of war without peace, right without wrong, black without white (and any colour of the spectrum without a contrasting one), a solid without a liquid, negative without positive, past without future... and so on. Similarly it is impossible to understand Darwin's theory without knowledge of Lamarck's. The establishment and juxtaposition of the concept of Lamarckianism brings out the full force of and essential difference of both Darwinian and post-Darwinian theory. It is otherwise impossible to conceive fully. If Lamarck had not existed, Darwin would have needed to create him![4]

But to press on. The emergence of Darwinism did not of course establish his pre-eminence in the field immediately. He had unlocked the door, as you might say, to the 'secret garden' of evolution, using the key of natural selection. Yet there were weak points concerning the mechanics of the hereditary process that worried him constantly. But help was to come from an unexpected source in the shape of a corpulent monk living in an Austrian monastery. Mendel opened that rather stiff and unyielding door a further inch or two by inventing and then using the crowbar of genetic inheritance. Others have now shouldered it open even further. With the science of genetics fully established, they have now got their heads round that door sufficiently to have a questioning and wondering look all around that astonishing garden. Levene, Todd, Wilkins, Crick and Watson and many more during their discovery of and research into RNA and DNA, have all contributed. They have described for us all a garden of incredible profusion and richness. They themselves have been dazzled by its complexity. And they leave us, as laymen, baffled by many of their provisional findings and not a little disturbed by all the possible ramifications.

One thing is certain though. After intensive work for over three quarters of a century, geneticists have now given Darwin's

---

[4] See Appendix 2.

theory greater strength and authority than ever before.

You see, it got off to a shaky start, especially when, through the blunders of its own supporters, it set all sorts of people marching down the wrong roads or into cul-de-sacs. In the early years, critics of the theory had a field day. In my own estimation, one of the most unfortunate of 'sound bites' set up by his supporters was the concept of the 'survival of the fittest'. It had the most unfortunate of overtones and was never sanctioned by the great man himself. Personally, I am convinced that being a half-truth it should have been altered into a rather more subtle form, such as 'fitness for survival'. This would surely be more in keeping with Darwin's philosophic stance.

And having made this distinction, shall we now go directly to the matter of the establishment of species (speciation) and the more delicate issue of further diversification (subspecies). In doing so we must take a closer look at the mechanism involved.

At once we must note the discovery of chromosomes. The German anatomist Walther Flemming was the first to observe and study them as the result of new techniques in microscopy in the 1870s. This was twenty years after Darwin's publication of the *Origin of Species* with its unfortunate inability to throw a clear light on the actual transmission of what one might call the 'seeds of heredity'. The actual method of creating the next generation was still a mystery. But Flemming was fortunate in that newly discovered synthetic dyes were able to stain transparent body cells and reveal their inner contents in some detail. He became fascinated by cell division which he named mitosis, and in the behaviour of thread-like objects (later to be named chromosomes) which pulled themselves apart and duplicated themselves – each to inhabit the new daughter cells. Unaware of Mendel's theory of inheritance, Flemming failed to see the true significance initially, but noted his findings in his published papers on cell division. This work was taken up and extended by the Belgian cytologist Beneden who discovered in 1887 that not only does each species have different numbers of chromosomes, but in the sexual production of ova and spermatozoa only half the number are present. Therefore male and female contribute half each of the full complement to their offspring. Had both Darwin and Mendel lived a little longer, then the advances made in microscopy and the technique of using synthetic dyes (ironically the English chemist Perkin was actually producing the first of these while Darwin was completing the *Origin of Species*) would have given them the extraordinary joy of being able to see with their own eyes the actual mechanics of heredity – a process they could only posit theoretically in their day. Unfortunately Darwin died in 1882 and Mendel only two years later. Yet by the opening of the twentieth century the newly established science of genetics had made sufficient headway to prove beyond a doubt the broad outline of the actual mechanics of gene transference.

The pace of discoveries quickened over the first half of the twentieth century. In the second half one could say that the final details of the wholly physical method of transference were triumphantly discovered by Crick and Watson – in 1953 to be precise. To an astonished and duly applauding scientific world, they made their famous demonstration of the DNA molecule, taking the form of a double helix.

So much then for one aspect of transference of genetic material from one generation to another! But it is not the only aspect. In this matter of passing on genetic material I believe there are other subtleties still to be explored. And these are connected with the specific issue of achieving speciation, and moreover lie beyond that of the pure mechanics of the thing. You see there is a bit more to the passing on of genetic material than the central role played by the double helix, utterly fascinating though it is. Unfortunately though it moves us on to a quite new aspect and into an entirely different area of investigation. What about the curious interlude *before* mating? What of this strange business of 'preferences' involved during the *individual* selection of mating partners? This of course comes well before the mechanics of gene transference even begins. More puzzling still comes the astonishing process of achieving full speciation. You see, if a newly created species (or subspecies) is to survive at all, then surely Nature must employ some mechanism to prevent miscegenation! If it doesn't, then the entire process of evolution itself grinds to a halt.

A mechanism of sorts has of course already been vaguely

posited. Geographical separation over a period of time clearly prevents interbreeding, and biologists use the term 'allopatric' to identify such species. But how does Nature prevent creatures interbreeding where they overlap geographically? This is a situation where biologists use the term 'sympatric'. However they do not attempt to explain it: they simply accept that it exists and leave it at that!

Creating a fully new species, or indeed the interim form we call subspecies, demands that a fully viable gene pool of the new form builds up quite quickly. What do I mean by fully viable? Quite simply one that is not too small. In a tiny gene pool the choice of partners is so restricted that mating becomes not just incestuous (which in itself is bad practice biologically speaking) but continues over too long a period. Can we concentrate on this point for a moment?

Among the species we choose to call *Homo sapiens*, the cautionary tale of the Egyptian pharaohs provides due warning of the drawbacks entailed by incest. For those who are unaware of its use in such an exalted society, it should be explained that because they had assumed the mantle of god-kings, it was considered beneath their sacred dignity to take as a wife anything less than the blood-royal line. Archaeologists have come across evidence that suggests that the eldest son of a pharaoh was expected to mate shortly after reaching puberty with his sister, solely to preserve the 'sacred' blood.

And it seems that this tradition was carried on generation after generation. Unfortunately the build-up of deleterious genetic material, while not unduly harmful in the initial stages of this pairing, certainly became more and more serious later. Many of the offspring of such pairing died of genetic disorders in infancy or early teens. The reason, of course, was not understood by the royal household. It would have been assumed to be misadventure and the usual toll taken by the grim reaper. That those other offspring who actually succeeded in reaching adulthood were often partial invalids was also assumed to be misadventure too. The baneful influence of incestuous relationships remained unrecognised. Sometimes, no doubt, as with royal families in other continents and over widely spaced historical periods in the remainder of the world, the problems associated with royal succession such as the early death of a royal infant would be kept secret: a healthy child (often born of a concubine) would be substituted. One way or another the royal succession would need to be, and be seen to be, achieved! But outside the peculiar circumstances of individuals holding supreme power, incest among the mass of human beings, and in the animal world generally, was (and is), under normal circumstances, a rare occurrence. There seems to be a quite strongly held taboo against it. This is instinctive, and has been acquired over a long period of time by the evolutionary processes: oddly though, such an instinct is often given further 'authority' by purely social taboos, usually engineered by religion or cultural tradition.

The build-up from long-term incestuous relationships, then, is an example of a gene pool which is not fully viable. Even so, the successful achievement of a fully viable gene pool anywhere within the animal kingdom (not excluding that of *Homo sapiens*) may well involve incest in its very earliest stages. But it must then proceed fairly rapidly to an expansion of partner choice, ranging from cousin, to second-cousin, to third and so on, until the deleterious genes are too well shuffled and thinly distributed to cause problems. Yet at the same time the advantageous genes must be safely preserved and concentrated. This you will agree is quite a tall order!

Therefore a stark question now presents itself: how can this come about if species and subspecies are not kept apart by geographical (allopatric) separation? How does the process of evolution continue when very similar species, or more significant still, subspecies are all milling around in the same area (sympatric) and, very often, in exactly similar habitats? At an extreme they may even fill the very same environmental niche!

The examples already given of so many species of duck, geese, and seabirds, together with so many small fish inhabiting coral reefs, should be more than enough to begin with. They prove that some kind of mechanism exists; they also underline an enormous question mark.

Once again then, how do species branch off from common ancestors and produce two or more species where there was formerly only one? More important still, how do subspecies subsequently recognise each other and refuse to interbreed?

Now this is an area of enquiry that nobody as yet has chosen to investigate. And if we ask ourselves why this should be, no clear answer emerges. One possibility is that in recent years various groups of fundamentalists have actively engaged themselves in attempting to discredit the very basis of Darwinian evolution itself – at least, that is, in the minds of the general public. They are aware, after all, that it presents a rather soft target! And in this respect they have had some success. Consequently many biologists have had their attentions diverted into the defence of the entire concept of evolution rather than the continuation of more detailed analysis.

When evolutionary theory was first introduced, the withdrawn and shy Charles Darwin was temperamentally unsuited to do battle with the mob of outraged critics who assailed him. Fortunately the medical scientist T H Huxley stepped into that breach and became what has since been commonly referred to as 'Darwin's bulldog'. A full century later Richard Dawkins has found it necessary to undertake something of the same role. To set the record straight and to frustrate so many pseudo-scientific exposures of 'errors' in the theory of evolution, he has not only summed up with remarkable clarity and brilliance much of the post-Darwinian research, but also added some remarkable insights of his own.

Dawkins first came into the public eye with the controversial and poignantly titled *Selfish Gene*.[5] Ten years later he produced the equally penetrating and absorbing work entitled *The Blind Watchmaker*.[6] This becomes particularly relevant to this essay in that it probes the 'blind' yet non-random (rather than random) process of evolution, together with the process by which different species are subsequently created.

Dawkins uses this subtle concept of a blind watchmaker with enormous success in the greater part of his thesis; however, in certain aspects of this matter of speciation there are curious lapses.

---

[5] Richard Dawkins, *Selfish Gene*, Oxford University Press, 1976
[6] Richard Dawkins, *The Blind Watchmaker*, Penguin Books, 1991. Permission for use given by Peters, Fraser & Dunlop.

For example he asserts that a single species is separated into two, then prevented from reverting back to its original state via interbreeding by lack of opportunity, rather than any definite preventative mechanism. He illustrates this by the following, and I quote a typical passage:

> Lions and tigers are now members of a different species, but they have both sprung from a single ancestral species, probably not very long ago.

He then goes on to explain that speciation would normally be impossible because miscegenation (interbreeding) would frustrate it. He gives the obvious and very necessary warning to the biological novice or the unwary, so that they may be prevented from falling into Darwinian heresy:

> Don't incidentally, read too much into my use of words like 'frustrate' as though the ancestral lions and tigers 'wanted' to separate from each other…

Dawkins then comes to the nub of the matter:

> …given that the single ancestral line spread to different continents …the ones that happened to be in Africa *could no longer* [my italics] interbreed with the ones who happened to be in Asia…

And of course reading this explanation of allopatric speciation our minds immediately supply the remainder of the Darwinian process. Here the differing habitat and variations in food supply offer scope for natural selection to favour changes in skin colour, skin markings, head and body shape. We visualise this automatically if we have any grasp of Darwinian theory at all, and do so without Dawkins's further aid. I would point out, however, that the differences between lions and tigers internally – that is their skeletal structure, musculature, and main organs – are all minimal. The changes are wholly on the outside, and are, you might say, 'cosmetic', though Dawkins fails to press this point. He is after all attacking from a different angle. Rather than pick lions and tigers, he could have made a far more dramatic (and less cosmetic) choice – for that matter he could also have shortened the timescale. The two carnivores he has chosen happen to involve their gradual geological separation by the formation of two distinct continents, Africa and Asia. And this geophysical event took a considerable time. But sudden climate change, brought about by large volcanic eruption spewing vast amounts of fine dust into the atmosphere, for example, can force animals to move, and do so rapidly. During such an enforced migration, animals can become separated much more dramatically from members of their own species than by geophysical change. It is unfortunate too (as I see it) that in later pages Dawkins happens to choose a shrew to further illustrate his case when moving on to consider the more tricky creation of subspecies. He certainly makes the point that barriers to interbreeding – at least in so small a creature – can be narrowed down progressively. I quote:

> Different sides of a desert, a mountain range, a river or even a motorway... nevertheless the idea of geographic separation as the key to speciation is clearer if we think in terms of an actual physical barrier, such as the sea or a mountain range.

Looking as I do at this issue from a rather different angle, I am shocked to find that Dawkins's contribution to this matter has failed to consider marine life where the larger and wide-ranging species and subspecies of fish have no obvious barriers to prevent interbreeding. It might be argued that varying sea temperatures and varying food supply create invisible barriers, but I would find this hard to accept. Then there is the problem with birds. Many species fly incredible distances during spring and autumn migrations. What geographical barriers do they face? Other than the murderous intent of many so-called 'sportsmen' with rifles and shotguns and occasional storm-force winds, they are never wholly frustrated in such forays. How can 'lack of opportunity' play a part here?

Take the example of various subspecies of duck and geese landing on the same stretch of water in the mating season. What prevents miscegenation under these conditions? Clearly something must have done in the past! And some subspecies are so alike (particularly the females) that it takes an expert to tell them apart. My own observations over the years of these closely related creatures milling about in highly crowded conditions in overlapping breeding times, have caused me to ask: how is the evolutionary process possible in such conditions? How can subspecies of duck or geese distinguish between one another, especially when in overall body shape and characteristics the variations are so tiny? These differences can be nothing more than a hardly noticeable blob of colour on the beak or cheek or the very last millimetres of a few feathers on the wing-tips! How does a velvet scoter know a common scoter or a surf scoter, a goldeneye a Barrow's goldeneye, a whooper swan a Berwick's, a light-bellied Brent goose a red-breasted? You might at this point be sarcastic and say that it 'takes one to know one'! Yet in such an apparently flippant answer there is a greater truth. Yes, they do know one, and there must be some mechanism to achieve this.

My own observation of duck and geese subspecies points to slightly differing mating displays as one possible mechanism. This could be one factor preventing interbreeding. And what about differing smell? Now here's an area where human beings are hopelessly inadequate. Shall we concentrate on this and forget about birds for a moment? Carnivores, herbivores and omnivores – with the exception of ourselves, of course – do incredible things with smell. If we take a subspecies of dog such as a bloodhound, for example, then it borders on the miraculous! Given even a cursory sniff at a piece of a person's discarded clothing, it can follow a trail hours old, and for an astonishing number of miles. And in smelling traces of their own species they must acquire an amazing amount of information beyond that of sex, age and mating potential. A bloodhound may be exceptional in this area, but all other animals certainly have a highly developed sense of smell also. Therefore, given the merest whiff of its own species or subspecies, creatures may well identify those of its own kind. Thus mating under these circumstances will be preferential, and *not* casual.

True, many animals also have somewhat less acute vision in comparison with that of *Homo sapiens* and seem to rely more heavily on smell in every aspect of their existence; this now seems well proven. During mating, smell seems to play a quite fundamental role. What then of creatures that appear to have acuity of vision far superior to ours? Take an eagle, or a buzzard hovering high over rough craggy ground; it looks for small birds and their chicks, field mice and shrews, in quite dense vegetation such as heather and bracken. Here vision obviously supersedes all other senses such as sound and smell. And that vision is incredible. But what sense is used in mating? How does a common buzzard distinguish the rare rough-legged variety? Does it use sight or hearing? Does it wait for a distinctive call? What causes an instinctive barrier to operate and prevent miscegenation? The answer is, we do not know. Research is wholly deficient in this area.

Most birds for that matter appear to have better sight compared with *Homo sapiens*. Probably they also have better hearing. But do they use sight almost exclusively, as we do? We always prefer to use sight, with hearing coming secondary. Even so, to the remainder of the animal world smell is still preferential in sexual matters – for that matter even to animals with excellent vision. As for purely male recognition of a female in oestrus – oh boy!

The question surrounding the mechanism by which species and subspecies recognise each other is, however, still not solved even supposing courtship-display or smell is the answer. It is still confounded by the awkward question: how did a different display or exclusive smell originate in the first place? It becomes a question of infinite regress. It is reminiscent of the story related by the philosopher and mathematician Bertrand Russell who, when probing an Asian gentleman on his religious beliefs, was assured by the said gentleman that the world was created instantly and was the centre of the universe. Further, it did not spin round the sun, but was held motionless on the back of an enormous elephant. When Russell questioned what the elephant stood on, the reply was a gigantic tortoise. When asked what the tortoise stood on, the conversation was hastily turned to another subject.

Now the concept of infinite regress is of course a genuine and useful philosophic tool. Clearly it can be a formidable aid to establish the reign of reason and logic when probing various hypotheses. And apart from Russell's use of it in exploring the curious logic employed by various religious sects – all too often some bizarre interpretation of what remains truly formidable insight propounded by the founder of that religion yet unfortunately in parable form – infinite regress can certainly help in bringing this problem of speciation into better focus. Using it, we must therefore return to our question: what caused minor differences in courtship-displays in the case of birds in the first place? Equally, for that matter, different courtship rituals in the case of land animals and similarly of course with marine life? The answer is we do not know. We have for the moment come up against something that is a mystery. Equally, if we ask why evolution should bother to produce a unique smell for each individual creature on this earth, what possible overall strategy is served by it? Again we find ourselves at a loss. Bloodhounds do not follow us about as a matter of habit; they do so only if induced to! All we are left with is the plain fact that recognition by smell happens! Ask one question, whether it be serious or silly, and you get serious or silly answers, with compound interest as you might say – an infinite regress, in fact. There are always a host of other questions lining up. Indeed you find that your original question, seemingly so triumphantly solved, was but a temporary resting place on the way to an ever-distant horizon!

Let us backtrack for a moment. In its broadest aspect, the mechanics of mutation were studied by the American geneticist Morgan as far back as 1907. He used the fruit fly *Drosophilia*, which was a wise choice. Why? Well, it has phenomenal reproductive rates. And when bred in a laboratory free from predators and all the hazards it would face in the wild, it exhibits a population explosion of staggering proportions. It does so, moreover, over a very short space of time! If ever Nature's system of checks and balances was more vital in preventing world takeover by countless billion *Drosophilia* then I find it hard to think of any other insect species that can better it. Locusts are not in the same league. Aiding Morgan's research still further – in this case by neatly reducing undue complexity – was the fact that *Drosophilia* has only four pairs of chromosomes. And research soon proved beyond doubt a truly fundamental issue (the one that gave Darwin so much angst): it proved that the process of evolution was achieved by mutation and that the role of the chromosome was central to it.

Morgan's assistant Muller, in what might seem a whimsical or frivolous state of mind, further speeded up *Drosophilia*'s mutation rate – this despite its already formidable and wholly natural prowess in this area! He did so by using X-rays. The results were impressive. By 1926 they proved that radiation, both natural and artificial, was the mysterious unseen agent in triggering extra rapid mutation. Later, other research workers found that a certain range of chemicals acted as agents also. Incidentally, Muller's experiments with X-rays demonstrate, for the purpose of this enquiry, that my extension of Newtonian law into biology is particularly apt. It underlines that 'pure advantage' does not exist: an advantage in one direction is almost always counterbalanced by disadvantages in another. This basic philosophical factor will be brought into play time and time again in later pages. However, it is a moot point whether Muller himself instinctively grasped that such a concept has universal application. What *is* proven is that in the specific and more restricted subject of radiation, he was one of the first to warn of the dangers of the ever increasing use of X-rays in medical diagnosis – not to speak of the excessive dosages often employed. Accelerated mutation in fruit flies, he proclaimed, could well mean cell damage in humans. This could in turn open up a range of serious developments from cancerous growths and leukaemia to abnormalities in later generations of offspring. His warning did not prevent the premature deaths of many doctors and technicians working in hospital X-ray departments. As for research workers using radioactive substances, Madame Curie, her daughter and many others succumbed also. Years later Muller also warned of serious consequences following radioactive fallout while testing nuclear devices. Tempting though it is to pursue this matter more fully, it is essential to move on.

A large part of fundamental research into mutation was carried out between the 1920s and 1950. And since the middle of the century, further research into the mechanics of accelerated mutation, either by radiation (natural or man-made) or by chemical agents, has proceeded with vigour. That vigour has at last achieved notable success. Yet research has somehow been directed away from the phenomenon that now becomes an essential part of this essay: the diversification of all life forms. The question we must now ask repeatedly is this: since there is one overwhelming and obvious difficulty in building up a viable gene pool after diversification, namely that of miscegenation, how is interbreeding with the original strain avoided? More to the point, how is it prevented, especially in the case of subspecies, and particularly when they are often forced, as are duck and geese, to use the same small stretch of water? Here, after all, individual males and females of different subspecies find themselves face to face. So what agency firstly provides recognition and secondly says, 'Danger! Not permitted!' Thus we now have two mysteries: the 'mystery of recognition' plus the added 'mystery of rejection'. How is this instinctive barrier achieved? Not that the barrier is absolute and *never* broken! But it holds in the main. Nine times out of ten, the differing subspecies simply will have nothing to do with each other, this despite close proximity and indeed every kind of temptation – not excluding an ongoing oestrus! If on the odd occasion a male is actually tempted, then the female screams the equivalent of 'rape' and feathers fly, both literally and metaphorically.

So however this comes about, and no matter what particular form it takes, this rejection of a 'different' racial partner is clearly instinctive and must have a genetic basis. All the incredible diversity we see about us, all the myriad forms that creatures have gradually assumed through the process of evolution, would have been impossible if miscegenation was the overall strategy ordained by Nature. To achieve a gene pool of sufficient size to make each species or subspecies viable, then clearly individuals within it cannot be promiscuous when they meet outsiders. Promiscuity may be the order of the day *within* their own group, but not outside it. Individuals in any significant number cannot revert back to mating with strangers or ancestral types. If they did then evolution would stop dead in its tracks. Indeed it could never have proceeded from the simple single-cell organism in the primeval sea in the first place!

Now this is something so fundamental that it must also have implications for that part of the animal kingdom we call the 'human' race. And indeed where mankind is concerned this must be equally true! Why? Because otherwise we would see none of the racial diversity in our own stock – a diversity that has lasted to the present day. Yet this too raises a problem and another question. Despite endless migrations, conquests and indeed some historical attempts to force racial integration by miscegenation, mankind is not a featureless amalgam of all types. What is more (and already touched on), there is ample evidence that sordid racial intolerance, racial hatred and racial violence have in no way decreased! Why? Optimists will immediately suppose that the answer lies in 'negative opportunity': they will claim that until the twentieth century with its leap forward in scientific and technical expertise, (which in turn has triggered an explosion in multiple and easier forms of travel), racial mixing was severely limited. They will further suggest, not without an amiable smile, that once intermixing has been achieved on a vast scale then these deplorable traits will disappear.

Shall we examine this more carefully? Initially, shall we probe the belief that racial mixing on any significant scale was prevented until very recently by primitive levels of transport. I would immediately challenge this and openly claim that it is untrue. I grant you the speed and efficiency of travel has increased enormously, but this in itself is not the significant factor. Considerable migrations were achieved in the past despite the fact that means of transport were primitive in the extreme. That extreme and that degree of primitiveness could and did extend in the earliest eras, right down to an individual's two feet. True, the later domestication of oxen and the horse gradually increased speed and range, though only to a pitiful degree by today's standards. However, the children's fable of the tortoise and the hare is relevant here and should not be ignored. Transport by water and the invention of the sail were once again a significant boost to travel. Overall it must be realised that decades of constant movement – more or less in one direction and in very early eras using only the sun for navigation – despite being slow, can achieve astonishing results.

I therefore believe that we can eliminate primitive transport from the equation. That leaves us with an instinctive taboo against miscegenation. You require even further evidence that races instinctively refuse to interbreed? Well, just ask yourself what empire or civilisation has ever achieved the wholesale integration of the races it has conquered? I am not for one moment suggesting that miscegenation never takes place. It does, but on a small scale. Clearly a minority will always interbreed either through force of circumstances or indeed because they are promiscuous by nature. Their actions will however be seen as a betrayal by the majority of their own racial group. Indeed the instinct for racial cohesion is so strong that, as has already been noted, those who stray outside the boundaries of their communities – either drawn by genuine love or by promiscuity – quickly bring down parental outrage onto their heads. It also stirs the passions of the community at large, and to such a pitch as to provoke physical assault, kidnap or even murder. This has happened time and time again throughout history. It happens particularly within countries with two or more competing religions, two or more differing clans, or even competing criminal gangs! Woe betide any young male or female having intimate contact with one another when they belong to competing Mafiosi in Sicily and Italy. And they do not even need to be competing criminal gangs. Competition between nobility, between government officials, between merchants – the list is endless. Thus the Romeo and Juliet 'syndrome' and, on a rather different plane, that of Caesar (not forgetting Anthony) and Cleopatra, are not isolated tragedies on the historical canvas. Nor were they simply dreamed up by Shakespeare. They were and still are representative of actual tragedies that were transformed by his genius into memorable explorations of conflict deep within the human psyche. He was after all a man hypersensitive to every type of human emotion. Nor is the bard alone in this, of course. From Ancient Greece onward, writers of every age have explored the unfolding tragedy that results when love, or alternately raw sexual passion, conflicts so painfully with one's instinctive loyalty to one's clan, tribe or race.

Nevertheless, shall we remind ourselves of the essential paradox? Such loyalty includes a willingness to co-operate with other humans of the same gene pool that can vary in degree from grudging support to unquestioned and heady altruism. This gives a measure of cohesion that has brought and continues to bring undoubted benefit to emerging civilisations. Unquestionably it is still very much an important factor in civilising us all to this very day. But, to repeat, there is no such thing as 'pure' advantage. Thus the Janus factor soon becomes evident. Advantage in one direction brings disadvantage in another – though usually these are initially hidden and rarely appreciated until much later.

Chapter IV
TWO FORMIDABLE PARADOXES

Proposition

The crisis of personal identity. Who are we? What are we?

Each individual human being, when faced by so many baffling and at times threatening aspects of reality is often transfixed by such thoughts. They ask first one, then the other question. Yet what seems rather a simple exercise becomes more difficult the further it is pursued. Initially human beings are prompted by a pressing need to establish some kind of latitude and longitude within the society they find themselves part of – then subsequently pinpoint with some accuracy their position within it. Why? It seems very curious and somewhat futile. After all they do so despite being given background knowledge in their early schooldays of their own personal insignificance. They are taught the wider realities. They are taught the biological and cosmological basics. Unless they are woefully deficient in attention-span and comprehension, they should be vaguely aware that they form but one individual life form among what is currently five thousand, six hundred and twenty million other human beings. Nor should one forget the countless billions of other life forms that exist beyond that of our own species on this planet. Equally in basic cosmology; they should be vaguely aware of the insignificance of this planet circling the star we call the sun, aware also of this star's total insignificance amongst at least one hundred thousand million other stars... this in our own galaxy alone! The further shattering reality centres round the fact that our galaxy is but one of at least one thousand million other galactic formations!

This, then, is just our spatial position! In the seemingly unending extent of that dimension we call Time, our individual life span is less than an instant. It measures virtually nothing in the unimaginable interlude since the beginning of Creation until the present day, let alone what may yet come after it. So, what then our momentary introduction to it? Hardly of any consequence. So why should our personal identity be of any importance? But then of course human nature is such an odd and paradoxical jumble of phenomena, a mere ragbag of conflicting signals.

EXPOSITION 1

That rather pathetic individual we see sporting red braces over a spotless white shirt, driving a very large high-powered car (quite empty except for a grey jacket carefully hung on a hook behind the driver's seat) and so often seen trapped in gridlock on our motorways, is of course displaying to the world his spatial position in it. Correction: he displays what *he* believes is his well-earned spatial position. He may, for example, be on the executive board of a firm that produces toilet paper, alternatively of a firm that creates advertisements for them. He may be one of any number of permutations on such a theme. All of them would be too tiresome to name in detail. Quite simply he arranges the production of goods, articles, services or foodstuffs that other people seem to want. At the end of the day it is *his* estimation of his important and indeed essential contribution to the basic needs of society that he wishes to display. And we are all guilty of attempting to mark out our own position and identity – this by displaying some kind of status symbol or other.

In essence though, most of it is a self-assessment, and there is seldom an input from others. Despite being coy about those gifts or strengths we have, and highly critical of others blowing their own trumpet, we are all to a differing degree anxious to build up our own sense of self-respect at the very least. Unfortunately though, in many cases this takes on a less than healthy aspect: it can so often extend into the realm of studied self-conceit and self-importance. Consequently, for those who are unable to afford the more vulgar and extravagant status symbols, such as a luxury yacht, a Rolls-Royce or Aston Martin, or a Thames-side penthouse, there are few other options but to be forced into the realms of make-believe. And in such a realm people buy themselves a mobile phone and assume the airs and graces of millionaires if nothing else. Fortunately though, the greater mass of mankind have few pretensions. They look at their position within society with far greater realism. Even so the questions as to who we are, and what are we, remain... if in less tangible and more sophisticated ways. To seek some kind of identity and to discover if one is an accepted (and indeed acceptable!) entity within one's immediate social fabric, seems to be a deep-seated urge in all of us. Even so the need for 'belonging' can demonstrate itself in something quite nebulous. It can be as absurd as to prompt young people to join a street gang, or prompt middle-aged hard men to act as bouncers at local raves. As for older people, they often settle for membership of a country and western club, or an old-style dance society. Admittedly this comes at the bottom end of the scale; yet it is quite enough for some. For others the sights are set a little higher: nomination as chairman of the local vigilante group, secretary of matchbox (collection) society; even reputation as the most saucy and pungent of critics at public hearings at the county council! On a slightly higher level there is the honour of being the invited speaker at local history societies, nomination as justice of the peace, treasurer (honest) of the local Tory, Labour or Social Democrat Party! These are all the rather trivial yet necessary aids when attempting to dispel feelings of essential strangeness in what is after all a most extraordinary and at times quite unreal world.

However, over and above all of these might well come an inter-meshing with society on a much more serious and wider footing. It takes the form of declaring one's 'loyalty' in its best sense to a concept on the grand scale. And it can involve active work in a political party or advancing the aims and aspirations of one's ethnic group, country or nation. It is, although few realise it, an extension to, and development of, the deep-seated instinct for territorial possession. It can reveal itself at an extreme in fanatical and aggressive acts wholly in the cause of an ethnic group, a country, or a nation state.

To further cement such a 'belonging', the individual may also take the last truly significant step – accept membership of an established religion! But that religion will be wholly associated with the particular ethnic group, country or state. Let it also be admitted, the deeper truths taught by that religion, together with some of its odd foibles may not be understood, or, indeed, investigated by that individual. Nevertheless the sense of brotherhood and belonging are the vital factors; these are enthusiastically taken on board. The disturbing 'Who am I?', together with 'What am I?' at last seems answered.

EXPOSITION 2

This ever comforting feeling of 'solidarity' with one's fellows or society at large (as the Polish interpretation of the word now has it) is seldom achieved without effort. In some cases it also means a good deal of heart-searching. This is because it is a gradual process and begins way back in our childhood; moreover is sought after in some anguish in that wretched fog that always surrounds childhood vision and comprehension.

Unhappily to the young child and indeed to those adults who never quite overcome the traumas of childhood, this world always begins as a hostile and bewildering place. The agonised cry of the newly born points to the extent of our initial trauma. Only those lucky enough (or perhaps unfortunate enough, depending on one's viewpoint and future circumstances), who later realise they are born into a particularly sheltered existence, are allowed to escape that basic trauma. Only these feel fully recognised as finite individuals in their own right. And to put jam on this particular cookie some also find complete happiness in the niche society has awarded them.

This is far from the case with the vast majority. For them, the age of five years, or thereabouts, marks the watershed. At this time most children actively begin to explore the immediate environment, then gradually come to terms with at least part of the world outside it. And it is then that the unusual complexity, and indeed threatening nature of so many facets of existence begin to make themselves felt.

If we can be induced to think back to our own childhood we become all the more aware of the true importance of those nagging questions: who are we? What are we? At the age of five we already know we are 'incomplete' as it were. We have yet to grow up and take our own place in the world. So when a stranger asks those basic questions, all we can do is to pipe up shrilly a name – that commonplace or cruelly outlandish name our parents have chosen to dub us with. We then breathlessly follow it with the surname. A few attach the 'station' of father and mother. In a class-ridden and highly structured society if our parents' names happen to be distinguished by titles or alternatively, (for one reason or another) have become household names, then we automatically receive the deference due to us... also of one kind or another. This remains true whether one has the surname Biggs or Kray and thus becomes indelibly associated with the monarchs of the criminal world. It also remains true whether one is the legitimate or illegitimate child of some god-awful movie or pop mogul, whether the child of a Cambridge don or Nobel laureate. Deference becomes especially marked however when name-dropping reveals close connection with hereditary titles: one need not be the actual child of a baronet, earl, viscount, or duke; even second or third cousins can make a claim to distinction. Most people have a weakness for titles, and deference becomes automatic and far-reaching. But for the vast majority, we are, socially speaking, an inert mass, an insignificant nobody, on a par with a bug that crawls out of the woodwork.

Thus from about the age of seven to ten years, we make pathetic attempts to bolster confidence and gain some sort of status. With it comes every effort to achieve a sense of belonging within our immediate community. We do so initially by wearing the local team's football colours, the T-shirt of the currently idolised pop group, or perhaps on a more socially useful note, by joining the Cubs or Brownies. Only at a later stage does one become sensitised to and aware of the wider status of one's ethnic group, country or nation state – that is, within wholly international terms. Thus the pride one might have had in the past may then become dented. It may be seen as parochial and misjudged. One's membership is then tempered by what may have become an uncomfortable realism. Yet for those determined to overcome unpleasant realities and retain the extremes of nationalism – the 'my country right or wrong' syndrome – one important additional factor is necessary: a blind loyalty! But this can seldom be sustained without the added influence and support of an established religion. Alternatively, one can embrace the equivalent of the Orwellian 'doublethink' found in extreme political faiths such as Communism or Fascism. Such a faith then becomes a religion in its own right.

Therefore at a quite tender age, and what seems a far more purposeful and dramatic level, some children might be initiated into membership of a sect, cult, or indeed the mainstream of a world religion. Achievement of loyalty and solidarity subsequently becomes a measure of belief rather than the deployment of logic. This, once again, can extend to other unquestioning beliefs, such as Communism or Fascism. A few may be initiated into Mafioso-type criminal gangs, where loyalty and the satisfaction of belonging are also attained by crude belief rather than logic.

True, a fair proportion of children who are given little choice but to adopt the religious beliefs of their parents, later rebel, or more quietly allow such a faith to fade away. If this should happen then they gradually adopt new identities and new senses of belonging.

Sadly though, some people grow into adulthood with a sense of identity and of belonging hardly developed beyond that of a ten year old. Essentially it is retained solely because the people whose company they keep happen to speak their own language not to mention bad language (or recognisable dialect of it both literally and metaphorically).Further they may not only share the same views and aims, but also a certain 'esprit de corps'.

This identity then becomes a kind of unofficial 'passport' giving the individual recognition and a sense of 'togetherness'. It also awards basic rights within the confines of the group. All this helps enormously in making the outside world less strange, less incomprehensive, less threatening.

*

Of the several factors that promote identity and sense of belonging, few will deny that tenacious and uncritical membership of a religious faith becomes, at the end of the day, the most potent and permanent influence of all. For this reason its

Janus-faced character, promoting social stability, co-operation and cohesion on the one hand, yet provoking discord, enmity and full-blown conflict on the other, must become an area that demands further enquiry. For any essay on human conflict such an enquiry is unavoidable.

*

Conflict generated by differing religious beliefs

Before one can begin an investigation into the malevolent aspects surrounding a blind and uncritical adoption of a religious belief, one must first define what is understood by the words 'religion' and 'belief' in the first instance.

Immediately one is partly frustrated by the fact that there are no commonly agreed definitions. The average dictionary or encyclopaedia will show subtle variations on the theme of 'recognition of a higher unseen controlling power'. Some will mention it is a term derived from the Latin 'religare', to bind. Others will introduce selected commentaries by theologians, and immediately embark on a study of comparative religion.

But few people will bother to open a series of dictionaries or encyclopaedias, there to note agreement or disagreement. Each individual *already has* his or her own private and very personal viewpoint. Having therefore to fall back on my own, I would say that it is a manifestation of human longing for a glimpse of perfection. Such perfection, moreover, is one that has eternal stability. It is a longing born out of a contrasting vision of a world clearly imperfect and in a constant state of flux. Arising out of this comes (for me) a tantalising question: from what source do we derive this intuitive feeling of 'perfection'? Does it suggest a state of bliss achieved in some previous existence? Was it somehow retained as a vague memory deep down within us? Or, alternatively, is it solely a product of our ever inventive minds? But this is no place to launch into a philosophic enquiry. This essay deals with human conflict, and, as with any essay, there is a duty imposed on an author not to put wings on other thoughts, no matter how intense the fascination or how persistent the temptation.

Having put forward this definition, it must stand: its function is, after all, to fill the gap to allow us to move on.

The next question is this: in response to such longing, what have the various codified and organised religions achieved for our world? Regretfully, we are forced to say they too are Janus-faced. One side is benign, comforting and serene, the other malignant and threatening. Indeed, when seen in certain shafts of light, the malign form expresses almost unimaginable evil!

However, in their benign mode, it can be seen as we glance at the historical record that most of our current world religions have at the very least *promoted* social cohesion. This ranges from a mere basic friendliness to an all-pervading and universal love. Taking religion (of any kind) as a single entity or force in aiding mankind's survival, it can be seen that it has brought stability to communal living, to tribal society, to nations – at times even to empires and complete civilisations. It thus plays a vital role in the 'survival factor'.

The other side of the Janus face? In their malignant mode, the various religions of the world have undoubtedly brought endless misery and conflict. That conflict usually begins as an internal cerebral struggle, but all too often is not contained there. Those gripped by an all-consuming religious zeal, in particular, are not content to live and let live. There is always a compulsion to convert others; there is a denial of the wisdom of maintaining a state of passive co-existence. In this lies so much of the world's troubles. Those burdened with religious mania profess to believe in an all-powerful God, one who is all-seeing and all-knowing, one who is the final Judge of every individual, who will reward or punish according to His unique knowledge of the circumstances involved. Yet by twisted logic there is an arrogant assumption that He is incapable of doing anything without help! But why should He require His earthbound and lowly followers' puny intervention? Can it really be that God requires mere mortals to help *him*? Surely this is sacrilege! Sacrilege of extraordinary proportions. It exposes minds of wholly inadequate intellect. Yet from this one impious assumption stems a host of physical acts that can only be described as the 'work of the devil'. All such acts – imbued as they are with religious zeal and absolute conviction of the rightness of the cause – excuse the most frightful of crimes and involve the most far-reaching consequences. Significantly though, these actions are always at variance with the general thrust of intention as proclaimed by the founder of that religion.

Thus it can be argued that we cannot blame religion in itself. Rather, we should place responsibility for such bestiality on those individuals who claim to be its followers. But can we really let organised religions off the hook so easily?

Shall we make a closer examination? Firstly, how do all the current mainstream world religions – all of whom have a central belief in a single omnipotent and omnipresent God – fail to belong to one perfectly unified structure? Why are there so many? Why in such diverse forms? And why are there splinter groups or subdivisions within each? Above all, why has there been such an appalling record of conflict between them? If fundamentally they all believe in one God, then surely this should be a unifying force, not a divisive one? Even allowing for minor interpretative differences based on the life and teachings of their founders, surely they should all be able to live peaceably with one another?

The fact that they do not demonstrates for me the power of the evolutionary 'thrust'. This thrust has the ability to overlap the realm of biology and enter into what we assume to be the purely compartmentalised affairs of men. It energises and directs the evolutionary process here as everywhere else. Nothing on this planet of ours remains static. As we already know, it affects not just living creatures, but the very ground we stand on: the plains, the mountains and the very continents – all are evolving. All are in flux. Therefore as with speciation in the biological sense, why shouldn't we find speciation, diversity and specialisation in the affairs of men? And indeed, nowhere is this more clearly shown than in the birth and development of the various religions. You require further evidence? Very well.

Can we agree initially that at their birth, the founders (or founder) of each religion gathered round them a small nucleus of followers which we may think of in biological terms as 'offspring'. These quickly built up a viable 'gene pool'. And even after the death of their founder(s) such a gene pool preserved the 'genetic message' in the chromosomes of written texts without any mutation – well, at least, that is, for a certain time. Faithful to both the biological and religious command not to stray and never, on any account, to allow promiscuity among their own offspring (which could destroy the purity of line) the new religions gradually achieves stability. Thus the cohesive factor attains its proper reward. Each religion may last decades, even entire centuries! Yet sooner or later mutations will occur!

Now biologically speaking, mutated genes can have a good, bad, or (to us) indifferent effect on the body that they find themselves creating. Some even fall by the wayside, as it were. They become what geneticists are tempted to call 'junk' genes! Even for those that *do* have a favourable influence, their full viability and consequent re-use in the next generation can only be guaranteed by the creation of a decent sized gene pool. Similarly with mutations in the sphere of world religions. History shows many minor variations, most of them purely cerebral; like 'junk' genes they never make any discernible impact. We know of them only by some fragments of information found on very early scrolls, or tattered manuscripts. Often too, our information is by third or fourth-hand at that. But other mutations certainly did succeed. They broke away from what was at that time the main body: and they did so no matter how well organised or impressive the original structure.

Proto-Judaism and Judaism

It is instructive to look at proto-Judaism to begin with, mainly because it displays the phenomenon of speciation so spectacularly! It has produced not just one, but actually *two*, new faiths – one called Christianity and the other called Islam.

Now Judaism traces its beginnings in any fully recognisable form to the proto-Judaism of Abram (later renamed Abraham). This patriarch born about 2300 BC and probably within the actual walled boundaries of the early city state of Ur in eastern Mesopotamia, received what he interpreted as a call from God. This call insisted that he should leave his homeland and migrate westward to a promised land. Obeying this, he journeyed with his extended family unit to several parts of both north-western and south-western Mesopotamia.

The presence of famine, however, forced him to migrate directly south toward Egypt. On reaching the Egyptian border he blotted his ethical copybook a little (at least, that is, for the purposes of this enquiry) insofar as he instructed his beautiful wife Sarai to pose as his sister. Now why should he do this? Reading further we find he feared his life was in danger. He assumed that all Egyptians were sex-starved and therefore reasoned that when recognised as her husband, sheer envy would provoke murderous assault. Sarai, as beautiful women do in such cases, accepted his concern. She agreed that he should pose as her brother. And amply proving Abram's fear, no less a person than Pharaoh himself became intoxicated by Sarai's beauty. The deception worked. Accepted as her brother, Abram came to no harm. Far from it: he was rewarded! Genesis 12:14 tells us: 'The woman was taken into Pharaoh's house. And for her sake he (Pharaoh) dealt well with Abram; he had sheep, oxen, he-asses, menservants, maidservants, she-asses and camels…'

In other words he did not receive a dagger in his ribs, but suitable treatment for the 'brother' of a recently added female possession! It was of course customary for pharaohs to have a range of concubines occupying the royal household. However, Abram's position became suspect when Egypt was visited by a series of plagues. Someone was surely cursed! Fortunately for all concerned at this point, divine intervention finally sorts out this sorry mess. Quite neatly Abram and his wife, not forgetting his brother Lot and their entire tribal group, were given passage out of Egypt. But the saga does not end here.

Later, after an adventurous journey, the tribe arrived at Bethel. Here an interesting separation – but not yet a 'speciation' either in the tribal or religious sense – took place. For the first time, biblical text actually recognises and even acknowledges the curse of overpopulation:

> And Lot who went with Abram, also had flocks and herds and tents, so the land could not support them dwelling together…

The biblical text then repeats itself as if to underline the fact:

> ...for their possessions were so great that they could not dwell together, and there was strife between the herdsmen of Abram's cattle and the herdsmen of Lot's cattle.

However, a pragmatic solution was immediately found by Abram:

> Separate yourself from me. If you take the left-hand [direction] then I will go to the right; or if you go to the right hand then I will go to the left.

Thus Abram found viable living space and grazing in Canaan while Lot found likewise in the Jordan valley. Later, however, Abram once more blotted his copybook. This time he did so on the pages of both his sexual and moral code, when he finally realised his beautiful Sarai was barren. Astonishingly at this point, and on his wife's suggestion – however one suspects without any undue protest or misgivings – he followed her advice to take her Egyptian serving maid Hagar as a concubine or mistress. The motive for each? They hoped to have issue. Somehow or other a child had to be produced. Once again deception seemed to be attempted, this time in hopefully passing off such a child as Sarai's own in the eyes of the tribal followers. But there were problems. Abram, so we are told, was eighty-six years old! However, we need not take this too seriously. We should remember that the story of Abram was passed on orally from one generation to another for some considerable time before scribes transferred it to written texts. Mutations of a story occur all too easily by word of mouth; they still occur, though infrequently, when texts are copied. Then again, wandering tribes had an uncertain grasp of chronology. A primitive system of marking each year on a rock or piece of stone is all very well for those who live out their lives in just one place. But for wanderers? In direct contrast, our twentieth-century unhealthy preoccupation with the passing of time demands absolute accuracy. Indeed the desire for exactness is such that physicists risk coronary thrombosis if their caesium clocks deviate more than one thousandth of a second! Such inaccuracy is seen as a form of mockery! As for our date of birth, even more disconcerting for us all, we now have to register it not just to the day but the very hour! Worse, it is all strictly documented on certificates; moreover, such data is held securely by central governments. Therefore we cannot confuse, lie about, or be vague about our age, still less the rapidity or otherwise of the passing of the years. To repeat: this tends to obscure the fact that early nomadic tribesmen had no such data banks or reliable means of counting the passing of time... at least worthy of mention. Indeed most had none whatsoever. However, it is often said with some justification that 'a man is as old as he feels'! And Abram, after all his various wanderings and adventures, may well have adopted this yardstick! At any event, the Egyptian maid Hagar duly became pregnant. Immediately, this suggests yet again that my theory regarding the instinctive urge against miscegenation is being undermined. Fortunately though, there are subtle twists in this story. Another highly discreditable interlude then took place. Sarai saw fit to become jealous! She reproached Abram. Genesis 16:5 tells us that she even nagged in the feminine way:

> I gave my maid to your embrace, and when she [Hagar] saw she had conceived, she looked on me with contempt. May the Lord judge between you and me. But Abram said to Sarai, 'Behold your maid is in your power; do to her as you please.' Then Sarai dealt harshly with her and she fled from here.

Our sensibilities are rightly shocked when picturing this development. In truth we become further committed in our sympathy for Hagar as the biblical text continues. Indeed in the very next sentence we learn that the poor girl, heavily pregnant, stopped to drink at a well in the wilderness – doubtless at the end of her tether! At this point came divine intervention. She was instructed by an angel to return and submit once more to Sarai. It can hardly be disobeyed. So at this point is my theory concerning racial cohesion being undermined, and of all things by divine intervention? However, we find the Creator of the Universe is always extremely subtle. Since he had ordained that species, subspecies and racial groups should instinctively keep apart to preserve their gene pool, it might seem to an eagle-eyed observer that He was about to frustrate His own universal design! Reject

His own laws? Not one bit of it! That is what divine intervention is all about! They mark the suspension or bypassing of natural law, but *momentarily* only! We call them miracles. And in this case, it seems divine intervention was wholly necessary. Abram and Sarai were promptly visited by the Almighty, swiftly renamed Abraham and Sarah, and promised – much to their disbelief – a child of their own. By these circuitous means Jewish blood was not 'defiled' by Egyptian.[1] Duly, and as promised, Sarah at the age of ninety years became pregnant.

Again we need not take her age literally. As with her husband, she no doubt felt the passage of a good many summers, if not winters. She would no doubt have remembered all her trials and tribulations, not least of them concubinage to Pharaoh! Joyfully, and in due time, she produced a son: Isaac. The line was finally saved! Incidentally, after Sarah's death, Abraham took another wife, Keturah, who bore him another six sons. I hesitate to make further comment at this point.

Biblical text, from this point, concentrates on the fortunes of Isaac. On reaching manhood this first-born was found a wife on the strict instructions of Abraham. She was selected – despite living a considerable distance away – from Abraham's original stock. Moreover, Rebekah was not just kosher, as you might say, but bloodline. The early chroniclers also touch on the saga of servant-girl Hagar's son Ishmael. She returned and gave birth to her son. Unavoidably enough she did so in Abraham's household. But difficulties soon arose. Sarah objected to her son having to play with poor non-kosher and only half-bloodline Ishmael. Abraham was distressed! Maybe he said something disparaging about all women at this display of such pettiness, but his words are not relayed to us. At any event poor Hagar suffered. Once more, accompanied by her son – this time fully in this world – she was sent on her way. And they soon found themselves yet again almost dying of thirst in the wilderness. Timely as always, God remembered his promise to Hagar. Natural law is once more suspended, momentarily! A miracle was performed in the shape of a well suddenly appearing in the desert. It contained pure water.

---

[1] This display of naked racial contempt finds an astonishing degree of repetition throughout the Old Testament.

Hagar and her son Ishmael were saved. Not only this, the boy was told that he would become a 'great nation' which he did! Indeed he became the father of all Arabs. This is why to this day, Abraham, as the progenitor of two distinct lines, is venerated by both Jews and Arabs. Further, the supposed final resting place of this patriarch, at Hebron, is a shrine considered especially significant to both. It is however equally true that such revered lineage, far from bringing Jews and Arabs into a harmonious relationship, seems to stimulate the very opposite. In the process of contesting rights over the shrine they are consumed by bitter hatred! The possession of the city and its tombs is subject to endless claims and counter-claims; worse, it constantly involves the spilling of blood. Indeed Hebron and Jerusalem alike form the nucleus of fierce territorial claims by both sides. So too, if to a lesser extent, do all other sites where, historically, both Jews and Arabs claim a traditional home.

But to return to the story of Isaac and Rebekah and our investigation of tribal cohesion. From their union came the twins Jacob and Esau. And the early chroniclers have an unusual story to tell when the twins reached manhood. Esau, the first twin to be delivered, had, by virtue of this, a claim of direct accession as leader to his father's tribal unit. But he was tricked out of such succession by Jacob. Oddly though, the second-born twin did not fall out of favour with the Almighty. The very reverse. Why? If you read the Old Testament with the fresh eye now given you by my thesis, you will find that Esau had the audacity to stray out of his gene pool. In Genesis 26:34 you may read: When Esau was forty years old he took to wife both Judith the daughter of Bereri the Hittite, and Basemath the daughter of Elon the Hittite; and they made life bitter for Isaac and Rebekah...' Regrettably however, it is not explained how this bitterness arose. There are three distinct possibilities: firstly, these two women being Hittite were automatically considered 'unsuitable' at best, or downright alien at worst; secondly, as Hittites they had been brought up under a different religious code and they may not have embraced the new religion of the patriarch Abraham with sufficient enthusiasm; thirdly, they were just temperamentally awkward or 'difficult', full stop! Of all three, the first is the most probable.

Despite being good neighbours and racially close, the Hittites were not considered 'kosher' in the tribal sense. And this alone put an immediate taboo on intermarriage! To most twentieth-century sensibilities this seems appalling snobbishness. The Hittites were, after all, by no means an 'inferior' people – if such description can ever be justified for any race. Their homeland, covering what is now Syria and much of Turkey, already had an advanced culture and was soon to become a notable civilisation from about 1400 to 1200 BC. Nor was there any noticeable difference in their racial characteristics. To make a suitable analogy, it would be comparable to an English farmer living in, say, north Yorkshire, selecting two Scottish farmer's daughters for his 'domestic comfort' (a common practice in biblical days) – moreover with both social status and actual wealth being wholly equal. Yet significantly for our thesis, it would seem that early chroniclers were at pains to show that the Almighty was not prepared to allow such alteration to His plan. To rectify matters, we see an instinctive reaction by Jacob and his mother to protect their recently created racial variation; their hostility was an attempt to prevent their gene pool being 'sullied'. Promptly, the chroniclers imply, God withdrew His favour from Esau and transferred it to Jacob. What is more, as a mark of this favour He renamed him 'Israel' and gifted him with fecundity! And of course at this point of the tortuous saga, the tribal reality of the Israelites was truly launched.

For twentieth-century sensibilities, however – especially for those born outside this racial stock and therefore not numbered among the so-called 'Chosen People' – this story raises awkward questions. Why should God interest Himself solely in the Children of Israel? And why at this historical juncture? It seems such an odd way for the mighty Creator of the Universe to establish Himself as the object of worship! Why such 'hole and corner' methods? And why concentrated on a tiny planet, circling a minor star, in a very ordinary galaxy? If we take the Old Testament at face value there is no answer to these questions. However, if we feel the need to be charitable, then we must look at this story as a product of the minds of very human chroniclers living in an age when the Earth was supposedly the centre of creation and where a very primitive anthropomorphic view of the Creator prevailed. Having made such allowances, we must accept that such a viewpoint, in the absence of deeper knowledge, is virtually inevitable. It is a saga of primitive people written by primitive people. But it has interesting relevance to our own era, nevertheless – particularly as the story progresses. You see, with the God of Israel and His worship now fully established, the future of His People was by no means a journey celebrated in constant joy and triumph. To our surprise we find God had a very precarious foothold in their thoughts, not to speak of their actions! The Israelites constantly sinned; worse, many reverted back to the worship of false gods. And although the Old Testament makes scant mention of other tribes it would seem in comparison that their neighbours prospered. In particular we are conscious of the ongoing saga of Ishmael and the successful emergence of what will later become the Arabic offshoot continuing in the background. Inevitably then, the stage had been set for a dramatic 'speciation' on two fronts, so to speak – the tribal division of Jew and Arab and the religious division of monotheistic and polytheistic. The Arabic tribes lagged behind in further religious speciation of their own until AD 622 when, in the person of Mohammed[2] (and the Hegira), Islam emerged and boldly made its own way.

Meanwhile shall we return to the fortunes of the Israelites. Early chroniclers as they wrote down the oral story did not balk at giving the full details of endless moral and sexual temptations – sins visited on all and sundry. Nor, as already noted, did they hesitate to mention periods of loss of faith and the chasing after false gods. Equally they make no bones about the devices used to re-establish tribal and religious unity and to minimise the number of 'drop-outs', Although they had no concept of genetics or of a gene pool in the twentieth-century scientific sense, they nevertheless had an intuitive feeling for the 'survival' factor of racial inheritance. There is, for example, constant mention of forced marriages (even occasional incest) as an aid to selective inheritance. And there are certainly detailed accounts of the

---

[2] Mohammed claimed to be a direct descendent of Ishmael.

serious consequences arising from miscegenation. Significantly, the 'Romeo and Juliet' or 'Caesar–Anthony and Cleopatra' syndrome, is evident almost two thousand years before Shakespeare's intuitive examination of this aspect of the human condition. Thus to counter any temptation for tribal members to breed outside tribal boundaries the leaders of Israelite society introduced various stratagems. Over and above the existing essentials of Israelite identity such as male circumcision and prescription against eating pork, came increasingly complex rituals and other 'identity' aids. Moses in particular saw to it that as much as possible was changed to make this tribe more and more distinctive from those inhabiting the immediate area. Every kind of visual, linguistic or ritualistic invention was adopted to accentuate their 'separateness'. Significantly, these are added to the ten Commandments and detailed by Moses himself. They begin in Exodus 19:10 and in several thousand words lay down exactly how temples should be built, how they should be furnished, how priests should be clothed, how many times, and in what way sacrifices should be carried out... far more than can be neatly summarised here. The list is exhaustive and indeed exhausting. Astonishingly too, we learn that these stratagems were by no means an unqualified success. Rather later, in the Book of Ezra, comes the proof. Something that had only been tacitly expressed throughout many earlier books of the Old Testament now becomes a directive. Here, in Chapter 10:1, it is explicit:

> While Ezra prayed and made confessions, weeping and casting himself down before the House of God, a very great assembly of men, women and children gathered to him out of Israel; for the people wept bitterly. And Shecanian son of Jehiel, of the sons of Elam addressed Ezra: 'We have broken faith with our God and have married foreign women from the peoples of the land, but even now there is hope for Israel in spite of this. Therefore let us make a covenant with our God to put away these wives and their children, according to the counsel of my lord...' And Ezra the priest stood up and said to them, 'You have trespassed and married foreign women and so increased the guilt of Israel. Now then make confession to the Lord the God of your fathers and do his will: separate yourselves from the peoples of the land and from the foreign wives...'

A long list of names of those who have 'transgressed' follows. It ends with the terse sentence: 'All these had foreign women, and they put them away with their children.' Unfortunately though as the entire Book of Ezra terminates at this point, we have no further information. Yet anyone with any sense of morality or ethical judgement is left with a tantalising question: what is meant by ' put away'? It is true that the dividing line between marriage and the taking of concubines was vague in these early days. The Old Testament quite openly suggests the presence of lust, and rarely does it celebrate or advocate the concept of love and lifelong commitment. Yet a proportion of these men must surely have had some feelings for these women and children! They were hardly mere chattels. Even so, there is no mention of the distressing consequences that must have followed. At best one must hope that 'put away' meant they were taken back to their tribal homeland and placed into the care of their immediate relatives. I hope also that it was done in a humane and civilised manner. At worst? One can only shudder. One can picture them being thrown out and left to survive as best they could!

By highly selective mating then, century after century, the Israelites maintained their essential tribal unity and their unique gene pool. But cracks or mutations began to appear in their religious cohesion. Varying interpretations of Mosaic Law, and of pronouncements by an ever lengthening line of prophets, began to create doctrinal 'subspecies'. For example, Moses had detailed the exact way in which animals should be sacrificed on an altar. The Commandments say in Exodus 29:10:

> You shall then bring the bull before the tent of meeting. Aaron and his sons shall lay their hands on the head of the bull and kill the bull before the Lord at the door of the tent of meeting, and shall take part of the blood of the bull and put it on the horns of the altar with your finger, and the rest of the blood you shall pour out at the base of the altar. And you shall take all the fat that covers the entrails, and the appendage of the liver, and the two kidneys and the fat on them and burn them on the altar. But the flesh of the bull and its skin and its dung, you shall burn with fire outside the camp: it is a sin offering. Then you shall take one of the rams and Aaron and his sons shall lay hands on the ram and

you shall slaughter it and take its blood and throw it against the altar round about. Then you shall cut the ram into pieces, wash its entrails and its legs, and put them with its pieces and its head and burn the whole ram on the altar: it is a burnt offering to the Lord; it is a pleasing odour, an offering by fire to the Lord.

As if that were not enough, Moses goes on to stipulate that a second ram should be killed and a smear of blood put on Aaron's right ear and of those of his sons, on the thumbs of their right hands, and great toes of their right feet and the remaining blood poured partly round the altar and partly mixed with oil. It is then sprinkled on their garments. A long and very detailed passage follows describing the further ceremony and the blessing of people, ending with a further command that two-year-old lambs be slaughtered each day continuously 'as a pleasing odour and an offering by fire to the Lord.'

Now to our twentieth-century minds this is quite shocking, even horrific. Turning a place of worship into a sanctified abattoir is beyond our comprehension. Any area supposedly consecrated to God, when used in such a fashion seems a mockery of what worship should entail. Especially those who are vegetarian and have concern for animal welfare have every right to be judgmental.

However, there is a tinge of hypocrisy in the show of horror by those unable to resist a diet of meat. Granted, in some (but not all) abattoirs in the West, animals are stunned before being slaughtered. And in buying meat on a supermarket shelf neatly packaged and 'sanitised' we are thereby spared watching animals having their throats cut and seeing their agonised death struggles. It was, however, a very normal part of life to a primitive farmer-herdsman, especially if his family was a large one. Meat comprised a significant proportion of their diet. Small animals were slaughtered almost every other day by the head of the household (no doubt with their children watching), and larger animals in turn were slaughtered as the need arose. Our horror would therefore be more wisely directed if we concentrated on a more important factor: the concept of expiation of sin merely through the agency of ritual. Here our horror has some legitimacy.

By attending lavish man-made ceremonial and participating in intricate ritual, many people were (and still are) encouraged to believe that their sins were forgiven. Thus, inevitably, individuals who happened to be wholly without conscience were tempted to sin repeatedly. They persuade themselves that provided ritual sacrifices are later observed in scrupulous detail, then total expiation followed! It was (and still is) a convenient system for the long-term sinner. Many saw (and see) no reason to change their ways. However, all this was to be challenged – if decades later. We find in the Book of Isaiah (1:11) a very significant passage, moreover reported as was customary in those days, as the voice of the Lord coming to the prophet in a vision:

> 'What to me is the multitude of your sacrifices?' says the Lord. 'I have had enough of burnt offerings of rams and the fat of fed beasts: I do not delight in the blood of bulls, or of lambs, or of he-goats. When you come to appear before me, who requires of you this trampling of my courts? Bring no more vain offerings; incense is an abomination to me. New moon and Sabbath and the calling of assemblies – I cannot endure iniquity and solemn assembly.'

Truly, these passionate words show us an astonishing volte-face, With these teachings, Isaiah presents us with implications that are quite direct and challenging. There is now a very different attitude to sin, to confession, to atonement and to mere mechanical lifting of conscience by elaborate ritual. And such diversification in actual doctrinal matters would become more noticeable – indeed would widen and deepen, as decade succeeded decade. It was a fundamental rift, bitterly contested by the group who remained conservatively minded. Yet the would-be reformers, in their longing for inner purity, persisted in trying to cut through the heavy chains of tradition.

As might be expected, the new morality was championed only by the thoughtful and introspective; it was resisted by the traditionalists and extroverts. But the break became so fundamental that it has further widened and deepened to this very day. Not that such a fundamental division – leading obviously, in the passage of time, to complete 'speciation' – remains a wholly Jewish phenomenon. Every other world religion has this fundamental rift. It is found between those who place their faith on the efficacy of ritual, and those who insist on inner purification.

Nothing has changed. Right up to the closing days of the twentieth century we are still faced with bitter infighting within all of the world religions. True, the rise of the so-called Evangelical and Charismatic movements, at least within the Christian Church, has obscured the issue; traditional ceremony has been thrown out of the window and a heady and rather dangerous raw emotionalism has taken its place. Those who are appalled by such a development and who see religion as a more personal and indeed quiet sanctuary for intellectual probing, are paradoxically, (and also ironically), forced back toward the older ritualistic traditionalism they were once so anxious to escape.

However, let us return to our examination of Judaism and the evolutionary thrust toward 'speciation'.

As we move through the centuries, we find that diversification and speciation do not always come from within. If we use the analogy of speciation taking place because of a change of climate or of habitat, we find that the Israelites also had to contend with many outside influences. These were especially traumatic when their territory was overrun, time and time again, by invading armies. For example, of all the many invasions, the Judaic purists found that of Alexander the Great and the subsequent inflow of Grecian culture the most alarming. The introduction into the circle of the educated Jewish elite of the teachings of Plato and Aristotle in particular proved the most unsettling and challenging to many traditionalists. Indeed the Hellenisation of a wide section of Jewry was seen as an impending disaster – a body blow in the making to the entire future of Judaism. Passions were so intense that they brought about the formation of a sect wholly dedicated to opposition; they were known as Pharisees. But as this sect emphasised pursuit of inner purity (rather than observance of mere ritual) they too came into conflict with the conservative priestly caste. This caste was later to be somewhat compartmentalised, or even stereotyped, as the Sadducees. Yet the Pharisees in time also suffered further diversification! As a result of their refusal to become deeply involved in the political scene, part of their group broke away to form a sect now known as the Zealots.

And the process of diversification failed to stop there. Shortly before the coming of Christ, a further group of ascetics given to meditation and living a communal life (where all goods and possessions were shared equally) also came into being. These were called the Essenes. Can we be surprised by the fact that to create a truly visible identity they were said to use the very simple ceremony of baptism as an aid to achieving inner purity. Further, John the Baptist is notable in that he was selected by Christ for His baptism. And at this point came full 'speciation'.

Christianity

It is all too easy to assume that, with the arrival of Christ, the new Church that bears His name quickly drew adherents, more promptly still established itself wholly within the lifetime of the Apostles. The facts of the matter are very different. After the crucifixion of Christ the Apostles were prevented in many ways from preaching the word and making rapid conversions. It was not in the interests of Rome or the Judaic High Priest that sections of their people should be tempted to follow a false Messiah. The Apostles were imprisoned for some time. Later came the stoning and martyrdom of Stephen. In every way Christianity had a difficult and dangerous emergence – much as any mutant has from any mainstream living species! And given that these numbers were so small, the gradual formation of a fully viable gene pool might never have been achieved. Indeed it would have probably resulted in the new religion's decline and oblivion. Significantly however Christ's crucial instruction to 'Go into all the world and preach the Gospel to the whole of Creation' changed everything. The opening up of membership to non-Jews may in this respect seem to destroy my central analogy with the purely biological theory of speciation! In fact it provides us with the reason why Christianity itself was to diversify and split into many differing sects so quickly after its foundation. Shall we now examine this saga in turn?

Gnosticism was an attempt by Greeks or Hellenists, who, having already been deeply influenced by Grecian philosophers, were nevertheless anxious to take on board certain aspects of the new teaching. It became a precarious balancing act. While progressively finding more and more merit in Christianity, they were unable to forget the achievements of the greatest of their own philosophers. Thus they persisted in attempts to merge one into the other. Equally Manichaeism was an attempt to graft some of the beliefs of Mani with that of Christ. In like manner the teachings of the Persian Zoroaster (or Zarathustra) onto Christianity – although all these efforts lacked the vigour of the Gnostics. St Paul was considerably exercised at one point to warn early converts to steer clear of both.

Nevertheless as the years passed Origen championed the Grecian cause and made some inroads into the early theology. Speciation *was* possible at this point. Yet it was delayed by a curious intervention. Temporary cohesion was won back in AD 312, unexpectedly enough in the person of a Roman Emperor! How did this come about?

During Christ's lifetime the Roman Empire was already overstretched and its unity was threatened in a variety of ways. From within came disunity through constant infighting by the elite of Roman society, struggling for succession to the title Emperor; equally, provincial disunity saw repeated revolt by conquered peoples who refused to part with their identity. If that were not enough, from wholly outside Roman borders came attacks by barbarians, particularly in the west. Already in AD 284, Diocletian was forced to divide the empire into four prefectura and twelve dioceses, with semi-autonomous rule. Incidentally he also increased the persecution of Christians who were destabilising the Roman Pantheon and thereby what remained of the rickety cohesion of the state. Progressively, over several decades, the focus of power moved away from Rome and was in danger of totally fragmenting – until that is, it was stabilised by the military prowess of the next notable emperor on the scene – Constantine. This personality has already made an appearance in earlier chapters. Nevertheless it is instructive to add further details. On the death of his father, de facto ruler of Gaul and Britain, Constantine was acclaimed by his troops as putative Emperor in AD 306. After consolidating his power, he defeated joint-emperor Maxentius in a battle outside Rome in AD 312. He is said to have gained that victory after he saw a vision of the cross superimposed on the sun. Constantine's subsequent friendliness to the new faith and recognition of Christianity (as a legal rather than a proscribed and persecuted sect) at first applied only to the sectors of the empire under his control. Moreover he did not outlaw worship of the old gods. Probably he believed they would wither on the vine. Nevertheless, as one might expect, his willingness to coexist with Christians (and his later conversion) set an example impossible to ignore. The gains were obvious, the losses less so. Churches were built, and bishops (formerly secretly appointed underground) were now openly consecrated for all to see. But on the less happy side of the balance sheet, deeply committed Christians, who had once been prepared to die for their beliefs, now found themselves increasingly rubbing shoulders with dubious converts – those who found it politically advantageous to embrace the new faith. Meanwhile Constantine went from strength to strength. With the defeat of the eastern Emperor Lucinius in AD 324, he became sole ruler of a now revitalised and reunited Roman Empire. Moving the centre of his power eastward, he found it convenient to set up his capital in Byzantium. Constantine may well have had hidden motives for his acceptance of Christianity, however. Some historians impute political advantages. My own viewpoint – deeply concerned as it is with the evolutionary advantages of social cohesion – would quickly support any further findings suggesting this. Constantine, being the man he was, had a deep concern for political unity. The worship of one wholly omnipotent and universal God (as opposed to a multiplicity of gods and goddesses) presented great social and political advantages. Each section of his Empire, after all, had their wretched little local pantheons, and these inevitably produced political 'deviants'. Certainly Constantine seemed unusually concerned when the newly established Church of Christ suddenly appeared to show deplorable signs of disunity. It all concerned an internal squabble over the relationship between God, Christ and what is confusingly called the Holy Ghost or Holy Spirit. Christians were now deeply agitated over a fundamental question: did God, Christ, and the Holy Ghost all have differences in status? Arius of Alexandria held that, as Christ himself had referred to God as the 'Father', it clearly implied that the son was not quite of equal status. Others held to a 'Three in One' relationship in which God and Christ were cemented into a single God-head by the Holy Spirit; others again held positions somewhere between the two. It was a doctrinal question which urgently required settling. Constantine *himself* called a synod in Nicaea in AD 325 and acted as chairman; this alone surely points to his concern in the matter.

After considerable debate, Arius's doctrinal proposition was defeated. And in what to us now seems a decidedly un-Christian and unduly acrimonious atmosphere, feelings became so heated that his doctrine was subsequently declared heretical. In its place a doctrine formulated by Athanasius was adopted. This asserted that Christ the Son was *one* (substance) with the Father. With this declaration, there can be little doubt that Constantine's hope for resuscitating religious unity was for the most part satisfied. Once more it had become for him the social and political asset that – as a dynamic, if new and virtually untried entity – he had originally visualised. Quietly in the background, and no doubt by occasionally knocking heads together, metaphorically speaking, the ageing Emperor managed to keep a semblance of unity. But it was not to last. With Constantine's death, disunity once again became progressively more serious. The process of diversification and eventual speciation had already taken too firm a hold; it could not be frustrated. The eastern half of the Roman Empire, became centred on territory once the homeland of Ancient Greece. Thus the pride of those with ancestral Grecian blood in their veins demanded an input from the Hellenic philosophers of old. This demand was not unreasonable. The greatest of her philosophers had already contributed much in paving the way for Christianity; they had also aided its rapid acceptance. Hellenic influences were given further impetus when, later, under a succession of weak or dissolute Roman Emperors, the Western section of the Empire came under increasing attack from barbarians. Decade after decade it became progressively weakened. Complete diversification of the early Church was achieved of course when most of Italy and the city of Rome itself finally fell to the invaders. The doctrinal division of what should have been a united Church of Christ was now accentuated both by physical distance and a politico-military divide. At this point full speciation was achieved. And the process did not end there. What had now become the Greek Orthodox Church was in due time to produce what one might call a 'subspecies': we now call this the Russian Orthodox Church. As for the Catholic Church of Rome, it too in later centuries was to split much more dramatically and bloodily into two warring factions, of course. Martin Luther, a Catholic priest deeply distressed by so much corruption, was to bring to a head a rebellion that rumbled on for centuries. Surviving the fall of Rome, the Western Church had now become a powerful and immensely influential body dominating the whole of Western and Northern Europe. But power had corrupted it. Refusing to turn a blind eye on such corruption, Luther was driven to nail his protestations to the door of his collegiate building. Significantly, Protestantism gained hold and achieved full speciation for quite a fundamental reason – a reason which had earlier created those grievous fissures within Judaism and Islam. This was the refusal to accept that forgiveness for sinful and corrupt ways could be bought with money and ostentatious ritual. Luther, as only one of many, believed passionately that inner purity could be achieved solely by reforming one's entire life or attitude to life. Surely sin can be forgiven solely by God Himself? It was sacrilege to presume that forgiveness could be received at the hands of a mere priest – an all-too-fallible and often corrupt one at that!

The shock of this schism eventually served in turn to achieve reform within the Catholic Church itself. It gradually swept away some of the worst excesses. Sadly though, a succession of popes of that era sought to reunify the Church by force: they rejected Christ's solution. They did not try to persuade their former flock by relying on reform and saintly example. Nor, for that matter, did they attempt an intellectual approach. Repression was used, and it brought the inevitable backlash. Attempting reconversion by force in what is now called the Counter-Reformation, the Roman Church committed appalling acts of savagery. These in turn stimulated newly established Protestant groups to pay back in kind. We are all aware of the ghastly sequence of events that followed. Echoes have reverberated along the corridors of European history to this very day. We are all aware too of the continuing diversification within the structures of both Roman and Protestant Churches. Groups of Catholics – with many priests among them – sensed that a degree of reform was entirely necessary. They saw the dangers inherent in rigid authoritarianism, combined with pomp and splendour and in ritual for its own sake. These now began forming themselves into campaigning groups. Latterly, despite a desperate rearguard action by traditionalists, changes were, (and still are) being made. The question of papal infallibility itself has seen a subtle shift in both definition and application. For example, the vexed question of birth control has caused, and still is causing, considerable anguish, leading in many cases to outright disobedience. So too the material wealth of the Church and the way in which it has been managed or mismanaged.

Similarly among Protestants the process of diversification goes on apace. There are today many sects and splinter groups, each of them having developed marginal differences stemming from the character and individual stance taken by their founders – Luther, Zwingli, Calvin and John Knox, to mention only the more obvious. And incidentally, as a direct consequence of Britain (especially!) having a huge overseas empire moreover encouraging missionaries to follow in the footsteps of its soldiers, there has been a proliferation of churches. Some have become, or may be thought of as a succession of subspecies, each of them with slightly variant characteristics. These are now surviving in outposts in every continent throughout the world!

So much for diversification within Christianity. What of the new world religion, Islam?

Islam

The Old Testament establishes the claim – and one that is fully accepted by Islam – that Abraham's son by Hagar, named Ishmael, began the process of both tribal and religious speciation from the original Semite stock.

Ishmael did so by physical separation: he set up a tribal unit of his own in the 'wilderness'.

At this point it should be observed (and indeed repeated

whenever necessary) that much of the Old Testament is written with generous poetic licence. Today few are prepared to take each word literally, the exception of course being those with rigid fundamentalist beliefs. Even so, if one is prepared for the sake of the pursuance of this investigation, to take the Old Testament at face value, then it does at the very least shine considerable light on the minds and attitudes of both the early scribes themselves and the people they wrote about – and wrote about with such vivid authority. Furthermore, every saga has a degree of historical truth running through it, embellished though it is! Significantly then, for the purpose of this enquiry, we are told that Ishmael, in his use of the wilderness as a barrier, remained fully isolated from the mainstream influence of what was shortly to become fully-fledged Judaism. In Genesis 21:20 we are informed:

> God was with the child [Ishmael] and he grew up; he lived in the wilderness and became expert with the bow. He lived in the wilderness of Paran; and his mother took a wife for him from the land of Egypt.

Hagar, the once much-abused servant girl, at last secured her own kind of triumph. We cannot but smile, and give her a wave of encouragement spiced with approval from what is now (hopefully) an unbiased historical distance.

Inevitably though, several questions are raised. For example, there has been some controversy regarding the evolution of the subsequent language we now call Arabic; after all, if Ishmael had been the progenitor of this racial group, one would expect greater retention of (at least) a recognisable dialect of Aramaic in its ancestral line. As this is not immediately obvious, linguistic scholars suggest the possibility that Ishmael's small band may have united originally (by the sheer social and political necessities of survival) with other wandering precursors of Bedouin tribesmen. These would have spoken their own dialect. This, they claim, accounts for a relatively unhindered and comparatively 'uncorrupted' speciation into the Arabic of today. Overall, what *is* certain in regard to the rapid physical evolution and distinctiveness of Arabian tribes (including, of course, their dialects) is that they must have achieved a viable gene pool with equal rapidity. As one would expect, therefore, full tribal speciation between Jews and Arabs suffered very little delay.

Nevertheless it is important to keep the basic biological processes in mind constantly and not to be tempted to suppose that human affairs are somehow rather different or set apart. As with all other diversifications in the animal world, our human racial stock, together with its languages and customs, continues to evolve. It is an endless process. It does not stop with just a single variant. True, a single variant can last unchanged for some considerable period of time, but this does not defy the all-powerful 'thrust' directing biological evolution and from which it cannot escape! Human diversification, as with that of all other creatures, does not flow to any supposed 'universal beat' of time. It does not, as is earlier demonstrated, mimic guardsmen marching strictly to time using the beat of specially composed evolutionary music and massed bands. Many species are out of step. Some are hardly in the march at all. Development is punctuated; in other words, evolutionary processes proceed in fits and starts. And at this point it is necessary to digress for a moment to explain more fully the impact of punctuationism on both the fields of biological evolution and similar evolution in human affairs.

Early opponents of Darwin's evolutionary theory attempted to discredit its basic proposition and discomfort its withdrawn and publicity-shunning founder by pointing out that some supposedly ancient species (more especially aquatic creatures) are still very much alive today. They hardly differ from their fossilised ancestors. The answer to this apparent rebuttal of Darwinism is that they did not require change. They happened to be so well adapted to their environment (or habitat) that changes were no more than minimal. While many other features of our planet have certainly changed, its oceans have not – at least not in any rapid and significant way. Land surfaces, in contrast, have – very much so! Volcanic eruptions, climate change, moving tectonic plates, the hot sun, moving sheets of ice, meteorites (which wiped out the dinosaurs), tiny rock and soil particles picked up by the wind-creating deserts, these and many more factors have all contributed to significant and sometimes violent change. Those land animals that were fortunate enough to be able to adapt to changing circumstances are still with us; those that could not are now extinct. In direct contrast, conditions in the sea were (and are) more equitable. Essentially though, one must emphasise that when basic circumstances change, then once more evolution and diversification are 'jolted into action'. This expression, enclosed as it is very carefully by inverted commas, is, mark you, a Darwinian heresy. Life forms do not change consciously; they change by fitness for survival or, in other words, by natural selection. I have used its heretical form merely because it serves to explain evolutionary punctuationism. More correctly then, Darwinian evolution – merely by happy accident – allows some living things, without their conscious knowledge (or help!), to avoid extinction.

But let us return to the emergence of Islam. In what we deem arrogantly as wholly 'human affairs', we find that an unseen punctuated evolution jolts a formerly cohesive tribal unit to diversify. By virtue of a rapid change of circumstances, and in a corresponding evolutionary 'burst of speed', a single breakaway tribe may splinter into several tribes, as in the case of the Bedouin. Despite long periods of isolation in the desert, these tribal units were at least loosely tied by their common language Arabic, but by very little else. And it comes as no surprise to find that in desert areas (themselves evolving quickly because of human exploitation of trees for fuel and overgrazing by their animals), where resources for the maintenance of life were severely restricted, tribal warfare was endemic and ruthless. Population control was more effectively achieved by man's own hand in these circumstances than by any other agency. Nature herself was spared the necessity. That is not to imply of course that, as a geographic whole, Arabia was lacking completely in relatively fertile areas; it did not *force* every tribe to live in conditions of utmost rigour. In earlier times especially there were some reasonably well-watered and productive areas; the huge sandy wastes we see today are the result of man's poor stewardship. But the jealous way with which these territorial possessions were guarded by their lucky inhabitants kept other tribes at bay, on the periphery. Beyond these small fertile areas, there were also convenient trading stations at intersections on well-established caravan routes. Found on some of these, and actually on the western borders of Arabia, was the thriving trading city of Mecca. It is important to add that a large proportion of its trade was augmented by the presence of an ancient temple called the Kaaba, built of black stones and having a meteorite as a corner stone. Bedouin tribes venerated this shrine, and it became dedicated to a large pantheon of gods and goddesses. What is more they made regular visits to it to perform pagan rites.

However by subtle irony it was in Mecca, in the year 610, that a merchant named Mohammed ibn Abdullah, received a series of visions that were later to bring him unparalleled reverence and the title Prophet – a title charged with the kind of significance the West rarely appreciates.

Most Bedouin tribes at that particular moment displayed a strange amalgam of religious beliefs. Homage was still paid among some tribes to the faith of their fathers – that is what had now become the 'ancient' religious rites stemming from Abraham and Ishmael. Among others a proliferation of pagan gods had taken over. Even for those still faithful to ancient rites, their faith was vague and becoming increasingly irrelevant. The dimly remembered patriarchs were now much diminished in status. Equally the status of the God they had worshipped. Monotheism was actively being edged out; in its place the usual jumble of pagan gods and goddesses had taken a strong foothold.

Mohammed himself, as with the minority living in or near Mecca, had retained a form of monotheism handed down through the centuries. But it was not focused in any truly dynamic way. And even within that minority there were some who, while fitfully acknowledging one supreme God, nevertheless hedged their bets in difficult times and made offerings at pagan altars. This was why the small number of Jews living in the area, who appeared (mistakenly!) to have no doubts or difficulties with their staunch support of Judaism, were rather envied. Many Arabs of that day toyed with the idea of accepting the strict monotheism of Judaism, but they were constantly deterred by a strong individualist streak in their character. Intuitively they desired true speciation from Judaism, but had no clear idea how this might be achieved. Until Mohammed's visions were made known to them, such diversification as they had achieved – and more or less acquired accidentally – had not as yet found an enclosed doctrinal gene pool. Until this was achieved, full speciation could not develop efficiently and unhindered. The God of Abraham, Isaac, Moses, and Jesus, together with an assembly of the Old Testament prophets, certainly formed the basis of the ancestral line. That much was accepted. But the precise way in which Arabs could branch out and find a suitable niche of their own still remained uncertain. To make matters more difficult still, they found that as they groped their way forward, they were constantly being jostled or tempted by others. These proclaimed, as always, the attractions of false gods and goddesses.

In his role as a merchant, Mohammed ibn Abdullah, the future Prophet, had access to all kinds of information on current affairs. Being a member of the Quraysh people – who themselves, prior to settling at Mecca, had led the kind of existence common to nomadic Bedouin tribes – he had ample scope to listen to and absorb accounts of his people's past and present history. In particular there was every opportunity to listen to the first-hand experiences of the murderous desert raids and vendettas. They were after all the accepted fabric of life endured by his clients. It is probable too that many of the petty chieftains who entered into conversation expressed their weariness of endless conflict. Most would have agreed that monotheism as a binding force had considerable social advantages.

The visions Mohammed subsequently experienced, and his recited descriptions of them, did not at first stir up undue controversy. There were some receptive individuals among his audience, but only a small number of true converts were made. Among them were those who believed that these inspired words should find a more permanent record: these duly set about making written copies. In this form the Prophet's words achieved much wider transmission. What should be emphasised too is the sharp contrast made with the Christian Bible. Most of the Old Testament and New Testament was written by observers some considerable time after the events described, and from the memory or the observation of others. Thus in the New Testament, for example, each Apostle had his own slightly differing approach, including the reportage of Christ's life and teaching. Thus, inevitably, controversy was later to arise over inconsistencies. With Mohammed's visions, however, his personal dictation of them to his followers neatly avoided textual differences. Of course that is not to suppose total exclusion of all errors. Unavoidably, when copies were made later by scribes, some few accidental 'mutations' occurred. But at least there was no controversy due to differing authors. Nor, for that matter, were there translator's errors, as in translations into (or from) Greek. By happy chance Arabic was for many centuries, and virtually right up to the present day, the sole language of transmission. Translations of the Bible, on the other hand, suffered continually from the inability to find exact equivalents of the text in different languages. Incidentally too, for those of us in the West who are not Moslem, it should be remembered that the Koran was intended to be recited and not read silently. Much of its power comes from a poetic quality, enhanced by reading aloud. There may be a reason for this. Mohammed, being an orphan, was actively employed in his youth in looking after camels and sheep in his uncle's household. As a boy he had no opportunity to become literate. However clerics and theologians over the centuries have found evidence that on reaching manhood he *did* become literate; despite being denied formal education. Nevertheless, the spoken word anyway was his *métier*, so why dilute or undermine it? This has its parallel with the poetic quality of the words of Christ in the New Testament. We suppose that Jesus as a boy was at least taught to read, because He was able to dispute with elders in the temple. It suggests He was also able to write. Even so He left none of his teachings written in his own hand. And speculation has failed to produce any cogent reasons other than yet another triumph for the spoken word. There is one further aspect one should note: Mohammed did not recite[3] his visions all in one short and uninterrupted period of revelation. A series of visitations took place. But all were at least documented more or less immediately by others, and certainly during his lifetime. This is in direct contrast with Christ's teachings.

---

[3] In Arabic recite is 'qur'an', which translates into 'Koran' in English.

Very well then. What was the impact of this new teaching? At first the reaction to Mohammed's words, either personally during recitation, or alternatively from the written word recited by others, was muted. Moreover it was at first restricted naturally enough to groups of inhabitants in and around Mecca, or to individuals among visiting camel trains. However, those who relied on the commercial trade brought mainly by pagan pilgrims to the Kaaba became increasingly hostile. Livelihoods were being put at risk. Converts at this time therefore came at a mere trickle. A larger number of sympathetic, but not wholly committed, individuals metaphorically sat on the fence and waited for further developments. Some believed in compromise – a fusion of paganism and monotheism. This was feasible in that many early civilisations had adopted this form. The early Greeks, for example, had a supreme god, Zeus, ruling the extremely varied major and minor gods and goddesses in a well populated Pantheon. But Mohammed insisted that his vision specified *one* supreme God and one only. This required of his followers absolute dedication – therefore a complete rejection of all other supposed deity, even if they were minor ones! Mohammed was in effect creating an enclosed and viable doctrinal gene pool. From this pool (and with such absolutism) he would have realised intuitively that it would be possible to fuel the process of full speciation from the God of Abraham into something far more dynamic. It is at this point, in AD 622 (a Christian date not recognised in the Moslem calendar), that he made his defiant proclamation. Significantly enough for our theme, it is singled out by his followers to mark the true beginning of the Islamic era!

Mohammed's unyielding insistence brought some further dedicated converts. Equally though, it brought to a head opposition amongst those who directly profited from pagan worship at the Kaaba. Feelings became so inflamed that his life was threatened and he was forced to flee. Finding greater sympathy at nearby Medina, he settled there and began to consolidate his position.

In due course his enemies were sufficiently alarmed by the continuing growth of this new religion and threatened open conflict. By 623 matters came to a head and resulted in the battle of Badr.

It is perhaps misleading to call this a battle. The numbers involved – at least that is in today's terms – were small. And, being small, the result was inconclusive – this despite Mohammed's initial success. With neither side having the decisive advantage, both regrouped and prepared for further conflict. Later battles were fought with greater numbers. These gradually brought the Prophet and his followers a degree of military prowess. With it came increasing success. Success breeds success, and in this instance a substantial increase in converts. As numbers increased so did the Prophet's prestige and military fortunes.

Eventually, in 630, he entered Mecca at the head of an army, now fully recognised as the founder of a vibrant new religion.

Two years later, after a brief illness, he died unexpectedly at Medina.[4]

The inevitable crisis that followed was made all the more serious in that the Prophet had failed to name any successor. Those who saw Mohammed as possessing a divine spirituality believed this quality would be inherited by a bloodline. But the nomination of one of his children was frustrated by the fact that Mohammed – despite having had several wives – had only one surviving daughter. All his sons had died in infancy. And in a wholly male-dominated society it was inconceivable for a woman to fill such a position.

Devoid of any clear indication as to who should be the new leader, and requiring a swift decision, those who opted for a pragmatic solution backed Abu-Bekr. There were several factors involved. He had been a true and early friend; he had been one of the first converts; he had given all of his considerable energies in establishing the faith; he was also the father of the Prophet's second wife. Closer links and proven spirituality could hardly be surpassed. They believed these must surely take precedence over the bloodline, such as it was. As pragmatists, they also had an

---

[4] Those of us in the West who are not Muslim must rely on information necessarily filtered through Western eyes. If there are any errors in this short description of the Prophet's life then these are due to centuries of misunderstanding yet to be rectified: they are not occasioned by prejudice on my part at least.

intuitive feel for the pitfalls of genetic inheritance; simple everyday observation would have told them that children of exceptional parents do not necessarily fulfil the promise expected of them. In point of fact there could be great variation between each of the offspring. In, say, a family of six to eight surviving children, common enough in those days, exceptional gifts, especially those of deep spirituality, did not necessarily flow to the eldest son. Nor, for that matter, did they become focused in any of the remainder. Worse, some offspring could well show lamentable faults. The attitude of the pragmatists was therefore not unreasonable.

In the event, Abu-Bekr proved to be an extremely able and vigorous successor. He added large sections of Mesopotamia to what was now a united Arabic nation. And it was a unity that contrasted so sharply with the endless feuding of petty chieftains that had gone before. Unfortunately, as he was already advanced in years, Abu-Bekr's leadership as the first caliph lasted only until 634. After his death the pragmatists succeeding in electing a second caliph, Omar ibn al-Khattabe. They did so once more by reason of merit and not of bloodline. Unfortunately this Caliph too, although extremely successful in his consolidation of what was rapidly becoming an Islamic empire, failed to live very long. Contemporary writers suggest that he may have been assassinated. When a third elected caliph, Uthman ibn Affan, also died in suspicious circumstances in 656, the pragmatists found themselves back in a crisis situation.

Despite the creditable record of the first three caliphs, there had remained a minority who passionately believed that the Prophet and his bloodline must surely retain some divine qualities. These now pressed their case with greater vigour. Remember only twenty-four years had elapsed since the Prophet's death!

Ali, the son of Abu Talib, uncle to Mohammed, if not in direct line could at least claim to be within the ancestral group. Perhaps of greater significance was the fact that he had married the Prophet's daughter Fatima. What is more, they had produced children. All in all this seemed sufficient. Ali was now proposed as Caliph. The matter provoked stormy debate. Ali and his associates eventually triumphed and he duly became the fourth caliph. His reign was however marked with growing dissension. Five years later, in 661, he was assassinated. A non-bloodline successor once more filled the gap. Stability of a sort was hurriedly achieved. Subsequently though, there occurred an even more poignant situation for the supporters of the bloodline. In 680 Husayn ibn Ali, who was Ali's son (Mohammed's grandson by his daughter) and an obvious contender for supreme power, was killed by the Ummayad Caliph Yazid.

It is difficult for those of us in the West to obtain a true picture of this unusually complex historical chapter, all the more so because those who chronicled it were themselves active supporters of one side or the other. But then, no historical event can ever receive absolute objectivity. Even Western historians writing long afterwards and supposedly totally uninfluenced are unconsciously swayed in one way or another. What cannot be disputed, however, is that this recurring problem of finding successors to the caliphate finally provoked a violently explosive schism. In fact the death of Ali and his son created two 'subspecies' within Islam virtually overnight; Sunnites and Shiites.

Even so, it would be misleading to suppose that this matter was driven by an Arabic form of Machiavellian power politics. The resulting schism involved a curious mixture of both political and religious doctrines. The Sunnites believed that the Prophet acted as the mouthpiece of God, and, although they revered him as such, they were reluctant to see the Prophet being given increasingly supernatural status. They fervently believed that God himself was beyond mere human comprehension! And while exceptional human beings, such as Mohammed, could at times partly interpret or be given just a hint of the essential mystery, there was always the danger of anthropomorphism creeping in. They feared too that for those with very little spirituality or depth of intellect, there was considerable danger of Mohammed himself becoming an idol and worshipped as such – something the Prophet himself had warned against at the battle of Badr. In the Koran we find him speaking of himself in these terms:

> Mohammed is no more than an apostle; the other apostles have

> already deceased before him: if he die therefore, or be slain, will ye turn back on your heels?

There is a clear implication of direct loyalty to God rather than to a mortal man – even one given the status of Prophet! In like manner, therefore, the elevation of Christ by Christians from that of a prophet to that of the very essence of God was (and still is) considered blasphemous by all Moslems. Thus the decoration of Christian churches with sculptures or paintings containing physical representations of God and His Son, together with that of the Virgin Mary, was (and is) held particularly reprehensible. These surely encouraged the worst kind of anthropomorphism! And it is an attitude that commands our respect. One cannot but admit that simple people are all too easily tempted to worship the statues and relics themselves rather than the concepts they represent.

However, to move on to the Shiite viewpoint: these conversely believed that the Prophet could at the very least pass on part of his divine guidance in the bloodline. Inevitably, of course, this belief proved to have difficulties of its own; indeed it provided yet another opportunity for diversification. As the decades rolled by, one Shiite group sought to venerate twelve descendants of Ali; another group believed there were only seven! By these means, Mohammed's gift of religious unity and social cohesion was in constant danger of disintegration, and this within the Shiite faction itself!

Ironically, the entire matter was later turned on its head when the pragmatists found to their dismay that as the Islamic empire rapidly expanded, the Caliph no longer concentrated on spiritual leadership: his role had become increasingly secularised! He had become no more than an administrator. Worse, increasing wealth and an unhealthy interest in power for its own sake suddenly produced caliphs who arrogantly assumed that their own bloodlines were solely fit for succession. And of course concentration of both power and wealth in one family dynasty tended to produce corrupt, dissolute and despotic rulers. These were in no way different in actual essence from the supreme rulers of all other empires in different continents round the world, both before and since.

Perhaps more ironically still, as later caliphs saw the Shiite veneration of the Prophet's bloodline as a threat and actively persecuted them, these descendants, no matter how diluted the line, became spiritually superior in every way. Adversity after all tends to assist in generating humility and introspection; absolute power, with all its attendant luxury and constant admiration from a fawning retinue can, unless the individual is unusually high-minded and gifted, promote decadence and self-delusion.

Whatever the merits or demerits of the respective Sunni and Shiia viewpoints, one basic fact remains: two subspecies had now been created within what was once a united Islam. Quite suddenly, unresolved and bitter recrimination led to open conflict between them. Indeed the schism has remained down through the centuries, lasting right up to the present day. In point of fact the fundamental nature of the dispute is emphasised in that it has exploded from time to time into extremely bloody conflicts. These have direct parallels with the slaughter achieved in Christendom by the extended conflict between Catholics and Protestants. More recently still, we must note that vicious infighting between Catholic and Greek Orthodox has exploded in the Balkans. It has produced actual warfare between Croats and Serbs. And over the centuries millions have died not just in conflict between main-line religions, but equally in internal disputes between competing sects.

Shall we return now to the conflict caused by succession to the Moslem caliphate? In areas where Shiia were in the majority came a succession of various imams who were venerated; indeed on some occasions they were raised to a status almost equal to the Prophet himself. What can Westerners make of this? In particular what can a biological viewpoint deeply concerned with the genetic input make of it? Our twentieth-century scientific probing of genetic inheritance shows that of the two viewpoints, the pragmatists may have the better case. It may seem unnecessary to point out that genetic input comes equally from the father and mother (half the chromosomes each), yet this is often overlooked. And while there is certainly a tendency for exceptionally gifted parents to pass on at least a proportion of their gifts to their children, then the lottery of genetic inheritance is such that it is by no means automatic. Thus our quite crude and unprofessional observation remains valid enough when we can confirm that not a few children of famous parents (in all walks of life and a variety of situations down through the ages) singularly fail to come up to expectations. Indeed a minority of these children are so disastrously 'out of line' that the cynical or downright bloody-minded can suggest they might not be 'bloodline' at all! But imputing bastardy merely throws dust in people's eyes. The science of genetics amply proves, and does so without a shadow of doubt a quite fundamental factor, that in the matter of accidental alignment of recessive genes, or for that matter in the endless computations available during the shuffling of genes from each parent, totally unexpected, unfortunate or even bizarre characteristics can result. In such cases bastardy would seem to have been proven, yet in reality such offspring have been quite legitimate!

But all this tends to apply only to the more 'political' aspects of the diversification of Islam. What of doctrinal divisions? Once again these mirror those found in Judaism and Christianity. There are those who believe that inner purity can only be achieved by constant self-examination and self-criticism. This, they argue, is the only hope we have of resisting temptation to sin. It is essentially an introvert approach. They are fiercely critical of those who believe that by effusive and very public beating of breasts – plus a little money given for 'good works', of course – forgiveness is theirs. It seems both blasphemous and a further encouragement of evil. Yet there is another aspect so easily overlooked. Those who are blessed with both sensitivity and an active conscience find it difficult to convince themselves that others may totally lack them. It seems inconceivable that people can be born *so* spiritually handicapped. They are perfectly able, of course, to accept that people can be born with physical deficiencies. There are such clearly visible defects as deformed legs or arms, or equally crippling internal conditions such as a weak heart: they may even perhaps push their credibility to the limit to involve mental illnesses such as schizophrenia – but they are unable to extrapolate further. Any neat take-off and short imaginative flight from the physical to the spiritual is somehow denied them. Time and time again they refuse to believe that physical qualities inherited at birth can actually jump the gap into another realm and produce spiritual deformity.

Nevertheless, if you are prepared to accept that life is full of inequalities and shortcomings, rather than be constantly pushed into those dangerous realms of make-believe (where the supremacy of 'what should be' dominates) then the matter takes on a different aspect. You just accept that many are born with grave disadvantages. And in finally recognising that their facilities for self-enquiry and rigorous soul-searching are cruelly restricted, you respond by adjusting your viewpoint. It is as simple as that.

Now many Islamic clerics, philosophers and mystics were (and their contemporaries still are) fully aware of this. Perhaps the best known of the early thinkers battling with this problem were Al-Ashari and Al-Baqillani. They brought copious energy, not to mention a degree of anguish and subtlety of thought to the matter. But unfortunately their very names, let alone details of their life's work, remain almost unknown in the West. In the absence of any understanding of their viewpoint, then perhaps a very crude analogy, plucked more conveniently from our own European heritage, might suffice. Briefly, perhaps Robert Burns's wholly unsophisticated but heartfelt cry, 'Oh may the Lord, the gift He gi' us, to see oorsel as ithers see us,' might offer itself as a candidate. It does at least meet our wretched twentieth-century demand for the 'instant' summing-up. Yet realists well know that the sad little cry Burns offers, in the vital cause of harmonious human relationships, is seldom answered. A very large section of mankind serves a life sentence trapped in the prison of self and egomania, and the remainder have to suffer for it. In the worst instances, this inability to pause and see oneself, even for a brief moment, in the very unflattering and all-too-truthful sight of others, can produce monsters. These have strutted over the historical stage throughout every century. The twentieth century in particular has seen not just such hideously deformed spiritual cripples such as Hitler and Stalin, but many lesser ones. And their restricted roles on the world stage have resulted from a lack of opportunity rather than talent. Pol Pot, Ceauşescu, Noriega,

Trujillo, Papa Doc, Mobutu, Idi Amin, Bokassa, Saddam Hussein – the list goes on and on and is too depressing to complete. Plumbing greater depths than Burns, we find Shakespeare making his own enquiry about the source of self-deception and crippled consciences. The bard's thoughts parallel those of the Islamic philosophers. And his absorption in the tragedy of this kind of cerebral imprisonment was total. It is to be found powerfully expressed in such plays as *Macbeth* and *Hamlet*; again in many of the sonnets he notes the self-deceptions so often generated during that passion called 'love'! Indeed the white heat generated by love or sexual desire often stimulates individuals to display either the very best or the very worst aspects found in human behaviour. As for Pascal in his *Pensées* and Spinoza in his *Ethics*, both express similar concerns. These and other probing minds, both East and West, have over the centuries provided some highly sophisticated answers. Yet to attempt some kind of rapid survey at this point would be foolish. The matter is too complex to allow a crude or hasty attempt at overview. And while it certainly has bearing on my theme, it remains beyond the scope of a restricted essay of this nature. Incidentally too, the matter is made all the more daunting in that these clerics, philosophers, mystics and poets fail to reach a consensus. Many of the solutions they offer vary, indeed vary considerably! Some even contradict each other.

Such an exercise is therefore fraught with endless difficulties. All one can say while rounding off this section of enquiry may, in direct consequence, sound banal. It is this: whatever the escape plan suggested to effect a breakout from imprisonment within the ego, then the demand in effort, courage and tenacity is exceptional. To strip one's soul naked before the sight of others, and indeed before all the world, is something most individuals will automatically shrink from attempting.

Given such an impasse, what is to be done? Do we merely accept that if we are born without sensitivity and a modicum of conscience, then we are beyond all human aid? Must we rely solely on 'road to Damascus' conversions, a kind of miracle that are essentially outside our own humble scope? Some say yes; some say no.

For those who say yes, no further comment is possible. Divine intervention in effect neatly absolves us from all further anguish and probing of conscience.

But what of those who say no? Their comment, after all, concerns itself with the stark question: why do people search after some sort of meaning or reason for living? Why do all the differing religions still remain a potent force in the world, this despite so many attempts, in the twentieth century in particular, to stifle or eradicate them. Many still feel a desperate need for guidance. More worrying still, a proportion of these still feel attracted to forms of worship that retain complex ceremonial and ritual.

Further examination of this aspect is thus wholly necessary. At once we become aware that down through the centuries Moslem, Christian and Jewish clerics have been as one in condemning pagan rites; all have been aware of the way in which simple people have been mesmerised and enslaved by mere ritual. It is all the more sensitive an issue therefore when these clerics in turn are accused of 'doublethink'! They too can be accused of using unethical forms of ceremony and ritual in their *own* places of worship. They too are in danger of using and abusing these 'spiritual aids' and marshalling them for their own dubious ends rather than for the salvation of their flocks.

The distinction and indeed the actual line drawn between helpful ritual and manipulative brainwashing is a fine one. Yet the case for the defence is not without vigorous support and respectable viewpoints.

Essentially such a viewpoint revolves round the very nature of God. It is surely neither an unreasonable nor untenable conviction that the Creator of the universe is beyond all human comprehension. Our miserably restricted intellects are wholly unable even to begin embracing such a concept. The picture given us by the science of astronomy in particular is so awesome that we recoil backwards in dismay. We feel overwhelmed by the immensity of time and space; we are dazzled by the spectacle of countless numbers of stars and of the constant flux entailed by their birth, life and death. We are dazzled by the nature and number of the galaxies and overwhelmed by questions about the nature and very purpose of the universe – indeed a number of universes! So how can we even begin to comprehend the essence of the Creator? And yet the founders of all the different world religions seem to offer us some hope. We are offered the prospect that this fog of incomprehension can at least be partly lifted; we might even catch a brief glimpse of what lies beyond.

If, then, for the most part, our intellect alone is incapable of grasping the nature of the Creator, it would seem that ceremony and ritual may be of some help in promoting this feeling of 'other worldliness'. Moreover, there are those too who value continuity and tradition especially in relation to the faith of their own earthly creators – that is their parents, grandparents and the long line of ancestors stretching backward to infinity. The Japanese people, for one, make an arresting comment when replying to criticisms of their traditionalism. They reply proudly: 'We do not spit in the faces of our ancestors!' Indeed the Japanese have elevated this to the status of a religion in its own right. Thus they and others are convinced that there is a place for symbolism in helping the unsophisticated to come to terms with the Creator of all things. And it becomes in itself a confession of inadequacy and a sign of humility before the face of a Being who is essentially beyond the grasp of our miserably cramped and fallible intellects.

This then is the case made by clerics who feel the necessity for large sections of humanity to watch complex ceremonies... or for that matter even in their own minor way to participate in ritual. They do not deny that it is an artificial solution. But, on the other hand, can anyone insist on withholding it from those who simply lack the courage to set out on a personal odyssey? Can one withhold it from those who are born without due sensitivity, who are born boisterously and selfishly extrovert rather than introvert?

Unquestionably though, the nature of this artificial aid does mean that it attracts considerable dangers. And it certainly requires the utmost sincerity if these are to be avoided. If due sincerity *is* achieved, then ceremony and ritual can possibly allow some brief moments of 'distance' from the self, moreover offer temporary escape from the tyranny of the ego.

However, nobody should doubt that the dangers are legion. For example, if the ceremony or the ritual is repeated too often, and without decently spaced intervals, it will quickly devalue the experience. The insensitive and the extrovert therefore have to achieve a very fine balancing act. This is made all the more difficult in that the tightrope provided is both very fragile and tends to sway when subjected to excessive emotion. Moreover it is not a one-off feat; it must be repeated at intervals over a lifetime.

But what of those incidental yet well-proven benefits that a shared religion can provide in purely social terms? As with their counterparts in Judaism and Christianity, we find that Islamic clerics, philosophers and mystics also emphasise the purely social benefits of religion. They stress that *only* a shared belief can bring about social justice, cohesion and responsibility. They constantly warn against self-indulgence and the spiritual emptiness that will accrue when individuals devote themselves to the constant pursuit of wealth and pleasure. Thus for those deeply committed to Islam, any lack of concern in things of the spirit becomes deeply shocking. It is this tradition that now, today, finds itself reacting so sharply to the apparently scandalous and decadent behaviour of the West. And in all honesty, those of us who happen to be born Westerners must admit that they have every right to express such concern, especially when they see evidence of this 'plague' or so-called Western 'cultural poison' beginning to move eastward. In our defence though, it must be said that the bulk of our Eastern brothers' perception of this lack of spirituality is not entirely accurate. Moslem vision, being necessarily so distant, tends to focus on those outrageous and outsize egos that constantly steal the limelight; consequently, they fail to see a whole 'underclass' of decent and responsible people – the bedrock of our ethnicity – who remain quietly in the background. There is, moreover, something of a tradition in the West of keeping one's deeper thoughts hidden and unexpressed. It is commonly felt to be vulgar and insensitive to voice them openly. It is therefore all too easy for those looking from some distance to receive a distorted picture. In point of fact there are sizeable proportions of decent and responsible people in the West who are equally horrified by the decadence of their own kith and kin. They too are deeply worried by current trends. Unfortunately, though, their voices are seldom heard. The irresponsible, the feckless and shameless members of Western society are always those too easily seen and heard. And this has given Islamic clerics in particular – and almost to a man – a wholly false impression.

One can only hope that more judicious thought in this matter will give Islamic leaders a more accurate picture. Surely Western society would have disintegrated years ago if the rottenness had not been balanced and indeed outweighed by other factors? To repeat, those factors embrace a solid mass of people dedicated to lasting values, to decency and to responsibility.

There is yet another aspect to Islam's inaccurate vision of the West. It is this: given that a great deal of the current hostility has been generated by years of misinterpreted information, there is a danger that such hostility may be easily fanned by extremists. After all, the West seems to be unaware of the appalling picture of greed, immorality and shamelessness it projects! The dangers building up have already resulted in isolated acts of terrorism at the hands of Islamic groups afflicted with religious mania. And if repeated on a larger scale, these could result in all-out conflict between East and West, bringing misery and horror to all. This very serious factor does of course come wholly within the remit of an essay dealing with causes of conflict, but it will be discussed more fully later.

Other religions

We must turn now to other world religions such as Hinduism, Buddhism, Confucianism and Shintoism. There are, of course, many more, but unfortunately they cannot be contained within the scope of this essay. There are obvious limitations to both the time and the space involved.

Doubtless though, it will give offence to those outside Christianity, Judaism and Islam, when they find I have grouped their cherished beliefs as 'other religions'. It will imply some kind of superficial and indeed outrageous downgrading on my part – even worse, confirm implication of lower status. This is to misunderstand the position entirely. It is done for pressing reasons. To repeat, the first is sheer lack of space in such an essay. Secondly, I am conscious that I address a mainly Western readership. It should be evident therefore that Judaism,

Christianity and Islam should receive the greater part of my attention as they have had far greater impact on events in the West than any of the other religions – moreover they will doubtless continue to do so for the conceivable future. And there is a third and rather delicate aspect. How exactly does one define a world religion? Is it solely determined by a very crude headcount?

Now surely it is outrageous to suggest that the status and value of any religion rests purely on the number of adherents it can muster? One would hope that the intrinsic value of anything rests within itself, not on how the fallible human mind might perceive it. Even so, in this crazy world of ours the reality of the situation seems to suggest that in defining a 'world religion' then sheer numbers do indeed count. And this factor does have some ugly consequences – ones that clash directly with claims of spirituality and enlightenment.

Crude Headcounts

With this in mind it becomes necessary to examine the stance taken by one major sect within Christianity to begin with – the Catholic Church. Here a succession of popes have given every evidence of their concern for sheer numbers. Messages to the faithful have continually insisted on the sheer joy of multiple births and the abhorrence of any effective form of birth control. Cynically, in response to many years of pleading for some relief, two birth control systems were finally announced. Realistically, however, they were non-starters: the first was complete sexual abstinence, the second a so-called 'rhythm method'. This stance has been maintained despite endless requests for more effective help. Indeed this single issue has raised such concern that it is in danger of creating a schism on its own account! A small body of rebellious Catholic theologians and priests now openly insist on a softening of attitude. Unfortunately though, very little has been achieved. Even so the reaction among educated and sensitive European laity has simply been to ignore papal ruling. Thus we now have the astonishing situation whereby the birth rate in Italy (the perceived bedrock of Catholicism) has actually fallen slightly below replacement level. The Italian average is now 1.3 children per family. As for the viewpoint on abortion, papal attitudes even in the instance of rape, are equally unbending. It is demanded that a woman must carry, give birth to and subsequently bring up such a child, despite her detestation of the father's act – not to speak of her fear that his violent character may well be inherited by his child!

Then again, there is the question of mixed marriages. Until very recently any Catholic who had the 'misfortune' to enter into marriage with a non-Catholic was duty-bound to see all subsequent children brought up in the Catholic faith. It mattered little if the other partner found this an insult to the integrity of his or her own beliefs. It mattered little either if this proved a basis for conflict within their future relationship. Securing a supply of children for a future headcount and denying them to other faiths seemed the only criteria operating in this matter. Urgent representations by several archbishops of Canterbury in meetings with successive popes on behalf of Protestants who were deeply distressed by such rulings were met with pointed silence. Only in the last decade has there been some relaxation and admission of the hurt and anguish involved.

These, combined with other more subtle yet equally unflattering and unworthy aspects of what one might call Catholic social engineering, point to the Vatican's unhealthy preoccupation with numbers.

Ironically though, it happens to be self-defeating in the long run. If the Vatican insists on thinking of its faithful as some kind of spiritual army, then they would be well advised to seek advice on recruitment policy from actual commanders of armies – that is the field marshals and five-star generals of nation states! Here I wager a guess that such commanders would point out a serious error of judgement. You see, in today's highly sophisticated conditions, the objective is to create a small but well-trained and generously supplied army. Above all, it must be motivated by the highest ideals. This is infinitely preferable to one that is over-large, poorly trained, badly supplied and lacking in what the French call *'elan'*. In a word, recruitment policy should embrace quality not quantity. Thus in this respect every effort to train, equip and motivate troops with the kind of spirit that knows no such word as 'defeat' is compromised by sheer numbers. These only serve to clog up all aspects of the training period, worse, to frustrate the logistics of supplying all the basic necessities of food, clothing and equipment. Attempting to spread supplies thinly to both the best military regiments or divisions *and* to the worst, is wholly disastrous!

Surely then if we translate the *elan* or fighting spirit of troops into wholly spiritual terms, and then apply it to the ranks of a world religion, a very different picture emerges. Every highly motivated member who is gained is a true advantage; every lip-serving or mere adherent who is virtually dragged in is a liability and a disadvantage.

One of the most horrific aspects of the 'numbers game' took place earlier this century in the Balkans when political leaders of a fascist regime in Catholic Croatia, blinded as they were by extreme religious zeal, tried to convert Orthodox Serbs by force. They slaughtered those who refused. Unbelievably, and in direct retaliation, Orthodox Serbs attempted similar conversions equally by force. These too resorted to slaughter when necessary. But in the history of religious conflict before the twentieth century the killing fields were much more extensive. As already noted, the Reformation, resulting so explosively in the creation of Protestant states or enclaves, was followed by the Counter-Reformation. Catholic emperors or princes, with the blessing of the popes of the day, sought to reclaim territory and the peoples within them not by displaying saintliness or more enlightened religious doctrines but by sheer force of arms. The Thirty Years War in Germany was preceded by convulsions in Poland, Hungary, Bohemia, Austria, the Netherlands, France and Britain. In areas retaken by Catholic forces, captured Protestants were considered lucky to be given the choice between recanting or death. The Spanish Count Alva, at the siege of Alkmaar in Holland, wrote to Phillip II: 'I am resolved to leave not a single creature alive; the knife shall be put to every throat'! Commanders of similar zeal often gave Protestants two choices – the slow torture of burning at the stake, or, if they recanted, the more merciful sentence of instant execution by beheading. Earlier, in sixteenth-century France, the number of Calvinist Protestants had reached perhaps one and a half million with large areas of southern France under their control. The massacre on St Bartholomew's night in 1572 saw hundreds cut to pieces in Paris, Rouen, Troyes, Orleans, Saumur, Bourges, Lyons, Bordeaux, Aix and Toulouse. But this frightful and carefully planned act failed to have its desired effect. In 1598 the Edict of Nantes gave the Protestants some measure of freedom and toleration. This lasted until 1685 when the Edict was revoked. Huguenots were then subjected to forcible conversion. Half a million fled France, many settling in Britain. Earlier still, in the fifteenth century, and a full century before the Lutheran revolt, followers of the Bohemian reformer John Huss (who was burnt at the stake in 1415) fought against the reimposition of Catholicism for almost two hundred years and suffered accordingly.

To recount the entire history of the Reformation and Counter-Reformation and details of the conflicts that ensued would once again require far more attention than I am prepared to give them in such an essay. Perhaps in summing up it is sufficient to say that diversification from Roman Catholicism was not a completely natural process, – that is if we think in biological terms. Rather it was one that was artificially accelerated by corruption within the Church. Punctuated evolution should have seen Catholicism last for a much longer period in its unchanged state. When the schism occurred, the counter measures, which incidentally included some much-needed reforms, were unable to reabsorb a large number of small but vigorous theological gene pools. And always the process of attempted reconversion of Hussites, Lutherans, Calvinists, (including Huguenots) and Anglicans was crudely seen as a numbers game. To repeat: it was played out by military means, not by demonstrating a superior and thereby more fulfilling spirituality. To those of us in Western Europe, where two centuries or more of reasonable levels of religious tolerance have been achieved, it now seems incredible that the teachings of Christ – which above all preach tolerance, forgiveness and love – could have been subverted and twisted so grotesquely. Where is the logic in trying to convert individual and supposedly 'free' and sacrosanct souls by force and not by saintly persuasion? What possible value is there in a mere headcount of supposedly active followers of a faith or sect if a large proportion of those individuals are reluctant, confused, hostile or even secretly determined to injure or destroy that faith? And this applies equally to all religions the world over, including, naturally, their various sects so often engaged in vicious internal conflict.

Perhaps we should move on to Judaism at this point and examine its particular position in this matter. Here, surprisingly, it would seem that, outwardly at least, there is no fixation with numbers or active attempts to gain converts by force. Judaism tends to be an exclusive 'club for members only' – conversions are rare. Moreover, this exclusivity is further protected by the belief that one is normally born into the faith. And even this is by restricted circumstances. The circumstance? Only if one has a Jewish mother can one be born Jewish. Thus added to the inevitable anguish that attends a mixed marriage (anguish which seems universal and not confined to Judaism any more than any other of the world religions), a Jewish father procreating with a non-Jewish mother results in children that are lost to Jewry! This could be later rectified by genuine conversion, but equally the child, having grown to adulthood and able to exercise thought for itself in the matter, might well choose not to enter Judaism. The point made is that an infant does not automatically become accepted into the faith through its father's line – only through its mother.

This might lead one to suppose that the reprehensible issue of crude headcount has far less importance. Unfortunately you would be mistaken. To be fair though, there happens to be a division of opinion within Judaism. Indeed the matter has different weight amongst the three main Jewish sects: Ultra-Orthodox, Orthodox and what are called, for want of a more dynamic title, Liberal. Moreover, this applies not only in the current state of Israel but also among the Diaspora scattered throughout the world.

Ultra-Orthodox Jews have a commitment to produce as many children as possible and totally reject birth control. Orthodox Jews have vague misgivings regarding population growth but are secretive regarding their attitude. Liberals, on the other hand, especially those who live in the state of Israel, see with stark realism the problems that accrue from a population explosion. Such realism focuses sharply on the physical size of Israel. It is after all a very small country hemmed in on all sides by either active or potential enemies. Clearly these already resent the Israeli success in the previous enlargement of territory. There is therefore a point beyond which the population cannot grow further without involving yet more territorial seizures.

Yet current population pressure has already meant that more and more Arabs are being forced off their land to make way for new Israeli settlements. Each time Arabs are threatened with eviction, tension is raised to breaking point. Successive attempts to broker a peace treaty have all run up against this basic obstacle. Despite this, such is the opposition to the concept of birth control that any open mention of explosive population pressure – clearly the fundamental cause of conflict – is neatly deleted from all verbal and written proceedings. It is a taboo subject. Delegations and heads of state from this country and that fly in, put their heads together, make announcements, go through the pantomime of handshakes and fixed smiles at cameras, then fly out again. The process is repeated endlessly. It has become an empty ritual. And being repeated so often, it has become a mockery. The fundamental cause is never discussed openly. Israel is urged not to proceed further with fresh housing settlements on Arab land, yet Orthodox Jews continue to produce children without restraint. In effect it makes a mockery of any peace plan.

To remark at this point that the existence of so many different world religions, together with splinter groups or 'speciation' within them, has been, and will continue to be, one of the major causes of human conflict would seem a superfluous exercise; it would appear merely to state the obvious. Nevertheless, humanity taken as a whole is now *so* submerged in excessive info flow and in digesting trivia that the obvious must be restated time and time again. Moreover, within the seemingly exclusive and clearly understood word 'religion' it must be understood that once again I also include communism and fascism. Belief in these 'faiths', as in all other religions, transcends the normal interplay of logic and reason. Also present is a belief in the superhuman qualities of their founders – at least in the minds of their devotees. Both communism and fascism become in effect truly 'religious experiences' and were (and are) acted on as such.

However, to overstate the influence of religions would be a grave error. Conflicts from this source only come to the fore when the very basic and central part of my thesis exert their grim and unyeilding influence. Conflict results from depleted resources coupled with the failure of the technology of the day (or the technology available in that particular region) to support excessive population increase. When people enjoy a high standard of living, they are unlikely to be swayed by a tiny minority of religious fanatics. This remains true despite such fanatics being found, unhappily, among every nation or ethnic group throughout the world. This cancerous minority see human beings of different beliefs as targets of their hatred, see them as ungodly people to be cleansed from the very face of the earth. Fortunately though – and to repeat yet again – religious fanatics of this extreme kind only begin to exert their malign influence when prosperity fades. Their hour comes when the pressure of population puts a premium on food or water supply together with basic materials and facilities for housing that population – above all, on the area of land available. One must never lose sight of this fact. Conflict stemming apparently from religious fanaticism is but symptomatic of a deeper problem: that problem remains population imbalance vis-à-vis the current resources available and the technological expertise applied.

Final summary

All the fragile knowledge that the human animal has gradually amassed – fragile in the sense that it is always no more than an approximation of the truth – has led to a partial understanding of the intricate nature of our world. Always remember it is provisional only. Shall we hurriedly pass over the further heroic attempts to begin to piece together knowledge of our galaxy and other distant galaxies because this is even more fragmentary and provisional. Nevertheless, what we have achieved has arisen solely from the remarkable ability to pass on precise and highly sophisticated pieces of information from one individual to another. It is an ability, even so, that in its amount of detail, versatility and flexibility seems to go far beyond that achieved by all other creatures in the animal kingdom.

Initially, among our primitive forebears this vital interchange of information was achieved solely by speech, though supplemented no doubt by expressive facial and hand movements. Later, what was essentially 'word of mouth' was supplemented by the more positive written word incised on clay, wood or stone; later still this was supplemented by printed text. Today all these forms have been overtaken and virtually superseded by a variety of sophisticated processes.

Unhappily however, it is a well-proven fact that even in the most primitive of eras the info flow generally could not always be relied upon to be truthful or accurate. It could be tampered with. Such tamperings were attempted more especially by those desiring to gain or maintain power over their fellow beings. These always found means whereby they could either withhold certain aspects of that information flow or indeed subvert it to provide subtle forms of misinformation.

And over many tens of thousands of years nothing has really changed!

In our contemporary world we seem to be entering an even more dangerous phase in that people have become so overawed by technical advances that they will refuse to believe that such sophisticated methodology can be subject to error! Such a delusion is created largely because so much of our present information is now stored or disseminated by computer and the Internet. And because it is such an imposing source it is casually supposed that it is free from inaccuracy or 'untruth'. To repeat: this is a highly dangerous assumption. The information is reliable only in relation to the degree of integrity maintained at the original source. Moreover there is an even worse danger: even supposing that all information could be made fully accurate and truthful, then there is still the frightening prospect of mankind being overwhelmed by mere weight of trivia.

★

TWO FORMIDABLE PARADOXES

Using the biologist's eye, rather than that of the blinkered historian, our view of world history can be radically altered.

Mankind, as all other creatures, is dominated by the instinct to procreate without restraint. Hence the historical panorama shows us endless examples of population pressure either outstripping available resources or overwhelming the capacity of the technology of the day to supply the basic needs. Such a pattern is repeated time and time again, and has been responsible for the fall of what seemed to be (for that era) the most powerful of nations or empire – sometimes entire civilisations.

*

There is a widely held assumption in the affluent West – an assumption tragically enough also held among Eastern nations who look on longingly from a distance – that stability and high standards of living are achieved by advanced technological know-how. This is completely false. Such a standard is achieved only by intelligent use of birth control and the limiting of population growth as near to bare replacement level as possible. To underline this, an overview has been taken of Victorian Britain at the turn of the century.

As the bells rang out the last day of 1899 and brought in the first of 1900, Britain was arguably the most advanced nation, technologically speaking, on Earth. Beyond that, and certainly beyond all argument, she had the largest empire the world had yet seen. This premier position was further bolstered by abundant energy supplies found in rich coal seams throughout large areas of her home territory. These both fuelled her industries and the largest mercantile fleet ever created. The latter established a formidable two-way process; it exported manufactured goods of high standard to what was virtually an open market at the far ends of the Earth and at the same time it brought back an enormous range of raw materials (not forgetting foodstuffs) previously in short supply. These all came at rock-bottom prices, or more truthfully were stolen from peoples who had no idea of their true value and were coerced into making cheap sales. On this basis the entire population of Britain should have lived in luxury. Yet in truth only a tiny minority enjoyed such wealth. The remainder lived in squalor, and often came near to starvation.

The political viewpoint sees only horrific social inequality. It supposes that the answer lies in a reformed social structure. The uncomfortable truth lies in the fact that an average family size of ten to twelve children was commonplace. At the same time the turn of the century happened to coincide with a period in which better sanitation and medical services had been provided: this cut back on what had once been high mortality rates and low life expectancy. Not surprisingly, Britain thus experienced an unsustainable population explosion. Under such enormous pressures no political structure, no matter what its ethos, organisational ability or transparency of motive, could possibly achieve a stable and sustainable future for its people. The crisis was solved only by accelerating the process of decanting all surplus people overseas. This in turn created misery and eventual conflict for the indigenous and 'primitive' peoples of those areas. But this is an aspect many British people would prefer to forget.

Affluence in Britain itself finally arrived only when a family size of two or three children became the norm. At the same time, and as a direct consequence, colonial acquisition became unnecessary. Britain could then have lived in peace with itself. However, as often happens, past misdeeds were to catch up on it. They did so in the form of a frustrated new nation brought into being by Bismarck.

★

The responsibility for the outbreak of the First World War (European Resource War) lies principally with Britain, France, Holland and tiny Belgium, rather than with Germany. By denying the newly created German nation a similar opportunity to establish the pattern of colonial conquests – providing, as it did, space to decant surplus population and the opportunity to exploit such colonies of their valuable resources – an explosive situation was created. Any spark would have brought about the horror of Total War, this either before 1914 or after it. Historians would be better employed examining the statistics for Germany's import of vital new energy sources, metals and ores, rather than recounting the tiresome and ridiculous antics of heads of state and political riffraff generally.

However, the responsibility for the Second World War (Second Resource War, which was in effect a mere continuation of unfinished business from the First) certainly lies with Germany – aided in this instance by Italy and Japan. Both the motivation and the means to wage aggressive war were present. In each of these countries birth control was discouraged so that the production of future cannon fodder could be ensured. This was in sharp contrast with the declining birth rates among the former colonial powers. It also contrasts sharply with a more liberal atmosphere in which freedom was gradually being given to women to run their own lives and have control over their own bodies.

★

The evolutionary 'thrust' or direction taken by every living creature or organism on this planet is toward greater and greater diversification. The human animal is in no way immune to, or indeed excluded from this thrust. Punctuated evolution, a state in which lack of environmental change allows a creature to remain more or less unchanged for hundreds of thousands (or at an extreme for millions) of years, in no way alters the overall picture which confronts us. Within this picture another basic scenario is firmly planted; it so happens that the biomass is a vast collection of interrelated and interdependent species, ensuring that no form of life within it can exist in haughty isolation.

Because of this extremely complex interrelationship, together with the interdependence so formed with every other living creature or organism, it should now be evident that man destroys flora and fauna and other organisms on a vast scale throughout the world ultimately to his own peril.

Nature employs a series of checks and balances throughout the biosphere; however, this is a system that man supposes he can now evade. It is a tragic error. This system can be ignored or supposedly bypassed only for a limited time. The riposte, when it comes, will be all the more severe if not catastrophic.

*

If we narrow our vision and begin to think of the human condition in purely political terms, then the greatest dangers now accruing from the population explosion in many areas of the world will come from conflicts caused by mass migrations. Many of what were formerly colonial territories and fragile emergent states in Africa, Asia, South and Central America are now being destabilised by either mass migration, or persistent immigration in the opposite direction. While it is impossible to lay blame on people attempting to escape from their present wretched state of destitution, it is even more difficult to prevent them from moving into areas which, for the moment at least, appear to enjoy prosperity. At the same time such massive movements cannot go on year after year. Sooner or later host countries will begin to resent the continual intake. Deep within the human psyche lie purely instinctive reaction patterns: the first of these and the most basic concerns personal survival; the second involves the bond formed with specific cultures, religions and traditions. Thus all well-meaning talk of a multiracial and multicultural society becomes possible in the host country only while relative prosperity lasts; as soon as a downturn becomes apparent then serious levels of conflict will become inevitable. Basically Nature employs a quite fundamental 'thrust'; this 'stimulates' (or, in evolutionary terms, produces by accident) a movement in which all creatures can be seen to progress toward greater and greater diversity. Such a 'thrust' wholly rejects amalgamation, absorption or integration, call it what you will, in which one subspecies could be expected to merge with another. And where the human animal is concerned, it remains an observable fact that people stubbornly persist in clinging on to their ethnicity – they cling to peculiarities of language, religion and distinctive customs, even when thousands of miles away from their homeland. It is an instinct that has survived purely because the ancestral line, stretching back as it does at least a million years, has used this to great effect as a survival factor. The human animal cannot now suddenly throw this instinct overboard. In the face of new circumstances it is simply retained. Each individual feels that ease of communication and of understanding are most readily achieved within small tightly knit communities speaking their own language and observing their own customs. They are not to be found within a huge and diverse mass; therefore, integration must be resisted.

However, recently some isolated instances of what appears to be the reversal of these powerful instincts would seem to disprove my thesis. It might therefore be profitable to look briefly at the example of South Africa and the collapse of a regime where the segregation of two very different peoples was actually enshrined in law. Here we suddenly see what appears to be sweetness and light emerging from an era in which very dark and demonic forces operated. The release of Nelson Mandela from a long prison sentence and his astonishing elevation within a short timescale to the presidency of new South Africa (I write these lines in 1995) has brought about worldwide euphoria. Black and white races with wholly different outlooks on life and cultural backgrounds, now seem to be setting out on a new path of hope and reconciliation. Yet unless a vital factor is solved all is doomed to failure. That factor is of course population control.

Here we find a fundamental difference between black and white races in the attitude they take to life as a whole. Generally speaking, black races have a fatalistic attitude; they accept life as it is, including all the disappointments, sorrows and often quite savage realities that from time to time make their presence felt in this world. And moreover – and this is crucial – they do not look into the future to anticipate such savagery. Whites (again generally speaking) resist fatalism. They fight against it. They do not lightly agree that 'what will be, will be'. If there seems some prospect of changing uncomfortable or decidedly unpleasant circumstances then they propel themselves into activities that attempt to change them. And, crucially, they look a little further ahead to anticipate trouble, though not always successfully. Certainly in the vital area of procreation they are not fatalistic: they do not accept that they must continue to produce large broods of children without any thought about their future. This is particularly true concerning available resources and the terrible risk of the unsustainability of their basic well-being. As a result they have successfully found methods to control fertility and have subsequently reaped the rewards.

In contrast, black races find such an attitude incomprehensible. If Nature has seen fit to make them unusually fertile, then so be it! Enjoy it! In South Africa particularly, the situation is all the more dangerous in that the black races now have such high expectations. They hope for access to high standards of living within the shortest possible time span. Yet at the same time they continue to have children well above the population replacement level. They appear to have forgotten that Nature still operates her checks and balances. A family size of eight to ten children is still commonplace and fails to raise an eyebrow. A crisis situation is therefore not far away.

Probably the first signs of the descent back into the horrors from which South Africans have so recently emerged will come in the farming areas. Here, workers on predominantly white-owned agricultural holdings will be tempted to seize land by force. They will see it as a basic survival strategy for themselves and their ever increasing number of children and grandchildren. Whites will be driven off by threats to their lives or by actual murder. And once this becomes an established pattern even the undoubted charisma and persuasive qualities of Nelson Mandela will fail to stop the drift to anarchy.

Turning to other areas of Africa where the presence of whites is minimal (and not in itself an obstacle to unity and co-operation), all attempts by black leaders to bring stability and some basic form of civilised living to their peoples will also be doomed to failure -- that is if the crucial factor of birth control is not seen as a top priority. Fatalism retained in this sector guarantees failure. It is significant that the horrific ethnic cleansing attempts by the Hutu against the Tutsi (and the reverse) have taken place in one of the most densely populated areas of Africa. It is hardly necessary to observe that it has one of the highest birth rates in the world. Many other African states have almost identical rates, but their populations are spread over larger areas. It is only a matter of time before similar ethnic cleansing incidents will occur. This is, after all, a continent both dominated and cursed by endless tribal rivalries; thus the process is made that much more vicious.

As for Northern Africa, in the swathe of land bordering the Mediterranean, the population pressures are only slightly less severe. The current regimes in Morocco, Algeria, Tunisia and Egypt will all have the greatest difficulty in maintaining stability. The poorest classes of society, as always, will fail to see that their misfortune and misery is self-inflicted; they will fail to see the correlation between their failure to restrict their birth rate with penury and social instability. They will turn to fundamentalist religious leaders who ask them simply to put their trust in God. This will in no way alter the basic situation. But it will at least slyly alter expectations; continued privation will then be excused as 'the will of God' or, more cunningly still, the lack of sufficient faith! Given such a scenario, fundamentalism will sweep through all these states unless rapid measures are taken to introduce acceptable birth control methods.

The situation in the Middle and Far East (with the exception of China and Japan) is hardly better. The present economic boom in rapidly developing countries such as South Korea, Indonesia, Burma and Thailand is not, after all, based on the discovery of valuable new-found resources (such as new oil fields, deposits of highly valuable ores such as chromium, uranium, platinum, etc.) but on an economic sleight of hand. It is an artificial economic boom. It is centred mainly on manufacturing what are no more than superfluous technological 'nick-nacks', even children's toys, games and other distractions already made in the West. The sole distinction is that these undercut Western price ranges. Shady entrepreneurs have also borrowed large sums of money from shallow-thinking bankers with which they have now transformed once beautiful and ancient cities into veritable Manhattans. Tall office blocks now dominate the skyline in servile imitation of what they suppose to be the most powerful natural force on Earth; indeed the triumph of the God Mammon is shouted out at every angle. It all looks so impressive to those who see only the outer shell of things. Inwardly it is all emptiness and a sham. The so-called 'Tiger Economies' will collapse sooner or later. Their foundations are built on the shifting sands of unsustainable population increase with its attendant social instability.

As for the Philippines, physically set at least in geographical terms within this new Eastern 'dynamism', it still sees the most extreme of pressures. Of course it never became a member of the Tiger Economy in the first place. And unless the malign influence of Cardinal Sin is somehow significantly diminished or bypassed, then the future for this nation can only be one of chaos and complete social disintegration.

Turning to the saga of the Israeli–Palestinian conflict, it is predictable that the charade of peace conferences will follow in quick succession. Leaders will line up for their photo opportunities, will give the usual empty speeches, and then depart with acclaim. Promises of Nobel Peace prizes will no doubt be whispered in the background. Yet the Gaza strip has the highest birth rate in the world and Ultra-Orthodox Jews come very close behind. Each claim the other's territory as population pressure inexorably mounts.

Turning to Europe, the only country which has failed to make any headway in restricting population increase is the formerly communist-ruled Albania. Here, the birth rate is not only by far the highest in Europe, but wins a very favourable position in the one-hundred-metre population sprint, as you might say, in the entire world. This, combined with a notable lack of any natural resources of any consequence, can only mean that it will become an equally notable trouble spot. Optimists may point to Japan. Here too there are no natural resources to speak of, but at least it has a docile population, highly regimented, industrious, inventive and imbued with an astonishing work ethic (not forgetting a sensible attitude to birth control), Albania seems to display the exact opposite. Those few Europeans who have visited Albania since the collapse of the communist regime, speak of an ill-disciplined people given to endless internal political feuding amongst themselves or pursuing age-old vendettas which have been passed down from generation to generation. These often end in murder. These reports may be biased or inaccurate; what is undeniable, however, is that large numbers of Albanians, in an attempt to avoid destitution, have (over three decades) crossed over into adjacent countries – the most notable of these being the former Yugoslavia. Choice of country is usually dictated by each individual's claim to religious affiliation. Although (as in Yugoslavia) the former communist regime attempted to erase all trace of religion, claiming it to be the first truly atheistic state, the population nevertheless retained (usually in secret) a tie with their ancestral religions. Thus Albania is said to be two thirds Moslem, with the remaining third being made up of Greek Orthodox, Roman Catholic and a few true atheists. Those Moslems who crossed into neighbouring countries therefore chose either Bosnia or Kosovo, where fellow Moslems made them welcome; Orthodox crossed into Macedonia or Greece, where fellow Greek Orthodox could be relied on for help; while Catholics crossed by very ancient and leaking cargo ships into Italy. Here fellow Roman Catholics were less accommodating. They suspected that a large proportion were in fact Moslem and an attempt was made to send the majority back across the Adriatic. And as one may now readily accept, the break-up of Yugoslavia into separate states was also dictated by ancestral religious affiliation. Tragically, Tito was dominated by political doctrines that minimised the problems inherent in a multicultural and multiracial society. Worse, having over the years of his rule partially achieved a mixed population, many now found themselves on the wrong side of invisible borders. Thus Serbian Orthodox found themselves the object of ethnic cleansing in Croatia; similarly, Catholic Croatians were ethnically cleansed from Serbia. In Bosnia there was a three way division. Here the majority were Moslem but with a substantial minority of Serbs and Croats living largely in rural areas, the conflict proved to be the most bitter and costly. The carnage would have continued until all sides were totally exhausted but for the intervention of European states, backed by the USA.

A temporary peace has now been secured (I write in 1996), but will last only until population pressures and suitable numbers of young men to act as cannon fodder subsequently react with the political aspirations of the various sectarian leaders.

In Kosovo – a province which the Serbs persistently claim to be their sacred territory and about which other Europeans are unable to make any informed decision either way – the influx of refugees from Albania coupled with the unsustainable population increase of the resident Moslems, remains a tinderbox where any stray spark will ignite further conflict. Fearing greater and greater sanctions imposed on them, these Kosovan Moslems now demand independence, or, at the very least, autonomous status. Up to this point the Moslem population has not taken up arms and provoked open conflict. But time is running out. However, few Europeans understand or seem to care – the British foremost among them. But then the British have never understood other people's territorial problems. They have after all been blessed by being an offshore island: here the sea makes a very distinctive marker of territorial boundaries. And who can quarrel with the sea? The terrible tragedy in Bosnia, for example was all the more incomprehensible to the British in that the Moslem population seemed identical, in outward physical appearance at least, to the Serbs and Croats. Many were and are blue-eyed, fair-haired and seemingly racially identical to northern Europeans. Moreover, few had truly fundamentalist religious devotion to Islam – the sort that might make them bigoted and fanatical. Thus the savagery that developed particularly during the siege of Sarajevo was all the more inexplicable. Yet the British have very convenient memory lapses. Only a few years previously, they themselves had sent a task force virtually to the other end of this earth to rescue British citizens and reclaim the Falkland Islands – this despite the fact that this territory was, geographically, more properly within the 'sphere of influence' of Argentina. How then can we be so critical of the Serbs? They may well be misguided in seeing themselves as a bastion against the creeping influence of Islam, but they can hardly be demonised simply for resenting illegal immigration. To make a crude comparison, imagine if the Asian population in and around Bradford in England, the majority ethnic group in that area, suddenly demanded autonomous status? What if they persistently encouraged illegal immigration from Asia generally? In point of fact a certain Dr Saddiki has already set up a so-called 'Moslem Parliament' and plans to organise Moslem schools in Britain to facilitate what he feels is the only proper educational regime suitable for his ethnic group. Who can blame him? He is after all only following his instinctive feelings regarding his cultural identity and devout religious beliefs. Nevertheless, he seems to remain blind to the immense harm that he may incur in the area of race relations – let alone the possible future repercussions should Britain see a sharp fall in her economic well-being. It could well be another Kosovo in the making should current trends be maintained.

Yet it is not really a close parallel if one tries looking at the matter from a different angle. Using such an angle it can be seen that most Islamic Kosovans – apart, that is, from their distinctive religion and their contempt for birth control – live a kind of life that is broadly European in outlook. In contrast, most British Asians seem determined to hang on to an outlook that is continents apart. For them, integration in its fullest sense is wholly rejected. And it is impossible for their Caucasian hosts to be critical of this 'decision'; it is after all only what the immigrant community's deeply felt instincts regarding identity demand of them. Nevertheless, herein lies a grave danger.

*

The greatest threat to stability among the affluent nations in the West – apart that is from continued immigration from destitute or warring countries abroad – is the rise in criminal activity from within. And nobody is prepared to consider a genetic and indeed eugenic alternative to the present policy of mere 'containment' of such criminality – if containment it is!

The futile policy of blindly going on as before clearly demands building and equipping yet more and more prisons. Sadly most nations follow this course despite every indication that it is a pathetically inadequate solution.

Criminals are mostly born, seldom made. They are the result of an unfortunate genetic handout that takes place even at conception. The chromosomes carry within them instructions that determine not just the moral character of the individual but the very construction and workings of the brain. And at the present level of our scientific expertise we cannot of course examine the workings of countless billion neurones. All we can observe is the outward manifestation of inner deficiencies; predictably these show themselves in the individual's attitude to life and in his or her general behaviour. Thus grossly inflated egos and fixation with one's own perceived needs and desires are seen to constitute the basis for criminality. What is more, these defects – to repeat ad nauseam if necessary – formed as they are within the structure of the brain itself, are the result of genetic material passed on from parents, grandparents or even several generations of them. Oddly enough, and in a rather circuitous manner, they reinterpret mediaeval religious concepts of Original Sin. But at the same time we must remember that despite the significance of genetic inheritance there is a further contribution. It is the unique reaction of each individual brain to circumstances and experiences that life happens to throw our way. And every individual has different ones, of course – even identical twins brought up in close contact with each other. These, while duplicating many experiences and feelings, still show some differing individual reactions in certain circumstances. Thus, among the vast majority born singly in a womb, the permutations attending the reactions that everyday chance throws their way is enormous. That is not to forget either that there are also what people like to call somewhat erroneously the 'formative influences' during nurture. Even so, formative or not, a proportion (but significantly smaller number) of criminals may indeed be unlucky enough to be exposed to the influence of criminal parents. In this sense, and this sense only, nurture can be thought of as formative.

Using cold logic, and avoiding all the pitfalls of mere emotional response, the only answer to ever rising crime statistics therefore is to sterilise the prison population should they have more than one child.

At this point one must always remember too that criminality is by no means confined to the lower echelons of society. Perhaps the most damage to a nation's social health comes from those in the upper class, where, as often as not, being in positions of trust and considerable influence, they are able to create the most havoc. The Robert Maxwell saga exemplifies both the mental condition and its syndromes perfectly. Possessing a grossly inflated ego which created unlimited expectations for personal wealth, power and influence, Maxwell seemed to believe at one and the same time that his seed would benefit the world in general. He had a large legitimate family and his many enemies or victims postulate other children out of wedlock. However, it is only fair to say the latter have not surfaced or been proven. The present lengthy investigation of at least two of his sons' activities, until it is finally closed[5], will still leave open the question of inheritance or nurture – that is if the sons' willing involvement in crime is proved. However, as one of Maxwell's sons already has large numbers of children of his own, it would seem that there is a pointer already swinging toward inheritance. He too seems to believe that the Maxwell seed in some abundance will be of benefit to this suffering world.

Beyond criminality posing as high-flying (and legal!) business practice, there is also a distinct danger of society being paralysed by highly organised criminal activities based on the Mafia model. Practitioners of this particular activity of course do not always bother to pose as legitimate business associates; indeed they tend to avoid the public eye rather than delight in its attention. And recently reports from Interpol and other police sources reveal that Russian rather than Italian-born 'executives' of this type have penetrated into areas of both Western Europe and North America. These have already been successful in bringing Russia itself near to a state of economic collapse. By continually and very successfully flouting the law they are also encouraging large numbers of otherwise law-abiding citizens to do likewise. The dictum, 'If you can't beat 'em, join 'em', has a certain unanswerable logic. Millions of Russians therefore engage in 'moonlighting' activities. Worse, even for their 'normal' work they attempt to evade all forms of state taxation. The position has become so desperate that in Russia today tax collectors have to engage a special force of well-armed paramilitary units simply to make some kind of inroad into massive tax evasion. Even then, they are only partially successful in their efforts. And due to such successful competition among their own kind, Russian Mafia members are constantly seeking new territories in which to further their leech-like activities. Meanwhile, if the average Russian fails to abandon the naive view that nobody should pay state taxes, it is only a matter of time before this state descends

---

[5] It is equally necessary to note that his sons have subsequently been found innocent.

into chaos, or the further dismemberment of its parts.

It can also be shown that a close connection exists in the criminal world with worldwide drug cartels. These come either from Asia or Central America, including of course the offshore Caribbean islands. And the small fry who work for the drugs barons ironically often pose as asylum seekers during entry into the affluent West – which of course they are in a sense, while evading the attentions of their own struggling and rarely successful law authorities.

*

The extended use of Newtonian laws of motion, in particular the third, which states 'to every action there is an equal and opposite reaction', and which I have now used in this essay to embrace all human activity, means that to every apparent advantage there are also grave disadvantages.

Making a further addition to Newtonian law, I have also observed that most of these disadvantages are hidden and unexpected; moreover, realisation of their presence takes some considerable time to penetrate human consciousness. This is because the starry-eyed originators of 'progress' adopt partisan attitudes. Not surprisingly, these are of course linked to overblown expectations of pure advantage. Subsequently, they then hold on to a form of Dickensian 'great expectations' with ever increasing desperation.

To offer an obvious example: forty years ago the euphoria that surrounded the first production of electricity by the nuclear industry, was starry-eyed in the extreme. Many scientists (but not all) were rash enough to support the view that the consumers' bills for electricity would become 'dirt' cheap. In fact euphoria reached a point where some predicted it would make metering to individual households unnecessary! The series of miscalculations or indeed realms of fantasy entered into at this time are extraordinary. As a further example, the problems surrounding the eventual build-up and final disposal of nuclear waste were not even touched on. As for the dangers of lung and skin cancer, which were almost inescapable for those who mined the uranium ore (not forgetting the physical and economic cost of refining) these too were completely overlooked.

Forgotten in like manner were the political factors surrounding the whereabouts of the most productive sources. Nobody gave them a second thought. In the latter case, some of the world's most productive mines happened (during the 1950s, 1960s and 1970s) to be the property of the apartheid government of South Africa. Concerning the latter and coming down to a narrow political aspect, it can be seen that Britain had to be especially circumspect simply because of this awkward fact. Having no uranium deposits of her own (at least none that were commercially viable) she therefore had to tailor her political relations with this government accordingly. Significantly, Britain did not join other nations in applying far-reaching economic sanctions to the apartheid government of the day!

In a different sphere, but still concerning the misuse of energy sources, if we look at the global picture, then it becomes apparent that the profligate use of fossil fuels, especially by the millions of cars and heavy transport vehicles now choking most roads, will create a crisis in the near future. Not only do they use such energy in the most inefficient manner, gridlocked as they are in every city and country throughout the world, but also there are additional and unforeseen threats. In the form of unused gases, this fuel is transformed into toxic agents emitted by exhausts. Subsequently, it enters countless millions of human lungs. However far more dangerously and indeed more subtly in the long run, it also causes so-called 'greenhouse gases'. These interact in the atmosphere to cause global warming; and this in turn stimulates climate change. There is a further unexpected factor: cars and lorries now also produce what is in effect a pandemic in the form of road deaths and serious injury – annually four thousand five hundred deaths and thirty thousand injuries in Britain alone! Yet these may well be dwarfed by greater calamities in the form of climate change in the future.

But perhaps the most cruel and ironic disadvantage of all concerns the end result of worldwide advances in medical science, together with a better understanding of hygiene. The temporary avoidance of Nature's checks and balances has resulted in a series of population explosions, particularly in Europe in the nineteenth century. This finally brought about in the early part of the twentieth century two world wars. And a riotous peace has graced the remainder of this century. It has also brought starvation and regional breakdowns in many of the world's social or political structures, thereby preventing aid from reaching those who most desperately need it. Need one mention obvious examples like Somalia and Afghanistan? And at this point one should also mention the resurgence of a new and particularly virulent form of disease such as tuberculosis. This disease ravaged Europe and North America for centuries, and indeed was still a major source for concern until the 1950s. Yet it was virtually wiped out in these affluent countries by the discoveries in the field of antibiotics – originally streptomycin. This has now been replaced by rifampicin, isoniazid, and ethambutol. And their use has been extended to other parts of the world where the disease is endemic. Once again these 'miracle' drugs have proved most effective. However the critical proviso is that the dosage must be maintained over an extended period of time, and properly supervised. When warfare or civil unrest of any kind disturbs the treatment regime, then the worst kind of scenario is brought into being – the disease not only returns but does so in new and much more virulent forms! All the triumphs achieved by the new 'wonder' drugs are thus negated. Currently there are now certain forms of TB that resist all that medical science can find in its armoury to fight them! Moreover displacement of refugees carrying these new forms means that the spread of untreatable TB to other parts of the world is almost unstoppable – not excepting affluent countries where it was thought to be totally eradicated!

But aside from open warfare or civil unrest, humanity has yet to accept that advances made by medical sciences also involve a price to pay. Quite simply it is this; death control must be accompanied by birth control. If this is rejected then the ultimate price will be the total elimination of all life on this planet. Nature's basic cyclic rhythms are already being seriously influenced by mankind's activities. Here we need only examine but one factor as an example. It is this: in the destruction of forests to meet our voracious demands for timber and its associated products (let alone its conversion to yet more agricultural land), the simple fact that green foliage, together with the all-too-thin film of green algae on the surface of the oceans, is vital for the recycling of oxygen from carbon dioxide, is wholly overlooked. Or at least it is ignored by the greater mass of the world population. Is it really necessary to mention other threats to the production of oxygen? Is it pertinent to observe that the cocktail of noxious gases that our chemical industries now spew out daily into the atmosphere – not to mention the dumping of waste into the sea, or the oil-spill from tankers – constantly interact with the fragile algae? If disease should ever strike these organisms, then all life on this planet will be slowly asphyxiated as the supply of oxygen is remorselessly depleted.

Given this overall scenario, it is particularly ironic that the well-meaning efforts by scientists such as Dr Norman Borlaug in developing high-yielding strains of dwarf wheat has in reality caused even greater problems. Dr Borlaug, commonly hailed as the 'father of the green revolution', has now brought a significant proportion of world agriculture into a truly perilous state. Not only have farmers everywhere become over-dependent on artificial fertilisers, but worse, the number of strains of wheat used has declined dramatically. Biodiversity, which happens to be the key to avoiding new crop diseases from sweeping unchecked through the vast monoculture systems throughout the world, has now been so drastically cut back that catastrophe can only be just round the corner.

Clearly Dr Borlaug and his co-workers had asked themselves the wrong question from the very start. They asked: how can we feed an exploding world population? This should have been seen as a senseless proposition from its first utterance. One can never feed a continually expanding population; the newly born quickly mop up any of the temporary surpluses that scientific 'breakthroughs' have obtained. All one does is to create for oneself a treadmill where increasingly desperate measures have to be applied merely to keep pace. Moreover, one should always remember the overall reality of the situation. We live on a finite planet. Production of food is finally limited by a finite area for agricultural products. Also to be taken into account is the uncertain nature entailed by temporary or permanent climate change, together the finite resources that must be applied for harvesting and fertilising. Attempting to increase the percentage of ground for agriculture at the expense of what remains of the world's forests, for example, threatens the already precarious and vital oxygen/carbon cycle. Here the greatly reduced green foliage, together with the extremely thin layer of green algae in the sea are responsible for the life-giving process of oxygen recycling. Each day logging companies throughout the world bring huge trees crashing down, while the extremely thin film of phytoplankton in the sea is under even greater threat of disease and final destruction by pollution. And it is foolish in the extreme to expect an increased metabolism in what is left of the photosynthetic organisms in the world's biomass to speed up their production of oxygen just to suit *our* requirements. To repeat therefore: Dr Borlaug asked a fatally flawed question from the very beginning. One can never feed an exploding population. The only relevant and correct question – one that should have been asked in the first instance is: how can we stabilise world population? After that had been answered, then the further question as to how we can give every human being total and lasting freedom from starvation – embracing, as it does, the further attentions of the other three Horsemen of the Apocalypse – becomes relevant.

That Dr Borlaug should receive a Nobel Prize for such short-sightedness is an indication of how pie-eyed even the normally well-informed Nobel committee can become; both they and much of the starry-eyed world never fail to react emotionally rather than rationally in such circumstances. When faced with what seems at first to be such a lifeline thrown to the starving millions, everyone throws their hands in the air and gives a deep-throated cheer for man's ingenuity! Such euphoria drowns out whispered questions and downbeat thoughts of disadvantages. Remember, for every apparent advantage there are always hidden (and delayed) disadvantages! And some not-so-hidden disadvantages are already evident among the rich nations of the West. Here the use of chemical fertilisers has become so over-generous and so unthinking as to do great mischief to all our rivers, including of course the living creatures and organisms that live in them. Other scientists who have subsequently discovered highly effective pesticides (and the commercial giants who have arm-twisted farmers all over the world into buying their products) will also have to learn the hard way that there is no such thing as an 'absolute advantage'. Slowly and surely the disadvantages will begin to appear. But it is a long-term process – so long term and so complex in its interaction with the incredibly subtle strands of interdependency throughout the biosphere, that it is impossible to predict what the final bill will be.

Seen in proper perspective, Dr Borlaug's 'green revolution' has simply brought temporary respite to the misery suffered by the starving millions. Once again the rejection of the principle that death control must be balanced by birth control, has meant that the so-called 'green miracle' has lasted but a single decade. As should have been foreseen, the advantages have been swept away by the remorseless rise in population levels. Misery has once more descended on the extra millions now enabled to be born into this suffering world.

As for the appalling error of sweeping away biodiversity and replacing it with complete dependency on but a few strains of wheat, this now puts the greater part of the world's wheat supply in the gravest danger.

Moving to the flash flooding of the productive lower reaches of so many Asian, African and American agricultural areas, this is caused by mass deforestation of upper reaches and an alteration of established weather patterns. It alone has brought death and destruction almost yearly throughout the 1970s and also in the 1980s. What will it bring in the 1990s?

My further predictions, based as they are on a new reading of Newtonian Law, are that abnormal weather patterns, produced directly from mankind's ever growing and ever mischievous influence on the cyclic rhythms, will cause far greater numbers of deaths and overall misery than have ever been saved by the 'green revolution'. All that Dr Borlaug has done is to delay Nature's riposte, and, by so doing, will surely make the delayed form even more vicious and terrible.

★

TWO FORMIDABLE PARADOXES

My predictions, written as they are in 1995, are naturally based on the proviso that present trends worldwide will be continued without fundamental change. And of course I keep good company with all those who attempt to look into the future, for we all inevitably risk being proven wrong. Some completely unforeseen new factor usually upsets the equation. However, as broadly speaking my predictions are so basic, it is difficult to visualise an unforeseen factor. After all they dare to concentrate simply on the life cycle of all life forms on this planet; moreover they remain within the area concerning the emergence of life and the subsequent fate of all living things to complete that cycle... by experiencing death. Therefore, all that I have pointed out is that, where human beings are concerned, Nature's checks and balances are aided by, and, in some cases superseded by, the Four Horsemen. Thus the life/death cycle has been, and will continue to be, influenced (sometimes spectacularly so) by these galloping figures. Visiting each continent, they will trim back the lives of millions. What is more, they will do so to children and young adults long before their natural life spans are completed. And I doubt very much whether any fundamental alteration is at all possible in such a scenario. After all is said and done, human populations are increasing at such a rate. Worse, the expectations for enhanced lifestyles are now so firmly ingrained. Remember that global communication and info flow generally have reached such fantastic levels that even the most deprived people on this earth have begun to dream of, and strive to attain, enhancement of their lifestyles. Moreover it is an enhancement exemplified by the most affluent nations in the fabled West.

My predictions concerning the future therefore embrace further resource wars, also mass migrations of people due to economic, ethnic, or religious factors. And as these migrations do not take place in a vacuum but necessarily involve making substantial additions to population levels into other areas, then destabilisation of those areas too is the only outcome.

*

Throughout this essay great stress has been put on birth control, implying that it is the sole means of limiting what can only be a further and ultimately catastrophic increase in the world's population. No doubt those who would wish to find as many points of criticism as possible will be quick to point out that taking the statistics for the birth rate in all the various countries alone, without reference to other factors, is totally misleading. One cannot obtain the full picture without reference firstly to infant mortality, secondly to the death rate among the population in general, thirdly the figures for life expectancy, fourthly the proportion of women of child-bearing age, etc. There are so many additional factors, which if ignored (as I appear to) can so easily falsify the picture. However, may I observe I am very well aware of this. There are two crucial reasons why I insist that the birth rate is by far the most significant factor in contributing to social instability and eventual conflict, which is after all the subject of my essay. They are as follows:

Among all young adults who have produced children, the bond formed within days of birth – coupled as they are with very strong instinctive feelings that the child must be protected at all costs – fosters an extreme reaction should their survival be threatened. It is a powerful instinct rarely equalled in the remainder of the animal world. It is, as I have carefully pointed out, proven to be (along with the second crucial factor of our exceptional communicative skills) the reason for mankind's almost miraculous survival in early eras. Again, as has been observed, most other creatures are extremely casual in this matter of offspring survival. A host of species in fact leave it solely to chance. Sheer fecundity alone is relied on to ensure that savage predation coupled with Nature's other means of creating a balance between species, allow just a few to survive. Incidentally too, in this matter of survival it is erroneous to believe that man is the only creature that kills those of its own kind during struggles for territory or the possession of females. In the sheer fight for survival there is now growing evidence that a large number of species – more particularly carnivores – are involved in killing both adults and young of their own kind. There is also growing evidence of cannibalism among some. And while infanticide is not unknown among humans, usually through lack of adequate food (or, in affluent countries, a temporary mental imbalance of the mother immediately following birth), the vast majority of us have been programmed by perhaps a million or more years of evolutionary development to regard the death of infants with feelings that seldom fall short of horror. To repeat, we cannot suppress such reactions.

Consequently if any regime in any area of the world is either unable or unwilling to promote the concept of birth control (and subsequently, in the face of rapid population growth, unable to organise a reasonable supply of the absolute basic necessities to maintain life), then there is only one outcome: public disorder and eventual chaos. Grave threats to survival, particularly of children, trigger off the most extreme of passions! This is instinctive; it cannot be controlled. Destabilisation of that country's social structure then becomes inevitable, and allows immediate entry of the Four Horsemen. And in such a situation it is impossible to convince those who have been the most productive and caring of young human life that they themselves are responsible for the tragedy that befalls them.

The overall debacle becomes the most painful of ironies. That such devotion, and at times supreme self-sacrifice given by most parents to their children – a devotion far surpassing that given by most other creatures in the whole of creation – should be so rewarded and rebound so cruelly, is truly heartbreaking. But the universal laws 'for every action an equal reaction' and 'for every apparent advantage a disadvantage – moreover one that is seldom evident until a considerable time later', still exert their rigid influence, endlessly!

Thus all sections of humanity in all parts of this extraordinary planet of ours must accept family limitation. And they must do so on the simple principle that a family size above that of mere replacement is grossly irresponsible. Failure to do so will ensure that not just human life, but *all* life in its entirety is doomed to extinction. It is as simple as that!

Postscript

The first two chapters of this essay were written in 1993. As the manuscript in its present form was finally submitted to a publisher as late as 1998, a postscript now becomes essential. Not that it is necessary to modify the various theories expounded in any way; the predictions however are a very different matter. These require additional comment, all the more so in that some have already proved accurate.

Essentially, the correlation I have made between high birth rate and social unrest, leading inevitably at a later stage to open conflict, is now, I would hope, impossible to dispute. The sole remaining uncertainty is the time factor involved. Therefore, we shall look briefly (lacking both time and opportunity for more detailed analysis) at those areas of the world that happen to be, as you might say, in the first division league table for exploding birth rates.

Gaza, with a birth rate of fifty-six per thousand, only partly balanced by a shocking infant mortality rate of forty-three per thousand, and an average family size of 7.7 children, has seldom been out of the world news. Coupled indissolubly as it is with the West Bank, which has only marginally smaller figures, both are destined to remain the subject of distressing events. Equally, the high birth rate among ultra-orthodox Israelis (as distinct from other citizens of their state), compounded by immigration mainly from Russia, ensures further conflict. Already it has put severe pressure on land resources and living space. And despite pleas from peace negotiators not to extend current settlements and to refrain from building new ones on Arab land, such work has gone ahead in open defiance. As may be expected, protesting Arabs have rioted. Loss of life, or severe injury, mainly among teenage Arabs, has thus been the set pattern year after year. In turn, Israel has suffered retaliation in the form of human bombers. These have brought carnage to its streets. And if one attempts to speculate on why such supreme sacrifices are made in the Arab cause, I suspect a pathological craving for personal recognition, probably involving teenagers from large families. There are, after all, many Arab families where twelve or more children are commonplace and certainly considerably above the 7.7 average. Thus martyrdom as a bomber may well be chosen among those, who as children sought, yet failed to receive, the attention or recognition they craved. I have no direct evidence for this: even so I find it difficult to believe that martyrdom would be an option within a small and tight family unit. With only two or three children, far closer emotional ties would make such sacrifice unlikely. As for the Israelis, it is significant that another teenager, this time from a large ultra-orthodox Jewish family, has chosen to murder Prime Minister Rabin. The motivation? Rabin was seen as a traitor. Too many concessions were assumed to have been made to the Palestinians. The young assassin typically craved the attention of his little world. And the legacy of this? The sharp divisions within the Israeli state that I, as a mere onlooker (and non-Jew) sensed five years ago, have now become acute. And it is wholly religious in origin. Fanatical ultra-orthodox factions accuse the 'liberals' of betraying their fundamental Jewish identity. They are seen as licentious 'outsiders'! And despite 'ultras' being a relatively small, if vociferous pressure group, it becomes evident that should their persuasive emotionalism gain wider acceptance, then yet another mass exodus will result – yet another Diaspora! This time, however, it will involve solely 'liberal' Jews from Palestine. Tired of endless vituperation they will be persuaded to leave the manic orthodox to fare as best they may.

Certainly my original prediction of continuing conflict between the Arab world (as distinct from Palestinian) and the Israelis, would hold – unless or until the taboo subject of population control is finally broached. The endless shuttle diplomacy has achieved only temporary solutions. The staged handshakes, the mandatory smiles at all those tiresome and endlessly repeated photo opportunities, have (and will) bring only temporary respite. The next atrocity, whether it be at the hand of Jew or Arab, will once more ensure ongoing conflict.

Moving to the next league player, Afghanistan. Here, all-out warfare has now ravaged the country for more than two decades.

This is hardly surprising given a birth rate of forty-nine per thousand. After all, there are ample supplies of cannon fodder. As each generation of children leave their all-too-brief childhood, they are immediately enrolled for military training by the warring factions. Nevertheless, what *is* surprising is the lack of any respite brought on by utter exhaustion of both parties. After all the country has been so ravaged! With food production virtually at a standstill and more homes reduced to rubble, one can only wonder where the opposing factions find 'ready money' to bring in imports of the basic necessities of life, let alone the military hardware. Herein lies a mystery that needs further investigation. While few doubt that Pakistan has, over the years, maintained generous supplies to the fundamentalist faction, while Russia has donated at least intermittently to the opposition, it is also plainly evident that both Pakistan and Russia have severe economic problems of their own. How then do they square the circle? The mystery deepens. There are whispers that some oil-rich Islamic states are propping up Pakistan. Significantly the USA, in a rather hysterical fit of denunciation, recently put a price on the head of the shadowy Islamic militant from that region. What then of the Russian contribution? What indeed? It would be ironic if the IMF's financial support of both Pakistan and Russia were found to be at least partly responsible for funds being siphoned off to sustain the Afghanistan conflict.[1] After all, such an incredible juggling act has been achieved among warring states in Africa, so why not Asia? This factor apart, the misery and suffering that has beset Afghanistan will continue, given the low status accorded women and their use as mere automated producers of cannon fodder.

Predictably too, the India/Pakistan dispute over Kashmir has waxed and waned. It is an ever useful distraction used by both governments when the basic problem of widespread poverty at home makes their surging populations restless and vengeful.

Moving further east, my predictions concerning the 'Tiger' economies of south-east Asia have also proved correct. They were

---

[1] Since these lines were written evidence has come forward of drug-trafficking becoming a factor beyond that of material help from Pakistan and oil-rich backers.

in truth but 'paper tigers'. Indonesia in particular, despite having extensive revenue from oil wells and the export of tin, timber, rubber and vegetable oils, is already a country of grave social inequality, ruled, as it has been by a corrupt military regime. Its future must inevitably be turbulent, given rapid and unsustainable population growth, given too its unusual geophysical structure. Composed of three large islands, three of medium size, and around three thousand small ones, set out like a string of pearls, the quite natural self-isolating tendencies are already present. There is an added religious factor operating in one sector known as East Timor in that it holds to the Catholic faith – this in a region dominated by Islam. However, if you accept my earlier observation that for those suffering social injustice, an alternative faith can be found in Communism, then there are other sectors of Indonesia destined for conflict. In the 1950s such a faith had already found favour in some areas. True, it has now been driven underground, but for how long?

Turning to Africa, here I can only echo my previous summing up: the entire continent is one great disaster area. As one vicious conflict is briefly halted, another erupts elsewhere. On top of this, it is now estimated that twenty million people are infected with AIDS. In some areas it has become pandemic. Worse, some research workers predict that new strains of AIDS will not just sweep through the remainder of Africa, but due to the ease of international travel, spread to the entire world. Personally I believe this to be overstated. However, it *will* have the tragic effect of displacing attention on, or even masking the presence of an even more potent killer! That killer? Tuberculosis! You see AIDS is essentially a sexually transmitted disease, and if one is in a happy, stable, pair-bond relationship (thereby not sexually promiscuous) then the danger is minimal. Rape is the only exception. But this risk can also be minimised if situations for opportunistic rape are avoided. Not so tuberculosis! The new strains of this disease are resistant to former 'miracle' drugs, which lamentably enough were supplied liberally by over-zealous aid workers in Africa and elsewhere. Why, lamentably? Well, despite knowing that strictly controlled medical regimes and correct doses were necessary, these drugs were nevertheless supplied without due caution – this either in war zones or during general civil unrest. The result? Partial or interrupted treatment has meant the emergence of new and far more virulent forms of TB. These cannot be countered by existing drugs. Moreover, in direct contrast to AIDS, one could be sitting next to an unidentified victim in an aircraft, train or bus, where a cough or a sneeze could form the pathway of infection! And while earlier strains of TB have been virtually wiped out by medical science in affluent countries, these new strains will change that triumph into a hollow victory.

One final comment concerning Africa, and an illuminating one! In a long and detailed report recently made by Oxfam, which investigated the causes of the decades-long conflict between Tutsi and Hutus in Rwanda, culminating as it did in the infamous massacre, at no point is any reference made to explosive population growth! Such an omission takes one's breath away. One can only suspect doublethink, closely identified with a way-out religious belief that 'God will always provide'. How such a belief can be maintained in the face of historical events which plainly show that God is unwilling to meddle in His own laws concerning biological 'carrying capacity' remains a mystery. With a population of 805 per square mile, and despite having the richest soils and highest agricultural production in the region, the birth rate of forty per thousand makes the population increase ('doubling time' of only thirty years) wholly unsustainable. Moreover, in general terms a similar picture exists throughout Africa.

Turning finally to Europe and the conflict in what was formerly Yugoslavia. Here again my predictions concerning Kosovo have proved accurate. Painful lessons that should have been learned in Croatia and Bosnia were jettisoned or ignored. Starry-eyed idealists persisted in their demands that a multicultural, multiethnic mix be maintained in the province. Partition, the only possible solution, given the circumstances, was seen as an evil. Yet such a mix can only be successfully achieved in countries where affluence and social stability are buttressed by low birth rates hovering round bare replacement level. But how did such a tragic situation develop in the first place?

During Tito's regime it was confidently expected that the Communist faith would replace what were seen as the outmoded Roman Catholic, Greek Orthodox and Islamic 'superstitions' through the whole of Yugoslavia. Coupled with efforts to create an industrial society out of a mainly agrarian one, Tito visualised a wholly new and vibrant state being born. It mattered little whether migrants from the desperately poor, high birth rate Albania trickled over the border year by year, attracted by the relatively higher standard of living. Quickly rising population totals throughout Yugoslavia were not seen as a problem. They surely underlined the triumph of communist doctrines. But Tito's death, followed by the collapse of Soviet Russia and her empire, quickly undermined the fragile stability. The older religious faiths, assumed to be in irreversible decline, now re-established themselves. Old hatreds were burnished, old ambitions revitalised. Catholic Slovenia, then Croatia, broke away. Blood ran copiously in Croatia. Bosnia, with a much more problematic mix, including as it did a large proportion of Muslims, subsequently saw rivers of blood. Gradual exhaustion, plus economic sanctions imposed by the remainder of Europe, brought an end to military conflict. Yet all efforts to re-establish the old ethnic mix have failed. Each group prefers to live in what are fast becoming rigidly fixed enclaves. Starry-eyed idealists however, still ignorant of underlying biological pressure, persist in their attempts at re-mixing.

Meanwhile Kosovan Albanians increased their pressure to achieve independence from Serbia – a vengeful Serbia where a crypto-communist regime was still smarting from its failure to dominate and maintain the old Yugoslavia. The more moderate and realistic Albanian Kosovans sought autonomy short of independence; the more militant demanded complete breakaway.

Formation of a Kosovan Liberation Army gave the Serbian regime the excuse it had been praying for. Large numbers of extra troops, police and paramilitary units were now sent in to protect Serbian Kosovans and to defend 'Holy Kosovo' from 'terrorists'. These were claimed to be, not without some justification, trained, armed and succoured by neighbouring Albania itself.

POSTSCRIPT

Within three short months, television screens throughout Europe and America began to show Islamic Kosovan farming folk driven from their homes, ever mounting victims of a deliberate policy of ethnic cleansing. They were filmed huddled in their farm carts, pulled by ancient tractors or decrepit horses making their way to the nearest town or border – any border! Covered by plastic sheets to protect them from atrocious weather, these pathetic people had a significant number of children amongst them. Sympathy and a feeling of outrage at their plight – the children in particular – was immediately expressed. Here, my theory of the vital part played by parenting skills during our early ancestry comes into play. We are *so* conditioned by this basic instinct: it immediately activates our response systems. Of all creatures in the biosphere, we alone suffer the greatest trauma when we see our offspring, or even those of total strangers, threatened by disease or physical attack. We never accept that we, as are all others in the biosphere, are subject to Nature's checks and balances; never acknowledge that an explosive population increase will inevitably see the arrival of the Four Horsemen of the Apocalypse. Serbian thugs and psychopaths, recruited, so it is alleged, from prisons, were now subconsciously carrying out the programme demanded by those horsemen. But do not misunderstand me: I am not for one moment suggesting these psychopaths should have been allowed to carry on with their massacres. Equally, this applies to the Kosovo Liberation Army. In like manner their own sprinkling of thugs should not be allowed to continue slitting the throats of Serbian farmers and their children – as they have done! Both children and adults of either ethnic group, once born into this world have an unalienable right to life. We would be less than human if we denied it, or indeed failed to protect them in every way. But prior to conception? That is a very different matter. If I say I regard contraception as the only way of saving life in the future, nobody should regard it as a sick joke, or a contradiction in term. And of course not just in Kosovo. Among exploding populations throughout the world.

As I write, troops from a variety of NATO countries have crossed into Kosovo and are rapidly occupying the province. Throughout Europe and America there is widespread feeling of relief, even a degree of triumphalism. This is wildly premature: it is only the beginning. The Kosovan crisis will remain, and will do so indefinitely, unless or until the basic problem of contraception is addressed. Those children we saw huddled so pathetically in farm carts, and who subsequently reached refugee camps across the border, will eventually return. In five, ten, fifteen years' time, depending on their present age, these will become sexually active. If, like their parents, they reject the concept of birth control, then where in such an impoverished country will they find the basic necessities of life for *their* children in turn? The resources within Kosovo are wholly inadequate. As for bringing in foreign capital and entrepreneurs to utilise that one remaining resource – the work ethic of the people – this too is an exercise rapidly coming to an end. Factories all over the world are churning out goods at such a rate that over production will cause all but the most efficient to go to the wall. A further factor: factories are becoming more and more automated, and workforces smaller. Affluent countries of the world are awash with consumer goods; poor countries less and less able to afford them.

By use of a mass doublethink, European politicians still declare that Kosovo remains within Serbia's territorial boundaries, this despite the fact that the few remaining Serbs will either be driven out, or find it prudent to leave. Thus, all the prior mouthing of 'restoring the ethnic mix' will then be seen for what it is – empty rhetoric. Croatia and Bosnia have already given the lie to this, but the starry-eyed, as always, are adept at looking the other way. Sadly they will continue to use the sterile political viewpoint: they will remain ignorant of all those subtle biological factors that continue to dominate what we claim to be a much vaunted human attribute – the facility to utilise logic and reason. It is this facility, we must remember, that supposedly lifts us into a state of consciousness triumphantly above the level reached by the remainder of the animal kingdom.

May, 1999

Appendix I

Berkeley and Hume expound a truly formidable 'immaterialist' and 'subjective idealism' doctrine, usually summed up by the term 'solipsism', which questions the entire existence of the 'real' world. Although they differ from each other slightly in content – Berkeley claiming all our sense data is provided directly from God, while Hume, circumventing any supernatural agency, doggedly insists the 'exterior' world may well be nothing more than a figment of our own imagination – it becomes apparent that both approaches are almost impossible to disprove. In the course of the philosophical argument Berkeley and Hume also question the entire basis for causality. Advances in scientific investigation almost two centuries later, more especially in the realms of nuclear physics, have tended to strengthen their position. Having considered the argument over a lengthy period I nevertheless believe there may be a tiny crack in this weighty structure; here a lever may be inserted to open the fissure a little further. However, this relates to 'normal' human affairs; it does not presume to enter the purely scientific debate concerning the activities of subatomic particles, where 'events' are so mysterious as to appear to defy all earlier laws of physics and all truly rational approaches. Moreover, even in the realms of day-to-day human affairs, I advance my argument with caution: I am not a professional philosopher and I am aware that those who are may well find my attempt amateurish; indeed, it may well be bedevilled at the very outset by a basic misunderstanding of the Berkeley/Hume position. Should this be so, then the professionals who have the advantage of an intimate knowledge of the field – certainly the solipsistic argument at their fingertips – will dismiss it immediately as worthless. Nevertheless I will persist because my argument revolves round one particular phenomenon common to the process of human thought that philosophers rarely attack with sufficient vigour. What is this phenomenon? Well, while all will agree that sense data (omitting the debate as to how it materialises)

Appendix I

must somehow be present within the mind as the basic essential to make conscious thought possible, then even so, there is this curious state of what one can only call 'partial' understanding of such sense data. And we come up against this curious phenomenon constantly and on a daily basis.

If we actually go back to the 'common sense' belief that the 'real' or' outside' world does in fact exist, then we have no difficulty in accepting 'partial' understanding. Thus, if we see such a basic thing as a tree or a house, and at which point some awkward person asks us what *kind* of a tree or house, then we may find ourselves at a loss. If we are not well informed on such subjects and can hardly distinguish between an oak tree and an ash tree, and certainly have no grasp of architectural styles, all we can say with certainty is that the shapes conform to our broad conception of trees and houses. If we are subsequently told that the tree is a maple and that the house is typically that of the seventeenth century, then we admit to our lack of specialised knowledge. But if we take the solipsist position seriously, then how is it that we may fail to know and interpret our sense data fully at one moment then be *completely* cognisant at the next? How do we fail to know a maple at one moment, but subsequently summon up the information at the next?

Going into the matter more deeply and at a more serious level: we know we receive from a wide variety of sources (equally what we believe to be 'real-life' people) a mass of sense data, which is not always precise and clear at its very source. Thus, for instance, should we happen to be in a military or highly structured organisation (such as the civil service) we may sometimes receive a direct order from those in authority over us which is so badly expressed that it can cause utter bewilderment. This in turn may lead to our confused and sometimes even anguished attempt to either question that order, or, by using our own initiative, take action that we think might well befit the circumstance. At other times we may be so totally confused as to fail to know how to interpret the sense data, or indeed what action we should subsequently take. And in fact, throughout history, emperors, kings or high-ranking officials have often given orders expressed in such a muddled way as to produce quite chaotic or indeed tragic consequences; equally, during times of open war, commanders on the field of battle have unfortunately given such imprecise or wholly ambiguous orders as to ensure their defeat – this, despite often having superior forces! And on an even more comprehensive scale, entire civilisations have fallen because both leaders and the population at large have totally misread data available to them.

Misunderstanding our sense data takes place all the time and in a variety of situations. For example, if we take a much more trivial and relaxed situation, say at a coffee break during the working day, then even here the exchange of information may be riddled with ambiguity. Simply because we *are* relaxed, this in itself tends to allow us to talk carelessly and without precision, so that we constantly misunderstand each other and have to correct our statements. Frequently one hears the earnest warning 'No, no, what I mean is...' Further down the slippery slope of incomprehension, one might receive a brief wave from someone at a distance, or even something as insubstantial as a nod and a wink! A proportion of these gestures we will understand immediately and we will act on such information in the appropriate manner; however, a very large proportion will cause surprise and confusion. Some data will be so lacking in any kind of direct meaning as to defy all understanding, like for instance, the wave from a distance. Here we might have only glimpsed the vague outline of the person who waved. Puzzled, we ask ourselves, 'Now who on earth was that?' As for the wink, it often leaves us completely at a loss.

Now why, on *any* level of importance, should *partial* understanding of sense data occur? It becomes especially curious when, as Berkeley argued, one's sense perceptions are directly donated by God himself! There is less difficulty with Hume. No longer troubling to us with the question of God's omnipotence and benevolence, Hume as a 'freethinker' and agnostic, insisted that all our perceptions and sense data were merely the collective figments of our own imaginations. To repeat; if so, then why should so much of our daily input of sense data be only partially understood? And why should it then be subject to so much error? Why do we persist in fooling ourselves that we only partially understand at one moment then fully understand the next?

To further illustrate why I find such imprecision of understanding – an inability to understand what is after all held to be essentially one's own internal perception – quite pivotal to the argument, I put forward the following counter-argument.

I believe the 'real' and 'outer' world exists beyond myself largely because I am also aware of an outpouring of genius in the fields of the sciences and the arts that make me feel acutely conscious of my own ignorance and lack of creative talent. These outpourings, I am convinced, could not possibly have been created within my own being and by my own intellectual capacity – given my consciousness of personal defects and restricted gifts of understanding. For example, during my schooldays there were intervals where one was forced to make choices between the arts and the sciences. And having chosen not to take mathematics at sixth form, I am now unable to deal with and fully comprehend advanced forms of mathematics. Consequently, I cannot follow in full detail much of the nineteenth- and twentieth-century bases for scientific development. Mathematical formulae produced by, say, Maxwell, Boltzmann, Lorentz, Planck or Einstein, inevitably become a foreign language. To have any kind of grasp of the scientific advances involved, I have to rely on other scientists operating at an intermediate stage and urgently concerned with passing on knowledge to students and a wider public generally. Thus these equations have to be translated into concepts embraced by language; moreover, they have to be expressed in simplified form via, as I have already touched on, the enthusiastic help of specialist scientists attempting to explain difficult concepts to a wider audience. This becomes essential before I can get to grips with the broader application and meaning. Thereby, I acknowledge a substantial debt to those dedicated scientific 'communicators' such as Professors Banesh Hoffman, Victor Weisskopt and others, who have been so eager to convey their own sense of bubbling joy and excitement over recent advances in physics; equally I am indebted to such people as Professors Richard Dawkins and Steve Jones who do likewise for biology and its associated subdivision of genetics. We all owe these people a great deal for their efforts in bringing the work of the specialist into some kind of generalised comprehension by others outside their field. Even so, I am sadly aware that I have only a patchy and imperfect concept of current scientific achievement. And again I find this curious and puzzling if I accept the Berkeley/Hume argument. Why should any sense perception be only partial or imperfectly understood? Yet, on the other hand, I immediately find this perfectly understandable if the 'real' world out there exists after all – if such scientists were real flesh and blood and their intellectual ability was not a figment of my own imagination. But returning to the solipsist position, how can I imagine a book in which such advanced and subtle forms of thought are fully expressed at one moment, but after reading some of its pages allow myself to imagine I can no longer either fully grasp or visualise the argument in detail – this especially when I come to difficult or unusually complex expositions? How can I, at one and the same moment, create out of my own mind the visual concept of a printed page containing highly complex information, yet equally at the selfsame moment convince myself I cannot understand it?

Pursuing this further, I feel on even safer ground in the realm of the arts, particularly that of music. Listening to, and sometimes performing music, happens to be an enthusiastic and welcome injection into my sense data perception almost daily. Here, the demonstration of pure genius, and the peaks of human achievement reached in outpourings by Bach, Handel, Haydn, Mozart, Beethoven, Schubert and Brahms for example, fill me with astonishment and reverence – so much so that I am convinced they reach out to make a tenuous contact with the Creator Himself... or what Einstein called the 'Sublime Intelligence'. I am quite sure that I myself could never have created such inspired work. And I believe I can prove this, at least to my own satisfaction, in the following way.

Now although I can play the less technically demanding sections of the Mozart and Beethoven piano sonatas, I can do so only with the aid of the scores. Should someone remove the score, then I immediately begin to stumble and falter. My memory of the music, unlike that of a professional concert pianist is not good. Now, if I happen to believe in the solipsist position,

Appendix I

which insists that Mozart's and Beethoven's sonatas are figments of my own imagination, then why should I chose to make life difficult for myself by imagining someone abruptly removing the scores – which renders me helpless and floundering – although I was perfectly able to see the notes and translate their musical meaning a moment earlier? Further, if I were asked to reproduce any of those sonatas on a blank sheet of manuscript paper, then while I might be able to write down the melody (which for me is the easier part, mostly written as it is for the right hand) I would have the greatest difficulty with the bass progression. The latter is, after all, written mostly for the left hand and forms either a rhythmic support, a subtle interaction or musical foil. Worse, if I were asked to write down the individual parts of a string quartet, even after being presented with the first few bars written for each instrument, I would flounder from the very beginning. As for a whole symphony, even those I know particularly well and especially love, the subtleties of their forms and the inventive nature of the parts given to each section of the orchestra are such that I would be completely flummoxed – this at the very first bar! For this reason I have the utmost admiration for those who have tried to complete (in as faithful a style as possible) the unfinished or partly sketched manuscripts left to us on the deaths of these towering musical geniuses.

Now surely if it is possible to hear and fully embrace musical statements produced by a hi-fi system and indeed be stimulated to reach states of exaltation or sheer ecstasy, how is it also possible to flounder helplessly when asked to write down such statements on blank manuscript paper? How is it that one can be intimate with say Bach's *St Matthew* or *St John's Passion*, then, as it were, be 'unknowing' when that musical statement comes to an end. Here, Berkeley's concept of 'immaterialism' may of course cover this objection. He may insist that my sense perception, although donated directly from God is such that He has not see fit to gift me with both an intense 'appreciation' and actual musical dexterity in performing – let alone composing. That particular obstacle though is not apparent in David Hume's argument, because he insists all my sense perception is created by my own whimsey. But I would argue with Berkeley that God would surely not tease me in such a way. Why, for example, should He allow me to believe I can actually hear Schubert's astonishing 'other world' *Quartet No. 15 in C Major D.887*, in its entirety and be so deeply moved by it as to be on the verge of tears; moreover, constantly strive to hear it again and again played by different performers, each with a different interpretation? And then why, after all this effort is made in one form of sense perception, should He disallow me from translating what I hear in my head into crotchets, quavers and semiquavers on manuscript paper?

Someone with a more agile mind than mine may find a counter-argument here, but I cannot.

Appendix II

The way in which the human mind identifies concepts and sense data needs fundamental rethinking. I am convinced we must reconsider the matter by referring back to the gradual formation of our individual perception of bits of sense data during our infancy. Only by such a dramatic regression (but hopefully not becoming a retrogression) can we reach the truth of the matter.

Put quite simply: here, during our first introduction to our world, the blurred images and sounds, those strange and frightening sensations, thrust on us as we emerge from the womb – sensations essentially outside our hazy sense of 'being' – cannot become meaningful and sensible unless, or until, we begin to recognise the existence of diametrically opposed phenomena. Probably the first of these is 'light' as opposed to the virtual 'darkness' of the womb. Coming within days of this, in all probability, is the feeling of 'wetness' as opposed to 'dryness' as we are repeatedly bathed. Coming shortly after, the sensation of warmth as opposed to cold, of hunger as opposed to fullness, movement as opposed to stillness. Later still, we begin to form the concept of silence by necessarily comparing it with the general cacophony that occurs during daylight hours (or the earlier sound of the mother's heartbeat in the womb) as opposed to the silence of night... and our isolation causes us to cry out in panic! And so the process goes on and becomes more and more complex.

Very much later, as we approach the age of three or four perhaps, there are many more subtle and complex comparisons to be made. These become what I will now call the process of making a 'quality establishment' between entities that are *not* exact opposites – but merely differences in kind. Take the problem of establishing colour difference for instance. Having earlier conceptualised the much more direct quality of tonal extremes – black as opposed to white – there may be difficulty in establishing the 'quality' of colours such as redness, blueness, yellowness. However, once this hurdle is overcome, and having mastered the essential differences between the primary colours, then comes the more difficult problem of secondary colours: green, brown, purple. Indeed some children are unable to distinguish between these for several years. As for tertiary mixtures, some are unable to establish, for example, what turquoise 'is' (that is, its essential spatial position between blue and green) until their teens – and here I am wholly excluding those with colour-blindness which is of course recognisably a medical condition. And, as with colours, so too with all other qualities and phenomena where we are unable to find *direct* opposites. In short, everything we establish as sense data can *only be achieved initially* by becoming aware of an exact *opposite*. Later, as we grow to adulthood, we refine this by establishing in our minds that not only are there, for example, shades of grey between intense black and intense white in the basic field of tonal range, but infinite gradations between them. These gradations within the totality of our sense data not only occur 'in their own right' so to speak, but often (sometimes very unkindly) influence every individual piece of sense data in every facet of our existence. To repeat: our ability to conceptualise anything depends on this very painfully acquired combination of processes – establishing exact opposites at first, then subsequently minor differences between related things. Equally of course, if we fail to establish the existence of these subtle differences then we *cannot know* and comprehend such data. They simply fail to exist – for those of us with blunted sensitivity at least!

This early establishment of basic opposites during infancy is, however, *such* a gradual process that we tend to forget the original spark of realisation and the essential process of differentiation that occurred. Thus, for some children, teenagers and mentally retarded adults, the realisation of truly 'abstract' ideas such as right and wrong, truth and falsehood, justice and injustice etc. remain in a fog of incomprehension. Worse, some perfectly normal individuals lack motivation and the sense of any urgency in attempting to dispel this fog. Consequently, the sum total of things remaining unperceived varies enormously between each individual. And I am convinced it has nothing to do with basic intelligence: it is simply a lack of sensitivity and receptivity. Admittedly, in the abstract field of concept-cognition and the setting up of parameters to define 'right' and 'wrong', 'justice' and 'injustice', it is difficult to prevent certain external factors coming into play. Whether we are aware of these or not, it must be remembered that religious, cultural and ethnic traditions (or taboos) can have undue influence on our judgement, thus hindering the establishment of 'qualitative' differences. Sadly, in some cases they can wholly prevent clear and unprejudiced thought in the matter. But fundamentally I firmly believe it is not lack of intelligence, just lack of sensitivity and receptivity.